WHATEVER HAPPENED TO...?

The Ultimate Pop & Rock 'Where Are They Now?'

BILL HARRY

BLANDFORD

A BLANDFORD BOOK

First published in the UK 1999
by Blandford
Cassell & Co.,
Wellington House
125 Strand
London WC2R 0BB

www.cassell.co.uk

A Cassell imprint

Reprinted 1999

Distributed in the United States by Sterling Publishing Co., Inc.,
387 Park Avenue South, New York, NY 10016-8810

A Cataloguing-in-Publication Data entry for this title is available and may be
obtained from the British Library

ISBN 0-7137-2675-X

Designed by Chris Bell

Printed in Great Britain by The Bath Press, Bath

CONTENTS

ROCK 'N' ROLL RETRO

A FEW YEARS AGO, watching television over a two-week period, it suddenly struck me that in the UK a number of acts from the original Mersey beat scene in Liverpool were still active and successful 30 years after that particular musical genre had come to an end. During that two weeks, I spotted several former Mersey 'beatsters' appearing on the small screen. I jotted down notes under the heading 'Whatever happened to the Mersey beatsters?', the point being that a number of them were still alive and kicking and finding a new career in television.

For instance, there was Geoffrey Hughes in the comedy *Keeping Up Appearances*. Geoff was a member of a Mersey band called the Travellers. He then got an acting break in the musical *Maggie May*, followed by parts in movies such as *Virgin Soldiers*, and went on to become a major soap star as Eddie Yates in *Coronation Street*.

One of the regular stars of *Brookside* – set in Liverpool – is Vince Earl, who plays Ron Dixon. Vince originally led his own bands, such as Vince Earl & the Talismen, before becoming a member of Rory Storm & the Hurricanes. He later changed careers to become a popular comedian, before settling down on Brookside Close. One episode he must have enjoyed was that in which a fictitious Mersey group called the Scottie Dogs appeared – with musicians such as Gerry Marsden and Pete Best playing together.

A third UK soap opera has provided steady work for yet another Mersey beatster: Clive Hornby has been appearing as Jack Sugden in the successful soap *Emmerdale* for many years. Clive was a member of a leading Mersey beat band, the Dennisons, who had a minor hit with 'Walkin' The Dog'.

During that two-week period I also saw several members of the Mersey scene who had become established comedians, following in the wake of other Liverpool stars such as Ken Dodd and Jimmy Tarbuck.

There was Faith Brown, who had her own television series. Faith – real name Irene Carroll – began singing on Merseyside in her early teens and became resident singer at the Rialto Ballroom when she was 16. She later teamed up with her brothers in the Carrolls before becoming a comedienne. Recently she, too, has popped up in *Brookside*.

Another comedy series featured Freddie Starr. Freddie is one of the most anarchic, funny and successful of all British comedians. As Freddie Fowell, he had a bit part in the movie *Violent Playground*. He then joined Howie Casey & the Seniors, who became the first Mersey beat group to make a record. Later he fronted several other bands, including Freddie Starr & the Delmonts and Freddie Starr & the Midnighters. His big break came when he was given a comedy spot on the television variety show *Sunday Night At The London Palladium*.

Russ Abbott is another group member who found himself with a career as a leading television comedian with his own series. He was a former member of the Black Abbotts.

Others have popped up on UK television over the years. These include artists such as Joe Fagin, former lead singer of the Strangers, who hit the chart with 'That's Livin' Alright' and 'Back With The Boys Again' from the series *Auf Wiedersehn, Pet*.

Freddie Starr

There was a period in the early 1980s when Clive Epstein, Brian Epstein's brother, became my partner in a venture to relaunch the newspaper *Mersey Beat*. Unfortunately, he died before we had completed our plans.

For the first issue, I had intended to do a complete round-up of the where-abouts of all the main groups from the Mersey scene. A number of them were still performing, and continue to do so today; these include Gerry & the Pacemakers, the Searchers, the Swinging Blue Jeans and the Merseybeats. Others, who had not quite achieved the big time but were established names on Merseyside, became part of an organization called Mersey Cats, donating all the proceeds of their shows to local children's charities. Within the last eight years they have raised £100,000 for these causes. These groups include Geoff Nugent's Undertakers, Faron's Flamingoes (Faron had to retire from active performing in 1997 due to heart trouble), Johnny & the Hurricanes, Karl Terry & the Cruisers, the Pathfinders and the Black Knights. As with the hit Mersey bands, they no longer comprise the full original line-ups.

Gerry & the Pacemakers is led by Gerry Marsden, but the Pacemakers themselves are all newcomers. Freddie Marsden, the original drummer, now runs a taxi firm, Pacemakers, in Liverpool and guitarist Les Chadwick settled in Australia in the 1970s.

The Undertakers moved to the US in the late 1960s, leaving Geoff Nugent behind in Liverpool. Jackie Lomax and Bugs Pemberton live in Los Angeles, where Jackie manages a club, while Chris Huston became a successful record-ing engineer and then a designer of recording studios. He now lives in Oregon. Sax player Brian Jones returned to the UK and joined Gary Glitter's band. Another group called the Undertakers is currently in existence, although they have no association with the original band – which is why Geoff has had to call his band Geoff Nugent's Undertakers. Similarly, the group called the Fourmost has no association with the original Fourmost who had their hits in the 1960s, and the same goes for the groups which call them-selves Vanity Fair and Unit 4 Plus 2.

This sort of situation has caused – and is still causing – controversy on the nostalgia circuit.

The Fourmost

THE NOSTALGIA CONTROVERSY AND TRIBUTE ARTISTS

Many of the groups from the 1960s and 1970s who are still performing include few, if any, of the original members. Some critics harp on this, others simply don't care – the audience is there to enjoy the music and if they are satisfied, that should be it. The general consensus seems to be that if at least one original member of the group remains, then keeping the group name is valid. After all, after a few decades have passed one can expect various per-sonnel changes and, sadly, fatalities.

However, when it comes to a group using an established hit name when not a single member of the original outfit is playing in it, that is a different matter. They could perhaps qualify the name by adding the word 'new' or the number '2' to it. Strictly speaking, though, they should call themselves a 'trib-ute' band rather than attempt to pass themselves off as the original hit artists.

The tribute band is a phenomenon which seems to have mushroomed in the 1990s. In this age of mass marketing, copycat bands and artists seem to be coming off the production line in ever-increasing numbers. Arguably, their origins lie in Australia, where many of the big names did not tour because of its geographical 'remoteness'. The Aussies simply decided to create their own versions and the term 'tribute band' was born.

Abba had been popular in Australia and a tribute band called Bjorn Again contacted British promoter Robert Reed in 1991. He booked them for the university circuit and on their first tour they grossed £120,000. Other Abba copycats include Abbacadabra and Voulez Vous. Further acts, such as the Australian Doors, were to follow.

The Bootleg Beatles are a prime example of a tribute band who can fill the Royal Albert Hall. They were even booked by Oasis to open for them at the Knebworth Festival in 1996, and by the winter of 1997 were embarked on a full-scale concert tour of the UK. It was the musical *Beatlemania* at London's Astoria Theatre that gave birth to the Bootleg Beatles. When the show ended in 1980, the copycat band continued to perform in their own right. Now there are literally hundreds of Beatle imitators – the Paperback Beatles, the Cavern Beatles, the Bandit Beatles, the Ludwig Beatles, the Silver Beatles, the Moondog Beatles, the Other Beatles, the Fab Four and numerous others. Oasis themselves, fairly new kids on the block, have already inspired several tribute bands, including Oasisn't and No Way Sis.

What is also amazing is the rapidity with which some of the tribute bands are formed. The Spice Girls only rose to fame in 1996, but within months there were six tribute bands on the road – some of them earning as much as £2,000 for each performance! They included Nice 'n' Spicy, the Wannabe Spice Girls, All Spice, the Spiced Girls, the Spicy Girls and the Spiceish Girls. Such bands vary, with some specializing in a lookalike appeal and others concentrating on sounding like their idols. Some camp it up, others take a more serious view of their performances.

In 1997 *Stage*, the British showbusiness newspaper, contained details of 160 separate tribute bands. They included Sgt Pepper's Magical Mystery Tour, Blurasis, Re-Genesis, the M People, Fake Us Quo, the Rolling Clones, Fabba and the Pretend Pretenders. An increase in lookalike tribute artists began to take place in 1995 with the growing popularity of *Stars In Their Eyes*, a UK television variety show in which contestants copied or parodied their favourite stars. (One of them looked so much like Errol Brown of Hot Chocolate that the group, sans Brown, hired him!) There are over 5,000 copycat Elvis Presleys in the States and other copycat bands in the UK include the Counterfeit Stones, the Pink Fraud, Zoo-2 and Wham Duran. The tribute bands have now joined the nostalgia circuit in holiday camps, cabaret, nightclubs and working men's clubs.

According to some pundits, it is simply a case of supply and demand. With complaints about the high price of concerts at venues such as Wembley Stadium, where touts can be hawking tickets for £150 a time, fans can be quite content to pay just a few pounds to see a good tribute band and actually get quite close to the copycats of their idols.

Yet there are signs that the price tag for tribute bands may be on the rise. In the UK, the Midland Bank sponsored a huge Bootleg Blitz Christmas party at the massive Battersea Power Station on 20 December 1997 with tickets priced at £27. Hosted by disc jockeys Emperor Rosko and Mike Read, the bill comprised:

> T. Rextasy (the one and only tribute to Marc Bolan and T. Rex), U Tour (a tribute to the sight, sound and songs of U2), Fleetwood Bac (adult-orientated rock at its best – the *Rumours* tribute line-up), Stayin' Alive (Saturday afternoon fever!), Australian Pink Floyd (probably the best tribute band in the world), Jean Genie (the David Bowie tribute band), Wonderwall (the supersonic Oasis tribute – roll with it!), the Counterfeit Stones (probably the second greatest rock 'n' roll band in the world) plus... the Ultimate Bootleg Band!

Tribute bands – whether paying homage to their heroes as do the Illegal Eagles, or playing it tongue-in-cheek like Guns 'N Moses, the Jewish heavy metal band – appear to be a facet of the rock landscape which is here to stay.

PAST STARS IN VOGUE

By 1997 another avenue had opened up for stars whose days of chart success seemed to have passed. Affluent businessmen and companies were booking numerous artists, particularly those from the 1970s, for birthday bashes.

Millionaire businessman Jim Melton booked Slade for his house-warming party, while Nigel Wray, owner of Saracens Rugby Club, booked the Village People for his forty-ninth birthday party – for the princely sum of £25,000. In 1997, booking agents were quoting £1,500 for Dozy, Beaky, Mick & Tich or Steve Ellis' Love Affair, £2,400 for Mud, £2,500 for the Tremeloes, £4,500 for the Drifters, £5,000 for Hot Chocolate, £6,000 for the Supremes, £10,000 for Gloria Gaynor and £50,000 for Tom Jones.

CHANGING TRENDS

At one time I did wonder why so many artists could not maintain their success. There would be a band or solo artist who had a string of hits, toured extensively and obviously improved as time went by – only to find that the hits had dried up and they were now unfashionable. Was it new trends that shortened the careers of so many artists? We know for sure that in the US the advent of the Beatles and the 'British Invasion' affected the careers of many solo singers drastically. Something similar happened in the UK when the beat movement swept the country, and artists ranging from Susan Maughan and Craig Douglas to Helen Shapiro and Eden Kane became unfashionable.

But that surely isn't the only answer, for why do some artists survive for decades while their contemporaries fade away?

If we look at the 1950s, there was a time when rock 'n' roll was almost nipped in the bud: Carl Perkins involved in an accident; Chuck Berry in jail; Elvis in the army; Buddy Holly, the Big Bopper and Richie Valens in an air crash; Jerry Lee Lewis in disgrace for marrying a young cousin and so on. Yet it puzzled me that when the artists survived the coming decades as performing acts, they had lost that chart magic. If Jerry Lee Lewis could provide such exciting rock 'n' roll classics as 'Whole Lotta Shakin' Going On', 'Great Balls Of Fire' and 'Breathless', why could he not repeat the success with at least one more rock 'n' roll classic in the three decades since?

Chuck Berry almost did it. His great classics of the 1950s were 'Maybellene', 'Roll Over Beethoven', 'School Days', 'Rock & Roll Music', 'Sweet Little Sixteen' and 'Johnny B. Goode', but he did come up with 'No Particular Place To Go' in 1964 and his biggest hit, 'My Ding-A-Ling', in 1972, but still did not produce the rock 'n' roll classics in the way that he had done in the 1950s. There were no more 'Blue Suede Shoes' from Carl Perkins, and although the Everly Brothers are still touring in 1998, virtually all their classics – 'Bye Bye Love', 'Wake Up Little Susie', 'All I Have To Do Is Dream', 'Bird Dog' – were produced in the 1950s, with a few in 1960 such as 'Let It Be Me', 'Cathy's Clown' and 'When Will I Be Loved'. But why no chart hits since?

Chuck Berry

7

The same applies to songwriters. Consider the number of British song-writers who had big hits in the 1960s: Mitch Murray, Geoff Stevens, Tony Macauley – did they lose the magic?

Time may pass some artists by, but others have great longevity – take, for example, the Rolling Stones, Elton John, David Bowie, Rod Stewart, Pink Floyd and the Moody Blues. So what does happen to the artists who have fallen by the wayside?

Initially, in the late 1960s, as music trends developed and beat groups became unfashionable, they turned to cabaret. The former young rebellious rock 'n' rollers donned their dinner jackets to entertain the chicken-in-the-basket audiences. This was the outlet for them until things began to change in the 1980s.

The nostalgia market then began to grow in the UK, continental Europe and the States, and the number of venues open to former hit parade stars expanded. In the UK, a new company called Flying Music began to promote large-scale theatre concert tours for artists of the 1960s – the Solid Silver Sixties Tours – which are still flourishing. Sixties weekends at holiday camps became fashionable; sixties acts could fill the Royal Albert Hall, the London Palladium – even Wembley Stadium. There was the Chelmsford Spectacular at Hylands Park, the Butlins specialist 'Music Break' holidays, the Salute To The Sixties at Wembley, festivals at stately homes and sixties bands on theme cruises. The market gradually began to provide an outlet for groups from the 1970s as well.

The 1950s were noted for the birth of rock 'n' roll in the US, the 1960s for the rebirth of rock 'n' roll with the British bands, led by the Beatles, and the early to mid-1970s for glam rock, disco and ludicrous fashions such as loon pants. Yet suddenly, in the late 1990s, the kitsch of the 1970s has become fashionable and glam rock is accepted more seriously now than the first time around.

Many different and varied music styles evolved in the 1980s – a plethora of genres including new romantics, techno, garage, hip hop, goth, rap and dance, all appealing to the young. But what had happened to the 'baby

Making a comeback? – Dave Berry (centre back), the Swinging Blue Jeans (back row) and the Searchers (front row)

boomers' – the huge mass of the population who were teenagers in the late 1950s and early 1960s, who sparked off the music boom in the first place and were the original rock 'n' roll generation? They were still around, of course. They had raised their children, who had now left the nest, paid off their mortgages, and now had time on their hands and money to spend – and they turned to the music that had originally turned them on. It is this that explains why the huge nostalgia market is sustainable.

THE COMEBACKS

Let us return to the question of why artists who undoubtedly had talent and chart success should fade away. Certainly, a number of them fight on, but rarely do they make a chart comeback.

For example, the Searchers – always an excellent group – almost grasped a second chance at record success when they made two albums for Sire Records. Great reviews, and healthy initial sales – but due to internal politics at the record company, no more albums were pressed to cater for the demand and the opportunity the Searchers had to return to the charts faded.

A new trend that appeared in the 1980s was the teaming up of a contemporary group with a former chart artist. Sandie Shaw had been an icon to Morrisey of the Smiths, so they teamed up on record and she found herself in the chart again. When Take That did the same for Lulu, she got a kick-start to her recording career and also re-entered the chart with new recordings on her own. The Happy Mondays teamed up with Karl Denver and he found his name on the chart lists once more, as did Dusty Springfield with the Pet Shop Boys and Shirley Bassey with Propellerheads. Marc Almond has recorded with Gene Pitney and P.J. Proby – and so it goes on. When Alan McGee of Creation Records, which houses hot acts such as Oasis, signed up Kevin Rowland, the former Dexy's Midnight Runners leader who had become bankrupt, he said he wanted to 'rehabilitate other pop icons'.

Sandie Shaw pictured here with Adam Faith

RETRO ROCK

The 1990s is the era of retro rock. More groups have re-formed in recent years than at any other time. Bands such as Yes have embarked on major tours and artists who have been out of the limelight for some time, such as Leo Sayer, have found they have a larger audience than imagined and can continue to sell out nationwide concert tours. Ten Years After, for instance, have re-formed to tour South America for the very first time.

The biggest effect of retro rock has been in the recording field, and this has been boosted by a group who disbanded over 25 years previously – the Beatles. When the Beatles issued their *Anthology* CDs, I was asked to comment. I said that the Beatles had done it once again – they had become trailblazers once more. They were pioneers in the field of stadium concerts, album sleeves and pop videos, and helped to introduce popular music into places it had never been before. Now that the Beatles had placed their recording career, warts and all, into an historical perspective in the *Anthology* collection, everyone else would follow. I predicted then that every major group would soon have its own equivalent of the Beatles' *Anthology*, and it has come to pass – groups are putting out boxed sets and CD collections containing out-takes, previously unreleased tracks, tracks without vocals, alternative takes and so on.

The market for artists of the 1950s, 1960s and 1970s, both for recording and performance, is colossal. There is a full back-up structure of agents and managers specializing in the nostalgia circuit, together with magazines such as *Record Collector* and *The Beat Goes On* covering the field.

Record Collector is probably my favourite music magazine at the moment. It is written by journalists who love the acts they write about, have incredible knowledge of their subject – and actually write about the artists rather than themselves, as is generally the case in the mainstream music mags. *The Beat Goes On* may not have the clout of a major publishing company behind it, but it has heart, and you can read reviews in which the critics are not impressed with their own cleverness but more concerned with informing the reader about the product.

Generally, when the UK press begin writing about the vintage stars who are still performing, we hear the old clichés about 'wrinklies' and zimmer frames. The articles or reviews all appear to be obsessed with the age of the performers. Yet this seems to apply only to the rock artists. Jazz, blues, R&B, country music artists and original American rock 'n' roll stars of the 1950s have careers that stretch over many years, yet reviews are generally positive and do not revert to the disparaging remarks British rock acts from the 1960s or 1970s have to put up with.

Another typically British obsession is the negative attitude towards success. The Americans have a different perception – they welcome and admire success. In many ways, the British seem to resent it and appear to take a perverse delight in seeing former idols on their way down. While the States welcomed the Spice Girls and showered them with awards, the UK press was constantly informing its readers that they were on their way out, despite evidence of increased record sales and their achieving the Christmas No 1 two years on the trot.

When I first began working on this book, people were under the impression that I was going to write about 'has-beens'. They seemed to think it would be crammed with stories of former stars who were now dustbin men, or confined to mental hospitals, or working as porters and so on. Although this may be the case with a handful of the artists mentioned, the great majority are still performing and their original audiences have rediscovered them.

When compiling this book, it has been frustrating to have to decide who to include and who to leave out. Naturally, I wished to cover as much ground as possible, but since there have been literally thousands of hit artists over the decades, such coverage would require several volumes. So, please excuse the omissions if you find your favourite artist absent – I hope you will still enjoy reading about the others.

Bill Harry
London

USING THE BOOK

WITHIN THE Where Are They Now? section of this book you will find the careers of literally hundreds of individual artists and groups described in detail. The In Memoriam section offers brief resumés of the lives of those who are now deceased, plus extended descriptions of major stars. In both sections, the artists are presented in alphabetical order. Within the text, artists and groups who have their own entries in either section appear in bold, for easy reference. Finally, alphabetical listings of fan clubs and fanzines for artists with entries in the book are provided, along with recommended sources of information regarding clubs and magazines for other artists mentioned in the text.

DEDICATION AND ACKNOWLEDGEMENTS

I WOULD LIKE to dedicate this book to Henry Henriod, who died in March 1998. Henry was one of those unsung heroes of the music scene who dedicated his life to the business and is much missed. At one time he worked for impresario Don Arden; he then began to manage Gene Vincent, before becoming involved in Hamburg's Star Club, where he booked numerous artists ranging from Ray Charles to the Everly Brothers.

Henry teamed up with Chas Chandler and Nigel Stander in the Newcastle Arena. Following Chas' death, he was attempting to set up a similar arena in Liverpool, a city he came to love. Henry and I were also hoping to establish a Mersey Beat Village, the world's first rock 'n' roll village, in tandem with the arena. We had been working on the project for two years when Henry was hospitalized and very sadly died.

Several people have aided me in this project, most notably Alan Clayson, who acted as a consultant. I would also like to thank Stuart Booth and Jane Birch of Blandford Press, and editor Sarah Widdicombe.

For photographs and permission to use them I have many sources to thank, including the Mersey Beat Archives, *The Beat Goes On* magazine, Flying Music, Hal Carter, Rotheray Management, BCM Management, EMI Records, Edsell Records, Rocket Records, Rak Records, Joey Dee, John Leyton, Spencer Leigh, Paul Cox, Acker's International Jazz Agency, John Martin Promotions Ltd, Sue Goodwin, Kenny Lynch, Brenda Brooker, Warner Home Video, Brent Walker Film Distributors, Channel 5, CIC Video, President Records, Michael Winner, Namara Films, Telstar Records, National Film Archives, RCA Records, Polydor Records, Atlantic Records, Arista, The Agency and Motown Records.

Bill Harry

ABBA This highly popular Swedish quartet achieved international superstardom. The four members were Bjorn Ulvaeus, Benny Andersson, Anni-Frid (Frida) Lyngstad and Agnetha Faltskog.

The quartet first rose to fame when they won the Eurovision Song Contest in 1974 with 'Waterloo'. Abba (their name derived from the initials of the first names of the members) then enjoyed incredible success throughout the 1970s, due to the brilliantly commercial melodic pop songs of Bjorn and Benny, and the glamour and infectious appeal of their two girl singers – one blonde, one red-haired.

Their hit singles stretched over a ten-year period and included: 'Ring Ring', 'I Do I Do I Do I Do I Do', 'SOS', 'Mamma Mia', 'Fernando', 'Dancing Queen', 'Money Money Money', 'Knowing Me Knowing You', 'The Name Of The Game', 'Take A Chance On Me', 'Summer Night City', 'Chiquitita', 'Does Your Mother Know, 'Angel Eyes/Voulez-Vous', Gimme Gimme Gimme', 'I Have A Dream', 'The Winner Takes It All', 'Super Trouper', 'Lay All Your Love On Me', 'One Of Us', 'Head Over Heels', 'The Day Before You Came', 'Under Attack' and 'Thank You For The Music'.

Album hits included *Waterloo*, *Abba*, *Greatest Hits*, *Arrival*, *The Album*, *Voulez-Vous*, *Greatest Hits Vol 2*, *Super Trouper*, *The Visitors*, *The Singles – The First Ten Years* and *Thank You For The Music*.

The group even starred in their own feature film *Abba – The Movie* in 1974, filmed during their Australian tour.

Benny and Frida, both of whom had been married previously, were wed in October 1978. They announced their divorce in February 1981 after Benny confessed he had fallen in love with Mona Norklit, a Swedish television announcer, whom he was later to marry.

Abba

Abba made their last live appearance in January 1982 and then announced various solo projects. Frida, who was born in Norvik, Norway, on 15 November 1945, moved to London and recorded the album *Something's Going On*. 'I Know There's Something Going On' from the album provided her with a minor hit, and she also had success with 'Time', which she recorded with B.A. Robertson. Frida later took an interest in environmental issues and moved to Switzerland, where she now lives. She also continues to record for Benny Andersson.

Blonde-haired Agnetha was the one whom admirers proclaimed had the sexiest bottom in the world! She was born on 5 April 1950 in Jonkopping, Sweden, and was a member of Abba when they first formed in 1970. She married fellow member Bjorn Ulvaeus in July the following year. Their daughter Linda was born in February 1973, and their son Peter in December 1977. Agnetha and Bjorn then separated and announced their divorce in December 1978.

In 1983 Agnetha made her acting debut in the Swedish film *Rakenstam* and recorded a solo album, *The Heat Is On*. She also had hit singles with 'The Heat Is On', 'Wrap Your Arms Around Me' and 'Can't Shake Loose'.

When Abba split, Agnetha bought a small Swedish island and retreated there with her children. She married surgeon Thomas Sonnefeld in December 1990, but they were later divorced. For a number of years she did not sing again, nor did she listen to any music. During this time she became interested in subjects such as yoga and astrology. Fifteen years after Abba disbanded, Agnetha decided to publish her biography, *As I Am: Abba Before And Beyond*, written with journalist Brita Ahman, which was published in October 1997.

When the group disbanded, Andersson, born in Stockholm on 16 December 1946, and Ulvaeus, born in Gothenburg on 25 April 1945, who both still live in Sweden, stayed together and co-wrote the hit musical *Chess* with Tim Rice. Bjorn was the subject of a *This Is Your Life* programme on Swedish television in 1986, and the group united once again for the occasion. Andersson and Ulvaeus also appeared on stage with **U2** in Stockholm, joining the Irish group on their version of 'Dancing Queen'.

Over the years, the various compilations of the Abba hits have proved to be steady sellers and the rise of tribute groups has also maintained the group's popularity. A 66-track 4-CD set, *Thank You For The Music*, was issued in 1995.

Stig Anderson, Abba's manager and 'fifth member', died on 9 September 1997. He was 66 years old.

ADGE CUTLER & THE WURZELS This novelty group from England's West Country initially surfaced with a minor chart hit called 'Drink Up Thy Zider' in 1967. Led by Adge Cutler, former manager of trad jazzer **Acker Bilk**, the other members were Tommy Banner, Tony Baylis and Peter Budd.

Exploiting the country yokel theme, they adapted three existing hits – 'Brand New Key', 'Uno Paloma Blanca' and 'I Was Kaiser Bill's Batman' – and turned them into comedy hits entitled 'Combine Harvester', 'I Am A Cider Drinker' and 'Farmer Bill's Cowman' respectively. The first of their releases topped the UK chart.

Since their hat-trick of UK Top 40 entries, and despite Adge Cutler's death in a road accident in 1974, the Wurzels still raise the roof at 'harvest home' dances in the West Country, with Budd and Banner joined by Amos Morgan and Squire Wintour.

AKKERMAN, Jan Born on 24 December 1946, Dutch guitarist Jan Akkerman was an original member of Johnny & The Cellar Rockers, then Brainbox, prior to joining Amsterdam-based group Focus. The band initially had success in continental Europe, then entered the UK chart with 'Hocus Pocus' in 1973, the year in which *Melody Maker* voted Akkerman the greatest guitarist in the world. The same year, the band climbed to No 4 in the UK chart with 'Sylvia'. Following the release of their album *Mother Focus* in 1975, Akkerman left to pursue a solo career. He performed mainly on the Continent and issued an album each year after turning solo, then settled in Scandinavia for several years and underwent an unhappy divorce.

In 1985, Akkerman joined fellow Focus member Thijs van Leer to record an album and in 1990 the original members of the group re-formed for an appearance on a Dutch television special. Plans for a tour of the States in 1992 were thwarted when Akkerman was involved in a car accident, in which he broke his back in two places. He was nursed back to health by a woman called Marian and married her in April 1993.

Akkerman released the album *Focus In Time* in 1996 and a new live album in 1997. In November 1997 he headlined the International Guitar Festival Of Great Britain on Merseyside. 1998 was Akkerman's fortieth year as a recording artist.

ALLISONS, The The members of this British vocal duo were John Alford, born in London on 31 December 1939, and Bob Day, born in Trowbridge, Wiltshire, on 2 February 1942.

Impresario Tito Burns saw his opportunity to create a British version of the **Everly Brothers** and they fooled the press and public into believing they were brothers, John and Bob Allison. They became the UK's entry in the 1961 Eurovision Song Contest and their number for the competition, 'Are You Sure', which was self-penned, became a UK chart-topper and came second in the competition. The group had only two further hits, 'Words' and 'Lessons In Love'.

Bob Day has retired and is now in poor health. John Alford lives in Lincoln and is still singing.

ALPERT, Herb Born on 31 March 1937, the American trumpeter-singer-songwriter-producer-record company boss Herb Alpert was also the manager of **Jan & Dean** and Lou Adler. Together with Jerry Moss, he founded A&M Records in 1962, initially in a garage, and the company grew into an international label.

Alpert assembled a group of musicians that he called the Tijuana Brass and made a number of records with them. His hits during the 1960s, 1970s and 1980s included: 'The Lonely Bull', 'Zorba The Greek', 'What Now My Love', 'Spanish Flea', 'The Work Song', 'Tijuana Taxi', 'Casino Royale', 'Flamingo', 'Mame', 'Wade In The Water', 'The Happening', 'This Guy's In Love With You', 'Without Her', 'Jerusalem', 'Rise Rotation', 'Keep Your Eye On Me', 'Route 101' and 'Diamonds'. These were primarily instrumentals, his first vocal disc being 'This Guy's In Love With You', a number which he sang to his wife Lani Hall in his own television special. At one time in the mid-1960s, Alpert had no less than four albums in the US chart at the same time, and international tours with the band included performances before Princess Grace in Monaco and at the Royal Albert Hall.

In 1969, Alpert had decided to cease performing and concentrate on recording and running A&M Records, but he resumed touring once again in 1974. In 1989, he and Moss sold their interest in A&M Records, and in 1996 the two of them founded a new label, Almo Sounds. Alpert immediately issued his first album in four years, *Second Wind*, and began his first tour in eight. In May 1997 he issued another album on the Almo label, *Passion Dance*.

ALTERED IMAGES Born in Scotland on 17 March 1962, Claire Grogan was an aspiring actress who appeared in the film *Gregory's Girl* in 1980. That same year she was invited to join Altered Images, a group comprising Tony McDaid on guitar, Jim McKinven on guitar and keyboards, John McElhone on bass and Michael 'Tich' Anderson on drums.

The band's first hit single was 'Dead Pop Stars', which proved controversial, charting in March 1981 only months after the death of **John Lennon**. This was followed by their biggest hit, 'Happy Birthday', which reached the No 2 spot. Other hit singles included 'I Could Be Happy', 'See Those Eyes',' Pinky Blue', 'Don't Talk To Me About Love', 'Bring Me Closer' and 'Love To Stay'.

McKinven and Anderson had left in 1982, to be replaced by multi-instrumentalist Stephen Lironi. The group broke up in 1983.

Claire Grogan continued to fare well as an actress, although she did not have as much success with her solo recordings. She was a host of *Night Network*, the UK television magazine show; appeared in Bill Forsyth's movie *Comfort And Joy*; and had dramatic roles in various television series and plays such as *Red Dwarf*, *Taggart*, *The Monocled Mutineer*, *Blott On The Landscape* and *EastEnders*.

Of the other ex-members, Johnny McElhone has been the most successful. He is now with the group Texas.

AMEN CORNER This group was formed in Wales in 1966 and took their name from the title of a play by James Baldwin. The members were Andy Fairweather-Low on vocals and guitar, Blue Weaver on organ, Neil Jones on guitar, Clive Taylor on bass, Mike Smith on tenor sax, Alan Jones on baritone sax and Dennis Bryon on drums.

Amen Corner's hit singles were: 'Gin House Blues', 'World Of Broken Hearts', 'Bend Me Shape Me', 'High In The Sky', '(If Paradise Is) Half As Nice' and 'Hello Suzie'. They appeared in the club scene in the horror movie *Scream And Scream Again* in 1969.

The group disbanded that year and their final single, a cover of the Beatles' 'Get Back', was issued in 1970. By that time Fairweather-Low, together with Weaver, Bryon, Taylor and Neil Jones had formed Fair Weather, with the addition of Andy Bown. They had one hit, 'Natural Sinner', and split by the end of the year. Alan Jones and Smith formed Judas Jump.

Weaver and Bryon, together with guitarist Alan Kendall, provided a rhythm section for the **Bee Gees** throughout the 1970s and early 1980s.

Known more as a guitarist than a singer these days, Andy Fairweather-Low appeared on the UK television programme *Top Of The Pops* in 1996, when a charity single that also featured Paul Rodgers reached the Top 40. He is also one of the backing musicians at Eric Clapton concerts. Blue Weaver is a highly paid session musician whose credits include 'Saturday Night Fever'.

AMERICA   Dewey Bunnell, Gerry Beckley and Dan Peek, who each played guitar and sang vocals, were all the sons of US Air Force officers based in England. They teamed up as a trio in 1970 and had their first hit, 'A Horse With No Name', in 1972. Following the success in the UK of their debut album *America*, they moved to the States and appeared on tour with the **Everly Brothers**. 'A Horse With No Name' was issued in the US, where it topped the chart.

The band continued to have hit singles on both sides of the Atlantic, including: 'I Need You', 'Ventura Highway', 'Don't Cross The River', 'Tin Man', 'Lonely People', 'Sister Golden Hair', 'Daisy Jane' and 'Today's The Day'.

Dan Peek left the band in 1977, when he became a born-again Christian and decided to record religious material as a solo artist. He had one hit, 'All Things Are Possible'. After he left, America had further hit singles with 'You Can Do Magic' and 'The Border'.

The trio's chart albums were *America*, *Homecoming*, *Hat Trick* and *History: America's Greatest Hits*.

After Peek left, Beckley and Bunnell continued their career, using various backing musicians. More recently, apart from their 1994 album *Hourglass*, they recorded on a tie-in album for *The Simpsons* television programme. Over the years, the two have also guested on recordings by a number of artists including Dan Fogelberg and the **Beach Boys**.

ANDREWS, Chris   Born in Romford, Essex, on 15 October 1938, singer-songwriter Chris Andrews began singing and playing guitar at the age of 11 and in the late 1950s he formed Chris Ravel & the Ravers.

As a songwriter, he penned several numbers for **Adam Faith** – including 'The First Time' and 'We Are In Love'– and three hits – 'Girl Don't Come', 'Long Live Love' and 'Message Understood' – for **Sandie Shaw**.

Andrews then had several successes in his own right as a singer with 'Yesterday Man', 'To Whom It Concerns' and 'Pretty Belinda'. His biggest hits came in Germany and he made many appearances there on television and as a performer.

Chris Andrews has returned to concert performances. In 1994, he and Sandie Shaw sang at a party in Hammersmith, west London, to celebrate RPM Records' first year in business.

ANIMALS, The   A band from Newcastle-upon-Tyne, the Animals originally formed in 1962. Eric Burdon and John Steel had first met at art school and they teamed up with Alan Price, Chas Chandler and Hilton Valentine. The group began to build a reputation locally in clubs such as the Club-A-Go-Go and the Downbeat. It was while they were appearing at the Cavern in Liverpool that they were spotted by Henry Henriod, who recommended them to Mickie Most and arranged for them to play at London's Scene Club.

The group settled in London in 1963 and hit the UK chart with their first release, 'Baby Let Me Take You Home', followed by their biggest hit, 'The House Of The Rising Sun'. They had a number of other hits before they disbanded in 1966: 'I'm Crying', 'Don't Let Me Be Misunderstood', 'Bring It On Home To Me', 'We've Gotta Get Out Of This Place', 'It's My Life', 'Inside-Looking Out' and 'Don't Bring Me Down'.

Alan Price had left the previous year, to be replaced by Dave Rowberry, while Steel left and was replaced by Barry Jenkins.

Following the group's break-up, Burdon settled in the States and formed Eric Burdon & the Animals with Jenkins, Vic Briggs and Danny McCulloch. By 1968 Briggs and McCulloch had been replaced by **Zoot Money** and Andy Summers, and the name changed to Eric Burdon & the New Animals. By 1970 he had teamed up with an American band called Night Shift who changed their name to War, and several further hits followed by Eric Burdon & War. Burdon continued to perform over the years with various different bands and line-ups. His autobiography, *I Used To Be An Animal, But I'm Alright Now*, was published in 1986.

Alan Price had considerable solo success over a 20-year period with hits such as 'I Put A Spell On You', 'Hi Lili Hi Lo', 'Simon Smith & His Amazing Dancing Bear', 'Honey I Need', 'Cry To Me', 'Midnight To Six Man', 'Come See Me' and 'A House In The Country'.

Chas Chandler also found success in his new career as a manager, discovering acts such as **Jimi Hendrix** and **Slade**.

In 1976 the original five members teamed up at Chas Chandler's house and cut an album in a mobile studio. 'House Of The Rising Sun' was re-released and charted again, and the group embarked on a world tour in 1983, before splitting once more.

Hilton Valentine had been working with a band called the Alligators, with singer Robert Kane. In 1993 he approached John Steel to form Animals II with Kane, plus Steve Hutchinson on keyboards, Steve Dawson on guitar and Martin Bland on bass. In 1997 they released an album on which they performed a number of the original Animals hits, and also toured Europe, Australia and the US.

Sadly, Chas Chandler died in 1996.

ANT, Adam   Adam Ant (real name Stuart Leslie Goddard) was born on 3 November 1954. He had originally played with outfits called Bazooka Joe and B-sides.

His initial Adam & the Ants group released their first single in January 1979. When it failed to register, most of the members were poached by Malcolm McLaren to form **Bow Wow Wow** and Adam gathered together another group of musicians. This time they were successful on record.

Adam developed 'antmusic', with its double drum sound, and his visual stage act, which was also appealing on television, presented himself and the group in pirate costumes, an American Indian look, a highwayman's outfit and so on.

The group's UK hit singles included: 'Kings Of The Wild Frontier', 'Dog Eat Dog', 'Antmusic', 'Young Parisians', 'Zerox', 'Cartrouble', 'Stand And Deliver', 'Prince Charming',' Ant Rap', 'Deutscher Girls', 'The Antmusic EP', 'Goody Two Shoes', 'Friend Or Foe', 'Desperate But Not Serious', 'Puss 'n' Boots', 'Strip', 'Apollo' and 'Vive Le Rock'.

After changing the personnel completely once again in 1985, Adam then concentrated on an acting career, appearing in stage, film and television productions ranging from *Entertaining Mr Sloane* to *Slam Dance* and *The Equalizer*.

While still appearing in film roles, Adam began recording again and hit the UK chart with 'Room At The Top' and 'Can't Set Rules About Love' in 1990, and 'Wonderful' and 'Gotta Be A Sin' in 1995.

Former Ant member **Matthew Ashman** died while in a diabetic coma in 1995.

APPLEJACKS, The   This group from Solihull, Warwickshire, included lead guitarist Martin Baggott, rhythm guitarist Phil Cash and drummer Gerry Freeman, all of whom were originally part of a skiffle group formed in 1960. They occasionally played at a youth club where Freeman was a Sunday school teacher. Another teacher was Megan Davies, who joined them in 1961. The following year organist Don Gould joined and in 1963 Al Jackson became their lead vocalist. They originally called themselves the Crestas, then the Jaguars and finally the Applejacks.

1964 was the year in which they had their only chart entries, three singles, the most popular of which was their first, 'Tell Me When'. The others were 'Like Dreamers Do' and 'Three Little Words'.

These days, an Applejacks group featuring Megan Davies and Gerry Freeman performs regularly in the Midlands, often backing Mike Sheridan.

ARCHIES, The   As well as being the name of the UK radio ventriloquist's dummy of the 1950s, Archie Andrews was a cartoon character in a series of US comics and syndicated television cartoon series. He first appeared in 1942, the creation of artist John I. Goldwater,

Don Kirshner, the director of the television series, selected a theme song, 'Everything's Archie', which would be played by a group of high-school characters. He then decided to release actual recordings of the fictitious group and gave them the name the Archies. The first single was 'Sugar, Sugar', which sold three million copies on its release in 1969.

The album *Everything's Archie* also went gold, followed by another single, 'Jingle, Jingle', and the album of the same name.

The Archies' other singles which appeared in the US chart were 'Bang-Shang-A-Lang' and 'Who's Your Baby?'.

Kirshner had the records produced behind closed doors using session men and the identities of the musicians was never revealed, although many believe that the lead singer was Ron Dante.

This most manufactured of pop groups has proved far less enduring than the flesh-and-blood **Monkees**, and their cartoon adventures have been seen only rarely since their 1969 apotheosis.

ARROWS, The This trio, originally formed in the UK in 1973, consisted of Jake Hooker on guitar, Alan Merrill on vocals and bass, and Paul Varley on vocals and drums.

Merrill and Hooker hailed from New York and Varley from Preston, Lancashire. Merrill had actually been a major recording star in Japan, but came to the UK at Hooker's request. Under the capable guidance of Mickie Most, they entered the Top 10 with their first release, 'A Touch Too Much', in 1974. With the benefit of Most's organization, they found things happening fast – including their own television series, a weekly comic strip and a paperback book about them. Their next hit was 'My Last Night With You'. It also proved to be their last.

The Arrows had engaged a manager who was at odds with the Mickie Most team and they soon vanished into obscurity.

It's a pity they didn't try a single with 'I Love Rock & Roll', a number that was penned by Hooker and Merrill, which provided Joan Jett

The Arrows

17

with a Stateside chart-topper. It was also re-recorded by other acts in 1998 and has provided the writers with decent royalties over the years.

Jake Hooker went on to marry Lorna Luft, daughter of Judy Garland, whom he also managed, but they became estranged. He is now in New York, acting in a management capacity to various acts.

Alan Merrill shunts between New York and Japan – a country where he is still popular and still charting. He has also been in Meatloaf's backing band and has made solo albums.

There was talk of reviving the Arrows in 1998.

ASIA This group was formed in 1981 by Steve Howe, who had just left **Yes**, and John Wetton, who had been a member of **Roxy Music** and **King Crimson**. Carl Palmer, a former member of Emerson, Lake & Palmer, joined them on drums, as did George Downes, who was formerly keyboards player with Yes.

Asia's hit singles included 'Heat Of The Moment', 'Only Time Will Tell' and 'Don't Cry'. Their chart albums were *Asia*, *Alpha* and *Astra*.

The original line-up did not last all that long despite tremendous success, with their debut album selling over four million copies and their television special, *Asia In Asia*, attracting over 20 million viewers.

Wetton left in 1983 and Greg Lake replaced him. By 1985 Howe had also left and was replaced by Mandy Meyer. At the same time Wetton returned and Lake left. The group disbanded the following year.

Asia was revived for a brief concert tour of Japan in 1990, with Pat Thrall as lead guitarist. In 1991 John Payne replaced Wetton and the group released another album, *Aqua*. Another album, *Aria*, was issued in 1994, the personnel by this time including Downes, Payne, Al Pitrelli and Mike Sturgis.

Steve Howe has joined a re-formed Yes.

ATOMIC ROOSTER This group was formed by organist **Vincent Crane** and drummer Carl Palmer in 1969, following the break-up of the **Crazy World Of Arthur Brown**, of which they were both members. Palmer left soon afterwards to join Emerson, Lake & Palmer.

Atomic Rooster lasted four years, during which time there were various changes in personnel. Drummers included Rick Parnell and John Hammond, and the guitarists were John Cann and Johnny Mandala. **Chris Farlowe** was lead vocalist.

The group issued five albums and had two hit singles in 1971, 'Tomorrow Night' and 'Devil's Answer'.

Crane (real name Vincent Rodney Chessman) was born on 21 May 1943. He was also a songwriter and penned the number 'Fire', which became a major hit for Arthur Brown. After Atomic Rooster folded, he joined **Dexy's Midnight Runners**. He committed suicide in February 1989, by overdosing on sleeping pills.

AVALON, Frankie Born Francis Avallone in Philadelphia on 18 September 1939, Frankie Avalon first began singing when he was only 14 years old. In 1957 he was a member of Rocco & His Saints and appeared that year in the movie *Jamboree*. In fact, his film career proved as fruitful as his recording one, as he appeared in nearly three dozen movies including *The Alamo*, *Voyage To The Bottom Of The Sea* and *The Haunted House Of Horror*. He is most noted for the series of 'beach movies' he made with Annette Funicello, which became a template for the entire genre. They included *Beach Party*, *Bikini Beach Party*, *Muscle Beach Party*, *Beach Blanket Bingo* and *How To Stuff A Wild Bikini*. Avalon was reunited with Funicello in 1989 in the final chapter – *Back To The Beach*.

Frankie Avalon made his chart debut in 1958 with 'Dede Dinah'. His other hits included 'Ginger Bread', 'I'll Wait For You', 'Venus', 'Bobby Sox To Stockings', 'A Boy Without A Girl', 'Just Ask Your Heart', 'Why', 'Swingin' On A Rainbow', 'Don't Throw Away All Those Teardrops', 'Where Are You', 'Togetherness' and 'You Are Mine'.

In 1979, Frankie Avalon had a part in the movie *Grease*. After that he recorded for a number of labels, but had more success on the US cabaret circuit.

BACHELORS, The This group was originally formed in Dublin in 1958 as the Harmony Chords, featuring brothers Con and Dec Cluskey and John Stokes. It was Decca's A&R man Dick Rowe who suggested the name Bachelors.

Following the name change, they had a major hit, 'Charmaine', and then a series of flops ('Far Away', 'Whispering', 'I'll See You'), before entering the UK chart again with a string of hits – 'Diane', 'I Believe', 'Ramona', 'I Wouldn't Trade You For The World' and 'No Arms Can Ever Hold You'. They also reached No 3 in the chart in 1966 with a cover of Simon & Garfunkel's 'The Sound Of Silence'.

Essentially balladeers, the Bachelors continued to be a popular turn on the UK cabaret circuit, although there was a major dispute in 1984 and the brothers asked Stokes to leave, despite the fact that they had been together for 25 years. Stokes then took them to court and was awarded compensation. The brothers replaced him with Peter Phipps.

There are currently two outfits appearing on the nostalgia circuit. The first is led by Con and Dec Cluskey; the other group is called John Stokes' Bachelors. John's two fellow members are Jonathon Young and Kevin Neill. Kevin played lead guitar with the Karl Denver Trio for almost 30 years.

BAD MANNERS This madcap British ska group, originally formed in 1980, had 12 hits between then and 1983: 'Ne-Ne Na-Na Na-Na Nu-Nu', 'Lip Up Patty', 'Special Brew', 'Lorraine', 'Just A Feeling', 'Can Can', 'Walking In The Sunshine', 'Buona Sera', 'Got No Brains', 'My Girl Lollipop (My Boy Lollipop)', 'Samson And Delilah' and 'That'll Do Nicely'.

The group's lead singer was the outrageous skinhead Buster Bloodvessel (real name Douglas Trendle), who was born on 6 September 1958. In 1990 he led a breakaway group called Buster's All Stars. He now runs a hotel in Margate, Kent.

Other members included Gus 'Hot Lips' Herman (trumpet), Chris Kane and Andrew 'Marcus Absent' Marson (sax), Winston Bazoomies (harmonica), Brian 'Chew It' Tuitti (drums), David Farrow (bass), Martin Stewart (keyboards) and Louis 'Alphonzo' Cook (guitar). Jimmy Scott, the group's conga player, died of pneumonia.

Bad Manners are still performing, but records – such as 1989's *The Return Of The Ugly* album – are intermittent.

BALDRY, Long John Born in Haddock, Derbyshire, on 12 January 1941, blues singer Long John Baldry began performing in London clubs and coffee bars in 1961. He appeared in bands such as Blues Incorporated and Cyril Davies' All Stars before fronting the Hoochie Coochie Men. He was also to appear with Steampacket and Bluesology.

The 6ft 7in singer topped the chart with 'When The Heartaches Begin' in 1967, following up with 'When The Sun Comes Shinin' Through'. In 1968 he entered the chart with 'Mexico', the Olympic Games theme, and his final chart entry was 'It's Too Late Now' in 1969.

Baldry left the UK and emigrated to Canada, initially appearing on the club scene there. Heavily bearded and a naturalized Canadian, he returned to the UK for a tour in 1993, the year in which he was heard as the voice of Captain Robotnick in the *Sonic The Hedgehog* cartoon.

BALL, Kenny The trad jazz boom in the UK spawned scores of jazz bands, but the field was dominated by the three Bs: Kenny Ball, **Acker Bilk** and Chris Barber.

Trumpeter Ball, who was born on 22 May 1931, formed his Jazzmen in 1958. Hits in the singles chart stretched from 1961 to 1967. They were: 'Samantha', 'I Still Love You All', 'Someday', 'Midnight In Moscow', 'March Of The Siamese Children', 'The Green Leaves Of Summer', 'So Do I', 'The Pay Off', 'Sukiyaki', 'Casablanca', 'Rondo',' Acapulco', 'Hello Dolly' and 'When I'm 64'.

Kenny Ball (centre) and his Jazzmen

Both Ball and Bilk were to have a major hit single in the US, Ball charting with his 'Midnight In Moscow' in 1962.

In 1985, Kenny Ball's was the first British jazz outfit to perform in Russia, a country that has been included on Ball's busy concert itinerary ever since – 'Midnight In Moscow' is no doubt one of his most requested numbers there!

BANANARAMA Sarah Dallin, Keren Woodward and Siobhan Fahey got together in 1981 and began singing in London pubs. They recorded an indie single that year, 'Ai A Mwana' and then signed with London Records.

Male vocal trio **Fun Boy Three** invited them to provide backing vocals to their single 'It Ain't What You Do, It's The Way That You Do It', which became a UK Top 5 hit. Fun Boy Three then provided backing vocals to the Bananarama single 'Really Sayin' Something', which also reached the UK Top 5.

The trio then enjoyed a huge chart run in the 1980s, during which their other hit singles were: 'Shy Boy', 'Cheers Then', 'Na Na Hey Hey Kiss Him Goodbye', 'Cruel Summer', 'Robert De Niro's Waiting', 'Rough Justice', 'Hotline To Heaven', 'Do Not Disturb', 'Venus', 'More Than Physical', 'Trick Of The Night', 'I Heard A Rumour', 'Love In The First Degree', 'I Can't Help It', 'I Want You Back', 'Love Truth And Honesty', 'Nathan Jones', 'Only Your Love', 'Preacher Man', 'Long Train Running', 'Goodbye Cruel World', 'Movin' On' and 'More More More'.

Siohban Fahey married Dave Stewart of the Eurythmics and left Bananarama in 1988, initially moving to Los Angeles. Jackie Sullivan replaced her in Bananarama.

Siobhan has since had big hits in the 1990s with Shakespear's Sister, (the missing 'e' is deliberate), a duo she formed in partnership with Marcella Detroit, a singer from New York. Their hits included 'You're History', 'Stay' (which topped the UK chart), 'Hello (Turn Your Radio On)' and 'I Don't Care'.

The two split in 1993, Detroit enjoying success as a solo artist while Fahey concentrated on family life, until she decided to launch her solo career in late 1996.

After Sullivan left, Dallin and Woodward continued Bananarama as a duo, entering the chart for the last time in November 1992 with 'Last Thing On My Mind' and then disbanding the group the following year.

BANGLES, The Sisters Vickie and Debbi Peterson, guitarist and drummer respectively and both vocalists, formed a group called the Bangs in Los Angeles in 1981. The other members were vocalist Susanna Hoffs and bass guitarist Annette Zilinskas. They then discovered that another group already existed called the Bangs, so they changed their name to the Bangles.

Prince, writing under the name Christopher, penned their hit 'Manic Monday', which reached No 2 in both the UK and US charts. They followed with 'If She Knew What She Wants' and 'Going Down To Liverpool'. 'Walk Like An Egyptian' topped the US chart and 'Eternal Flame' became their second US chart-topper. Other hit singles included 'Walking Down Your Street', 'Following', 'Hazy Shade Of Winter',' In Your Room' and 'Be With You'.

In 1989 the group announced they were splitting, as Hoffs intended to pursue a solo career. In 1991 her solo album was released, and she also charted with the single 'My Side Of The Bed'. 1995 saw Hoffs and her husband M. Jay Roach celebrating the birth of their son, Jackson.

Bangles Greatest Hits was issued in 1989 and went gold, and by 1995 their album *A Different Light* had notched up three million sales.

BARCLAY JAMES HARVEST The members of this group, originally formed in Oldham, Lancashire, in 1967, were Stuart John Wolstenholme, Melvin John Pritchard, John Lees and Les Holroyd. Appropriately, they signed with the Harvest label in 1967.

The band charted with their EP 'Live' in 1977 and followed with 'Love On The Line', 'Life Is For Living' and 'Just A Day Away' in the singles chart.

Their album entries included: *Barclay James Harvest, Time Honoured Ghost, Otoberon, Gone To Earth, Barclay James Harvest XII, Turn Of The Tide, A Concert For The People, Ring Of Changes, Victims Of Circumstance, Face To Face* and *Welcome To The Show*.

Since peaking in the UK in 1982 with *A Concert For The People* at No 15 in the album chart, Barclay James Harvest have consolidated their far greater popularity in Europe – particularly in Germany, but with concert performances in France, Belgium, Denmark, Austria, Switzerland, Spain and Portugal as well. They ended the 1980s with their album *Glasnost (Live)*, which was recorded in East Berlin in 1987.

In 1992 the group celebrated their twenty-fifth anniversary with a concert in Liverpool, and during that year three retrospective albums were issued: *The Best Of Barclay James Harvest*, *Alone We Fly* and *The Harvest Years*.

1995 saw the release of a new album, *Caught In The Light*.

BARRON KNIGHTS, The   Originally formed in 1960, the Barron Knights received a Gold Award from BASCA (British Academy Of Songwriters, Composers And Authors) in 1995 acknowledging their lifetime achievement in music.

The original group members were Duke D'mond (vocals and rhythm), Butch Baker (guitar, banjo and vocals), P'nut Langford (guitar, vocals), Barron Anthony (bass and vocals) and Dave Ballinger (drums). A comedy-music act, with a wide-ranging performance taking in styles from Tamla Motown to classical to rock 'n' roll, they made their chart debut in 1964 with 'Call Up The Groups', a spoof on the then current beat boom.

The group continued to have hits throughout the 1960s, 1970s and 1980s. These included: 'Come To The Dance', 'Pop Go The Workers', 'Merry Gentle Pops', 'Under New Management', 'An Olympic Record', 'Live In Trouble', 'A Taste Of Aggro', 'Food For Thought', 'The Sit Song', 'Never Mind The Presents', 'Blackboard Jumble' and 'Buffalo Bill's Last Scratch'.

Before health problems hastened Anthony's departure from the group, Rick Huxley (ex-**Dave Clark Five**) deputized for him on at least one occasion.

When Ballinger was hospitalized, the group found a replacement – and Ballinger later sued them in the High Court.

Still a popular live performing act, the Barron Knights currently appear regularly in theatres, cabaret and sixties revival shows, with the original members Duke, P'nut and Butch joined by Gareth Watt-Roy on bass and Lloyd Courtnay on drums.

BARRY, John   Born Jonathan Barry Prendergast in York on 3 November 1933, this musician-composer formed the John Barry Seven and enjoyed several UK chart hits, including 'Hit And Miss', 'Walk Don't Run', 'Black Stockings', 'The Magnificent Seven' and 'Cutty Sark'.

Then, as simply John Barry or with the John Barry Orchestra, his hits included 'Beat For Beatniks', 'Never Let Go', 'Blueberry Hill', 'The James Bond Theme', 'From Russia With Love' and 'The Persuaders'. It was Barry's version of 'Hit And Miss' which was used as the theme tune to the UK television series *Juke Box Jury*.

Barry became noted for creating the James Bond theme music and for the incidental music in the Bond films. This in turn led to him becoming one of the most prolific composers of film soundtracks and his music has accompanied literally scores of movies, including *Born Free*, *The Knack*, *The Ipcress File*, *The Lion In Winter*, *Out Of Africa* and *Dances With Wolves*.

In 1997, Barry masterminded *Shaken Not Stirred*, a collection of interpretations of James Bond themes by artists as diverse as Pulp and **Iggy Pop**. He also began recording an all-new non-film album entitled *The Beyondness Of Things*. In the same year *The Best Of John Barry: Themeology*, a 23-track CD, was issued.

During 1998 Barry embarked on a UK tour, which included a Royal Albert Hall appearance on 18 April, performing his film music with the 87-piece English Chamber Orchestra.

BARRY, Len   This American singer was born Leonard Borisoff in Philadelphia, Pennsylvania, on 12 June 1942. For a number of years he was lead singer with the Dovells, but left the group for a solo career, making his recording debut as Len Barry with 'Lip Sync'. He hit No 2 in the US chart with his second release, '1-2-3'. His other hits – 'Like A Baby', 'Somewhere' and 'It's That Time Of Year' – were all released within a 12-month period. Later in the 1960s he concentrated on songwriting and production.

Len Barry was struck down by a bout of salmonella poisoning during a nostalgia tour of the UK – the first of many – in 1991.

BART, Lionel   Born Lionel Begleiter in London on 1 August 1930, this composer was an original member of Tommy Steele's backing band the Cavemen and wrote 'Rock With The Caveman', along with other Steele hits such as 'A Handful Of Songs', 'Water Water' and 'Little White Bull'. He also composed songs for the stage shows *Lock Up Your Daughters* and *Fings Ain't Wot They Used To Be*, in addition to writing hits such as 'Living Doll' for **Cliff Richard**.

Bart's biggest success was composing the music for *Oliver!* in 1960. He became rich on the proceeds, although his other musicals – which included *Blitz!*, *Maggie May* and *Twang* – did not

21

fare so well. He suffered from alcoholism, spent his money and was declared bankrupt in 1972.

From his home in Acton, west London, Bart attempted comebacks, composing musicals such as *Gulliver*, which was never staged, and from 1965 on he had been working on *Quasimodo*, a musical based on the story of the hunchback of Notre Dame. Another brief moment of fame occurred in 1989, when he recorded a television advertisement for the Abbey National Building Society with a cute song called 'Happy Endings'.

In 1995, *Oliver!* was staged once more in the West End of London and became a hit all over again. However, Bart had sold his rights to the show in 1966 when he had originally faced financial ruin. Cameron Mackintosh, producer of the 1990s West End version, decided to give Lionel a percentage of the profit made by the musical, which assured him of an income for life.

BASIL, Toni

Born in 1950, American choreographer Toni Basil had a very successful career in the US, particularly in association with popular music, and was involved in films such as *Head*, which starred the **Monkees**, and *American Grafitti*. She also had her own dance troupe, the Lockers.

In 1981 Basil ventured into the realm of song and recorded a successful album, *Word Of Mouth*. The following year she had two chart hits, 'Mickey' and' Nobody', hitting the bestseller lists on both sides of the Atlantic. After a further album, *Toni Basil*, released in 1983, she returned to her former lucrative profession.

Within the entertainment industry, these days Toni Basil is better known as an in-demand choreographer than chart contender.

BASS, Fontella

A soul singer and pianist, Fontella Bass was born in St Louis, Missouri, on 3 July 1940. At the age of five she began singing and playing piano with a church choir. She was heard performing in church by Little Milton and was invited to play in his band. After performing with Milton for four years, she teamed up on record with Bobby McClure. The duo entered the US chart with 'Don't Mess Up A Good Thing' and 'You'll Miss Me (When I'm Gone)'.

Bass then had two hits as a solo artist, the million-selling 'Rescue Me' in 1965, followed by 'Recovery' in 1966. She also toured the UK in 1965 and 1966. In 1972 she recorded the album *The Art Ensemble Of Chicago With Fontella Bass*.

After her recording collaborations with her husband, the jazz trumpeter Lester Bowie, she now concentrates on gospel singing.

BASSEY, Shirley

Born in Tiger Bay, Cardiff, on 8 January 1937, this singer was the youngest of the seven children of a Nigerian seaman and Yorkshire-born woman, who were divorced when Shirley was two years old.

She recorded her first hit, 'The Banana Boat Song', in 1957. Her other chart entries included: 'Fire Down Below', 'You You Romeo', 'As I Love You', 'Kiss Me Honey Honey Kiss Me', 'With These Hands', 'As Long As He Needs Me', 'You'll Never Know', 'Reach For The Stars/Climb Every Mountain', 'I'll Get By', 'Tonight', 'Ave Maria', 'Far Away', 'What Now My Love', 'What Kind Of Fool Am I?', 'I (Who Have Nothing)', 'My Special Dream', 'Gone', 'Goldfinger', 'No Regrets', 'Big Spender', 'Something', 'The Fool On The Hill', 'Love Story', 'For All We Know', 'Diamonds Are Forever' and 'Never Never Never'.

Following 'Never Never Never' in 1973, 14 years were to pass before 'The Rhythm Divine' entered the chart in 1987. There was then another gap of several years before 'Diso' La Passione' in 1996.

Shirley's powerful voice, used to dramatic effect in the delivery of a number of her songs, her glamorous wardrobes and her sheer vocal passion have maintained a huge fan following over the years. She is also an icon of the gay community. Her success was international and she is best remembered for the James Bond movie theme songs 'Goldfinger', 'Diamonds Are Forever' and 'Moonraker'. She has had hits with numbers from several musicals, some of which she has made uniquely her own, including 'Big Spender' from *Sweet Charity*. She received a Brittania Award in 1977 as the Best Female Solo Singer In The Last 50 Years.

Shirley's first husband, film producer Kenneth Hume, committed suicide soon after their divorce in 1965. Of her three children, tragically, her daughter Samantha drowned, reputedly after jumping off the Clifton Suspension Bridge in Bristol. Her surviving daughter, Sharon, has three children and Shirley also has an adopted son, Mark, who lives in Spain with his daughter Tatjana. Shirley's second marriage to Italian hotelier Sergio Novak also ended in divorce in 1981.

The Welsh diva announced her semi-retirement in 1981, initially emerging only for television specials and a tour to celebrate her fortieth anniversary in the business in 1994. In January 1996, stars gathered for a television tribute, *An Evening With Shirley Bassey*, on her sixtieth birthday.

Of her almost 50 albums, Shirley's chart releases have included: *Fabulous Shirley Bassey, Shirley, Shirley Bassey, Let's Face The Music, Shirley Bassey At The Pigalle, I've Got A Song For You, Twelve Of Those Songs, Golden Hits Of Shirley Bassey, Live At The Talk Of The Town, Something, Something Else, Big Spender, It's Magic, The Fabulous Shirley Bassey, What Now My Love, The Shirley Bassey Collection, I Capricorn, And I Love You So, Never Never Never, The Shirley Bassey Singles Album, Good Bad But Beautiful, Love Live And Feelings, Twenty-fifth Anniversary Album, The Magic Is You, Love Songs* and *I Am What I Am*.

Shirley's album *The Birthday Concert* was released in November 1997, and the following month a television documentary, *Shirley Bassey: This Is My Life*, was screened. It covered her appearance at the Carnegie Hall, New York, in October 1996 and her 1997 appearances in Antwerp, Atlantic City and Hollywood. It also showed her entertaining friends at her Monte Carlo home, where she had lived for the previous six years. In addition, she was featured during her recording session for 'History Repeating', the 1997 single that she made with the Propellerheads.

Shirley began a UK tour, called the Diamond Tour, in June 1998.

BAY CITY ROLLERS, The

This Scottish group became massive stars in the 1970s with a string of hits and their own television series. Edinburgh-born Derek Longmuir on drums and his brother Alan on bass originally formed a band in 1967, but it wasn't until the early 1970s and the inclusion of three other musicians from Edinburgh that they achieved teenybopper stardom, dressed in their tartan scarves and trousers.

With singer Les McKeown, and guitarists Stuart Wood and Eric Faulkner, the Bay City Rollers had a dozen hits, including two consecutive chart-toppers, between 1971 and 1977. They were: 'Keep On Dancing', 'Remember (Sha-La-La)', 'Shang-A-Lang', 'Summerlove Sensations', 'All Of Me Loved All Of You', 'Bye Bye Baby', 'Give A Little Love', 'Money Honey', 'Love Me Like I Love You',' I Only Wanna Be With You', 'It's A Game' and 'You Made Me Believe In Magic'. The group even topped the US chart in 1975 with 'Saturday Night'. They were also joined by two other members, Ian Mitchell and Billy Lyall.

The group then suffered several strokes of ill fortune before they split.

Their manager Tam Paton was gaoled for three years in 1982 for committing indecent acts with under-age teenagers.

'Post-fame syndrome' is a state of depression suffered by stars whose career is on the wane, and Faulkner and Alan Longmuir both attempted suicide.

Bad luck continued to dog the members and McKeown killed a 75-year-old woman in a car accident and was charged with reckless driving.

In 1989 Lyall died from an AIDS-related illness.

It was a distressing time for McKeown to find himself virtually penniless. He said: 'One day this man turned up at my house, told me my bank account had been emptied and instructed me to move out. My mum and dad lived with me and they suddenly found themselves without a home.' He added: 'People who used to be your friends melt away. Betray you.'

However, he formed Les McKeown's Bay City Rollers with Mitchell and continued to sing. The group have become popular in Europe and appeared before an audience of 24,000 in Berlin.

Alan Longmuir, together with Eric Faulkner, his girlfriend Kass and Stuart Wood, re-formed as the Bay City Rollers and toured Japan in 1996. Alan's brother Derek decided not to join them, preferring to become a registered nurse in Edinburgh instead.

B. BUMBLE & THE STINGERS

This group originally charted in 1961 with 'Bumble Boogie', which was an instrumental pop version of Rimsky-Korsakov's *Flight Of The Bumble Bee*.

In 1962 they produced their most noted release, 'Nut Rocker', based on Tchaikovsky's *Nutcracker Suite*, which topped the chart in the UK. It also re-entered the UK chart exactly ten years later in 1972.

Producer Kim Fowley had conceived the group, using pianist Ernie Freeman as the 'B. Bumble' in the studio. Due to their chart-topper, a UK tour was hastily arranged with various musicians, including R.C. Gamble, who took on the name of B. Bumble. The Stingers who toured with him were Terry Anderson (guitar), Jimmy King (rhythm) and Don Orr (drums).

The musicians on the celebrated 'Nut Rocker' returned to session work in Los Angeles, while producer Kim Fowley maintained a higher profile via his involvement with all manner of chart acts over the next 30 years.

BEACH BOYS, The   This group was originally formed in 1961 by the brothers Brian, **Carl** and **Dennis Wilson**, together with their cousin Mike Love and friend Al Jardine. In 1962 Jardine left, to be replaced by David Marks. On completing a course in dentistry, he returned to the group in mid-1963 and Marks left.

Over the years, the Beach Boys' hit singles have included: 'Surfin' Safari', 'Surfin' USA', 'Shut Down', 'Surfer Girl', 'Little Deuce Coupe', 'Be True To Your School', 'In My Room', 'Fun Fun Fun', 'I Get Around', 'Don't Worry Baby', 'When I Grow Up (To Be A Man)', 'Dance Dance Dance', 'Do You Wanna Dance', 'Help Me Rhonda', 'California Girls', 'The Little Girl I Once Knew', 'Barbara Ann', 'Sloop John B', 'Wouldn't It Be Nice', 'God Only Knows', 'Heroes And Villains', 'Wild Honey', 'Darlin'', 'Do It Again', 'I Can Hear Music', 'Rock And Roll Music', 'It's OK', 'Good Timin'' and 'Come Go With Me'.

Album hits included: *Surfin' USA*, *Beach Boys Party*, *Beach Boys Today*, *Pet Sounds*, *Summer Days*, *Best Of The Beach Boys*, *Surfer Girl*, *Best Of The Beach Boys Vol 3*, *Smiley Smile*, *Wild Honey*, *Friends*, *20/20*, *Greatest Hits*, *Sunflower*, *Surf's Up*, *Carl and The Passionate Tough*, *Holland*, *15 Big Ones*, *The Beach Boys Love You*, *La (Light Album)*, *The Very Best Of The Beach Boys* and *Beach Boys*.

In late 1964, Brian Wilson, who suffered from partial deafness, collapsed from a nervous breakdown and decided he would no longer make live appearances with the group. **Glen Campbell** replaced him for a few months, then Bruce Johnson took over. Johnson remained with the group until 1972, when Blondie Chaplin replaced him. Chaplin, together with another short-term member Ricky Fataar, left the group in 1974 and Dennis Wilson, who had been involved in a solo career, re-joined, this time as drummer. Tragically, he drowned in 1983.

In 1990 a television movie biopic, *Heroes & Villains: The True Story Of The Beach Boys*, was aired, and in 1991 Brian published his autobiography, *Wouldn't It Be Nice*.

The Beach Boys appeared in the UK once again in 1996. In October 1997 EMI issued a boxed set called *Pet Sounds Sessions*, consisting of four CDs that included the original mono mix, previously unreleased instrumentals, vocals-only renditions and a new stereo mix. Carl Wilson died from liver cancer in February 1998.

In December 1998 their album *Ultimate Christmas* was issued, containing 26 original songs which had never been released previously.

BE-BOP DE LUXE   This group was formed in Wakefield, Yorkshire, in 1971 by guitarist Bill Nelson. Ian Parkin, Rob Bryan and Nicholas Chatterton-Dew joined him.

They made their album debut with *Axe Victim* in 1974, but Nelson was disappointed with the result and changed the group completely,

The Beach Boys

dispensing with the services of Parkin, Bryan and Chatterton-Dew and bringing in Charlie Tummahai on bass, Simon Fox on drums and Andrew Clarke on keyboards. Their next album, *Futurama*, proved more satisfactory to Nelson. Their third album was *Sunburst Finish* and one of the tracks, 'Ships In The Night', gave them their first hit single, which was followed by an EP, 'Hot Valves', which also charted.

Nelson once again became disillusioned and the group disbanded in 1978. Throughout the years he has resisted all offers to re-form it.

Nelson still resides in Yorkshire where, via his own studio and record label, he issues all manner of retrospective and new collections. Scheduled for release in 1998 was the second in a trilogy of albums based loosely on the theme of childhood.

BECK, Jeff Born in Wallingford, Surrey, on 24 June 1944, guitarist and reluctant singer Jeff Beck was a member of **Screaming Lord Sutch** & the Nightshift and the Tridents, and replaced Eric Clapton in the **Yardbirds** in 1965. He left the following year to form a trio, the Jeff Beck Group, with Ron Wood on bass and Aynsley Dunbar on drums. In 1967 Mickie Most produced him singing and performing on 'Hi Ho Silver Lining', which became his biggest hit in the singles chart.

When Dunbar left to form his own band Ray Cook replaced him, and was himself replaced by Mickie Waller, who was then replaced by Tony Newman. Nicky Hopkins also joined on keyboards. They released their debut album, *Truth*, in 1968, followed by *Beck-Ola* the next year.

After a period in hospital following a car accident, Beck re-formed his band with Bobby Tench on vocals, **Cozy Powell** on drums, Clive Chaman on bass and Max Middleton on drums. They issued two albums, *Rough And Ready* and *Jeff Beck Group*.

Beck then teamed up with American musicians Tom Bogart and Carmine Appice to form Beck, Bogert & Appice in 1973, and they issued the album *Jeff Beck, Tom Bogert & Carmine Appice*. The trio split the following year

Over the years Beck continued to perform with various line-ups, teaming up with different musicians and issuing a series of albums, including: *Blow By Blow*, *Wires*, *Jeff Beck With The Jan Hammer Group Live*, *There And Back*, *Flash*, *Jeff Beck's Guitar Shop With Terry Bozzio And Tony Hymas* and *Crazy Legs*. In 1995 he promoted his new *Greatest Hits* release on a US tour.

Jeff Beck now lives in Sussex. He contributed musically to the UK television series *Glam Metal Detectives*, and has appeared in cameo in Comic Strip productions. A new album is currently in preparation.

BEE GEES, The Barry Gibb and his twin brothers Robin and Maurice were all born on the Isle of Man and raised in Chorlton-cum-Hardy. Their mother Barbara was a singer, their father Hugh the leader of an orchestra. Six months after their brother **Andy** was born in 1958, the family emigrated to Australia.

The three elder Gibb boys had already been performing as a trio in Manchester, with their first professional performance taking place in 1955. In Brisbane, Bill Good introduced them to disc jockey Bill Gates, who began playing their tapes on his radio show. Good named the group the B.G.s after the initials of himself and Gates. By 1962 they had moved to Sydney and changed their name to the Bee Gees.

After several chart entries in Australia, the group moved to London in 1967. They approached **Brian Epstein's** office to see if he would manage them and met up with Robert Stigwood, who worked for Epstein at the time. Young Australian actor Colin Peterson joined them on drums. They were signed to Nems Enterprises and their hit streak began. When Epstein died, a deal was made which included Stigwood taking acts such as the Bee Gees and **Cream** with him.

The Bee Gees' recording success has been phenomenal and their hit singles have included: 'New York Mining Disaster', 'To Love Somebody', 'Massachusetts', 'World', 'Words', 'Jumbo', 'I've Gotta Get A Message To You', 'First Of May', 'Tomorrow Tomorrow', 'Don't Forget To Remember', 'I.O.I.O.', 'Lonely Days', 'My World', 'Run To Me', 'Jive Talkin'', 'You Should Be Dancing', 'Love So Right', 'How Deep Is Your Love', 'Stayin' Alive', 'Night Fever', 'Too Much Heaven', 'Tragedy', 'Love You Inside Out', 'Spirits (Having Flown)', 'Someone Belonging To Someone', 'You Win Again', 'E.S.P.', 'One', 'Ordinary Lives', 'Secret Love' and 'Paying The Price Of Love'.

Album successes have included: *Bee Gees First*, *Horizontal*, *Idea*, *Odessa*, *Best Of The Bee Gees*, *Cucumber Castle*, *Spirits Having Flown*, *Bee Gees Greatest* and *Living Eyes*.

1969 proved an eventful year, with Peterson being sacked, Robin embarking on a solo career

– which resulted in Stigwood suing him – and Maurice marrying **Lulu**. They were separated in 1973 and later divorced, and he then married Yvonne Spencely in 1975. Robin's hits included 'Saved By The Bell', 'August October' and 'Another Lonely Night in New York'.

Barry was also to prove very successful as a songwriter and producer, penning and producing **Barbra Streisand's** 'Woman In Love' and her album *Guilty*. He was to write many hits for other artists such as **Dionne Warwick** and Diana Ross, and also had a solo hit with 'Shine Shine'.

The brothers were reunited as the Bee Gees in 1971 and continued as a trio.

Their younger brother Andy was also to embark on a singing career and his hits included: 'I Just Want To Be Your Everything', '(Love Is) Thicker Than Water', 'Shadow Dancing', 'An Everlasting Love', '(Our Love) Don't Throw It All Away', 'Desire', 'Time Is Time' and 'Me (Without You)'. Sadly, Andy became a drug addict and was declared bankrupt, owing over $1m; he died from heart failure in 1988 in hospital in Oxfordshire.

On Sunday, 2 March 1997 an edition of the UK television programme *The South Bank Show* was dedicated to the group. In October that year, the brothers Gibb stormed off camera five minutes into an interview on *Clive Anderson All Talk* after an altercation with the host. At the time, their latest single, 'Still Waters', was dropping out of the UK Top 20.

BELAFONTE, Harry   Born in New York on 1 March 1927, actor-singer-songwriter Harry Belafonte moved to Jamaica with his family when he was five years old and returned to New York, where he joined the US Army in 1944. After his two-year tour of duty he joined a drama workshop.

It was in 1950 that he began performing as a folk singer, backed by two guitarists, Millard Thomas and Craig Work. During the 1950s he had several hits, which were to bring him the nickname 'King Of Calypso'. His records included: 'The Banana Boat Song', 'Island In The Sun', 'Mama Look At Bubu' and 'Mary's Boy Child'. His strong film roles during the decade included parts in *Bright Road*, *Carmen Jones* and *Island In The Sun*.

Over the years Belafonte appeared in numerous other films, including *The World, The Flesh And The Devil*, *Odds Against Tomorrow*, *The Angel*

Harry Belafonte

Levine, *Buck & The Preacher* and *Uptown Saturday Night*. He also became an ambassador for the Peace Corps.

In the 1980s, Belafonte was a leading light in the USA For Africa appeal and was heard on the organization's million-selling 1985 single, 'We Are The World'. In the 1990s, his continuing charity activities were mainly for UNICEF, but he also returned to the big screen scene, accepting film roles once again.

Belafonte has four children: two girls, Adrienne and Shari, by a former marriage, and David Michael and Gina with his wife, Julie Robinson. Harry and Julie currently live in a house in New York City and a farm in upstate New York. In 1998, his daughter Shari appeared in a *Babylon Five* US television movie.

BENNETT, Cliff   Born in Slough, Berkshire, on 4 June 1940, singer Cliff Bennett first formed the Acme Skiffle Group with some friends. The end of the skiffle boom led to a change of music and a new name. Inspired by the Duane Eddy hit, Cliff called his band the Rebel Rousers.

The group first came to the attention of **Brian Epstein** at the Star Club in Hamburg. Members included Frank Allen (bass), Sid Phillips (piano and sax), Mick King (lead) and Moss Groves (sax). In 1964 Allen left them to replace Tony Jackson in the **Searchers**. The group signed with Epstein and celebrated their first hit, 'One Way Love'. They followed with a minor hit, 'I'll Take You Home', then sped up the charts with the Lennon & McCartney track from the *Revolver* album, 'Got To Get You Into My Life'.

The Rebel Rousers disbanded in 1969 when Cliff changed direction and called his new outfit Toe Fat. They were not successful, so he formed a new group, Rebellion, three years later and another outfit, Shanghai, three years after that.

Cliff decided to leave showbusiness and found a job with the P&O shipping line. He did so much business with Middle Eastern clients that he eventually formed his own shipping company, whose customers include the Emir of Bahrain.

After being enticed to perform at a charity concert at the Odeon, Hammersmith, in the mid-1980s, he made occasional appearances in various clubs, including a **Joe Meek** tribute show at the Odeon, Lewisham, in 1991 along with **Mike Berry**, **Heinz**, the **Honeycombs**, **Screaming Lord Sutch**, the **Tornados** and Danny Rivers.

Although still continuing with his business, Cliff has re-formed the Rebel Rousers and is now on the road, with his son-in-law attending to the business during his absences. Performing on the sixties nostalgia circuit, his 1997 repertoire included: 'One Way Love', 'I'll Take You Home', 'Back In The USSR', 'Soul Man', 'If You Gotta Make A Fool Of Somebody', 'Got To Get You Into My Life' and 'Hold On I'm Coming'.

BENNETT, Tony Born Anthony Domenick Benedetto on 3 August 1926 in New York, Tony Bennett made his debut appearance as a singer in a church minstrel show at the age of seven. His career was put on hold during World War II when he was posted to Europe as an infantryman.

A post-war appearance on the *Arthur Godfrey Talent Show* led to a television contract. In 1953 he recorded 'Stranger In Paradise', from the musical *Kismet*. Bennett's version of the number topped the UK chart when the show opened in London in 1955.

His other hits have included: 'Can You Find It In Your Heart', 'From The Candy Store On The Corner To The Chapel On The Hill', 'The Autumn Waltz', 'In The Middle Of An Island', 'Ça, C'est L'Amour', 'Young And Warm And Wonderful', 'Firefly', 'I Left My Heart In San Francisco', 'I Wanna Be Around', 'The Good Life', 'Who Can I Turn To' and 'If I Ruled The World'.

Bennett, who lives in New York, is still an active performer and recording artist. His 1996 album, *For The Ladies*, received a Grammy Award and he issued a new album, *On Holiday*, in May 1997. In recent years, Tony Bennett's re-evaluation by a young audience was exemplified by releases that embraced a duet with **Elvis Costello**.

BERN ELLIOTT & THE FENMEN The members of this group, originally formed in Erith, Kent, in 1961, were Bern Elliott (vocals), Alan Jump (lead), Wally Allen (rhythm), Eric Willmer (bass) and John Povey (drums). It was while they were at the Star Club in Hamburg that they heard the **Searchers** performing 'Money' and decided to record it. The number gave them their first hit in 1963 and they also charted with 'New Orleans' in 1964. The group split from Bern Elliott in 1964, but neither had any further success of note on record, although the Fenmen reached the lower reaches of the chart with 'Rag Doll'.

Elliott formed another group called the Klan with Dave Cameron (organ and guitar), Tim Hamilton (rhythm), John Silby-Pearce (bass) and Pete Adams (drums). They had a minor hit with 'Voodoo Woman' in 1965.

Two former Fenmen, Wally Allen and John Povey, are members of the present-day **Pretty Things**, having joined the group in 1968.

BERRY, Chuck The legendary rock singer-songwriter was born Charles Edward Berry in San Jose, California, on 18 October 1926. In 1955 he recorded some of his songs on an audition tape and took them to Chess Records. As a result, 'Maybellene' was released.

Berry then came out with a stream of rock classics: 'Brown-eyed Handsome Man', 'Roll Over Beethoven', 'Sweet Little Sixteen', 'School Day', 'Johnny B. Goode', 'Rock 'n' Roll Music', 'Reelin' And Rockin'' and 'Memphis Tennessee'. During his live performances he developed a style of hopping across the stage, which became known as his 'duck walk'. He also began to appear in movies such as *Go Johnny Go*, *Rock Rock Rock* and *Jazz On A Summer's Day*.

27

In 1959 Berry was gaoled for taking an under-age girl across state lines. On his release from prison in 1964 he issued further hit singles – 'Nadine', 'No Particular Place To Go', 'You Never Can Tell' – and then toured the UK with Carl Perkins. He toured the UK again in 1972 and had another huge hit with 'My-Ding-A-Ling', which topped the charts on both sides of the Atlantic.

Throughout his career, Berry has received many honours from the music industry and has also been involved in various tangles with the law. In 1989, action was brought against him by over 200 women regarding allegations that he had secretly installed video-recording equipment in the ladies' toilets of his restaurant. In 1990, his house was raided by the police who seized weapons, drugs, cash and homemade pornographic videos. He was involved in further legal tussles in 1993.

1987 saw the publication of *Chuck Berry: The Autobiography* and also the release of a film biography, *Hail! Hail! Rock & Roll*.

Chuck Berry still tours the world regularly.

BERRY, Dave Born in Woodhouse, Yorkshire, on 6 February 1941, David Grundy was asked by a local outfit, the Chuck Fowler Band, to become their lead singer in 1961, when their leader joined the army. They decided to rename the band Dave Berry & the Cruisers, with Dave adopting the surname of his idol, **Chuck Berry**. The other members of the group were Frank Miles (lead), Alan Taylor (rhythm), John Fleet (bass) and Kenny Slade (drums).

In 1963 their debut single, 'Memphis Tennessee', was released. Chuck Berry's original version was swiftly reissued and both versions entered the Top 20. Dave developed a specific image for his performances, dressing completely in black and creating a theatrical style of delivery when singing.

Following hits with 'My Baby Left Me', 'Baby It's You' and 'The Crying Game', Dave then split with the Cruisers and formed a new band, which he also called the Cruisers. His other hits included 'One Heart Between Two', 'Little Things', 'This Strange Effect' and 'Mama'.

Dave Berry lives in Derbyshire. He remains an active recording artist and an enormous star in the Netherlands, while working the sixties nostalgia circuit at home. He still names his backing band the Cruisers, although they have undergone many personnel changes over the years.

His policy is to employ young musicians and the most recent member is 21-year-old Chris Firminger, who joined in September 1997, prior to Berry's appearance on the *QE2* on a Caribbean nostalgia cruise.

During 1997, when Dave Berry appeared on a nationwide tour with Peter Noone, **Gerry & the Pacemakers** and **Wayne Fontana**, he also celebrated his thirtieth wedding anniversary. He met his wife, Marthy Van Lopik, when he first went to Belgium for the Knokke Song Festival in 1965, following which he topped the Belgian charts with 'This Strange Effect', which became that country's biggest-ever singles seller. Marthy and Dave, who were married in 1967, have a daughter, Tania.

BERRY, Mike Born Michael Bourne in Hackney, east London, in 1943, this singer first led Kenny Lord & the Statesmen and was given the name Mike Berry by **Joe Meek**, who produced his first Decca single, 'Will You Love Me Tomorrow'. His 'Tribute To Buddy Holly' almost charted in 1961. Among the musicians in Berry's backing band, the Outlaws, were Ritchie Blackmore and Chas Hodges.

Mike Berry

1963 saw Berry hit the chart with another Joe Meek production, 'Don't You Think It's Time', followed by 'My Little Baby', which charted the same year.

During the 1970s, he pursued a career as an actor, appearing in UK television series such as *Worzel Gummidge* and *Are You Being Served?*.

Berry returned to the charts in 1980, 17 years after his last hit, with his biggest-selling record of all, 'The Sunshine Of Your Smile', which was produced by a former Outlaw, Chas Hodges. He followed with two further chart entries, 'If I Could Only Make You Care' and 'Memories'.

Mike Berry is still singing and is back on the sixties nostalgia circuit with a new band, also called the Outlaws. He maintains a foot in the acting world, mostly in television commercials. During the spring of 1997 he was touring in the musical *Stupid Cupid*.

BEST, Pete   The original drummer with the Beatles, Pete Best was born in Madras, India, on 24 November 1941. The Quarry Men began playing at his mother's club, the Casbah, in 1959. When they changed their name to the Beatles the following year and were set to appear in Hamburg, they asked Best to join them in August. Over the next two years, in Liverpool and Hamburg, they forged the sound which was to make them famous, but dumped Best when they were on the brink of success and brought in Ringo Starr.

Best had no success with Lee Curtis & the All Stars or his own group, the Pete Best Four. He eventually hung up his drumsticks and became a civil servant, settling down in West Derby Village in Liverpool with his wife Kathy and daughters Beba and Bonita. He took early retirement in 1993.

In the meantime, he had made his first live appearance in 20 years at a Beatles convention at the Adelphi Hotel, Liverpool, in August 1988, and decided to become a musician once more. *Live At The Adelphi*, an album recorded at the gig, was released, followed by *Back To The Beat*, recorded at the Cavern in 1994 and *Once A Beatle, Always*, issued in October 1996.

He also formed the Pete Best Band, with himself and his younger brother Roag on drums. Other members are Vince Hagen (lead), Paul Davies (keyboards), Andrew Cawley (vocals) and Andrew Kirk (bass). The group embarked on a series of world tours and Pete became something of a celebrity when several tracks he recorded with the Beatles were issued on the first *Anthology* CD. His autobiography, *The Best Years Of The Beatles*, was published in 1996.

BEVERLEY SISTERS, The   The vocal trio consisting of Joy Beverley, born in 1929, and her twin sisters Teddie and Babs, born in 1932, had a number of chart entries between 1953 and 1960 – 'I Saw Mommy Kissing Santa Claus', 'Willie Can', 'I Dreamed', 'Little Drummer Boy', 'Little Donkey' and 'Green Fields'.

The girls were a popular cabaret draw, but decided to retire in 1967 to raise their children. Joy married soccer star Billy Wright and they had two children, Vicky and Babette. Teddie had a baby girl, Sasha.

The three daughters followed in their mothers' footsteps and formed a vocal trio called the Little Foxes. Following an appearance at the hip venue the Hippodrome in London, club owner Peter Stringfellow decided to book their mothers and the Beverley Sisters re-formed to appear at a Monday night residency at the club. They were the high spot of the 'gay night', and joined several other female stars such as **Shirley Bassey** and Judy Garland who were classed as gay icons.

Since that remarkable resurgence of interest in the mid-1980s, the Beverley Sisters have appeared in cameo in the UK television sitcom *Girls On Top*. In 1996, it was reported that a pensioner clapped so hard at a more typical Sisters concert that he needed treatment to damaged tendons in his hands.

B52s, The   This group, formed in Georgia in 1976, consisted of Fred Schneider (keyboards and vocals), **Ricky Wilson** (guitar), his sister Cindy (guitar and vocals), Kate Pierson (organ and vocals) and Keith Strickland (drums). The girls wore beehive hairdos as a gimmick and the band took its name from a Southern nickname for the hairstyle.

The group recorded and pressed 2,000 copies of a number called 'Rock Lobster', which came to the attention of Island Records supremo Chris Blackwell, who signed them. Their debut album, *The B52s*, entered the charts on both sides of the Atlantic, and their hit single 'Rock Lobster' was released in 1979. This number was credited with inspiring John Lennon to record again.

On 12 October 1985, Ricky Wilson died from an AIDS-related illness.

The group's other hit singles, recorded after Wilson's death, included: 'Give Me Back My Man', 'Future Generation', 'Rock Lobster/Planet Claire', 'Love Shack' and 'Candy'.

Cindy Wilson left the group in 1990 to embark on a solo career and Julee Cruise replaced her.

In 1995, the B52s appeared in the feature film *The Flintstones* performing '(Meet) The Flintstones' and charted with the number, which was issued under the credit the BC52s.

In 1996, the group began a long sabbatical so that its members could work on individual projects, with Keith Strickland issuing the album *Just Fred*.

BILK, Acker The renowned jazz musician was born Bernard Stanley Bilk in Somerset on 28 January 1929. The name Acker is a Somerset expression meaning 'mate'.

His career as a blacksmith was interrupted by British Army service, and he was placed in an army gaol in Egypt for three months in 1947 as a result of falling asleep on guard. It was while he was in gaol that Acker whiled away the hours learning to play the clarinet. On returning to civilian life, he gave up his job as a blacksmith and took up jazz, forming a group he called the Paramount Jazz Band in 1957. Initially they played around the Bristol area, and then in the beer cellars of Dusseldorf.

Acker had composed a number that he called 'Jenny', after one of his children. In 1961, when he was invited to play a tune on a UK children's television series called *Stranger On The Shore*, he changed the title of his tune to that. The record was eventually to sell over four million copies and topped the charts on both sides of the Atlantic.

Acker Bilk and his Jazz band

Acker's hit run had begun in 1960, and prior to 'Stranger On The Shore' his UK chart entries were: 'Summer Set', 'Goodnight Sweet Prince', 'White Cliffs Of Dover', 'Buona Sera', 'That's My Home' and 'Stars And Stripes Forever'. Following 'Stranger On The Shore', his hits were: 'Frankie And Johnny', 'Gotta See Baby Tonight', 'Lonely', 'A Taste Of Honey' and 'Aria'.

Acker Bilk was the star turn at the televised party for Eurovision Song Contest entrants in 1994. As is the case everywhere else he performs, he was not allowed to quit the stage without giving them 'Stranger On The Shore'.

He currently has homes in London and in the Somerset village of Pensfold, where he was born.

BLACK SABBATH This group originally formed in 1967 and made their recording debut with 'Evil Woman (Don't Play Your Games With Me)' in 1970. The same year, their eponymous debut album was issued. The members were Tony Lommi (guitar), Terry 'Geezer' Butler (bass), Ozzy Osbourne (vocals) and Bill Ward (drums).

Black Sabbath's hit singles included: 'Paranoid', 'Never Say Die', 'Hard Road', 'Neon Knights', 'Die Young', 'Mob Rules' and 'Turn Up The Night'.

Chart albums included: *Black Sabbath, Paranoid, Master Of Reality, Black Sabbath Vol 4, Sabbath Bloody Sabbath, Sabotage, We Sold Our Soul For Rock 'n' Roll, Technical Ecstasy, Never Say Die, Heaven And Hell, Black Sabbath Live At Last, Mob Rules, Live Evil* and *Born Again*.

The heavy metal band became enormously successful on both sides of the Atlantic and embarked on several major tours.

Gradually, the relationship between Osbourne and the other members of the band became strained and he left in 1979 to form Blizzard Of Oz. The group replaced him with Ronnie James Dio. In 1980 Ward also left the band due to ill health and Vinnie Appice replaced him.

More internecine conflicts followed, resulting in Dio quitting and taking Appice with him to form a group called Dio. Dave Donato became lead vocalist for a short time, but he in turn was replaced by Ian Gillan. Ward also returned for a while, but due to ill health had to leave once again, to be replaced by Bev Bevan of the **Electric Light Orchestra**. Within a few months Ward was back, although Gillan was to leave in 1984.

For the Live Aid benefit in July 1985, the original line-up gathered together for the single appearance, then went their separate ways. In 1986 Lommi was the only original member remaining, and the band was billed as Black Sabbath With Tony Lommi. Over the next ten years there were numerous personnel changes.

On 4 and 5 December 1997, for the first time since 1974 (apart from the Live Aid concert), the original members of the group re-formed for two major shows at Birmingham National Exhibition Centre. Black Sabbath had actually re-formed earlier in 1997 to tour the US, but Ward wasn't with them and Mike Bordin of Faith No More occupied the drum seat. The 49-year-old Ward had been reluctant to appear on tour with them, due to his continuing health problems, but finally agreed to perform at the Birmingham concerts.

BLIND FAITH This supergroup, formed in 1969, consisted of Eric Clapton (guitar and vocals), **Stevie Winwood** (keyboards, guitar and vocals), **Rick Grech** (bass, violin and vocals) and Ginger Baker (drums).

Blind Faith were to last for only a very short time, cutting one chart album, *Blind Faith*, in 1969 and making their debut in June of that year at an open-air festival in Hyde Park in front of 100,000 people.

After their only tour, the group split up in 1969. Grech died in 1989. In the subsequent decade, Baker has been on the road again with Jack Bruce in a re-formed **Cream** in all but name, and Clapton and Winwood have continued to consolidate successful solo careers.

BLONDIE This group was formed in New York in 1974. Guitarist Chris Stein spotted Deborah Harry appearing as one-third of a girl group called the Stilettos and asked the former Playboy Club 'bunny' to join a new group he was founding. They recruited Fred Smith on bass and Billy O'Conner on drums. Clem Burke soon replaced O'Connor.

They named the group Blondie due to the colour of Debbie's hair and cut a demo called *Platinum Blonde*. Before making their record debut in 1976 with 'X-Offender' they found a new bass player, Gary Valentine, and added Jimmy Destin on keyboards.

The group signed to Chrysalis and their chart reign began. There were other personnel changes, with Frank Infante replacing Valentine

31

on bass. They then recruited an English bassist, Nigel Harrison, so Infante moved to guitar.

Blondie's first hit was 'Denis' in February 1978 and stretched ten years to a re-mix in December 1988. In between, their singles charts entries were: '(I'm Always Touched By Your) Presence Dear', 'Picture This', 'Hanging On The Telephone', 'Heart Of Glass', 'Sunday Girl', 'Dreaming', 'Union City Blue', 'Atomic', 'Call Me', 'The Tide Is High', 'Rapture', 'Island Of Lost Souls' and 'War Child'.

Their album entries included: *Plastic Letters*, *Parallel Lines*, *Blondie*, *Eat To The Beat*, *Autoamerican*, *Best Of Blondie* and *The Hunter*.

The band split in 1982 and Debbie Harry began appearing in films such as *Gigolo*, *Roadie*, *Hairspray* and *Videodrome*. Clem Burke did session work with the Eurythmics, Destri made some solo albums, including *Heart On The Wall*, and Stein went into production and founded Animal Records in 1983. The previous year, Debbie and Stein's book, *Making Tracks: The Rise Of Blondie*, was published.

In the meantime, Debbie went solo under her full name Deborah Harry. She was born in Miami, Florida, on 1 July 1945 and was raised by adoptive parents. As a solo artist, she had hits

with the singles 'Backfired', 'French Kissin' In The USA', 'Free To Fall' and 'In Love With Love'. She also charted with the albums *Koo Koo* and *The Hunter*.

Stein developed a serious illness and was forced to retire from the business. Debbie, who was living with him, also retired for a while to tend him over a three-year period up to 1986, when he recovered. In 1989 she embarked on a US tour with a band comprised of Stein (guitar), Leigh Fox (bass), Jimmy Clark (drums), Carla Olla (rhythm) and Suzy Davis (keyboards).

Since then, Debbie has appeared in a number of television movies and shows, continues to tour and record, and in 1995 formed a new band comprising Stein (guitar), Joe McGinty (keyboards), Greta Brinkman (bass) and Don Kline (drums). The same year she also appeared in the film *After Midnight*.

Chart action returned in 1995 with the re-mixes of 'Atomic', 'Heart Of Glass' and 'Union City Blue'. 1997 saw the release of *Blondie: The Essential Collection*.

BLOOD, SWEAT & TEARS Originally conceived by Al Kooper, this group made their debut in New York in 1967. From there, they moved to San Francisco and by 1969 there had been several personnel changes, with vocalist David Clayton-Thomas now leading the group.

The other members were Steve Katz (guitar, harmonica and vocals), Jim Fielder (bass), Bobby Colomby (drums, percussion and vocals), Fred Lipsius (piano and alto), Dick Halligan (keyboards, trombone and flute), Chuck Winfield and Lew Soloff (trumpet and flugelhorn) and Jerry Hyman (trombone and recorder).

The group's hit singles included: 'You've Made Me So Very Happy', 'Spinning Wheel', 'And When I Die', 'Hi-De-Ho', 'Lucretia Mac Evil', 'Go Down Gamblin'', 'Lisa Listen To Me', 'So Long Dixie', 'Tell Me That I'm Wrong' and 'Got To Get You Into My Life'.

1968 saw the release of the band's debut album, *The Child Is Father To The Man*. Their album successes included: *Blood, Sweat & Tears*, *Blood, Sweat & Tears 3*, *BS&T 4* and *Greatest Hits*.

David Clayton-Thomas and Fred Lipsius left Blood, Sweat & Tears in 1971, with Clayton-Thomas embarking on a solo career and releasing albums such as *David Clayton-Thomas*, *Tequila Sunrise* and *Harmony Junction*.

Bobby Doyle replaced him and other new members included Georg Wadenius and Joe

Deborah Harry of Blondie

Henderson. This line-up was brief, with another original member, Dick Halligan, leaving the group and the introduction of new lead vocalist Jerry Fisher, plus other new members Lou Marini Jnr and Larry Willis.

Further changes took place and Clayton-Thomas returned in 1974. The personnel changes continued until 1980, when the band broke up and ceased to exist for almost eight years. They were revived by Clayton-Thomas for a 1988 tour and continued to perform on the nostalgia circuits.

As Clayton-Thomas and Bobby Columby owned the name, when other former members – Kooper, Lipsius, Randy Brecker, Fielder, Katz, Soloff and Tom Malone – teamed up in 1993, they adopted the name the Child Is Father To The Man Band.

Blood, Sweat & Tears continued to perform as a nostalgia act in 1998.

BOBBY FULLER FOUR, The Bobby Fuller was born in Baytown, Texas, on 22 October 1943. He settled in Los Angeles, where he formed the Bobby Fuller Four with his brother Randy (bass), Jim Reese (rhythm) and DeWayne Quirico (drums). The group had two major hits with 'I Fought The Law' and 'Love's Made A Fool Of You'.

Shortly after going solo, Bobby Fuller was found badly beaten and suffocated in his car in front of his house on 18 July 1966. The police initially assumed suicide, but there were so many unexplained circumstances surrounding his death that murder was also suspected. Before the inquest, *The Bobby Fuller Memorial Album* was being loaded on to delivery vans.

Bobby's brother Randy attempted to carry on with the band, but was unsuccessful.

BONEY M This group was the brainchild of record producer-composer Frank Farian. Farian had recorded a single called 'Baby Do You Wanna Bump?' and needed a group to promote it on television, so he engaged the services of four West Indian singers – Bobby Farrell, Marcia Barrett, Liz Mitchell and Maisie Williams – dubbing them Boney M. Although they initially mimed to the product, they sold over 50 million records in Europe and enjoyed a string of disco hits between 1976 and 1981. These included: 'Rivers Of Babylon', 'Brown Girl In The Ring', 'Ra-Ra-Rasputin', 'Mary's Boy Child/Oh My Lord', 'Ma Baker', 'Sunny', 'Daddy Cool',

'Belfast', 'Painter Man', 'Hooray Hooray It's A Holi-Holiday', 'My Friend Jack' and 'Gotta Go Home'. Their final hit record was 'We Kill The World (Don't Kill The World)'.

The group eventually split up in 1986. Liz Mitchell re-formed Boney M in 1991, hiring three new members to appear on the nostalgia circuit in the UK and on the Continent, where they still perform.

A distinctive visual appeal of the original group was the animated dance movements of Barry Farrell, although the last to be heard of him was that he had fallen on hard times and was living on benefits in a council house in Amsterdam.

Farian continued to write and produce, working with other acts such as Far Corporation.

BONZO DOG DOO DAH BAND, The This band was formed at Goldsmiths' College, London, in 1965. The Beatles hired them to appear in the film of Magical Mystery Tour, in which they performed 'Death Cab For Cutie' in a strip club. This led to a Liberty Records contract and their debut album, *Gorilla*, in 1967.

The group comprised **Vivian Stanshall** (vocals and trumpet), Roger Ruskin Spear and Rodney Slater (sax), Legs Larry Smith (drums), Neil Innes (piano and guitar), Sam Spoons (spoons) and Vernon Dudley Bohey-Nowell (banjo and double bass).

Paul McCartney produced their single 'I'm The Urban Spaceman' under the pseudonym Apollo C. Vermouth and it reached No 5 in the UK chart. The band also issued an album of the same name.

Legs Larry Smith became a close friend of George Harrison, who wrote a song about him – 'Ladies And Gentlemen His Name Is Legs' – which was included on Harrison's 1975 album *Extra Texture, Read All About It*.

The group broke up in 1970. For a time, Stanshall led a band called the Bonzo Freaks, then recorded *Sir Henry At Rawlinson's End*, which was turned into a film starring Trevor Howard. He later became a voice-over artist. Sadly, he perished in a house fire in his north London home in 1995.

Neil Innes became involved with the Monty Python team, then participated in a wonderful Beatles parody called the Rutles. Now living in East Anglia, he writes for children's television and for commercials, and is a popular guest at US Beatlefests. Oasis borrowed the tune of one of his compositions for their hit 'Whatever'.

33

Legs Larry Smith lives near Henley-on-Thames, Rodney Slater lives in Bedford. The remaining members live in London.

BOOKER T. & THE MGs Booker T. Jones was born in Memphis, Tennessee, on 12 November 1944 and became the pianist and organist in a school group at the age of 14. Two years later he auditioned for Stax Records and became friendly with the musicians there, and formed the vocal and instrumental group Booker T. & the MGs. Together with drummer-guitarist Al Wilson, another drummer called Lewis Steinberg and lead guitarist Steve Cropper, he composed an instrumental, 'Green Onions', which brought Jones his first gold disc while he was still only 16.

Other hits for the band included: 'Hip Hug Her', 'Groovin'', 'Soul Limbo', 'Hang 'Em High', 'Time Is Tight' and 'Mrs Robinson'.

There were various personnel changes in the group, but Booker T. had three particular musicians – Steve Cropper, **Al Jackson** and bassist Donald Dunn – as part of the band for most of the time. Other musicians who appeared with the band included Andrew Love (baritone sax), Wayne Jackson (trumpet), Joe Arnold (tenor sax) and Isaac Hayes (piano).

Steve Cropper went on to pen hits for several artists. They included: 'Dock Of The Bay' for **Otis Redding**, 'Midnight Hour' for **Wilson Pickett** and 'See Saw' for Aretha Franklin.

The band broke up in 1972 and the members became involved in composing and producing. Booker T. went on to team up with Priscilla, his second wife, who was Rita Coolidge's sister. They had a chart success with their album *Booker T. And Priscilla* and a single, 'Home Grown'.

Al Jackson and Donald Dunn re-formed the group in 1974. Since the murder of Jackson in 1975, they have managed to continue in a recognizable form for periodic tours and, less frequently, new albums.

BOOMTOWN RATS, The Former music journalist Bob Geldof formed the Nightlife Thugs, although they changed their name soon afterwards to the Boomtown Rats. They took the name from a gang of thugs featured in the Woody Guthrie biopic *Bound For Glory*.

Apart from Geldof on vocals, the members were Johnnie Fingers (keyboards), Gerry Cott and Gerry Roberts (guitar), Pete Briquette (bass) and Simon Crowe (drums). The group had 14 hits between 1977 and 1984.

Geldof was born in Dun Laoghaire, Eire, on 5 October 1954 and the group was formed in 1975. Bob played the leading roll in the Pink Floyd film *The Wall* in 1982. The Rats split up in 1984.

Together with Midge Ure, Geldof organized a project for Band Aid with the record 'Do They Know It's Christmas', which was released in November 1984 and became the biggest-selling single in the UK up to that time. He then organized the Live Aid concert in 1985 to raise aid for Ethiopia. The Rats re-formed in 1984 in order to perform at Live Aid.

Geldof was knighted for his services and began to make solo records in 1986, having a hit with 'This Is The World Calling'. He married Paula Yates in 1987, but the marriage ended acrimoniously when she went to live with INXS singer **Michael Hutchence**.

Since then, Pete Briquette's session work has included Tricky's *Maxiquaye* album in 1995. In July 1995, Bob Geldof joined Bon Jovi on stage at Wembley Stadium to sing 'I Don't Like Mondays', before entering a period of what he called 'creative paralysis'.

BOONE, Pat Born Charles Eugene Boone in Jacksonville, Florida, on 1 June 1934, this major American singer of the 1950s is the great-great-great-great grandson of the famous pioneer Daniel Boone. During his heyday he had 60 hits, including six chart-toppers, sold more than 45 million records and holds a record for more than 200 consecutive weeks in the charts, with 'Love Letters In The Sand', his biggest-selling record, spending 34 weeks in the bestseller lists.

Between 1955 and 1962, when Boone outsold every other artist with the exception of **Elvis Presley**, his hits included: 'Two Hearts', 'Ain't That A Shame', 'At My Front Door', 'No Other Arms', 'Gee Whittakers!', 'I'll Be Home', 'Tutti Frutti', 'Long Tall Sally', 'I Almost Lost My Mind', 'Friendly Persuasion', 'Chains Of Love', 'Don't Forbid Me', 'Anastasia', 'Why Baby Why', 'I'm Waiting Just For You', 'Love Letters In The Sand', 'Bernadine', 'Remember You're Mine', 'There's A Gold Mine In The Sky', 'April Love', 'A Wonderful Time Up There', 'It's Too Soon To Know', 'Sugar Moon', 'If Dreams Came True', 'That's How Much I Love You', 'For My Good Fortune', 'Gee, But It's Lonely', 'I'll Remember

Tonight', 'With The Wind And The Rain In Your Hair', 'For A Penny', 'Twixt Twelve And Twenty', 'Fools Hall Of Fame', '(Welcome) New Lovers', 'Moody River', 'Big Cold Wind', 'Johnny Will', 'I'll See You In My Dreams' and 'Speedy Gonzales'.

Incidentally, the clean-cut singer – who was so particular about correct grammar that he refused to sing 'Ain't That A Shame?', preferring his own rendition of 'Isn't That A Shame?' – was once dubbed 'Elvis Without The Pelvis'!

He appeared in several films, including *Bernadine*, *April Love*, *State Fair* and *The Main Attraction*, although he turned down a film role with Marilyn Monroe because he wouldn't kiss a woman other than his wife.

Boone married Shirley Foley, daughter of country music artist Red Foley, in 1955 and the couple had four daughters. He later changed his style to record country, gospel and Christian music, and formed the Boone Family Singers to record several Christian albums with his wife and daughters. His third daughter, Debby, made her solo debut with 'You Light Up My Life' in 1977, which topped the US chart for ten weeks, becoming the biggest hit of the year.

By 1997, Boone had settled in a large Beverly Hills mansion with his wife Shirley. The host of Christian television and radio shows provided a major surprise at the American Music Awards early that year. He turned up wearing a studded collar and leather waistcoat, and had a tattoo on his chest. He said he had turned to heavy metal after listening to a tape of music by Metallica, **Deep Purple** and Van Halen. Confessing he loved the genre, he produced an album of heavy metal classics set to a big band sound on *Pat Boone In A Metal Mood: No More Mr Nice Guy*, which was a major seller in the US. There was a backlash, which resulted in his Christian television series being cancelled.

BOSTON Tom Scholz was born in Toledo, Ohio, on 10 March 1947 and founded the group Boston in 1975. The other members were Fran Sheehan (bass), Brad Delp and Barry Goudreau (guitar) and Sib Hashian (drums), all of whom were born in Boston.

They had a hit in 1977 with 'More Than A Feeling' and followed up with 'Don't Look Back' the following year.

Eight years after their second hit, Boston re-entered the US chart in a big way in 1986, reaching No 1 with 'Amanda'.

Guitarist Tom Scholz is still at the helm of Boston who, with three huge-selling albums to their credit, have tended to be choosy in the 1990s about when and where they tour, and how often they release new material.

BOW WOW WOW This band was created by Malcolm McLaren, the man behind the **Sex Pistols.** He formed Bow Wow Wow in 1979 with some former members of Adam & the Ants – **Matthew Ashman** (guitar), Lee Gorman (bass) and Dave Barbarossa (drums) – adding a 14-year-old schoolgirl, Annabella Lwin, as lead singer.

Controversy was created over the cover of their first album, *See Jungle! See Jungle! Go Join Your Gang! Yeah, City All Over! Go Ape Crazy!* in 1981, when the 15-year-old girl was pictured nude in a photo which recreated Manet's famous *Luncheon In The Grass*. Annabella's mother accused McLaren of exploiting her daughter and called him a pornographer.

The group enjoyed a run of hits between 1980 and 1983: 'C30', 'C60', 'C90', 'Go', 'Your Cassette Pete', 'W.O.R.K. (N.O. Nah No No My Daddy Don't)', 'Prince Of Darkness', 'Chihuahua', 'Go Wild In The Country', 'See Jungle', 'I Want Candy', 'Louis Quatorze' and 'Do You Wanna Hold Me.'

The band split up in 1984. Annabella embarked on a solo career, initially recording for RCA without much success and signing to Sony for a short time in 1993. Gorman, Ashman and Barbarossa stayed together as a group, calling themselves the Chiefs Of Relief, but also disbanded when success didn't come their way.

Ashman turned down the offer of re-forming Bow Wow Wow shortly before his death in 1994.

Annabella lives in London and is believed to be forming a new group with Lee Gorman, who co-produced a 1993 album for his previous employer, **Adam Ant**, in 1992. He also composes jingles and film soundtracks. Barbarossa is now a member of Beats International.

BRIGHTMAN, Sarah This English singer was born on 14 August 1961. Her childhood ambition was to become a ballet dancer. Sarah was a former member of the sexy dance troupe Hot Gossip and during her spell with them had her first hit, a disco favourite, 'I Lost My Heart To A Starship Trooper'. Her other hits included 'The Adventures Of A Love Crusader' and 'Him'.

Sarah appeared in the hit musical *Cats*, and married its composer Andrew Lloyd Webber in

1984. The marriage lasted six years. She appeared in the television version of Lloyd Webber's *Song and Dance* and starred in his musicals *Phantom Of The Opera* and *Aspects Of Love*.

Brightman entered the chart again in 1985 with 'Pie Jesu', a duet with 12-year-old Paul Miles-Kington. The following year she had two further hits, both from the musical *Phantom Of The Opera*, The first was the title song, which she sang in a duet with Steve Harley, former leader of **Cockney Rebel**. The second was 'All I Ask Of You', a duet with **Cliff Richard**. She was to have a third hit from the same musical, 'Wishing You Were Somehow Here Again'.

In 1992 her duet with opera singer José Carreras, 'Amigos Para Siempre', entered the chart, and in 1997 she had a further UK chart entry with 'Timeless'. Her album Eden was issued at the close of 1998.

BROOKS, Elkie   Elkie Brooks (real name Elaine Bookbinder) was born in Salford, Lancashire, on 25 February 1945. Her brother Tony Mansfield became the drummer with the Dakotas.

Elkie started singing at the age of 15 and in 1964 began recording, although she was not to have any success on record for several years. In 1970 she joined a band called Dada and in 1972 was a member of Vinegar Joe, sharing vocal honours with Robert Palmer.

As a solo artist, she had her first hit with 'Pearl's A Singer' in 1977. Her other hit singles included: 'Sunshine After The Rain', 'Lilac Wine', 'Only Love Can Break Your Heart', 'Don't Cry Out Loud', 'The Runaway', 'Fool If You Think It's Over', 'Our Love', 'Nights In White Satin', 'Gasoline Alley', 'No More The Fool', 'Break The Chain' and 'We've Got Tonight'.

Her hit albums included: *Two Days Away*, *Shooting Star*, *Live And Learn*, *Pearls*, *Pearls II*, *Minutes* and *Screen Gems*. In 1978 Elkie married sound engineer Trevor Jordan and the couple had a son, Jermaine, the following year.

Elkie now lives in North Devon. She undertook a 50-date UK tour in 1994, the year in which three of her albums – *Bookbinder's Kid*, *Inspirations* and *Nothin' But The Blues* – reached modest positions in the chart. Her UK tour in 1998 stretched from 23 March to 30 April.

BROS   Twin brothers Matt and Luke Goss were born on 29 September 1968. The brothers, a singer and a drummer respectively, began their career in 1984 under the name Gloss. They were a trio, the additional member being bassist Craig Logan. They signed a recording deal in April 1987 and achieved spectacular fan worship in the late 1980s.

Their chart hits within a 12-month period included: 'When Will I Be Famous', 'Drop The Boy', 'I Owe You Nothing', 'I Quit', 'Cat Among The Pigeons/Silent Night', 'Too Much', 'Chocolate Box' and 'Sister'. Apart from their ten hit singles, their debut album *Push* sold 5½ million copies worldwide in 1988. The trio's career collapsed a year later when much of their £12 million fortune was lost through lack of business acumen. It was also the year that their stepsister Carolyn was killed in a car crash.

Following the group's demise in 1991, Luke formed Luke Goss & The Band Of Thieves in 1993 and had a minor hit that year with 'Sweeter Than The Midnight Rain'. The group disbanded and he penned a book, *I Owe You Nothing*. He also became an actor, initially appearing in the stage plays *Plan 9 From Outer Space* and *What A Feeling*, and in 1997 made his debut in the West End of London, starring as Danny in the musical *Grease*.

Matt, who had settled in a flat in Maida Vale, west London, went solo and entered the chart in 1996 with 'If You Were Here Tonight'.

Craig Logan became international marketing manager at EMI Records in London in September 1995.

BROTHERHOOD OF MAN   This vocal quartet comprised two males and two females. They were originally launched in 1969 with **Tony Burrows** as lead singer and made their chart debut with 'United We Stand', followed by 'Where Are You Going My Love'. The group were chosen to represent the UK in the Eurovision Song Contest in 1976. Six years after their last chart entry, they were now led by Martin Lee and Lee Sheridan, with Sandra Stevens and Nicky Stevens, and won the competition with 'Save Your Kisses For Me', their biggest hit and first UK chart-topper. They also topped the chart with 'Angelo' and 'Figaro'. Other hits included 'My Sweet Rosalie', 'Oh Boy (The Mood I'm In)', 'Beautiful Lover' and 'Middle Of The Night'. After a four-year gap, they had a minor hit with 'Lightning Flash' in 1982 and spent the rest of the decade on the chicken-and-chips circuit.

As a member of the Hit Squad, Tony Burrows returned to the stage in the 1997 Festival Of The Sixties at Bognor Regis, West Sussex. Sue Glover,

another former member, is married to recording engineer Nick Horne, and lives near Newbury, Berkshire.

BROWN, Errol Singer-songwriter Errol Ainsworth Brown was born in Kingston, Jamaica, on 12 November 1948. His mother Edna went to England when he was three, leaving him behind while she sought a better life for them, and he was able to join her when he was ten. Determined that he would have a chance to succeed in life, she took on two jobs in order to have him educated at a private school. She died from cancer when Errol was 18. He was later to write the hit 'Emma' in her memory.

After a spell in the civil service, Brown teamed up with Tony Wilson in 1969 and they made their recording debut with a reggae version of 'Give Peace A Chance' on the Beatles' label, Apple. They adopted the name Hot Chocolate. Wilson left the band to embark on a solo career, which was unsuccessful. The line-up now consisted of Brown (vocals), Harvey Hinsley (guitar), Larry Ferguson (keyboards), Patrick Olive (percussion) and Tony Connor (drums).

During the next 15 years the group had 22 Top 30 hits, including chart-toppers such as 'Every One's A Winner' and 'You Sexy Thing'. Among their other hits were: 'Brother Louie', 'Emma', 'Disco Queen', 'Heaven Is In The Back Seat Of My Cadillac', 'So You Win Again', 'Put Your Love In Me' and 'I'll Put You Together Again'.

The band finally split in 1987 and Brown embarked on a brief solo career, with hits such as 'Personal Touch' and 'Body Rockin'', before retiring in 1989.

Brown now lives in Esher with his wife Ginette, a former model and dancer, and his daughters Colette and Leonie. In 1997 he decided to make a comeback with a new album and an on-the-road tour.

'You Sexy Thing' was used on the soundtrack of the 1997 movie *The Full Monty* and it entered the Top 10 once again, bringing Brown back into the limelight with performances on high-audience UK television shows such as the *National Lottery Live*. A Hot Chocolate album compilation was also released and re-charted. In May 1998 Brown began a nationwide tour, promoted by Flying Music.

Other members of the original group still perform under the Hot Chocolate name, with a new lead singer, Greg Bannis.

BROWN, James Known as the 'Godfather Of Soul', James Brown was born in Barnwell, South Carolina, on 3 May 1928. At the age of 16 he was convicted of theft and incarcerated at the Alto Reform School, but was given an early release to join a gospel group. They were to evolve into James Brown & the Famous Flames.

The group entered the US R&B chart in 1957 with 'Please Please Please' and topped it the following year with 'Try Me'. Between 1960 and 1974, Brown had 43 singles enter the Billboard chart. They included: 'Papa's Got A Brand New Bag', 'I Got You (I Feel Good)', 'It's A Man's Man's Man's World', 'Cold Sweat' and 'Say It Loud – I'm Black And I'm Proud'.

Over the years, Brown has continued to experience highs and lows in his recording career, with occasional hits such as 'Payback' and 'How Do You Stop'.

Following a massive tour in 1973, he was hospitalized due to exhaustion. A week later his eldest son, Teddy, was killed in a car crash. The Inland Revenue Service then insisted he owed them $4.5 million in back taxes and he spent the rest of the decade fighting the case.

Brown's next problem period occurred in 1988, when his wife Adrienne accused him of assault and battery, although she dropped the charges after she herself was arrested for possession of PCP. Brown was also arrested for possessing the drug after a dramatic high-speed police car chase through Georgia and Carolina. Adrienne was sent to a drug rehabilitation centre and Brown was fined and given a two-year suspended sentence.

In September of that year, he burst into an insurance meeting armed with a pistol and shotgun, and the following day was in another car chase with the police, who arrested him once again for possession of PCP. In December he was sentenced to six years in prison. He spent two-and-a-half years in custody and ten months in a community work centre, and remained on parole until October 1993. He remains on probation until the end of 1998, is banned from driving and has to face regular drugs tests.

Brown's *Universal James* album was issued in 1993 and *Live At The Apollo* in 1995, the year in which his wife Adrienne died, following cosmetic surgery. Recently, his contribution to music has been acknowledged with a series of awards and honours, including a star on the Hollywood Walk Of Fame and a Lifetime Achievement Award in the R&B Foundation Pioneer Awards.

In January 1998, at the age of 69, Brown was in hospital fighting an addiction to painkillers. His dependency on the drugs developed followed the incident in which he hurt his back trying to do the splits during a show in Florida. While he was in hospital, police seized two guns from his South Carolina home.

BROWN, Joe Born in Swarby, Lincolnshire, on 13 May 1941, this singer-guitarist first found acclaim on Jack Good's *Boy Meets Girl* UK television series in 1959. He led his own band, Joe Brown & the Bruvvers, signed with Larry Parnes and had a string of hit singles between 1960 and 1973, including: 'Darktown Strutters Ball', 'Shine', 'What A Crazy World We're Living In', 'A Picture Of You', 'Your Tender Look', 'It Only Took A Minute', 'That's What Love Will Do', 'Nature's Time For Love', 'Sally Ann', 'With A Little Help From My Friends' and 'Hey Mama'.

Brown then branched out as an all-round entertainer, appeared in the movie *What A Crazy World* and also featured in the stage musical *Charlie Girl*.

Joe Brown

He married Vickie Haseman, former member of the **Vernons Girls**, who became a prolific backing vocalist on recording sessions. She was also to join Joe in his country-rock band Home Brew. Sadly, Vickie died from cancer in 1991. Their daughter, Sam Brown, became a hit singer in her own right, and father and daughter joined forces for the first time to tour the UK in 1996.

Joe decided on the year 1997 to make a comeback, issuing his first album in several years, *Fifty-six And Taller Than You Think*. He also began a lengthy tour, which spanned the whole of the UK throughout 1997.

BROWNE, Jackson   This singer-songwriter-instrumentalist was the son of US Army parents and was born in Heidelberg, Germany, on 9 October 1948.

Browne began his musical career in Los Angeles and initially played with the Nitty Gritty Band, in 1966. During the 1960s he also appeared with Tim Buckley and **Nico**. He became successful as a songwriter, penning hits for artists such as Linda Ronstadt and the Byrds. As a solo artist, he enjoyed his first hit in 1972 with 'Doctor My Eyes'. His other hits included: 'Here Come Those Tears Again', 'Running On Empty', 'Stay', 'The Load-Out', 'Boulevard', 'That Girl Could Sing', 'Somebody's Baby', 'Lawyers In Love' and 'Tender Is the Night'.

Jackson Browne's most recent album was *Looking East*, released in 1996. The following year he supervised the compilation of *The Next Voice You Hear*, a 'best of' retrospective.

BRUCE, Tommy   A former truck driver's mate at Covent Garden vegetable market, who had been orphaned in 1949 at the age of ten, Londoner Tommy Bruce was persuaded by songwriter Barry Mason to make a demo disc in 1960. As a result, he got a record deal with Columbia Records and reached No 2 in the chart with his version of the Fats Waller hit 'Ain't Misbehavin''. Two other chart entries, 'Broken Doll' and 'Babette', followed, but his brief spell in the chart was over.

Bruce was noted for his distinctive raspy voice, which was once compared to the sound of a steam hammer and gravel polisher. He appeared on various television shows and toured with his backing band the Bruisers.

Married at one time to a member of the **Vernons Girls**, Tommy Bruce remains an in-demand performer on the club and cabaret circuit for an act that hinges as much on comedy as on his singing.

BUCKS FIZZ   Formed in 1981, Bucks Fizz comprised four former session vocalists: Cheryl Baker, Jay Aston, Mike Nolan and Bobby Gubby. The group was formed expressly to win the Eurovision Song Contest, which they did with 'Making Your Mind Up'. Cheryl had previously tried her luck with Eurovision as a member of another outfit called Co-Co.

Bucks Fizz became a popular television show and also a cabaret club act, particularly as the two pretty female singers had a routine in which their short skirts were whipped off during 'Making Your Mind Up'.

Other hits for the quartet included: 'Piece Of The Action', 'One Of Those Nights', 'The Land Of Make Believe', 'My Camera Never Lies', 'Now Those Days Are Gone', 'If You Can't Stand The Heat', 'Run For Your Life', 'When We Were Young', 'London Town', 'Rules Of The Game', 'Talking In Your Sleep', 'Golden Days', 'I Hear Talk', 'You And Your Heart So Blue', 'Magical Peak', 'New Beginning', 'Love The One You're With', 'Keep Each Other Warm' and 'Heart Of Stone'.

In 1984 the group were involved in a road accident, during which singer Bobby G. was left in a comatose state, suffering from brain damage. He eventually returned to the group, which was dissolved in 1989.

In 1985, Jay Ashton left Bucks Fizz and sold a story to the tabloids alleging that she had had an affair with the group's producer, Andy Hill. Shelley Preston replaced her.

After 12 years and 20 top-selling hits, Cheryl Baker stepped down to concentrate on a television career, which began in 1984 with a UK children's show called *How Dare You*, and in 1997 she was into her eleventh year as co-presenter of the programme *Record Breakers*. Cheryl, who was born Rita Crudgington on 8 March 1954 in London, has now settled in a converted oast-house near Sevenoaks, Kent, with her husband, bass guitarist Steve Stroud, and their twin daughters Kyla and Natalie, born in 1995. She has also published a recipe book, *Cheryl Baker's Low Calorie Cook Book*, which has become a best-seller.

Jay was with the band from 1981 to 1985, and after she split from them she was involved for four years in lawsuits with the Bucks Fizz management and her ex-lover Hill, husband of the group's founder Nichola Martin. She was left penniless, living in a squalid bedsit. In 1998 she decided to relaunch her career with a new band called Zen Shoppers with live-in boyfriend, guitarist Dave Colquhoun.

Bucks Fizz reunited in 1991 and recorded an album, *Bucks Fizz Live At The Fairfield Hall, Croydon*. Bobby G. continues to appear on the cabaret circuit with the group, but is the only original member remaining. The outfit participated in a show in aid of the Princess Diana Memorial Fund in Cornwall in the autumn of 1997.

In 1998 Mike Nolan appeared in a re-formed Bucks Fizz, Cheryl Baker was presenting the television programme *The Really Useful Show* and Andy Hill was still writing songs and running a studio with his wife Nichola.

BUFFALO SPRINGFIELD   The members of this group, formed in 1966 and named after a steamroller, were Stephen Stills, Neil Young, Dewey Martin, Richie Furay and Bruce Palmer.

Being Canadian, Palmer experienced continuing problems with the immigration authorities and eventually had to be replaced by Jim Messina.

The group received acclaim for their album releases, which included *Buffalo Springfield*, *Buffalo Springfield Again* and *Last Time Around*. They had one Top 10 single in 1967, 'For What It's Worth (Stop, Hey What's That Sound)', and a minor hit with 'Rock 'n' Roll Woman'.

They split up in 1967, such a brief lifespan no doubt adding to their legendary status.

Martin attempted to launch another band under the Buffalo Springfield name with Randy Fuller, Bill Darnell, Peter Bradstreet, Terry Gregg and Buddy Emmans, but he was then legally prevented from using the name and later formed Dewey Martin's Medicine Ball.

In 1987, Palmer and Martin did manage to gather together other musicians and launch a tribute band, Buffalo Springfield Revisited. By 1991 they were still performing on the US nostalgia circuit, with the personnel now comprising Martin, Michael Curtis, Bill Darnell and Robin Lamble.

Stephen Stills is a member of the presently still-functional **Crosby, Stills & Nash**. Neil Young has had a more fruitful solo career than Bruce Palmer, who managed only an eponymous 1971 album, while Richie Furay formed Poco with Buffalo Springfield's latter-day bass player, Jim Messina (who was to have better luck with **Loggins & Messina**).

BURROWS, Tony   Born 14 April 1942, this singer-songwriter was present on numerous hit records. He was a member of the Kestrels, the **Ivy League**, the **Flowerpot Men**, Edison Lighthouse, First Class and the Pipkins, in addition to singing as a backing vocalist for Elton John, **Chris Spedding**, **John Barry**, **Kiki Dee** and Matthew Fisher. On one edition of the UK television show *Top of the Pops* in 1970 he appeared no less than three times!

Burrows was lead singer on 'Love Grows' with Edison Lighthouse, 'My Baby Loves Loving' with White Plains, and even 'United We Stand' with **Brotherhood Of Man**. In 1973 he was also in a band called First Class with Robin Shaw and John Carter. They had a hit with 'Beach Baby'.

Burrows now lives in Finchampstead, Berkshire, and apart from singing on a number of television commercials, he continues to sing in two groups, one called the Hit Squad and the other, formed in 1997, named after a previous band, First Class.

CAMEL This progressive rock group was formed in London in 1972. The members were Peter Bardens (vocals), Doug Ferguson (bass), Andy Ward (drums) and Andy Latimer (vocals, guitar and flute). Over a ten-year period they had a succession of chart albums, which included: *The Snow Goose*, *Moon Madness*, *Rain Dances*, *Breathless*, *I Can See Your House From Here*, *Nude*, *The Single Factor* and *Stationary Traveller*.

Following the release of *Moon Madness*, Ferguson left and was replaced by Richard Sinclair, a former member of Caravan. When Bardens left, another ex-member of Caravan, Jan Schelhaas, replaced him.

By the beginning of the 1980s, the only original member of the band was Andy Latimer, who had been joined by Tom Scherpenzeel (keyboards), Christopher Rainbow (vocals), Paul Bass (bass) and Paul Burgess (drums). Following the release of their album *Pressure Points* in 1984, the group disbanded. Latimer then re-formed the band in 1992, issuing the album *Dust And Dreams*, which was based on John Steinbeck's noted novel *The Grapes Of Wrath*.

In 1994 Bardens returned to team up with Camel once again, performing a series of live gigs and cutting an album, *Mirage*.

In 1996 Latimer was still fronting the group and yet another concept album, *Harbour Of Tears*, based on the Irish emigration to the US, was released.

CAMPBELL, Glen This country music artist was born in Billstown, Arkansas, on 22 April 1936. He moved to California in 1960, performing in studio sessions and occasionally appearing with the **Beach Boys** as a replacement for Brian Wilson.

Campbell's first major hit as a solo artist was 'By The Time I Get To Phoenix' in 1967. His other hit singles included: 'I Wanna Live', 'Dreams Of The Everyday Housewife', 'Gentle On My Mind', 'Wichita Lineman', 'Galveston', 'Where's The Playground Susie', 'True Grit', 'Try A Little Kindness', 'Honey Come Back', 'Oh Happy Day', 'It's Only Make Believe', 'Dream Baby', 'Rhinestone Cowboy', 'Country Boy', 'Don't Pull Your Love', 'Southern Nights', 'Sunflower' and 'Can You Fool'.

The winner of five Grammy Awards, he became known as the 'Rhinestone Cowboy' following his hit of that name.

Campbell continues to perform and tour the UK regularly. He appeared in concert in the UK with Kenny Rogers and **Tammy Wynette** in November 1996 and returned to headline a tour in April 1997.

CANNED HEAT The first line-up of Canned Heat consisted of **Bob 'The Bear' Hite** (harmonica and vocals), **Al 'Blind Owl' Wilson** (harmonica, guitar and vocals), Frank Cook (drums) and Stuart Brotman (bass).

The second line-up, between 1966 and 1967, consisted of Hite, Wilson and Cook with Henry 'Sunflower' Vestine on guitar and Mark Andes on bass (who was soon replaced by Larry 'The Mole' Taylor). Their third line-up saw Hite, Wilson, Vestine and Taylor joined by Adolpho 'Fito' de la Parro on drums. This line-up, which lasted from the summer of 1967 to the summer of 1969, had hits with 'Boogie With Canned Heat', 'Living The Blues' and 'Hallelujah'.

Al Wilson died in September 1970 and Bob Hite in April 1981, although the group continued recording and performing.

Their tenth incarnation in 1995 comprised Junior Watson (guitar), Ron Schumake (bass), Fito de la Parro (drums), Henry Vestine (guitar) and James Thomberry (vocals, harmonica and guitar).

Larry Taylor has a heart condition, but still records with the group. Henry Vestine had an alcohol problem, but toured occasionally until his death from cancer on 20 October 1997. Fito de la Parro is the only remaining original member of Canned Heat who toured Europe in 1996 to plug their latest album, *Internal Combustion*.

CANNON, Freddie Born Freddie Picariello in Massachusetts on 4 December 1940, this singer was the son of a dance-band leader. He began his career leading Freddie Karmon & the Hurricanes. Bob Crewe and Frank Skay spotted him, changed his name to Freddie Cannon and gave him 'Tallahassee Lassie' to record. The number was a major hit and he followed with several further chart entries, including: 'Way Down Yonder In New Orleans', 'Chattanooga Shoe Shine Boy', 'Jump Over', 'Transistor Sister', 'Palisades Park', 'Abigail Beecher' and 'Action', the latter a theme song from the US television series *Where The Action Is*.

The album *The Explosive! Freddie Cannon* was said to be the first rock 'n' roll album to top the UK chart when it became a massive hit in 1960.

Cannon worked in the promotions department of United Artists before teaming up in the 1980s with the Belmonts, **Dion's** old backing group, for a crack at the nostalgia market.

CAPTAIN BEEFHEART Born Don Van Vliet on 15 January 1941 in Glendale, California, the man who was to become known as Captain Beefheart originally formed a band with his school friend **Frank Zappa**, called the Soots. It was unsuccessful, and he joined other bands before calling himself Captain Beefheart and forming a group he called the Magic Band with Alex St Clair and Jeff Cotton (guitar), Jerry Handley (bass) and John French (drums).

Over the years, Beefheart changed the line-up of his backing band several times and recorded a number of albums. His most famous LP, a double set released in 1969, was called *Trout Mask Replica* and is his most successful record.

In 1986, Beefheart reverted to his given name Don Vliet and announced to the world that he was withdrawing from the music business to return to his love of painting. Together with his wife Jan, he moved to the Mojave desert and his work has since been exhibited all over the world. He continues to live in his desert home, although he is currently in poor health.

CARROLL, Ronnie Born Ronald Cleghorn in Belfast, Northern Ireland, on 18 August 1934, Ronnie Carroll took a variety of jobs before he began singing professionally. He made his first entry into the hit parade in 1956 with 'Walk Hand In Hand'.

Other hits which followed included: 'The Wisdom Of A Fool', 'Footsteps', 'Ring A Ding Girl', 'Roses Are Red', 'If Only Tomorrow' and 'Say Wonderful Things'.

Carroll married Millicent Martin in 1959. Lean times in the 1980s led him to bankruptcy, but he eventually became a restaurateur.

A 26-track CD, *The Ronnie Carroll Story*, was released in October 1996.

CASSIDY, David Born in New York on 12 April 1950, this singer was the son of actor Jack Cassidy and his younger brother Shaun also became a successful singer.

David first found fame as a member of the Partridge Family, a fictitious television family which also featured David's stepmother, singer-actress Shirley Jones. They had a number of hit records, although David and Shirley were the only two members of the television family group who actually sang on the records.

The Partridge Family television series made its debut in September 1970 and their hits included: 'I Think I Love You', 'It's One Of Those Nights', 'Breaking Up Is Hard To Do', 'Looking Through The Eyes Of Love' and 'Walking In The Rain'.

David began to record in his own right and had a string of hits, which continued after *The Partridge Family* series ended in 1974, stretching up to 1985. They included: 'Could It Be Forever', 'How Can I Be Sure', 'Rock Me Baby', 'I'm a Clown', 'Daydreamer', 'If I Didn't Care', 'Please Please Me', 'I Write The Songs', 'Darlin'', 'The Last Kiss' and 'Romance'.

Realizing his teenybopper days were over, Cassidy had switched to acting and starred in the stage musical *Joseph And The Amazing Technicolor Dreamcoat*. In 1987 he took over the lead in the musical *Time* from **Cliff Richard**. More recently, he appeared on Broadway in Willy Russell's *Blood Brothers* and also wrote a book, *Come On, Get Happy – Fear And Loathing On The Partridge Family Bus*.

CHAD & JEREMY Chad Stuart and Jeremy Clyde were two former public schoolboys who teamed up as a duo. The singer-songwriters recorded for the Ember Records label between 1963 and 1965 and had one minor hit in the UK with 'Yesterday's Gone'.

However, in 1964 in the wake of the Beatles and the 'British Invasion' in the US, they enjoyed a series of hits in the US chart with 'Yesterday's Gone', 'A Summer Song', 'Willow Weep For Me', 'If I Loved You', 'Before And After', 'I Don't Wanna Lose You Baby' and 'Distant Shores'.

When the US hits dried up, Chad & Jeremy decided to disband in 1967, by which time other duos such as **Peter & Gordon** and **David & Jonathan** were proving successful.

Jeremy Clyde has pursued an acting career and played the lead role in the UK televsion series *Sexton Blake* in 1978. Chad Stewart has concentrated on composition, chiefly for stage musicals.

CHARLES, Ray Born Ray Charles Robinson in Albany, Georgia, on 23 September 1930. At the age of six this singer was blinded by glaucoma and sent to the State School For The Blind until he was 15.

In 1954 Charles had an R&B hit for Atlantic, 'It Should Have Been Me'. In 1959 his 'What'd I Say' became a Top 10 single and was followed by 'Georgia On My Mind'. In 1962 he released a country album, *Modern Sounds In Country And Western*.

Over his career Charles has enjoyed nearly 70 US chart singles. They include: 'Hit The Road Jack', 'I Can't Stop Loving You', 'You Are My Sunshine', 'Take These Chains From My Heart', 'Busted' and 'Crying Time'. In 1973 he formed his own record label, Crossover.

Over the years, Charles has received numerous prestigious awards from his peers and has performed at many special events. He sang 'Let It Be' at a **John Lennon** tribute concert in Liverpool in 1990, and in 1995 attended Frank Sinatra's eightieth birthday, at which he sang 'Ol' Man River'. A US television tribute, *The Genius Of Ray Charles*, was transmitted in 1992.

Ray Charles released the album *Strong Love Affair* in 1996 and Rhino Records issued a 5-CD boxed set entitled *Genius & Soul* in 1997.

CHAS & DAVE This duo first hit the UK chart with 'Strummin'' in 1978. During the next five years their chart entries included: 'Gertcha', 'The Sideboard Song', 'Rabbit', 'Stars Over 45', 'Ain't No Pleasing You', 'Margate', 'London Girls' and 'My Melancholy Baby'. In 1986 they had a further hit, 'Snooker Loopy', credited to the Matchroom Mob With Chas & Dave, and they also provided the vocals and instrumental backing to two Tottenham Hotspur Football Club hits, 'Ossie's Dream' and 'Tottenham Tottenham'.

Bassist Dave Peacock from Edmonton and pianist Chas Hodges from Ponders End first met in 1963. Dave was a member of the Raiders (a group whose original name was the Rolling Stones, which they dropped because they thought it was silly) and Chas was about to join **Cliff Bennett** & the Rebel Rousers. They became firm friends and would often

Ray Charles

43

join in singalong sessions at Chas's aunt's pub in Dunmow, Essex. By the early 1970s they were both members of a group called the Tumbleweeds. They then decided to become a duo and perform rock 'n' roll in their own London accents, a style that they called Rockney (a blend of rock and cockney). At one time the group owned their own pub, Chas & Dave's.

Although their hits dried up, they continued to perform, and still do today. In 1997 they enjoyed one of their busiest years since the 1980s, with a large number of gigs to celebrate '25 Years On The Road'. They also penned the songs for a Johnny Speight musical about London East End life.

Late in 1997 *Chas & Dave: The Early Years* was released. This included all the tracks from their first album, plus ten extra tracks of previously unreleased material.

CHECKER, Chubby Ernest Evans was born in South Carolina on 3 October 1941. After originally performing as a singer under his own name, he changed it to Chubby Checker after a comment that he resembled a teenage **Fats Domino**.

At the age of 20, the former chicken plucker found fame. The number 'The Twist' was originally recorded by Hank Ballard. When Checker covered the song, he received such major promotion on the television show *American Bandstand* that his version became a million-seller. The single set off a dance craze and Checker recorded other dance and twist numbers, including 'Let's Twist Again' and 'The Hucklebuck'.

'The Twist' has continued its popularity over the decades and has undergone several revivals and re-entered the charts on a number of occasions. As a result, Checker has never stopped performing and in 1997, at the age of 57, he was still playing with his band, Chubby Checker & the Wildcats.

CHICKEN SHACK This British blues band was formed in Birmingham in 1965 by guitarist-vocalist Stan Webb. The other members were Paul Hancox (bass) and John Glasgow (drums).

The group moved to London and signed with the Blue Horizon label, a company run by Mike Vernon which specialized in British blues bands. By that time the personnel had changed and Webb was joined by Christine Perfect (vocals and piano), Andy Sylvester (bass) and Dave Bidwell (drums). They found initial success with their two albums *40 Blue Fingers Freshly Packed And Ready To Serve* and *OK Ken*.

In 1969 they entered the singles chart with 'I'd Rather Go Blind', followed by 'Tears In The

Stan Webb of Chicken Shack

Wind'. Christine Perfect's distinctive voice was a great asset to the band and she was to receive a Best Female Singer Award from *Melody Maker*. Christine was married to John McVie of **Fleetwood Mac** and when the records entered the chart that year, she left Chicken Shack to join her husband's group.

This signalled the end of Chicken Shack's potential in the singles chart. Christine's replacement was Paul Raymond. The group continued to be popular at major outdoor festivals, particularly since Stan Webb entertained the crowds by leaving the stage and mixing with them, using a 60m (200ft) guitar lead!

Their subsequent albums were not successful and the group disbanded in 1973. Webb joined **Savoy Brown** for a while, then formed another group called Broken Glass. Later, he was to revert to the Chicken Shack name.

With Stan Webb still at the helm, Chicken Shack remains a club and festival draw in Europe, particularly in Germany.

CHICORY TIP   This band was formed in 1968. The members were Peter Hewson (vocals), Barry Mayger (bass), Brian Shearer (drums) and Dick Foster (guitar). Rod Cloutt replaced Foster in 1972. The group entered the chart with three records: 'Son Of My Father', 'What's Your Name?' and 'Good Grief Christina'.

Foster originally left the group to join Edison Lighthouse. On New Year's Eve 1996 he left Edison Lighthouse, and in 1997 decided to re-form Chicory Tip with Mayger and Shearer, performing as a trio.

CHRISTIE, Lou   This American singer was known for his trademark falsetto voice. He was born Lugee Alfredo Giovanni Sacco in Glen Willard, Pennsylvania, on 19 February 1943. The first outfit he joined was called the Classics, but they were unsuccessful. He then led Lugee & the Lions, which also failed. It was when he decided to turn solo as Lou Christie that success came his way with a series of hit singles between 1963 and 1969. These included: 'The Gypsy Cried', 'Two Faces Have I', 'Lightnin' Strikes', 'Rhapsody In The Rain' and 'I'm Gonna Make You Mine'.

In the 1970s Christie became a UK resident when he married a former Miss Great Britain, Francesca Winfield. He moved back to the US, but has returned to Europe during the 1990s for well-received spots at sixties nostalgia festivals.

CHRISTIE, Tony   Born Anthony Fitzgerald in Conisborough, Yorkshire, on 25 April 1943, this singer had five entries in the UK chart in the first half of the 1970s: 'Las Vegas', 'I Did What I Did For Maria', 'Is This The Way To Amarillo', 'Avenues And Alleyways' and 'Drive Safely Darlin''. His chart debut came via a song by Mitch Murray and Peter Callender, a team who also aided **Paper Lace** in achieving chart success.

Married with three children, Tony Christie lives in the West Midlands and continues to pursue his career on the cabaret circuit.

CLARK, Petula   One of the UK's most successful female singers, who began her stage career at the age of seven, Petula Clark was still performing on stage – starring in the hit musical *Sunset Boulevard* – in 1997.

As a child, she enjoyed a career in radio and films, appearing in more than 20 movies. During the 1950s her hits included: 'The Little Shoemaker', 'Majorca', 'Suddenly There's A Valley', 'With All My Heart', 'Alone' and 'Baby Lover'.

In 1959 Petula married Claude Wolff, press agent for the French label Vogue Records.

Her most successful decade was the 1960s, when her major hits included: 'Sailor', 'Something Missing', 'Romeo', 'My Friend The Sea', 'I'm Counting On You', 'Ya Ya Twist', 'Casanova', 'Downtown', 'I Know A Place', 'You Better Come Home', 'Round Every Corner', 'You're The One', 'My Love', 'A Sign Of The Times', 'I Couldn't Live Without Your Love', 'This Is My Song', 'Don't Sleep In The Subway', 'The Other Man's Grass' and 'Kiss Me Goodbye'.

Petula appeared in two major musical movies: *Finian's Rainbow* with Fred Astaire and *Goodbye, Mr Chips* with Peter O'Toole. She also had her own television shows on both sides of the Atlantic.

Her hits in the 1970s were 'The Song Of My Life', and 'I Don't Know How To Love Him'. Her re-mix 'Downtown '88' hit the charts in 1988.

In addition to concerts, Petula set her sights on the West End stage and featured as Maria in *The Sound Of Music* in 1981–2. In 1990 she wrote her own West End musical, *Someone Like You*, in which she starred.

Petula also proved successful in her appearances as Norma Desmond in the hit Andrew Lloyd Webber musical *Sunset Boulevard*.

CLIFF, Jimmy   Born James Chambers in St Catherine, Jamaica, on 1 April 1948, Jimmy Cliff began his musical career leading Shakedown Sound and had a number of hits in Jamaica before appearing on a US tour with other artists, promoted by the Jamaican government. He was spotted by Island Records supremo Chris Blackwell who brought him to the UK, where he had a series of hits in the singles charts: 'Wonderful World Beautiful People', 'Vietnam' and 'Wild World'.

Cliff was also a songwriter and his composition 'You Can Get It If You Really Want' became a major hit for **Desmond Dekker**.

In 1973 he starred in the movie *The Harder They Come*, which has since become a cult favourite, and the following year he converted to Islam and was moved to visit Africa. He then began appearing regularly in Africa, pulling in huge audiences in South Africa, Nigeria, Senegal, Cameroon, Zambia, Lesotho and Zimbabwe.

Cliff's recording of 'I Can See Clearly Now', featured in the film *Cool Runnings*, became a hit on both sides of the Atlantic in 1994.

Jimmy Cliff remains a stadium-filling attraction in South America and Africa. In 1997,

wheels were in motion for the filming of his script of *The Harder They Fall*, a sequel to his film *The Harder They Come*.

CLOONEY, Rosemary   Born in Maysville, Kentucky, on 23 May 1928, Rosemary Clooney was one of the most popular female singing stars of the 1950s. On her first chart hit, 'You're Just In Love', she duetted with Guy Mitchell. Her other hits included: 'Come On-A-My House', 'Tenderly', 'Half As Much', 'Botch-A-Me', 'Hey There', 'Where Will The Baby's Dimple Be', 'This Ole House', 'Mambo Italiano' and 'Mangos'.

Rosemary also found success on the big screen, appearing in more than 50 films, including *The Stars Are Singing* and *White Christmas*.

Married to actor José Ferrer, personal problems affected her career during the 1960s, but she returned to form late in the 1970s, primarily as a jazz singer.

Although semi-retired for more than a decade, Rosemary Clooney has written her autobiography, *This For Remembrance*, which was turned into a television movie called *Escape From Madness*. She has also made occasional stage appearances, including a 1991 concert at Carnegie Hall, usually within easy distance of her home in New York, and has released the occasional new album of mostly jazz material.

COCKER, Joe   Born in Sheffield, South Yorkshire, on 20 May 1944, Joe Cocker began his career in 1959 as a member of the Cavaliers. The group later changed their name to Vance Arnold & the Avengers and then became the Grease Band.

Cocker's first solo effort was a cover of the Beatles' 'I'll Cry Instead', which was unsuccessful. His hit singles include: 'Marjorine', 'With A Little Help From My Friends', 'Delta Lady', 'The Letter', 'Unchain My Heart' and 'When The Night Comes'. He also had a major hit singing with Jennifer Warnes on 'Up Where We Belong', a theme song from the movie *An Officer And A Gentleman*.

Produced by Don Was, and containing several re-recordings of old material, Joe Cocker's latest album, *Organic*, was issued in late 1996. A television documentary about his 30-year career called *Joe Cocker: Have A Little Faith* was screened on UK television in December 1997 and featured interviews with **Ray Charles**, Eric Clapton and Tom Jones.

Rosemary Clooney

COCKNEY REBEL   This group was formed by Steve Harley (real name Steven Nice) in 1973. The other members were Milton Reame-James (keyboards), Jean-Paul Crocker (violin), **Paul Avron Jeffreys** (bass) and Stuart Elliot (drums).

The band's debut album was *Human Menagerie*, from which their first single, 'Sebastian', was taken. They followed with a succession of hits: 'Judy Teen', 'Mr Soft', 'Make Me Smile', 'Mr Raffles', 'Here Comes The Sun', 'Love's A Prima Donna', 'Freedom's Prisoner' and 'Ballerina'.

Their album hits included *The Psychomodo, The Best Years Of Our Lives, Timeless Flight, Love's A Prima Donna* and *Face To Face*.

During this time, Harley had broken up the band and renamed it Steve Harley & Cockney Rebel. Elliot remained on drums and the new members were Jim Cregan (guitar), Duncan Mackay (keyboards) and George Ford (bass).

Harley disbanded the group again and went solo, moving to the US for a while. He returned to the UK – and the charts, when he duetted with **Sarah Brightman** on the title song from the musical *Phantom Of The Opera* in 1986. He was even offered the lead role in the musical, but it went to Michael Crawford.

Harley recorded a solo album in 1995, *Yes You Can*, the same year that *The Best Of Steve Harley & Cockney Rebel* was released. The following year he issued another album, *Poetic Justice*, and promoted it during an extensive tour.

Original bassist Paul Avron Jeffreys was a victim in the Lockerbie air disaster in December 1988.

COHEN, Leonard   Canadian poet-singer-songwriter-author Leonard Cohen was born in Montreal on 21 September 1934. His first book of poetry, *Let Us Compare Mythologies*, was published in 1956 and his first novel, *The Favourite Game*, in 1963. Other novels include *Beautiful Losers* and *Parasites Of Heaven*, while his poetry collections include *The Spice Box Of Earth, Flowers Of Hitler, The Energy Of Slaves, Death Of A Ladies Man, Book Of Mercy* and *Stranger Music*.

Cohen's debut album, *Songs of Leonard Cohen*, was issued in 1968 and his other album releases include: *Songs From a Room, Songs of Love and Hate, Live Songs, Death of a Ladies' Man, Recent Songs, Leonard Cohen, The Future* and *Cohen Live*.

Many artists have recorded Cohen's songs and there have been a number of tribute albums. The most recent was the 1995 release

Tower Of Song: The Songs Of Leonard Cohen, which featured various artists singing his material, including Elton John, Bono, Tori Amos, the Chieftains, Suzanne Vega and Peter Gabriel.

Cohen lived with the actress Rebecca DeMornay for some time, but the couple split in 1994 when Cohen gave up his career to become a Buddhist monk.

Currently, in 1997, at the age of 63, he lives in a Zen monastery high on Mount Baldy in California. Although unmarried, he has two children, and his son Adam is a musician who signed to Sony in 1997.

COLLINS, Judy   This singer-songwriter-pianist-guitarist was born in Seattle, Washington, on 1 May 1939. At the age of 18 she married her teacher, Peter Taylor, and they went to live in the Rocky Mountains, where she gave birth to their son Clark.

Judy first began to sing in clubs in 1959 and the family moved to Chicago. She made her recording debut in 1961 with an album, *A Maid Of Constant Sorrow*, and went on to become one of the most popular female folk artists of the decade.

Judy's hit singles in the US chart include: 'Both Sides Now', 'Amazing Grace', 'Cook With Honey' and 'Send In The Clowns', the latter entering the chart in both 1975 and 1977. Her album hits include: *Whales And Nightingales, Judith* and *Amazing Grace*.

Her autobiography, *Trust Your Heart*, was published in 1988.

Tragedy struck in 1992, when Judy's son Clark died from carbon monoxide poisoning. His body was discovered in a garage belonging to his estranged wife.

Judy toured the US in 1994, the year in which her album of **Bob Dylan** covers, *Judy Sings Dylan... Just Like A Woman*, was issued. The followed year her first novel, *Shameless*, was published.

Judy Collins continues to record and is also very involved in political causes, particularly for UNICEF.

COLOSSEUM   Some former members of **John Mayall's** Bluesbreakers got together to form Colosseum in 1968. The original line-up of the band was Jon Hiseman (drums), Dick Heckstall-Smith (sax), Dave Greenslade (keyboards), Tony Reeves (bass) and James Litherland (guitar and vocals).

Litherland left, to be replaced by Dave 'Clem' Clempson, while Chris Farlowe joined as vocalist. When Reeves left, Mark Clarke replaced him. The group disbanded in 1971.

Hiseman and Clarke formed Colosseum II in 1975 with Gary Moore (guitar), Neil Murray (bass), Don Airey (keyboards) and Mike Starrs (vocals). Later, Hiseman decided he wished to return to his first love – jazz music – and he joined his wife Barbara Thompson in her jazz band Paraphernalia.

During their career Colosseum had a number of albums enter the charts: *Colosseum*, *Valentyne Suite*, *Daughter Of Time* and *Colosseum Live*.

The original line-up (Hiseman, Heckstall-Smith, Clempson, Greenslade and Clarke) re-formed in 1995. Fronted by vocalist **Chris Farlowe**, they undertook a 40-date European tour and released an in-concert album and video.

COMO, Perry Born Pierino Como on 18 May 1912, this singer's original profession was as a hairdresser, but in 1933 he decided to become a singer and joined the Freddy Carlone Band. By 1943 he had decided on a solo career and began an incredible run of hit records – almost 150 of them over a 30-year period. He also had his own television show.

Among Perry Como's numerous hits were 'Ko Ko Mo (I Love You So)', 'Tina Marie', 'Hot Diggity', 'Juke Box Baby', 'More', 'Glendora', 'Round And Round', 'Catch A Falling Star', 'Magic Moments', 'Kewpie Doll' and 'It's Impossible'.

In the late 1980s, Perry Como was still singing in Las Vegas seasons. Fulsome media tributes on the occasion of his eightieth birthday in 1992 tied in with the issue of *The Living Legend* CD retrospective.

COMSAT ANGELS This group was formed in Sheffield, South Yorkshire, in 1978. The members were Stephen Fellows (vocals and guitar), Kevin Bacon (bass), Andy Peake (keyboards) and Mik Glaisher (drums).

Three of the group's albums entered the charts: *Sleep No More*, *Fiction* and *Land*. They also had a solitary singles hit, 'Independence Day', in 1984.

The American Com Sat Corporation forced the band to change their name for US releases or appearances to CS Angels, and when they changed record labels and signed with Island Records, the label talked them into changing

their name to Dream Command. By this time Bacon had left the band.

The group reverted to their original name and recruited Simon Anderson on guitar and Terry Todd on bass, with Thunderbird Records releasing a new album, *The Glamour*, in 1995.

CONRAD, Jess Actor-singer Jess Conrad (real name Gerald James), was born in Brixton, south London, in 1935. He made his acting debut in the television play *Rock-A-Bye-Barney* in 1959. The following year he appeared on the television pop shows presented by Jack Good, which included *Oh Boy!*, *Wham!* and *Boy Meets Girl*.

Conrad then made his recording debut with 'Cherry Pie'. His only hit record was 'Mystery Girl' in 1961. He has appeared in a number of films including *Serious Charge*, *The Ugly Duckling*, *Too Young To Marry*, *The Queen's Guard*, *Rag Doll*, *The Boys*, *Konga* and *The Great Rock 'n' Roll Swindle*.

During the 1970s he appeared in a number of stage musicals, including *Joseph And The Amazing Technicolor Dreamcoat* and *Godspell*.

Conrad is married to former Dutch model girl Renée Bergman and they have two daughters. He is still actively performing.

CONWAY, Russ This British pianist had a six-year reign in the charts. He was born Trevor Stanford in Bristol on 2 September 1927, and during a stint with the Royal Navy had an accident in which the top of the third finger of his right hand was cut off. By the time he left in 1955 he had been awarded a Distinguished Service Medal. While at sea he had taught himself to play piano and when demobbed he began playing in clubs.

Signed up by A&R man Norman Newell, Conway made his recording debut with 'Party Pops', the first of a huge string of hits. He also created a record by becoming the only instrumentalist to have two consecutive No 1 hits – with 'Side Saddle' and 'Roulette'.

He had a number of bestselling albums and his singles hits included: 'Got A Match', 'More Party Pops', 'The World Outside', 'China Tea', 'Snow Coach', 'More And More Party Pops', 'Royal Event', 'Fings Ain't Wot They Used To Be', 'Lucky Five', 'Passing Breeze', 'Even More Party Pops', 'Pepe', 'Pablo', 'Toy Balloons', 'Lesson One' and 'Always You And Me'.

Conway's hits stopped coming in 1963, although he kept on working until he had a nervous breakdown and went into retirement for several years. In 1989 he was diagnosed as having stomach cancer. Six years later he lost the thumb on his left hand when his car door slammed on it. Nevertheless, he still manages to give over 20 concerts each year.

COOPER, Alice This singer, son of a preacher man, was born Vincent Damon Furnier in Detroit, Michigan, on 4 February 1948. He formed a group called the Earwigs, who then became the Spiders, then the Nazz and finally Alice Cooper. He claimed that the name was chosen because he believed he was the reincarnation of a seventeenth-century witch, and was later to adopt the name officially.

The members of the band included Mike Bruce (lead), Dennis Dunaway (bass), Glen Buxton (guitar) and Neal Smith (drums).

Wearing thick eye make-up, Alice performed bizarre acts during the heavy rock performance, using a live snake, bloodied dolls, live chickens, mock hangings and stage props which included an electric chair and guillotine.

The group's hit albums included *Love It To Death*, *School's Out*, *Billion Dollar Babies* and *Muscle Of Love*.

Cooper sacked his band in 1974 – they went on to form a group called Billion Dollar Babies. His solo career was affected by his alcoholism and his albums in the 1980s did not match the success of the band's 1970s releases, until a revival of fortunes came with *Trash* in 1989 and *Hey Stoopid* in 1991.

Cooper appeared in the movie *Wayne's World* in 1992 and recorded a new album, *The Last Temptation*, in 1994. He continues to tour and records regularly. In 1998 he opened his own sports bar in Phoenix, Arizona. Glen Buxton lives in Iowa, where he works at Goodyear Aerospace constructing radar units. Michael Bruce is a songwriter, living in Arizona, where he plays in local groups. Dennis Dunaway lives in Connecticut, where he owns an arts and crafts shop, and Neal Smith is a realtor in New England.

COSTELLO, Elvis Declan Patrick McManus was born on 25 August 1954 and moved with his mother to Liverpool in 1968. Inspired by the local music scene and having seen a performance by Nick Lowe at the Cavern Club, he moved to London and formed a band called Flip City. The singer-songwriter-guitarist then began

performing solo as D.P. Costello, the surname being his grandmother's maiden name, but was persuaded by Jake Riviera of Stiff Records to call himself Elvis Costello. He formed his group the Attractions in 1977, the other members being Steve Nieve (keyboards), Bruce Thomas (bass) and Pete Thomas (drums).

The band notched up a formidable string of hits, including: 'Watching The Detectives', '(I Don't Wanna Go To) Chelsea', 'Pump It Up', 'Radio Radio', 'Oliver's Army', 'Accidents Will Happen', 'I Can't Stand Up For Falling Down', 'Hi Fidelity', 'New Amsterdam', 'Clubland', 'A Good Year For The Roses', 'Sweet Dreams', 'I'm Your Toy', 'You Little Fool', 'Man Out Of Time', 'From Head To Toe', 'Party Party', 'Everyday I Write The Book', 'Let Them All Talk', 'I Wanna Be Loved/Turning The Town Red', 'The Only Flame In Town', 'Green Shirt', 'Don't Let Me Be Misunderstood' and 'Tokyo Storm Warning'.

Costello began extensive tours of the UK and US, and in 1986 married Caitlin O'Riordan, bassist with the **Pogues**. The same year he appeared in the movie *No Surrender*, filmed in Liverpool. The following year he collaborated with Paul McCartney on various recordings. He also began to perform increasingly with other artists and bands, apart from the Attractions.

Costello has made various other acting appearances in, for example, the 1987 movie *Straight To Hell*, directed by Alex Cox, and Alan Bleasdale's television series *Scully*. He also made an appearance in the Spice Girls' 1988 film *Spiceworld*.

Elvis Costello currently lives in Dublin, Eire, and is involved in all manner of (often iconoclastic) artistic undertakings, such as a 1995 reunion with the original Attractions, which led to their release of *All This Useless Beauty* the following year. Although his last four albums have not been commercial successes, we have not heard the last of Elvis Costello. In late 1998 the album *Painted From Memory* by Elvis Costello with Burt Bacharach was released.

COUNTRY JOE & THE FISH Joseph McDonald formed Country Joe & the Fish in San Francisco in 1964 after spending four years in the US Navy, although the band did not make their debut album, *Electric Music For The Mind And Body*, until 1967. The other members of the group were Bruce Barthol (bass), Barry Melton (guitar), David Cohen (keyboards) and Gary Hirsch (drums).

The band became a big concert draw, toured Europe, issued several albums and had various changes in personnel, before ending with an album finale, *C.J. Fish*, in 1969.

McDonald eventually re-formed the group as Country Joe & His All-Star Band in 1972. The group split two years later and McDonald and Melton became a duo, touring France for a while. In 1975 McDonald was once again touring abroad with Country Joe & His Band. In 1977 he returned to the studio with various ex-Fish to record the aptly titled *Reunion*. Over the years he has alternately continued to go solo, and then form a new band using the old Country Joe name.

COVINGTON, Julie This actress-singer was born in 1950 and made her recording debut in the late 1960s with the album *Beautiful Changes*.

She entered the UK chart with 'Don't Cry For Me Argentina', from the musical *Evita*, in 1976. The following year her second single, 'Only Women Bleed' was a hit and Julie's version of 'Don't Cry For Me Argentina' re-entered the chart in 1978.

Another success in 1977 was her appearance as part of a female group in the UK television drama series *Rock Follies*. This resulted in a chart entry with 'OK', credited to Julie Covington, Rula Lenska, Charlotte Cornwall and Sue Jones-Davies.

Julie's 1989 single, 'When Housewives Had The Choice', was the theme of a UK radio series. The lady herself is still seen on the theatre stage, and heard occasionally as a radio broadcaster.

CRAZY WORLD OF ARTHUR BROWN, The
Arthur Brown, an Oxbridge graduate, was born in Whitby, North Yorkshire, on 24 June 1944. He formed the Crazy World Of Arthur Brown in 1966 with Sean Nicholas (bass), Vincent Crane (keyboards) and Drachen Theaker (drums). His single 'Fire' was a hit, topping the UK chart and reaching No 2 in the US. Brown used to perform the number wearing a flaming fire-helmet, proclaiming 'I am the god of hell fire'.

His debut album, *The Crazy World Of Arthur Brown*, was produced by Pete Townshend, but unfortunately Brown was sued for stealing the tune of 'Fire', which resulted in him losing most of his royalties. By this time Carl Palmer had replaced Theaker, but halfway through the band's first US tour he left to join **Atomic Rooster**.

Brown was to form a new band called Kingdom Come with guitarist Andy Dalby and keyboards player Mike Harris, but they were unsuccessful and folded in 1973, with Brown moving to Texas, where he set up in business as a carpenter.

He appeared again to perform on a tour in 1993 and returned to the road once more in 1995.

When Brown appeared at the Institute of Contemporary Arts in London during the first weekend in December 1997, the *London Standard* erroneously reported that it was his first appearance in 20 years. The occasion was called The Recurring Technicolour Dream and was a celebration of the thirtieth anniversary of the original Technicolour Dream at the Alexandra Palace in 1967.

Brown remains a full-time carpenter with his painting and decorating business in Texas, in partnership with Jimmy Carl Black, a former member of the Mothers Of Invention. Drachen Theaker spent a number of years in Los Angeles as a session musician but has returned to the UK to join a jazz trio called Hazchem.

CREAM A trio that was hailed as one of the world's top bands, Cream comprised Eric Clapton (guitar), Jack Bruce (bass) and Ginger Baker (drums). Their hits included: 'Wrapping Paper', 'I Feel Free', 'Strange Brew', 'Anyone For Tennis', 'Sunshine Of Your Love' and 'White

Ginger Baker, drummer with Cream

Room And Badge'. Their hit albums were *Fresh Cream*, *Disraeli Gears*, *Wheels Of Fire*, *Goodbye*, *Best Of Cream*, *Live Cream* and *Live Cream Vol 2*.

Despite their huge following and success on record, in 1968 Cream announced that they would be disbanding, as they had taken their music as far as it would go. Their farewell concert took place at the Royal Albert Hall in November of that year and was filmed by Tony Palmer for a television documentary.

Clapton and Baker then went on to form **Blind Faith**, while Bruce embarked on a solo career.

Eric Clapton remains an international star, whose albums are bought *en masse* almost out of habit. He has carved a second career with psychiatrist-couch discussions to the media about his life, his soul and his torment.

Tragedy seemed to dog him for a number of years. His five-year-old son Conor, the result of an affair with Italian model Lori del Santo, fell to his death from a fifty-third floor apartment window in New York. Clapton was to express his grief in the song 'Tears In Heaven'. In 1990 a helicopter crash claimed the life of his close friend Stevie Ray Vaughan, who had just performed on stage with him. Other victims of the crash included Clapton's agent, his tour manager and his bodyguard. His former girlfriend Alice Ormsby-Gore became hooked on drugs and he helped her enter rehab, but she died from an overdose.

Clapton himself was hooked on drugs for 20 years, and sex and drugs featured prominently in his life. He married Pattie Boyd, ex-wife of his best friend George Harrison, and his lovers and girlfriends have included a variety of models, film stars and singers, including Sheryl Crow, Michelle Pfeiffer, Paula Hamilton, Stephanie Beacham and Susannah Doyle.

Clapton's grief for Conor received some consolation when he rediscovered his daughter Ruth, born from a liaison in 1984.

His own childhood was rather strange. He was reared by his grandparents in Sussex, believing that his mother was his elder sister. He never knew his father, a Canadian soldier who returned home to his wife. His mother Pat also married a Canadian soldier and went to live abroad.

For several years Clapton held regular concert seasons at the Royal Albert Hall, but in 1998 announced that he was ending them as music was now only third on the list of his priorities.

By 1998 the 53-year-old superstar was spending most of his days working with counsellors to help drug addicts and alcoholics in a London centre. He had also established a 36-bed clinic in Antigua, where he has a home.

1998 also saw the release of a new CD, *Pilgrim*.

The recorded output of Jack Bruce and Ginger Baker is more intermittent, although both of them joined up with guitarist Gary Moore in 1994 for a global tour with a set centred on Cream numbers.

CREATION   This group were originally called the Mark Four, when the members were **Kenny Pickett** (vocals), Eddie Phillips (lead), Mick Thompson (rhythm), John Dalton (bass) and Jack Jones (drums).

Dalton left to join the Kinks and Thompson abandoned music. The others decided to remain together with the addition of former **Merseybeats** member Bob Garner, and they changed their name to Creation in 1966.

The group had two hit singles that year, 'Making Time' and 'Painter Man'. The group broke up in 1968.

Eddie Phillips released a solo album, *Riffmaster Of The Western World*, in 1990. The original line-up of Creation re-formed in 1993. Kenny Pickett died in 1996.

CREEDENCE CLEARWATER REVIVAL
Multi-instrumentalist John Fogerty first formed a band while at high school in California. Other members included Stu Cook (bass), Doug 'Cosmo' Clifford (drums) and his brother Tom (rhythm).

They initially formed as Tom Fogerty & the Blue Velvets, but changed their name to the Visions in 1964 and later that year, when they signed to Fantasy Records, were renamed the Golliwogs. Under this name they made several records without success, until John and Clifford entered national service. They returned to the band in 1967 and the new name Creedence Clearwater Revival was chosen. They took the word Creedence from a friend of Tom's called Creedence Nuball and Clearwater from a beer commercial.

From 1968 the band were to begin a hit streak with chart singles including: 'Suzi Q (Part One)', 'Proud Mary', 'Bad Moon Rising', 'Green River',

'Commotion', 'Down On The Corner', 'Fortunate Son', 'Travelin' Band', 'Up Around The Bend', 'Lookin' Out My Back Door', 'Have You Ever Seen The Rain', 'Sweet Hitch-Hiker' and 'Someday Never Comes'.

Their album hits included: *Creedence Clearwater Revival*, *Bayou Country*, *Willie And The Poorboys*, *Cosmo's Factory* and *Pendulum*.

Following the lack of success of their album *Mardi Gras*, the group split at the end of 1972.

John Fogerty began recording as a one-man band under the name the Blue Ridge Rangers and hit the chart with 'Jambalaya' and 'Hearts Of Stone'. He then began to record and perform under his own name, releasing the album *John Fogerty* in 1975, *Centrefield* in 1984 and *Eye of the Zombie* in 1988.

In the meantime, Clifford and Cook had been appearing with the Don Harrison Band, while various Creedence records were re-released as compilations. The group re-formed in 1980 to perform at John's wedding and at a reunion event at their old high school.

Tom had been suffering from tuberculosis for some years and finally died from respiratory failure in September 1990.

John continued to perform, but his relations with the other two surviving members of the band were obviously strained. When the group were inducted into the Rock & Roll Hall Of Fame in 1993, Fogerty would not allow Clifford and Cook to join him on stage when a selection of Creedence hits were performed.

Clifford and Cook have continued as backing musicians to Don Harrison and also Doug Sahm. John Fogerty played solo concerts in the UK as recently as October 1997.

CREOLE, Kid This entertainer was born Thomas Darnell Browder on 12 August 1950. He was also known as Argyle Knept. In the mid-1960s he led Dr Buzzard's Original Savvana Band, which he ran until 1976. He then emerged in 1979 as Kid Creole with his troupe the Coconuts, although he also made solo records.

Between 1981 and 1983 his hits included: 'Me No Pop I', 'I'm A Wonderful Thing Baby', 'Stool Pigeon', 'Annie I'm Not Your Daddy', 'Dear Addy', 'There's Something Wrong In Paradise' and 'The Lifeboat Party'.

Kid Creole performed a couple of his old hits on UK television as recently as October 1997 for the programme *Night Fever*.

CROSBY, STILLS, NASH & YOUNG This group was originally formed in 1968 as Crosby, Stills & Nash with members David Crosby (guitar), Stephen Stills (vocals and guitar) and Graham Nash (vocals and guitar). Crosby had been a member of the Byrds, Stills of **Buffalo Springfield** and Nash of the **Hollies**.

They made an impact the following year with their album *Crosby, Stills & Nash*, followed by *Marrakesh Express*, and their chart singles included: 'Marrakesh Express', 'Suite: Judy Blue Eyes', 'Just A Song Before I Go', 'Wasted On The Way' and 'Southern Cross'.

Neil Young, another former member of Buffalo Springfield, joined them, and this combination hit the singles chart with 'Woodstock', 'Teach Your Children', 'Ohio' and 'Our House'.

Album releases included *Déjà Vu* and *Four Way Street*. The group then folded in 1971.

Crosby and Nash continued as a duo during the 1970s, while Stills and Nash opted for solo careers. Stills had hits with 'Love The One You're With' and 'Sit Yourself Down', while Young's hits included 'Only Love Can Break Your Heart', 'Heart Of Gold' and 'Old Man',

In 1977 Crosby, Stills & Nash reunited for an album, then split again, but came together once more in 1982.

Crosby was jailed for a drugs offence in 1985 and released in 1987, when the group once again resumed their career.

Crosby, Stills & Nash remain a popular concert attraction and had a minor chart entry with their *After the Storm* album in 1993, the year Crosby underwent a liver transplant.

Neil Young has long resumed a successful solo career.

CRUSH, Bobby Pianist Bobby Crush entered the UK chart with 'Borsalino', the catchy theme tune to a French film starring Alain Delon and Jean-Paul Belmondo, in 1972. He has since been a successful instrumentalist on variety bill, although he has not revisited the singles chart, his albums are steady sellers and include chart entries such as *Bobby Crush* and *The Bobby Crush Incredible Double Decker Party*.

To coincide with a tour by Gene Pitney in 1995, *Reel Music*, Bobby Crush's fourteenth album, did brisk business. Also a singing actor, Crush has appeared in remakes on stage and on disc of *Hair* and *Joseph And The Amazing Technicolor Dreamcoat*, as well as in the role of Dr Frank N. Furter in *The Rocky Horror Show*.

However, just as jaw-dropping in its way was Bobby on UK television's *Viva Cabaret!* giving 'em a piano medley of punk evergreens.

CULTURE CLUB This group was formed in 1981, led by the androgynous Boy George (real name George O'Dowd) on vocals. The other members were Jon Moss (drums), Roy Hay (guitar and keyboards) and Michael Craig (bass).

They made their recording debut with 'Kissing To Be Clever' in 1982. Other hits which followed included: 'Do You Really Want To Hurt Me', 'Time (Clock Of The Heart)', 'Church Of The Poison Mind', 'Karma Chameleon' and 'Victims'.

Boy George's proclaimed homosexuality and transvestite dress initially created waves, particularly in the States, but he managed to overcome the prejudice and the group had three US Top 20 entries.

Boy George, the obvious focal point of the band, then went solo and topped the UK chart in 1987 with 'Everything I Own'. He followed this with a series of hits, including: 'Keep Me in Mind, 'Sold', 'To Be Reborn', 'Live My Life', 'No Clause 28', 'Don't Cry', 'Everything Starts With An E', 'After The Love', 'Bow Down Mister', 'Generations Of Love', 'Sweet Toxic Love', 'The Crying Game' and 'More Than Likely'. Albums included *The Martyr Mantras*, *The Devil in Sister George* and *Cheapness and Beauty*.

George was born in Eltham, Middlesex, on 13 June 1961. He initially made guest appearances with **Bow Wow Wow** under the name Lieutenant Lush. His solo career was even more outstanding than his success with Culture Club, and apart from maintaining his position as a chart artist he also became a successful disc jockey and newspaper columnist.

George's autobiography, *Take It Like A Man*, was published in 1995 and is due to become a major feature film. He topped the bill at the Royal Albert Hall in June 1998, when he celebrated his thirty-seventh birthday.

Culture Club re-formed in 1998 following a multi-million dollar offer for a 100-date tour of the US midway through the year.

CUPID'S INSPIRATION This group was led by vocalist Terry Rice-Milton, the other members being Wyndham George (guitar), Laughton James (bass) and Roger Gray (drums). They later added pianist Garfield Tonkin to the line-up. They had two chart singles in 1968 – 'Yesterday Has Gone' and 'My World' – the former a Top 5 entry, the latter a minor hit.

Having no further success on record, the group split up at the end of that year. Rice-Milton immediately re-formed it with himself and two new members, Gordon Haskell (bass) and Bernie Lee (guitar). They attempted a new musical direction, but their endeavour to 'go progressive' failed and they disbanded in 1969.

Gordon Haskell joined **King Crimson**.

In the 1990s, a Cupid's Inspiration was rumoured to be in rehearsal for an assault on the UK nostalgia scene.

CURVED AIR This band was formed in 1970 with Sonja Kristina, who was born in Brentwood, Essex, on 14 April 1949, as singer, guitarist, pianist and songwriter. Other members included Darryl Way (violin), Florian Pilkington Miska (guitar), Francis Monkman (keyboards) and Ian Erye (bass).

They made their recording debut with the album *Air Conditioning*, one of the first picture discs, and had a sole singles chart entry with 'Back Street Luv'. There were various changes in the line-up and by 1972 Sonja was the only original member left. The group disbanded for two years while she appeared in the musical *Hair* and they then re-formed, cut two more albums and disbanded for the last time in 1977.

Sonja is still active on the theatrical and musical stage as a performer and promoter and is married to ex-**Police** man Steward Copeland, who had replaced Miska on drums. Miska himself quit the music business after an unsuccessful recording studio venture. Monkman and Way are still working musicians, but tend towards modern interpretations of classical works rather than pop.

DAMNED, The When this group was formed in 1976 during the punk explosion, with Dave Vanian on vocals and Brian James on guitar, bassist Ray Burns called himself Captain Sensible and drummer Chris Miller dubbed himself Rat Scabies. The following year, Robert Edmunds joined them on guitar.

The group disbanded at the beginning of 1978 and all four of the original members joined different bands. They got together again a few months later for a farewell gig, then three of them – Scabies, Sensible and Vanian – decided to stay together as a trio and performed under different names until they officially acquired the Damned name from Brian James. They then added Alistair Ward on bass. Ward left in 1980 and was replaced by Paul Gray. Keyboards player Roman Juggs joined them in October 1962.

Members of the group also pursued solo projects, and Captain Sensible had hits with 'Happy Talk', 'Glad It's all Over', 'There Are More Snakes Than Ladders' and 'Wot'. By 1984 he had left the band once again.

The band broke up again following their farewell tour in 1989, then reunited once more in 1991.

The Damned's hit singles included: 'Love Song', 'Smash It Up', 'I Just Can't Be Happy Today', 'History Of The World', 'Friday 13th', 'Lovely Money', 'Thanks For The Night', 'Grimly Fiendish', 'The Shadow Of Love, 'Is It A Dream', 'Eloise', 'Anything', 'Gigolo', 'Alone Again Or' and 'In Dulce Decorum'.

Album hits included: *Damned Damned Damned*, *Machine Gun Etiquette*, *The Black Album*, *Best Of The Damned*, *Strawberries* and *Phantasmagoria*.

The former members of the Damned are content to embark on individual projects – such as Dave Vanian and Roman Jugg's membership of the Phantom Chords – while reuniting for periodic mortgage-paying engagements that have an air of nostalgia about them.

DAMONE, Vic Born Vito Farinola in Brooklyn, New York, on 12 June 1928, Vic Damone first began recording in 1947 and had considerable success in the heyday of the crooners, with almost 40 hits, including: 'On The Street Where You Live', 'An Affair To Remember', 'You Were Only Fooling', 'Again', 'You're Breaking My Heart', 'Tzena Tzena Tzena', 'Eternally', 'Ebb Tide', 'My Heart Cries For You' and 'My Truly Truly Fair'.

Damone had his own US radio and television shows during the 1950s and appeared in several films, including *Rich, Young And Pretty*, *Athena*, *Deep In My Heart* and *Kismet*.

Since the early 1980s, Vic Damone has recorded several new albums to be sold in theatre foyers on his regular concert tours around the world.

DANA This Irish singer was born Rosemary Brown in the Bogside area of Londonderry, Northern Ireland, on 20 August 1951. While still a schoolgirl, she won the Eurovision Song Contest for Eire in 1970 with 'All Kinds Of Everything', which went on to top the UK chart. Her other hits included: 'Who Put The Lights Out', 'Please Tell Him That I Said Hello', 'It's Gonna Be A Cold Cold Christmas', 'Never Gonna Fall In Love Again', 'Fairytale', 'Something's Cookin' In The Kitchen' and 'I Feel Love Comin''.

Over the years, Dana performed regularly in cabaret and in pantomimes. In 1990 she moved to the States, where she married a preacher and hosted her own radio show, *Mother Angella*, for several years, before returning to Eire in 1997 to stand for President in the elections on 30 October. Despite being backed by the Roman Catholic church, the odds of her winning were quoted by bookmakers at 25-1. She surprised everyone by coming in third.

DANNY & THE JUNIORS The members of this vocal outfit from Philadelphia were **Danny Rapp** (lead vocals), Joe Terranova (baritone), Frank Mettei (second tenor) and Dave White (first tenor).

It was entrepreneur Artie Singer who spotted the boys, became their manager and co-penned their biggest hit with them, 'At The Hop'. The number topped the US chart in 1958. Two other big hits, 'Rock And Roll Is Here To Stay' and 'Dottie', followed.

During the early 1960s the group recorded 'Twistin' USA', 'Pony Express', 'Back On The Hop', 'Twistin' All Night Long' and 'Doin' The Continental Walk'. They disbanded in 1963.

In 1971 Dave White recorded a solo album, *Pastel, Paint, Paper And Ink*, under his real name, David White Tricker.

A reissued 'At The Hop' returned the group to the UK Top 40 in 1976, seven years before leader Danny Rapp's apparent suicide in his Arizona home.

D'ARBY, Terence Trent   Singer-songwriter Terence Trent D'Arby was born on 15 March 1962 in New York. The son of a Pentecostal preacher, he experienced a variety of jobs, including as a journalist and as a boxer, before he joined the US Army and was posted to Germany. While there, he joined a group in Frankfurt called Touch.

By 1987 D'Arby had moved to London, where he launched a solo career. His hit singles included: 'If You Let Me Stay', 'Wishing Well', 'Dance Little Sister', 'Sign Your Name', 'Do You Love Me Like You Say', 'Delicate', 'She Kissed Me', 'Let Her Down Easy' and 'Holding On To You',

His debut album, *Introducing The Hard Line According To Terence Trent D'Arby*, topped the UK chart. His second album, *Neither Fish Nor Fowl*, reached No 12 in the chart, followed by a No 4 position for his third album, *Terence Trent D'Arby's Symphony Or Damn Exploring The Tension Inside The Sweetness*.

Having also enjoyed chart and performance success in the States, D'Arby has appeared on many leading television shows on both sides of the Atlantic and made an impressive appearance at the John Lennon tribute concert in Liverpool in 1990.

Now sporting blond locks, he continues in an attempt to reclaim further popularity with albums such as his 1995 release *Terence Trent D'Arby's Vibrator*, which was issued to tie in with his UK tour that year.

D'Arby has always experienced a volatile relationship with the press, who regarded him as a loudmouth due to his extravagant claims about his talent. His girlfriend Mary Vango gave birth to their daughter Seraphina at the close of 1998.

DAVE CLARK FIVE, The   This group from Tottenham, north London, first found success with the single 'Do You Love Me' and topped the UK chart with their next release, 'Glad All Over'. The band comprised Dave Clark (drums), Mike Smith (keyboards and vocals), Rick Huxley (bass), Denis Payton (tenor sax and guitar) and Len Davidson (guitar).

Danny and the Juniors

They were to have 22 hits in the UK over a ten-year period during the 1960s and 24 singles in the US chart. These included: 'Bits And Pieces', 'Can't You See That She's Mine', 'Because', 'Everybody Knows (I Still Love You)', 'Any Way You Want It', 'Come Home', 'Reelin' And Rockin'', 'I Like It Like That', 'Catch Us If You Can', 'Over And Over', 'At The Scene', 'Try Too Hard', 'Please Tell Me Why', 'You Got What It Takes' and 'You Must Have Been A Beautiful Baby'.

Leading contenders in the 'British Invasion' of the US following the success of the Beatles, the Dave Clark Five even starred in their own film, *Catch Us If You Can*, in 1965. The group disbanded in August 1970.

Dave Clark is a successful businessman and theatrical impresario. Mike Smith still lives in London and writes and produces jingles. Denis Payton is a partner in a Bournemouth estate agency. Lenny Davidson is believed to be a greyhound trainer in north London. Rick Huxley runs a musical equipment shop in Middlesex.

DAVE DEE, DOZY, BEAKY, MICK & TICH

This group was originally formed in 1963 as Dave Dee & the Bostons. The lead singer was David Harmon, who adopted the name Dave Dee. The other members were Trevor Davies (bass), known as Dozy; John Dymond (guitar), known as Beaky; Michael Wilson (lead guitar), known as Mick; and Ian Amey (drums), known as Tich.

During a tour supporting the **Honeycombs**, they were spotted by Ken Howard and Alan Blaikley, who managed the band and began to pen their songs. The group's hit singles stretched from 1965 to 1969 and included: 'You Make It Move', 'Hold Tight', 'Hideaway', 'Bend It', 'Save Me', 'Touch Me Touch Me', 'Okay', 'Zabadack!', 'Legend Of Xanadu', 'Last Night In Soho', 'Wreck Of The Antoinette', 'Don Juan' and 'Snake In The Grass'.

Dave Dee then left the band to embark on a solo career, while the others continued as a quintet. He did not succeed as a solo artist and became an A&R man. The rest of the band had a minor hit with 'Mr President' and a chart album, *Fresh Ears*, before breaking up.

Over the years there were occasional reunions, and during the 1970s and 1980s Dozy, Beaky, Mick & Tich toured extensively in Europe and the Middle East. In the late 1980s they entertained the rich and famous at their Club 60s bar in Marbella, Spain.

Dave Dee settled in Cheshire and released a solo album in 1995, produced by Sandy Newman of **Marmalade**. He has now teamed up with Marmalade and currently lives in Queens Park, London.

From their base in Salisbury, Wiltshire, Dozy and Tich continue to work as Dozy, Beaky, Mick & Tich, with a new Beaky and Mick. John Dymond, the original Beaky, lives in Marbella and leads his own group, the Beakles, while Michael Wilson has a driving school in Salisbury. Ian Amey runs an old people's home in Salisbury with his wife and sister.

DAVID & JONATHAN This vocal duo brought together Roger Cook and Roger Greenaway. Greenaway had previously been a member of another vocal group, the Kestrels. The two initially teamed up as a songwriting duo and penned the hit 'You've Got Your Troubles' for the **Fortunes**. With Greenaway as David and Cook as Jonathan, they recorded the Lennon & McCartney number 'Michelle' and reached No 11 in the UK chart. Another Lennon & McCartney song, 'She's Leaving Home', made no chart impact, although they were to be successful with their self-penned hit 'Lovers Of The World Unite'.

The pair had no further record success under that name, but they composed several numbers which various artists took into the charts. They also collaborated with a number of session musicians in the band Blue Mink, with Cook and singer Madeline Bell fronting the group. This outfit had seven chart entries, including 'Melting Pot' and 'Stay With Me'.

Roger Cook currently commutes between Nashville and London for numerous songwriting projects and has penned numbers for the likes of **Crystal Gayle** and Don Williams. Roger Greenaway is an executive with the Performing Rights Society. The two join forces occasionally for charity events.

DAVIS, Billie Born Carol Hedges in Woking, Surrey, in 1945, this singer made her chart entry duetting with **Mike Sarne** on the 1962 hit 'Will I What'. The following year she charted in her own right with 'Tell Him'. Her third hit was 'He's The One'.

Billie's romance with **Jet Harris** ended following a car crash in which they were both involved. She next had a minor hit in 1968 with 'I Want You To Be My Baby', then began appearing regularly on the Continent, particularly in Spain.

For a number of years her name was linked romantically with **P.J. Proby**. She still performs regularly and also has her own floral design business.

DEE, Kiki Born Pauline Matthews on 6 March 1947, Kiki Dee's first hit single was 'Amoureuse' in 1973, followed by 'I've Got The Music In Me'. She duetted with Elton John on the international hit 'Don't Go Breaking My Heart'.

Her acoustic album, *Almost Naked* – notable for the nudity on the cover – was released in 1996. She is also one of the actress-singers who appeared in stage presentations of Willy Russell's *Blood Brothers*.

DEEP PURPLE This progressive British heavy metal band made their recording debut with 'Hush' in 1968. The record sold a million and reached No 4 in the US chart. In 1969 they performed *Concerto for Group and Orchestra* at the Royal Albert Hall with the London Philharmonic Orchestra and in the US at the Hollywood Bowl with the Los Angeles Philharmonic.

Edinburgh-born Rod Evans was the group's lead singer and composed original music for the band with Jon Lord, who played organ. Other members were Nicky Simper (bass), Ritchie Blackmore (lead guitar) and Ian Paice (drums). Roger Glover and Ian Gillan were to replace Evans and Simper in 1969.

Deep Purple made their first inroads in the States, having three singles in the chart that were not even released in the UK. Following 'Hush', their first album, *Shades Of Deep Purple*, charted in the US, followed by hit singles such as 'Kentucky Woman' and 'River Deep Mountain High', and further albums such as *The Book Of Taliesyn* and *Deep Purple In Concert*.

Their hit singles in the UK over two decades included: 'Black Night', 'Strange Kind Of Woman', 'Fireball', 'Never Before', 'Smoke On The Water', 'New Live And Rare', 'Perfect Strangers', 'Knocking At Your Back Door', 'Strangers' and a re-recorded version of 'Hush', which hit the UK chart in 1980.

Album hits were many and included: *The Gemini Suite*, *Deep Purple In Rock*, *Fireball*, *Machine Head*, *Purple Passages* and *Who Do We Think We Are*.

Gillan and Glover left the group in 1973, to be replaced by Dave Coverdale and Glenn Hughes. Blackmore quit in 1975 to form Rainbow and American musician Tommy Bolin replaced him.

Deep Purple disbanded in 1976, with Coverdale forming Whitesnake, Lord and Paice forming Paice, Ashton & Lord with Tony Ashton, Hughes rejoining his former band Trapeze and Bolin returning to the US to form the Tommy Bolin Band.

Blackmore, Gillan, Glover, Lord and Paice re-formed in 1984 and began to record and to tour again. Gillan quit once again in 1989 to go solo.

The group reunited again in 1992 with Blackmore, Lord, Paice, Glover and Gillan, releasing a new album, *The Battle Rages On*, in 1993.

A new Deep Purple album, *Purpendicular*, was released in 1996. It featured original members Jon Lord, Ian Gillan, Ian Paice and Roger Glover. The group which began a UK tour that year included Gillan, Glover, Lord, Paice and an American musician, Steve Morse.

DEKKER, Desmond Born Desmond Dacres in Jamaica on 16 July 1942, singer-songwriter Desmond Dekker made his recording debut in 1963 with 'Honour Your Mother And Father'. In his home in Kingston he was recognized as a leading musician and dubbed 'King Of The Blue Beat'. He formed his own band, the Aces, who regularly topped the Jamaican chart.

Dekker found success in the UK chart and his hit singles included: '007', 'The Israelites', 'It Miek', 'Pickney Gal', 'You Can Get It If You Really Want' and 'Sing A Little Song'. 'The Israelites' actually charted on three different occasions in the UK.

In 1993, Desmond Dekker, who tours the UK on a regular basis, recorded the album *King Of Kings* with British musicians. The same year, Rhino Records issued a retrospective, *Rockin' Steady – The Best Of Desmond Dekker*.

DENE, Terry Born Terry Williams in London on 20 December 1938, this singer was discovered at the famous 2 I's club in Old Compton Street, Soho, and appeared on the UK television pop show *6.5 Special*. He was later to star in the film *The Golden Disc*.

Decca's Dick Rowe signed him up and his hits in the 1950s included' A White Sport Coat', 'Start Movin'' and 'Stairway Of Love'.

57

In 1959 Dene was called up for national service, but was released two months later as being 'medically unfit'. His marriage to singer Edna Savage broke up and he had problems with alcohol. His promising career virtually in tatters, he became an evangelist, singing on street corners and recording three gospel albums.

Dene then went to Sweden for five years and in 1978 issued an album and an autobiography, both called *I Thought Terry Dene Was Dead*.

In the 1980s he became a rock 'n' roll singer again and formed a group called the Dene-Aces.

In April 1997, Terry Dene was among the guests at a star-studded skiffle evening at London's 100 club.

DENVER, Karl Leader of his eponymous trio, Karl Denver was born Angus MacKenzie in Scotland on 17 December 1934. He lived in Nashville for three years before returning to the UK, where he was discovered by Jack Good and had 11 chart hits between 1961 and 1964 including: 'Marcheta', 'Mexicali Rose', 'Wimoweh', 'Never Goodbye', 'A Little Love A Little Kiss', 'Blue Weekend', 'Can You Forgive Me', 'Indian Love Call', 'Still My World Of Blue' and 'Love Me With All Of Your Heart'.

The Karl Denver Trio were resident on the UK radio series *Side By Side*, on which the Beatles appeared as guests, and they were also booked to appear on the special Beatles edition of the television show *Shindig*.

In 1989, Karl Denver remade 'Wimoweh' with the Happy Mondays. A year later, the amalgam tried again with 'Lazyitis' and were rewarded with a Top 50 entry.

DE PAUL, Lynsey This singer-composer-producer was born on 11 June 1950. Her hits in the 1970s included: 'Sugar Me', 'Getting A Drag', 'Won't Somebody Dance With Me', 'Ooh I Do', 'No Honestly' and 'My Man And Me'. She also appeared with Mike Moran singing 'Rock Bottom' on the Eurovision Song Contest in 1977.

Lynsey had a four-year relationship with actor James Coburn and her name was also romantically linked with Dudley Moore, Ringo Starr and Sean Connery. She currently lives in St John's Wood, London, and in 1996 produced a children's album, 'How Do You Do, I'm Marcus'.

DE SHANNON, Jackie Born Sharon Myers on 21 August 1944, this singer-songwriter initially started recording under the name Sherry Lee Myers in 1959 and began composing in 1960. She was included on the bill of a Beatles tour of the States in 1964 and has penned over 600 songs during her career, among them many hits for artists ranging from the Byrds to **Brenda Lee**.

Jackie was also to have hits in her own right with 'What The World Needs Now Is Love', 'Put A Little Love In Your Heart' and 'Love Will Find A Way'.

In more recent years, as always, California-based Jackie has concentrated more on songwriting than performing. In 1988, Al Green and Annie Lennox's version of her 'Put A Little Love In Your Heart' reached the UK Top 30.

DEXY'S MIDNIGHT RUNNERS This group was formed in 1978 and made their recording debut the following year with 'Dance Stance', which entered the UK chart, and followed with 'Geno', a tribute to Geno Washington, the soul singer.

'There There My Dear', 'Plan B', 'Show Me', 'The Celtic Soul Brothers', 'Come On Eileen', 'Jackie Wilson Said', 'Let's Get This Straight (From The Start)' and 'Because of You' were other chart entries.

The group comprised Kevin Rowland (vocals and guitar), Al Archer (guitar), Pete Williams (bass), Pete Saunders (organ), Andy Growcott (drums), Big Jimmy Patterson (trombone), Steve 'Babyface' Spooner (alto sax) and Jeff Blythe (tenor sax).

They split in two in 1980, with Rowland and Patterson recruiting new members and continuing as Dexy's Midnight Runners, while the others called themselves the Bureau.

By 1982 Rowland was the only surviving original member. The band finally split in 1985, and in the 1990s Rowland found himself in financial trouble and was declared bankrupt in 1991. By 1994 a Sunday newspaper was reporting that he was on the dole and had checked into a drug rehabilitation clinic. However, he had a hand in *It Was Like This*, a 1996 Dexy's Midnight Runners retrospective album. That December, he was signed as a solo artist to Creation Records.

DIAMONDS, The This vocal group originally formed in 1954 and comprised Stan Fisher (lead vocals), Ted Kowalski (tenor) and Bill Reed (bass). The same year Stan Fisher left, to be replaced by Dave Somerville.

After recording 'The Stroll' in 1955, Kowalski

and Reed left. Evan Fisher and John Felton replaced them on tenor and bass voices respectively.

The group then had hits with 'Why Do Fools Fall In Love', 'Church Bells May Ring', 'Love Love Love' and 'Ka-Ding-Dong'. In 1957 their biggest hit, 'Little Darlin'', reached No 2 in the US chart and No 3 in the UK.

Other singles which made the US chart included: 'Zip Zip', 'Silhouettes', 'The Stroll', 'Walking Along' and 'She Say (Oom Dooby Doom)'.

There were various personnel changes before the group split up in 1961. The original band held a reunion in 1973 on a US television special.

John Felton died on 18 May 1982.

In the 1990s, a version of the Diamonds is still working the clubs and state fairs of the US.

DICKSON, Barbara   Born in Dumfermline, Scotland, on 27 September 1947, this singer-songwriter began her career as a folksinger in a trio, along with Rab Noakes and Archie Fisher.

She made her solo debut with the album *From the Beggar's Mantle*. Barbara then appeared in the musical *John, Paul, George, Ringo & Bert* and began to find success as a solo artist with hits such as 'Answer Me', 'January February', 'Another Suitcase in Another Hall', 'Caravan Song', 'In The Night' and 'I Know Him So Well', a duet she sang with Elaine Paige. This number, from the musical *Chess*, topped the UK chart.

Barbara also found success on stage and won an award for her role in *Blood Brothers*. She also appeared in dramatic roles on television and received acclaim for her appearance in *Band Of Gold*. She is married to Oliver, a UK television production manager, and has three children – Colm, Gabriel and Archie. In 1995 she was received a Lifetime Achievement Award from BAFTA (British Academy Of Songwriters, Composers And Authors).

During 1997 Barbara appeared in Melbourne, Australia, in *Chess*. From October 1997 she starred in *The Seven Ages Of Women* at the Playhouse Theatre, Liverpool, Chelmsford Civic Theatre, Lincoln Theatre Royal and Oldham Coliseum Theatre.

DIDDLEY, Bo   Otha Ellas Bates was born on 30 December 1928 in Mississippi. Raised by relatives, he was given the name McDaniels. His sister Lucille bought him his first guitar and he began a career as a blues performer. While in his teens he also trained as a boxer, which is when he adopted the name Bo Diddley.

His biggest US hit was 'Say Man' in 1959. Diddley then became an inspiration to British acts such as the **Rolling Stones**, and in 1963 he arrived in the UK to tour with the **Everly Brothers** and the Stones, backed by the 'Duchess' – Norma Jean Wofford – and Jerome Green. During that year he had two hits in the UK chart: 'Pretty Thing' and 'Hey Good Lookin''.

Over the years, Diddley has continued to star at rock 'n' roll revival concerts and in 1973 recorded the album *The London Bo Diddley Sessions* with British guest musicians. During that year he also appeared in the film *Let The Good Times Roll*.

Diddley has been particularly active in the 1990s and appeared on tours with **Chuck Berry** and the Rolling Stones. He was inducted into the Rock & Roll Hall Of Fame in 1987 and received a Lifetime Achievement Award at the Rhythm & Blues Foundation Awards in 1996.

Produced by Mike Vernon, a new Bo Diddley album, *A Man Amongst Men*, was released in 1996. Among the various stars guesting on it were Keith Richards, Ron Wood and Johnny 'Guitar' Watson.

DION   Vocalist Dion DiMucci was born in the Bronx, New York, on 18 July 1939. He made his debut disc, 'The Chosen Few', in 1959 with a group of singers called the Timberlanes, but preferred to have his own backing band and found various singers on the street corners in his neighbourhood. He engaged Fred Milano and Angelo D'Aleo (tenor vocals) and Carlo Mastrangelo (bass vocals) to join him as the Belmonts. When D'Aleo was conscripted, the group continued as a trio. The group then split in 1960, with Dion going solo and the Belmonts continuing to record on another record label.

The hits by Dion & the Belmonts were: 'I Wonder Why', 'No One Knows', 'Don't Pity Me', 'A Teenager In Love', 'When Or Where', 'When You Wish Upon A Star' and 'In The Still Of The Night'.

Hits by the solo Dion included: 'Lonely Teenager', 'Runaround Sue', 'The Wanderer', 'The Majestic', 'Lovers Who Wander', 'Little Diane', 'Love Came To Me', 'Ruby Baby', 'Sandy', 'This Little Girl', 'Be Careful Of Stones That You Throw', 'Donna The Prima Donna', 'Drip Drop' and 'Abraham, Martin And John'.

The Belmonts had a number of hits on their own, including: 'Tell Me Why', 'Come On Little Angel' and 'Anne-Marie'.

Dion co-wrote one of his biggest hits, the chart-topper 'Runaround Sue', and then married the real-life Sue who had inspired the song. During the height of his popularity in the 1960s he was appearing in films such as *Teenage Millionaire*, *Don't Knock The Twist*, *Twist Around The Clock* and *Ten Girls Ago*. Dion also became the only popular music artist apart from **Bob Dylan** to appear on the cover of the Beatles' album *Sgt Pepper's Lonely Hearts Club Band*.

In 1972 he was reunited with the Belmonts for a concert at Madison Square Garden. The concert was recorded and issued as an album called *Reunion*. As a solo artist, he recorded his new calling-card number, 'King Of The New York Streets'.

Dion was inducted into the Rock & Roll Hall Of Fame in 1989. He is still an active concert performer, evoking interest in his latest releases as well as a back catalogue of hits.

DISTEL, Sacha This French guitarist-singer was born in 1933. His uncle was the band leader Ray Ventura. He lived through the occupation, when the Nazis took his mother to an extermination camp. Fortunately, she was to survive after 19 months of imprisonment.

Distel joined Ventura's music publishing company, became a jazz instrumentalist and had his first hit in France in 1956 with 'Scoubidou'. As a jazz guitarist he recorded with Lionel Hampton, Stan Getz, Dizzy Gillespie and the Modern Jazz Quartet. In 1959 he became romantically involved with Brigitte Bardot.

During the 1960s, **Petula Clark** and her husband Claude Wolff brought Distel to England, where he toured clubs throughout the decade and appeared on most of the major television variety shows. Distel's biggest international hit was 'Raindrops Keep Falling On My Head'.

In 1985 the car he was driving crashed and his passenger, soap opera actress Chantel Nobel, was seriously injured and fell into a coma. She was later confined to a wheelchair. Distel received a one-month suspended sentence, later overturned.

Distel has survived two bouts of cancer. He was diagnosed with thyroid cancer and had a tumour removed, then later developed skin cancer and underwent chemotherapy for a year.

Now a grandfather, he has been married to his wife, former skiing champion Francie Breaud, since 1962 and their two sons are Laurent and Julien.

In November 1997 *The Very Best Of Sacha Distel*, his first UK album release for 15 years, was issued to catch the Christmas market. During the year he had continued to appear on UK television on programmes such as *The Mrs Merton Show* and *The Last Chance Lottery*.

DIXIE CUPS, The Singer Joe Jones discovered this female trio in New Orleans. Jones took sisters Barbara Anne and Rose Lee Hawkins and Joan Marie Johnson to New York, and they were signed to the new Red Bird record label founded by hit songwriters Jerry Leiber and Mike Stoller.

The trio's US hits included: 'Chapel Of Love (which topped the chart), 'People Say', 'You Should Have Seen The Way He Looked At Me' and 'Iko Iko'.

After an unsuccessful spell with RCA, the group broke up in the mid-1970s. Barbara Anne and Rose Lee later re-formed the trio with another singer and are still performing, although they have had no further new record releases.

A compilation CD, *The Dixie Cups Meet The Shangri-Las*, was issued in 1986.

DR FEELGOOD When this band was formed in 1971 the members were **Lee Brilleaux** (vocals and harmonica), Wilko Johnson (guitar), John B. Sparks (bass), John Potter (piano) and 'Bandsman' Howarth (drums). When Potter and Howarth left the band, drummer John Martin joined them.

The group were to have a series of hit albums: *Malpractice*, *Stupidity*, *Sneakin' Suspicion*, *Be Seeing You*, *Private Practice* and *As It Happens*. Hits in the singles chart were: 'Sneakin' Suspicion', 'She's A Wind Up', 'Down At The Doctor's', 'Milk and Alcohol', 'As Long As The Price Is Right' and 'Put Him Out Of Your Mind'.

Johnson left and was replaced by John 'Gypie' Mayo, who was himself replaced by Johnny Guitar in 1981. The next year both Sparks and Martin left the band.

Brilleaux died from pancreatic cancer in 1994. Martin and Sparks are now the mainstays of an Essex-based group, the Practice, while Wilko Johnson leads an eponymous band and is a popular attraction on Europe's R&B circuit. The current line-up of Dr Feelgood features none of the original members.

DR HOOK This seven-piece band was formed in 1968, led by lead vocalists Dennis Locorriere and Ray Sawyer – who wears an eye patch. The other members were Jance Garfat (bass), George Cummings (steel and lead guitar), Bill Francis (keyboards), Rik Elswit (guitar) and John Wolters (drums). They were originally known as Dr Hook & the Medicine Show, but the group truncated it to Dr Hook in 1975.

Their hit singles in the US chart include: 'Sylvia's Mother', 'The Cover Of Rolling Stone', 'Only Sixteen', 'A Little Bit More', 'Sharing The Night Together', 'When You're In Love With A Beautiful Woman', 'Better Love Next Time', 'Sexy Eyes', 'Girls Can Get It' and 'Baby Makes Her Blue Jeans Talk'.

After Dr Hook's farewell tour in 1985, Dennis Locorriere became a songwriter in Nashville and issued a solo album, *Running With Scissors*, in 1996. The group's other mainstay, Ray Sawyer, leads a Dr Hook on the nostalgia circuit.

1996 also saw the release of *Pleasure And Pain: The History Of Dr Hook*, a three-CD boxed set of 63 tracks, 14 of which had never previously been released.

DR JOHN Born Malcolm John 'Mac' Rebennacle in New Orleans on 21 November 1941, this singer began his career backing strippers in the Latin Quarter of New Orleans and started singing with a Dixieland band in 1961.

He moved to Los Angeles and formed his own band, Grit's & Gravy. He then developed his new identity, with a mixture of voodoo, Creole, African and R&B influences, calling himself Dr John Creux, The Night Tripper, and dressing in exotic costumes. His first album, *Walk On Gilded Splinters*, was produced by **Sonny Bono**, while Mick Jagger and Eric Clapton were among the guests on his 1971 album, *Sun, Mood And Herbs*. His biggest singles hit was 'Right Place Wrong Time' in 1973.

Over the years, Dr John has had a number of album releases and has played alongside scores of major artists – including Willie Dixon, Etta James, **Ray Charles**, B. B. King and Eric Clapton – at numerous concerts.

Following a stint with Ringo Starr's All Starr Band, Dr John returned to solo concerts. These included a week at London's Ronnie Scott's club in 1996, which drew famous fans like **Steve Winwood** and Van Morrison. At the close of 1997, Dr John was among the numerous guest singers on the hit record 'A Perfect Day'.

DOLLAR This successful male-female singing duo enjoyed a decade of hits from November 1978 until July 1988. Their chart successes included: 'Shooting Star', 'Who Were You With In The Moonlight', 'Love's Gotta Hold On Me', 'I Wanna Hold Your Hand', 'Takin' A Chance On You', 'Hand Held In Black And White', 'Mirror Mirror (Mon Amour)', 'Ring Ring', 'Give Me Back My Heart', 'Videotheque', 'Give Me Some Kinda Magic', 'We Walked In Love', 'O L'Amour' and 'It's Nature's Way (No Problem)'.

The two members of Dollar were David Van Day and Thereze Bazaar. The 17-year-old David was just out of stage school when he joined the six-piece vocal outfit Guys & Dolls. Thereze was also a member of the group and the two began living together. When David was fired because he was in conflict with another member, he took Thereze with him and they formed Dollar.

Eventually the couple split. Despite an album which cost £500,000 to make, Thereze had no further hits, went to live in Sydney, Australia, and is a single mother to her son Alexander.

David re-formed Dollar with a new partner, Karen Logan, and continues to appear at functions, much of the duo's work involving entertaining the employees of a large network marketing company, Amway.

DOMINO, Fats Born Antoine Domino in New Orleans on 26 February 1928, this singer-pianist made his first professional appearance at the age of 14. He then became a member of the Billy

Fats Domino

61

Diamond Dance Band, before turning solo with a record called 'The Fat Man'. By that time he was leading the Fats Domino Band.

Domino's hits during the 1950s included: 'Blueberry Hill', 'Ain't It A Shame', 'Poor Me', 'I'm Walking', 'Please Leave Me' and 'All By Myself'. In 1963 he had another major hit with 'Red Sails In The Sunset'.

Domino first appeared in the UK in 1967, when the Beatles' manager **Brian Epstein** booked him for concerts in London. **Gerry & the Pacemakers** and the **Bee Gees** supported him on the bill of the six concerts at the Saville Theatre. He featured in the movie *Let The Good Times Roll* in 1972.

The father of eight children, Domino lives with his wife in New Orleans and appears regularly in cabaret in Las Vegas.

In 1995 he began a UK tour with Little Richard and **Chuck Berry**. Fifteen minutes into his act at Sheffield Arena he had to leave the stage due to a throat infection and was taken to hospital. He was then advised not to continue with the tour and had to return to the States.

DONEGAN, Lonnie Affectionately known as the 'King of Skiffle', Lonnie was born Anthony Donegan in Glasgow, Scotland, on 29 April 1931. From 1956, he had an amazing six-year chart run with 32 hits ranging from 'Rock Island Line' to 'My Old Man's A Dustman'.

Following a heart attack in 1976, Lonnie decided to live in semi-retirement and moved to the Costa del Sol with his second wife Sharon and their three sons Peter, David and Andrew. He also bought a house in Lake Tahoe, California. In 1978 **Adam Faith** recorded Lonnie's tribute album, *Putting On The Style*, in which the veteran singer was joined by a host of guest artists including Ringo Starr, Elton John and Brian May of Queen.

In 1988 Lonnie formed Donegan's Sunshine Band and in 1996 began recording another tribute album with several big-name guests. He appeared in several acting roles, which included the UK television cop series *Rockcliffe's Babies*, but missed out a regular role in the UK soap opera *EastEnders* due to a technician's strike, which meant he was out of the country for tax

Lonnie Donegan (centre)

reasons while the first three episodes were filmed.

During the early 1990s, Lonnie undertook a 100-concert fortieth anniversary tour across Europe and later began to film a number of television shows in which he read from children's stories.

DONOVAN This folk singer was born Donovan Phillip Leitch in Glasgow on 10 May 1943. When he became resident on the UK television programme *Ready, Steady, Go!* he was touted as the UK's answer to Bob Dylan. He was also inspired by the legendary **Woody Guthrie**, who had a guitar with the slogan 'This guitar kills fascists'. Donovan's guitar sported the slogan 'This guitar kills'.

His singles between 1963 and 1968 included 'Catch The Wind', 'Colours', 'Sunshine Superman', 'Mellow Yellow', 'There Is A Mountain', 'Jennifer Juniper' and 'Hurdy Gurdy Man'. He had a dozen singles in the US chart, which he topped in 1966 with 'Sunshine Superman'.

His album releases included: *What's Bin Did And What's Bin Hid, Fairy Tale, Sunshine Superman, Universal Soldier, A Gift From A Flower To A Garden, Open Road* and *Cosmic Wheels*.

Donovan's inspiration in the mid-1960s had been Linda Lawrence. They renewed their romance in 1970 and married. She had a son, Julian, by the late **Brian Jones** of the **Rolling Stones**, and she and Donovan were to have two daughters, Oriole and Astrella.

In the early 1970s, Donovan composed film scores for *If It's Tuesday, It Must Be Belgium, The Pied Piper* and *Brother Son, Sister Moon*. He then decided to retire from music and he and Linda went to live a simple life in a place in California called Joshua Tree. After a gap of six years he decided to enter the recording studio once more and the couple returned to the UK to raise their children, where Donovan cut three more albums. He then suffered a period of ill health and they moved back to the desert at the end of the 1980s.

In 1996 Donovan released a new album, *Sutras*.

DOORS, The This group was fronted by vocalist **Jim Morrison**, the son of a rear admiral, who was born on 8 December 1943 in Melbourne, Florida. The other members were Ray Monzarek (keyboards), John Densmore (drums) and Bobby Krieger (bass).

The group were formed in 1964 and took their name from Aldous Huxley's book *The Doors Of Perception*. They issued their debut album, *The Doors*, on the Elektra Records label in 1967 and it contained their huge singles hit 'Light My Fire', penned by Krieger. Two more LPs, *Strange Days* and *Waiting For The Sun*, followed, along with another hit single 'Hello I Love You'.

Dubbed the 'Lizard King', Morrison began to take the drug LSD and in 1969, at a concert in Miami, was accused by the police of lewd behaviour on stage, which resulted in the loss of $1 million-worth of bookings.

Two further albums, *Morrison Hotel/Hard Rock Café* and *L.A. Woman*, were released.

Late in 1970, Morrison and his wife went to live in Paris, where he professed an intention to write poetry. The band continued without him and issued 'Love Her Madly', a US Top 20 entry.

Morrison died from a heart attack in his bath on 3 July 1971.

The Doors continued with their career and charted that year with 'Riders on the Storm'. They issued two further albums, *Other Voices* and *Full Circle*, but disbanded in 1973.

Monzarek was unsuccessful in his attempts to re-form the band, and issued solo albums such as *The Golden Scarab* and *The Whole Thing Started With Rock 'n' Roll*.

Initially, Krieger and Densmore became record producers, then teamed up in the Butts Band. Krieger then turned to jazz and issued an album, *Bobby Krieger And Friends*, in 1977.

'Riders On The Storm' entered the UK chart for a second time in 1976.

A film biopic, *The Doors*, directed by Oliver Stone, was released in 1991 and spawned a soundtrack album hit, also leading to the release of a *Greatest Hits* CD that year.

The surviving Doors – still California residents – were inducted into the Rock & Roll Hall Of Fame in 1993. Four years later, they collaborated on a well-received boxed set containing a majority of previously unreleased material. Called simply *Doors*, the 4-CD boxed set was issued in October 1997.

DOUGLAS, Craig Born Terence Perkins in Newport, Isle of Wight, on 12 August 1941, this singer had a string of hit singles which stretched from 1959 to 1963. He then suffered the same fate as many young solo peformers on both sides of the Atlantic, once the Beatles and the

63

beat group scene came into force. At this time Douglas went on to tour the world, before settling into the cabaret circuit. Ironically, the Beatles had been his backing band for one night at the Liverpool Empire on 28 December 1962.

Douglas' hits included: 'A Teenager In Love', 'Only Sixteen', 'Pretty Blue Eyes', 'The Heart Of A Teenage Girl', 'Oh! What a Day', 'A Hundred Pounds Of Clay', 'Time', 'When My Little Girl Is Smiling', 'Our Favourite Melodies', 'Oh Lonesome Me' and 'Town Crier'.

These days, Douglas divides his time professionally between intimate supper-club cabaret and nostalgia packages.

DOWLANDS, The This British vocal duo had one minor hit in January 1964 with a cover version of the Lennon & McCartney number 'All My Loving'. Gordon and David Dowland are both graphic designers in Bournemouth, albeit for different companies. David is still a semi-professional entertainer.

DOWNLINERS SECT This group was originally formed by rhythm guitarist Don Craine and drummer Johnny Sutton in 1962 as Downliners. Johnny and Don changed the name to Downliners Sect when they disbanded the original line-up and brought in Keith Grant (bass) and Terry Gibson (lead). By the time they made their recording debut in 1964 with 'Baby What's Wrong' they had also recruited the harmonica player Ray Sone.

The band failed to achieve success on record and continually changed personnel. Sone left and Gibson and Sutton were replaced by Bob Taylor and Kevin Flanagan. At one time, Matthew Fisher played piano with the band. Craine himself decided to leave and Grant and Sutton then went with the band to Sweden, where they made a few records before they disbanded.

Craine and Grant re-formed the band in 1976 and they began to appear on the nostalgia circuit. With these two still at the helm, Downliners Sect are still based in London and are very much a going concern both in the studio and on the boards.

DRIFTERS, The An American vocal group, the Drifters have been in existence since 1953 and still perform today, although there have been numerous changes of personnel through the years.

The original Drifters line-up was **Clyde McPhatter** (lead tenor), Gerhart Thrasher (tenor), Andrew Thrasher (baritone) and Bill Pinckney (bass), and at one time they were billed as Clyde McPhatter & the Drifters with their first chart entry being 'Money Honey'. Hits with McPhatter singing included 'Lucille', 'Such A Night', 'Honey Love' and 'Bip Bam'. The group continued to perform when McPhatter was called to serve in the armed forces, with Johnny Moore taking over lead vocals. McPhatter did not rejoin when he was discharged. At one time Ben E. King was lead singer with the group, performing on a number of their major hits, but he left after arguing with the manager over the fact that the group received only modest wages despite their incredible record sales and sell-out concert tours.

With so many different members over the years, there have been several groups who have toured using the Drifters name, including the New Drifters, the Original Drifters, Bill Pinkney & the Originals and so on.

The classic lead singers with the outfit were the late McPhatter, King and the late Rudy Lewis. The current lead singer is Johnny Moore, the longest-serving member of the group, who has been in and out of the line-up for over 30 years.

The Drifters' hit singles include: 'There Goes My Baby', 'Dance With Me', 'True Love', 'This Magic Moment', 'Save The Last Dance For Me', 'I Count The Tears', 'Some Kind Of Wonderful', 'Please Stay', 'Sweets For My Sweet', 'When My Little Girl Is Smiling', 'Up On The Roof', 'On Broadway', 'I'll Take You Home', 'Under The Boardwalk', 'I've Got Sand In My Shoes' and 'Saturday Night At The Movies'.

The Drifters continue to perform around the world, with seasons in Australia and Bermuda, months spent in Las Vegas and Lake Tahoe, and regular tours of the UK.

DRISCOLL, Julie Born in London on 8 June 1947, Julie Driscoll had previously been involved in the running of the **Yardbirds** fan club. It was Giorgio Gomelsky who suggested she become a singer, making her recording debut in 1965 with 'Didn't Want To Have To Do It'. She joined Steam Packet, along with **Rod Stewart**, **Long John Baldry** and the Brian Auger Trinity. When Stewart and Baldry left, Julie remained a member of the Brian Auger Trinity and they had a major hit in 1968 with 'This Wheel's On Fire'. She then left for a solo career, without much success, and issued an eponymous album in 1971, which featured backing from a number of musicians – including pianist Keith Tippett, whom she married.

Julie retired from the business, although she performed on a number of her husband's jazz albums. Currently she lives in a small village in the Bristol area and continues to make the occasional appearance with her husband's avantgarde jazz outfit, mainly in Europe. Her remake of 'This Wheel's On Fire' was used over the credits of the UK television comedy series *Absolutely Fabulous*.

Brian Auger, former leader of the Trinity, now lives in Los Angeles, although he returns to the UK occasionally to perform. He has appeared in sixties extravaganzas in Europe and in a reconstituted **Spencer Davis Group**.

DUBLINERS, The   This Irish folk group was formed in Dublin in 1962. They entered the UK chart with 'Seven Drunken Nights' in 1967, followed by 'Black Velvet Band' and 'Maids When You're Young Never Wed An Old Man'. They made several albums of Irish folk and rebel songs, including *A Drop Of The Hard Stuff* and *Drinkin' And Courtin'*.

The Dubliners' line-up comprises Luke Kelly, Barny McKenna, Ronnie Drew, Ciaron Bourke and John Sheahan, although Bourke had to leave the group in 1974 following a brain haemorrhage.

After a hit version of 'The Irish Rover' with the **Pogues** in 1987, the group resumed its schedule of standing-room-only concerts and record releases.

DUNCAN, Johnny   American country singer Johnny Duncan was born on 5 October 1938. A former disc jockey, he became a successful performer with over 40 hits in the country chart, including: 'Thinkin' Of A Rendezvous', 'I Couldn't Have Been Any Better' and 'She Can Put Her Shoes Under My Bed (Anytime)'.

Johnny Duncan returned to Nashville to reinvent himself as a C&W singer. After a decade of minor hits, in 1976 he climbed high in the US country chart with 'Stranger', and reached No 1 with its follow-up, 'Thinkin' Of A Rendezvous'.

DURAN DURAN   This group from Birmingham was formed in 1978 and took their name from the villain in the cult movie *Barbarella*, played by actor Milo O'Shea.

After various changes in personnel, they settled down in 1980 with Simon Le Bon (lead vocals), Andy Taylor (guitar), John Taylor (bass), Roger Taylor (drums) and Nick Rhodes (keyboards). Initially, they were labelled with the movement of 'new romantics', a group of flamboyant bands who dressed in colourful and stylish outfits and included **Visage** and **Spandau Ballet**.

Duran Duran charted with their debut disc, 'Planet Earth', in 1981, and succeeding hit singles included: 'Careless Memories', 'Girls On Film', 'My Own Way', 'Hungry Like The Wolf', 'Save A Prayer', 'Rio', 'Is There Something I Should Know', 'Union Of The Snake', 'New Moon On Monday', 'The Reflex', 'Wild Boys', 'A View To A Kill', 'Notorious', 'Skin Trade', 'Meet El Presidente', 'I Don't Want Your Love', 'All She Wants Is', 'Do You Believe In Shame', 'Burning The Ground', 'Violence Of Summer', 'Serious', 'Ordinary World', 'Too Much Information' and 'White Lines'.

Hit albums included: *Duran Duran*, *Rio*, *Seven And The Ragged Tiger*, *Arena*, *Big Thing*, *Decade*, *Liberty*, *Duran Duran (The Wedding Album)* and *Thank You*.

They achieved international success, with major hits in the US and tours which included Japan, Australia and Canada.

In 1985 John and Andy Taylor, together with Robert Palmer and Tony Thompson, formed a group called Power Station, whose hits included 'Some Like It Hot', 'Get It On' and 'Commun-cation'. Later that year Duran Duran disbanded and Le Bon, Roger Taylor and Rhodes formed a band called Arcadia, whose hits included 'Election Day', 'The Promise' and 'The Flame'.

By this time the various members of the group had married: Andy in 1982 to the group's hairdresser Tracey Wilson, Roger to Giovanna Cantonne and Nick to model Julie Anne, both in 1984, and Simon to model Yasmin Parvanah in 1985. John and his girlfriend Amanda de Cadenet, a television presenter, had a daughter in 1989.

In 1986 Duran Duran decided to re-form to record, although Roger had left the band for good. The group began live appearances again and the trio recruited drummer Sterling Campbell to join them in 1988.

They were back as a trio again with Simon, Nick and John when they recorded *Thank You*, an album of cover versions, in 1995.

65

A five-piece Duran Duran, which included two original members, Simon LeBon and Nick Rhodes, embarked on a UK tour in December 1998. They were also promoting a *Greatest Hits* album and video, and their new album *Hallucinating Elvis* is being issued in 1999.

DURY, Ian Born in Billericay, Essex, on 12 May 1942, singer-songwriter Ian Dury was struck down by polio at the age of seven and spent several years in an institution for the disabled. In his late teens he attended Walthamstow Art College. He later became a teacher, a profession in which he continued until the age of 28, when he began performing on the pub rock scene in London with a group he had formed called Kilburn & the High Roads, but they had no success on record.

Dury formed a new group, which he called the Blockheads. The members were Chas Jakel (guitar), Mickey Gallagher (keyboards), Davey Payne (sax), Norman Watt-Roy (bass) and Charley Charles (drums).

They signed with Stiff Records and issued *New Boots And Panties*, an album which spawned their track 'Sex And Drugs And Rock And Roll'. The album was a critical and commercial success, and Dury also recorded a single in tribute to his idol **Gene Vincent**, 'Sweet Gene Vincent'.

The band's hit singles included: 'What A Waste', 'Hit Me With Your Rhythm Stick', 'Reasons To Be Cheerful', 'I Want To Be Straight', 'Superman's Big Sisters' and 'Profoundly In Love With Pandora'. 'Hit Me With You Rhythm Stick' was Dury's most noted number and charted in both 1978 and 1985.

In 1986 Dury began an acting career in the television drama *Talk Of The Devil* and has since appeared in a number of television plays. He also wrote a musical play, *Apples*, in 1989.

Ian Dury also hosted a late-night UK television show in the 1990s, and in 1996 he made a rare concert appearance as the headlining act at the Bracknell Music Festival.

DYLAN, Bob One of the giants of popular music, Bob Dylan (real name Robert Allan Zimmerman) was born on 24 May 1941 in Duluth, Minnesota. In 1960 he travelled to New York to visit the dying folk legend **Woody Guthrie** in hospital, and then began appearing in Greenwich Village clubs. His debut album, the eponymous *Bob Dylan*, was released the following year.

The 1960s was Dylan's most productive decade, with hit singles such as: 'Times They Are a-Changin'', 'Subterranean Homesick Blues', 'Maggie's Farm', 'Like A Rolling Stone', 'Positively Fourth Street', 'Can You Please Crawl Out Your Window', 'One Of Us Must Know (Sooner Or Later)', 'Rainy Day Women Nos 13 & 35', 'I Want You', 'I Threw It All Away' and 'Lay Lady Lay'.

His albums of that decade included: *The Freewheelin' Bob Dylan*, *The Times They Are A-Changin'*, *Another Side Of Bob Dylan*, *Bob Dylan*, *Bringing It All Back Home*, *Highway 61 Revisited*, *Blonde On Blonde*, *Greatest Hits*, *John Wesley Harding* and *Nashville Skyline*.

Of course, Dylan's hits have continued since that time, but the 1960s was an era when he achieved so much and influenced so many.

Dylan married Sara Lowndes on 22 November 1965 and in July 1966 was involved in a motorcycle crash in which his neck vertebrae were broken, causing him to remain inactive for an 18-month period.

In addition to his recordings and concerts, Dylan penned the book *Tarantula*, appeared in the documentary *Eat The Document*, covering his UK tour with the Band, and featured in the film *Pat Garrett And Billy The Kid*. Another film, *Renaldo And Clara*, covered his Rolling Thunder Revue, a major tour in which he was joined by guest artists such as Joan Baez, **Joni Mitchell** and Roger McGuinn.

Sara filed for divorce in 1977, and by the close of the decade Dylan had become a born-again Christian.

In 1987 he appeared in the UK movie *Hearts of Fire,* and in 1988 he recorded with George Harrison, **Roy Orbison**, **Tom Petty** and Jeff Lynne in the **Traveling Wilburys**.

In 1996 Dylan nearly died from histoplasmosis, an infection caused by airborne spores from bird and bat droppings.

1997, his fifty-sixth year, became one of his most active for decades, with a world tour during which he played for the Pope in Bologna and made an appearance at Wembley Arena in London in October, which coincided with the release of his forty-first album, *Time Out Of Mind*, issued on 29 September. His son Jakob also embarked on a mini-tour of the UK with his band the Wallflowers in October 1997.

EAGER, Vince   One of several young rock 'n' roll stars in the Larry Parnes stable, Vince Eager made his debut in 1958 and began appearing on UK television shows such as *Oh Boy!* and *Drumbeat*, but never achieved success on record.

In the 1990s, Vince Eager participated in the West End musical, *Elvis*.

EAGLES, The   This American band was formed in 1971 and played as the backing band to Linda Ronstadt for a short time before spreading their wings as the Eagles.

That same year they were spotted by David Geffen, then running Asylum Records, who signed them up. They recorded their debut album in London and entered the US chart with their first single, 'Take It Easy'.

The basic quartet consisted of Glenn Frey (guitar and vocals), Bernie Leadon (guitar and vocals), Randy Meisner (bass and vocals) and Don Henley (drums and vocals).

The Eagles US chart singles included: 'Take It Easy', 'Witchy Woman', 'Peaceful Easy Feeling', 'Already Gone', 'Best Of My Love', 'One Of These Nights', 'Lyin' Eyes', 'Take It To The Limit', 'New Kid In Town', 'Hotel California', 'Life In The Fast Lane', 'Please Come Home For Christmas', 'Heartache Tonight', 'The Long Run', 'I Can't Tell You Why' and 'Seven Bridges Road'. They had several No 1 records and 'New Kid In Town' and 'Hotel California' were consecutive chart-toppers for them.

The group's early recordings and tours were in the UK and their album chart entries included: *On The Border*, *One Of These Nights*, *Desperado*, *Their Greatest Hits 1971–1975*, *Hotel California*, *The Long Run*, *Live* and *Best Of The Eagles*.

Leadon left the Eagles at the beginning of 1976 and was replaced by Joe Walsh. He played in various other outfits, including the Nitty Gritty Band. Meisner left in 1978 to be replaced by Timothy B. Schmit. He wanted to continue recording, but could not stand life on the road. He had a minor chart entry with 'One More Song', on which he was backed by Frey and Henley, and also charted with the eponymous album *Randy Meisner*. He later joined bands such as Poco and Black Tie.

The Eagles effectively disbanded in 1981, with the individual members pursuing solo projects.

Don Henley, in particular, enjoyed a successful career and had a major hit in 1982 with 'Dirty Laundry'. He also charted with 'Leather And Lace', a single he cut with singer Stevie Nicks, and he even duetted with the Muppets on 'Kermit Unpigged'. In his personal life, he married model Sharon Summerall in March 1995. At one time he was involved in a scandal: late in 1980 he was arrested when a 16-year old naked girl was found in his house suffering from a drugs overdose. He was fined, put on probation and entered into a drugs counselling scheme.

Joe Walsh was a former member of chart band the James Gang. When the Eagles disbanded he continued recording and performing, tried his hand at producing and was also a disc jockey. His solo hits included 'Rocky Mountain Way', 'Life's Been Good', 'All Night Long' and 'A Life Of Illusion'.

Claiming the band would only play again 'when hell freezes over', when Frey, Henley, Schmit and Walsh re-formed the Eagles it was for Hell Freezes Over, a 1996 world tour and tie-in album.

When the group were inducted into the Rock & Roll Hall Of Fame in New York on 12 January 1998 they mentioned that although the Hell Freezes Over comeback tour had been a big success, they would never tour again without a new album. As their last album of all, *The Long Run*, had taken more than three years to complete, they did not envisage recording another LP.

All six members of the country-rock group were present at the induction: Bernie Leadon, Joe Walsh, Don Henley, Timothy B. Schmit, Don Felder, Glenn Frey and Randy Meisner.

EARTH, WIND & FIRE   This Chicago group was formed in 1969. They disbanded in 1984 but re-formed in 1987.

Earth, Wind & Fire were a jazz-funk band formed by Maurice White, who sang and played drums and kalimba. The other main vocalist was Philip Bailey. White's two brothers joined them – Verdine on bass and Fred on drums. The other members were Larry Dunn (keyboards), Andrew Woodfolk (horns), Roland Bautista (guitar) and Ralph Johnson (drums and percussion).

Their chart singles included: 'Mighty Mighty', 'Devotion', 'Shining Star', 'That's The Way Of The Wind', 'Sing A Song', 'Can't Hide Love', 'Gateway', 'Saturday Nite', 'Serpentine Fire', 'Fantasy', 'Got To Get You Into My Life', 'September', 'After The Love Has Gone', 'Let's Groove' and 'Fall In Love With Me'.

Earth, Wind and Fire

The group was still a concert attraction in the 1990s, buoyed partly by a merchandising hook-up with the fast-food chain Burger King. They embarked on their first tour for six years in 1994 and toured Japan the following year. During 1995 they also signed to the Avex label and were given a star on the Hollywood Walk Of Fame.

EAST OF EDEN   This band from the West Country of England comprised Dave Arbus (violin and flute), Ron Gaines (alto sax), Geoff Nicholson (guitar), Andy Sneddon (bass) and Geoff Britton (drums).

After signing with the progressive Deram label in 1969, they issued two albums, *Mercator Projected* and *Snafu*, and had a Top 10 hit with the instrumental single, 'Jig-A-Jig'.

The group then moved on to the Harvest label to record two more albums, *East Of Eden* and *New Leaf*, before disbanding.

A few years later, Britton had a brief spell with Paul McCartney's group Wings.

In 1997, original members Arbus, Nicholson and Gaines were the core of an East of Eden reformed to record a new album, *Kalipse*.

EAST 17   This band was first formed by vocalist and keyboards player Tony Mortimer in 1990. The other members were Brian Harvey (lead vocals), John Hendy (vocals, bass and keyboards) and Terry Coldwell (drums). They originally called themselves E17 after the local postcode, but then changed their name to East 17 and celebrated a Top 10 hit with their debut single 'House Of Love'. Other hits followed: 'Deep', 'West End Girls', 'It's Alright', 'Around The World', 'Steam', 'Stay Another Day', 'Let It Rain', 'Hold My Body Tonight', 'Thunder' and 'Do U Still'.

There were problems relating to Harvey's arrest for possession of cannabis and his announcements on television, apparently in support of drugs, caused such a media backlash that he was sacked from the group, who eventually disbanded. In January 1998 they announced that they were on the verge of re-forming.

EASYBEATS, The   This Australian band originally formed in 1963, with one Scots, two English and two Dutch members. They were Stevie Wright (vocals), Harry Vanda and George

Young (guitar), Dick Diamonde (bass) and Gordon Fleet (drums).

They became the resident band at the Beatle Village club in Sydney, taking their name from the UK radio pop music programme *Easybeat*. In 1965 they topped the Australian chart with 'She's So Fine', and followed with four further Australian chart singles.

After moving to the UK in 1966, the band had a Top 10 hit with 'Friday On My Mind', which also topped the Australian chart and entered the US Top 20. The following year Fleet left and was replaced by Tony Cahill.

The Easybeats' final hit was 'Hello, How Are You?' in 1969 and heralded the end of the group, with Vanda and Young moving back to Australia to open a studio in Sydney, where they were to produce bands such as AC/DC. The two also called themselves Flash & the Pan, and under that name entered the UK chart with 'And The Band Played On (Down Among The Dead Men)' in 1978 and 'Waiting For A Train' in 1983.

An Easybeats was formed in the 1980s to milk the sixties nostalgia market in Europe.

ECHO & THE BUNNYMEN
To Liverpool, Eric's in the 1970s was what the Cavern was in the 1960s. It became a showcase for a range of new Mersey groups, including Echo & the Bunnymen, who began appearing there at the end of 1978. They originally began as a trio with Ian McCulloch on vocals, Les Pattison on bass and Will Sergeant on guitar. They had a drum machine which they called 'Echo'.

In 1979 the group released their debut single, 'Pictures On My Wall', and later that year were joined by drummer **Peter De Freitas**. They had a minor hit with 'Rescue', followed by an album *Crocodiles*, which entered the UK Top 20.

Hit singles included: 'Crocodiles', 'A Promise', 'The Back Of Love', 'The Cutter', 'Never Stop', 'The Killing Moon', 'Silver', 'Seven Seas', 'Bring On The Dancing Horses', 'The Game', 'Lips Like Sugar' and 'People Are Strange'.

In 1988 McCulloch left to embark on a solo career, but the group decided to continue without him. A few months later, De Freitas was killed in a road accident and was replaced by Damon Reece.

McCulloch was successful with some of his record releases, but Echo & the Bunnymen were not and disbanded. They got together again in 1997 and began a UK tour in March 1998.

EDDIE & THE HOT RODS
From Southend in Essex, this group was formed in 1975 and comprised Barrie Masters (vocals), Lew Lewis (harmonica), Paul Gray (bass), Dave Higgs (guitar) and Steve Nicol (drums). The band established a reputation in clubs such as the Marquee in London and on the pub rock circuit.

Lewis was eventually sacked and guitarist Graeme Douglas, a former member of the Kursaal Flyers, joined the band. Various other changes in personnel followed, with both Douglas and Gray leaving. The group disbanded in 1981, then Masters re-formed the outfit in 1984 to appear in further pub gigs. They were to disband once again, and re-formed in 1995.

The group's hits included the EP 'Live at The Marquee' and the singles 'Teenage Depression', 'I Might Be Lying', 'Do Anything You Wanna Do' and 'Quit This Town'.

These days, Masters is a glazier in London, while Douglas and Higgs each run their own recording studios in Essex. Paul Gray is a member of the **Damned** and Nicol is a builder in Essex.

EDGAR BROUGHTON BAND, The
This group first started performing together at school in Warwickshire. The original members were Edgar Broughton (guitar and vocals), his brother Steve (drums), Arthur Grant (bass and vocals) and Victor Unitt (guitar and vocals). Edgar was born on 24 October 1946 and Steve on 20 May 1950, and until 1970 the group were actually managed by the brothers' mother, Ma Broughton.

They performed on the London underground circuit, making their debut album, *Wasa Wasa*, in 1968. Their singles successes included 'Out Demons Out' and 'Apache Dropout', and they are also remembered for 'Hotel Room'. Their music included a great deal of political comment and they performed at numerous free concerts. When Warwick Council prevented them from holding a free concert in a local park, they began playing from the back of a moving lorry.

Unitt left the band following their 1973 album, *Oora*. When the group disbanded, Steve became a session musician, appearing on recordings by artists such as Mike Oldfield and **Roy Harper**. The group re-formed in 1986 for tours of the UK and Europe, in addition to recording again.

Edgar currently runs music workshops in a youth centre in Wandsworth, south London.

Steve runs a recording complex in Barnet, Hertfordshire, and drums with the 22-piece Soul Power. Arthur Grant designs, builds and customizes recording studios. Victor Unitt is the only member of the group not to take part in the re-formation. He designs and manufactures lingerie and night attire.

EDMUNDS, Dave   Born in Cardiff, south Wales, on 15 April 1944, singer-guitarist-songwriter-producer Dave Edmunds was a member of Love Sculpture, a group who entered the UK chart in 1968 with 'Sabre Dance'. They disbanded the following year and in 1970 Dave had his first solo hit with 'I Hear You Knocking'. His other hit singles included: 'Baby I Love You', 'Born To Be With You', 'I Knew The Bride', 'Girls Talk', 'Queen Of Hearts, 'Crawling From The Wreckage', 'Singing The Blues', 'Almost Saturday Night' and 'Slipping Away'.

He also had success in partnership with artists such as Nick Lowe and Rockpile, and has enjoyed a fruitful career as a producer for a wealth of acts including **Dion**, **Elvis Costello**, the **Everly Brothers**, **Shakin' Stevens**, the **Stray Cats**, **Status Quo**, k.d. lang and the Flamin' Groovies.

Although employed mainly as a backing musician, Dave Edmunds was one of the few artists to emerge with credit at a John Lennon tribute extravaganza staged in Liverpool in 1990. Since then, he has recorded with Steve Cropper, **Dion** and George Harrison, among others.

ELECTRIC LIGHT ORCHESTRA   The first Electric Light Orchestra was formed in Birmingham in 1971 and consisted of various members of Brumbeat groups. They made their debut the following year but Roy Wood, one of the principal members, left the band to form Wizzard.

Their first single, by Jeff Lynne, was '10538 Overture', which became a UK Top 10 hit. They were to enjoy over 30 chart singles, which included 'Roll Over Beethoven', 'Evil Woman',

*Dave
Edmunds
(centre
front)*

'Rockaria!', Don't Bring Me Down', 'Twilight', 'Hold On Tight' and 'Calling America'.

They also had a dozen album hits, which included: *Queen Of The Hours*, *Out Of The Blue*, *Three Light Years*, *Time* and *Secret Messages*.

The group became more familiarly known as ELO and their basic personnel comprised Jeff Lynne (vocals and guitar), Richard Tandy (vocals and keyboards), Kelly Groucutt (vocals and bass), Bev Bevan (drums), Mik Kaminski (violin), and Hugh McDowell and Melvyn Gale (cello).

In 1980 they topped the chart when they collaborated with **Olivia Newton-John** on 'Xanadu'.

In addition to releasing a solo album, *Armchair Theatre*, for the next decade Jeff Lynne became increasingly involved with writing and producing for a host of major artists including **Tom Petty**, George Harrison, **Randy Newman**, Brian Wilson, **Roy Orbison** and **Del Shannon**. He also became a member of the supergroup the **Traveling Wilburys** and was selected to produce the Beatles single 'Free As A Bird'.

Bev Bevan headed a committee that procured cash for Birmingham Children's Hospital via charity concerts such as Heartbeat '86, in which Brumbeat exponents such as Robert Plant, Denny Laine, Ace Kefford – and Jeff Lynne – participated.

Due to his heavy committments, Lynne left ELO, who in 1992 became ELO II, led by Bevan and comprising Groucutt and Kaminski with Eric Lockwood on keyboards, Peter Haycock and Neil Lockwood on guitars and Lewis Clark. There was an immediate album release, *Electric Light Orchestra II*, and a European tour.

1994 saw the release of *The Very Best Of The Electric Light Orchestra*, which entered the Top 5 of the UK album chart.

ELECTRIC PRUNES, The

ELECTRIC PRUNES, The   This American band made their recording debut in 1967 with 'Ain't It Hard'. That single failed to register, but their next release, 'I Had Too Much To Dream (Last Night)', entered the chart.

The group consisted of John Lowe (guitar, autoharp and vocals), Ken Williams (lead), Weasel Spagnola (rhythm), Mark Tulin (bass) and Michael Weakley (drums). Preston Ritter soon replaced Weakley. They had a minor hit with their album *The Electric Prunes* and charted again with their single 'Get Me To The World On Time'.

In 1969, together with other musicians, they recorded a rock version of a Catholic Mass called *Mass in F Minor*, and disbanded soon after.

John Lowe became a studio engineer, working with the likes of Foghat, **Sparks** and **Todd Rundgren**, before producing and directing television commercials. Mark Tulin is now a psychologist and Ken Williams an air-conditioning salesman. Michael Weakley changed his surname to Fortune but, like the other ex-Prunes, still lives in California.

EQUALS, The   Eddie Grant, the lead guitarist from Guyana, Derv and Lincoln Gordon, twins from Jamaica on vocals and rhythm guitar respectively, and Patrick Lloyd and John Hall from London on rhythm and drums respectively, began playing together as a group in 1965.

Their major hit, 'Baby Come Back', recorded the following year, was originally issued as a B-side in the UK. Due to its success on the Continent, it was reissued as the A-side and topped the UK chart. Other hits which followed included 'Viva Bobby Joe' and 'Black Skinned Blue-eyed Boys'.

Eddie Grant, who penned the songs, left the group in 1971 to embark on a solo career. The rest of the group began to appear regularly on the cabaret circuit, although there were numerous changes in personnel.

Grant (real name Edward Montague) was born on 5 March 1948. He set up his own production company when he left the band and as a solo artist his hits included 'Do You Feel My Love', 'Don't Wanna Dance', 'Electric Avenue' and 'Gimme Hope Jo'Anna'.

Derv Gordon and Patrick Lloyd, still based in north London, are the only original members left in the current line-up, which performs on the sixties nostalgia circuit. They have also been tremendously successful in Germany.

Eddie Grant returned to the West Indies, where he has his own recording complex.

EVERETT, Betty   Born in Greenwood, Mississippi, on 23 November 1939, soul singer-pianist Betty Everett made her singing debut at the age of eight as a member of a church choir.

She moved to Chicago and her recording career began, with hits such as 'You're No Good', 'The Shoop Shoop Song', 'Let It Be Me' and 'There'll Come a Time'.

She was to continue as a draw in soul circles, and also maintained a steady stream of hits in

71

the R&B charts into the late 1970s with numbers such as 'Hold On', 'Maybe' and 'Unlucky Girl'.

Betty Everett has continued to be a strong draw on the club circuit in the US and Europe.

EVERLY BROTHERS, The The Everly Brothers were the most popular duo of the rock 'n' roll era. Don Everly was born in Brownie, Kentucky, on 1 February 1937 and his brother Phil in Chicago on 19 January 1939. They began their showbiz career as children, appearing on their parents' radio show, and made their first recordings in 1955.

Their initial releases in 1956 failed to sell, but they hit the chart in 1957 with 'Bye Bye Love'. Their other hit singles included: 'Wake Up Little Susie', 'This Little Girl Of Mine', 'All I Have To Do Is Dream', 'Claudette', 'Bird Dog', 'Devoted To You', 'Problems', 'Love Of My Life', 'Take A Message To Mary', 'Poor Jenny', ''Till I Kissed You', 'Let It Be Me', 'Cathy's Clown', 'When Will I Be Loved', 'So Sad', 'Lucille', 'Like Strangers', 'Walk Right Back', 'Ebony Eyes', 'Temptation', 'Don't Blame Me', 'Crying In The Rain', 'That's Old Fashioned', 'Gone Gone Gone' and 'Bowling Green'.

By the late 1960s the Everly Borthers had decided to change musical direction and specialize in country-rock music, resulting in the end of their hit records streak.

The brothers were in conflict and eventually split up in 1973, with both continuing in solo careers. Exactly ten years later they made up and appeared in the Everly Brothers Reunion Concert at the Royal Albert Hall in London on 23 September 1983.

They continued to record and perform during the 1980s, the decade in which they were inducted into the Rock & Roll Hall Of Fame and received a star on Hollywood Boulevard.

In 1962 Don had married his first wife Venitia Stevenson, who had previously been married to the actor Russ Tamblyn, and in 1990 their daughter Erin married Axl Rose of Guns 'N Roses.

In May 1996 Don and Phil arrived in the UK for a six-week concert tour, which included two appearances at the Royal Albert Hall. They then commenced a tour of the States in July. The same year saw the release of *Golden Years Of The Everly Brothers – Their 24 Greatest Hits*, and a television documentary, *The Life And Times Of The Everly Brothers*.

At the age of 60, Don married songwriter Adela Garza in Nashville and soon afterwards set off on another UK tour midway through 1997.

The Everlys are turning a lodge near their home into a hotel filled with memorabilia of their 50-year career.

The Everly Brothers

FAITH, Adam Born Terence Nelhams in Acton, west London, on 23 June 1940, singer Adam Faith topped the chart with his debut disc, 'What Do You Want', and followed with another chart-topper, 'Poor Me'. By 1966 he had spent 260 weeks in the chart, with 24 hits over a seven-year period, including: 'Someone Else's Baby', 'When Johnny Comes Marching Home', 'How About That', 'Lonely Pup', 'This Is It', 'Easy Going Me', 'Don't You Know It', 'The Time Has Come', 'Lonesome', 'As You Like It', 'Don't That Beat All', 'Baby Take a Bow', 'What Now', 'Walkin' Tall', 'The First Time', 'If He Tells You', 'I Love Being In Love With You', 'Message To Martha', 'Stop Feeling Sorry For Yourself', 'Someone's Taken Maria Away' and 'Cheryl's Going Home'.

Faith's hit streak ended in 1966, but by 1970 he had married and begun a second career as a television actor, appearing in the successful UK series *Budgie*. He continued with film appearances, which have included roles in *Beat Girl*, *Never Let Go*, *What A Whopper*, *Mix Me A Person*, *Stardust*, *McVicar* and *Yesterday's Hero*.

Over the years Faith involved himself in various business enterprises, launching a celebrity financial management consultancy called Faith and contributing financial columns to the *Daily Mail* and *Mail on Sunday* newspapers. For a time he also managed **Leo Sayer**.

A fraudster caused Faith's businesses to crash, but he did not declare himself bankrupt, opting to pay off his £2 million debts over a period of years – which he managed to do. His marriage also ended following a two-year affair with tennis star Chris Evert.

After another successful television series, *Love Hurts*, Faith decided to return to the stage by taking the lead, as Zach The Choreographer, in a nine-month tour of the musical *A Chorus Line*, which opened on 30 June 1997. He commented: 'It's taken me 30-something years to realize that I actually belong in showbusiness.'

Faith was one of the first British pop artists to have a book devoted to him – *Poor Me*, in 1962. In 1996 his autobiography, *Acts Of Faith*, was published.

In May 1997, the 57-year-old singer announced that he would be leaving his 450-acre farm in Kent to emigrate to South Africa, commenting: 'I would still work over here, but it is my dream to breed animals over there.' Faith had originally set up the Faith Foundation Rhino Rescue in 1989 to protect the rare species, which was in danger of extinction from poachers.

FAITHFULL, Marianne Born in Hampstead on 29 December 1946, Marianne Faithfull was a 17-year-old convent-educated girl when **Rolling Stones** manager **Andrew Loog Oldham** discovered her at a party. He was to dub her 'an angel with a big bust'. Mick Jagger wrote 'As Tears Go By' for her and the two embarked on a lengthy affair, even though she was married and had a son. He was eventually to leave her for Chrissie Shrimpton.

'As Tears Go By' was one of four Top 10 chart hits for Marianne, the others being 'Come And Stay With Me', 'This Little Bird' and 'Summer Nights'. She also entered the chart with 'Yesterday', 'Is This What I Get For Loving You' and 'The Ballad Of Lucy Jordan'.

For a time she became an actress, appearing on stage and in the film *Girl On A Motorcycle*.

Marianne became a heroin addict, had several broken relationships, made a number of attempts at suicide and entered detox clinics on several occasions.

In 1979 she issued a critically acclaimed album, *Broken English*, but spent her £90,000 royalties on a three-month binge.

Marianne Faithfull

In 1990 her marriage to American writer Giorgio della Terza collapsed and she went to live in isolation in Shell Cottage in Eire.

In 1995 Island issued her album *A Secret Life*, and the following year Marianne issued *20th Century Blues*, an album of songs by Kurt Weill and Bertholt Brecht. In 1997 she began appearing in a series of concerts with a 90-minute show featuring the songs of Weill and Brecht, supported only by pianist Paul Truebland. She performed songs such as 'Mack The Knife', 'Falling In Love Again' and 'The Ballad Of Sexual Perversity'.

In December 1997 Marianne was the subject of a UK television documentary, as part of the series *Britgirls*. March 1998 saw the release of a two-album retrospective, *The Decca Anthology*, that included all her 1960s singles, B-sides and EPs, selected tracks from her albums, three Italian language songs and 11 previously unreleased tracks.

FAMILY Guitarist John 'Charlie' Whitney had originally formed this group in 1962 at Leicester Art College under the name the Farinas. This was changed to Family in 1967, at the suggestion of American producer Kim Fowley. Apart from Whitney, the line-up then comprised Roger Chapman (vocals), Jim King (sax and flute), **Rick Grech** (bass) and Harry Ovenall (drums).

When they signed to Reprise Records in 1968 a new drummer, Rob Townsend, had joined them. In 1969 Grech left to join **Blind Faith** and was replaced by John Weider. Weider left in 1971 to form Stud and was replaced by John Wetton, and the following year Palmer and Wetton left to join **King Crimson**, being replaced by Tony Ashton and Jim Cregan. 1973 saw Family's Farewell Tour, following which Chapman and Whitney joined Streetwalkers, Cregan became a member of Cockney Rebel prior to joining **Rod Stewart's** band and Townsend joined Medicine Head.

During the group's career, their hits in the singles chart were: 'No Mule's Fool', 'Strange Band', 'In My Own Time' and 'Burlesque'. Their chart albums were: *Music In The Doll's House*, *Family Entertainment*, *A Song For Me*, *Anyway*, *Fearless*, *Bandstand* and *It's Only A Movie*.

Backed by the Short List, Roger Chapman is still filling stadiums in Germany after a big hit there in 1984 with 'Crisis'. Rob Townsend is in the Blues Band. Rick Grech became a furniture salesman in Leicester and died on 17 March 1990. Jim King retired from the music business. John Whitney does sessions in London, while John Palmer works mostly in Germany with Chapman's Short List and for the Fairlight Music Computer company.

FARLOWE, Chris Born John Henry Deighton in London on 13 October 1940, this R&B singer's first foray into music came with the John Henry Skiffle Group, followed by the Thunderbirds. Appearing on the London R&B circuit, he established his reputation and Mick Jagger produced his version of the **Rolling Stones** number 'Out of Time', which topped the UK chart. Other hits included 'Ride On Baby' and 'Handbags And Gladrage'.

During the mid-1960s Farlowe's band the Thunderbirds featured Albert Lee (guitar), Dave Greenslade (organ), Bugs Waddell (bass), Ian Hague (drums) and Jerry Temple (congas). There were some line-up changes and then Chris formed a band called the Hill, before joining **Colosseum**. After a brief spell with **Atomic Rooster**, the man **Otis Redding** hailed as a 'soul brother' gave up singing to run a shop in Islington, north London, specializing in selling Nazi memorabilia.

He made an album, *The Chris Farlowe Band, Live*, in 1975 and guested on some Jimmy Page sessions in the 1980s, but concentrated mainly on the military memorabilia business. By 1986 it was experiencing financial problems with the waning demand for Nazi souvenirs, and Farlowe was declared bankrupt.

He was finally discharged in 1990 and commented: 'Whenever I heard "Out of Time" I knew the official receiver got a bit more. From now on the royalties will come to me.' He was also to embark on a major tour fronting Colosseum in 1995.

Chris Farlowe continues to live at home with his mother in Islington and concentrates on selling 1950s furniture in Camden market, although he has resumed making occasional live appearances as a singer.

FELICIANO, José This singer was born in Puerto Rico on 10 September 1945 and was blind from birth. His family moved to New York when he was five years old. After appearing in Greenwich Village, he was signed to RCA Records and made his recording debut in 1964 with 'Everybody Do The Click'.

During his lengthy career, Feliciano was to have only two hits in the US chart, 'Light My Fire' and 'Hi-Heel Sneakers', both in 1968, although he was more successful as an album artist.

In 1981 he began specializing in the Hispanic market, recording in Spanish, and in 1984 he received the Best Latin Pop Performance award at the Grammys for 'Me Enamore', an award he also received in 1987 and 1990 for 'Tu Immenso Amor' and 'Cielito Lindo' respectively.

In 1995 José Feliciano made his first appearance in the UK for 13 years. He returned in 1996 for a residency in London's Jazz Café. The same year, continuing to record in Spanish, he issued his latest album, *El Americano*.

FELIX, Julie Born in Santa Barbara, California, on 14 June 1938, folk singer Julie Felix moved to the UK in the early 1960s. With the growing interest in folk music, she soon became an established name and appeared regularly on television, being resident on *The Frost Report* and hosting her own shows, *Once More With Felix* and *The Julie Felix Show*.

Mickie Most produced her one Top 20 singles entry in 1970, 'El Condor Pasa'. Her only other success was 'Heaven Is Here', which reached No 22 in the chart.

Founder of the New Age Folk Club, Julie once received a conviction for possessing marijuana. She still lives in the UK and currently remains a fixture on Europe's folk club circuit.

FLEETWOOD MAC When they originally formed in London in April 1967, this group comprised Peter Green (guitar), Mick Fleetwood (drums), John McVie (bass) and Jeremy Spencer (guitar). A third guitarist, Danny Kirwan, joined the following year and in 1969 they topped the chart with their instrumental 'Albatross'. Peter Green could not stand the strain of stardom and left the band in 1970.

Green was born Peter Greenbaum in London on 29 October 1946. He took LSD and went on a 25-year trip, during which he was incarcerated in the psychiatric unit of Brixton Prison after allegedly threatening his manager with a shotgun. This was the beginning of ten years of psychiatric treatment. For a time he became a

Julie Felix

gravedigger, then a hospital porter. At one time he married a member of the Jews For Jews sect, but it didn't work out. He then went back to live with his parents and was sleeping for up to 20 hours a day.

Michelle Reynolds, Green's ex-manager's wife, persuaded the now fat and balding guitarist to stay with her at weekends. He met her brother, Peter Watson, who encouraged him to pick up a guitar for the first time in nearly 25 years. As a result, he was confident enough to play in public with the Splinter Group in 1996. In 1997 an album, *The Peter Green Splinter Group*, was released, with drummer **Cozy Powell** as one of the musicians.

1969 was also the year in which Christine Perfect, singer with **Chicken Shack**, who had married McVie, joined the band. Spencer left in 1971 to be replaced by American musician Bob Welch. Kirwan was fired from the band in 1972 and later ended up in a psychiatric hospital.

In 1975 their tenth line-up included Americans Lindsey Buckingham and Stevie Nicks, and this Anglo-American line-up, with Fleetwood and John and Christine McVie, became the most popular Fleetwood Mac combination.

Their 1977 album *Rumours* topped both the UK and US charts, remaining in the latter for more than 130 weeks and selling in excess of 25 million copies. It also stayed in the UK chart for 400 weeks.

In 1997, on the band's thirtieth anniversary and the twentieth anniversary of *Rumours*, the Buckingham, Fleetwood, Nicks and McVies line-up re-formed for a reunion album, *The Dance*, which shot straight to the No 1 position in the US in September 1997 and entered the UK chart at No 15. *Rumours* also re-entered the UK chart at No 19.

In January 1998 the group received a Lifetime Achievement award at the Brit Awards.

FLOWERPOT MEN, The During the height of the 'flower power' boom which blossomed among the hippie community in San Francisco in the late 1960s, the British songwriting team of Carter & Lewis penned 'Let's Go To San Francisco' and recorded it with session singers – the ubiquitous Tony Burrows plus Neil Landon and Perry Ford, all of whom also became involved in the Ivy League. John Carter and Ken Lewis had originally led Carter Lewis & the Southerners, before becoming writers and session singers.

Other singles releases by the Flowerpot Men – 'Am I Losing You' and 'Young Birds Fly' – were not successful. When making live appearances, they were augmented by Jon Lord (organ), Nick Simper (bass), Ged Peck (guitar) and Carlo Little (drums).

Neil Landon later became lead singer with Noel Redding's Fat Mattress, while Perry Ford was involved in a re-formed Ivy League, but has since left the group. Tony Burrows is still an active entertainer.

FLYING BURRITO BROTHERS, The Gram Parsons decided to leave the Byrds prior to a South African tour due to his views on apartheid. When the Byrds themselves split up soon afterwards, he recruited two other members of the band, Chris Hillman and 'Sneaky' Pete Kleinow, to join him. With the addition of bassist Chris Etheridge and drummer Joe Corneal, he formed the Flying Burrito Brothers in 1968. Several weeks later, Corneal left to join Dillard & Clarke and another ex-Byrd, Michael Clarke, joined them.

Parsons left the group in 1970 and spent two years in London. His replacement was Rick Roberts. Over the years there were numerous other personnel changes and the group split in 1972. The following year Parsons was found dead from heart failure, due to drug abuse.

Kleinow and Etheridge revived the group in 1974 with various other musicians and another former Byrd member, drummer Gene Parsons. By 1981, with other personnel changes and the continuation of album releases which were not major hits, they truncated their name to the Burrito Brothers. By 1985 they were calling themselves the Flying Brothers.

Pete Kleinow is now a record producer in California. Chris Ethridge returned to session work. Chris Hillman is recording a new album, set for release in 1998.

FONTANA, Wayne Born Glynn Ellis in Manchester on 28 October 1945, this singer's entry into the musical world began with a skiffle group called the Velfins, who then evolved into the Jets. When Wayne made a demo record for the Fontana label in 1963, he adopted the name of the label and was backed by a group called the Mindbenders, named after a recent Dirk Bogarde film.

As Wayne Fontana & the Mindbenders, their hits included: 'Hello Josephine', 'Stop Look &

Listen', 'Just A Little Bit Too Late', 'She Needs Love', 'Um Um Um Um Um Um' and 'Game Of Love'. Wayne then turned solo in 1965 and charted with 'It Was Easier To Hurt Her', 'Come On Home', 'Goodbye Bluebird' and 'Pamela Pamela'.

The Mindbenders continued as a trio, with Eric Stewart taking over lead vocals, and hit the chart with 'A Groovy Kind Of Love', 'Can't Live With You', 'Ashes To Ashes' and 'The Letter'. Stewart was later to team up with Paul McCartney for a time.

Wayne Fontana still leads a new Mindbenders on the sixties nostalgia circuit. They currently comprise Julian Latimer (bass), Craig Newhouse (lead) and Dave Alexander (drums).

FOREIGNER This group was originally founded in New York by two English musicians – guitarist Mick Jones, formerly of Spooky Tooth and the Leslie West Band, and keyboards player Ian McDonald, a former member of **King Crimson**. They were joined by British drummer Dennis Elliot, also formerly with King Crimson. The three American members were Lou Gramm (vocals), Al Greenwood (keyboards) and Ed Gagliardi (bass). The group released their debut album in 1977.

Their hits included: 'Feels Like The First Time', 'Cold As Ice', 'Long Long Way From Home', 'Hot Blooded', 'Double Vision', 'Blue Morning Blue Day', 'Dirty White Boy', 'Head Games', 'Urgent', 'Waiting For A Girl Like You', 'Juke Box Hero' and 'Break It Up'.

Jones decided to stop the band recording and touring in 1980. McDonald, Greenwood and Gagliardi left. The group was then re-formed as a four-piece with Rick Wills on bass and they topped the album chart with *4* in 1981.

As a solo artist in 1987, Lou Gramm had a Top 10 single, 'Midnight Blue', and an album hit, *Ready Or Not*.

While every member of Foreigner embarked on solo projects in the 1980s, the group has never announced a disbandment.

The Very Best Of Foreigner was released in 1992.

FORTUNES, The This group was formed in 1963 and consisted of Glen Dale and Barry Pritchard (guitar and vocals), David Carr (keyboards), Rod Allen (bass and vocals) and Andy Brown (drums). They made their recording debut with 'Summertime, Summertime', and their follow-up, 'Caroline', was adopted by the pirate radio station Radio Caroline as its signature tune.

Five of the group's singles were chart entries: 'You've Got Your Troubles', 'Here It Comes Again', 'This Golden Ring', 'Freedom Come Freedom Go' and 'Storm In A Teacup'.

In 1966 Dale left the band to turn solo and was replaced by Shel MacRae. Carr left the group in 1968 and they remained a quartet until George McAllister joined them in 1971.

David Carr now lives in the US and is a record producer. Andy Brown works in a Worcester post office. Glen Dale resides in Tenerife and performs solo locally. Barry Pritchard has retired from the music business on health grounds. Rod Allen still leads the Fortunes on the sixties nostalgia circuit. The other members are Mike Smitham (guitar), Paul Hooker (drums) and Bob Jackson (keyboards).

FOUNDATIONS, The Originally formed in 1967 with members from Ceylon, Jamaica, Barbados and Dominica, this group consisted of Alan Warner (guitar), Clem Curtis (vocals), Pat Bourke (sax), Eric Allendale (trombone), Peter MacBeth (bass) and Tim Harris (drums).

Their debut hit was 'Baby, Now That I've Found You', penned by songwriter Tony Macauley, who was their original manager.

Curtis then moved to the States as a solo artist and was replaced by Colin Young. The group next had a US chart-topper, 'Build Me Up Buttercup', followed by 'In The Bad Bad Old Days'. Curtis returned to the UK and there are now two groups, one led by him, the other by Young. In between his Foundations gigs, Curtis runs an antique business near Milton Keynes.

FOUR FRESHMEN, The This vocal group was formed at Butler University, Indianapolis, in 1948. The members were Bob Flanigan, Ross and Don Barbour, and Hal Kratzsch.

The outfit made their chart debut with 'It's a Blue World' in 1952 and followed with singles such as 'It Happened Once Before' and 'Mood Indigo'. Their big hit was 'Graduation Day' in 1956. The popular vocal team also has seven chart albums.

Kratzsch left in 1953 and was replaced by Ken Errair, who was himself replaced by Ken Albers in 1955. Barbour left in 1960, only to be killed in a car crash the following year. Errair died in a plane crash in 1968 and Kratzsch died from cancer in 1970.

With only a shadowy connection to the original line-up, the Four Freshmen toured the UK in 1992, backed by Ray McVay's All-Star Big Band.

FOURMOST, The   This Liverpool band, part of the **Brian Epstein** stable of artists, was originally formed in 1959 as the Four Jays. By the time they signed up with Epstein, the line-up consisted of Billy Hatton (vocals and bass), Brian O'Hara (lead and vocals), Mike Millward (vocals and rhythm) and Dave Lovelady (drums).

The group's hits were: 'Hello Little Girl', 'I'm In Love', 'A Little Loving', 'How Can I Tell Her', 'Baby I Need Your Lovin'' and 'Girls Girls Girls'.

Mike Millward died from leukaemia in 1966 and was eventually replaced by a founder member of the Four Jays, Joey Bowers. Paul McCartney found a song for them called 'Rosetta' and produced the record with them, but it failed to hit. They became a cabaret attraction during the 1970s, but one by one the original members left, until only Brian O'Hara was left, performing with new members. Eventually he retired, and the Fourmost which currently performs has no original members in it.

Three of the original members – Joey Bowers, Billy Hatton and Dave Lovelady – formed a quartet called Clouds, along with Joey's wife.

The members of the Fourmost announced their retirement from music in 1996, but agreed to re-form to appear at special concerts for the Mersey Cats (a group of original Mersey Beat bands who raise money for children's charities) in 1998.

FOUR PENNIES, The   Originally formed in Blackburn in 1962 as the Lionel Morton Four, this quartet comprised Lionel Morton (vocals and rhythm), Fritz Fryer (lead), Mike Wilsh (bass) and Alan Buck (drums).

They changed their name to the Four Pennies the following year and made their chart debut in 1964 with 'Do You Want Me To', then topped the chart with their second release, the self-penned 'Juliet'.

The Four Pennies' other 1960s hits were: 'I Found Out The Hard Way', 'Black Girl', 'Until It's Time For You To Go' and 'Trouble Is My Middle Name'. They also released two albums: *Two Sides Of The Four Pennies* and *Mixed Bag*.

When the group disbanded, Fryer originally formed a trio – Fritz, Mike and Mo – then went into record production and later opened Fritz Fryer's Antiques in Ross-on-Wye, Herefordshire, a successful business which he still runs.

Wilsh penned a number of songs, such as 'Champs Elysées', which were popular on the Continent, and he continued to perform over the years in various incarnations of the group. Buck went into music publishing.

Morton, then married to actress Julia Foster, became a children's television presenter on *Playschool* and appeared as the lead in the West End musical shows *Hair*, *Jesus Christ, Superstar* and *West Side Story*. He composed the signature tune to the UK televsion series *Playaway* and eventually, in 1990, moved to Bath with his third wife.

In 1996 he embarked on a solo career with a one-man singalong show: 'With instant access to hundreds of all-time classic favourites via a laptop computer linked to a giant wide screen, an entire audience is transformed into a bonafide choir with a master singer/entertainer at the helm.'

The original members of the Four Pennies gathered again in 1993 to appear on a UK television special, but attempts to keep the group together in its original line-up fell apart when a promoter failed to pay them for a number of appearances, and there were quarrels and 'I-told-you-sos' from Morton. That same year, Buck hanged himself.

Wilsh had been running a group called the Pennies for a number of years from his base in Bristol, but, with the blessing of the other original members, has now been allowed to call them the Four Pennies. He is on double bass and vocals and is supported by John Ozoroff (lead and vocals) and Charles Hart (drums and vocals). John 'Duff' Lowe was on keyboards and vocals for five years until 1997, when he left the group. Lowe was an original member of John Lennon's first skiffle group, the Quarry Men, and decided to team up with another original Quarry Men member.

FOX, Samantha   This glamorous singer, born on 15 April 1966, began her career as a 'page three girl' – a topless model in the *Sun* newspaper – and rapidly became the most famous topless model in the UK.

She then graduated to pop stardom and since the mid-1980s has had a string of hits which include: 'Touch Me', 'Do Ya Do Ya', 'Hold On Tight', 'I'm All You Need', 'Nothing's Gonna Stop Me Now', 'I Surrender', 'I Promise You',

'True Devotion', 'Naughty Girls', 'Love House' and 'I Only Wanna Be With You'.

She also has aspirations as an actress and was a huge success in the 'Bollywood' film *Rock Dancer* – so much so, that at the end of 1997 she was offered the part in another Indian blockbuster, *Love Story 98*.

FRAMPTON, Peter   This singer-songwriter-guitarist was born in Beckenham, Kent, on 22 April 1950. At the age of 16 he formed the Herd, whose hits included 'From The Underworld', 'Paradise Lost' and 'I Don't Want Our Loving To Die'. In 1969 he formed Humble Pie, who charted with 'Natural Born Boogie'. In 1972 he formed the band **Camel** and in 1974 turned solo.

Frampton then decided to leave the music business and staged a farewell concert. His double album *Frampton Comes Alive* subsequently became a huge seller, spawning the hit singles 'Show Me The Way' and 'I'm In You', causing him to change his mind. His other hits included 'Baby I Love Your Way' and 'Do You Feel Like We Do'.

Frampton appeared in the film *Sgt Pepper's Lonely Hearts Club Band* and based himself in the States, where he had some further hits, including 'Signed, Sealed, Delivered (I'm Yours)' and 'I Can't Stand It No More'.

The hits then began to fade away and the 1980s were not a fruitful period.

In 1991 Frampton considered re-forming Humble Pie, but a week after meeting **Steve Marriott** to discuss it, Marriott died in a fire.

Appositely titled *Comes Alive II*, a second in-concert Peter Frampton album was issued in 1996 shortly before its maker moved from Los Angeles to Nashville.

FRANCIS, Connie   Born Concetta Maria Franconero in Newark, New Jersey, on 12 December 1938, this singer entered the chart with her tenth record release, 'The Majesty Of Love', in 1957. Between 1958 and 1964 she had 35 chart hits, which included: 'Who's Sorry Now', 'Stupid Cupid', 'My Happiness', 'Lipstick On Your Collar', 'Among My Souvenirs', 'Mama', 'Where The Boys Are', 'Second Hand Love' and 'Vacation'. She featured in four films, including *Where The Boys Are* and *When The Boys Meet The Girls*.

Connie fell in love with singer **Bobby Darin**, and although they wanted to get married, their romance was marred by the attitude of Connie's father, who broke off their relationship.

In fact, her personal life was full of drama, revealed in her autobiography *Who's Sorry Now*, published in 1984. She revealed how she was raped at knifepoint in a motel, a horrifying incident which left her emotionally crippled and caused her to retreat from the public eye for a number of years. She was eventually awarded over $3 million in damages. When she underwent nasal surgery, the operation went wrong and it took her a number of years to recover. Then her brother George was murdered by gangsters in 1981.

After spending some time in a rest home, Connie began to work again in 1988 and she went on to record 'Something Stupid' with Boy George.

Now more C&W than mainstream pop, Connie was signed to Sony in 1993, but it was a

Connie Francis

hits compilation, *The Singles Collection*, rather than any new material that was to restore her to the UK album chart, where it reached No 12 in May 1993.

FRANKIE GOES TO HOLLYWOOD

This group was formed in Liverpool in 1980 by vocalists Holly Johnson and Paul Rutherford, together with guitarists Brian 'Nasher' Nash and Mark O'Toole and drummer Peter Gill. Three years later they had a major hit with 'Relax', a number banned by the BBC radio and television, which helped to place it in the spotlight – where it sold two million copies and topped the chart.

They also reached No 1 with their two follow-up singles, 'Two Tribes' and 'The Power Of Love', equalling the record of fellow Liverpudlians **Gerry & the Pacemakers** of topping the charts with their first three releases.

Other releases include: 'Welcome To The Pleasure Dome, 'Warriors Of The Wasteland' and 'Watching The Wildlife'.

The group disbanded in 1987 when Johnson, who was born in Khartoum, Sudan, on 19 February 1960, turned solo. Their record company ZTT sued him, but he took them to the High Court the following year and won artistic freedom and substantial compensation. Rutherford also turned solo, without much success, and formed a group called Pressure Zone in 1991. The other members of the group, with new lead singer Dee Harris, also failed to match previous glories.

Brian Nash returned to work as an electrician in 1990, but then teamed up with Grant Boult in a group called Low. Peter Gill works for a production company called Love Station. Mark O'Toole moved to Los Angeles for a time, but returned to Liverpool in 1992.

In 1991 Johnson revealed he had the AIDS virus, but he is still performing today and sang 'Ferry 'Cross The Mersey' before an audience of 32,000 at Anfield Stadium in May 1997 during a special concert in aid of the families of the victims of the Hillsborough football disaster.

Several of the group's hits were re-released in 1993.

FREDDIE & THE DREAMERS

This beat group was originally formed in Manchester in October 1961. The members were Freddie Garrity (vocals), Derek Quinn (lead), Roy Crewsdon (rhythm), Pete Birrell (bass) and Bernie Dwyer (drums).

They appeared at Liverpool's Cavern club and also performed in Hamburg, Germany. The success of the Beatles led to record companies signing up numerous groups and the Dreamers were contracted to Columbia, making their debut with 'If You Gotta Make A Fool Of Somebody'. Freddie next co-wrote 'I'm Telling You Now' with songwriter Mitch Murray.

The group had a comedy act in which Freddie pranced and danced around in a gawky fashion, creating a dance called 'Do The Freddie', which resulted in a single of the same name specially for the US market.

The group found international fame and also appeared in a number of films, including *What A Crazy World*, *Just For You* and *Every Day's A Holiday*.

Their other hit singles included: 'You Were Made For Me', 'Over You', 'I Love You Baby', 'Just For You', 'I Understand', 'A Little You' and 'Thou Shalt Not Steal' – all between 1963 and 1965.

The original line-up eventually split in 1968 with Freddie finding a new backing band, which he also called the Dreamers, to appear on the cabaret circuit.

Freddie and Birrell also appeared regularly on the weekly UK television children's show *Little Big Time*. In 1988 Freddie appeared in a stage production of *The Tempest*.

He continues to appear with different line-ups of the Dreamers. The other original members are no longer performing: Birrell became a taxi driver, Crewsdon has his own bar in the Canary Isles and Quinn works for a soft drinks company.

For a number of years Freddie has also been appearing in pantomimes during the Christmas season in roles such as Silly Billy in *Jack & The Beanstalk*. In 1996 he played a drug-pushing disc jockey in the hit UK television series *Heartbeat*. The following year, his house was the subject of an edition of *Through The Keyhole*.

FUGS, The

This group was formed in New York's Greenwich Village in 1965 and comprised Ed Sanders (guitar and vocals), Tuli Kupferberg (vocals) and Ken Weaver (drums).

As a live band, their performances were sometimes labelled outrageous due to the controversy of their lyrics. They recorded the number 'Out Demons Out', by which they are now most popularly identified. They also had some minor chart album hits with *The Fugs' First Album* and *The Fugs*.

*Freddie
and the
Dreamers*

The group disbanded in 1969, although Sanders and Kupferberg re-formed the group in 1980 and continued recording until 1989, when they released *Fugs Live In Woodstock*.

Ed Sanders is also an author. His best-known book is *The Family* (1972), an account of the Manson murders. Tuli Kupferberg continues a sporadic solo recording career.

In 1993, Kupferberg and Sanders regained the rights to the entire Fugs catalogue, and instigated a comprehensive reissue schedule.

FUN BOY THREE In 1981, three members of the successful two-tone band the **Specials** decided to break away as a trio, calling themselves Fun Boy Three. They were vocalists Terry Hall and Neville Staples, and guitarist Lynval Golding.

The trio made their chart debut with *The Lunatics (Have Taken Over The Asylum)*, and then had two hits when they teamed up with the female vocal group **Bananarama** for 'It Ain't What You Do (It's The Way That You Do It)' and 'Really Saying Something'.

Other hits included: 'The Telephone Always Rings', 'Summertime', 'The More I See (The Less I Believe)', 'Tunnel Of Love' and 'Our Lips Are Sealed'.

After two years the three went their separate ways, with Hall forming other groups, including Colourfield, before turning solo in a career which has ploughed an erratic furrow but always commanded media attention. Staples formed the short-lived Sunday Best in the mid-1980s and seems to have disappeared from the music scene, while Golding is reputed still to be in the music business as a session guitarist.

GALLAGHER & LYLE Benny Gallagher and Graham Lyle were the members of this Scots singing-songwriting duo. They moved to London to further their songwriting career and joined the group McGuinness Flint in 1969, penning the hits 'When I'm Dead And Gone' and 'Malt And Barley Blues' for the band.

The pair left McGuinness Flint to pursue their own career on record. As Gallagher & Lyle, they first charted in 1976 with 'I Wanna Stay With You', followed by three further chart entries: 'Heart On My Sleeve', 'Breakaway' and 'Every Little Teardrop'.

The two later split and Graham Lyle teamed up with another songwriter, Terry Britten, and penned 'What's Love Got To Do With It' for Tina Turner.

With ex-members of **Manfred Mann**, Benny Gallagher is a member of the seven-piece Manfreds, who toured Europe in the spring of 1998 and have a new album due for release.

GARRICK, David Born Phillip Darryl Core, this Liverpool singer of the Mersey Beat era was a former choirboy who also had operatic training. He began singing with local groups in 1965, when he adopted the name of the eighteenth-century actor.

Garrick made his record debut with 'Go', which didn't register, but hit the chart with his next two singles, 'Lady Jane' and 'Dear Mrs Appleby', in 1966.

These proved to be his only hits, despite several further singles, including: 'Don't Go Out In The Rain Sugar', 'I've Found A Love', 'Ave Maria', 'A Little Bit Of This (A Little Bit Of That)' and Maypole Mews', and an album, *A Boy Called David*.

While his name means little in the UK, David Garrick remains a draw in sixties nostalgia festivals on the Continent.

GAYLE, Crystal Born Brenda Gail Webb in Paintsville, Kentucky, on 9 January 1951, this singer was raised in Wabash, Indiana.

She began singing with Loretta Lynn's roadshow when she was only 16 and it was Loretta who gave her the name Crystal, so as not to confuse her with record label stablemate **Brenda Lee**.

In addition to her own hit singles, which included 'I'll Get Over You', 'Don't It Make My Brown Eyes Blue' and 'Cry', she had a series of chart-topping duets, which included 'You And I' with Eddie Rabbitt and 'Making Up For Lost Time' with Gary Morris.

In 1979, Crystal became the first country artist to appear on a tour of China.

A huge star in C&W circles in the States, she was signed to Capitol in 1990 and reunited with her old mentor, Allen Reynolds. She lives with her husband and two children in Tennessee.

GAYNOR, Gloria Born Gloria Fowles on 7 September 1949, Gloria Gaynor originally sang with a vocal group called the Soul Satisfiers in the early 1970s. She then made her solo debut with 'Never Can Say Goodbye'. Other hit singles included: 'Reach Out I'll Be There', 'All I Need Is Your Sweet Lovin'', 'How High the Moon', 'I Will Survive', 'Let Me Know' and 'I Am What I Am'.

Her album *Never Can Say Goodbye* became an international hit and was particularly popular in discos, leading to Gloria being dubbed the 'Queen Of The Discos' by the International Association Of Disc Jockeys in 1975.

Her career eventually became overshadowed by that of Donna Summer, although the impact of 'I Will Survive' has continued as one of the most popular disco numbers of all time – and the most popular karaoke number.

For a number of years Gloria disappeared from the scene completely. Initially, she could only find work in the UK and took a job with BBC radio presenting *Gospel Train*. She also appeared in Christmas shows at the Hippodrome in London in the early 1990s. In 1990 her album *Gloria Gaynor '90* was issued, but could not find an outlet in the US. One of the tracks was a gospel version of 'I Will Survive', which went on to become a massive hit in Italy.

In her personal life, Gloria went through financial problems and drug troubles, and separated from her husband, Lindwood Simon.

In 1994 she was rediscovered in the US with the explosion of interest in the 1970s and acts such as Donna Summer, **Abba** and the **Bee Gees**. Gloria was suddenly appearing on television talk shows and was again in demand for seventies concerts.

A born-again Christian, Gloria sings regularly at the Christian Life Centre in New York. She has been reconciled with her husband and has updated her biography, *I Will Survive*. She has also completed a new disco album, *The Answer*, for release in 1998.

GENESIS In 1965, singer Peter Gabriel and keyboards player Tony Banks were in a band called the Garden Wall. The following year they joined a group called the Anon, which had guitarist Mike Rutherford in it. The next year they renamed themselves Genesis. The group was signed to Charisma Records; drummer Phil Collins joined them in August 1970 and Steve Hackett three months later.

Genesis became a major act with more than 20 hit singles, including: 'I Know What I Like (In Your Wardrobe)', 'Your Own Special Way', 'Spot The Pigeon', 'Follow You Follow Me', 'Many Too Many', 'Turn It On Again', 'Duchess', 'Misunderstanding', 'Abacab', 'Keep It Dark', '3x3', 'Mama', 'That's All', 'Illegal Alien', 'Invisible Touch', 'In Too Deep', 'Land Of Confusion', 'Tonight Tonight Tonight' and 'Throwing It All Away'.

Their album hits have included *Foxtrot*, *Genesis Live*, *Selling England By The Pound*, *Nursery Cryme*, *The Lamb Lies Down On Broadway*, *A Trick Of The Tail*, *Wind And Wuthering*, *Seconds Out*, *And Then There Were Three*, *Duke*, *Abacab*, *3 Sides Live*, *Genesis* and *Trespass*.

Gabriel left the band in May 1975 to pursue a successful solo career. Steve Hackett left the band in June 1977 and also had a stream of hit albums on both sides of the Atlantic. By 1980

Phil Collins of Genesis

Collins had also embarked on a solo career, although he still performed as a member of Genesis, which had trimmed down to a trio. Rutherford also appeared in another band, Mike & the Mechanics, although he too still performed with Genesis.

Genesis seemed to fade from the scene in the 1990s and there was a six-year silence. Collins announced in 1996 that he was quitting the band. Genesis re-emerged with the release of their fifteenth album, *Calling All Stations*, in September 1997. This was built around the Mike Rutherford/Tony Banks combination, with a new front singer, 28-year old Ray Wilson, a former member of Stiltskin.

Coincidentally, a new Steve Hackett LP was released. *Genesis Revisited: Steve Hackett & Friends* was a Genesis-oriented album, which contained contributions from many musicians who had performed or recorded with Genesis over the years, such as Bill Bruford, John Wetton, Ian McDonald, Colin Blunstone, Tony Levin, Paul

Carrack and Chester Thompson. When asked why he had released it at the same time as the new Genesis album, Hackett pointed out that Genesis had been dormant for some time and he had begun working on the album in 1995.

GERRY & THE PACEMAKERS Gerry Marsden was born in Liverpool on 24 September 1942. He led his first skiffle group at the age of 14 and in 1959 transformed it into a rock 'n' roll band with his brother Freddie on drums, Les Chadwick on guitar and Les Maguire on piano.

They were placed at No 2 to the Beatles in the 1961 *Mersey Beat* poll and signed with Brian Epstein. The manager attempted to repeat his success with the Beatles by following each of the steps taken by that band. He had the group record with George Martin for the Parlophone label, got a *Gerry & The Pacemakers* magazine launched by the publishers of *Beatles Monthly*, had their photographs taken by Dezo Hoffman and their suits made by the Beatles' tailor

Gerry and the Pacemakers

Douggie Millins, put on a *Gerry's Christmas Cracker* stage show to emulate the *Beatles Christmas Show*, arranged an appearance on *The Ed Sullivan Show* and even had the group star in a film, *Ferry 'Cross The Mersey*.

Gerry & the Pacemakers hit the No 1 spot in the UK with a number the Beatles had turned down, 'How Do You Do It'. They then topped the chart with their two subsequent releases, 'I Like It' and 'You'll Never Walk Alone', making them the first artists ever to reach No I in the UK chart with their first three records. As a result of Gerry's recording, 'You'll Never Walk Alone' became a British football anthem.

Gerry & the Pacemakers had four further hits: 'I'm the One', 'Don't Let The Sun Catch You Crying', 'Ferry 'Cross The Mersey' and 'I'll Be There'.

The group disbanded and Gerry appeared in the stage musical *Charlie Girl* in London's West End. He then began appearing in children's television programmes.

In the 1970s, he re-formed Gerry & the Pacemakers with different personnel and has been touring ever since. His brother Freddie launched a minicab company in Liverpool in 1996 called Pacemakers, and Les Chadwick has been living in Australia since the early 1970s.

Following the Bradford City Football Club disaster in May 1985, in which 55 people were killed when a fire destroyed a stand, Gerry recorded 'You'll Never Walk Alone' again as a charity disc to raise funds for the relatives of the victims. Under the name the Crowd, he enrolled 50 artists to join him on the record, including Paul McCartney and Zak Starkey. The record reached No 1 – the first time an artist had topped the chart with two different versions of the same number.

Gerry's autobiography, *You'll Never Walk Alone*, was published in 1993. He has been appearing on the Flying Music Solid Silver Sixties Tours almost annually and in 1996 featured in a stage musical based on his life, *Ferry 'Cross The Mersey*.

There were some further changes in the personnel of Gerry & the Pacemakers in 1997. Bass player Andy Cairns remained in the outfit while Kevin Jackson and Sean Fitzpatrick left, to be replaced by Tony Young on keyboards and Colin Garth on drums.

In 1998 Gerry & the Pacemakers began to tour the UK in a concert version of the stage play *Ferry 'Cross The Mersey*.

GLITTER, Gary   Gary Glitter was born Paul Gadd in a workhouse in Banbury, Somerset, on 8 May 1940. He was an illegitimate child, son of a young working-class girl, Marguerita, and a munitions factory worker who was married with six children. The singer has never met his father and does not wish to. For a time he moved in with his mother and half-brother, but she could not cope with working and bringing up the two boys at the same time, so he was put into care when he was 11 years old.

Paul moved to London to play in the clubs, but it wasn't until the onset of the 1970s that he found success. Mike Leander came up with the name Gary Glitter and had him record 'Rock 'n' Roll Part One' and 'Part Two', which went to the top of the chart. Other hits included: 'I Didn't Know I Loved You (Till I Saw You Rock 'n' Roll)', 'Do You Wanna Touch Me', 'Hello Hello I'm Back Again', 'I'm The Leader Of The Gang', 'I Love You Love Me Love', 'Remember Me This Way', 'Always Yours', 'Oh Yes! You're Beautiful', 'Love Like You And Me', 'Doing Alright With The Boys', 'Papa Omm Mow Mow', 'You Belong To Me, 'It Takes All Night Long', 'A Little Boogie Woogie In The Back Of My Mind', 'Gary Glitter', 'And Then She Kissed Me', 'All That Glitters', 'Dance Me Up' and 'Another Rock And Roll Christmas'.

Glitter married his childhood sweetheart Ann Merton and the couple had two children, Paul and Sarah. They divorced after nine years.

In his autobiography, *Leader*, Glitter revealed how he had struggled with alcohol and drug addictions and with bankruptcy, and how he had twice attempted suicide.

At the height of his career he had sold 18 million records, and in October 1997, his twenty-fifth year in show business, he received a Gold Award from BASCA (British Academy Of Songwriters, Composers And Authors).

Things were looking good in November 1997. Glitter was about to embark on his annual Christmas tour, this one called A Night Out With The Boys, and was celebrating the release of a double album of his greatest hits. Several of his numbers had been used in the hit British film *The Full Monty* and he had filmed a duet with the Spice Girls for their movie, *Spiceworld*. In addition, he had been cast in a film due to be made in 1998 called *Iloveyoulovemelove*, which tells the story of a bigamous taxi driver from Blackpool whose wives fall in love with Glitter.

Disaster struck during the month, when a computer he had taken to be repaired was discovered to have child pornography stored on the hard drive. The store phoned the police and Glitter was arrested. He denied any knowledge of it and was released, but the allegation had a dramatic effect on his career and Ugly Bug Productions, the producers of *Iloveyoulovemelove*, immediately recast Noddy Holder in the role and the Spice Girls decided to cut the sequence with Glitter from their movie. He has now been charged with the offence.

Gary Glitter's autobiography, *Leader*, was updated and reissued in 1998.

GOLDEN EARRING This Dutch group was originally formed in the Hague, Netherlands, in 1961. The members were George Kooymans (guitar and vocals), Rinus Gerritsen (bass and vocals), Hans Van Herwerden (guitar) and Fred Van Der Hilst (drums).

There were various changes in personnel before their first hit in the Dutch chart with 'Please Go' in 1965 – Herwerden and Hilst had been replaced by Peter De Ronde on guitar and Jaap Eggermont on drums, with Frans Krassenburg also joining on vocals.

In 1966 Barry Hay replaced Krassenberg and Golden Earring topped the Dutch chart with 'Dong-Dong-Di-Ki-Gi-Dong'.

1969 saw Eggermont leave to become a producer, with Cesar Zuiderwijk as his replacement.

The band supported the **Who** on a European tour in 1972 and the following year topped the Dutch chart again with 'Radar Love'. The number also entered the UK chart twice, first in 1973 and then again in 1977. They had an album, *Moontan*, in the UK chart in 1974.

'Radar Love' also entered the US Top 20. They next entered the US Top 10 with 'Twilight Zone' and toured there and in Canada. The group disbanded in 1986.

Of all the ex-members of Golden Earring, Barry Hay enjoyed the most success as a soloist with the 1989 album *Victory of Bad Taste*, but was involved once again when the group reformed to issue their fortieth album in 1996.

GOLDIE & THE GINGERBREADS After disbanding the Gingerbreads in 1969, Goldie (Genjya Zelkowitz) sang in various jazz combos before joining the otherwise all-male Ten Wheel Drive. Next came two solo albums attributed to Genya Ravan, before she reverted to Goldie Zelkowitz for three more. From the late 1970s to the present, the former name has been the one most used for sleeve credits for session work on albums by Gamma and Lou Reed, among others, and for her duet (on 'Mr Music') with Ellen Foley. As a record producer, she has been responsible for the Dead Boys 'Young Loud And Snotty' and an attempt to relaunch Ronnie Spector as a punk star with 'Siren' from 1980.

GORE, Lesley Lesley Gore was born in New York on 2 May 1946. In 1962 she began singing with a jazz group, and made her recording debut the following year with 'It's My Party', which topped the US chart.

Her other hit singles included: 'Judy's Turn To Cry', 'She's A Fool', 'You Don't Own Me', 'That's The Way Boys Are', 'I Don't Wanna Be A Loser', 'Maybe I Know', 'Look Of Love', 'Sunshine', 'Lollipops And Rainbows', 'My Town', 'My Guy And Me' and 'California Nights'.

Lesley graduated from high school in 1964, the year in which she appeared in the film *Girls On The Beach* and was named the year's Best Female Vocalist in all three US music trade papers.

She appeared as Pussycat in the *Batman* television series and made her stage debut in the musical *Half A Sixpence* in 1967.

Lesley began to appear regularly on the nightclub circuit in the States and also in summer stock musicals such as *Finian's Rainbow* and *Funny Girl*.

In 1995 she appeared at a charity function at New York's Copacabana with Michael Bolton, prior to a month-long residency at the city's Rainbow Room.

GRANT, Julie This British singer had three chart hits between 1963 and 1964: they were 'Up On The Roof', 'Count On Me' and 'Come To Me'. A pretty, dark-haired youngster with a bouffant hairstyle, she appeared on several tours, including the **Rolling Stones'** first major sortie.

Julie moved to the States where she married David Connelly, who was tour manager to Isaac Hayes, the Carpenters and several other leading acts. She currently resides in Connecticut.

GRAPEFRUIT Brothers Pete and Geoff Swettenham, a guitarist and a drummer respectively, together with guitarist John Perry, were members of Tony Rivers & the Castaways. They left that group in 1966 and decided to form a band of their own. Terry Doran, manager of Apple Music, introduced them to George Alexander, a bass player and songwriter, who became their fourth member. **John Lennon** gave the band their name – it was the title of a book by Yoko Ono – and they signed to RCA Records.

Two of their singles – 'Dear Delilah' and 'C'mon Marianne' – entered the chart, but their best song, 'Deep Water', and album releases were unsuccessful and Pete Swettenham left early in 1969, to be replaced by Bobby Ware and Mike Fowler. However, the group disbanded by the end of the year.

Alexander revived Grapefruit in 1971 with two members of the **Easybeats**, Harry Vanda and George Young. They recorded a single, 'Sha Sha', but disbanded once again.

John Perry joined the Only Ones in 1997.

GROUNDHOGS, The In 1963 the Dollarbills changed their name to John Lee's Groundhogs. They comprised Tony McPhee (guitar), John Cruickshank (vocals and harp), Bob Hall (piano), Pete Cruickshank (bass) and Dave Boorman (drums). There was no John Lee in the group – the prefix had been added in honour of John Lee Hooker, whom they backed on tour. The group then broke up in 1966.

They were to re-form in 1968, with McPhee and Pete Cruickshank adding new musicians Steve Rye on vocals and harmonica and Ken Pustelnik on drums. They became a trio when Rye left, and in 1972 Pustelnik was replaced by Clive Brooks.

Between 1970 and 1974 the group had a number of album entries, including *Thank Christ For The Bomb*, *Split*, *Who Will Save The World* and *Solid*.

The trio broke up in 1975, although McPhee continued to use the name for a short time, when he issued two unsuccessful singles.

McPhee revived the name again in 1984 and continues to lead the group, who remain a firm fixture on the club circuit of the UK and Germany. In addition, McPhee continues to play well-received concerts of acoustic blues.

GUESS WHO This Canadian group was originally formed in Winnipeg in 1962 as Chad Allan & the Reflections. They began performing in the style of British groups such as the Shadows and then adopted the style of the Mersey Beat bands. They topped the Canadian chart in 1965 with

their cover of Johnny Kidd & the Pirates' 'Shakin' All Over', with the record company changing the group's name to Guess Who.

In 1966 they became a quartet, comprising Burton Cummings (vocals and keyboards), Randy Bachman (guitar), Jim Kale (bass) and Garry Peterson (drums).

Their US hits included: 'Shakin' All Over', 'These Eyes', 'Laughing', 'Undun', 'No Time', 'American Woman', 'No Sugar Tonight', 'Hand Me Down World', 'Share The Land', 'Albert Flasher', 'Rain Dance', 'Star Baby', 'Clap For The Wolfman' and 'Dancin' Fool'.

Bachman, a Mormon, left the group in 1970, as his beliefs conflicted with their lifestyle. He later formed a group with original member Chad Allen plus two of his brothers, which he called Brave Belt. This group, sans Allen, developed into Bachman-Turner Overdrive, with C.F. Turner, and their hits included: 'Let It Ride', 'Takin' Care Of Business', 'You Ain't Seen Nothing Yet', 'Roll On Down The Highway', 'Hey You' and 'Take It Like A Man'.

When Bachman left Guess Who, Cummins added two guitarists, Kurt Winter and Greg Leskiw. There were various other personnel changes before Cummins eventually disbanded the group in 1975.

As a solo artist, Burton Cummins had hits with 'Stand Tall' and 'You Saved My Soul', and released a number of albums, including his chart album debut *Burton Cummins*.

Guess Who re-formed in 1979, but personnel changes continued throughout the next ten years and the line-up in 1989 comprised Jim Kale (bass), Ken Carter (vocals), Dale Russell (vocals and guitar), Garry Peterson (drums) and Mike Hanford (keyboards). By 1995, when the group issued the album *Lonely One*, Hanford had been replaced by Leonard Shaw and Carter by Terry Hatty.

HAGGARD, Merle This leading country music artist was born on 6 April 1937 in an abandoned railroad car near Bakersfield in California. Over the years he has had almost 40 No 1 records in the country chart, although only one entry in the popular music chart – 'If We Make It Through December' in 1974. His many country hits include 'Okie From Muskogee', 'Mama Tried', 'The Fugitive' and 'Branded Man'.

Haggard's dramatic life was highlighted in his 1981 autobiography, *Sing Me Back Home: My Life*. He had spent three years in San Quentin for attempted burglary, but was given a full pardon by Ronald Reagan, then Governor of California, in 1972.

Merle Haggard was inducted into the Country Music Association's Hall Of Fame in 1994. At present he is seeking a new recording contract – with a 1995 5-CD boxed set of old material as a bargaining tool.

HAIRCUT 100 This pop group had a spate of hits between 1981 and 1983 with the singles 'Favourite Shirts', 'Love Plus One', 'Fantastic Day', 'Nobody's Fool' and 'Prime Time'. Lead singer Nick Heyward turned solo and had a further string of hits in his own right up to 1988, including: 'Whistle Down The Wind', 'Take That Situation', 'Blue Hat For A Blue Day', 'On A Sunday', 'Love All Day', 'Warning Sign', 'Laura', 'Over The Weekend' and 'You're My World'. He signed to Columbia in 1990 and is still making records.

Percussionist Mark Fox became A&R manager for the independent label East West and was responsible for contracting the Beloved and Jimmy Nail. Guitarist Graham Jones is a tree surgeon in Cornwall. Drummer Blair Cunningham, bass guitarist Les Nemes and saxophonist Phil Smith are all session players in London.

HALLYDAY, Johnny The leading French rock 'n' roll singer for more than three decades, Johnny Hallyday was born Jean Phillipe Smet in Paris on 15 June 1943 and made his first impact on the French chart in 1960 with 'Souvenirs, Souvenirs'. He was able to sing French versions of hits in the English language, such as 'Viens Dancer Le Twist', his version of 'Let's Twist Again', which became his first million-seller in 1961. That year he also starred in his first feature film, *Les Parisiennes*.

Hallyday married the beautiful French singer Silvie Vartan and the couple had a son, David.

In 1986 he was still notching up the hits in France with 'Quelque Chose De Tennessee', but despite his superstar status in that country, Hallyday has had no recording success in English language countries, particularly the UK and US, despite many attempts.

Johnny Hallyday was still hammering on foreign doors in the 1990s, with an all-English album and a concert debut at London's Royal Albert Hall.

HAMILTON IV, George This country artist was born in Winston-Salem in North Carolina on 19 July 1937. He was to tour with artists such as **Buddy Holly**, **Gene Vincent** and the **Everly Brothers**, and found success with 'A Rose And A Baby Ruth' in 1956. His other hits included: 'Only One Love', 'Why Don't They Understand', 'Now And For Always' and 'Abeline'.

In 1974, Hamilton became the first US country star to record an album in Eastern Europe and perform in Russia and Czechoslavakia. He was also the first C&W star to have his own UK television series, hosting nine of his own shows. Since then, he has hosted his own television series in South Africa and New Zealand, and has headlined a summer season in Blackpool.

HARPER, Roy This folk artist was born in Manchester on 12 June 1941. After being discharged from the Royal Air Force by pretending to be insane, he was placed in mental institutions and also spent some time in gaol. After a period travelling as a busker, he recorded his debut album, *Sophisticated Beggar*, in 1966. Although chart success eluded him, his series of albums sold well and he built a respectable following. Jimmy Page recorded with him, he made a guest appearance on Pink Floyd's *Wish You Were Here* album and for a short time in 1975, when he released his *HQ* album, he formed a backing group with **Chris Spedding** (guitar), Dave Cochran (bass) and Bill Bruford (drums).

During the 1990s, Roy Harper was able to obtain the rights to most of his previous work and began releasing his back catalogue on his own label, Science Friction. In 1995 he was back in the recording studios, making a new album. His son Nick Harper is recording in his own right.

HARRIS, Anita Anita Madeleine Harris was born in Midsomer Norton, Somerset, on 3 June 1944. She began to take lessons in song and dance at the age of eight. The attractive singer became noted for the length of her hair, which cascaded down her back. She appeared with the vocal group the Grenadiers, then sang with the Cliff Adams Singers before turning solo in 1961.

Anita went on to represent the UK at song contests in Montreux, Knokke-Le-Zoute and San Remo.

Her biggest hit was 'Just Lovin' You' in 1967, which reached No 6 in the UK chart. It sold more than a million copies and was penned by Tom Springfield. She followed this with 'Playground', 'Anniversary Waltz' and 'Dream A Little Dream Of Me'.

Anita was a popular entertainer on numerous television shows from the 1960s to the 1980s and also branched out as an actress, appearing in the film *Carry On Doctor* and in several stage shows. In 1990 she featured in the touring stage show *Nightingale*, based on the life of Florence Nightingale. She also appeared in the musical *Bertie*, based on the life of Vesta Tilley.

Married to Mike Margolis, a writer-director, Anita earns a good living in cabaret and is in great shape for a woman in her late fifties. She was the central figure in a promotional campaign for Slendertone keep-fit equipment in 1997, appearing in the advertisements and demonstrating the equipment on QVC, the television shopping channel.

HARRIS, Jet   Bass guitarist Jet Harris was originally a member of **Cliff Richard's** backing group the Drifters. When it was discovered that there was an established American group of that name, Harris suggested they call themselves the Shadows. During his spell with the group he appeared on a number of their hit instrumentals, including 'Apache', 'Man Of Mystery', 'FBI', 'Frightened City', 'Kon Tiki' and 'Wonderful Land'.

In 1962 Harris left the group to embark on a solo career and hit the chart with 'Besame Mucho' and 'Main Title From The Man With The Golden Arm'. The following year he teamed up with another former Shadows member, Tony Meehan, and the duo topped the chart with 'Diamonds', following up with 'Scarlett O'Hara' and 'Applejack'.

Harris was then involved in the car crash that changed his life. He and his girlfriend, pop singer **Billie Davis**, were badly hurt when their chauffeur-driven car was in a collision with a bus. Harris suffered head injuries. Of the crash,

he was to comment: 'It happened only a few hours after I had been voted Britain's top instrumentalist. It shook me terribly. I became a physical wreck and it's no secret I turned to the bottle – or rather, two bottles of vodka a day.'

Jet Harris

Harris then went missing and was spotted at a wrestling match in Brighton. He began to appear in court frequently over the years. In 1963 he came before the Brighton magistrates on a charge of being drunk and disorderly. Two years later he appeared before the Marylebone magistrates, also accused of driving while drunk. He was fined and disqualified from driving for two years.

By that time Harris was living in Portsea Hall in Paddington, west London. Soon after the drunk-driving charge he was in court again, where he pleaded guilty to assaulting a man. The police told the magistrate that Harris had not been 'quite sound in the head' since the car accident: he had been found pointing a shotgun at five people in the flats where he lived, although the gun had been used in a pantomime and wasn't loaded. From the dock, Harris said: 'Look – I'm a musician. I don't shoot people, my lord.' The court was told that he was undergoing psychiatric treatment and the magistrate commented: 'On the face of it, it looks like some mental trouble.'

Harris then appeared at Marlborough Street court pleading guilty to being in charge of a car while unfit to drive through drink, and of possessing cannabis and LSD. He was given a suspended sentence.

Harris said that he would have married Billie Davis but for the car accident. Over the years he has married four times. During one of his divorce hearings, the judge was told that he was currently having affairs with three women.

In 1974, after a variety of jobs, including periods as a barman, he began working as a conductor for the Bristol Omnibus Company, but was sacked for arguing with a passenger. At the time he was living in a £9-a-week caravan at Little Witcombe, near Cheltenham in Gloucestershire. He said: 'Ten years ago I was earning £1,000 a week with a luxury flat near Hyde Park. These days I'm lucky if my take-home pay touches £35. And I'm living in a caravan.' Other jobs he has undertaken over the years include working as a hospital porter, as a trawlerman, a cockle seller, a restaurant chef and a window cleaner.

In 1996 Harris went to Bournemouth to see a show by Hank Marvin. He went into the bar and met the caterer, Janet, who became his fourth wife. He was also given a lot of help by Barry Gibson, managing director of Burns, the London guitar makers, who arranged for Jet to travel to Milan to see psychologist Amadeo Maffi. Harris said that the treatments had a remarkable effect. He gave up drinking.

Currently, Harris lives in a flat in Gloucester with Janet, who is 20 years his junior. He has four children by his previous marriages, Janet has three.

Jet Harris now performs with his own band, the Diamonds, and also makes guest appearances with Local Heroes, whose other members include former Shadows members Alan Jones and Cliff Hall, along with former **Tornados** drummer Clem Cattini.

HARRIS, Richard This Irish actor was born on 1 October 1930 in Limerick, Eire. After studying at the London Academy Of Music And Dramatic Art, he made his stage and film debut in 1958. He was married to the Hon Elizabeth Rees-Williams, who later married Rex Harrison; his second wife was actress Ann Turkel, but they divorced in 1982. Among his 50-plus films are *The Heroes Of Telemark*, *Camelot*, *The Molly Maguires* and *A Man Called Horse*. He received Oscar nominations for his appearances in *This Sporting Life* and *The Field*.

As a singer Harris recorded 'MacArthur Park', which entered the chart in both 1968 and 1972. Songwriter Jim Webb, who also produced the record, penned the number. He had originally offered it to the Association, who turned it down. The track was a full seven minutes long; Webb produced it in Los Angeles and Harris recorded the vocals in London. It was the actor's sole chart entry.

Since the 1970s, Harris has concentrated on thespian projects, such as a re-run of *Camelot* on the West End Stage in the late 1980s. He also continues to appear in films, taking roles in *The Field*, *Patriot Games* and *The Unforgiven*.

Richard Harris lives partly in London's Savoy Hotel and partly on his own island in the West Indies.

HARRIS, Rolf This Australian singer-comedian-cartoonist was born on 30 March 1930 in Perth, and had his first UK chart hit in 1960 with 'Tie Me Kangaroo Down Sport'. He moved to the UK and among his early appearances was one as a guest on the 1963 *Beatles Christmas Show*.

His other hits included 'Sun Arise', 'Johnny Day', 'Bluer Than Blue' and his chart-topper, 'Two Little Boys', which entered the chart twice – in 1969 and 1970. He also joined Gerry Marsden as one of the Crowd on the recording of 'You'll Never Walk Alone', which topped the UK chart in 1985.

Harris became something of a cult figure with his unique cover version of Led Zeppelin's 'Stairway To Heaven' in 1993, which entered the UK Top 10. For some years he has been the popular host of the hit UK television series *Animal Hospital*.

In 1997 Harris recorded a new album of cover versions called *Can You Tell What It Is Yet?*. They included covers of Alanis Morissette's 'One Hand In My Pocket', the Beatles' 'Hey Bulldog', Lou Reed's 'Perfect Day' and the **Kinks'**

'Dedicated Follower Of Fashion'. He also issued a remix of a re-recording of his old hit 'Sun Arise'.

Rolf Harris lives in Berkshire.

HARRIS, Wee Willie Born Charles William Harris in Bermondsey, London, in 1933, this pianist first began performing in pubs under the name Fingers Harris.

Harris was an outrageous British rock 'n' roll performer of the late 1950s and early 1960s, who concentrated on recording cover versions of US hits such as 'Riot In Cell Block Number Nine', 'Love Bug Crawl', 'Wild One', 'Got A Match', 'I Go Ape' and 'Back To School Again'.

A comedy rock 'n' roll act who dyed his hair in livid hues and wore clothes in colours such as shocking pink or green, when performing 'I Go Ape' Harris would wear a leopardskin costume and a bowler hat. He made a number of appearances on television pop shows such as 6.5 Special.

Wee Willie Harris was mentioned in **Ian Dury's** hit 'Reasons To Be Cheerful Part Three'. He is still performing after 40 years and supported **Fats Domino** on a UK tour in 1993.

HARTLEY, Keef This well-respected British drummer, born on 8 March 1944, started out as a member of the legendary Liverpool band Rory Storm & the Hurricanes. He next appeared with the Artwoods and **John Mayall**, before forming his own Keef Hartley Band in 1968. The group changed its name to Dog Soldier in 1973.

Keef Hartley now has a building business in Berkshire.

HATCH, Tony This record producer-songwriter was born in Pinner, Middlesex, in 1939. He had one hit in his own right, supported by his orchestra, with 'Out Of This World' in 1962, which reached a modest No 50 in the UK chart.

His early recording successes as a producer were with Mersey Beat bands such as the **Searchers**, the Undertakers and the Chants. He also recorded and wrote several hits for **Petula Clark**.

Hatch co-wrote 'Where Are You Now (My Love)' with Jackie Trent, who took the number to the top of the UK chart. The couple were then married and became a team. Jackie had two further hits as a solo singer, 'When The Summertime Is Over' and 'I'll Be There'.

In the 1970s Hatch was contracted to pass acerbic but well-qualified comments on the acts arrayed in New Faces, a long-running UK television talent show. He also penned and produced 'Sad Sweet Dreamer' for Sweet Sensation, a chart-topper in 1974.

Reportedly, his marriage to Jackie Trent floated into a choppy sea in the 1990s, but the couple was seen together at a recent Performing Rights Society awards dinner.

HAWKWIND This science-fiction heavy metal group was formed in 1969. They made their recording debut the following year, although there were numerous personnel changes in the band, a situation that was to continue throughout their career.

Hawkwind eventually made their chart debut in 1972 with 'Silver Machine', and other entries in the singles chart included 'Urban Guerrilla' and 'Shot Down In The Night'. 'Silver Machine' actually entered the chart on three occasions – in 1972, 1978 and 1983.

The group had a formidable number of chart albums: In Search Of Space, Doremi Fasol Latido, Space Ritual Alive, Hall Of The Mountain Grill, Warrior On The Edge Of Time, Road Hawks, Astonishing Sounds, Amazing Music, Quark Strangeness And Charm, 25 Years On, PXR 5, Live 1979, Levitation, Sonic Attack, Church Of Hawkwind, Choose Your Masques, Zones, Hawkwind, Chronicle Of The Black Sword and Space Bandits.

The basic personnel who contributed to the chart and live performance success were Dave Brock (guitar and vocals), Nick Turner (sax, flute and vocals), Mick Slattery (guitar), John Harrison (bass), Terry Ollis (drums) and Dik Mik (electronics).

The fluid changes continued throughout. In 1971 poet Robert Calvert became lead vocalist and Stacia joined as a dancer, but left when she married in 1975. Science-fiction author Mike Moorcock also took an interest in the band and made numerous appearances with them.

Over the years, musicians who have been members of Hawkwind include Huw Lloyd Langton, Viv Prince, Dick Taylor, Dave Anderson, Del Dettmar, Lemmy, Simon King, Simon House, Alan Powell, Paul Rudolph, Adrian Shaw, Paul Hayles, Martin Griffiths, Steve Swindell, Harvey Bainbridge, Tim Blake, Ginger Baker, Keith Hale, Alan Davis, Danny Thompson, Mick Kirton, Richard Chadwick and Steve Bemand.

Lyricist Robert Calvert died as the result of a heart attack in August 1988. Del Dettmar emigrated to Canada. Stacia is married and now lives in Germany. Nick Turner has a farm in West Wales. Lemmy is resident in Los Angeles. Dave Brock and Simon House were still in the line-up of a Hawkwind who issued the album *Electric Tepee* and toured the States in 1993.

By 1995, when the album *The Business Trip* was released, Brock was the only original member remaining in the group.

HAYSI FANTAYZEE

Kate Garner and Jeremy Healy formed their vocal duo in the early 1980s. Their biggest hit was their first, 'John Wayne Is A Big Leggy'. Their further hits which followed included 'Holy Joe', 'Shiny Shiny' and 'Sister Friction'.

Kate is currently a photographer, living in Los Angeles, while Jeremy has become one of the highest-paid disc jockeys in Europe. He works regularly in London as a club DJ and also records music for advertisements and fashion shows.

HEDGEHOPPERS ANONYMOUS

This group was originally formed in 1963 as the Trendsetters, the members being Mick Tinsley, Ray Honeyball, Alan Laud, Leslie Dash and John Stewart. Jonathan King became their manager and wrote and produced their sole hit, 'It's Good News Week', in 1965. Their follow-up, 'Don't Push Me', failed to register.

Singer Mike Tinsley pursued a solo recording career, initially under the aegis of Jonathan King.

In 1993, Alan Avon issued a version of 'Over The Rainbow' on a cassette single. With only the most tenuous connection with the 1965 one-hit-wonders, a Hedgehoppers Anonymous roamed the UK in the mid-1990s.

HEINZ

Heinz Burt was born in Hagen, Germany, on 24 July 1942. In 1960 he became the bass player with the **Tornados**, an instrumental outfit who started out as **Billy Fury's** backing band. They became the first British band to top the US chart – with 'Telstar' in 1962.

Heinz left the group the following year and had tremendous initial success, with chart hits including: 'Just Like Eddie', 'Country Boy', 'You Were There', 'Questions I Can't Answer' and 'Diggin' My Potatoes'.

With his good looks and peroxide-blonde hair, Heinz was also featured in several British pop movies during the 1960s. By the end of the decade he had left the music business, although he attempted to launch a new career as an actor in the mid-1970s.

Heinz lives in Southampton and performs in sixties nostalgia packages.

HERBIE GOINS & THE NIGHT TIMERS

A former US serviceman living in the UK, Herbie Goins joined Alexis Korner's Blues Incorporated and then went on to form his own outfit, the Night Timers, in 1964. They were signed to Parlophone and their singles included 'The Music Played On' and 'Incredible Miss Brown'. In 1967 they recorded an album, Number One In Your Heart, by which time Herbie was sharing vocal honours with another American singer, Ronnie Jones.

Although the group disbanded in 1970, a copy of 'Number One In Your Heart' found its way on to the turntable at Wigan Casino, to become a much-requested northern soul classic. It was included on *Soultime*, a CD retrospective issued by the See For Miles label in 1992.

HERMAN'S HERMITS

Originally known as the Heartbeats, this group was formed in Manchester in 1963. They comprised Peter Noone (vocals), Karl Green (bass), Keith Hopwood (rhythm), Lek Leckenby (lead) and Barry Whitwam (drums).

They made their chart debut with the No 1 hit 'I'm Into Something Good'. Between 1964 and 1970 their hits included: 'Show Me Girl', 'Silhouettes', 'Wonderful World', 'Just A Little Bit Better', 'A Must To Avoid', 'You Won't Be Leaving', 'This Door Swings Both Ways', 'No Milk Today', 'Easy West', 'There's A Kind Of Hush', 'I Can Take Or Leave Your Loving', 'Sleepy Joe', 'Sunshine Girl', 'Something's Happening', 'My Sentimental Friend', 'Here Comes The Star', 'Years May Come', 'Years May Go' and 'Bet Yer Life I Do'. As Peter Noone & Herman's Hermits, they had a chart hit with 'Lady Barbara' in 1970. The following year Noone, who had married a French girl, Mireille Strasser, in 1968 (the couple were to have a daughter, Natalie, 18 years later), had his one solo hit under his own name, 'Oh You Pretty Thing'.

Noone was also an actor who had appeared as Len Fairclough's son Stanley in the UK television soap opera *Coronation Street* and, together with the group, starred in the films *Mrs Brown*

Peter Noone of Herman's Hermits

You've Got A Lovely Daughter, *When The Boys Meet The Girls* and *Hold On!*.

Having gone solo in 1970, Noone did reunite with the band for one last time during a 'British Invasion' concert at Madison Square Garden in New York in 1973. He appeared on the cabaret circuit for some years, before settling in Los Angeles in 1980 where, for a time, he formed a group called the Tremblers, although they had no success on record. He returned to London in 1983 to star in the stage musical *The Pirates Of Penzance*, before returning to the US where he became a successful disc jockey and television presenter, running his own show, *My Generation*, for five years. He appeared on his first UK tour in 25 years in 1995 and it was a sell-out. In April 1997 he returned to star in the Solid Silver Sixties Tour along with Gerry Marsden, **Wayne Fontana** and **Dave Berry**.

Following their initial split with Noone, Herman's Hermits spent some time in the States and began appearing on the nostalgia circuit. On their return to the UK they became a regular act on the cabaret circuit, where they have continued to perform into the 1990s, although there were various personnel changes. By 1997 there was only one original member of Herman's Hermits in the line-up: drummer Barry Whitwam.

In March 1997, Mega Records in the US issued the group's new album, *That Was Then – This Is Now*, followed by a single, 'Dust My Hot Rod Down'.

On 8 June 1997, the final date of the Solid Silver Sixties Tour at the London Palladium, Peter Noone was joined on stage by three former members of the original Hermits – Barry Whitwam, Carl Green and Keith Hopwood.

HILL, Vince   This British singer was born in Coventry on 16 April 1939. He began his career as a big-band singer and then became part of the Raindrops vocal group, who had a regular spot on the UK radio programme *Parade Of The Pops*.

Hill turned solo in 1962 and entered the chart with 'The River's Run Dry'. He then had a nine-year chart life with hits such as: 'Take Me To Your Heart Again', 'Heartaches', 'Merci Cheri', 'Edelweiss', 'Roses Of Picardy', 'Love Letters In The Sand', 'Importance Of Your Love', 'Doesn't Anybody Know My Name', 'Little Blue Bird' and 'Look Around'.

Hill hosted his own television series, *They Sold A Million*, in 1973 and continued his career as a popular entertainer. In 1995, he had a season in the Green Room at London's prestigious Café Royal.

Vince Hill currently lives near Henley-on-Thames.

HILTON, Ronnie   This major British singing star of the 1950s had a run of hits which continued until 1965. He was born Adrian Hill in Hull, Humberside, on 26 January 1926. During World War II he joined the Highland Light Infantry and later worked in a factory in Leeds.

After undergoing an operation to rid himself of a hair lip, he changed his name to Ronnie Hilton, had a successful radio series, was popular in stage performances in city theatres and celebrated 11 years in the charts.

His hits included: 'I Still Believe', 'Veni Vidi Vici', 'A Blossom Fell', 'Stars Shine In Your Eyes', 'Yellow Rose Of Texas', 'Young And Foolish', 'No Other Love', 'Who Are We', 'Woman In Love', 'Two Different Worlds', 'Around The World', 'Wonderful Wonderful'. 'Magic Moments', 'I May Never Pass This Way Again', 'The World Outside', 'The Wonder Of You', 'Don't Let The Rain Come Down' and 'A Windmill In Old Amsterdam'.

Hilton topped the chart in 1956 with 'No Other Love', a number from the Rodgers & Hammerstein musical *Me And Juliet*.

Ronnie Hilton is still engaged for summer seasons, particularly in the north of England, and presents programmes about 1950s pop on UK radio.

HOLLIES, The   This Manchester group was noted for vocal harmonies. Alan Clarke and Graham Nash had already been performing as a duo. With the addition of Eric Haydock on bass and Don Rathbone on drums, they became the Fourtones.

The group became known as the Hollies in 1962, and were spotted performing at Liverpool's Cavern club the following year by A&R man Ron Richards. With the addition of Tony Hicks on guitar, they made their recording debut with '(Ain't That) Just Like Me'. After this, Bobby Elliott replaced Rathbone on drums.

The Hollies had more than 30 singles in the UK chart and have topped it twice – with 'I'm Alive' in 1965 and 'He Ain't Heavy, He's My Brother' in 1988. Among their other major hits were 'Just One Look', 'Here I Go Again', 'On A Carousel', 'Carrie-Anne' and 'The Air That I Breathe'. They also had a number of album successes.

Nash left the group at the end of 1968 because he had become dissatisfied with their musical direction, and immediately teamed up with David Crosby and Stephen Stills. Terry Sylvester, a former member of Mersey Beat groups the Escorts and the Swinging Blue Jeans, replaced him.

Clarke also decided to leave and was replaced by Mikael Rickfors, a singer from Sweden. Clarke's solo efforts proved unsuccessful and he rejoined the group in 1973.

During the 1980s there were various line-up changes, and the original members got together again with Graham Nash for a reunion recording of an album, *What Goes Around*, in Los Angeles in 1983. Allan Clarke, Tony Hicks and Bobby Elliott continued during the decade, with the addition of Alan Coates and Ray Stiles.

A 3-CD boxed set, *Treasured Hits And Hidden Treasures*, was released in 1993, and the Hollies got together again with Graham Nash for a recording at Abbey Road in late 1995, which resulted in the single 'Peggy Sue Got Married'.

The Hollies toured the UK from 1 October to 30 November 1997 and during March, April and May 1998.

The Hollies At Abbey Road '66–'70 was issued on 23 February 1998. This CD featured a previously unreleased track, 'Schoolgirl', written by Graham Gouldman. Extra guitars had been added by Tony Hicks and mixed down by his son, Abbey Road engineer Paul Hicks.

Former bass player Eric Haydock leads the Eric Haydock Band.

HONEYBUS   Honeybus had a single Top 10 hit, 'I Can't Let Maggie Go', in 1968, a number which has since become inextricably linked with a television commercial for Nimble bread.

'I Can't Let Maggie Go' was written, produced, arranged and sung by Peter Dello (real name Peter Blumson), who also played guitar on the record. He had originally wanted Honeybus to be strictly a studio band, but following their chart hit they were briefly a performing band as well, the line-up being Dello, Ray Cane, Colin Hare and Peter Kircher. Alas, they proved to be one-hit-wonders – their follow-up, '(Do I Figure) In Your Life', failed to make the charts. This was actually a very strong tune, and although the Honeybus version failed to make it, it brought strong sales when covered by **Dave Berry** and **Joe Cocker.**

Dello left the group, who released another single, 'Girl Of Independent Means', before disbanding in 1969. Following the band's demise, a final release, 'Story', was issued in 1970.

Dello, a former member of the 1960s beat group Grant Tracy & the Sunsets, shunned the limelight and worked anonymously on various studio recordings, before returning to his original profession as a music teacher. Aged 55 in 1997, he now lives in Wembley where he teaches classical, blues and rock music for guitar and keyboards, both privately and in a school.

In 1997 a 25-track CD, *Honeybus... At Their Best*, was issued by the See For Miles label.

HONEYCOMBS, The   This beat group was formed by lead guitarist Martin Murray in 1963. The other members were Denis D'Ell (vocals and harmonica), Alan Ward (rhythm and keyboards), John Lantree (bass) and his sister Honey Lantree (drums). The initial name for the band was the Sherabons, but they swiftly changed it to Honeycombs. Some say this was based on Honey's nickname, others that it was chosen by Pye Records MD Louis Benjamin after a track by Jimmie Rodgers.

The band received a great deal of press from the novelty of having a girl drummer. Their debut single, 'Have I The Right', penned by Ken

Howard and Alan Blaikley, topped the UK chart in 1964. The group embarked on a UK concert tour, their single reached No 5 in the US chart, selling a million copies, and their follow-up, 'Is It Because', became a minor UK hit.

Murray was temporarily replaced in the group by Peter Pye following a fall in which he broke bones in his leg and hand. He left the group at the end of 1964, prior to their tour of Australasia, and formed a new band called the Lemmings.

The Honeycombs' next release was 'Something Better Beginning', followed by 'That's The Way'. During 1965 they toured Japan. In 1966 their singles failed to chart and D'Ell, Ward and Pye left. They were replaced by Colin Boyd, Rod Butler and Eddie Spence and the band changed their name to the New Honeycombs. Honey Lantree left the group in 1967, but her attempts to launch a solo career failed and she rejoined, although the group was soon to disband.

In 1991 the Honeycombs reunited for a tribute concert in honour of their late recording manager, **Joe Meek**.

Currently, while moonlighting in the Southside Blues Band, Essex resident Denis D'Ell leads the present-day Honeycombs. This group included hairdresser Honey Lantree and signwriter Peter Pye in the line-up for a special anniversary concert in an Islington pub in 1995. Alan Ward is the proprietor of a Walthamstow musical equipment shop and manufacturer of his own make of speaker cabinets. John Lantree lives in London.

HOPKIN, Mary Born in Pontardawe, Wales, on 3 May 1950, this singer came to the attention of Paul McCartney after the fashion model Twiggy spotted her on the UK television talent show *Opportunity Knocks*.

McCartney signed her to Apple Records and picked and produced her first single, 'Those Were The Days', which sold five million copies after its release in 1968, reaching No 1 in the UK and No 2 in the US. He wrote and produced her second single, 'Goodbye', which reached No 2 in the UK and was also a US Top 20 entry.

McCartney produced Mary's album, *Postcard*, and next single, 'Que Sera Sera'. She then chose her sister Carol to be her manager and within a year had left Apple. Her next releases were produced initially by Mickie Most and then by Tony Visconti, whom she married. She then gave birth to the first of her two children, a daughter, Jessica.

After she left Apple, Mary's hits were: 'Temma Harbour', 'Knock Knock Who's There', 'Think About Your Children', 'Let My Name Be Sorrow' and 'If You Love Me'.

Having spent time raising her family, she appeared in a group called Sundance in the early 1980s and then another band called Oasis.

Now divorced from Visconti, Mary Hopkin lives less than five miles upriver from George Harrison's spread in Henley-on-Thames.

HUMAN LEAGUE, The Formed in Sheffield, South Yorkshire, in 1977, this group took their name from that of a computer game.

The members who were to achieve a number of hits were Phil Oakey (vocals and synthesizer), Joanne Catherall and Susan Sulley (vocals), Ian Burden (bass) and Jo Callis (synthesizer). Adrian Wright appeared with them, providing slides and films for their stage performances.

The group's hit singles include: 'Holiday '80', 'Empire State Human', 'Boys And Girls', 'The Sound Of The Crowd', 'Love Action', 'Open Your Heart', 'Don't You Want Me', 'Being Boiled', 'Mirror Man', 'Fascination', 'The Lebanon', 'Life On Your Own', 'Louise', 'I Need Your Loving' and 'Love Is All That Matters'.

Their album hits included: *Travelogue*, *Reproduction*, *Dare* and *Hysteria*.

Boiled down to Oakey, Sulley and Catherall, the Human League began a chart comeback in 1995 with 'Tell Me When', followed by the album *Octopus* and another hit single, 'One Man In My Heart'. In 1996 they entered the chart with 'Stay With Me Tonight'.

HUNT, Marsha Born on 15 April 1949, this singer played a leading part in the successful West End stage version of the tribal-rock musical *Hair*. Despite the many attempts to find success on record in various groups and as a solo artist, she succeeded in having only one minor hit, 'Keep The Customer Satisfied' in 1970. She was to become the mother of Mick Jagger's daughter, Karis.

In 1986, Marsha's autobiography, *Still Life*, was published. Since then she has written two novels, and still pops up occasionally in television dramas.

IAN, Janis Born Janis Eddy Fink in New York on 7 May 1951, this singer began performing in folk clubs in New York in 1995, adopting her brother Ian's first name as her stage surname. Her debut single, 'Society's Child', was issued in 1966 and became her first entry into the singles chart the following year. Seven years were to pass before her second hit, 'At Seventeen', which reached No 3 in the US chart. The number was taken from her album *Between The Lines*, which also charted. Her UK hits included 'Fly Too High' and 'The Other Side Of The Sun'.

Janis remains an active recording artist who, since undertaking her first London concert in ten years in 1991, has been a regular visitor to the UK.

While promoting her first album in a decade, *Breaking Silence*, in 1993, she came out and talked openly about the fact that she was a lesbian.

Janis Ian returned to Europe in 1995 for a two-week promotional tour to plug her album *Revenge*, and later the same year a 42-track CD called *Society's Child: The Anthology* was issued.

IFIELD, Frank This singer was born in Coventry, West Midlands, on 30 November 1936. His family emigrated to Australia when Frank was nine, and he first found success recording the theme song to the Australian television series *Whiplash*.

He returned to England, signed with EMI and had a series of major hits, beginning with 'Lucky Devil' in 1960. Over the next six years his chart entries included: 'Gotta Get A Date', 'I Remember You', 'Lovesick Blues', 'Wayward

The Ivy League

Wind', 'Nobody's Darlin' But Mine', 'Confessin'', 'Mule Train', 'Don't Blame Me', 'Angry At The Big Oak Tree', 'I Should Care', 'Summer Is Over', 'Paradise', 'No One Will Ever Know' and 'Call Her Your Sweetheart'. His gimmick, if such it could be called, was the yodel.

Ifield became the first artist to notch up three consecutive No 1 records in the UK chart. He appeared in the film *Up Jumped A Swagman*, and his fortunes as a recording artist began to wane with the emergence of the Beatles. He then began to appear on the cabaret circuit.

Frank Ifield's singing career ended in 1988 following a serious illness. However, he now comperes a C&W series on Australian television and is writing his autobiography.

INCREDIBLE STRING BAND, The This Scottish folk outfit first formed as a trio comprising Mike Heron, Robin Williamson and Clive Palmer in Glasgow in 1965. The following year saw the release of their first album, the eponymous *The Incredible String Band*. The group split following the album release, although Heron and Williamson teamed up again the following year.

Heron was born in Glasgow on 12 December 1942 and Williamson in Edinburgh on 24 November 1943. The two continued recording and performing as the Incredible String Band, with various back-up members. They recorded over a dozen albums, including *Wee Tam And The Big Huge*, *Be Glad For The Song Has No Ending* and *Earthspan*. In 1974 the two found themselves incompatible following differences in both their musical and personal outlooks, and announced their split.

After a period of 23 years, they decided to perform on stage again together, beginning with concerts in Glasgow in September and London in December 1997. However, the pair have decided to use their own names rather than invoking that of the Incredible String Band.

Robin Williamson enjoys a thriving folk career as a Celtic harpist and storyteller.

IVY LEAGUE, The This group was originally formed in 1964 by songwriters John Carter and Ken Lewis. The duo were joined by Perry Ford and charted with 'Funny How Love Can Be', 'That's Why I'm Crying' and 'Tossing and Turning'. **Tony Burrows** replaced Carter in 1966 and Lewis left a few months later. The group

then underwent various changes of personnel before finally disbanding.

An Ivy League containing no original members works on the European sixties nostalgia circuit with a mixture of the old hits and a risqué brand of comedy. The members are John Brennan, Dave Buckley and Michael Brice.

JACKSON, Joe Singer Joe Jackson was born in Burton-upon-Trent, Staffordshire, on 11 August 1954. He initially joined a pub band called Edward Bear in 1974, and by 1976 was a member of Arms & Legs. He penned three numbers for the group, but their records failed to chart. He left the band in 1977 to become house pianist at Portsmouth's Playboy Club.

As a solo artist, Jackson made his recording debut with 'Is She Really Going Out With Him' in 1978, and followed with 'It's Different For Girls', 'Jumpin' Jive', 'Steppin' Out', 'Breaking Us In Two', 'Happy Ending' and 'Be My Number Two'.

Joe Jackson's 1994 album *Night Music* revealed the influence of classical music, and he continued to venture into the classical field with his November 1997 album, *Heaven And Hell*. He also appeared in two concerts at London's Queen Elizabeth Hall in December 1997 accompanied by violin, keyboards and digital orchestration.

JAM, The This group was formed in Woking, Surrey, in 1973 and took their name from the phrase 'jam session'. They originally comprised Paul Weller, bassist Bruce Foxton, drummer Rick Buckler and guitarist Steve Brookes. Brookes left at the end of 1976 and the group continued as a trio. They were to have three No 1 singles, then disbanded at the height of their career in 1982 when Weller told his two associates that he was leaving the group.

The band's chart singles were: 'In The City', 'All Around The World', 'The Modern World', 'News Of The World', 'David Watts/'A' Bomb In Wardour Street', 'Down In The Tube Station At Midnight', 'Strange Town', 'When You're Young', 'The Eton Rifles', 'Going Underground', 'Start', 'That's Entertainment', 'Funeral Pyre', 'Absolute Beginners', 'Town Called Malice', 'Just Who Is The Five O' Clock Hero', 'The Bitterest Pill' and 'Beat Surrender'.

Their album hits were: *In The City*, *This Is The Modern World*, *All Mod Cons*, *Setting Sons*, *Sound Affects*, *The Gift*, *Dig The New Breed* and *Snap*.

Weller then formed the Style Council, while Foxton had a number of hits as a solo artist – 'Freak', 'This Is The Way' and 'It Makes Me Wonder' – before joining Stiff Little Fingers. Buckler eventually set up his own furniture restoration business.

Hits in the singles chart for the Style Council were: 'Speak Like A Child', 'Money Go Round', 'Long Hot Summer', 'Solid Bond In Your Heart', 'My Ever Changing Moods', 'Groovin'', 'Shout To The Top', 'Walls Come Tumbling Down', 'Come To Milton Keynes', 'The Lodgers', 'Have You Ever Had It Blue', 'It Didn't Matter', 'Waiting', 'Wanted', 'Life At A Top People's Health Farm' and 'How She Threw It All Away'.

Their chart albums were *Café Bleu* and *Our Favourite Shop*.

The Style Council disbanded in 1989, following their record company Polydor's rejection of their latest album. Weller retired from the business for two years, then returned as a solo artist with some powerful albums. He has been recognized as a 'godfather' of Britpop, and is still a chart contender. Rick Buckley continues to run his antiques business in Surrey.

JAMES, Tommy This singer-songwriter-group leader was born Thomas Gregory Jackson in Dayton, Ohio, on 29 April 1946. By the age of 13 he had cut his first record, 'Long Pony Tail'. He later led Tommy James & the Shondells, who included Eddie Gray (guitar), Ronnie Rossman (keyboards), Mike Vale (bass) and Pete Lucia (drums).

James' hit 'Mony Mony' topped the UK chart in 1968.

The group's hit singles in the US were: 'Hanky Panky' (which topped the chart), 'Say I Am (What I Am)', 'It's Only Love', 'I Think We're Alone Now', 'Mirage', 'I Like The Way', 'Getting Together', 'Mony Mony', 'Do Something To Me', 'Crimson And Clover (another chart-topper), 'Sweet Cherry Wine', 'Crystal Blue Persuasion', 'Ball Of Fire' and 'She'.

James went back to his farm in 1970, then returned the following year with a solo album and the big hit single 'Draggin' the Line'. Following a minor hit with 'I'm Coming Home', he returned to the Top 20 in 1980 with 'Three Times in Love'.

The Shondells had continued recording under the name Hog Heaven, but soon split up.

Interestingly enough, several artists have had hits reviving numbers by the band, including Joan Jett with 'Crimson and Clover', Billy Idol with 'Mony Mony' and Tiffany with 'I Think We're Alone Now'.

Preceding the Beatles' *Anthology*, a collection of recordings covering Tommy James & the Shondells' career, also called *Anthology*, was issued in the States by Rhino Records in 1989.

During the 1990s Tommy James was performing on the US nostalgia circuit.

JAN & DEAN Jan Berry, born on 3 April 1941, and Dean Torrence, born on 10 March 1940, both in Los Angeles, originally formed a group called the Barons with Bruce Johnson and Sandy Nelson.

The group split and Jan and Dean, together with Arnie Ginsburg, continued as a trio, recording 'Jennie Lee'. The group split, but Jan and Dean were later to team up as a duo and recorded the hit 'Baby Talk'. In 1963 they recorded 'Linda', in which they had developed their vocal sound, which was similar to that of the **Beach Boys**. It was Brian Wilson who co-wrote their chart-topper 'Surf City', and their following hits included 'Drag City', 'Dead Man's Curve' and 'Ride The Wild Surf'.

In April 1966 Jan was involved in a serious road accident when his car crashed into a parked truck. He went into a coma and was completely paralysed for several months. He also suffered severe brain damage. After several years in which Jan had to undertake a learning process in order to recover, the duo were to reunite in 1970 when they appeared on a Beach Boys tour.

Dean Torrence now runs Kittyhawk Graphics in California, a company specializing in record covers, which he founded in 1967. Jan Berry's health has improved greatly since he was injured almost fatally in the accident and in 1995 he married Gertie Filip.

A biopic entitled *Dead Man's Curve* was shown on television in 1978, with Bruce Davison and Richard Hatch as Jan and Dean.

Jan and Dean amalgamate for sixties revival shows, making about 50 appearances a year, and new Jan & Dean records still appear in the shops occasionally, ranging from *Surf City – The Best Of Jan & Dean* to *Teen Suite 1958–1962*, both issued in 1995.

JAPAN This group was formed by David Sylvian (real name David Blatt), who was born on 23 February 1958. David and his brother Steve (who called himself Steve Jansen) formed Japan in the mid-1970s. The other members were Mike Karn (real name Anthony Michaelides) on sax and Richard Barbieri on keyboards. Steve played drums.

The group made their recording debut with the German label Hansa in 1978. They were initially unsuccessful, but a 1979 release, 'Life In Tokyo', was a huge hit in Japan.

It was when the band signed with Virgin Records in 1980 that success came their way and led to Hansa re-releasing their earlier records – 'Quiet Life', 'European Son', 'I Second That Emotion', 'Life In Tokyo' and 'All Tomorrow's Parties' – all of which became hits. Their Virgin successes were 'Gentlemen Take Polaroids', 'The Art Of Parties', 'Visions Of China', 'Cantonese Boy', 'Night Porter' and 'Canton (Live)'.

When the group disbanded in 1984, David recorded with Japanese actor-singer Ryuichi Sakamoto, under the name Sylvian Sakamoto, on 'Bamboo Houses' and 'Forbidden Colours'. As a solo artist, he charted with 'Red Guitar', 'The Ink In The Well', 'Pulling Punches', 'Words With The Shaman' and 'Let The Happiness In'.

In 1991, the four original members reunited unexpectedly as Rain Tree Crow for an eponymous album, before going their separate ways once again. In 1997 the group re-formed again specially for concert performances under the name Jansen/Barbieri/Karn.

JEFFERSON AIRPLANE This popular group from San Francisco was formed in 1965 by Ohio-born guitarist Marty Balin. There were a number of personnel variations throughout the group's early span. The original female singer was Signe Tole Anderson, who was replaced by Grace Slick in 1966. The original drummer was Skip Spence, who was replaced by Spencer Dryden, who was replaced by Joey Covington, who in turn was replaced by John Barbata. Balin left the band in 1971 and Papa John Creach joined, while David Freiberg was added to the line-up the following year.

The other basic members of the original band were guitarist Paul Kantner, bass guitarist Jack Casady and lead guitarist Jorma Kaukonen.

Bill Graham, who ran the popular Fillmore Auditorium, became their manager and they made their debut with the album *Jefferson Airplane Takes Off*, which went gold. Their second album, *Surrealistic Pillow*, produced two Top 10 hits – 'Somebody To Love' and 'White Rabbit'.

The band enjoyed healthy sales with albums such as *After Bathing At Bester's*, *Crown Of Creation*, *Bless Its Pointed Head* and *Volunteers*, and singles such as 'Ballad Of You And Me And Poonell', 'Watch Her Ride', 'Greasy Heart', 'Crown Of Creation' and 'Volunteers'.

In 1970, an album entitled *Blows Against The Empire* was issued under the name Paul Kantner & Jefferson Starship.

In 1971 Grace Slick gave birth to Kantner's baby, which they named God – but later changed this to China. The couple split after living together for seven years and Grace married the group's lighting engineer, Skip Johnson.

The band continued with different permutations of personnel through the 1980s and 1990s, generally utilizing different names including Jefferson Airplane, Jefferson Airplane The Next Generation, Jefferson Starship and Starship. There were several chart singles and albums from the various combinations.

The first Starship single in 1985 was a US chart-topper, 'We Built This City'. In 1995 the members of Starship were Kantner, Balin, Casady, Tim Gorman, Prairie Prince, Slick Aguilar and Darby Gould, who issued a new album, *Deep Space/Virgin Sky*.

As Jefferson Airplane, the group was inducted into the Rock & Roll Hall Of Fame in 1996.

Marty Balin, Paul Kantner and Jack Casady were members of Jefferson Starship for an appearance at London's Bottom Line in late 1994. Skip Spence is an institutionalized paranoid schizophrenic in San José. In March 1994 Grace Slick was the central figure in a disturbance that involved drunkenness, a shotgun and the arrival of police at her California home. The resulting court case ended with her being ordered to enter a detoxification programme.

JETHRO TULL This group was formed in 1963 by Edinburgh-born Ian Anderson, singer and flautist with the band. The other members were Mick Abrahams (guitar), Glenn Cornick (bass) and Clive Barker (drums).

With Anderson the obvious leader, focal point and composer of the band's material, the personnel were to change over the years until the group became basically his backing band.

Their hit singles included: 'Love Story', 'Living In The Past', 'Sweet Dream', 'The Witch's Promise', 'Life Is A Long Song', 'Ring Out Solstice Bells', 'Lap Of Luxury' and 'Said She Was A Dancer'.

The group are primarily a performing and album-selling band with over 20 chart LPs to their credit, including their debut, *This Was*, and *Stand Up*, *Benefit*, *Aqualung*, *Thick As A Brick* and *Living In The Past*. Anderson himself charted with his solo album *Walk Into Light* in 1983.

Now a backing outfit for Ian Anderson – the wealthiest and only remaining original member,

Jethro Tull

who possesses his own Scottish island – the group issued *Roots To Branches*, their twenty-seventh studio album, in late 1995, and embarked on a 13-month world tour. The same year saw the release of another solo album from Anderson, *Divinities: Twelve Dances With God*.

JILTED JOHN   This actor-singer had one hit in 1978, the eponymous 'Jilted John'. His real name was Graham Fellows. He appeared in the UK television soap opera *Coronation Street*, and created and played would-be pop star John Shuttleworth in the comedy series *500 Bus Stops* and in *The Shuttleworths* on radio. He now performs in the assumed-name role and adopted persona, and undertook a UK tour in late 1997.

JIMMY JAMES & THE VAGABONDS   Jimmy James was born in Jamaica in 1940 and had two hits in this own country, 'Bewildered In Blue' and 'Come Softly To Me', before travelling to the UK in 1964. He appeared with various R&B outfits before forming his own band, the Vagabonds, in 1965.

The group recorded an album, *New Religion*, and several singles, before making their first chart impact in 1968 with 'Red Red Wine'. There were various personnel changes in James' backing band over the years, and even new chart entries in 1976 with 'I'll Go Where Your Music Takes Me' and 'Now Is The Time'.

In recent years, Jimmy James has concentrated on the European cabaret circuit.

JIMMY POWELL & THE FIVE DIMENSIONS   Jimmy Powell had two singles released on Decca in 1962 – 'Sugar Babe' and 'Tom Hark'. The next year he formed his London-based R&B band the Five Dimensions, who at one point included **Rod Stewart** playing harmonica. In 1955 they released two Pye Records singles – 'That's Alright' and 'I've Been Watching You'.

The band broke up in 1965 and Powell formed several other outfits named the Dimensions, performing primarily in the Midlands. In 1966 he recorded 'I Can Go Down'.

Jimmy Powell himself was still releasing singles in the 1970s, and a CD compilation, *The R&B Sensation*, was issued in 1992.

JOEL, Billy   This singer-pianist-songwriter was born William Martin Joel on 9 May 1949 in Hicksville, Long Island. Like many an aspiring teenage American musician, he was inspired by watching the famous Beatles debut on *The Ed Sullivan Show* and decided to form a band. He joined a group called the Echoes, followed by a local Long Island band called the Hassles.

After the group split, he became a rock critic and later moved to Los Angeles, where he married his girlfriend Elizabeth Weber in 1973, the year he signed with Columbia Records. He charted the following year with the album *Piano Man* and the single of the same name taken from it. The track was autobiographical.

Since then, Joel has had more than 30 chart singles and several album hits. His US hit singles included: 'Just The Way You Are', 'My Life', 'You May Be Right', 'It's Still Rock And Roll To Me', 'Tell Her About It', 'Uptown Girl', 'An Innocent Man', 'The Longest Time', 'Modern Woman', 'A Matter Of Trust', 'We Didn't Start The Fire', 'The River Of Dreams' and 'All About Soul'.

Major album hits included: *The Stranger*, *52nd Street*, *Glass Houses*, *Songs In The Attic*, *The Nylon Curtain*, *An Innocent Man*, *The Bridge*, *Kohyept*, *Stormfront* and *River Of Dreams*.

In his personal life, Joel divorced Elizabeth in 1982 and met the stunning model Christine Brinkley later the same year. The two became engaged and he featured her on his video of 'Uptown Girl'. The two were married in 1985 and divorced in 1995.

During his career Joel received many prestigious awards, held concerts in Leningrad and played before an audience of more than 100,000 when he became the first rock star to appear at the Yankee Stadium in New York.

In 1995 he teamed up with Elton John for US dates and the two superstars began to write songs together. The pairing proved such a success that in June 1998 Joel began a UK tour, called Face To Face, sharing the bill with Elton John. However, he had to back out of concerts due to throat problems and Elton continued on his own, with Billy announcing that he would retire from touring due to his age.

JOEY DEE & THE STARLITERS   Joey Dee was born Joseph DeNicola on 11 June 1940 in Passaic, New Jersey. He led the house band at the Peppermint Lounge in New York in 1961 and first entered the chart in January 1962 with a number he had co-written, 'Peppermint Twist' – the Peppermint Lounge was a club associated with the twist.

101

Apart from this chart-topper, Dee and his group had several other US hits: 'Shout', 'Hey Let's Twist', 'Ya Ya', 'Hot Pastrami With Mashed Potatoes' and 'What Kind Of Love Is This'. Dee himself also appeared in the films *Hey Let's Twist* and *Two Tickets To Paris*.

In 1964 he opened his own club, the Starliter. His new band comprised Felix Cavaliere, Gene Cornish and Eddie Brigati, who left him later that year to form the **Young Rascals**. **Jimi Hendrix** was also guitarist with the Starliters for a spell in 1965.

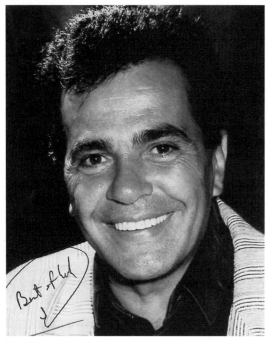
Joey Dee

The Starliters never toured the UK, but appeared at the Star Club in Hamburg with Liverpool bands the Beatles, the **Searchers** and Kingsize Taylor & the Dominoes. They also appeared in France and topped the bill above the Beatles at a concert in Sweden.

After a regular run of releases, further records were issued sporadically on a variety of labels in the US.

In 1987 Dee founded the Starlite Starbrite Foundation For The Love Of Rock 'n' Roll.

Although he no longer records, Joey Dee still performs regularly in the States with a new version of the Starliters, which includes his wife Lois Lee and his son Ronnie on sax.

JOHN FRED & HIS PLAYBOY BAND This American group in the one-hit-wonder category topped the US chart in January 1968 with 'Judy In Disguise (With Glasses)', a parody of 'Lucy In The Sky With Diamonds'. John Fred Gourrier from Baton Rouge, Louisiana, led the group. The other members were Jimmy O'Rourke (guitar), Harold Cowart (bass), Tommy DeGeneres (organ) and Joe Micili (drums). The horn section comprised Charlie Spinosa and Ronnie Goodson on trumpet with Andrew Bernard on sax.

The group continued to record, but had no further success and disbanded in the early 1970s. John formed a new Playboy band between 1975 and 1977, then disbanded it and returned home to Baton Rouge, where he settled down as a record producer for RCS.

JOHNNY & THE HURRICANES Born in Walbridge, Ohio, in 1940, tenor saxophonist Johnny Paris formed this instrumental outfit in 1957. He continued to change the personnel of the band over the years, including the times when the hits dried up and he carried on performing in cabaret venues.

The group's hits between 1959 and 1961 included: 'Red River Rock', 'Reveille Rock', 'Beatnik Fly', 'Down Yonder', 'Rocking Goose', 'Ja-Da' and 'Old Smokey/High Voltage'. They topped the bill at Hamburg's famous Star Club when the Beatles made their debut there in 1962.

Johnny Paris was seen at London's Stringfellows club in 1994 at the launch party for the ill-fated *Gold* nostalgia journal.

JONES, Aled A former Welsh choirboy, Aled Jones had three singles in the UK hit parade in 1985 and 1986: 'Memory', 'Walking In The Air' and 'A Winter Story'. 'Walking In The Air' was used on the soundtrack of the animated version of *The Snowman*, a popular children's book which was adapted for television.

In 1994, Aled graduated from the Old Vic Theatre School.

In 1995, thanks to modern recording technology, he was able to re-record 'Walking In The Air' as a duet with his younger self. He has also attempted to make it as a rock singer and, rather more successfully, as a host on children's television.

JONES, Howard A singer-keyboards player, Howard Jones was born on 23 February 1955 in Southampton, Hampshire. On leaving Music

College in Manchester he became a piano teacher for a while, then formed several bands.

With compensation he received following an accident, Jones bought a synthesizer, made a demo tape and was signed by WEA Records in 1983.

Between 1983 and 1987 his hits included: 'New Song', 'What Is Love', 'Hide And Seek', 'Pearl In the Shell', 'Like To Get To Know You Well', 'Things Can Only Get Better', 'Look Mama', 'Life In One Day', 'No One Is To Blame', 'All I Want', 'You Know I Love You... Don't You?' and 'A Little Bit Of Snow'.

Jones opened a vegetarian restaurant in New York in 1987, but within a year it burned down. When his 'In The Running' failed to chart in 1992, WEA dropped him. He initially thought his career was at an end, but decided to place his future in his own hands. In 1994 he produced a CD, *Working In The Backroom*, which he recorded at home and sold at his gigs, reaching sales of 20,000.

In 1996 he went out on the road performing acoustic tours and promoting a new album, *Live Acoustic America*, and later in the year began work on a new recording project, *Angels And Lovers*.

JONES, Janie The life of this blonde singer, with undoubted sexual chemistry, has been awash with controversy.

In the 1960s she was arrested for appearing topless at a film premiere. She recorded numbers such as 'Tickle Me Tootsie Wootsies' and hit the chart with 'Witches Brew'. She hosted decadent parties at her London home, where disc jockeys and celebrities watched various antics through two-way mirrors. This led to her being dubbed 'London's Vice Queen'. She ran 120 prostitutes, was sentenced to a prison term of seven years in 1973 and was dubbed by the judge 'an evil woman'.

It was while Janie was in jail that Moors murderess Myra Hindley fell in love with her.

The Clash featured Janie on their debut album and backed her, using the name Lash, when she recorded 'House Of The Ju Ju King'.

In 1993 she published her autobiography, *The Devil And Miss Jones*.

Late in 1997 Janie issued an album entitled *We're In Love With The World Of Janie Jones*, which featured a cover photograph of her wearing her topless dress.

JOY DIVISION Formed in Manchester in 1977, this group consisted of **Ian Curtis** (vocals), Bernard Albrecht (guitar), Peter Hook (bass) and Stephen Morris (drums). They took their name from that of a group of musicians in a concentration camp also featured in the novel *House Of Dolls*.

The band began to build up a cult following and were championed by disc jockey John Peel. Their single 'Love Will Tear Us Apart' entered the chart – but this was the only recording success Curtis was to see. An epileptic, he had been suffering deteriorating health, and various appearances began to be cancelled. In 1980, following the completion of a new album, he fell ill again, resulting in further cancelled gigs. His last appearance with Joy Division took place on 23 May, when he had to be helped off the stage. Two weeks later, just prior to the start of the band's debut tour of the US, Curtis hanged himself.

'Love Will Tear Us Apart' re-entered the chart in 1983 and Joy Division also charted with 'Atmosphere' in 1988, although the group no longer existed.

They had enjoyed three album hits – *Closer*, *Unknown Pleasures* and *Still* – the latter released after Curtis' death.

In 1980 the surviving members renamed themselves New Order. Albrecht now began to call himself Barney Sumner.

New Order became highly successful in their own right, with a host of hit singles including: 'Ceremony', 'Procession', 'Temptation', 'Blue Monday', 'Confusion', 'Thieves Like Us', 'The Perfect Kiss', 'Sub-Culture', 'Shellshock', 'The Peel Sessions', 'State Of The Nation', 'Bizarre Love Triangle', 'True Faith', 'Touched By The Hand Of God', 'Blue Monday 198', 'Fine Time', 'Round And Round', 'Run 2', 'Disappointed', 'Regret', 'World (The Price Of Love)', 'Spooky', 'True Faith '94' and 'Blue Monday '95'.

Album hits included: *Movement*, *Power Corruption And Lies*, *Low-Life*, *Technique*, *BBC Radio 1 Live In Concert* and *Republic*.

The group recorded 'World In Motion', a UK No 1 record, with the England World Cup Squad in 1990.

1995 saw a re-mix of 'Love Will Tear Us Apart' enter the chart, with the album *Permanent: Joy Division 1995* also charting. During the same year, Curtis' widow penned a biography of Ian called *Touching From A Distance*.

KALLEN, Kitty This American singer was dubbed the 'US Sweetheart Of Song'. Kitty was born in 1922 in Philadelphia and became the vocalist with a number of big bands, including those of Harry James, Artie Shaw, Jack Teagarden and Jimmy Dorsey. She had a major hit in the UK with 'Little Things Mean A Lot' and recorded with Bing Crosby.

Kitty duetted with Richard Hayes on the single 'Our Lady Of Fatima', which became a Top 10 hit in the US in 1950, but her biggest success there was 'Little Things Mean A Lot', which topped the chart in May 1954. Her next major hit was in July of the same year – 'In The Chapel In The Moonlight'.

Kitty entered the UK chart with 'Little Things Mean A Lot' in 1955, the year in which she topped the bill at the London Palladium.

Her final hit, in 1962, was 'My Coloring Book'.

Kitty Kallen was still performing in 1997 – at the age of 71.

KANE, Eden Singer Eden Kane (real name Richard Sarstedt) was born on 29 March 1942 in Delhi, India. During the 1950s he formed a skiffle group with his brothers Peter and Robin. As a solo artist he won a national talent contest and was signed by managers Michael Barclay and Philip Waddilove, who decided to change his name. He recalled: 'One of the guys was a fan of the film *Citizen Kane*, hence the surname and Eden was added to complete a strong biblical connection.'

Kane had five chart hits between 1961 and 1964, after which the success of the Beatles affected the recording fortunes of many solo singers. His hits were: 'Well I Ask You', 'Get Lost', 'Forget Me Not', 'I Don't Know Why' and 'Boys Cry'.

When the UK music scene became so dominated by groups, Kane attempted to comply with the new trend and recorded 'Rain Rain Go Away' in the beat group style. He then recorded 'Do You Love Me Like I Love You', on which he was backed by a Liverpool group, Earl Preston & the TTs. It wasn't successful, so he emigrated to Australia, where his 'Boys Cry' had become a major hit.

Kane had his own successful television series there before deciding to relocate to the US, and he moved to Hollywood, where he got married. He has lived there ever since and owns a ranch in Arizona.

Kane teamed up with his brothers Peter and Robin to complete an album, *Worlds Apart Together*, in 1973.

Back in Hollywood, he joined the team at *Star Trek: The Next Generation* and has been involved with the Star Trek universe ever since, He is currently working on *Star Trek: Voyager*.

In between times, Kane still takes time to make appearances on the nostalgia circuit, and in 1997 returned to the UK to embark on a nationwide Flying Music promotion, The Solid Gold Rock 'n' Roll Tour with **Marty Wilde**, **Joe Brown**, **John Leyton** and the **Vernons Girls**.

K.C. & THE SUNSHINE BAND This funky disco band with a Caribbean, gospel and rock foundation was formed by Harry Wayne Casey and Richard Finch in 1973. Other members included Jerome Smith (guitar), Robert Johnson (drums) and Fermin Goytisolo (congas and percussion).

The group were later to augment their sound with further musicians and also a horn section. They originally found record success in the UK chart before their eventual entry into the US hit list.

Casey also teamed up with Teri DeSario in 1979 for the No 2 US chart placing of 'Yes, I'm Ready', credited to 'Teri DeSario with K.C.'.

The band's UK hit singles included: 'Queen Of Clubs', 'Sound Your Funky Horn', 'Get Down Tonight', 'That's The Way (I Like It)', 'I'm So Crazy', '(Shake Shake Shake) Shake Your Booty', 'Keep It Comin' Love', 'I'm Your Boogie Man', 'Boogie Shoes', 'It's The Same Old Song', 'Please Don't Go', 'Give It Up' and '(You Said) You'd Gimme Some More'.

A 1982 road accident left K.C. paralysed for several months. On recovery, he and a reconstituted Sunshine Band topped the UK chart in 1983 with 'Give It Up'. A year later, this number entered the US Top 100, where it was credited to K.C. alone. That same year Casey set up his own record company, Meca Records.

There were no further chart hits for the group, but K.C. continued to tour the States and in 1991 Rhino Records issued the CD *Best Of K.C. & The Sunshine Band*.

In 1995 various record companies issued other compilations, including the albums *Oh Yeah!* and *Get Down Live!*. A revival of 'That's The Way (I Like It)' by the Clock made the UK Top 20 in 1998.

KENNY Confusion was caused by this name as it applied to both an Irish solo singer and an English band, both of whom were recording around the same time on Mickie Most's Rak Records label in the 1970s.

Singer Kenny's hits were 'Heart of Stone' and 'Give It to Me'. The group Kenny had hits with 'The Bump', 'Fancy Pants', 'Baby I Love You OK' and 'Julie Ann'. An album by the band rounded off their chart run when tracks were lumped together on *The Sound Of Super K*. Nevertheless, the group soldiered on until it drowned in the rip-tide of punk.

Initially, the members were Richard Driscoll (vocals), Chris Redburn (bass), Yan Style (guitar) and Andy Walton (drums). When recording at Rak Studios, Mickie Most included top session men **Chris Spedding** and Clem Cattini on their hit tracks.

When the group disbanded following their album release, Driscoll appeared in **Cockney Rebel** and Classix Nouveaux, Redburn went on to run a haulage company and Style a hire firm called Kane Green, and Walton took a job with a computer company.

KING Singer-songwriter Paul King was born on 20 January 1960. He formed the group King in 1984 and they enjoyed five hits in their two years of existence: 'Love & Pride', 'Won't You Hold My Hand Now', 'Alone Without You', 'The Taste Of Your Tears' and 'Torture'. When they disbanded in 1986, Paul King went solo and charted the following year with 'I Know'.

He later joined MTV and is currently a presenter on the music channel VH1 – and a very creditable one, with his great insight into the music scene.

KING BROTHERS, The These three brothers from Hornchurch, Essex, were a highly popular vocal group in the late 1950s. They comprised Michael on guitar, Tony on bass and Denis on piano, and actually made their television debut in 1953 on *Shop Window* when Denis was only 14 years old. Appearances at fashionable London nightclubs, plus the Windmill Theatre and the London Palladium, followed.

The brothers signed to the Parlophone label and between 1957 and 1961 their hits were: 'A White Sports Coat', 'In The Middle Of An Island', 'Wake Up Little Susie', 'Put A Light In The Window', 'Standing On The Corner', 'Mais Oui', 'Doll House' and '76 Trombones'.

They also appeared in the pop film *6.5 Special*.

Of the group, Denis King has been the most successful artistically. Today, he is one of the UK's foremost composers of television themes, including those for *Within These Walls*, *Lovejoy* and *Black Beauty*.

KING, Carole This singer-songwriter-pianist was born in Brooklyn, New York, on 9 February 1942. She married lyricist Gerry Goffin and they became a writing team.

By the time she was 20, Carole and her husband were in great demand. In 1961 they had their first major hit when the **Shirelles** recorded 'Will You Love Me Tomorrow'. The **Drifters** then recorded 'Up on the Roof'. Other songs by the duo included 'Natural Woman', 'Locomotion', 'One Fine Day', 'Halfway To Paradise', 'Just Once In My Life', 'I'm Into Something Good', 'Chains', 'Take Good Care Of My Baby' and many others.

Carole also began to record some of their songs in her own right, including 'It Might As Well Rain Until September'.

Following their divorce, Carole went into semi-retirement while she raised their two young daughters, Louise and Sherry, in Los Angeles. By the late 1960s she had begun to write again. She also formed a group in 1968 called the City, before becoming a solo performer. Of particular merit was her 1971 album *Tapestry*, from which her chart-topping single 'It's Too Late/ I Feel The Earth Move', was taken. She also scored with a third track from the LP, 'You've Got A Friend'.

Since that time Carole has issued a number of singles and albums which have charted, and has been on numerous tours with artists ranging from **James Taylor** to Bob Dylan. She released the albums *Color of Your Dreams* and *In Concert*. There was also an album by various artists paying tribute to her songs, *Tapestry Revisited: A Tribute To Carole King*.

Carole is still an active recording artist, but her stage appearances are restricted to charity events.

Her second husband, Rick Evers, was also her manager. He died in March 1978 from an accidental drugs overdose.

KING CRIMSON This group was formed in 1969 and comprised Robert Fripp (guitar), Greg Lake (guitar and vocals), Ian McDonald (sax), Mike Giles (drums) and Pete Sinfield (lyricist).

The same year they toured the US and charted with their debut album, *In The Court Of The Crimson King*.

Following the tour, McDonald and Giles left the band; McDonald was to help form **Foreigner** in 1979. In 1970 Greg Lake left to form Emerson, Lake & Palmer. Fripp and Sinfield engaged other musicians, including Gordon Haskell, Mel Collins and Andy McCulloch, although Haskell and McCulloch left after the release of the group's third album, *In the Wake Of Poseidon*. Various personnel changes continued, until Fripp announced that the group had disbanded for good in 1974.

Fripp, who married singer Toyah Willcox in 1986, joined with other original members Sinfield, Giles, McDonald and Lake for a one-day event at a London conference hall in March 1997 to promote the release of a King Crimson boxed set, *Epitaph*.

1997 saw the new King Crimson line-up, formed by Fripp, which included singer-songwriter Adrian Belew, drummers Bill Bruford and Pat Masteletto, and Tony Levin and Trey Gunn.

During the same year Giles began working on a new album, as did McDonald. Lake was touring Europe and South America with a re-formed Emerson, Lake & Palmer, and Sinfield, who had written hits for Celine Dion such as 'Think Twice' and 'Call the Man', was planning a new solo album.

In December 1997 Bruford, Fripp, Gunn and Levin teamed up as Project One for three live London appearances.

Fripp and his wife live in Wiltshire; she is now a television holiday programme presenter and also presents music shows for VH1. Her biggest successes came in the early to mid-1980s, when she was known simply as Toyah. Her hit singles included: 'I Want To Be Free', 'Thunder In The Mountains, 'Brave New World', 'Leya', 'Be Loud Be Proud (Be Heard)', 'Rebel Run', 'The Vow', 'Don't Fall In Love (I Said)', 'Soul (Passing Through Soul)' and 'Echo Beach'. Two of her EPs also entered the singles chart – 'Four From Toyah' and 'Four More From Toyah'.

KING, Jonathan   Born Kenneth King on 6 December 1944, this artist made his recording debut in 1965 with 'Everyone's Gone To The Moon', a Top 5 entry in the UK which also registered in the US Top 20.

His other UK hits were: 'Let It All Hang Out', 'Lazy Bones', 'Hooked On A Feeling', 'Flirt', 'Una Paloma Blanca', 'One For You One For Me', 'You're The Greatest Lover' and 'Gloria'.

But this extraordinary man's recording career didn't end there. He had a succession of hits under numerous different names, including Bubblerock, 53rd & 3rd, Sakkarin, Shag, 100 Ton & A Feather, Weathermen, Sound 9418, and Father Abraphart & the Smurps.

Hits under these names included: '(I Can't Get No) Satisfaction', 'Loop De Love', 'Sugar Sugar', 'In The Mood' and 'It's The Same Old Song'.

King was also a record producer, launched his own record label (UK Records), was a leading columnist in the national press and hosted a popular television series, *Entertainment USA*.

He was the man behind the UK's 1997 Eurovision Song Contest win by Katerina & the Waves.

In January 1998, the 53-year old former singer and disc jockey was contracted by the media group Sanctuary Music to sign up potential stars of the future.

KING, Solomon   This American singer was to find success in the UK. In 1968 he had two singles in the UK chart, 'She Wears My Ring' and 'When We Were Young'.

His 1970 version of Aretha Franklin's 'Say a Little Prayer' became a northern soul classic later in the decade, although the artist himself was ensconced firmly in the supper clubs.

KINGSTON TRIO, The   This major American folk group was originally formed in San Francisco in 1957 with members Bob Shane, Nick Reynolds and Dave Guard. They made a huge impact in 1958, when their single 'Tom Dooley' topped the US chart.

Their other hit singles included: 'The Tijuana Jail', 'M.T.A.', 'A Worried Man', 'El Matador', 'Bad Man Blunder', 'Where Have All The Flowers Gone', 'Greenback Dollar', 'Reverend Mr Black' and 'Desert Pete'. The trio also had several successful albums.

In 1961 John Stewart replaced Guard. He remained a member of the trio until 1967 and then turned solo, his hits including 'Gold', 'Midnight Wind' and 'Lost Her In The Sun'.

In 1987 the Kingston Trio were back on the road, albeit with only Bob Shane remaining from the original line-up.

The Kinks

KINKS, The Formed in 1962, this group comprised Ray and Dave Davies (vocals and guitar), Peter Quaife (bass) and Mick Avory (drums).

Since they topped the UK chart in 1964 with 'You Really Got Me', they have continued to chart over three decades. Their hit singles have included: 'All Day And All Of The Night', 'Tired Of Waiting For You', 'Everybody's Gonna Be Happy', 'Set Me Free', 'See My Friend', 'Till The End Of The Day', 'Dedicated Follower Of Fashion', 'Sunny Afternoon', 'Dead End Street', 'Waterloo Sunset', 'Autumn Almanac', 'Wonderboy', 'Days', 'Plastic Man', 'Victoria', 'Lola', 'Apeman', 'Supersonic Rocket Ship', 'Better Things', 'Come Dancing' and 'Don't Forget To Dance'.

They have also had numerous chart albums, including: *Kinks, Kinda Kinks, Kinks Kontroversy, Well Respected Man, Face To Face, Something Else* and *Sunny Afternoon*.

Raymond Douglas Davies, born in London on 21 June 1944, is acknowledged as one of the UK's premier songwriters. In recent years, the leader of the Kinks has been touring with a very successful three-hour, one-man show, presenting an evening of music and anecdotes. The show is called The Storyteller: An Evening With A Twentieth Century Man. He plays acoustic versions of old Kinks hits – 'L-O-L-A', 'Autumn Almanac', 'Sunny Afternoon', 'You Really Got Me', 'Waterloo Sunset', 'Dedicated Follower Of Fashion' – and specially written new material, together with tracks from the Kinks' latest CD release, *To The Bone And Animal*.

Ray, whose autobiography is called *X-Ray*, has had an event-filled life. He has suffered a couple of drugs overdoses, left his wife and children in 1973, and divorced his second wife Yvonne in 1981 when he began an affair with singer Chrissie Hynde, who gave birth to the couple's daughter, Natalie. Hynde then left Ray in 1984 to take up with Jim Kerr of Simple Minds.

Ray Davies currently lives in London and in October 1997 published a book of his short stories, entitled *Waterloo Sunset*.

Dave Davies is based in California, where he writes screenplays and composes movie soundtracks. His recent autobiography was called *Kink*.

Peter Quaife – now Peter Kinnes – emigrated to Canada, where he is a self-employed fine artist in Ontario whose exhibition in 1994 contained work of an autobiographical nature. He also teaches classical guitar.

Mick Avory left the group in 1984 and was replaced by Bob Henrit, but he met up again with Ray and Dave when the group was inducted into the Rock & Roll Hall Of Fame in 1990. He also appeared on a 1993 album for the Kinks called *Phobia*. He is a mainstay of a group called Shut Up Frank, is a keen golfer and continues to work in an administrative capacity for Konk, the Kinks' organization. He also occasionally appears with an outfit called Kast Off Kinks, which includes John Dalton and various other members of the group from the 1970s.

Both Davies brothers are still leading an increasingly seldom-seen Kinks.

KIRBY, Kathy Pop music's Marilyn Monroe look-alike was born in Ilford on 20 October 1940. The beautiful, convent-educated strawberry blonde trained as an opera singer between the ages of 10 and 13. Band leader Ambrose discovered her when she was only 16. He invited her to sing with his band and also took over the management of her career. By the time she was 18 she was appearing at the Flamingo Room in Madrid, and in 1958 was singing with the Danny Bryce Orchestra at the Lyceum in London, in addition to appearing in cabaret at venues such as the Astor, the Blue Angel and Le Condor.

Kathy made her Pye Records debut with 'Love Can Be', and between 1963 and 1965 had five chart entries with 'Dance On', 'Secret Love', 'Let Me Go Lover', 'You're The One' and 'I Belong', the latter being her entry in the 1965 Eurovision Song Contest, in which she came second.

Kathy was voted Top British Female Singer in a *New Musical Express* poll and even had a brief entry in the US chart with 'The Way Of Love'. She also toured with artists such as **Cliff Richard** and Duane Eddy. She made her television debut in 1960 in *Cool For Cats* and starred in the popular series *Stars And Garters*. She also appeared in shows such as *Big Night Out* and *Sunday Night At The London Palladium*, and had her own television series in 1964.

Following the death of her manager and mentor Ambrose in 1971, her career seemed to go to pieces. Ill fortune plagued the beautiful star and she became a bankrupt, owing £30,000 to the Inland Revenue. Later, she was arrested for allegedly deceiving a London hotel over her bill of £304. She was remanded on bail on condition that she attend a mental hospital. She was found innocent and all charges were dropped, but such publicity tends to stick.

Kathy hit the headlines again when she was found to be living with a lesbian, Laraine McKay, who proposed marriage to her. McKay was arrested on a deception charge and sent to Holloway Prison.

By 1979 Kathy was singing in between games at a London bingo hall, and the following year she sold her story to a Sunday newspaper in a three-week series, in which she wrote: 'I am not going to write off my career. The stage is in my bloodstream. If I am no longer the glossy-lipped Golden Girl Of Pop, I still have one asset left – that's my voice.'

Following the 'wilderness years', during which she was also hospitalized, Kathy managed a qualified comeback on the nostalgia circuit, with her 1996 CD compilation, *The Very Best Of Kathy Kirby*, doing brisk business in the foyers.

KISS This group was formed in 1973 and comprised Gene Simmons (vocals and bass), Ace Frehley and Paul Stanley (guitar) and Peter Criss (drums).

Their outrageous glitter rock and heavy metal act was a very visual one, as they wore flamboyant costumes and make-up which hid their identities, and refused to be photographed without their make-up. Their live shows were full of explosive action and set pieces, and they were particularly popular in Japan.

The group's hit singles included: 'Rock And Roll All Nite', 'Shout It Out Loud', 'On And On', 'I Feel A Song (In My Heart)', 'The Way We Were' and 'Part Time Love'.

They were far more successful as an album band and their album hits ranged from *Destroyer* to *Asylum*.

Eric Carr replaced Criss; Vince Cusano replaced Frehley, and was himself replaced by Mark Norton. As Norton began to suffer from a debilitating illness, Bruce Kulick took over from him.

All four members of the band had solo albums issued on the same day in October 1978.

In 1997 Mercury reissued all 13 of the group's albums in re-mastered form, with sleeve notes by the group. The albums were: *Dressed To Kill, Destroyer, Double Platinum, Hotter Than Hell, Love Gun, Dynasty, Kiss, Rock And Roll Over, Unmasked, Alive, Alive II, Music From The Elder* and *Creatures Of The Night*.

KISSOON, Mac & Katie This brother and sister duo (real surname Farthing), both of whom were born in Trinidad – Mac on 11 November 1943 and Katie on 11 March 1951 – emigrated to the UK with their parents in the 1950s.

They had a five-year chart run in the 1970s with 'Chirpy Chirpy Cheep Cheep', 'Sugar Candy Kisses', 'Don't Do It Baby', 'Like A Butterfly' and 'The Two Of Us'.

Since being the only homegrown act on a round-Britain soul package – headlined by the Supremes – in 1976, Mac and Katie Kissoon have been hired for cabaret, and as backing singers on record and on stage for others. Katie was in the employ of Van Morrison in the 1980s.

KITT, Eartha Born in Columbia, South Carolina, on 26 January 1928, Eartha May Kitt – the singer Orson Welles once described as 'the most exciting woman in the world' – was brought up in abject poverty and in her early life was subjected to racial abuse.

After moving to New York, she joined the Katherine Dunham Dance Company, then spent time as a solo artist in Paris.

Her career has included films, theatre, television and recordings, for which she has received numerous awards.

She has had a number of bestselling albums, including 'Old Fashioned Girl', 'I'm Still Here' and 'Santa Baby'. Her films have included *St Louis Blues* with **Nat King Cole** and *Anna Lucasta* with **Sammy Davis Jnr**.

Eartha was once blacklisted by the CIA, who dubbed her 'a sadistic nymphomaniac', which almost destroyed her career overnight. When asked to describe her life, she said: 'Rejected. Ejected. Dejected. Used. Accused. Abused.' Her autobiography, *I'm Still Here*, was published in 1989.

While Eartha collaborated on record with Bronski Beat in 1989, a more typical venture in the autumn of her career was a 1992 tour of the UK with the Ink Spots.

KNIGHT, Gladys Born on 28 May 1944 in Atlanta, Georgia, Gladys Knight's parents were gospel singers and she began to sing from an early age. When she was only ten years old she formed a vocal group with her brother Merald, sister Brenda and cousins William and Elenor Guest. In 1957 another cousin, James 'Pips' Woods, encouraged her to become professional and took over their management. The group was then dubbed Gladys Knight & the Pips.

Both Brenda and Elenor left the group in 1959 to get married and were replaced by Edward Patten and Langston George.

Their first hit was 'Every Beat Of My Heart' in 1961 and they followed with: 'Letter Full Of Tears', 'Giving Up', 'Everybody Needs Love', 'I Heard It Through The Grapevine', 'The End Of Our Road', 'It Should Have Been Me', 'The Nitty Gritty', 'Friendship Train', 'You Need Love Like I Do (Don't You)', 'If I Were Your Woman', 'I Don't Want To Do Wrong', 'Make Me The Woman That You Go Home To', 'Help Me Make It Through The Night', 'Neither One Of Us', 'Daddy Could Swear – I Declare', 'Where Peaceful Waters Flow', 'Midnight Train To Georgia', 'I've Got To Use My Imagination' and 'Best Thing That Ever Happened To Me'.

When George left the group in 1962 they remained a quartet.

Gladys starred in a US television sitcom, *Charlie & Co*, along with Flip Wilson, in 1985–6.

She split with the group in 1989, although Merald continued to tour with her. The other two members of the band, Edward Patten and William Guest, then went on to work in the ice-cream business. In 1995, Patten suffered a stroke and is now confined to a wheelchair. Guest later became the vice president of Crew Records.

As exemplified by her leading role in *Charlie & Co*, nowdays Gladys Knight is almost as much a US television personality as a singer, although as recently as 1989 she had a global smash with the James Bond theme, 'Licence To Kill'. The following year she reunited with the Pips for Tamla Motown's thirtieth anniversary concert.

In 1996 Motown Records issued *The Lost Live Album*, a recording made of the group in 1974 which had recently been discovered. The same year, Gladys Knight & the Pips were inducted into the Rock & Roll Hall Of Fame.

KRAFTWERK This group was formed in Germany in 1970. They chose the name Kraftwerk, which in German means 'power plant'.

The members consisted of Ralf Hutter (keyboards, drums, vocals, woodwind and strings), Florian Schneider-Esleben (keyboards, drums, vocals, woodwind and strings), Wolfgang Flur (electronic drums) and Klaus Roeder (violin and guitar).

Eventually, their music found success outside Germany and their UK hit singles included: 'Autobahn', 'Neon Lights', 'Pocket Calculator', 'Computer Love', 'Showroom Dummies', 'Tour De France', 'Musique Non-Stop', 'Telephone', 'The Robots' and 'Radioactivity'.

Their album successes included: *Autobahn*, *The Man-Machine*, *Computer World*, *Trans-Europe Express*, *Set*, *Electric Café* and *The Mix*.

In 1975 Karl Bartos replaced Roeder, and by 1991 Bartos and Flur had left to form Elektric. Kraftwerk recruited Fritz Hijbert and Fernando Fromm-Abrentes to replace them.

Ralf Hutter and Florian Schneider-Esleben, the group's mainstays, are still based professionally in Dusseldorf's Kling Klang Studio. In the years since 1981's *Computer World*, Kraftwerk have released only two albums – and these include a remixed compilation. Some claim that Hutter's dedication to competition cycling leaves him little time for music.

KRAMER, Billy J. This singer from the Bootle area of Liverpool was born William Howard Ashton on 19 August 1943. From Billy Forde & the Phantoms he went on to lead Billy Kramer & the Coasters, managed by local pensioner Ted Knibbs, in the early 1960s. After the group was voted No 3 in a *Mersey Beat* poll, Ted sold Billy's management to **Brian Epstein** for a nominal sum. The Coasters refused to turn professional, and other Mersey groups such as the Remo Four turned down the position of backing band, so Epstein teamed Kramer with Manchester's the Dakotas. They comprised Mike Maxfield (lead), Robin MacDonald (rhythm), Ray Jones (bass) and Tony Mansfield (drums). The group were to have one solo hit without Billy, the instrumental 'The Cruel Sea'.

It was **John Lennon** who suggested adding the 'J.' to Kramer's name to give it some distinction (it stood for **Julian**, John's son).

The group topped the chart with 'Do You Want To Know A Secret?'. Their second release, 'Bad To Me', also topped the chart, and they had hits with two further Lennon/McCartney numbers, 'I'll Keep You Satisfied' and 'From A Window'. Kramer then insisted on recording 'Little Children', which gave him his third No 1 hit. The group also charted with 'Trains And Boats And Planes'. Paul McCartney offered him 'Yesterday', but he turned it down.

Billy J. Kramer

No further hits followed, but Kramer pursued a solo career, married, had two sons and settled in Crewe, Cheshire, appearing mainly on the cabaret circuit.

Due to his problems with alcohol, Kramer's first marriage broke down and he moved to the States, remarrying and settling on Long Island, New York, in 1984. He gave up drinking and, in between stage appearances, worked as an alcohol counsellor.

After 12 years in the US, during which time he obtained dual nationality, he returned to the UK to appear on the sixties circuit, which had grown throughout the late 1980s and early 1990s. He had been backed by a group called the Coustiks, but was approached by members of his former backing group the Dakotas and they teamed up once more for the Chelmsford Spectacular in 1996. They then decided to work together once again as Billy J. Kramer & the Dakotas.

The Dakotas are now a four-piece, with the two original members, Mike Maxfield and Tony Mansfield, joined by Toni Baker on keyboards and Eddie Mooney on vocals.

Billy J. Kramer With The Dakotas At Abbey Road was released on 23 February 1998. On its release, Mike Maxfield recalled: 'On one occasion, John (Lennon) said that he had written our next single. He sat at the piano and played "Bad To Me" and then went straight into another song, "I Wanna Hold Your Hand". We thought "Bad To Me" was very good, but Billy said "Can I have the other one?" John said,"'It's going to be our next single, so you can't have it!"'

KRISTOFFERSON, Kris   The actor-singer-songwriter Kris Kristofferson was born on 22 June 1936 in Brownsville, Texas. He became a Rhodes scholar and moved to England to study literature at Oxford University in 1957–8. While there, he began to write songs and became a performer under the name Kris Carson.

He moved to Nashville in 1965 and enjoyed a No 1 country hit, which he co-wrote, called 'Why Me'. Other country hits included: 'Me And Bobby McGee', 'Help Me Make It Through The Night' and 'For The Good Times'.

For a time he was married to singer Rita Coolidge.

Kristofferson found success as a film actor, but in 1978 declared he was quitting to concentrate full time on his music. However, he continued to appear in movies, although not as successfully as before.

Among his dozens of films are *Pat Garrett & Billy The Kid*, *Alice Doesn't Live Here Anymore*, *A Star Is Born*, *Convoy* and *Heaven's Gate*.

Kris Kristofferson is currently a member of the Highwaymen, a country rock 'supergroup', with Johnny Cash, Waylon Jennings and Willie Nelson.

LAINE, Frankie This American singer was born Frank Paul Lo Vecchio, of Sicilian immigrant parents, in Chicago on 30 March 1913. He left Chicago and moved to California, taking a variety of jobs ranging from dancing instructor to shipping clerk.

In 1932, together with dancing partner Ruth Smith, he danced for 3,501 hours – the all-time marathon dance record.

It was Hoagy Carmichael who arranged for Laine to make a test record, which also turned out to be his first hit, 'That's My Desire', in 1947. He was to have a further seven entries in the US chart, but a staggering two dozen in the UK chart, with three of his hits charting twice. They included: 'High Noon', 'Girl In The Wood', 'I Believe', 'Where The Wind Blows', 'Hey Joe', 'Answer Me', 'Blowing Wild', 'Granada', 'The Kid's Last Fight', 'My Friend', 'There Must Be A Reason', 'Rain Rain Rain', 'In The Beginning', 'Cool Water', 'Strange Lady In Town', 'Humming Bird', 'Hawkeye', 'Sixteen Tons', 'Hell Hath No Fury', 'A Woman In Love', 'Moonlight Gambler', 'Love Is A Golden Ring', 'Rawhide' and 'Gunslinger'.

Laine was also noted for singing the theme songs for movies and television series such as *Man Without A Star*, *Gunfight At The OK Corral* and *Champion The Wonder Horse*.

He married screen actress Nan Grey in 1950 and the two settled in an opulent ocean-front house in San Diego, close to where he keeps his boats. In 1971 Frankie secured commercial fishing licences and started a fishing business.

Since the 1970s, Laine has concentrated on religious material and remakes of his old hits, although in more familiar clippety-clop character was his 'Blazing Saddles' in its lyricist Mel Brooks' 1974 spoof western movie of the same name. By the mid-1980s, he was in virtual semi-retirement.

From his San Diego home, Frankie Laine has set out occasionally for limited concert appearances and occasional performances on US television, such as in an *American Bandstand* anniversary concert in 1988. He also organizes the San Diego Composers Festival.

LAST, James Born in Germany on 17 April 1929, this orchestra leader-composer originally began writing arrangements for a host of artists, including Caterina Valente and Helmut Zacharias.

He signed to Polydor Records in 1964 and has been touring and recording successfully ever since. He has had more than 100 hit albums in the German chart, but also more than 50 album chart entries in the UK, and achieved considerable success in the States. Although primarily an album artist, Last hit the US and UK charts with the single 'The Seduction' in 1980.

While his relentless touring and recording schedule has eased off in recent years, James Last and his musicians remain at large in concert halls throughout the globe.

LEANDROS, Vicky This singer was born in Greece in 1950, although she was raised in Hamburg, Germany.

Vicky made her recording debut in 1965 and represented Luxembourg in the 1967 Eurovision Song Contest with 'Love Is Blue', which was a major hit throughout Europe.

After 'Come What May' almost topped the UK chart in 1972, 'The Love In Your Eyes' and 1973's 'When Bouzoukis Played' were lesser UK hits.

LEE, Brenda This American rock 'n' roll singer was dubbed 'Little Miss Dynamite'. She was born Brenda Mae Tarpley on 12 December 1944 in Lithonia, Georgia, and made her showbusiness debut at the age of 11 on the *Ozark Jubilee* television show.

Brenda initially made an impact in the country music charts with singles such as 'Jambalaya' and 'I'm Gonna Lasso Santa Claus', before entering the Top 50 with 'One Step At A Time'.

Her hits in the singles chart included: 'Sweet Nothin's', 'I'm Sorry', 'That's All You Gotta Do', 'I Want to Be Wanted', 'Just a Little', 'Rockin' Around The Christmas Tree', 'Emotions', 'I'm Learning About Love', 'You Can Depend On Me', 'Break It To Me Gently', 'Everybody Loves Me But You', 'Heart In Hand', 'It Started All Over Again', 'All Alone Am I', 'Your Used To Be', 'Losing You', 'My Whole World Is Falling Down', 'I Wonder', 'The Grass Is Greener', 'As Usual', 'Think', 'Is It True', 'Too Many Rivers', 'Rusty Bells', 'Coming On Strong' and 'Ride, Ride, Ride'.

At one point Brenda came to the UK to record a number of singles with Mickie Most.

In April 1963 she married Ronnie Shacklett in Nashville.

After family commitments led Brenda to cease touring and record only sporadically, she rose anew as a country star, guaranteed work for

as long as she could stand. In 1988, she guested on k. d. lang's *Shadowlands* album.

Brenda appeared in the UK in 1993 on a nostalgia tour with other American stars of the same vintage, including **Chris Montez**, **Johnny Tillotson** and **Len Barry**. Currently she hosts a syndicated US television programme, *Nashville Today*, with Johnny Tillotson.

LEE, Leapy This singer was born Lee Graham in Eastbourne, East Sussex, on 2 July 1942. His one major hit was 'Little Arrows' in 1968. He followed with a minor chart entry, 'Good Morning', but his career was seriously compromised when he was gaoled.

Lee and Diana Dors' husband Alan Lake were involved in an altercation in a pub in Sunningdale in Berkshire, during which the publican's wrist was slashed by a flick knife. Following his gaol term, Lee tried his hand at producing and then moved to Spain, where he currently runs a nightclub in Majorca.

LEFT BANKE, The Keyboardist Michael Brown, a former classically trained musician, teamed up with vocalist Steve Martin, guitarist Jeff Winfield, bassist Tom Finn and drummer George Cameron to form the Left Banke in 1964, inspired by the 'British Invasion'.

They were to have a handful of chart hits, the most notable being 'Walk Away Renée', inspired by Finn's girlfriend Renée Fladen. The others were 'Pretty Ballerina' and 'Desirée'.

Due to a lack of further recording success, the band split up in 1968.

Michael Brown, together with guitarist Steve Love, vocalist Ian Lloyd and drummer Brian Madey, formed Stories, who topped the US chart with their cover of Hot Chocolate's 'Brother Louie'.

Three members of the original band – Martin, Finn and Cameron – briefly re-formed in 1978 to cut an album, *Voices Calling*, which eventually saw the light of day in 1986.

Tom Finn, George Cameron and vocalist Steve Cameron reunited for concerts and one single in the late 1970s. Keyboards player Michael Brown writes mostly for other artists, although there have been intermittent solo releases.

LENNON, Julian The elder son of **John Lennon**, Julian was born in Liverpool on 8 April 1963. John spent very little time with Julian during his upbringing, and even less once he had married Yoko Ono. However, as if to make up for it, he spent five years devoting his time to raising Sean, his son by Yoko.

Following in his father's footsteps, Julian formed a group called the Lennon Drops, then for a short time he was a member of Quasa. However, he found his biggest successes as a solo artist, experiencing a major hit with his debut album, *Valotte*, in 1984.

His recording success lasted less than 18 months, during which four of his singles entered the UK chart – 'Too Late For Goodbyes', 'Valotte', 'Say You're Wrong' and 'Because'.

Julian Lennon

For a time he had problems with drink and drugs, which seriously hindered his musical career, but was able to rid himself of the addictions.

Finally, in 1996 Julian received a hard-won – and considerable – portion of his late father's fortune. He flits between homes in Monte Carlo, California and London, not forgetting to visit his mother Cynthia, who now lives in Normandy, France.

Julian Lennon's recording career was revived in May 1998 with the release of his album *Photograph Smile*, which was issued on the same day as Sean Lennon's album *Into The Sun*. Unfortunately, both half-brothers promoted their albums with interviews in which they disparaged their father. Of the two, Julian was most successful, with his album entering the chart.

LEVEL 42 This group was formed in London in 1980, the line-up being Mark King (vocals and bass), Mike Lindup (keyboards and vocals), Boon Gould (guitar) and Phil Gould (drums).

They chose their name after enjoying the cult book *The Hitch-Hiker's Guide To The Galaxy*, in which the answer to the meaning of life was the number 42.

Throughout the 1980s the band's hits included: 'Love Meeting Love', 'Love Games', 'Turn It On', 'Starchild', 'Are You Hearing (What I Hear)?', 'Weave Your Spell', 'The Chinese Way', 'Out Of Sight – Out Of Mind', 'The Sun Goes Down (Living It Up)', 'Micro Kids', 'Hot Water', 'The Chant Has Begun', 'Something About You', 'Leaving Me Now', 'Lessons In Love', 'Running In The Family', 'To Be With You Again', 'It's Over', 'Children Say', 'Heaven In My Hands' and 'Take A Look'.

In December 1987 Boon and Phil Gould left the group, both suffering from ill health. Neil Conti of Prefab Sprout deputized on drums for a short time. By 1988 the new replacements were Alan Murphy on guitar and Gary Husband on drums. Murphy died the following year from AIDS. They found a new guitarist, Jakko Jakszyk, in 1991.

Phil Gould rejoined for the group's eleventh studio album, *Forever Now*, in 1994. Leader Mark King lives on the Isle of Wight. In 1990 he ran off with his wife Pia's best friend, who was also nanny to their children, and Pia obtained a divorce.

LEWIS, Jerry Lee This legendary rock 'n' roll singer-pianist was born in Ferriday, Louisiana, on 29 September 1935. He first began recording in 1954 and found success with his second record on the Sun label, a cover of Roy Hall's 'Whole Lotta Shakin' Goin' On'. His next record, 'Great Balls Of Fire', was an international hit, and he followed this with 'Breathless'.

Scandals and tragedies then entered Lewis' life. His UK tour of 1958 had to be cancelled after three dates, due to the hostile press that

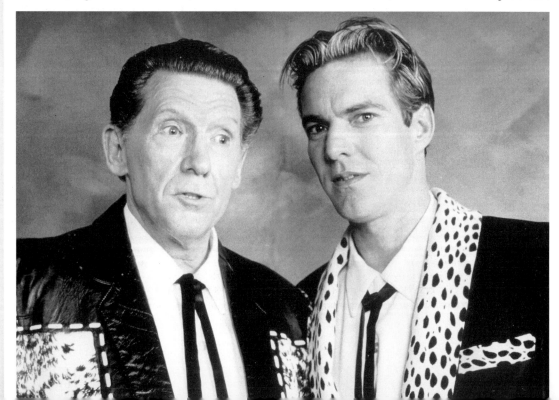

Jerry Lee Lewis (left) with actor Dennis Quaid

resulted when it was discovered that his third wife, Myra, – his 13-year-old second cousin, whom he had married bigamously on 11 December 1957 – accompanied him. Two other hits followed, 'High School Confidential' and 'What'd I Say'.

From the mid-1960s Lewis turned his attention to country music, with a great deal of success. He topped the country chart with several numbers, including 'There Must Be More To Love Than This' and 'Would You Take Another Chance On Me'.

Plagued by alcohol and drugs problems, Lewis suffered a personal tragedy when his son, Jerry Lee Jnr, was killed in a road accident in 1973. Lewis was then sued when he accidentally shot his bass guitarist in the chest. A gun also led to his arrest when he was found waving one outside **Elvis Presley's** home, Graceland, in 1976.

In 1981 Lewis nearly died from a bleeding ulcer, and the following year his fourth wife was found drowned in a swimming pool. The very next year his fifth wife was found dead from a drugs overdose. He married yet again and continued to have problems with bleeding ulcers, drugs and alcohol, but carried on performing. Actor Dennis Quaid portrayed the rock star's turbulent life in the 1989 biopic *Great Balls Of Fire*. Lewis' autobiography, *Killer*, was published in 1993.

Jerry Lee Lewis now lives in Eire with his sixth wife and their son, Jerry Lee Lewis III. During 1997 he embarked on a world tour to celebrate his fortieth anniversary in showbusiness.

LEYTON, John Born in Frinton-on-Sea, Essex, on 17 February 1939, John Leyton made his professional acting debut at the Theatre Royal in York. This brought him to the attention of the UK television company Granada, who cast him in the series *Biggles*. He next appeared in the series *Harpers, WI* as a pop singer, who sang a number called 'Johnny Remember Me'. Leyton released it as a single and it topped the chart, becoming a million-seller.

He followed this with another chart-topper, 'Wild Wind', and his further hits became successful in various parts of the world. These included: 'Son This Is She', 'Lone Rider', 'Lonely City', 'Down The River Nile', 'Cupboard Love', 'I'll Cut Your Tail Off' and 'Make Love To Me'.

Leyton then concentrated on a movie career, appearing in films such as *The Great Escape* and *Von Ryan's Express*. Stage performances as well as various roles in television dramas and series followed. Leyton also guest-starred in a dozen major US television shows, including *The Man From U.N.C.L.E*, *Lost In Space* and *Mission Impossible*.

Apart from his work as an actor, writer and film producer, John Leyton also became a successful businessman and was chairman and managing director of the well-known London restaurant Meridiana. He later sold it and in 1993 opened up a new venture, the Market Bar & Restaurant in London's Portobello Road. That same year he decided to re-enter show business and has since been appearing on nostalgia bills throughout the UK.

LIND, Bob This folk-rock singer was born in Baltimore, Maryland, on 25 November 1942. He made his recording debut with 'Cheryl's Going Home'. It failed to register, but the B-side of the record, a song Lind had penned called 'Elusive Butterfly', became a major hit. It was also his only hit in the US, although he had a minor hit in the UK with the follow-up, 'Remember the Rain'. Lind's recording of 'Elusive Butterfly' reached the Top 5 in the UK, as did Val Doonican's cover version.

As a songwriter, Bob Lind penned numbers for a variety of artists. Currently, he is still working on the folk and C&W circuit in the States.

LITTLE FEAT After appearing with various outfits, singer-songwriter **Lowell George**, born in Hollywood on 13 April 1945, decided to form his own band, Little Feat, in 1970. The line-up comprised Paul Barrere (lead guitar), Bill Payne (keyboards), Fred Tackett (guitar), Kenny Gradney (bass), Richie Hayward (drums) and Sam Clayton (percussion).

The group broke up in 1973, but Lowell was persuaded by Warner Bros to re-form it the following year. They recorded 'Feats Don't Fail Me Now' with Bonnie Raitt, Emmylou Harris and Van Dyke Parks.

The band continued recording and began to tour extensively, until they broke up again in 1979, with George going solo. Two months after the split, George was found dead following a heart attack, allegedly caused by drug abuse. A benefit concert in his memory was held in California, with the remaining members of Little Feat joined by **Jackson Browne**, Emmylou Harris, Bonnie Raitt and Linda Ronstadt. It raised $230,000 for Lowell's widow.

115

Payne, Hayward, Barrere, Gradney and Clayton still record and perform as Little Feat, with various musicians joining them from time to time; they are now managed by Peter Asher. The members also pursue parallel careers as solo artists and session musicians.

LLOYD COLE & THE COMMOTIONS

This group was formed in 1984, the members being Lloyd Cole (vocals and guitar}, Neil Clark (guitar), Lawrence Donegan (bass}, Blair Cowan (keyboards) and Steven Irvine (drums).

Their debut single, 'Perfect Skin', entered the UK chart and they followed this with 'Forest Fire', 'Rattlesnakes', 'Brand New Friend', 'Lost Weekend', 'Cut Me Down', 'My Bag', 'Jennifer She Said' and 'From The Hip'. Their chart albums included *Rattlesnakes* and *Easy Pieces*.

Cowan left the band in 1987 and the group split up two years later, with Cole basing himself in New York from 1990. After the split, all the Commotions except Cowan returned to session work.

Cowan also went to New York, where he joined Cole, who continued a schedule of album releases, the most recent being *Love Story* in 1994.

LOGGINS & MESSINA

Born in Maywood, California, on 5 December 1947, Jim Messina was a member of various groups, including **Buffalo Springfield** and Poco. Kenny Loggins, born in Everett, Washington, on 7 January 1948, had toured with the Electric Prunes. The two singer-guitarists teamed up for the first time in 1971, when they recorded *Kenny Loggins With Jim Messina Sittin' In*. Their hit singles as a duo included 'Your Mama Don't Dance', 'Thinking Of You' and 'My Music'.

After the duo split in 1977, Jim Messina reached the US album list with *Oasis* and 1981's *Messina*. He then rejoined Poco in 1989.

However, of the two, Kenny Loggins has amassed the most commercial acclaim, getting off the runway with the million-selling 'Footloose' – a movie theme – in 1984. His other hit singles include: 'Whenever I Call You Friend', 'This Is it', 'Keep The Fire', 'I'm Alright', 'Heart To Heart', 'Welcome To Heartlight' and 'I'm Free (Heaven Helps The Man)'. He also had a chart hit with Steve Perry that was called 'Don't Fight It'.

Loggins & Messina reunited in 1992 for a series of benefit appearances.

LOPEZ, Trini Singer Trini Lopez was born in Dallas, Texas, on 15 May, 1937.

His most successful recording period was the 1960s, which saw him celebrate his biggest international hit with 'If I Had A Hammer'. Other chart entries included 'Kansas City', 'I'm Coming Home Cindy' and 'Gonna Get Along Without Ya Now'. His chart albums included *Trini Lopez at PJ's* and *Trini Lopez In London*.

Lopez shared the bill with the Beatles at the Olympia, Paris, but was mainly a cabaret artist and has continued to perform on the international cabaret circuit for decades. In 1981 he returned to the chart with a minor hit, *Trini Hits*.

New records from Trini Lopez are less frequent than his seasons in the supper clubs of Las Vegas.

LOVE This group was originally formed in Los Angeles as the Grass Roots with members Arthur Lee, Bryan McLean, John Echols, Johnny Fleckenstein and Don Conka. The same year they had to change their name because there was another LA band called the Grass Roots and they became Love, sans Conka and Fleckenstein, who were replaced by Ken Forssi and Alban 'Snoopy' Pfisterer.

Love became the first rock band to sign with Elektra Records and they had some minor hit singles and albums, the most memorable being the 1967 album release *Forever Changes*.

Lee changed the personnel of the band in 1968 and also in 1970, when they comprised Frank Fayad (bass), George Suranovich (drums) and Gary Rowles and Nooney Rickett (guitar). He was to form yet another version of the band in 1974 with Melvan Whittington and John Sterling (guitar), Joe Blocker (drums) and Sherwood Akuna and Robert Rozelle (bass). The group disbanded soon afterwards. Lee was persuaded to re-form it in 1977, but the band failed to release any records. Lee and McLean appeared on various Love reunions throughout the 1980s.

Lee released his *Arthur Lee* album in 1981, and another solo album, *Arthur Lee And Love*, in 1992, while Rhino Records issued a double-disc anthology, *Love Story*, in 1995. In 1996 Lee was sentenced to 12 years on a firearms charge and is in prison California. Don Conka died in the 1970s.

LOVE AFFAIR This group was originally formed in 1966 with members Steve Ellis (vocals), Morgan Fisher (keyboards), Rex Brayley (guitar),

Mick Jackson (bass) and Maurice Bacon (drums). In 1976 Ellis, backed by session musicians, recorded 'Everlasting Love', which topped the UK chart.

Other hits followed – 'Rainbow Valley', 'A Day Without Love', 'One Road' and 'Bringing Back The Good Times' – before Ellis left to form his own band. Fisher joined **Mott The Hoople**, while Bacon became a music publisher.

The Love Affair name was kept alive over the years by various formations appearing on the cabaret circuit, led by Martin Lyon. Original member Maurice Bacon managed this outfit. Then Steve Ellis appeared with his own version of Love Affair. A dispute began, which was eventually resolved when it was agreed in 1997 that both parties could retain the name. Lyon's group continues under the title Love Affair, while Ellis parties on with Steve Ellis' Love Affair.

LOVE, Courtney This controversial American singer was born Love Michelle Harrison in San Francisco on 9 July 1965. Her parents separated when she was a year old and her mother renamed her Courtney. She was reputed to have taken LSD when only four years old, and following an arrest for theft she was incarcerated in a number of reform schools. She became a stripper for a time, then visited Liverpool and mixed with several of the Mersey groups, before returning to the US where she continued to perform as a stripper.

Courtney formed her first band in 1989 and also married a transvestite musician, James Moreland. With her band Hole, she became known as a 'Queen Of Grunge' and had a UK chart entry in 1991 with 'Pretty On The Inside'.

In 1991 she married **Kurt Cobain** and gave birth to a baby girl, Frances Bean Cobain. Her husband committed suicide in 1994. That same year, Hole's album *Live Through This* became a big chart hit and the group was also to enjoy singles hits with numbers such as 'Doll Parts' and 'Violet'.

Courtney began 1995 by being arrested for offensive behaviour on an internal Australian flight and a few months later was charged with assaulting Kathleen Hanna, singer with Bikini Kill, and was given a one-year suspended sentence. Allegedly, Courtney also had an affair with Trent Reznor, the female lead singer of Nine Inch Nails.

She appeared in minor roles in movies such as *Straight To Hell* and *Sid And Nancy*, before receiving more substantial parts, appearing with Keanu Reeves in *Feeling Minnesota* in 1996. She then appeared as a heroin-addicted stripper in *The People vs Larry Flint*, which won her a Best Actress nomination in the 1997 Golden Globe Awards.

Courtney's new friend, actress Sharon Stone, helped her transform herself from grunge queen into glamour puss and taught her how to dress and present herself. She attended the Golden Globe Awards wearing £2,500 worth of diamonds and a Valentino dress, and then turned up at the Academy Awards in a Versace gown. Donatello Versace then chose her to star in her spring and summer advertising campaign, and leading fashion photographer Richard Avedon featured her in a series of classy photographs.

Despite the reinvention of Courtney, as she escaped from her hellraiser image other problems arose. The controversial documentary producer Nick Broomfield produced an unflattering film about the singer that was due to be shown at the Sundance Festival in the US. Love's lawyers forced the organizers to omit it from the showcase, although it was shown at another festival, Slamdunk, and the BBC also scheduled a screening in the UK in 1998.

That year saw the publication of a lurid biography of Courtney Love by horror writer Poppy Z. Brite, and on the recording front Hole's third album was due to be issued in 1998.

LOVIN' SPOONFUL This American group was formed in 1965 with John Sebastian (vocals, guitar and harmonica), Zal Yanovsky (guitar and vocals), Steve Boone (bass and vocals) and Joe Butler (drums and vocals). They began a residency at the Night Owl in Greenwich Village and their first single, 'Do You Believe In Magic', also issued that year, entered the Top 10 – their album of that name also charted. They had nine further hits, including: 'You Didn't Have To Be So Nice', 'Daydream', 'Did You Ever Have To Make Up Your Mind?', 'Summer In The City', 'Rain On The Roof' and 'Nashville Cats'.

Yanovsky left the group in 1967 following a dispute. It was alleged that in order to avoid prosecution following a drugs bust, he incriminated other people. Jerry Yester replaced him.

Sebastian himself left the group the following year to go solo. After numerous releases, he finally topped the US chart in 1976 with 'Welcome Back', the theme tune from the television series *Welcome Back Kotter*, which starred John Travolta.

In 1980 the four original members of the group reunited for an appearance in the **Paul Simon** film *One Trick Pony*.

The group, minus Sebastian, re-formed in 1991 to appear on the nostalgia circuit, together with Yester's brother, and are still performing.

Sebastian continues to perform in concerts and issued a new album, *I Want My Room*, in 1996. Yankovsky retired from the music scene to open a restaurant called Chez Piggies, but now also acts as a record producer.

LULU Born Marie McLaughlin Lawrie on 3 November 1948 in Lennoxtown, Scotland, at the age of 15 this young Scot was singing with a band called the Gleneagles when Marion Massey signed her to a management deal and changed the group's name to Lulu & the Luvvers.

They entered the Top 10 with their debut record, 'Shout', and other hits followed – 'Here Comes the Night', 'Leave A Little Love' and 'Try To Understand'.

Lulu went solo in 1966 and appeared in the movie *To Sir With Love*, recording the title song which topped the US chart, although it wasn't issued in the UK.

Her other hits included: 'The Boat That I Row', 'Let's Pretend', 'Love Loves To Love Love', 'Me The Peaceful Heart', 'Boy', 'I'm A Tiger', 'Boom Bang-A-Bang', 'Oh Me Oh My (I'm A Fool For You Baby)', 'The Man Who Sold The World', 'Take Your Mama For A Ride' and 'I Could Never Miss You (More Than I Do)'. In 1986 she charted with another version of 'Shout', causing Decca to re-release the original Lulu & the

Luvvers version – and the combined sales placed her in the Top 10.

Lulu's Eurovision Song Contest appearance in 1969 resulted in a win for her with 'Boom-Bang-A-Bang', but she shared joint first place with the entries for France, Spain and the Netherlands. She had her own UK television series and David Bowie produced her when she recorded his 'The Man Who Sold The World'.

In her personal life, Lulu married Maurice Gibb of the **Bee Gees** in April 1969, but they separated in 1973 and she married hairdresser John Frieda in 1976. They were also to split up.

In 1993 Barry Gibb produced Lulu's album *Independence*, and the title track from it was issued as a single and reached No 1 in the chart. A second single from the album was 'I'm Back For More'. She then recorded 'Relight My Fire' with Take That, which also topped the chart. She continued to have hits with 'How 'Bout Us', 'Goodbye Baby and Amen' and 'Every Woman Knows'.

Lulu

LYNCH, Kenny This popular British entertainer, the youngest in a family of 13, was born in Stepney, east London, on 18 March 1939. A singer, comedian, actor and television personality, he made his singing debut in a nightclub at the age of 12. By 1955 he was singing with the Ed Nichol Band. He was also an apprentice tailor and boiler insulator, before entering his national service in 1957.

Lynch made his chart recording debut in 1960 with 'Mountain Of Love'. His streak of hits, which lasted until 1965, included: 'Puff', 'Up On The Roof', 'You Can Never Stop Me Loving You', 'Stand By Me', 'What Am I To Do' and 'I'll Stay By You'. He was the first artist, apart from the Beatles, to record a Lennon/McCartney number, but 'Misery' failed to produce a chart entry for him.

As a songwriter, Lynch penned numbers for various artists including Cilla Black, the **Small Faces**, **Elkie Brooks** and **Mike Sarne**. He appeared in the films *Just For Fun* and *Dr Terror's House Of Horrors*, and in the television series *Room At The Bottom* and *Curry And Chips*.

He has continued to record over a 30-year period for various record labels and actually returned to the chart in 1983 with 'Half The Day's Gone And We Haven't Earned A Penny'.

Lynch, who was awarded an OBE, currently lives in Henley-on-Thames, Oxfordshire. George Harrison is a neighbour.

In 1996 he had just completed a tour with Jimmy Tarbuck and a season in Blackpool. He then recorded a jazz album, *After Dark*, and formed a new band called Stash, with former members of Bad Company. Recently, he has also been recording with a children's choir using material based around a children's concept called the Bunniboos. In 1998 he continues to make appearances with Jimmy Tarbuck.

LYNN, Vera This legendary British singer, known as the 'Forces Sweetheart', celebrated her eightieth birthday in March 1997 with Princess Margaret and Margaret Thatcher among her guests.

Born in London on 20 March 1917, Vera was the most popular singer in the UK during World War II and proved to be an inspiration to the armed forces with her performances of songs such as 'The White Cliffs Of Dover' and 'We'll Meet Again'. Obviously, since no charts existed at the time, such records are not to be found in any listing.

When the charts were first established in the UK, Vera's hits began to appear, and between then and 1957 they included: 'Homing Waltz', 'Auf Wiedersehen', 'Forget Me Not', 'Windsor Waltz', 'My Son My Son', 'Who Are We', 'A House With Love In It', 'The Faithful Hussar' and 'Travellin' Home'.

Vera Lynn became much more than a singer and is something of a British institution. Pink Floyd wrote 'Vera' in their album and film *The Wall* in honour of her, and she was awarded an OBE and made a Dame of the British Empire.

LYNTON, Jackie This British singer first appeared in the famous 2 Is coffee bar in the 1950s. He was spotted by impresario **Larry Parnes** and signed to his stable of artists.

Lynton did not achieve success, but for many years he compered the Reading Festival and continued performing. Lynton currently appears on the London pub rock scene. In 1997 a 28-track CD of his recordings was released, entitled *Why Not Take All Of Me*.

MADNESS This group was originally formed in 1977 as the Invaders in the midst of the British 'two-tone' movement, a mixture of reggae, ska and pop.

They changed their name to Madness in January 1979 – the members were Suggs (vocals), Mike Barson (keyboards), Chrissie Boy Foreman (guitar), Bedders (bass), Lee Kix Thompson (sax), Woody Woodgate (drums) and Chas Smash (horns). Suggs' real name is Graham McPherson, Bedders is Mark Bedford, Chrissie Boy is Christopher Foreman, Woody is Daniel Woodgate and Chas Smash is Cathal Smyth.

In 1979, following their debut disc, the ska number 'The Prince', which also became their first chart entry, they signed to Stiff Records.

Over the next ten years their chart singles included: 'One Step Beyond', 'My Girl', 'Work Best and Play', 'Baggy Trousers', 'Embarrassment', 'The Return Of The Las Palmas Seven', 'Grey Day', 'Shut Up', 'It Must Be Love', 'Cardiac Arrest', 'House Of Fun', 'Driving In My Car', 'Our House', 'Tomorrow's Just Another Day', 'Wings Of A Dove', 'The Sun and The Rain', 'Michael Caine', 'One Better Day', 'Yesterday's Men', 'Uncle Sam', 'Sweetest Girl', '(Waiting For) The Ghost Train' and 'I Pronounce You'.

In 1981 Madness appeared in the Two-Tone film *Dance Craze* and the movie *Take It Or Leave It*.

Barson left in 1984 and moved to the Netherlands with his Dutch wife, Sandra, and the group split up in 1986.

The following year they re-formed as a quartet, calling themselves the Madness, and signed with Virgin Records.

The members also became involved in various solo projects, and the group re-formed again in 1992 to hold a Madstock! open air concert at Finsbury Park in London, which was filmed. They returned to Finsbury Park for another Madstock! concert in 1994, and Madstock IV took place at the same venue on 7 June 1998. There have also been reunion tours by more or less the original line-up, most recently in 1995.

Suggs, who married singer Bette Bright in 1982, has found success as a solo artist with his album *The Lone Ranger* and the Top 10 hit singles 'I'm Only Sleeping', 'Camden Town', 'The Tune' and 'Cecilia'. In 1997 he became the host of *Night Fever*, a celebrity karaoke television show.

MADONNA This enormously successful singer-songwriter was born Madonna Louise Veronica Ciccone in Bay City, Michigan, on 16 August 1958. As a girl she was interested in dance and took lessons in ballet, jazz and modern dance.

Madonna moved to New York, took dance lessons, spent several months dancing in Paris, and then returned to New York to join a group called the Breakfast Club. She then formed her own band, Emmenon, in 1980, the year she appeared in a low-budget film called *A Certain Sacrifice*.

Her single 'Everybody', released in 1982, was a hit in clubs and 'Holiday' was the beginning of an avalanche of hit singles and albums.

These included singles such as: 'Borderline', 'Lucky Star', 'Like a Virgin', 'Material Girl', 'Crazy For You', 'Into The Groove', 'Dress You Up', 'Gambler', 'True Blue', 'Open Your Heart', 'La Isla Bonita', 'Who's That Girl', 'The Look Of Love', 'Like A Prayer', 'Express Yourself', 'Cherish', 'Oh Father', 'Keep It Together', 'Vogue', 'Hanky Panky', 'Justify My Love', 'Rescue Me', 'This Used To Be My Playground', 'Erotica', 'Deeper and Deeper', 'Bad Girl', 'Fever', 'Rain', 'I'll Remember', 'Secret', 'Take A Bow', 'Bedtime Story', 'Human Nature', 'You'll See', 'One More Chance' and 'Love Don't Live Here Anymore'.

Album hits included: *Madonna*, *Like A Virgin*, *True Blue*, *Who's That Girl*, *You Can Dance*, *Like A Prayer*, *I'm Breathless*, *The Immaculate Collection*, *Bedtime Stories* and *Something To Remember*.

Madonna has also pursued a movie career, appearing in *Desperately Seeking Susan*, *Shanghai Surprise*, *Who's That Girl*, *Dick Tracy* and *A League Of Their Own*. Her biggest screen role was as Eva Perón in the 1997 version of the musical *Evita*, in which she had the opportunity to sing the popular hit 'Don't Cry For Me Argentina'.

Madonna's videos have often been controversial, some of them of a torrid and steamy nature, and a number censored in various countries. She also posed nude for photographs and eventually published an erotic book of photographs of herself called *Sex*. Her film documentary *In Bed With Madonna* also raised eyebrows.

Madonna's tours were sensational and included The Virgin Tour – Madonna Live, and Blonde Ambition World Tour '90.

In her personal life, she was married for a time to actor Sean Penn, but the relationship proved volatile. After the divorce she had many swains, including actor Warren Beatty.

After taking a year out in 1997 for motherhood, looking after her baby Lourdes, she was back in action in 1998.

The March 1998 issue of *Vanity Fair* pictured her on the cover, trailering an interview in which she discussed her daughter, whom she calls Lola. The father is Madonna's former boyfriend, Carlos Leon.

She was a guest on BBC television's *National Lottery Live* on 21 February 1998, performing her new single, 'Frozen'. It was her first live television performance in the UK for 15 years.

During 1998 she agreed to accept a low fee to appear in an independent film directed by Mattia Karel called *Red Door*. During the same year she may also be starring in a film of the hit musical *Chicago*.

In addition, 1998 saw the release of the 39-year-old singer's new album, *Ray Of Light*.

Madonna has a beach house in Coconut Grove, Miami, but lives mostly in Los Angeles.

MANFRED MANN Originally launched in London in 1962 as the Mann-Hugg Blues Brothers, this group changed their name to Manfred Mann the following year. In 1964 the group were asked to write a theme tune for the UK television pop music series *Ready, Steady, Go* – '5-4-3-2-1' gave them their first hit.

The group featured Manfred Mann on keyboards; he was born Michael Lubowitz on 21 October 1940 in Johannesburg, South Africa. The vocalist was Paul Jones, born Paul Pond on 24 February 1942. Guitarist Mike Vickers was born on 18 April 1941, bass player Tom McGuinness on 2 December 1941, and drummer Mike Hugg on 11 August, 1942.

During the 1960s they had 17 hits, including: 'Hubble Bubble Toil And Trouble', 'Do Wah Diddy-Diddy', 'Sha La La', 'Come Tomorrow', 'Oh No Not My Baby', 'If You Gotta Go Go Now', 'Pretty Flamingo', 'You Gave Me Somebody To Love', 'Just Like A Woman', '

Manfred Mann

Semi-Detached Suburban Mr James', 'Ha Ha Said The Clown', 'Sweet Pea', 'Mighty Quinn', 'My Name Is Jack', 'Fox On The Run' and 'Ragamuffin Man'.

Vickers left in 1965 and was replaced by Jack Bruce. He left the following year to join **Cream**, at the same time as Jones quit to concentrate on a solo career and was replaced by Mike D'Abo. Klaus Voormann also joined on bass.

Jones reached the Top 5 with his first solo release, 'High Time'. His other hits included 'I've Been A Bad Bad Boy', 'Thinkin' Ain't For Me' and 'Aquarius'. He appeared in the film *Privilege* with model Jean Shrimpton and then quit the music scene for more than a decade to concentrate on acting work, mainly in the theatre.

Manfred Mann disbanded in June 1969 and Mann formed Emanon, which didn't last for very long. He then began to compose advertising jungles with Mike Hugg.

McGuinness formed McGuinness Flint with drummer Hughie Flint, guitarists Benny Gallagher and Graham Lyle, and Dennis Coulson on keyboards, while Mann and Hugg formed Manfred Mann Chapter Three, but disbanded it after a few months.

McGuinness Flint had big hits with 'When I'm Dead And Gone' and 'Malt & Barley Blues'. They were to split up in 1975.

In 1972 Manfred Mann formed Manfred Mann's Earth Band with guitarist Mick Rogers, bassist Colin Pattenden and drummer Chris Slade. Their chart hits included: 'Joybringer', 'Blinded By The Light', 'Davy's On The Road Again', 'You Angel You' and 'Don't Kill It Carol'.

Paul Jones and Tom McGuinness reunited in 1979 to form the Blues Band.

Manfred Mann still leads Manfred Mann's Earth Band, working mostly on the Continent. He says he rarely plays in the UK because the overheads of touring are too expensive. His band features original members Chris Slade and Mick Rogers.

Paul Jones, Mike D'Abo, Tom McGuinness, Mike Hugg, Mike Vickers, Benny Gallagher and Rob Townsend (ex-member of **Family**), regrouped as the Manfreds in the late 1980s. They are an on-going in-concert recreation of the protagonists' most familiar moments. Each member, however, pursues other projects within the entertainment industry. D'Abo, for example, is a West Country radio presenter, and Jones and McGuinness are mainstays of the Blues Band.

Manfred Mann records still sell well and at the close of 1996 EMI issued a 26-track CD called *Groovin' With The Manfreds*. The multi-talented Manfreds produce a tremendous concert performance, with 26 numbers from the huge hit repertoire of the various members.

MANILOW, Barry   This American singer was born Barry Allen Pinkus on 17 June 1946 in Brooklyn, New York. His parents separated when he was a child and his late mother, Edna, raised him. He was married at the age of 21, but the marriage lasted less than a year. His first job was in the mailroom at CBS Records, but his big break came in 1972 when Bette Midler had him produce her hit album *The Divine Miss M*. He then went on to top the US chart with 'Mandy' in 1975.

Manilow's other hit singles include: 'It's A Miracle', 'Could It Be Magic', 'I Write the Songs', 'Tryin' To Get The Feeling Again', 'This One's For You', 'Weekend In New England', 'Looks Like We Made It', 'Daybreak', 'Can't Smile Without You', 'Even Now', 'Copacabana (At the Copa)', 'Ready To Take A Chance Again', 'Somewhere In The Night', 'Ships', 'When I Wanted You', 'I Don't Want To Walk Wthout You', 'I Made It Through The Rain', 'The Old Songs', 'Somewhere Down The Road', 'Let's Hang On', 'Oh Julie', 'Memory', 'Some Kind Of Friend' and 'Read 'Em And Weep'.

He has also had numerous hit albums, including: *Even Now, Manilow Magic, One Voice, Barry, Gift Set, If I Should Love Again, Barry Live In Britain, I Wanna Do It With You, A Touch More Magic, 2am Paradise Café* and *Manilow*.

Primarily a ballad singer, Manilow enjoys international success, headlines major tours, has Broadway shows, composes and performs songs for films, and stars in his own television specials, in addition to having won numerous awards.

He penned the stage musical *Copacabana*, which opened in London's West End in June 1994 and was a sell-out hit.

At the age of 51 he began a 12-date UK tour called The New Concert on 13 January 1998. By that time he had been at the top for 20 years, sold over 50 million records and written both film scores and complete musicals.

The UK press gave major coverage to the tour and pointed out that 40 women, known as Maniloonies, paid over £100,000 (taking hotels and all other costs into consideration) between them to attend all his UK concerts.

Barry Manilow currently lives in Los Angeles with his long-time partner Linda Allen, a production designer. His new musical, *Harmony*, opened on Broadway late in 1998.

MARCELS, The Formed in Pittsburgh in 1961, this vocal quintet took their name from a local hairstyle. They were a multi-racial group comprising Cornelius Harp (lead vocal and guitar), Ronald Mundy (first tenor vocal), Gene Bricker (second tenor vocal), Dick Knauss (baritone vocal) and Fred Johnson (bass vocal).

The Marcels had two major hits, their US chart-topper 'Blue Moon' and 'Heartache'. In the UK their hits were 'Blue Moon' and 'Summertime'.

Bricker and Knauss, the two white vocalists, left the group following their recordings of the latter two numbers. Walt Maddox and Allen Johnson, Fred's brother, replaced them.

Their final US chart entry was 'My Melancholy Baby', after which Mundy and Harp left.

The five original members of the group reunited on several occasions during the 1970s for revival shows and have remained together on the nostalgia circuit in the US.

A compilation, *The Best Of The Marcels*, was released in 1990.

Allen Johnson died in 1995.

MARMALADE This Glasgow group began life as Dean Ford & the Gaylords in 1961. They moved to London in 1967 and changed their name to Marmalade. The members then were Dean Ford and Willie 'Junior' Campbell (vocals), Graham Knight (bass), Pat Fairley (rhythm) and Alan Whitehead (drums).

They had a string of hit singles between 1968 and 1976. Following their chart entry with their debut disc, 'Lovin' Things', they topped the chart with their version of the Lennon/McCartney number 'Ob-La-Di Ob-La-Da'.

Their other hits included: 'Wait For Me Marianne', 'Baby Make It Soon, 'Reflections Of My Life', 'Rainbow', 'My Little One', 'Cousin Norman', 'Back On The Road', 'Radancer' and 'Falling Apart At The Seams'.

Campbell, who was the groups' main songwriter and producer, left in 1971 to study at the Royal College Of Music. Hugh Nicholson replaced him.

There were various other personnel changes over the years, and Graham Knight and Sandy

Newman are mainstays of the present-day Marmalade who are fixtures on Europe's sixties nostalgia circuit, sometimes backing Dave Dee.

In 1997, Glen Taylor replaced Charlie Smith, who had been their drummer for a number of years.

Dean Ford and Pat Fairley both live in Los Angeles. Ford drives executive limousines and Fairley is mine host of a bar called Scotland Yard. Alan Whitehead runs Secrets, a London nightclub.

Junior Campbell is currently writing the music for a new series of *Thomas The Tank Engine*, the television adaptation of a series of children's books.

MARTELL, Lena This middle-of-the road performer had released no less than 13 albums by 1979, when her version of the Kris Kristofferson song 'One Day At A Time' spent three weeks at No 1 – her sole entry in the UK singles chart. An ill-advised crack at 'Don't Cry For Me Argentina' and the title track of *Beautiful Sunday*, issued in 1980, were among subsequent misses, but her album still hovered around the middle of the Top 50.

Lena Martell retired from singing in the late 1980s.

MATCHBOX This group was founded in 1971 by bass guitarist Fred Poke. The other members were Wiffle Smith (vocals), Rusty Lipton (piano), Steve Bloomfield (guitar) and Bob Burgos (drums).

During the 1970s they were beset by problems with the different record companies they signed to and there were various personnel changes.

By the time Matchbox had their first hit, a number penned by Bloomfield called 'Rockabilly Rebel', Smith and Lipton had left. Gordon Waters, Jimmy Redhead and vocalist Graham Fenton joined them.

Their other hits were: 'Buzz Buzz a Diddle It', 'Midnite Dynamos', 'When You Ask About Love', 'Over the Rainbow/You Belong To Me', 'Babes In The Wood', 'Love's Made A Fool Of You' and 'One More Saturday Night'.

Known as Major Matchbox in certain overseas territories, the group has used the pseudonym Cyclone on a late 1980s A-side, a revival of **Freddie Cannon's** 'Palisades Park'. Steve Bloomfield also started a parallel solo career with an eponymous album.

MAYALL, John   John Mayall was born in Manchester on 29 November 1933 and first launched a band called the Powerhouse Four there in 1955. The other members were John McVie (bass), Bernie Watson (guitar) and Keith Robertson (drums). They changed their name to the Blues Syndicate and moved to London in 1961, where they teamed up with **Alexis Korner** in the Bluesbreakers, the first of many bands Mayall was to feature using this name.

1964 saw his debut album, *Mayall Plays Mayall*, with McVie, Roger Dean on guitar and Hughie Flint on drums. Eric Clapton joined and was included on their album *The Bluesbreakers*, but by 1966 Clapton had left to form **Cream** with former Mayall bassist Jack Bruce.

Blues Alone in 1966 featured Mayall overdubbing on several instruments, with only drummer Keef Hartley to accompany him.

Other albums, including *A Hard Road*, *Crusade*, *Bare Wires* and the live LPs *Diary Of A Band Vol I* and *Vol 2*, followed.

During the 1960s an incredible array of leading musicians passed through the Bluesbreakers including Peter Green, Mick Fleetwood, Aynsley Dunbar, Andy Fraser and Mick Taylor.

Mayall ended the Bluesbreakers in 1969 and moved to Los Angeles for a short time, returning to cut the album *Blues From Laurel Canyon*. He then cut an album, *Turning Point*, without using a drum sound.

He next moved to California and continued recording albums which were a fusion of jazz and blues.

Still based in Los Angeles, where he has lived for 25 years, John Mayall issued a new album, *Spinning Coin*, in 1995, and was in London for its promotion and the wedding of his son Gaz. He also released a new album in 1998, entitled *Blues For The Lost Days*.

MAYFIELD, Curtis   This multi-talented soul artist was born in Chicago on 3 June 1942. A singer, songwriter, producer and guitarist, Curtis Mayfield began his career with his own band at college, the Alphatones. He joined the Roosters in 1957. The group changed its name to the Impressions and hit the chart with 'Gypsy Woman' and 'It's All Right'. Several other hits followed, and Mayfield was also penning songs for artists such as Gene Chandler and Major Lance.

He left the Impressions in 1970 and his debut solo album was the eponymous *Curtis*. He hit the singles chart in the UK with 'Move On Up'.

Mayfield's 1972 album for the film *Superfly* went platinum and resulted in two million-selling singles, 'Superfly' and 'Freddie's Dead'.

In the 1980s he changed his style to R&B and continued writing for other artists. In August 1990, during a concert in Brooklyn, a lighting rig fell on him, paralysing him from the neck down. Unable to sing, he continued running his own record label, Conquest. Recovery has been slow, but he released *New World Order*, his first album since the accident, in 1996. The same year saw the release of a three-CD boxed set, *People Get Ready! The Curtis Mayfield Story*.

McGOWAN, Cathy   Dubbed 'Queen Of The Mods' for her appearances on the UK television pop music series *Ready, Steady, Go!*, with her fringed hair, mini-skirts and high profile of interviewing the top pop stars of the day, Cathy McGowan soon became a role model for teenage girls nationwide.

When the television company Rediffusion merged with ABC in 1968, the series was taken off the air. Cathy then enjoyed success in a business producing clothes for teenagers.

She married film actor Hywel Bennett and the couple had a daughter, although they separated in 1975.

In the late 1980s, Cathy surfaced from motherhood in Twickenham, Middlesex, to present an afternoon television chat show.

McGUIRE, Barry   Singer-songwriter Barry McGuire was born in Oklahoma City on 15 October 1935. He started his career singing in coffee houses, made his professional debut in a Beverly Hills club and his television debut in *Route 66*, and formed a duo, Barry & Barry, with singer Barry Kane. He was also a member of the New Christy Minstrels, who were formed in 1961, and he co-wrote their hit 'Green Green'.

McGuire left the Minstrels in 1964 to become a solo singer and discovered a protest song called 'Eve Of Destruction' penned by 19-year-old P.F. Sloan, which he recorded. It topped the US chart in 1965, reached No 3 in the UK and sold over two million copies. It was his only chart hit.

In the mid-1970s McGuire became evangelically Christian, as evidenced by his religious *Seeds* and *Lighten Up* albums, as well as a guest appearance on *Come Together*, described as 'a musical experience in love', which was an album featuring various artists of the same persuasion, including **Pat Boone**. In 1998 Barry McGuire toured the UK from January to March as a member of the Mamas & Papas, along with Scott McKenzie and two female singers.

McKELLAR, Kenneth This singer's one UK singles hit was 'A Man Without Love' in 1966.

Although McKellar is all but retired, the issue of *The Very Best Of Kenneth McKellar*, a CD collection, was considered a worthwhile market exercise in 1996.

McKENZIE, Scott Scott McKenzie was born in Alexandria, Virginia, on 1 October 1944 and had previously been a member of the Journeymen, a folk group in which John Phillips also performed. It was Phillips who wrote 'San Francisco (Be Sure To Wear Flowers In Your Hair)', which gave McKenzie a UK chart-topper in 1967. The number also reached the US Top 5 and was No 1 in several countries, including Germany, Belgium and Denmark. Phillips also produced the disc and played guitar on it, with his wife Michelle playing bells.

McKenzie's only other hit was 'Like An Old Time Movie'. Currently he is a member of the present-day Mamas & Papas, who began a UK tour early in 1998.

McLEAN, Don This singer-songwriter was born in New Rochelle, New York, on 2 October 1945.

His self-penned 'American Pie', from his album of the same name, was released in 1971 and topped the US chart at the beginning of the following year. His next single, 'Vincent', based on the life of painter Vincent Van Gogh, was also a major hit that year, along with another album, *Tapestry*. McLean himself became the subject of a song, 'Killing Me Softly With His Song', which was recorded by Roberta Flack.

His version of **Buddy Holly's** 'Everyday' also charted. Other singles hits included 'Crying' and 'Castles In The Air'.

In the late 1980s McLean married and now lives in Maine with his wife and two children.

In recent years he has moved towards the C&W market. However, in 1991 his 'American Pie' managed an unexpected return to the UK Top 20.

Don McLean's latest album, *River Of Love*, was issued in 1995 and he is currently writing his autobiography.

McTELL, Ralph This British folk singer was born Ralph May on 3 December 1944. He changed his surname to that of his inspiration, Blind Willie McTell.

His only two entries in the singles chart were 'Streets Of London' and 'Dreams Of You'.

As well as working as a folk music presenter on radio, Ralph McTell was still filling European theatres as well as folk clubs in 1997 when *Streets Of London*, his official biography by Chris Rockenhull, was published. He also plans an autobiography of his early years.

MEDICINE HEAD This duo, comprising John Fiddler (vocals, guitar, keyboards and bass drum) and Peter Hope-Evans (harmonica and Jew's harp), was formed in Stafford in 1968. The two friends from art college had begun by playing at parties and their career took a new path when they met up with disc jockey John Peel, who became their champion. Former Yardbird Keith Relf produced their album *Heavy On The Drum* in 1971 and joined them for a brief time. Their hit singles included: '(And The) Pictures In The Sky', 'One One One Is One', 'Rising Sun' and 'Slip And Slide'.

For a time Roger Saunders augmented them on guitar, Rob Townsend on drums and George Ford on bass, but in 1976 they reverted to a duo and signed with Chas Chandler's record label, Barn. However, the punk explosion had begun and they disbanded later in the year.

Fiddler teamed up with some former members of **Mott The Hoople** to form the British Lions, but by the early 1980s had joined A Box Of Frogs, which mainly comprised ex-members of the Yardbirds. He then participated in an ill-fated musical with former Thin Lizzy guitarist Scott Gorman. In 1990 Fiddler turned solo and returned to the concert stage, also recording a critically acclaimed album, *Return Of The Buffalo*, released in 1995. During his solo career, Hope-Evans performed on two Pete Townshend albums, *Empty Glass* and *White City*. He is currently a journalist specializing in the paranormal, corresponds for *The Fortean Times* and teaches adult literary classes in London.

MELANIE This singer-songwriter was born in New York on 3 February 1948. She spent her teen years in New Jersey and was impressed by the folk movement scene, although her first professional performances were as an actress in summer stock productions.

As a singer, Melanie signed with Columbia in 1967 and made her debut with 'Beautiful People', which was not a success.

She began recording for Buddah Records in 1969 and had a hit with 'What Have They Done To The Rain', followed by 'Lay Down' and 'Peace Will Come'. Some bestselling albums followed – *Candles In The Rain*, *Leftover Wine* and *The Good Book*.

By this time Melanie was touring and appearing on television shows.

Her next move was to Neighbourhood Records, who issued 'Brand New Key', which topped the chart, and an album, *Gather Me*, which went gold. Buddah were also successful releasing Melanie product at this time with the albums *Garden In The City* and *Four Sides Of Melanie*, plus the single 'Nickel Song'.

Other chart entries in 1972 included 'Ring The Living Bell', 'Together Alone' and the LP *Stoneground Words*. The following year, *Melanie Live At Carnegie Hall* entered the chart.

She continued issuing albums until 1977, then ceased recording for five years, although she carried on with her live performances.

A new album, *Arabesque*, was issued in 1983 and more releases followed, although they did not sell in the quantities of her early record successes. In 1989 she composed the music to the *Beauty & The Beast* television series.

During the early 1990s she issued the albums *Precious Cargo* (1991), *Freedom Knows My Name* (1993) and *Silver* (1994).

These days, the release of new Melanie records is sporadic at best, and her stage performances are restricted mainly to fundraising concerts.

MERSEYBEATS This Liverpool band were originally called the Mavericks. They approached Bill Harry, copyright holder of the name Mersey Beat, for permission to call themselves the Mersey Beats.

The Mavericks had formed in 1960, although members Dave Elias and Billy Butler were to leave the band before the name change. Former insurance clerk Tony Crane was lead guitarist and former shipping clerk Billy Kinsley the bass guitarist. Aaron Williams joined them on rhythm guitar and John Banks joined them on drums.

The Merseybeats

The band later truncated their name to Merseybeats and had a number of hit singles, including: 'It's Love That Really Counts', 'I Think Of You', 'Don't Turn Around', 'Wishin' And Hopin'', 'Last Night', 'I Love You', 'Yes I Do' and 'I Stand Around'.

At one point Kinsley left, to be replaced by Johnny Gustafson. The group then disbanded in 1996. Crane and Kinsley teamed up as the Merseys and enjoyed one hit – 'Sorrow'. They then split up; Crane re-formed the Merseybeats and has led the group since.

Kinsley rejoined the band in the 1990s and the line-up is currently a five-piece, the other members being Bob Packham (bass guitar and sax), Alan Cosgrove (drums and trumpet) and Dave Goldberg (keyboards and guitar).

In 1995 and 1996, the readers of *The Beat Goes On* magazine voted them the Best Sixties Act.

MIDDLE OF THE ROAD The original members of this Scottish quartet were Sally Carr, Ian Lewis, Eric Lewis and Ken Andrew. Initially performing Latin-American style music under the name Los Caracas, they changed their name to Middle Of The Road after hearing a song in Italy, which they then recorded. This was 'Chirpy Chirpy Cheep Cheep', and it became a major summer hit throughout Europe and also a chart-topper in the UK and several other countries.

They followed with 'Tweedle Dee Tweedle Dum', 'Soley Soley', 'Sacramento' and 'Samson & Delilah'. The group were to disband, but after years in ordinary jobs back in their native Scotland, Sally Carr and Ken Andrew decided to re-form Middle Of The Road especially for a television show in Germany in 1991. They were immediately booked for a German tour, then a Dutch television show, and soon found themselves in demand throughout Europe, 25 years after the group was originally formed.

In 1997 they issued a CD, *Middle Of The Road*, containing newly recorded, newly arranged versions of their hits, and they intend to record fresh material in the future.

MINNELLI, Liza The daughter of legendary singer Judy Garland and movie producer Vincente Minnelli, Liza was born in 1946. She seemed to have inherited her mother's talent and appeared set for a brilliant future when she won the Best Actress Oscar for her role as Sally Bowles in *Cabaret*. Sadly, her career and personal life became as troubled as her mother's had been.

Three of Liza's marriages failed and she remained childless. She married Australian Peter Allen in 1967, but the couple parted three years later and he died from an AIDS-related illness in 1991. Her second marriage, to Jack Haley Jnr, lasted five years and they divorced in 1979. Her third marriage, to Mark Gero, also ended in divorce in 1992.

Things started going downhill when the critics savaged her Broadway appearance in 1984. Her show folded and she entered the Betty Ford Clinic for alcohol and drugs dependency. She did not appear on Broadway again until 13 years later, when she deputized for Julie Andrews, who was on holiday, in *Victor/Victoria*, but was accused of fumbling her lines. The 50-year-old singer received another pummelling from the critics.

In 1995 Liza had begun to suffer from degenerative arthritis and was in constant pain, and she then underwent a hip replacement operation.

Liza Minnelli was due to appear in a series of concerts in the UK in June 1998, but she cancelled them at the last minute due to ill health.

MINOGUE, Kylie This petite singer was born in Melbourne, Australia, on 28 May 1968. She made her acting debut in the Australian soap opera *The Sullivans* when she was only ten years old, followed by appearances in *Skyways* and *The Hendersons*.

Kylie first came to fame as Charlene in another soap, *Neighbours*. She made her recording debut with 'The Locomotion', which topped the Australian chart, and was then invited to England by producer Peter Waterman to record 'I Should Be So Lucky', which notched up two million sales and topped the UK chart in 1987. Her debut album became the most successful by a female solo act in UK chart history. Other hits included 'Got To Be Certain' and 'Je Ne Sais Pas Pourquoi'.

Kylie had a well-publicized affair with **Michael Hutchence**, but in 1997, at the age of 30, her beau was French fashion photographer Stephane Sednaoui, although their romance came to an end in October of that year.

The girl who was once known as the 'Singing Budgie' had a new album entitled *Impossible Princess*, due for release in September 1997, but due to the death of Diana, Princess of Wales, the title was hastily changed to *Kylie Minogue*. When a single from the album did not achieve major sales, the album release was postponed until January 1998.

Kylie's image began to change over the years, from the clean-cut little soap star appealing to the pre-teens to a sexy singer who wore erotic costumes, posed for raunchy publicity stills and had a breast enhancement.

Kylie had begun to gain credibility when Nick Cave invited her to sing a duet on his *Murder Ballads* album, and the Manic Street Preachers wrote two songs specially for her *Kylie Minogue* album.

In the meantime she began filming a drama for UK television, *The Misfit*, screened in November 1997, in which she played a young male castrati choirboy.

MITCHELL, Guy   Guy Mitchell was born Al Cernik in Detroit, Michigan, on 27 February 1927. At one time he sang with the Carmen Cavallero Band and he began recording in the early 1950s. His first hit was 'Feet Up' in 1952. For the rest of the decade he had a series of hits, several of which charted more than once.

These included: 'She Wears Red Feathers', 'Pretty Little Black Eyed Susie', 'Look At That Girl', 'Chicka Boom', 'Cloud Lucky Seven', 'Cuff Of My Shirt', 'Sippin' Soda', 'Dime And A Dollar', 'Singing The Blues', 'Knee Deep In The Blues', 'Rock-A-Billy', 'In The Middle Of A Dark Dark Night', 'Call Rosie On The Phone' and 'Heartaches By The Number'.

'She Wears Red Feathers', 'Look At That Girl', Singing The Blues' and 'In The Middle Of A Dark Dark Night' topped the US chart.

In addition to having his own television series, Mitchell appeared in several movies, including *Those Redheads From Seattle* and *Red Garters*.

Guy Mitchell still appears in concert throughout the world and regularly appears in the UK. He had an acting role in Johnny Byrne's television drama *Your Cheatin' Heart* in 1990 and continues to have a very active British fan club.

MITCHELL, Joni   This American folk singer was born Roberta Joan Anderson on 7 November 1943 in Fort McLeod, Alberta, Canada. Appearing on the Toronto folk scene, she became pregnant, then had the baby adopted and has never seen her since. She married folk singer Chuck Mitchell in 1965 and they worked as a duo, moved to Detroit and then parted company.

Joni then relocated to New York late in 1966 and signed with Reprise, although she was to chop and change between different record companies over the years. Her hit singles were to include: 'You Turn Me On', 'I'm A Radio', 'Help Me', 'Free Man In Paris' and 'Big Yellow Taxi'.

Her biggest recording successes came with her album releases, many of which entered the chart, and include: *Ladies Of The Canyon*, *Blue*, *Court And Spark*, *Miles Of Aisles*, *The Hissing Of Summer Lawns*, *Hejira*, *Don Juan's Reckless Daughter*, *Mingus*, *Shadows And Light*, *Wild Things Run Fast* and *Dog Eat Dog*.

Joni also succeeded as a songwriter, with artists ranging from **Judy Collins** to Matthew's Southern Comfort recording her compositions, which include 'Both Sides Now', 'Chelsea Morning' and 'Woodstock'.

In her personal life, she lived with Graham Nash of **Crosby, Stills & Nash** for some time, before marrying musician Larry Klein in 1982. They were later to separate, but remain good friends.

Joni returned to the Reprise label with her new LP, *Turbulent Indigo*, in 1994, for which she received a Grammy Award for Best Pop Album. She then undertook a brief and low-key promotional tour of Europe.

MOJOS, The   This Liverpool band, formed in 1963, were initially known as the Nomads – they changed their name when they heard of a London band calling themselves the Nomads.

The original group consisted of Stu James (vocals), Adrian Wilkinson (guitar), Keith Karlson (bass) and John Konrad (drums). Terry O'Toole joined as pianist and Nicky Crouch, former member of Faron's Flamingoes, replaced Wilkinson.

The Mojos had three chart hits: 'Everything's Alright', 'Why Not Tonight' and 'Seven Daffodils'. The group then disbanded, but was re-formed by Stu James and Nicky Crouch as Stu James & the Mojos. Lewis Collins on guitar and Aynsley Dunbar on drums joined them. They released 'Coming On To Cry' and 'Wait A Minute', but failed to find success on record and Dunbar left, to be replaced by Stan Bennett, former member of Mersey band the Denims.

Their final release was 'Goodbye Dolly Gray' in 1967 and they disbanded once again.

Stu James became an executive with Chrysalis Music, Nicky Crouch a computer programmer in Liverpool. Terry O'Toole and John Konrad

The Mojos

also returned to Merseyside for jobs outside the music business. Adrian Wilkinson launched a building firm, Aynsley Dunbar went on to become a major drum star with bands such as the Mothers Of Invention, Jefferson Starship and Journey, while Lewis Collins found fame as an actor and is particularly known for his role as Bodie in the UK television series *The Professionals*.

Keith Karlson, who had lived in the US for some time, returned to Liverpool and re-formed a group which he called the Mojos, who made their debut at the 1994 Mersey Beatle Convention in Liverpool. It was to be a short-lived venture and Karlson joined another Mersey band, the Black Knights, in 1966. In 1997, since Karlson was now in the band, the Black Knights decided to change their name to the Mojos. They made their debut as the Mojos at the Albion Hotel, New Brighton, for the Mersey Cats, a rock 'n' roll charity comprising a number of original Mersey groups from the 1960s who devote themselves to raising funds for local children's causes.

MONEY, Zoot This vocalist-organist was born George Bruno in Bournemouth, Dorset, on 17 July 1942. He played with Blues Incorporated before forming his Big Roll Band in 1964. They were resident at the Flamingo and became a popular draw at various other London clubs.

Apart from Zoot, the other members were Andy Somers (guitar), Nick Newall (tenor sax), Johnny Almond (baritone sax) and Colin Allen (drums).

They released a number of singles: 'Uncle Willie', 'Bring It Home To Me', 'Please Stay', 'Something Is Worrying', 'Many Faces Of Love', 'Let's Run For Cover', 'Big Time Operator', 'Star Of The Show' and 'Nick Nack', but without success.

Zoot disbanded the group in 1967 and briefly joined Eric Burdon & the New Animals. He then formed a new band, Dantalion's Chariot, who released one single, 'Madman Running Through The Fields'. Zoot joined Ellis, with former **Love Affair** singer Steve Ellis, for a time and also appeared with Grimms.

Zoot Money has been a central figure in Blues Reunion packages of British musicians at large in the UK and Europe from the late 1980s. He is also an accomplished actor who has been sighted in bit parts on the cinema screen, in Shakespeare plays on stage, and in the soap opera *EastEnders* and various television sitcoms and commercials.

MONKEES, The This band was 'manufactured' by corporate Americans as their answer to the Beatles. Bob Rafelson and Bert Schneider decided to create a television sitcom to match the Beatles' movie *A Hard Day's Night* and interviewed 437 actors.

They chose Mancunian Davy Jones (guitar and vocals) and three Americans: Mike Nesmith (guitar and vocals), Pete Tork (vocals, keyboards and bass) and Mickie Dolenz (vocals and drums).

As the Monkees, they recorded 58 episodes of their television series, their nine albums sold 16 million copies and their 14 singles sold seven and a half million. These included three No 1 hits: 'I'm A Believer', 'Daydream Believer' and 'Last Train To Clarksville'. The original group lasted 39 months.

Peter Tork left and the Monkees recorded a television special in 1969.

Davy, Mike and Mickie continued as a trio for a time, then disbanded, to re-form occasionally many years later for several reunion tours, including one of the UK in 1989.

In the summer of 1996, all four reunited for the first time since 1968 to record a new album, *Justus*. In 1997 they began a nine-date tour of the UK, culminating in a concert at Wembley Arena on 19 March. This was the first reunion tour in which all four of the original members of the group appeared together.

Nesmith had paid $150,000 to get out of his original Monkees contract and had always refused to join the group when they had re-formed for any appearances and recordings. When he was asked why he had finally come out of retirement to join them, he said: 'I just wanted to.'

Following the original disbandment of the group, Nesmith recorded an album in 1970 with the First National Band. He has recently completed a novel, due to be published in the US by St Martin's Press.

The Monkees are currently set for an anniversary tour, sans Nesmith. He pulled out, claiming he was writing the next movie for the group. Davy Jones commented: 'We made a new album with him, he toured Great Britain with us, then all of a sudden he's not here. Later I hear rumours he's writing a script for our next movie. Oh, really? That's bloody news to me. He's always been this aloof, inaccessible person – the fourth part of the jigsaw puzzle that never quite fits in.'

MONTEZ, Chris This American singer was born Christopher Montanez in Los Angeles on 17 January 1943. He enjoyed an international hit with 'Let's Dance' in 1962, which led him to co-headline a UK tour with Tommy Roe on which the Beatles were a support act. His next hit was 'Some Kinda Fun', but it was to be a further three years before he entered the chart again with 'Call Me'. Other hits included 'The More I See You', 'There Will Never Be Another You' and 'Time After Time'.

However, he will be remembered particularly for 'Let's Dance', which entered the Top 10 once again when it was released in the UK in 1972. It also charted when reissued in 1979.

Chris Montez has been a frequent visitor to Europe during the 1990s, appearing on the bill of various sixties package shows. In 1991 he recorded an album of new material.

MOODY BLUES, The Vocalist Denny Laine (real name Brian Hines), formerly of Denny Laine & the Diplomats, teamed up with Ray Thomas, Mike Pinder, Graeme Edge and Clint Warwick to form this group in Birmingham in 1964. Their debut single was 'Lose Your Money'; their second release, 'Go Now', in 1965, topped the UK chart.

Warwick left the group – and the music business – in 1966, and Rod Clarke replaced him. A few months later the group split up, with Laine embarking on a solo career.

Within a matter of weeks Thomas, Pinder and Edge had re-formed with the addition of John Lodge and Justin Hayward.

1968 was an important year, opening with the release of 'Nights in White Satin', penned by Hayward, plus the album *Days Of Future Passed*. The same year saw the release of a second album, *In Search Of The Lost Chord*, plus the singles 'Voices In The Sky', 'Tuesday Afternoon' and 'Ride My See Saw'.

Over the years, the Moody Blues' albums have included: *To Our Children's Children, A Question Of Balance, Every Good Boy Deserves Favour, Seventh Sojourn, This Is The Moody Blues, Caught Live + 5, Octave, Out Of This World, Long Distance Voyagers, The Present, Voices In The Sky/The Best Of The Moody Blues, The Other Side Of Life, Greatest Hits, Keys Of The Kingdom, Sur La Mer, Live At Red Rocks* and *The Story Of The Moody Blues... Legend Of A Band*.

1994 saw the release of an 80-track boxed set, *Time Traveller*.

Singles hits included: 'Question', 'The Story In Your Eyes', 'Isn't Life Strange', 'I'm Just A Singer (In A Rock 'n' Roll Band)', 'Steppin' In a Slide Zone', 'Driftwood', 'Gemini Dream', 'The Voice', 'Talking Out Of Turn', 'Blue World', 'Sitting At The Wheel', 'Your Wildest Dreams', 'I Know You're Out There Somewhere', 'No More Lies' and 'Say It With Love'.

The classic 'Nights In White Satin' has entered the chart on several different occasions.

Denny Laine appeared on a nationwide UK tour in 1996 and the following year, in partnership with businessman John Ashworth, opened a club called the Rhythm Station, near Manchester.

MOTLEY CRUE This heavy metal band was formed in Los Angeles in 1981 and comprised Vince Neil (vocals), Mick Mars (real name Bob Deal; guitar), Nikki Sixx (real name Frank Carlton Serafino Ferrano; bass) and Tommy Lee (drums).

Their album releases include: *Too Fast For Love*, *Shout At The Devil*, *Theatre Of Pain*, *Girls Girls Girls*, *Dr Feelgood*, *Decade Of Decadence* and *Circus*.

Lee, obviously imbued with animal magnetism, married the beautiful actress Heather Locklear in 1986. They were later divorced and in 1995 he married the television sex symbol Pamela Anderson of *Baywatch* fame.

Lee's life was not without its elements of drama. He was arrested in 1990 for performing a lewd act on stage, and in 1994 was charged with possession of a concealed and loaded weapon, for which he was fined and sentenced to a year's probation. That same year he was arrested on two further occasions: firstly, after an affray in a bar, and then for beating up his live-in girlfriend Bobbie Brown. In 1998, a judge sentenced him to six months in gaol after he had attacked his wife while still on probation for attacking a photographer.

Vince Neil was involved in a car crash that resulted in the death of Nick 'Razzle' Dingley of Hanoi Rocks. He was charged with manslaughter and ordered to pay $2.6 million in damages, serve 20 days in gaol and perform 200 hours of community service. The group fired him in 1992. He then turned solo and released his debut single, 'You're Invited But Your Friend Can't Come', a minor UK chart entry, followed by an album, *Exposed*, which entered the US Top 20 in 1993. His next album was *Carved In Stone*, released in 1995.

Neil's replacement in the group was John Corabi, a former member of the metal band Scream.

MOTT THE HOOPLE This band was formed in Herefordshire in 1969. While working as an A&R man at Island Records, Geoff Stevens became interested in some demos submitted by an outfit called the Doc Thomas Band. He told them that if they replaced their lead singer, Stan Tippens, he would sign them. The band auditioned for a new singer and chose Ian Hunter, former bass guitarist with **Screaming Lord Sutch**. Stevens then changed their name to Mott The Hoople, the title of a 1967 book by Willard Manus. The other members of the band were Dale 'Buffin' Griffin (drums), Pete 'Overend' Watts (bass), Verden 'Phally' Allen (organ) and Mick Ralphs (guitar and vocals).

Their Island releases were unsuccessful and they were dropped from the label in 1972. The band were due to split up, so Watts wrote to David Bowie asking if he needed a bass player. Instead, Bowie offered to produce an album and single with them, gave them one of his songs – 'All The Young Dudes' – and fixed a deal for them with CBS Records. The single hit the Top 5 and the album also charted. Allen became disenchanted with the band's musical policy and left, and was soon followed by Ralphs. New members were Luthor Grosvenor from Spooky Tooth, who was now calling himself Ariel Bender, on guitar, and Morgan Fisher, former member of **Love Affair**, on piano. Mick Ronson replaced Bender.

Internal squabbles led to the band splitting up in 1974, the same year that Ralphs' new band, Bad Company, found chart success. Hunter teamed up with Ronson in the Hunter-Ronson Band, and the remaining members of the band took on vocalist Nigel Benjamin and guitarist Ray Majors and dubbed themselves Mott.

Ian Hunter continued his career as a solo artist and issued a new album, *The Artful Dodger*, in 1997, which he promoted on a 20-date UK tour. Morgan Fisher writes technical instruction books for Yamaha keyboards. Dale 'Buffin' Griffin produces sessions for the BBC's Radio 1 music station, principally for John Peel. Verden Allan lives in Hereford and plays in a duo. Guitarist Luthor Grosvenor lives in London but is no longer associated with the music business. Pete Watts runs antique shops in London and

131

Gloucester, and Mick Ralphs lives near Henley-on-Thames, Oxfordshire.

MOUSKOURI, Nana This Greek singer was born on 10 October 1936 in Athens. She met composer Manos Hadjidakis in 1958 and he provided her with material. She made her debut disc the following year and was soon established as a leading singer in her homeland.

Nana moved to Germany, where she recorded 'Weisse Rosen Aus Athen', an adaptation of an old Greek song, 'The Water And The Wine'. She recorded it in English and, as 'White Rose Of Athens', it became a million-seller following its release in 1961.

Nana's biggest UK hit came 25 years later with 'Only Love', which reached No 2 in the UK chart in 1986.

Although less frequently than before, Nana Mouskouri is still heard in concert around the globe as one of Greece's foremost musical ambassadors.

MOVE, The A Brumbeat band, the Move were originally formed in 1965 from members of various Birmingham outfits. They included Roy Wood (vocals and guitar), Carl Wayne (vocals), Chris 'Ace' Kefford (bass), Trevor Burton (guitar) and Bev Bevan (drums).

Carl, born Carl Tooley in Birmingham on 18 August 1946, originally led Carl Wayne & the Vikings. Roy, born on 8 November 1946, was a former member of Mike Sheridan & the Nightriders. Chris was born on 10 December 1946. Bev, born on 24 November 1944, was a former member of Carl Wayne & the Vikings, and Trevor, born on 9 March, 1944, was a former member of Danny King & the Mayfair Set. All five were born in Birmingham.

Tony Secunda, a young man bursting with innovative ideas, managed the Move. They hit the chart with numbers such as 'Night Of Fear' and 'I Can Hear The Grass Grow'. Their 'Flowers In The Rain' became the first record to be played on the BBC Radio 1 music station, in 1967. It proved controversial, as Secunda utilized a saucy postcard featuring Prime Minister Harold Wilson on the cover. Wilson sued, with the result that the royalties were donated to charity.

Following their 1968 hit 'Fire Brigade', Kefford suffered a nervous breakdown and the group continued as a quartet, with Burton taking over on bass. Roy Wood penned their chart-topping 'Blackberry Way' and following their next release, 'Curly', Burton left the band. Soon after that Carl Wayne departed, opting for a solo career, mainly on the cabaret circuit.

Other releases such as 'Brontosaurus' and 'When Alice Comes Down To The Farm' followed, and the band were joined by Jeff Lynne, former member of the Idle Race. After a series of further releases, including 'Tonight', 'Chinatown' and 'California Man', the group split into two other bands, Wizzard and the **Electric Light Orchestra** (ELO).

In 1995 Ace Kefford, together with members of Fairport Convention, recorded songs reflecting his born-again Christianity. He currently lives in a drugs rehabilitation centre in Warwickshire.

Carl Wayne, who left the Move in 1970, began appearing on the cabaret circuit and television variety shows. He even had a small part in the soap opera *Crossroads*. Carl married actress Susan Hanson, who played the part of Diane in *Crossroads*. The couple now live in Pyrford, Surrey, with their son Jack. Wayne spent six years appearing in Willie Russell's long-running West End musical *Blood Brothers*, finally leaving his role as narrator in 1996.

Roy Wood, who turned 50 in 1997, fronts his own band, the 12-piece Roy Wood Big Band, on tours that mingle new material with the hits he wrote for the Move, ELO and Wizzard. The outfit, which features a sensational seven-piece all-female horn section, completed a theatre tour of the UK in late 1997.

Bev Bevan leads a re-formed ELO. Trevor Burton is the mainstay of a blues outfit that works the Midlands pub/club circuit.

The Move: Movements: 30th Anniversary Anthology, a 3-CD set, was issued in 1997 and contained three complete albums, A- and B-sides of singles, alternate takes, the 'Something Else' EP, and previously unissued live and studio product.

MUD Mud was originally formed in 1968 and comprised Les Gray (vocals), Rob Davis (lead and vocals), Ray Stiles (bass and vocals) and Dave Mount (drums and vocals). They released a series of singles without much success, and it was only after they had signed with Mickie Most and Rak Records that they first entered the chart with 'Crazy' in 1973.

Rak songwriters Nicky Chinn and Mike Chapman penned several major hits for the band. Their chart entries on Rak were: 'Hypnosis', 'Dyna-Mite', 'Tiger Feet', 'The Cat

Crept In', 'Rocket', 'Lonely This Christmas', 'The Secrets That You Keep', 'Oh Boy', 'Moonshine Sally', 'One Night' and 'L-L-Lucy'. They then signed with Private Stock and their hits were: 'Show Me You're A Woman', 'Shake It Down' and 'Lean On Me'.

In 1987 Gray, who had signed as a solo artist with Warner Bros, had a minor hit with 'A Groovy Kind Of Love'.

The group's hit days seemingly over, they began to perform on the cabaret circuit. By the 1990s there was a revived nostalgia circuit on which the group performed.

1n 1997 Mud embarked on what they said was to be their final tour of the UK. Gray, now aged 51, said: 'I was getting more and more tired, but I thought it was just old age. Then I had a few tests and they whisked me into hospital and began testing me for diabetes. I was so weak I was forced to walk on crutches.'

Gray found he had a crippling illness and his weight dropped dramatically. His last appearance with the band took place in May 1997. Les, who lives in Portugal, said he hoped that he would be able to complete what was to be their last tour sometime in 1998. 'I hope I'll be fit again and I might be able to work again,' he said.

MUDLARKS, The A family trio from Bedford, Mary, Fred and Jeff Mudd began singing as the Mud Trio in 1951. Twelve-year-old Mary sang soprano, fourteen-year-old Fred baritone and sixteen-year-old Jeff tenor.

They were signed to the Columbia label and reached the UK Top 10 with their second release, 'Lollipop'. They followed up with two other chart hits, 'Book Of Love' and 'The Love Game'.

Appearances on UK television shows such as *6.5 Special* enhanced their image and they were voted Top British Vocal Group two years on the trot in the *New Musical Express*. When Jeff had to serve his term in national service in 1959, David Lane replaced him. On his return two years later, Jeff found that interest in the band's style of music had waned and they folded.

Mary Mudd is married and still lives in Bedford.

MUNGO JERRY This group comprised Ray Dorset (vocals and guitar), Colin Earl (piano and vocals), Paul King (banjo, jug, guitar and vocals) and Mike Cole (bass). Leader Dorset, with his distinctive curly hair, came to be seen in the public's eyes as 'Mungo Jerry'.

The group's UK chart presence was felt over a four-year period in the early 1970s, when their hit streak began with the chart-topper 'In The Summertime'. Their second release, 'Baby Jump', also topped the UK chart. They followed with further hit singles: 'Lady Rose', 'You Don't Have To Be In The Army To Fight In The War', 'Open Up', 'Alright Alright Alright', 'Wild Love' and 'Long Legged Woman Dressed In Black'.

1972 saw the departure of King and Earl to form another outfit, the King Earl Boogie Band. The band wasn't successful and now King, who lives in Cornwall, has left the music business, as has Earl, who lives in Weybridge, Surrey, where he repairs vintage cars.

The departure of King and Earl caused a break in the continuity of Mungo Jerry, during which Dorset cut a solo album, *Cold Blue Excursions*. He then formed a new Mungo Jerry with John Godfrey, John Pope and Tim Reeves, whose first hit was 'Alright Alright Alright'.

Dorset continued to make live appearances with different personnel over the years and found some success as a songwriter, penning television themes and 'Feels Like I'm In Love', a No 1 hit for Kelly Marie in 1980.

The father of five children and now resident in Bournemouth, the group's mainstay, Ray Dorset – who has now assumed the stage alias Mungo Jerry – sang over the credits of *Prospects*, a 1990s UK television drama series. He enjoyed a hit by proxy when Shaggy revived 'In The Summertime' – also the theme of a drink-driving public service television clip.

The group currently enjoys regular work on the sixties nostalgia circuit all over Europe.

NASHVILLE TEENS, The This R&B outfit was formed in Weybridge, Surrey, in 1962 with members Art Sharp (vocals), John Allen and Pete Shannon (guitar), John Hawkens (piano), Ray Phillips (bass) and Barry Jenkins (drums). Phillips later switched to vocals and they toured with the unusual two singers up front.

After a spell in Hamburg, they backed **Bo Diddley** on a UK tour and were spotted by Mickie Most, who produced their debut single, 'Tobacco Road'. They followed with 'Google Eye', 'Find My Way Back Home', 'This Little Bird' and 'The Hard Way'.

The group backed artists such as **Carl Perkins** and **Chuck Berry**, and continued recording until 1969 before disbanding. They were to re-form many years later.

With Ray Phillips the only remaining original member, the Nashville Teens were the toast of a Festival Of The Sixties at Butlin's Southcoast World in Bognor Regis, Dorset, in November 1997.

NATURALS, The Formed during the beat music era in the 1960s under the name the Blue Beats, this British group comprised Ricki Potter (vocals), Curt Cresswell (guitar), Bob O'Neale (harmonica), Nick Wakelin (bass) and Roy Heather (drums). They changed their name to the Naturals when they signed to Parlophone.

The group had only one chart entry, a cover of the Beatles' 'I Should Have Known Better', in 1964. Two unsuccessful singles, 'It Was You' and 'Blue Roses', followed, but the group had become a 'one-hit wonder' and disbanded.

In 1995, the original personnel of the Naturals regrouped for engagements local to their native Essex.

NAZARETH Formed in Dunfermline in 1968, this Scots group evolved from a band called the Shadettes. The members were Dan McCafferty (vocals), Manny Charlton (guitar), Pete Agnew (bas) and Darrell Sweet (drums).

They moved down to London and found success with a series of hit singles, beginning with 'Broken Down Angel' in 1973. Their other chart entries were: 'Bad Bad Boy', 'This Flight Tonight', 'Shanghai'd In Shanghai', 'My White Bicycle', 'Holy Roller', 'Hot Tracks', 'Gone Dead Train', 'Place In Your Heart', 'May The Sun Shine' and 'Star'.

Their album hits included: *Razamanaz*, *Loud 'N' Proud*, *Rampant*, *Greatest Hits*, *No Mean City*, *The Fool Circle* and *Nazareth Live*.

Zal Cleminson, former member of the Sensational Alex Harvey Band, joined them for a while, as did keyboard player John Locke. Soon after that Billy Rankin joined on guitar, then Locke left, so Rankin replaced him on keyboards.

The group decided to suspend their career for a while in the late 1980s and work on some solo projects, but they produced an album, *No Jive*, in 1992.

Manny Charlton quit to become a record producer in 1987. Vocalist Dan McCafferty has a parallel recording career as a soloist, atthough he, Pete Agnew and Darrell Sweet are the three original members who remain in Nazareth – and the band, surprisingly, is still going strong, with regular world tours and new albums.

NENA After an international breakthrough in 1984 with '99 Red Balloons', the German group fronted by Gabriele ' Nena' Kerner notched up a minor hit with 'Just A Dream' before returning to the West German orbit of engagements.

NERO & THE GLADIATORS This instrumental group signed to Decca Records in the early 1960s. In 1961 they had two minor hits with 'Entry Of The Gladiators' and 'In The Hall Of The Mountain King'.

The group is no more, but most of its former members are still in the business, including guitarist Ritchie Blackmore in a reunited **Deep Purple** and keyboard player Mike O'Neill in the 1950s rock 'n' roll revivalists Houseshakers.

NEWBEATS, The Mark and Dean Mathis and Larry Henley made up this group from Georgia. Henley had originally seen the brothers performing with a band in Shreveport and asked if he could sing with them. They added him to the group, which broke up soon afterwards.

Henley continued as a solo artist and the brothers as a duo, but they teamed up as a trio in 1963 and recorded 'Bread And Butter', which became a hit on both sides of the Atlantic. Their next release was 'Everything's Alright', also a Top 20 entry in the States, and in 1965 they had two further singles in the US chart, 'Break Away (From That Boy)' and 'Run, Baby Run'.

Other releases followed, but were relatively unsuccessful. In 1971, their original version of 'Run, Baby Run' was released in the UK and became a Top 10 hit, giving them a new lease of life.

When the Newbeats eventually split in 1974, Larry Henley functioned as a solo vocalist and, more successfully, as a songwriter. His biggest commercial strike was with 'Wind Beneath My Wings', a hit for Bette Midler in 1989.

NEWMAN, Randy This singer-songwriter-pianist was born in New Orleans, Louisiana, on 28 November 1943. He was the nephew of composers Alfred, Emil and Lionel Newman.

He issued his first single, 'Golden Gridiron Boy', in 1961 and that year began writing music for other artists. Over the next few years numerous British and American acts recorded his songs, including the Fleetwoods, Gene McDaniels, Cilla Black, Alan Price, the **Walker Brothers**, Gene Pitney, **Judy Collins**, Harpers Bizarre, **Jackie De Shannon**, **Frankie Laine**, **Three Dog Night** and **Manfred Mann**.

Newman's biggest hit in his own right was 'Short People', which reached No 2 in the US chart in 1978.

With his uncles being executives at 20th Century Fox, Newman was able to enter the film world, composing various soundtracks for films which included *Ragtime*, *The Natural*, *The Three Amigos*, *Awakenings* and *The Paper*.

In 1995 Newman played his first UK concert in six years. Later that year, he premiered a concept CD of Goethe's *Faust* with a cast that included himself as the Devil, with **James Taylor**, Elton John, Linda Ronstadt and Bonnie Raitt. The project was also staged in San Diego.

1996 saw Randy Newman receive an Oscar nomination for his song 'You've Got A Friend', which was featured in Walt Disney's *Toy Story*. The same year he penned songs for the film of *James And The Giant Peach* and received a Henry Mancini Award for a lifetime achievement in music.

NEW SEEKERS, The When Australian hit band the Seekers closed their career with a farewell performance for television in 1969, founder member Keith Potger then established a new group, the New Seekers, and became their manager. They comprised Eve Graham and Lyn Paul, both former singers with a group called the Nocturnes, with Paul Layton and Marty Kristian.

Between 1970 and 1979 the group's hits included: 'What Have They Done To My Song Ma', 'Never Ending Song Of Love', 'I'd Like To Teach The World To Sing', 'Beg Borrow Or Steal', 'Circles', 'Come Softly To Me', 'Pinball Wizard', 'Nevertheless', 'Goodbye Is Just Another Word', 'You Won't Find Another Fool Like Me', 'I Get A Little Sentimental Over You', 'It's So Nice (To Have You Home)', 'I Wanna Go Back' and 'Anthem (One Day In Every Week)'.

The group enjoyed success in the US chart, entered the Eurovision Song Contest in 1972 and had two UK chart-toppers, but decided to appear on a farewell tour of the UK and disband in 1974. A new contract with CBS had them re-form and they continued, sans Lyn Paul, who had had a minor solo hit in 1975, until they finally broke up in 1978.

With the success of the nostalgia circuit internationally, original members Kristian and Layton decided to revive the outfit and recruited three other members – Donna Jones, Vikki James and Mick Flynn.

Donna had enjoyed a successful solo career in Australia, where she had a No 1 hit with 'The Way You Do It', while Mike was a former member of the Mixtures, who topped the charts with the 'Pushbike Song'.

NEWTON-JOHN, Olivia Blonde, wholesome and extremely pretty, this singer was born in Cambridge on 26 September 1948. At the age of five she moved to Australia with her parents, where she took up folk singing and won a talent contest in which the prize was a trip to England. She decided to remain in the country and met Bruce Welch of the Shadows, resulting in a booking to appear with **Cliff Richard** and the group in their London Palladium pantomime, *Cinderella*. She moved in with Welch and was cited in his divorce hearings. In 1977 she featured in the film *Toomorrow*, a science-fiction musical about a group, which resulted in the formation of an actual group of that name with members Olivia, Ben Thomas, Karl Chambers, Vic Cooper and Chris Slade. They issued two singles, but were unsuccessful and disbanded.

In 1971, Olivia duetted with Cliff Richard on the flipside of one of his records and toured Europe with him. Her solo single 'If Not For You' entered the UK Top 10 and was the first of a string of hits, which included: 'Banks Of The Ohio', 'What Is Life', 'Take Me Home Country Roads', 'Long Live Love', 'I Honestly Love You', 'Sam', 'Hopelessly Devoted To You', 'A Little

135

More Love', 'Deeper Than The Night', 'Magic', 'Physical', 'Landslide', 'Make A Move On Me', 'Heart Attack' and 'Twist Of Fate'.

Olivia and Bruce were engaged for a time, but split up in 1972. This did not affect her association with Cliff Richard and the Shadows, who were closely involved in her career, with members of the group producing her records. She was also the resident guest on Cliff's UK television series in 1972.

Olivia was the UK's representative in the 1974 Eurovision Song Contest, although **Abba** won the competition with 'Waterloo'.

She moved to the States, settling in Malibu, California, in 1975 on the advice of her new manager Lee Kramer, with whom she was also romantically involved. The 1970s proved to be a successful decade for her, with numerous awards from the US record industry. It was also the decade in which she starred with John Travolta in the smash-hit movie musical *Grease*, with her duet with Travolta, 'You're The One That I Want', topping the US chart, followed by another duet with Travolta, 'Summer Night', hitting the No 5 position.

Olivia's next movie, *Xanadu*, was a flop, although the title song, which she recorded with the **Electric Light Orchestra**, hit the No 2 spot in the UK. She also had hits with the soundtrack album and 'Suddenly', a ballad from the movie in which she duetted with Cliff Richard. Another film, *Two Of A Kind*, in which she also co-starred with John Travolta, failed to make much impact.

Olivia married Matt Lattanzi in 1985 and gave birth to a daughter, Chloe, the following year. She took time off to concentrate on marriage and motherhood before being diagnosed with breast cancer in 1992. She made a full recovery, but separated from her husband in 1995.

That same year she released her first studio album in five years, *Gala (One Woman's Journey)*, and teamed up with Cliff Richard once again for a duet from his musical *Heathcliffe*, returning her to the UK chart.

Olivia Newton-John now divides her time between appearing in movies such as *It's My Party*, and

Olivia Newton-John

championing environmental issues. Despite lengthening periods away from the public eye, she has entered middle age as a showbusiness evergreen with an OBE.

NEW VAUDEVILLE BAND, The This group was originally formed in 1966 by drummer Henry Harrison, a former member of Cops 'n' Robbers. They developed a jazzy style based on sounds of the 1920s and 1930s, and registered big with 'Winchester Cathedral'. They followed with 'Peek A Boo', 'Finchley Central' and a minor hit, 'Green Street Green'.

Reportedly, an entity calling itself the New Vaudeville Band can still be heard in the States, the scene of the group's greatest triumph with 'Winchester Cathedral' in 1966. Geoff Stevens, the song's composer – and singer on the record – collected a large royalty cheque in 1992 when his opus 'The Crying Game' was revived as the main theme for a movie of the same name.

NICE, The This group began life as a backing band for singer P.P. Arnold. They were: Keith Emerson (keyboards), Brian 'Blinky' Davison (drums), Lee Jackson (bass and vocals) and David O'List (guitar).

Leaving Arnold in 1967, they made their recording debut with 'The Thoughts Of Emerlist Davjack', although their only hit single was 'America', their version of the tune from the musical *West Side Story*. When they performed it at the Royal Albert Hall, the group burned the United States' flag on stage, resulting in censure from the Albert Hall authorities and complaints from the composer, Leonard Bernstein. A trio of album hits comprised *Nice*, *Five Bridges* and *Elegy*.

O'List left to join **Roxy Music** and the band continued as a trio. However, despite their innovation and showmanship they never achieved the heights their potential warranted, and Emerson was later to form the more successful Emerson, Lake & Palmer. Jackson formed Jackson Heights and Davison formed Every Which Way, but both bands proved unsuccessful. Jackson and Davison teamed up briefly in 1974 to form Refugee, which went the same way as their previous bands.

Keith Emerson is based in California and has a Nice/ELP-style instrumental group there consisting of local musicians. David O'List lives in London and is involved in the film business. Lee Jackson is also in London, working for an architecture and design conglomerate. Brian Davison lives in north Devon, where he teaches drums, runs 'rhythm and improvisation' workshops and plays in local jazz combos. He is a near-neighbour of Charlie Watts.

NICOL, Jimmy Drummer Jimmy Nicol was working with Georgie Fame & the Blue Flames when he was asked to act as a replacement for Ringo Starr in the Beatles in 1964. Ringo had suddenly been taken ill with tonsillitis and Jimmy was hired to join them for ten days. The 25-year old from south London insisted on playing the drums himself, although **Brian Epstein** had wanted him to mime to tapes of Ringo.

Nicol earned less than £2,000 from the tour and says it ruined his life. On his return he led a band called the Shubdubs, but they were unsuccessful and he joined the house band on the television programme *Come Dancing*. He later joined a Scandinavian instrumental act, the **Spotniks**, and while touring Mexico he met and married a Mexican Indian girl, Josephina.

The couple returned to the UK, penniless, in 1987 and initially lived with Jimmy's mother Edith in her tiny flat. By 1996 they had a small flat of their own in south London, with Jimmy trying to eke out a living through carpentry work.

Ironically, Howard, Jimmy's son from his first marriage, became a sound engineer and won a BAFTA award for his work on the television series *The Beatles Anthology*.

NIRVANA Formed in Aberdeen, Washington, in 1986, this group comprised **Kurt Cobain** (guitar and vocal), Chris Novoseli (bass) and Chad Channing (drums). Their debut single was 'Love Buzz', issued in June 1988. For a brief time they were joined by guitarist Jason Everman, who left the band following a major US tour. Channing also left and was replaced by Dave Grold. This trio recorded the album *Nevermind*, released in 1991, which thrust the band into the limelight. In 1993 their next album, *In Utero*, was released and guitarist Pat Smear joined them on tour.

After Kurt Cobain committed suicide in April 1994, the group disbanded. Dave Grohl formed a new band called Foo Fighters, with Smear on guitar, and Novoselic joined a new band, Sweet 75, in 1996.

NOLANS, The   Irish couple Tommy and Maureen Nolan were originally a duo until, following their move from Eire to Blackpool in England in 1962, they introduced their offspring into their act in 1963. These included Anne, Denise, Maureen, Brian, Linda, Coleen and Bernadette.

The girls turned professional and, as the Nolan Sisters, moved to London. They now comprised Anne, Denise, Linda, Bernadette and Maureen. Denise then left to pursue a solo career and the other sisters continued as a quartet. When Anne married and left the group, Denise re-joined. They truncated their name to the Nolans and hit the chart with 'I'm In The Mood For Dancing'.

Other hits included: 'Spirit Body And Soul', 'Don't Make Waves', 'Gotta Pull Myself Together', 'Who's Gonna Rock You', 'Attention To Me', 'Chemistry' and 'Don't Love Me Too Hard'.

When Linda left to get married, Anne re-joined. The various sisters have recorded solo singles, and Linda and Coleen had a minor hit with 'Don't Do That' under the name the Young & Moody Band.

Linda hosted her own *Linda Nolan And Friends* television show in 1989. Since then, she has been a regular guest on the *James Whale Radio Show* (on television!), and still comperes the cabaret on Blackpool's Central Pier each summer. Denise is seen mostly in variety and pantomime, while Maureen, Bernadette and Coleen still perform and record under the group's name.

NUMAN, Gary   Born Gary Webb in Hammersmith, west London, on 8 March 1958, this singer took the surname 'Numan' from a plumber in listed in the telephone directory.

Numan first entered the chart in 1979 with his group Tubeway Army and the single 'Are Friends Electric'. He dropped the Tubeway Army name the same year and continued to have a string of hit records until 1988. They included: 'Cars', 'Complex', 'We Are Glass', 'I Die, You Die', 'This Wreckage', 'She's Got Claws', 'Love Needs No Disguise', 'Music For Chameleons', 'We Take Mystery (To Bed)', 'White Boys And Heroes', 'Warriors', 'Sister Surprise', 'Berserker', 'My Dying Machine', 'The Live EP', 'Your Fascination', 'Call Out The Dogs', 'Miracles', 'This Is Love', 'I Can't Stop', 'I Still Remember', 'Cars Are Electric', 'New Angel' and 'America'.

After an eight-year low in his career, Carling Premier Lager used 'Cars' in its television commercials in 1996, resulting in the re-release of the single. This gave Numan his first hit in several years and sparked off a Numan revival. In May 1997 a tribute album, *Random*, was issued, in which a number of contemporary bands performed Numan numbers, including Blur's Damon Albarn, Beck, the Orb, St Etienne and Republica. André Deutsch published Numan's autobiography, *Praying To The Aliens*, written with Steve Malins, in the autumn of that year. Gary also made his film debut as a villainous nightclub owner in the movie *The Kinsman*. There was even a tribute band called the Numan Principle.

In October 1997 Gary released a new album, *Exile*, and began an autumn tour. In November of that year another tribute album, *Random 2*, was issued.

Gary Numan lives in a large house called Dunvegan in Essex.

OCEAN, Billy   This singer was born Leslie Sebastian Charles in Trinidad on 21 January 1950. When he was four the entire family moved to the East End of London.

Ocean took on a variety of jobs, including working for a tailor and joining the Ford car plant at Dagenham. He left in 1976 to sign with GTO Records and began his 12-year streak of hit record releases. They included: 'Love Really Hurts Without You', 'L.O.D. (Love On Delivery)', 'Stop Me (If You've Heard It All Before)', 'Red Light Spells Danger', 'American Hearts', 'Are You Ready', 'Caribbean Queen', 'Loverboy', 'Suddenly', 'Mystery Lady', 'When The Going Gets Tough The Tough Get Going', 'There'll Be Sad Songs (To Make You Cry)', 'Love Zone', 'Bittersweet', 'Love Is Forever', 'Get Outta My Dreams Get Into My Car', 'Calypso Crazy', 'The Colour Of Love', 'Licence To Chill', 'I Sleep Much Better (In Someone Else's Bed)' and 'Pressure'.

Ocean also became hugely successful in the States, receiving several Grammy Awards and achieving three No 1 hits.

Since his global smash with 'When The Going Gets Tough' in 1986, for the soundtrack of the film *Jewel Of The Nile*, Ocean has released albums and spin-off singles regularly, and the possibility of him notching up further million-sellers is far from laughable.

O'CONNOR, Hazel   This blonde British vocalist was born on 16 May 1955 and began her career as an actress, making her movie debut in the soft-porn flick *Girls Come First*. In 1980 she was given the starring role in the feature film *Breaking Glass*.

For a two-year period from 1980 Hazel enjoyed a series of hit singles: 'Eighth Day', 'Give Me An Inch', 'D-Days', 'Well You', '(Cover Plus) We're All Grown Up', 'Hanging Around' and 'Calls The Tune'.

Since her hits dried up, Hazel O'Connor has made albums in Germany and has been seen in television dramas and on the stage in London's West End. She currently lives in Wicklow in Eire.

O'CONNOR, Sinead   This controversial singer was born in Glengeary, Eire, in 1966. She initially joined a local band, Ton Ton Maconte, then sang on the solo album by **U2's** the Edge and cut her own solo album, *The Lion And The Cobra*, in 1987.

Moving to London at the age of 17, she had made an impressive television appearance on *Top Of The Pops* sporting a shaven head, which led to her being dubbed the 'Bald-headed Banshee'.

Sinead's second album, *I Do Not Want What I Haven't Got*, sold over six million copies and she

Hazel O'Connor with Phil Daniels in the film Breaking Glass

139

become a major star on both sides of the Atlantic.

Problems began when she was in the States and refused to perform at a show because it opened with that country's national anthem. Her records were burned in public, her concerts cancelled and Frank Sinatra threatened to 'kick her ass'.

Sinead miscarried in 1990, but by 1996 had given birth to Roisin, the second of her two children.

When she appeared on the US television show *Saturday Night Live*, she ripped up a photograph of the Pope, which led to her being jeered by the audience when she appeared at a **Bob Dylan** tribute event a few weeks later.

In 1993 Sinead suffered a breakdown and attempted suicide, and in 1995 resolved never to talk to the press. She went into therapy.

By 1997 she had regrown her hair and publicly apologized to the Pope, but in October of that year announced that she would appear as the Virgin Mary in a shocking new film, Neil Jordan's *The Butcher's Boy*, based on a novel by Patrick McCabe. In it, she would appear in a vision to a boy and suggest he go on a killing spree. This involved Sinead in further controversy, as a spokesman for the Catholic Church stated: 'We will ask them not to distribute this movie, and not to release anything that mocks the Virgin Mary in any way.'

In November 1997 Sinead O'Connor moved into a luxury five-bedroomed house in Highgate, north London. That year her new single, 'This Is A Rebel Song', was issued, along with the album *Gospel Oak*. Chrysalis also issued a compilation album, *So Far: The Best Of Sinead O'Connor*.

OFARIM, Esther & Abi   This husband-and-wife team of hitmakers comprised Esther, born Esther Zaled in Safed, Israel, on 13 June 1943, and Abi, born Araham Reichstadt in Tel Aviv, Israel, on 5 October 1939.

They became a popular singing duo in their home country and Esther appeared in the 1963 Eurovision Song Contest – but representing Switzerland.

The duo began appearing in Europe and became popular in the UK, where their single 'Cinderella Rockefella' topped the chart for three weeks in 1968. They followed up with another Top 20 entry, 'One More Dance', but it was to be their last hit.

Now divorced, Esther still sings professionally, while Abi runs a record production company in Munich.

OLDHAM, Andrew Loog   A former press agent, Andrew Loog Oldham took over management of the **Rolling Stones** in April 1963. He developed their image and they became the major rivals to the Beatles. He also discovered **Marianne Faithfull**.

The Stones replaced Oldham with Allen Klein in 1967. For a time Oldham formed a new record label, Immediate Records, in partnership with Tony Calder. He relocated to Bogata, Columbia, in 1982 and has lived there ever since, managing a band called Ratones Paranoiacos. Together with Tony Calder and Colin Irwin, he penned the book *Abba – The Name Of The Game*, in 1995.

O'SULLIVAN, Gilbert   A singer-songwriter from the 1970s, Gilbert O'Sullivan resumed his career in the 1990s. Born Raymond O'Sullivan in Eire on 1 December 1946, he had 15 hit singles between November 1970 and September 1980. They were: 'Nothing Rhymed', 'Underneath The Blanket', 'We Will', 'No Matter How I Try', 'Alone Again (Naturally)', 'Ooh-Wakka-Doo-Wakka-Day', 'Claire', 'Get Down', 'Ooh Baby', 'Why Oh Why Oh Why', 'Happiness Is Me And You', 'A Woman's Place', 'Christmas Song', 'I Don't Love You But I Think Like You' and 'What's In A Kiss'.

O'Sullivan broke away from his manager Gordon Mills and his success faltered. In 1982 he sued Mills, and received substantial damages and had all his tapes and copyrights returned.

However, despite his obvious talent as one of the UK's leading singer-songwriters of the 1970s, he failed to reach the hit parade again.

Gilbert O'Sullivan continues to perform, took part in a Flying Music concert tour of the UK and also appeared alongside Oasis at the Glastonbury Festival in 1995.

PAIGE, Elaine   This petite singer was born in Barnet on 8 March 1948. Her principal success has been in musical roles in the theatre and her chart hits have included 'Don't Walk Away Till I Touch You', 'Memory', 'Sometimes' and 'The Second Time'. Her biggest hit was the chart-topper 'I Know Him So Well', from the musical *Chess*, on which she duetted with **Barbara Dickson**. It became the all-time bestselling single by a female duo in the UK.

Elaine, who made her London debut in *Hair*, also starred in major shows such as *Cats*, *Evita*, *Piaf* and *Chess*. She received an OBE in 1995.

Elaine returned to London in October 1997 following nine months on Broadway, starring as Norma Desmond in the musical *Sunset Boulevard*, for which she was reputedly paid £25,000 per week. She declared she was selling her Chelsea home of 11 years. The 49-year-old star is still single following an 11-year affair with lyricist Tim Rice. She called off the romance in 1990.

In 1998 she appeared at the Royal Albert Hall in the Andrew Lloyd Webber Fiftieth Birthday Celebration on 7 April, and on 18 June appeared at the Hampton Court Palace Festival, performing in her first concert for three years.

1998 also saw Elaine appear in her first West End play, Moliere's *The Misanthrope*, with the Peter Hall Company.

PAPER LACE   Formed in Nottingham in 1969, this group named themselves after their city's most famous product – lace. The line-up comprised Mike Vaughan, Chris Morris and Carlo Santanna (guitar), Philip Wright (drums) and Cliff Fish (bass).

The group appeared on the UK television talent show *Opportunity Knocks*. They then recorded a number penned by Mitch Murray and Peter Callender, which topped the UK chart. It was immediately covered in the States by the Heywoods, which prevented Paper Lace from emulating its UK success there. Their songwriting managers then followed up with 'The Night Chicago Died', which took Paper Lace to the UK No 3 spot, and a third hit was 'The Black-eyed Boys'. The group broke away from the Murray/ Callender team and never had another hit in their own right.

Paper Lace's last taste of Top 30 fame was a merger with local soccer heroes Nottingham Forest Football Club, for the 1978 singalong 'We've Got The Whole World In Our Hands'.

The original group split up in 1980. A different set of personnel using the name emerged in 1983 and continues to perform on the nostalgia circuit.

PARTRIDGE, Don   Known as the 'King Of The Buskers', Don Partridge was born in Bournemouth, Dorset, in 1945. He began busking in London in the 1960s, initially in Berwick Street Market, and was spotted by Don Paul, former member of vocal group the Viscounts, who became his manager. Partridge then found success on record: first with 'Rosie', which reached No 4 in the chart, followed by 'Blue Eyes' at No 3 and 'Breakfast On Pluto' at No 26. He also gathered together a number of fellow street singers to record the album *The Buskers*.

Partridge performed as a 'one-man band' in the days when busking was illegal and, following his stint on the streets in London in 1963, he played in Paris, the South of France and Germany. When Paul became his manager, he took the singer into Regent B Studio in Denmark Street in London and, at a cost of £8, recorded the singer's performance of Paul's own composition, 'Rosie'.

Following his third and final chart entry, Partridge opened Don Partridge's Stew & Wine Shop in Camden Passage, but the business collapsed within 18 months and he bought himself a horse and wagon and began to travel around the UK. He then moved to Sweden and settled in Stockholm, where his Swedish wife became pregnant.

His marriage broke down in 1977 and he moved to Switzerland, then on to Germany and Denmark before returning to the UK.

With his new girlfriend Pam he launched a wine factory, which also failed, then the couple moved to Sussex in 1993 where he organized the Seaford Festival.

Don Partridge then returned to London and began performing on the streets once again.

PAUL, Les   Born Lester Polfus in Waukesha, Wisconsin, on 9 June 1923, this guitarist originally formed the Les Paul Trio in the late 1930s. In 1941, while in hospital recuperating from a car crash, he developed the famous Gibson Les Paul model guitar, which eventually went on the market in 1952.

Paul teamed up with singer Mary Ford (real name Colleen Summer) and the two were married in 1948. The duo were successful on record and their hits included: 'Mockin' Bird Hill', 'How High The Moon', 'The World Is Waiting For The Sunrise', and their chart-topper, 'Vaya Con Dios'.

The couple were divorced in 1963 and Mary died in 1977.

Les Paul was still releasing records in the late 1970s before taking a sabbatical. In 1980, a US television documentary, *The Wizard Of Waneska*, about his life and work led to a return to both studio and stage in 1984. In 1992, he was the star turn at a guitar festival in Seville, Spain. He also conducts guitar workshops.

PAUL & PAULA   Ray Hildebrand and Jill Jackson, two college students, recorded a tune called 'Hey Paula', penned by Hildebrand. It leapt into the No 1 position in the US and was also a big hit in the UK in 1963. That was the year it all happened for them. They had two further hit singles – 'Young Lovers' and 'First Quarrel' – and cut no less than three albums – *Paul And Paula Sing For Young Lovers*, *We Go Together* and *Holiday For Teens*.

The duo had no further chart success, although they reunited in 1982 to record a C&W album.

PAXTON, Tom   This folk singer-songwriter was born in Chicago on 31 October 1937. He began performing in Greenwich Village, New York, at the beginning of the 1960s and issued his album *Ramblin' Boy* in 1965. He was to become a prolific album artist, issuing more than two dozen LPs.

Paxton never had a hit single, but was more successful as a songwriter, with artists ranging from **Judy Collins** and **John Denver** to the **Kingston Trio** recording his material.

For one part of his career he relocated to London. He then returned to the US, where he continues to write and record.

Tom Paxton toured Europe as recently as 1997.

PEDDLERS, The   This highly regarded jazz/pop trio performed for more than a decade. Drummer Trevor Morais had been a member of Mersey outfit Faron's Flamingoes, who had originally recorded 'Do You Love Me' in the UK. The group became disillusioned and split up when the record company placed the number on the B-side, providing an opportunity for Brian Poole & the **Tremeloes** and the **Dave Clark Five** to record it.

Morais teamed up with keyboards player Roy Phillips and bassist Tab Martin to form the Peddlers, and they had a minor hit with 'Let The Sunshine In' in 1965, a Top 20 entry with 'Birth' in 1969 and another chart entry the following year with 'Girlie'.

During their career they recorded a dozen albums, with 'Birthday' entering the charts. The trio disbanded in the mid-1970s.

Tab Martin lives in Pangbourne, Berkshire and Roy Phillips in Germany. Trevor Morais joined Quantum Jump and, in the 1980s, Wildlife. He was also heard on albums by Mike Batt and Jim Capaldi.

PEPSI & SHIRLIE   This female duo provided backing vocals and danced with **Wham!** in their live performances and travelled the world, including China, with George Michael and Andrew Ridgeley.

Shirlie Holliman joined Wham! to promote their debut single, 'Wham Rap!', with Mary Washburn, who was soon replaced by Diane Sealey, known as Dee C. Lee. The latter left to join Style Council in October 1983 and Pepsi replaced her.

Pepsi & Shirlie also recorded in their own right and had four chart hits: 'Heartache', 'Goodbye Stranger', 'Can't Give Me Love' and 'All Right Now'. The two also had their own range of clothing sold through the Top Shop chain. The sales waned, then faded away when Wham! split, but the two became regulars on UK children's television for a while.

Shirlie married Martin Kemp of **Spandau Ballet** and now lives in north London with her husband and two children. She nursed Martin during 1996 when he became seriously ill with a brain tumour. Shirlie also continues her association with George Michael by running his web site on the Internet.

When Pepsi & Shirlie split, Pepsi appeared in the musical *Hair* and decided to become an actress.

PETER & GORDON   Gordon Trueman Riviere Waller was born in Braemar, Scotland, on 4 June 1945 and Peter Asher in London on 22 June 1944. The two first met up at Westminster School and teamed up as a folk duo, Gordon & Peter.

One of Peter's sisters was Jane Asher, who was Paul McCartney's girlfriend at the time. Peter asked him to provide them with a song and he gave them 'World Without Love', which became their debut disc and a UK chart-topper. By that time they were billed as Peter & Gordon. Paul then provided them with 'Nobody I Know', which was another million-seller. The duo then flew to the States to appear on the *Ed Sullivan Show*. Their third disc, 'I Go To Pieces', was given to them by **Del Shannon**, and although it did not make much of an impact in the UK, it reached No 9 in the US chart. Their next hits were 'True Love Ways', followed by 'To Know You Is To Love You' and 'Baby I'm Yours'.

Paul McCartney then gave the duo another number, 'Woman', which was published under the pseudonym of Bernard Webb and was again a transatlantic hit for them. They had one further UK hit, 'Lady Godiva', and two other singles, 'Sunday For Tea' and 'The Jokers'.

Due to the ever-changing tastes in music, in 1967 Peter suggested to Gordon that they split.

Gordon Waller never had another chart placing. He released the solo singles 'Rosecrans Boulevard' and 'Weeping Analeah' and an album on Bell. In 1973 he appeared in *Joseph And The Amazing Technicolor Dreamcoat* at the Edinburgh Festival and in London and Australia. He later worked as a photocopier salesman, before settling down in Northamptonshire and becoming a partner in a company making radio commercials.

Peter Asher became head of A&R at Apple Records in 1968. In 1970 he moved to the States and became a manager and producer with artists such as **James Taylor** and Linda Ronstadt. He was nominated for Grammys in 1975, 1977, 1978 and 1989, and received his Producer Of The Year Grammy in 1977.

PETER, PAUL & MARY Formed in Greenwich Village, New York, in 1961, this folk trio consisted of Peter Yarrow, Paul Stookey and Mary Travers. They first entered the US chart in 1962 with 'Lemon Tree'. Their other hit singles included: 'If I Had A Hammer', 'Puff The Magic

Peter and Gordon

143

Dragon', 'Blowin' In The Wind', 'Don't Think Twice – It's Alright', 'Stewball', 'Tell It On The Mountain', 'For Lovin' Me', 'I Dig Rock And Roll Music', 'Too Much Of Nothing', 'Day Is Done' and 'Leaving On A Jet Plane'.

They also had a number of hit albums, including: *Peter Paul & Mary*, *In The Wind*, *In Concert Vol I* and *Ten Years Together*.

Since their sundering in 1971, the trio re-formed periodically for tours and occasional albums, mainly in 1972 and again in 1978, but found that the music scene had moved on. Mary also released three solo albums during the 1970s, and Yarrow recorded in German and had some success as a songwriter, penning the 1976 Mary McGregor chart-topper 'Torn Between Two Lovers'.

PETERS & LEE   This duo were popular British cabaret artists of the 1970s. Lennie Peters, born in London in 1939, had aspirations to become a boxer. It was only after he was rendered blind following an accident that he decided to become an entertainer and began singing and playing piano in London pubs.

During a tour of clubs he met Dianne Lee, who at the time was a dancer. Dianne, a miner's daughter born in Sheffield in 1950, agreed to become his partner and the duo won several heats on the television talent show *Opportunity Knocks*. They then topped the UK chart with their debut disc, 'Welcome Home', issued in 1973, simultaneously topping the album chart with their debut LP, *We Can Make It*.

Their other chart singles were: 'By Your Side', 'Don't Stay Away Too Long', 'Rainbow' and 'Hey Mr Music Man'.

The duo split up in 1980 but re-formed six years later and became a leading cabaret attraction, also appearing regularly in holiday camps.

Sadly, Lennie Peters died from cancer in 1992. Dianne Lee functions as a solo turn on the cabaret circuit and also appeared in the 1990s as 'Sinderella' in comedian Jim Davidson's bawdy pantomime of that name.

PETTY, Tom   Singer-songwriter Tom Petty was born on 20 October 1952 in Gainesville, Florida. He formed a band called the Sundowners in 1971. They underwent various name changes, including Mudcrutch. He moved to Los Angeles and formed a new band, the Heartbreakers, whose eponymous debut album was issued in 1976.

Petty composed songs for a number of artists, including Roger McGuinn, Roseanne Cash and Del Shannon, and collaborated on recordings with artists such as **Bob Dylan** and Stevie Nicks.

His hit singles have included: 'Breakdown', 'Don't Do Me Like That', 'Refugee', 'The Waiting', 'You Got Lucky', 'Change Of Heart', 'Don't Come Around Here No More', 'Make It Better (Forget About Me)', 'Jammin' Me', 'I Won't Back Down', 'Runnin' Down A Dream', 'Free Fallin'', 'A Face In The Crowd', 'Learning To Fly', 'Into The Great Wide Open', 'Too Good To Be True', 'Something In The Air', 'Mary Jane's Last Dance', 'You Don't Know How It Feels' and 'It's Good To Be King'.

In 1987 Petty became a member of the **Traveling Wilburys**, along with George Harrison, **Bob Dylan**, **Roy Orbison** and Jeff Lynne, assuming the recording identity of Charlie T. Wilbury Jr.

After the issue of his soundtrack album to the film *She's The One* in autumn 1996, Tom Petty broke his hand and was obliged to cancel the rest of the year's concert schedule. However, he managed to fulfil 20 dates early in the New Year.

PICKETT, Bobby 'Boris'   This singer-songwriter was born on 11 February 1940 in Somerville, Massachusetts. Inspired by the Boris Karloff horror movies he used to watch in his father's cinema, he recorded 'Monster Mash' in time for the 1962 Hallowe'en celebrations. The record topped the US chart that year, but his only other chart entry was a minor one, 'Monster's Holiday' reaching No 30.

When a re-promoted 'Monster Mash' sold a million all over again in 1973, Bobby 'Boris' Pickett reappeared on US television with a reconstituted Crypt-Kickers, and recommended touring. The record also entered the UK Top 5 that year.

Later, with no further record success, Bobby Pickett became a taxi driver.

PICKETT, Wilson   Soul singer-songwriter Wilson Pickett was born in Prattville, Alabama, on 18 March 1941. He first joined the Detroit R&B quintet the Falcons in 1959 and during his stint as lead vocalist they had a chart hit with 'I Found Love'.

Pickett turned solo in 1963, but it wasn't until 1965 that he made a chart impact, with 'In The Midnight Hour'. This was followed by: '634-5789 (Soulsville USA)', 'Land Of 1,000 Dances', 'Mustang Sally', 'Everybody Needs Somebody To

Love', 'I Found A Love Part I', 'Funky Broadway', 'Stag-O-Lee', 'She's Lookin' Good', 'I'm A Midnight Mover', 'Hey Jude', 'Sugar Sugar', 'Engine Number 9', 'Don't Let The Green Grass Fool You', 'Don't Knock My Love Part 1' and 'Fire And Water'.

Pickett has had numerous problems with the law over the years and was arrested in New York in 1974 for pulling out a gun during an argument. In 1987 he faced a five-year gaol term for the gun incident. In 1992 he was arrested for assault and for driving with open bottles of alcohol. He agreed to pay damages and enter a rehabilitation programme. In 1993 he pleaded guilty to assault charges and was sentenced to a year in gaol, plus five years' probation for the drink-driving offence, was fined and agreed to treatment for alcoholism and to undertake 200 hours of community service. His sentence began in January 1994 and he was released in 1996, still on probation – and was arrested for drugs offences.

Wilson Pickett has received many awards, was inducted into the Rock & Roll Hall Of Fame in 1992 and Rhino Records issued a compilation tribute, *A Man And A Half – The Best Of Wilson Pickett*, in 1993. His professional career since the mid-1980s has been a steady if unremarkable mixture of 'soul revues' in cabaret and remakes of his hits, such as a 1987 'dub' version of 'In The Midnight Hour'.

PICKETTYWITCH This group featured on the UK television show *Opportunity Knocks* in 1969. The two main vocalists were Polly Brown and Maggie Farren. The talent show brought them to the attention of hit songwriters Tony Macauley and John McLoud, who penned 'That Same Old Feeling' for them. It was followed by two further chart singles, '(It's Like A) Sad Old Kinda Movie' and 'Baby I Won't Let You Down'.

Other releases – 'Bring A Little Light Into My World', 'Summertime Feeling' and 'Waldo P. Emerson Jones', together with a *Pickettywitch* album – didn't register and they disbanded.

Pretty, blonde-haired Polly Brown, with a smoky, nasal voice not unlike that of **Dionne Warwick**, hit the headlines with her romance with disc jockey Jimmy Saville. She had a brief success as a solo artist with her 1974 hit 'Up In A Puff Of Smoke', which registered in both the UK and US Top 20s.

Polly lives in London and is, principally, a blues singer. Maggie Farran runs a successful publicity agency in London.

PINKERTON'S ASSORTED COLOURS The members of this group were Samuel 'Pinkerton' Kemp (vocals and autoharp), Tony Newman and Tom Long (guitar), Barrie Bernard (bass) and Dave Holland (drums). They had a minor hit with their debut disc, 'Mirror Mirror', followed by 'Don't Stop Loving Me Baby'.

Stuart Colman then replaced Bernard, and they truncated their name to Pinkerton's Colours, then simply Pinkerton.

In the 1970s, the remnants of the group became Flying Machine – who had a US Top 5 entry with 'Smile A Little Smile For Me'. Stuart Colman's book, *They Kept On Rockin': The Giants Of Rock 'N' Roll*, was published in 1982. He was also a London-based radio presenter and record producer (notably for **Shakin' Stevens** and an ailing **Billy Fury**) before moving to Nashville in the 1990s.

An attempt was made to relaunch Pinkerton's Assorted Colours on the sixties nostalgia circuit in the 1980s.

PINK FAIRIES, The Originally called the Social Deviants, then the Deviants, this group was formed in west London in 1967. The main members were Mick Farren (vocals), Duncan Sanderson (bass and vocals), Paul Rudolph (guitar and vocals) and Russell Hunter (drums). Various other artists sat in with them from time to time, including **Marc Bolan**, Peregrine Took and members of Group X.

As the Deviants, they cut three albums and toured the States. Farren quit the band to become a journalist and they were then joined by John Alder, known as 'Twink', a former member of the **Pretty Things**, who changed the band's name to the Pink Fairies.

Like many of the London-based underground outfits, they appeared on a number of gigs for free. Following their album release *Never Never Land*, Twink left the group (although he was to reappear occasionally during their various incarnations) and they continued as a trio, having minor chart success with their album *What A Bunch Of Sweeties*.

The group disbanded in 1973 and have been re-forming and disbanding ever since. With one of their revivals in 1987 they issued another album, *Kill 'Em And Eat 'Em*.

In 1994 John 'Twink' Alder released a solo album, *Mr Rainbow*, and he now works for Demon Records' distribution department. Duncan Sanderson is a freelance photographer

145

in London. Paul Rudolph lives in Canada and in 1990 was working in a Vancouver cycle shop. Russell Hunter is a London bus driver while Larry Wallis, a guitarist who joined one of their later line-ups, was house producer for Stiff Records before going freelance.

PIRATES, The This group started life as Johnny Kidd & the Pirates in 1959. They were led by Frederick Heath, known as **Johnny Kidd**, and made an impact with their first single, 'Shakin' All Over'. There was a shuffle in the personnel of the group soon after the record's release and the new outfit comprised Kidd, Johnny Spence on bass, Frank Farley on drums and Johnny Patto on guitar. Mick Green replaced Patto and the group had further hits with 'A Shot Of Rhythm & Blues', 'I'll Never Get Over You' and 'Hungry For Love'. Green left to join the Dakotas in 1965 and in 1966 Kidd was killed in a car crash.

Green, who was born in Matlock, Derbyshire, on 22 February 1944, was then to join **Cliff Bennett** & the Rebel Rousers. For a time he backed Engelbert Humperdinck and then formed a new band, Shanghai, with Cliff Bennett, Pete Kircher and Brian Alterman.

In 1976 the Pirates re-formed with Mick Green, Frank Farley and Johnny Spence, but disbanded again after a while. Green then backed various artists, including Paul McCartney and **Rod Stewart**, before re-forming the Pirates in

1996 with bass guitarist Bjorn Anders and drummer Romek Patrol.

PLATTERS, The This American vocal group was originally founded in 1953. Co-founder Tony Williams sang lead vocals on the group's major hits, which included: 'Only You', 'The Great Pretender', 'My Prayer', 'Twilight Time' and 'Smoke Gets In Your Eyes'. The other members of the band were David Lynch, Paul Robi, Herb Reed and Zola Taylor.

There was a major scandal in 1959, when the four male members of the group were arrested after being caught in compromising circumstances with four 19-year-old girls, three of them white. They were later acquitted in court.

Williams left the group to embark on a solo career in 1961 and was replaced by Sonny Turner. The following year Taylor and Robi also left to become solo singers and were replaced by Sandra Dawn and Nate Nelson. Their final US chart entry was 'Sweet, Sweet Lovin'' in 1967, which only reached No 70.

Over the years the Platters had enjoyed over 20 major hits, others including: 'The Magic Touch', 'You'll Never Know', 'Harbor Lights' and 'Red Sails In The Sunset'.

The Platters continued to appear in nightclubs throughout the world and are still performing, although none of the original members is in the current line-up.

The Platters

POETS, The The members of this Glasgow group were George Gallagher (vocals), Tony Miles (rhythm), Hume Paton (lead) and John Dawson (bass). **Andrew Loog Oldham** became their manager and they made their recording debut in December 1964 with 'Now We're Thru'. They followed with 'That's The Way It's Got To Be' and 'I Fly So Blue'.

The group then moved from Decca Records to Oldham's Immediate label and released 'Baby Don't You Do It'. There were various personnel changes, with Jim Breakey joining on drums and Fraser Watson playing rhythm, then lead, and Andi Mulvey on vocals. Their last single was 'Wooden Spoon' in 1967 and by the time that they disbanded in 1973 there were no original members left in the group.

POGUES, The This Irish folk-based band was formed in London in 1983. The group comprised Shane MacGowan (vocals and guitar), Jem Finer (banjo), Philip Chevron (guitar), James Fearnley (accordion), Spider Stacey (tin whistle), Caitlin O'Riordan (bass) and Andrew Ranked (drums).

Among their hit singles were: 'A Pair Of Brown Eyes', 'Sally Maclennane', 'Dirty Old Town', 'Poguetry In Motion', 'Haunted', 'Fairytale Of New York', 'If I Should Fall From Grace With God', 'Fiesta' and 'Yeah Yeah Yeah Yeah'.

Their album hits included *Red Roses For Me* and *Rum Sodomy And The Lash*.

Caitlin married **Elvis Costello** in May 1986 and left the group a few months later. Darryl Hunt replaced her on bass.

In 1991, MacGowan was sacked and new singer Joe Strummer stepped in. The Pogues continued to have success on record and on tour – and MacGowan was also to forge himself a creditable solo career, forming his own band, the Popes, in 1994, and making his debut with the album *The Snake* the following year. The LP included MacGowan singing one duet with Maire Brennan of Clannad and another with **Sinead O' Connor**. MacGowan also had a hit when he recorded 'My Way' in 1996.

The Pogues are still chart contenders, entering the UK Top 40 as recently as December 1997.

POLICE, The This trio was founded in 1977 by drummer Stuart Copeland, a former member of **Curved Air**, and managed by his brother Miles Copeland.

Stuart contacted Sting (real name Graham Sumner) in Newcastle and asked him to join, together with guitarist Henri Padovani. They released a single, 'Fall Out', then Padovani left to form the Flying Padovani Brothers. He was replaced by Andy Summers. The three gained some visual identity by all having blonde hair.

The Police then had tremendous success on record with a formidable array of chart singles, including: 'Can't Stand Losing You', 'Roxanne', 'Message In A Bottle', 'Fall Out', 'Walking On The Moon', 'So Lonely', 'Six Pack', 'Don't Stand So Close To Me', 'De Do Do Do, De Da Da Da', 'Invisible Sun', 'Every Little Thing She Does Is Magic', 'Spirits In The Material World', 'Every Breath You Take', 'Wrapped Around You Finger', 'Synchronicity' and 'King Of Pain'.

Their major album sellers included: *Outlandos D'Amour*, *Regatta De Blanc*, *Zenyatta Mondatta*, *Ghost In The Machine* and *Synchronicity*.

In the meantime, Sting was obtaining work as an actor, appearing in the movies *Quadrophenia*, *The Bride*, *Plenty* and *Dune*, and the UK television productions *Artemis '81* and *Brimstone & Treacle*. He also began to work on solo projects: his first solo single, 'Spread A Little Happiness', was

The Police

issued in 1982 and his debut album, *Dream Of The Blue Turtles*, in 1985.

The last gig the Police performed as a trio was Amnesty '86, although they did not officially split up.

Sting was to become a major superstar and continues to produce regular hit singles and albums.

Stuart Copeland had been composing film and television scores for some time, including for the movie *Rumble Fish* in 1982, the same year he issued an instrumental album, *I Advance Masked*.

Other movie scores included those for *Wall Street*, *Talk Radio*, *Hidden Agenda*, *First Power*, *Men At Work* and *Boys*, and for the television series *The Equalizer*.

Andy Summers issued his *XYZ* album in 1987, and succeeding albums included: *Mysterious Barricades*, *Golden Wire*, *Charming Snakes* and *World Gone Strange*. He also became involved in composing movie scores for films such as *2010* and *Weekend at Bernie's*.

Attributed to Sting and the Police, a re-mix of 'Roxanne' was in the UK Top 20 in December 1997.

POOLE, Brian Brian Poole is back on the nostalgia rock circuit. The former leader of the **Tremeloes** now fronts a new band called Brian Poole & Electrix.

Born in Barking, Essex, on 2 November 1941, Poole formed his first band in the late 1950s. The group signed with Decca in 1960 and, as Brian Poole & the Tremeloes, had their first hit with 'Twist and Shout', followed by 'Do You Love Me', 'I Can Dance', 'Candy Man', 'Someone Someone', 'Twelve Steps To Love', 'The Three Bells' and 'I Love Candy'. Poole left the group in 1966 to go solo, but had no further success on record.

The Tremeloes attended Brian's wedding to his fan club secretary Pamela Rice on 7 October 1968. When their first daughter, Karen, was born, Brian left the music business to work as a butcher in his brother's shop. Their second daughter, Shellie, was born a year later.

Although Pam works for an American computer software firm, she has decided also to take on a new fan club – that of Alisha's Attic. Karen and Shellie Poole are the lead singers and songwriters in this band, whose debut album, *Alisha Rules The World*, went gold following its release in November 1996. By mid-1997 they had had a string of hit singles, including: 'I Am, I Feel,' 'Alisha Rules The World', 'Indestructible' and 'Air We Breathe'. Following the release of his eponymous CD/album *Brian Poole*, their father recorded a new single penned for him by his daughters.

At one time, Brian Poole formed his own recording company, Outlook Records. One of his recent recording projects saw him recruit four other stars of the sixties – Reg Presley of the **Troggs**, Mike Pender of the **Searchers**, Tony Crane of the **Merseybeats** and Clem Curtis of the **Foundations** – in an outfit called the Corporation. Their first single was the old Showstoppers hit 'It Ain't Nothin' But A Houseparty'.

POP, Iggy Born James Jewel Osterberg on 21 April 1947, on joining the Iguanas in 1964 this singer-songwriter-drummer changed his name to Iggy. For a time he played drums for various musicians and groups, including the Shangri-Las and Buddy Guy. He joined the Prime Movers in 1965 and the Butterfield Blues Band in 1966. The following year he formed the Psychedelic Stooges, but truncated their name to the Stooges later on. Iggy left the band at the beginning of 1974.

In the 1970s, he disappeared from the music scene for almost two years, being treated in a psychiatric clinic for his drugs addiction. His only visitor was David Bowie, who had developed a friendship with him following their first meeting in 1972. Both musicians moved to Switzerland, where they spent a great deal of time recording.

Iggy emerged in 1977 with his first solo album, *The Idiot*, produced by Bowie, and the two also collaborated on a number called 'China Girl'.

Over the years, Iggy has had numerous album releases, including: *Lust For Life*, *New Values*, *Soldier*, *Party*, *Brick By Brick* and *American Caesar*. His singles include: 'Bang Bang', 'Cry For Love', 'Real Wild Child', 'Livin' On The Edge' and 'Beside You'. He has also recorded duets with Kate Pierson and Debbie Harry.

Guest spots in movies graduated to fatter parts, and his film appearances include roles in *Sid And Nancy*, *Cry Baby*, *Dead Man* and *City Of Angels*.

In 1997, Iggy Pop was at the console for the re-mixed release of the Stooges' 1973 album, *Raw Power*.

POWER, Duffy One of the original stable of acts managed by impresario **Larry Parnes**, Duffy Power gained a reputation as a powerful performer, but never achieved any success on record.

Over the past five years, three CDs of Duffy Power's old recordings have been issued. In 1995 he taped a new album, produced by Peter Brown and featuring Jack Bruce, Danny Thompson, Dick Heckstall-Smith and Clem Clempson.

PRESTON, Johnny This singer was born John Preston Courville in Port Arthur, Texas, on 18 August 1939. While at Lamar State College of Technology in Beaumont, he formed the Shades with Mike Akin, Butch Crouch and Johnny Wilkson.

In 1957 they were spotted appearing at a nightclub by Bill Hall and the disc jockey **J.P. Richardson**, who was known as the Big Bopper. Hall took over management of the singer and renamed him Johnny Preston, while the Big Bopper produced him, recording the number 'Running Bear', a tale of ill-fated Indian lovers, which the Bopper also wrote.

Soon afterwards, Richardson died in the air crash which killed **Buddy Holly** and **Ritchie Valens**, and the record was postponed. When it was eventually released, initially it did not do well. The record company then noticed it had been pushed in St Louis by a local jukebox operator and had sold 15,000 in that city alone, so they re-promoted it and it topped the US chart.

Preston initially began touring the States on bills with artists such as **Brenda Lee** and **Freddie Cannon**, dressed in Indian costume. Preston's next release, 'Cradle Of Love', was also a major seller, and he toured the UK on a bill with **Conway Twitty** and Freddie Cannon. His third and final Top 20 hit was 'Feel So Good'.

Preston continued to record, without much success, with numbers such as 'Charming Billy', 'I Want A Rock 'N' Roll Guitar', 'Little Blue', 'Leave My Kitten Alone' and 'Broken Hearts Anonymous'.

A family man, Johnny Preston currently works as a contract pipe fitter. He says he does not intend to join any further nostalgia tours, having decided not to go on the road again. His income is supplemented by a regular royalty bonus, as he secured the rights to all of his own recordings.

PRETENDERS, The This group was founded in the UK in 1978 and comprised Chrissie Hynde (lead vocals), **James Honeyman-Scott** (keyboards, guitar and vocals), **Pete Farndon** (bass) and Martin Chambers (drums).

Chrissie was born in Akron, Ohio, on 7 September 1951 and moved to London in the late 1960s. She became an artist's model at St Martin's School of Art, worked in Malcolm McLaren's sex shop and joined the *New Musical Express* as a rock journalist. In 1974 she moved to Paris to join the Frenchies, then returned to the States to join Jack Rabbit. She returned to France and eventually ended up back in London, where she became a backing singer on the Stiff Records nationwide tour.

In 1978 she teamed up with a group of musicians and they cut their first record as the Pretenders. Their debut single, 'Stop Your Sobbing', charted and was followed by 'Kid', while their third release, 'Brass In Pocket', topped the UK chart, as did their album debut, *Pretenders*.

The group's other hit singles included: 'Talk Of The Town', 'Message Of Love', 'Day After Day', 'I Go To Sleep', 'Back On The Chain Gang', '2000 Miles' and 'Thin Line Between Love And Hate'.

Honeyman-Scott died in 1982, Farndon the following year. Chrissie had a baby with Ray Davies of the **Kinks** in 1983, then married Jim Kerr of Simple Minds the following year and gave birth to another baby. For a time it looked as if the Pretenders' chapter was over, but she became guest singer on UB40's reworking of Sonny & Cher's 'I Got You Babe' in 1985.

The following year Chrissie re-formed the Pretenders, still with Mike Foster, but adding Robbie MacIntosh and Blair Cunningham of **Haircut 100** and T.M. Stevens and Bernie Worrell of **Talking Heads**. Another hit run began with 'Don't Get Me Wrong', 'Hymn To Her' and 'If There Was A Man'.

The Pretenders recorded *Isle Of View*, an 'unplugged' album in front of a studio audience, in 1995, and the documentary *The Pretenders: No Turn Left Unstoned*, was screened on UK television.

PRETTY THINGS, The This group was formed in 1963 with Dick Taylor, a founder member of the **Rolling Stones**, on guitar, Phil May (vocals), Brian Pendleton (rhythm), John Stax (bass) and Peter Kitley (drums). Kitley was

149

replaced by Viv Andrews, who was swiftly replaced by Viv Prince prior to their debut single, 'Rosalyn'.

The Pretties were certainly more outrageous than the Rolling Stones and produced a powerful series of singles and albums that, although they achieved a degree of chart success, did not bring them the fame their talent warranted. Their singles included 'Midnight To Six Man' and 'Come Up And See Me' and their albums were also influential, particularly *SF Sorrow*, *Parachute* and *Freeway Madness*.

Throughout the group's career there were constant changes in personnel, Prince being replaced in 1965 by Skip Alan. Stax and Pendleton left to be replaced by Wally Allen and John Povey. Alan was replaced by John Alder, but later rejoined the band, and Dick Taylor left in 1969. The group disbanded in 1971, then reformed a few years later, and they have continued to disband and re-form ever since, usually with May and Taylor in the line-up. Their 1990 incarnation saw them issue 'Eve Of Destruction' and in 1995 they released a retrospective album, *Unrepentant*.

By 1996 Phil May and Dick Taylor were still leading the group. Taylor lived in the Isle of Wight, but his house fell into the sea. May has continued to live in west London. Of the varous other former members, Viv Prince lives in Portugal, where he breeds dogs, Brian Pendleton is 'something in the City', John Stax lives in Australia, Skip Alan was the inventor of the Swivelwalker, a mobility aid for paraplegics, John Povey is a Buddhist and Wally Allen lives in Sussex.

PRINCE   Prince Rogers Nelson was born in Minneapolis, Minnesota, on 7 June 1961. He started out as lead singer with a group called Grand Central while he was still at high school. They later changed their name to Champagne. When the group split, he took tapes of his songs to Warner Bros and was given a recording contract, making his debut with the album *For You* in 1978, from which the single 'Soft & Wet' was taken.

In 1981, Prince created a backing group that became known as the Revolution and the following year added a girl group, Vanity 6. Later another all-girl group, Apollonia 6, replaced them.

Prince also starred in two movies, the semi-autobiographical *Purple Rain* in 1984, for which

he received an Oscar for Best Original Score, and *Under The Cherry Moon* in 1986.

By 1991 he had a new backing band, New Power Generation, the same year that the documentary *The Prince Of Paisley Park* was shown on UK television.

Prince's achievements as a recording artist have been considerable. Singles hits include: 'Little Red Corvette', 'Delirious', 'When Doves Cry', 'Let's Go Crazy', 'Purple Rain', 'I Would Die 4 U', 'Take Me With You', 'Paisley Park', 'Raspberry Beret', 'Pop Life', 'Kiss', 'Sign O' The Times', 'I Could Never Take The Place Of Your Man', 'Alphabet St', 'I Wish U Heaven', 'Batdance', 'Partyman', 'Thieves In The Temple', 'Cream', 'Money Don't Matter 2 Night', 'My Name Is Prince', 'The Morning Papers', 'The Most Beautiful Girl In The World', 'Letitgo', 'Prince Medley' and 'Gold'.

He also has a formidable run of album hits stretching from *For You* to *The Gold Experience*.

On his thirty-fifth birthday in 1993, Prince announced that he had changed his name to a symbol, which, due to its design, resulted in his being referred to as 'the artist formerly known as Prince'.

Prince married Mayte Garcia, once a dancer in his troupe, on St Valentine's Day 1996 and their first child was born in 1997. A new album – Prince's first since *The Gold Experience* in 1995 – is understood to be in preparation.

PRINCE BUSTER   Born Cecil Bustamante Campbell in Kingston, Jamaica, on 28 May 1938, this singer-producer-entrepreneur abandoned his career as a boxer to take part in the development of the ska sound in Jamaica and launched record companies, ran record shops, discovered artists and recorded in his own right as Prince Buster.

Among his many releases were 'Oh Carolina', 'Al Capone', 'Madness', 'Judge Dread' and 'Ten Commandments'.

Still resident in Jamaica, Prince Buster returned to live work in the 1980s as a prelude to a relaunch as a recording artist in 1992.

PROBY, P.J.   This singer-songwriter-cabaret artist was born James Marcus Smith in Texas on 6 November 1938. He attended a military academy and his sister dated **Elvis Presley**. **Eddie Cochran's** girfriend dubbed him P.J. He chauffeured Paul Newman around Hollywood and also dated **Dean Martin's** daughter. Jack Good invited him to the UK to appear on the television special *Around The Beatles*, and he hit No 3 in the chart with the single 'Hold Me'. He followed up with two further Top 10 hits – 'Together' and 'Somewhere' – and also charted with 'I Apologise' and 'Maria'.

Proby's entire career crumbled due to an incident on stage in Croydon in January 1965, when his trousers split and Tom Jones replaced him. Due to the incident, he was also banned from touring by a number of the theatre chains. His recording career foundered and he later became bankrupt for the second time – he had already been declared a bankrupt in the States.

Controversy dogged Proby over the years. He loosed off an air pistol at his third wife and pursued a farmer's 14-year-old daughter, who later became his fifth wife. In addition to his legal marriages, he had six common-law wives.

In 1968 Proby became engaged to Vanessa Forsyth, but discovered he already had two wives. On learning his second marriage was probably bigamous, he said: 'How the hell was I to know the divorce had not come through?' Forsyth then left him.

Proby moved north and became a shepherd in Bolton and a muck spreader in Huddersfield, before returning to London and a job as a janitor in Hammersmith.

He once faced a possible stiff sentence for firing an air gun with pellets and was fined £60 for taking an axe to his unpaid, live-in secretary. The flamboyant singer drank five bottles of bourbon a day, but renounced alcohol when he had a heart attack.

Jack Good came to his rescue in 1970 when he featured Proby in the musical *Catch My Soul*. He later appeared as Elvis in the stage production *Elvis On Stage*, but was sacked due to his eccentric behaviour. In 1978 he was hired to appear in *Elvis The Musical* in London's West End, but was fired for trying to rewrite the script. In 1984 Proby fell off the stage during a Rock & Roll Legends concert.

Appearing on the cabaret circuit for a time, he based himself in the north of England and began recording for a record label in Manchester. One of his singles was a version of 'Tainted Love', the **Soft Cell** hit.

After more years in the wilderness, Proby stepped back into the limelight in the 1990s when he appeared in the West End in another stage musical as Elvis Presley. He also appeared in the **Roy Orbison** tribute show *Only The*

Lonely, singing old hits. For a while he was linked romantically to **Billie Davis**.

In January 1997 Proby had his first major album release in 20 years with *Legend*, a 12-track production which included collaborations with St Etienne and Marc Almond. In 1996, 'Yesterday Has Gone', a single recorded with Almond, was released and entered the chart. Later, in 1997, P.J. Proby began touring as the Godfather in *Quadrophenia*.

P.J. Proby

PROCOL HARUM This group had their biggest hit in 1967 with their debut single, 'A Whiter Shade Of Pale', composed by Gary Brooker and lyricist Keith Reid. The other members of the band were Matthew Fisher (organ), Dave Knights (bass), Ray Royer (guitar) and Bobby Harrison (drums). The record was eventually to sell six million copies.

Harrison and Royer were replaced by Robin Trower and B.J. Wilson, and the group's second hit was the single 'Homburg'. Fisher and Knights left in 1969, to be replaced by Chris Copping on bass and keyboards. By this time the band consisted of all the members of a previous band called the Paramounts, who had had a minor hit with 'Poison Ivy' in 1964. Trower left in 1971 to be replaced by Dave Ball, who in turn left the band in 1972, his replacement being Mick Grabham.

American songwriters Leiber & Stoller produced Procul Harum's ninth album. There were then more personnel changes, before the group disbanded following a farewell tour in 1977, although they reunited briefly the same year to appear at the BPI Awards ceremony, where 'A Whiter Shade Of Pale' was voted Best British Hit Single 1952–1977.

Gary Brooker pursued a solo career, his album *No More Fear Of Flying* being produced by George Martin, and he also collaborated with Eric Clapton. A keen angler, he became Europe's fly fishing champion in 1987. Brooker had also bought himself a public house in Godalming, Surrey, and formed a pub band called No Stiletto Shoes. At the end of 1990 he decided he wanted to record another Procol Harum album and contacted Keith Reid, who by then was living in New York.

The group re-formed in 1992 with the Brooker, Trower, Fisher and Reid combination and issued a new album, *The Prodigal Stranger*, although it did not become a chart hit. In 1995 they recorded a CD of symphonic versions of their hits, *The Symphonic Procol Harum*, with a full orchestra and 50-piece choir. The group carried on touring and in 1996 teamed up with the London Symphony Orchestra to perform at the Barbican Centre.

In November 1997 the 52-track triple CD set *Procol Harum: 30th Anniversary Anthology* was released. This contained their four complete albums, A- and B-sides of singles, demo discs and the first-ever stereo release of 'A Whiter Shade Of Pale'. In 1998 the eponymous *Procol Harum* was issued – their debut album from the original mastertapes, plus ten bonus tracks.

PUCKETT, Gary Gary Puckett was the leader of a group who were formed in San Diego but were named after the town of Union Gap in Washington, the site of a famous Civil War battle.

Puckett, who was born in Hibbing, Minnesota, on 17 October 1942, led a band that comprised Dwight Bennett (tenor sax), Kerry Chater (bass), Gary Withem (woodwind and piano) and Paul Whitbread (drums). Initially their gimmick was to dress in Civil War outfits and they termed themselves in military fashion: General Pucket, Sergeant Bennett, Corporal Chater and Privates Withem and Whitbread.

Their hit singles included: 'Woman Woman', 'Young Girl', 'Lady Willpower', 'Over You', 'Don't Give In To Him' and 'This Girl Is A Woman Now'.

The group split in 1971 and Puckett continued as a solo artist, releasing six singles and an album between 1970 and 1972. He also appeared on the **Monkees'** twentieth anniversary tour.

Kerry Chater is now a songwriter in Nashville.

Paul Whitbread plays drums occasionally and books bands. He lives in San Diego, where Gary Withem teaches music at a talent school.

Only one original member, Dwight Bennett, is playing regularly – on sax in Flash Cadillac & the Continental Kids.

QUATRO, Suzi The 'Queen of Glam Rock' was born in Detroit, Michigan, on 3 June 1950. Discovered by producer Mickie Most, Suzi had 15 chart hits during the 1970s and sold over 40 million records. The singer-bass guitarist, who dressed in black leather jump suits, topped the charts with numbers such as 'Can The Can' and 'Devil Gate Drive'. Her last hit was 'Heart Of Stone' in 1982.

Suzi enjoyed a degree of success as an actress, appearing on television as Leather Tuscadero in *Happy Days* and in UK dramas such as *Minder* and comedies like *Absolutely Fabulous*. She also starred in the 1986 stage production of *Annie Get Your Gun*.

By the mid-1980s Suzi was appearing in seventies revival shows with artists such as **Gary Glitter**, and was recording for continental companies.

She married Len Tuckey, lead guitarist with her band, and the couple had two children, Richard and Laura. They settled in a sixteenth-century house in Essex.

Len and Suzi were later divorced and she married Rainer Haas, a German millionaire promoter. She continues to live in Essex during the week, commuting to stay with her husband at weekends at their home in Hamburg.

Suzi re-recorded her hits for the Scandinavian label CNC in 1996 and released an album, *What Goes Around*.

Suzi Quatro continues to appear at festivals and pops up regularly on television and radio. During 1998 she was celebrating the silver anniversary of her first hit by recording an album of new material.

In the same year, Suzi was pleased to see her 15-year-old daughter following in her footsteps as a singer.

QUICKSILVER MESSENGER SERVICE

This group was formed in San Francisco in 1964. The members were Gary Duncan and John Cipollina (guitar), David Freiberg (bass) and Greg Elmore (drums).

The band were part of the big West Coast Sound movement in San Francisco, appearing regularly at the Fillmore and Avalon Ballrooms, the first Human Be-in in Golden Gate Park and the Monterey Pop Festival.

They made their debut album, *Quicksilver Messenger Service*, in 1968, followed by *Happy Trails* the next year. Other album releases included *Just For Love*, *What About Me* and *Comin' Thru*. Nicky Hopkins joined them in 1969.

The group eventually folded and there were various attempts to revive it during the 1980s.

Since the failed re-formation, the group has been no more, and former members John Cipollina and Nicky Hopkins have since died, but a 1993 compilation album, *The Ultimate Journey*, was well received.

Suzi Quatro

RADHA KRSNA TEMPLE George Harrison of the Beatles was impressed by Swami Prabhupada, a 70-year-old Indian holy man who had travelled to New York in 1965 to bring a holy maha-mantra to the West. George decided to record the devotional chant, and the final recordings were made at Abbey Road Studios. A group of devotees chanted the mantra, Paul and Linda McCartney operated the control console and George played organ.

The result was the single 'Hare Krisna Mantra' by Hare Krsna Temple, issued on the Apple label. It reached No 17 in the UK chart. Their second single, 'Govinda', reached No 23 and George also produced an album, *The Radha Krsna Temple*.

The first single enjoyed international success, particularly in the European charts, and reached No 1 in Germany and Czechoslovakia and the Top 10 in Japan.

Swami Prabhupada died on 17 November 1977. He was 81 years old and left a gold ring with a disciple, saying: 'Please give this to George Harrison. He was a good friend to us all. He loves Krsna sincerely, and I love him. He was my archangel!'

RAFFERTY, Gerry This singer-songwriter was born in Paisley, Scotland, on 16 April 1947. He was originally a member of the Humblebums, a folk trio which also included Billy Connolly and Tam Harvey, in 1968. The band issued two unsuccessful albums, then split up in 1970, with Rafferty releasing his first solo album, *Can I Have My Money Back*, the following year.

Rafferty formed Stealers Wheel in 1972 with guitarist Paul Pilnick, bassist Tony Williams and drummer Rod Coombes. They issued an album, *Stealers Wheel*, which spawned the 1973 hit single 'Stuck In The Middle With You'.

The group was beset by legal problems between Rafferty and his manager, and his record company kept him out of the studio until these were resolved in 1978. He then moved to a different company and recorded the album *City To City*. Two of its tracks, 'Baker Street' and 'Night Owl', became hit singles.

Rafferty continued to issue records during the 1980s, but without success.

In the 1990s, 'Stuck In The Middle With You' was utilized during a particularly gruesome scene in Quentin Tarantino's cult movie *Reservoir Dogs*.

In 1993, Gerry Rafferty's album *On A Wing And A Prayer* was accompanied by a rare tour by its creator.

RAMONES, The This band was formed in New York in 1974. The members were Joey Ramone (real name Jeffrey Hyman; vocals), Tommy Ramone (real name Thomas Edrelyi; drums), Johnny Ramone (real name John Cummings; guitar) and Dee Dee Ramone (real name Douglas Colvin; bass). Allegedly, they took their name from the pseudonym Paul McCartney used when he toured Scotland with the Silver Beatles in 1960 – Paul Ramone.

The band made their recording debut in 1976 with 'Blitzkrieg Bop'.

The Ramones appeared frequently in the UK and had more success in the UK chart than in the US. Their UK hit singles included: 'Sheena Is A Punk Rocker', 'Swallow My Pride', 'Don't Come Close', 'Rock 'n' Roll High School', 'Baby I Love You', 'Do You Remember Rock 'n' Roll Radio' and 'Somebody Put Something In My Drink'.

Their UK chart albums were: *Leave Home*, *Rocket To Russia*, *Road To Ruin*, *It's Alive*, *End Of The Century* and *Too Tough To Die*.

Tommy left the band in 1978, but continued to produce their records. Other producers for the group were to include Phil Spector and Graham Gouldman. Marky Ramone (real name Marc Bell) took Tommy's place. Marky left in 1983 and was replaced by Richard Beau, who called himself Ritchie Ramone.

Personnel changes continued, with Dee Dee leaving in 1989 to become a rap artist under the name Dee Dee King. In 1992 he formed a band called Dee Dee Ramone & the Chinese Dragons. His replacement was Christopher Joseph Ward, who adopted the name C.J. Ramone.

Tommy Ramone is now a full-time record producer. Following a so-called farewell tour in 1995, the remaining Ramones and a replacement drummer were still a functioning group for a London concert in the summer of 1996.

REA, Chris Singer-songwriter Chris Rea was born in Middlesbrough, Cleveland, on 4 March 1951. He began his solo career in 1977 and was successful in the international charts.

His UK hits included: 'Fool (If You Think It's Over)', 'Diamonds', 'Loving You', 'I Can Hear Your Heartbeat', 'I Don't Know What It Is But I Love It', 'Stainsby Girls', 'Josephine', 'It's All Gone', 'On The Beach', 'Let's Dance', 'Loving

You Again', 'Joys Of Christmas', 'Que Sera', 'On The Beach Summer '88', 'Driving Home For Christmas' and 'Road To Hell'.

In 1994, during a trip to France to buy a house, Rea was struck down with peritonitis and put into intensive care. His weight fell drastically and he had to undergo five major operations.

In January 1998 Rea celebrated the twentieth anniversary of his career with a new album, *The Blue Café*, and a single from it, 'Square Peg, Round Hole'. The 47-year-old singer-songwriter had been with his wife Joan since 1968, although they didn't marry for 11 years. Their two daughters, Josephine and Julia, were now fourteen and eight years old respectively.

REGAN, Joan Born in Romford, Essex, on 19 January 1928, this singer was a major star in the 1950s and enjoyed a string of hit records, including: 'Ricochet', 'Someone Else's Roses', 'If I Give My Heart To You', 'Prize Of Gold', 'Open Up Your Heart', 'May You Always', 'Happy Anniversary', 'Papa Loves Mama', 'One Of The Lucky Ones' and 'Must Be Santa'.

In her personal life, Joan suffered many problems. When her first husband Harry Claff was sentenced to five year's imprisonment for fraud, she suffered a nervous breakdown. She divorced him and married Martin Cowan, and moved to Florida. A domestic accident in her home there in 1984 left her paralysed and speechless. She was involved in speech therapy, and when visiting the UK in 1987 was invited to sing again.

As a result, in the 1990s Joan Regan was well enough to undertake summer shows in the UK.

REPARATA & THE DELRONS American female vocal group Reparata & the Delrons had their origins in 1962 when four girls – Mary Aiese, Nanette Licari, Anne Fitzgerald and Regina Gallagher – formed the Del-Rons. There were some personnel changes by time they recorded their first single, 'Whenever A Teenager Cries', but the group eventually settled down to a trio consisting of Aiese, Licari and Lorraine Mazzola. It was not until 1968 that they had a big hit in the UK with 'Captain Of Your Ship'. By this time they were known as Reparata & the Delrons, with Mary assuming the name Reparata.

When Mary Aiese left in 1970, the group continued for another three years with Lorraine assuming the name Reparata – she also retained this alias for her subsequent sojourn in **Barry**

Manilow's backing combo. However, there was a dispute over her rights to the name after Mary Aiese resumed a singing career that peaked commercially with 'Shoes' – attributed to Reparata – in the UK Top 50 in 1975.

RICHARD, Cliff The UK's greatest solo pop star was born Harry Rodger Webb on 14 October 1940 in Lucknow, India. Cliff Richard & the Shadows were formed in 1958 and they became the UK's leading group prior to the Beatles.

Cliff has issued in excess of 100 singles, virtually all of them chart hits. He follows the Beatles and **Elvis Presley** with the largest number of UK chart-toppers. These include: 'Travellin' Light', 'Living Doll', 'Please Don't Tease', 'I Love You', 'The Young Ones', 'Bachelor Boy', 'Summer Holiday', 'The Minute You're Gone', 'Congratulations', 'We Don't Talk Anymore' and 'Mistletoe And Wine'.

Cliff Richard

155

The 'Peter Pan Of Pop' continues to make headlines. He was knighted by the Queen and in 1996, during a rainy spell at Wimbledon, entertained the crowds with an impromptu performance of 'Congratulations'. He then broke theatre records with his stage musical *Heathcliffe*.

In July 1997 the 56-year-old star announced he might no longer continue recording. He cited the radio stations that were preventing his music from reaching an audience because they refused to play his hits. He told the *Evening Standard* newspaper: 'If EMI can't get airplay, it's not worth doing any more records. Capital say that I'm not the right market for them and that young people don't like my music. Even Phil Collins isn't getting any airplay.' Cliff's agent Bill Latham commented: 'Cliff is frustrated that Radio 1 won't play his records. The listeners don't get the opportunity to judge for themselves.'

In December 1997, EMI issued a 4-CD boxed set entitled *Cliff Richard: The Rock 'n' Roll Years 1958–1963*.

In 1998, having had 13 No 1 hits and sold 250 million records over four decades, Cliff Richard celebrated the fortieth anniversary of the start of his career with a series of concerts at the Royal Albert Hall in November and December. He also issued his fifty-eighth album and formed a new record label with former EMI managing director Clive Black.

RIGHTEOUS BROTHERS, The
This vocal duo comprised Bill Medley, born in Santa Ana, California, on 19 September 1940, and Bobby Hatfield, born in Beaver Dam, Wisconsin, on 10 August 1940.

They decided to team up in 1962, and it was during a performance before black marines at the Black Derby in Santa Ana that they were dubbed the Righteous Brothers.

Following a hit with 'Little Latin Lupe Lu' and an appearance on the bill of a Beatles tour in the US, they were spotted by producer Phil Spector and became the first white act on his Philles label. Their first release for him, 'You've Lost That Lovin' Feelin'', topped the chart on both sides of the Atlantic.

In the UK, it looked as if Cilla Black would beat them to the top with her cover version, but the **Rolling Stones'** manager **Andrew Loog Oldham** took an advertisement in the music press praising the Righteous Brothers' version – which then leap-frogged Cilla's into the top position.

'Just Once In My Life', 'Unchained Melody' and 'Ebb Tide' entered the charts, then Spector sold their contract to MGM Records for a million dollars. They had a series of three chart hits with MGM's Verve label: '(You're My) Soul And Inspiration', 'He' and 'Go Ahead And Cry'.

Medley left in 1968 to pursue a solo career and Hatfield replaced him with Jimmy Walker. However, for legal reasons they had to wait a year before they were allowed to use the name the Righteous Brothers. 1974 saw them with another trio of hits, 'Rock And Roll Heaven', 'Give It To The People' and 'Dream On'.

Medley's wife Karen was murdered in 1976 and Bill retired from the business for a five-year period. When he resumed his recording career in 1981, 'You've Lost That Lovin' Feelin'' had been re-released once again.

In 1982, Medley reunited with Hatfield for an anniversary special of the television show *American Bandstand*. In 1984 he notched up a solo hit in the US C&W chart with 'Still I Do', and topped the pop chart three years on with '(I've Had) The Time Of My Life', a duet with Jennifer Warnes from the movie *Dirty Dancing*.

In 1990 the Righteous Brothers topped the chart again with 'Unchained Melody', which had been featured in the Demi Moore film *Ghost*, and yet another re-issue of 'You've Lost That Loving Feeling' then entered the Top 20. A year later another film, *Rambo III*, returned Medley to prominence via a revival of 'He Ain't Heavy He's My Brother'.

Bill Medley and Bobby Hatfield teamed up once again in 1994 for a season in Las Vegas and have remained together since for similar engagements.

RIVERS, Johnny
Singer-songwriter-producer John Ramistella was born in New York on 7 November 1942, although he was raised in Baton Rouge.

He first began recording in 1956, but it was not until he moved back to New York and met disc jockey Alan Freed, who aided him in obtaining a recording contract – and also encouraged him to change his name to Johnny Rivers – that he experienced success.

Rivers moved to Los Angeles and became hugely popular as a rock performer during his residency at the Whiskey A Go-Go, which resulted in his album chart debut with *Johnny Rivers At The Whiskey A Go-Go*. A stream of chart albums was to follow.

Rivers' singles hits, which stretched from 1964 to 1977, included: 'Memphis', 'Maybelline', 'Mountain Of Love', 'Midnight Special', 'Seventh Son', 'Where Have All The Flowers Gone', 'Under Your Spell Again', 'Secret Agent Man', '(I Washed My Hands) In Muddy Water', 'Poor Side Of Town', 'Baby I Need Your Lovin'', 'The Tracks Of My Tears', 'Summer Rain', 'Rockin' Pneumonia', 'Blue Suede Shoes', 'Help Me Rhonda', 'Swayin' To The Music' and 'Curious Mind'.

Rivers was also to prove an astute businessman, setting up his own music publishing company and record label, for which he signed up acts such as 5th Dimension. He was to produce their hits, such as 'Up, Up And Away', for which he received a Grammy Award.

Having sold his publishing company for more than $1 million and discovered and produced a host of major acts, Rivers went into semi-retirement in 1983.

In 1990, Rhino Records issued the hit compilation *Johnny Rivers: Anthology 1964–1977* and Rivers decided to perform on occasional tours of the US. Recently he was said to have been recording in Sun Studios with **Carl Perkins** and James Burton. Carl has since died.

ROBINSON, Smokey Born William Robinson on 19 February 1940 in Detroit, Michigan, in 1954, this singer-songwriter founded the vocal group the Matadors, which evolved into the Miracles. They became the first act to sign with Tamla Motown and made their recording debut with 'Way Over There' in 1960. The following year, Robinson and Motown boss Berry Gordy co-wrote 'Shop Around', which became a Miracles hit and Motown's first million-seller.

Other hit singles by the Miracles included: 'What's So Good About Goodbye', 'I'll Try Something New', 'You've Really Got A Hold On Me', A Love She Can Count On', 'Mickey's Monkey', 'I Gotta Dance To Keep From Crying', 'I Like It Like That', 'That's What Love Is Made Of', 'Ooo Baby Baby', 'The Tracks Of My Tears', 'My Girl Has Gone', 'Going To A Go-Go', 'I'm The One That You Need', 'The Love I Saw In You Was Just A Mirage', 'More Love', 'I Second That Emotion', 'If You Can Want', 'Yester Love', 'Special Occasion', 'Baby Baby Don't Cry', 'Abraham Martin And John', 'Doggone Right', 'Here I Go Again', 'Point It Out', 'The Tears Of A Clown', 'I Don't Blame You At All', 'Do It Baby' and 'Love Machine'.

During the 1960s, Robinson became a prolific Motown songwriter, spinning hit after hit for artists ranging from the Temptations to Mary Wells. He also became involved in administrative duties for the label and became vice president of Motown, a position that later affected his songwriting output. He also left the Miracles to pursue a solo career in 1972.

Robinson's solo hits included: 'Baby Come Close', 'Baby That's Backatcha', 'The Agony And The Ecstasy', 'Cruisin'', 'Let Me Be The Clock', 'Being With You' and 'Tell Me Tomorrow'.

In recent years, Robinson has been the recipient of many awards from his peers, and has also been inducted into the Rock & Roll Hall Of Fame and the Songwriters Hall Of Fame. He has performed duets with other artists, among them Aretha Franklin, Manhattan Transfer, **Tammy Wynette** and Bryan Adams, and last toured the UK in 1992.

In 1996 Motown issued a 4-CD boxed set, *The 35th Anniversary Collection*.

Despite marital problems and his bout of drug addiction during the 1980s, Smokey Robinson and his wife, Claudette Rogers, a former member of the Miracles, are still together. They married in 1959 and have two children, Berry and Tamla. Robinson's snail-paced recording itinerary has resumed.

ROCKIN' BERRIES, The This Brumbeat comedy group were noted for their impressions of other pop artists. They comprised Chuck Botfield, Roy Austin and Geoff Turton (guitar), Clive Lea (vocals), and Clive Bond (drums).

They had a two-year spate of hits in the 1960s with 'I Didn't Mean To Hurt You', 'He's In Town', 'What In The World's Come Over You', 'Poor Man's Son', 'You're My Girl' and 'The Water Is Over My Head'.

The group had a smoother transition into the cabaret field than other beat groups, as their forte of comedy and impressions was more suited to that circuit.

Chuck Botfield is the *de facto* leader of the present-day Rockin' Berries. Although Geoff Turton still appears with the group, he has invested in the hotel business following a lucrative solo windfall in the US in 1969 with the Top 10 hit 'Baby Take Me In Your Arms', under his Jefferson pseudonym. Keith Smart, former drummer with Roy Wood, and impressionist Stevie Riks have joined the two original members in the current line-up.

157

After leaving the group, Clive Lea functioned as a comedy impressionist with the Black Abbotts.

RODGERS, Clodagh

This attractive, long-limbed singer was born in Northern Ireland. She made her chart debut in 1969, reaching No 3 in the chart with 'Come Back And Shake Me'. Other hits which followed included: 'Goodnight Midnight', 'Biljo', 'Everybody Go Home The Party's Over', 'Jack In The Box' and 'Lady Love Bug'.

In 1969, Clodagh won the Best Legs In British Showbusiness trophy, had her voice insured for £1million and won the 1971 Eurovision Song Contest with 'Jack In The Box'.

After her hits dried up in 1972, Clodagh toured for a while and then decided to give up appearing on one-nighters. She preferred to spend time at home raising her two sons – Matthew, from her marriage to her first husband, her former manager John Morris, and Sam, from her second marriage to guitarist Ian Sorbie.

For a while Clodagh and Ian ran a wine and restaurant business in Paignton, Devon, but it collapsed and they ended up in the bankruptcy court in 1992.

Tragically, Ian died from a brain tumour in 1995. He was only 43 years old.

After this, Clodagh rarely appeared in pop shows but occasionally starred in pantomime, often playing the Fairy Godmother in *Cinderella*.

Clodagh Rodgers began recording again and in 1997 issued a CD, *You Are My Music*. There was something of a revival for her during the year, as she also starred as Mrs Johnstone in the West End production of Willy Russell's *Blood Brothers* at the Phoenix Theatre.

ROGERS, Julie

This glamorous singer was born Julie Rolls in London on 6 April 1943. After a variety of jobs, she sang with a dance band led by Teddy Foster and made her recording debut in 1963 with 'It's Magic'. Her next release, 'The Wedding', became her biggest hit, reaching No 3 in the UK chart and also entering the US Top 10. It was a cover version of an Argentinian song, 'La Novia'. Julie commented: 'My only regret was use of the words "Ave Maria" for I thought it might be too sickly and religious for the fans. My big problem is this: most of the hit discs are bought by girls, so it's extra important they should like me, not regard me as a sort of opponent.'

Julie's other hits were 'Like A Child' and 'Hawaiian Wedding'. She also enjoyed a very successful career on the cabaret circuit.

Julie Rogers continues to perform and appeared on the Salute To The Sixties bill at Wembley Stadium late in 1996, when reviews once again remarked on her beauty.

During 1997 thieves seriously injured her husband when they raided her home.

ROLLING STONES, The

In rock circles, this group is second only to the Beatles. Their origins lay in 1960, when Mick Jagger and Keith Richards were together in R&B groups.

Brian Jones, from Cheltenham, arrived in London and advertised that he was forming an R&B band. Pianist **Ian Stewart** joined him. They later teamed up with Jagger, Richards and Dick Taylor, and formed a band call the Rollin' Stones. They had a variety of drummers before settling on Charlie Watts, who had been a member of **Alexis Korner's** Blues Incorporated. Bill Wyman joined them in 1962.

The Beatles saw them perform in Richmond and George Harrison mentioned them to Decca A&R man Dick Rowe, who immediately signed them. Young **Andrew Loog Oldham**, who had recently handled publicity for the Beatles, signed them to a management deal and decided to build up an image the reverse of that of the comparatively clean-cut Beatles. Oldham also changed their name to the Rolling Stones and got rid of Stewart. The line-up now comprised Jones, Jagger, Richard (having dropped the 's'), Wyman and Watts.

They made their recording debut with 'Come On', a minor hit, but scored a bigger impact with their second release, the Lennon & McCartney number 'I Wanna Be Your Man'. Their hits have continued ever since, with the majority of their material penned by Jagger and Richard. This placed Jones on the sidelines and he left the group disillusioned; he was later found dead in his swimming pool.

Among their numerous hits were: 'Not Fade Away', 'It's All Over Now', 'Little Red Rooster', 'The Last Time', '(I Can't Get No) Satisfaction', 'Paint It Black', 'Let's Spend The Night Together' and 'Jumping Jack Flash'. All these were released in the 1960s, and despite all their other singles hits, this seemed to be their most successful singles decade, with seven reaching the No 1 spot.

They were also incredibly successful in the

albums field, with over 35 album hits stretching from their debut *Rolling Stones* in 1964 to their recent *The Bridges Of Babylon*.

The group's entire history has been littered with exposed skeletons – drug busts, romantic affairs and so on.

The Rolling Stones' tours continued to gross higher and higher figures, the most recent earning hundreds of millions of dollars. Despite their continuing ability to dredge in the cash, however, Bill Wyman – himself no stranger to scandal and tabloid gossip – left the group in 1993 and now runs a successful chain of restaurants called Sticky Fingers.

The one who has created

most headlines over the years is, of course, Mick Jagger. Romances with **Marianne Faithfull** and others have provided numerous newspaper column inches. On 9 December 1997, Jagger's wife Jerry Hall gave birth to their fourth child, Gabriel Luke Beauregard Jagger. The couple had been living together for 20 years and married for six. Jagger wasn't present at the birth as he was still in the US completing the Rolling Stones' latest tour, which coincided with the release of their album *Bridges To Babylon*. The tour began in 1997 and ran through 1998, although the band caused further controversy by cancelling their UK appearances in August due to changes in the tax laws.

The Rolling Stones

ROMEO, Max This Jamaican singer (real name Max Smith) was born in 1947. He had one major success in the UK in 1969 with the reggae number 'Wet Dream', which entered the chart twice that year.

Nothing much has been heard of him since as, following a few tours in UK at the time of his single's success, he concentrated on recording and producing in Jamaica.

However, two Max Romeo albums were released in the 1990s – *Far I Captain Of My Ship* in 1992, and *On The Beach* in 1993. Both were recorded in Jamaica.

RONETTES, The Sisters Veronica and Estelle Bennett teamed up with their cousin Nedra Talley as resident dancers at the Peppermint Lounge in New York.

They then appeared as the Dolly Sisters in the film *Twist Around The Clock*, and with their first record, 'I Want A Boy', in 1961 they called themselves Ronnie & the Relatives. In 1962 they changed their name to the Ronettes and issued 'Silhouettes'.

Record producer Phil Spector was impressed by Veronica's voice (she was more popularly known as Ronnie) and so he signed them to his label, releasing the trio singing the songs 'My Baby' and 'Baby I Love You'. In 1963 they appeared on his compilation album *A Christmas Gift For You*.

The Ronettes' other hit singles included '(The Best Part Of) Breakin' Up', 'Do I Love You' and 'Walking In The Rain'.

In 1965 the Ronettes toured with the Beatles, but Ronnie (who married Phil Spector that year) had left the group and was replaced by another cousin, Elaine. The trio disbanded the following year.

Nedra married New York radio presenter Scott Ross, later a church minister, while Estelle wed a Joe Dong. Neither was involved in Ronnie's later re-formation of the Ronettes. They were actually called Ronnie & the Ronettes and the two back-up singers were Denise Edwards and Chip Fields.

Ronnie separated from Spector and their divorce came through in 1974. By 1981 she had turned solo again and in 1995 her autobiography, *Be My Baby*, was published.

In 1997 Ronnie was recording a new album and she, Nedra and Estelle were still in litigation over the rights to songs the Ronettes had recorded with Spector.

ROSE-MARIE This flame-haired Irish singer had 18 hit albums to her credit.

Rose-Marie had four sisters and a brother, and when she left school at the age of 15 she became a hairdresser. Her big break came on the UK television talent show *New Faces*, the week that comedian Jim Davidson won. She also appeared on *Search For A Star* and had a hit single with 'When I Leave My World Behind' in 1983. Two years later she had a chart album with *Rose-Marie Sings Just For You*.

Rose-Marie became a UK television regular, appearing on numerous shows ranging from *Tonight* to *Shooting Stars,* and her awards include Most Popular Country Singer and Best International Concert Star.

At the age of 35, she ended 1997 by completing a tour to promote her new album, *Rose-Marie At Christmas*, issued by Crimson Records. It was a mix of traditional songs and contemporary ballads. During 1998 Rose-Marie appeared on a UK tour with comedians Reeves & Mortimer.

ROSE, Tim This American singer was born in September 1940. His recording of 'Hey Joe' in 1966 was said to have inspired **Jimi Hendrix's** version, and his follow-up was 'Morning Dew', which he co-wrote with Bonnie Dobson.

Rose's major album was the eponymous *Tim Rose*, and during the 1970s he based himself in London for a time.

Rose dropped out of the music scene for many years and became a priest, among other things. He resurfaced to tour in the summer of 1997, and following his sell-out concerts he made an appearance in London for a one-off gig at the Jazz Café in December of that year. His new work is a collaboration with Nick Cave, released in 1998.

ROUSSOS, Demis This singer was born in Alexandria, Egypt, on 15 June 1942. His family moved to Athens in Greece, where he began performing in a band called Idols, followed by a group called Aphrodite's Child, whose other members were **Vangelis** Odyssey Papathanassiou and Lucas Sideras. They had a modest hit in the UK with 'Rain And Tears' in 1968.

When the group split up, Roussos was to enjoy a fruitful career as a middle-of-the-road singer and Papathanassiou achieved fame as an instrumentalist who was commissioned to compose various movie scores, including that for *Chariots Of Fire*.

Roussos' solo hits included: 'Happy To Be On An Island In The Sun', 'Goodbye My Love Goodbye', 'Can't Say How Much I Love You', 'The Roussos Phenomenon' (an EP), 'When Forever Has Gone', 'Because' and 'Kyrila'.

Incidents in Demis Roussos' life in recent years have included a hijacking by Lebanese terrorists and the shedding of 51kg (8 stone/112lb)in weight.

ROXY MUSIC

Originally formed in 1970, the initial line-up of this group was Bryan Ferry (vocals and keyboards), Graham Simpson and Andy Mackay (bass), Brian Eno (synthesizer), Roger Bunn (guitar) and Dexter Lloyd (drums).

There were various changes in personnel during the group's career, and musicians who passed through included Phil Manzanera, David O'List, Rik Kenton, John Porter, Eddie Jobson, Paul Thompson, Johnny Gustafson and John Wetton. The band simply ceased to exist by 1976. Ferry then re-formed it in 1978 and they continued touring and recording.

Roxy Music had a canon of singles hits between 1972 and 1982, including: 'Virginia Plain', 'Pyjamarama', 'Street Life', 'All I Want Is You', 'Love Is The Drug', 'Both Ends Burning', 'Trash', 'Dance Away', 'Angel Eyes', 'Over You', 'Oh Yeah', 'The Same Old Scene', 'Jealous Guy', 'More Than This', 'Avalon' and 'Take A Chance On Me'. 'Virginia Plain' entered the charts in both 1972 and 1977, and their only chart-topper was their cover of **John Lennon's** 'Jealous Guy'.

The group also had a dozen hit albums, including *Roxy Music, For Your Pleasure, Stranded, Siren* and *Manifesto*, a number of them noted for the sexy ladies featured on visually erotic album sleeves.

Roxy Music disbanded again in 1983.

Bryan Ferry was listed among the UK's richest 500 people in a 1997 survey in the *Sunday Times* newspaper. His most recent album was *Mamouna* in 1994.

Phil Manzanera and Andy Mackay remain in demand for session work, television themes and incidental music. Brian Eno is a colossus of ambient music, but has developed other areas of interest such as the publication of his 1995 diary (as *A Year With Swollen Appendices*) and advanced computer science. He has also worked with Ferry again. Paul Thompson returned to the northeast of England and his present activities are unknown.

ROZA, Lita

Singer Lita Roza was born in Liverpool in 1926. Early in her career she sang with big bands in the UK and US, and during the 1950s she was a singer with the Ted Heath Band over a four-year period.

Lita recorded successfully with titles such as 'Allentown Jail', 'Half As Much', 'I Went To Your Wedding' and 'Hi-Lili Hi-Lo'. She then hit the top of the chart with '(How Much Is) That Doggie In The Window'. She was to experience only two further chart hits – 'Hey There' and 'Jimmy Unknown'.

Lita continued with a successful career on radio and television and in cabaret over the years. Together with other members of the Ted Heath Band, she received a Gold Award from BASCA (British Academy Of Songwriters, Composers And Authors) in 1995.

Lita Roza is still making albums – in much the same style as her 1950s hits – in the 1990s.

RUBETTES, The

Initially, in 1974, the Rubettes were a group of session musicians created by Liverpool songwriters Wayne Bickerton and Tony Waddington. Their debut record, 'Sugar Baby Love', with a lead vocal by Paul Da Vinci, entered the charts and Bickerton and Waddington formed a group to mime to the song on television. The line-up comprised Alan Williams (vocals and guitar), Tony Thorpe (guitar), Bill Hurd (keyboards), Mike Clarke (bass) and John Richardson (drums).

The five stayed together, and began live appearances and recording in their own right. Their other hit singles were: 'Tonight', 'Juke Box Jive', 'I Can Do It', 'Foe-Dee-O-Dee', 'Little Darling', 'You're The Reason Why', 'Under One Roof' and 'Baby I Know'.

After completing their eighth and last album for Polydor in 1979, the Rubettes recorded for CBS for a further year before retiring in 1981. The various members of the group then pursued a natural progression of solo projects and productions, until in 1984 they were invited to tour Germany.

John Richardson is now a regressive hypnotherapist, and a member of New Age outfit called Pilgrim. Tony Thorpe had a hit in 1982 with 'Arthur Daley'. All former members contributed to a 1994 Rubettes biography by Alan Rowett, published by Alan Williams – who also led the Rubettes during a headlining 49-date twenty-first anniversary package tour in the spring of 1995.

161

The group continues to perform actively as a quartet on the nostalgia circuit with three of the original members in the current line-up: Alan Williams on lead vocals and guitar, Mike Clarke on bass and Bill Hurd on keyboards. Alex Bines is the drummer.

RUNDGREN, Todd Born in Upper Darby, Pennsylvania, on 22 June 1948, Todd Rundgren formed the Nazz in 1987 and the band made their debut supporting the **Doors**.

He found solo success in 1970 with his album *Runt* and single 'We Gotta Get You A Woman'. Over the years, his hit singles have included 'I Saw The Light', 'Hello It's Me', 'Good Vibrations' and 'Can We Still Be Friends'. In addition to his own recordings, as a producer and engineer Rundgren was involved in the production of records by a number of other acts, including Meatloaf's *Bat Out Of Hell*. He also scored the music for Joe Orton's *Up Against It*, once intended as a film project for the Beatles.

In 1974 he formed another band, Utopia, who charted with 'Set Me Free'.

That year, four masked men broke into Rundgren's home in Woodstock and tied up him, his girlfriend and guests, while they ransacked his house.

Rundgren became very involved with exploring the potential of interactive multi-media and became a consultant for the on-line service CompuServe, while still continuing his musical career as both an artist and a producer.

Following a major tour of the States in 1995, Todd Rundgren released a multi-media CD called *The Individualist*, and in 1997 released *With A Twist*, an album of recordings of his best-known songs – in bossa nova style!

RYAN, Marion A popular British female vocalist of the 1950s, Marion Ryan was born in Middlesbrough, Cleveland, and became a television entertainer, appearing on numerous shows including *Music Story*, *Oh Boy*, *Off The Record*, *Gerry's Inn* and *6.5 Special*. She made various records, including 'Hot Diggity', 'Mr Wonderful' and 'Mangos', but had only one major hit – with her Top 5 entry 'Love Me Forever' in 1958. Her twin sons, Paul and Barry, became hit artists in their own right in the 1960s.

Marion Ryan retired from showbusiness in 1965 and married leading impresario Harold Davidson. She and her husband have been settled in the States for a number of years now and Harold represents a number of major artists, which included Frank Sinatra until his death in 1998.

RYDELL, Bobby Born Robert Ridarelli in Philadelphia on 26 April 1942, this singer became such a success on record that he was financially independent for life by the time he was 21.

His first chart record was 'Kissin' Time' in 1959, and he followed with another 17 hits stretching until 1963.

Among Rydell's chart singles were 'We Got Love', 'Wild One', 'Swingin' School', 'Volare' and the 'Cha-Cha-Cha'. He also had a hit duetting with **Chubby Checker** on 'Jingle Bell Rock'.

Like many other solo singers, he then found the chart dominated by groups, following the emergence of the Beatles in the States in early 1964.

Bobby Rydell is now a familiar figure on the US nostalgia circuit. The high school in the 1978 movie *Grease* was named after him.

ST PETERS, Crispian This singer was born Robin Peter Smith in Swanley, Kent, on 5 April 1939. He initially joined a skiffle outfit called the Hard Travellers, followed by the group Beat Formula Three. He was spotted by David Nicolson, who became his manager and christened him with the more colourful name of Crispian St Peters. He recorded 'At This Moment' and 'No No No', then had chart hits with 'You Were On My Mind', 'Pied Piper' and 'Changes', all in 1966.

St Peters tended to blot his copybook with extravagant claims to the music press about his vocal and songwriting talents, although he was later to say that these were just flippant comments made to a single paper, which were then blown up out of all proportion.

When the pop hits dried up he turned to a country style, even dubbing himself Country Smith for one release in 1968. He also issued a country-style album in 1970 called *Simply – Crispian St Peters*.

He remained in the wilderness for years, until a feature in *The Beat Goes On* magazine in 1996 attracted attention and he decided to emerge as a performing artist again.

1997 saw the release of *Crispian St Peters: The Anthology*, a 29-track CD.

The singer still lives in his native Kent.

SAINTE-MARIE, Buffy This Canadian singer-songwriter was born on 20 February 1941. Among the songs she penned were 'Universal Soldier', 'Until It's Time For You To Go' and 'Up Where We Belong'. Among her own hits were 'Soldier Blue' and 'I'm Gonna Be A Country Girl Again'. Her songs were recorded by numerous artists including **Elvis Presley**, **Barbra Streisand**, Chet Atkins and Dottie West.

Buffy gave up recording, although she continued performing, when her son was born, and joined the cast of the children's television show *Sesame Street* for five-and-a-half years. She restricted her performances for a number of years, but is likely to begin touring again now that she has signed with the Ensign label.

Buffy Sainte-Marie has been living in Hawaii for the past 25 years.

SAM & DAVE This soul duo coupled Samuel David Moore, born in Miami, Florida, on 12 October 1935, and Dave Prater, born in Ocilla, Georgia, on 9 May 1937. The two teamed up in 1961. They joined the Memphis-based Stax Records in 1965, making their chart debut with 'You Don't Know Like I Know'. Other hits which followed included: 'Hold On! I'm Coming', 'Soul Man', 'Soothe Me', 'Soul Sister Brown Sugar' and 'I Thank You'.

In 1968 Dave shot his wife during an argument, but escaped imprisonment.

The duo split in 1970 when their relationship deteriorated and embarked on solo careers, without much success. They were encouraged to team up again in 1972.

Sam & Dave have not performed together since 1980. In 1987 Dave was arrested for selling crack, and was fined and sentenced to community work, but was killed in a road accident the following year.

Sam continued recording and performing, and added vocal harmonies to **Bruce Springsteen's** *Human Touch* in 1992.

In 1993 a 2-CD retrospective, *Sweet 'n' Soul: The Anthology*, was issued. The following year Sam recorded 'Rainy Night In Georgia' with Conway Twitty, shortly before Twitty's death, and the record entered the US Top 20.

SAM THE SHAM Sam the Sham (real name Domingo Samudio) was born in Dallas, Texas. After a four-year stint in the US Navy, he worked on a building site and saved enough money to go to college. He began playing with various bands and eventually led a group called the Pharoahs, comprised of Ray Stinnet (guitar), Butch Gibson (sax), David Martin (bass) and Jerry Patterson (drums). They made their recording debut with 'Haunted House', which was unsuccessful, but followed with 'Wooly Bully', penned by Sam, which topped the US chart in 1965, and followed that with 'Lil' Red Riding Hood'.

Sam parted from his Pharoahs in 1970 to go solo. He says he adopted the term 'Sham' – which was rhythm-and-blues jargon for shuffling, twisting or jiving to music – as that's what he did when he sang. The singer has remained a popular concert attraction in his native Texas.

SANTANA Singer-songwriter-guitarist Carlos Santana was born on 20 July 1947 in Autlan, Jalisco, Mexico. He formed his own band, Santana, in San Francisco in 1966. The other musicians included Mike Carrabello (congas), Jose 'Chepito' Areas (percussion), Gregg Rolie (keyboards), David Brown (bass) and Mike Shrieve (drums).

His younger brother Jorge Santana formed his own band, Malmo, who had a hit with 'Suavecito'.

The Latin flavour he brought to rock music caught on and Santana's hits in the singles chart included: 'Evil Ways', 'Black Magic Woman', 'Ye Como Va', 'Everybody's Everything', 'Samba Pa Ti', 'She's Not There', 'Winning' and 'Hold On'.

The group was also successful in the album field, making their debut with *Santana* and following with *Abraxas* and *Santana 3*. By the time of the third album there had been personnel changes, with Neil Schon joining the group on guitar and Coke Escovedo on percussion.

Carlos Santana made several further albums and collaborated with a number of jazz musicians. He toured with Buddy Miles, which resulted in the 1972 album *Carlos Santana And Buddy Miles Live*.

His subsequent albums have not sold in the volume of his earlier releases, but he continues to record, receiving a Grammy Award for his 1989 release 'Blues For Salvador'. He changed labels to Polydor in 1992 and issued *Cuts And Grace*.

Peter Sarstedt

Carlos Santana became a convert to the doctrines of Bengal holy man Sri Chimnoy. He still leads the group – who appeared at Wembley Stadium in 1995.

SARNE, Mike Born Michael Scheur on 6 August 1939, Mike Sarne began his career as an actor in 1957 and made his first record in 1962. This was a novelty single, 'Come Outside', which he recorded with actress Wendy Richard (later to be noted for her roles as Miss Brahms in the UK television comedy series *Are You Being Served?* and Pauline Fowler in the soap opera *EastEnders*). This record topped the UK chart in May 1962. His second chart hit that year was another novelty item, 'Will I What', recorded with **Billie Davis**.

Two more chart hits followed in 1963, with Sarne performing solo; they were 'Just For Kicks' and 'Code Of Love'.

Sarne then directed the movie *Joanna* and in 1970 went to Hollywood to direct the controversial *Myra Breckinridge*, which starred Mae West and Raquel Welch.

Nothing much was heard in the years that followed, although he continued work as an actor and producer. His most recent film production was *The Punk And The Princess* in 1995.

Of German extraction, Sarne then appeared as a German drug smuggler in the 1997 television series *The Knock*.

Interestingly enough, Wendy Richard re-recorded 'Come Outside' in 1986, along with actor-singer **Mike Berry** who also featured in *Are You Being Served?*, although the number did not register second time around.

SARSTEDT, Peter This British singer-songwriter was born on 10 December 1942. He originally played guitar in **Eden Kane's** backing band – Eden (real name Richard) is actually Peter's elder brother. Peter topped the chart with his self-penned 'Where Do You Go To My Lovely', an evocative, elegant song with an effective denouement. He followed this with a Top 10 entry called 'Frozen Orange Juice', but failed to make any further dents in the chart. For a time he formed the Sarstedt Brothers with Richard and their brother Robin, but they were unsuccessful.

Peter currently lives in Wiltshire and still performs new material in clubs, although much of his income is derived from Europe's sixties nostalgia circuit, where he sometimes appears with one or both of his brothers.

All three Sarstedt brothers received a Special Award from BASCA (British Academy Of Songwriters, Composers And Authors) in 1996.

At the beginning of 1998 Peter Sarstedt toured the UK as support to the Mamas & Papas.

SAVOY BROWN Kim Simmonds formed this funky British blues band in 1966. His brother Harry, who was also the manager of Chicken Shack, managed them, and blues maestro Mike Vernon originally recorded their songs.

Apart from Simmonds, the basic personnel comprised Dave Peverett (guitar and vocals), Rivers Jobe (bass) and Roger Earl (drums). Tony Stevens replaced Jobe and singer Chris Youlden was recruited. The group had success on album and toured the US regularly.

In 1970, after Peverett, Stevens and Earl had left to form Foghat, Simmonds moved to the States. He decided to concentrate on the US market as the leader of new editions of Savoy Brown – including the one on the road today.

SAXON This British heavy metal band was originally formed in 1977. The line-up comprised Bill Byford (vocals and lyrics), Paul Anthony Quinn (lead), Graham Oliver (guitar) and Nigel Durham (drums).

Their hit singles include: 'Wheels Of Steel', '747 (Strangers In The Night)', 'Big Teaser/Rainbow Theme', 'Backs To The Wall', 'Strong Arm Of The Law', 'And The Bands Played On', 'Never Surrender', 'Princess Of The Night', 'Power And The Glory', 'Nightmare', 'Back On The Streets', 'Rock 'n' Roll Gypsy', 'Waiting For The Night', 'Ride Like The Wind' and 'I Can't Wait Anymore'.

They also had several hit albums, including: *Wheels Of Steel*, *Strong Arm Of The Law*, *Denim And Leather*, *Power And The Glory*, *Crusader* and *Innocence Is No Excuse*.

Saxon undertook a promotional world tour in 1992 to tie in with a new album, *Solid Ball Of Rock*.

SAYER, Leo Singer-songwriter Leo Sayer (real name Gerard Hugh Sayer) was born in Shoreham-by-Sea, Sussex, on 21 May 1948. On leaving school, he became a magazine illustrator and began performing as a singer in the evenings. **Adam Faith** signed him and in 1973 he made his debut with 'Everybody Going Home'. The same year he married his girlfriend, Joan.

Sayer's second single, 'The Show Must Go On', was a hit, as was his debut album, *Silver Bird*.

He initially performed wearing a clown costume, but eventually the pierrot image began to pall and he abandoned it.

Sayer's hits included 'One Man Band' and 'Long Tall Glasses', and in 1976 'You Make Me Feel Like Dancing' topped the US chart. In 1978 he had his own weekly UK television series, *Leo*, and in 1983 began another series, this time entitled *Leo Sayer*.

1993 saw him release his first album in seven years, *Cool Touch*, and he began his comeback.

In December 1997 Sayer appeared on *Freddie Starr's Christmas Special* and was voted Comeback Of The Year in the *Sun* newspaper. The *Sun* also referred to this as the 'reinstatement of a legend'.

In February 1998 Leo Sayer began a three-month concert tour of the UK.

SCAFFOLD, The This Liverpool trio was formed in 1962 with members Mike McGear, Roger McGough and John Gorman. Mike was Paul McCartney's younger brother. Noted for their satirical wit, they appeared regularly on the UK television show *Gazette*. George Martin produced their debut single, '2 Day's Monday'.

Their hits during the 1960s included 'Thank U Very Much', 'Do You Remember', 'Lily The Pink' and 'Gin Gan Goolie'. In 1970 they merged with a group called the Liverpool Scene to become Grimms. Mike McGear recorded a solo single, 'Woman', and then an album with Roger called *McGough & McGear*, which was produced by Paul McCartney.

The Scaffold re-formed for a time and entered the chart with 'Liverpool Lou', also produced by McCartney.

When the group disbanded, John Gorman became a television personality, appearing on several children's shows, in addition to the controversial *OTT* series. He was a member of the Four Bucketeers, who had a hit with 'The Bucket Of Water Song' in 1980. Gorman then moved to France, but returned to the UK in the 1990s.

Roger McGough became a bestselling poet, settling in London and giving frequent poetry readings at major venues, in addition to appearing regularly on television.

Mike McGear, the father of six children, remains at his home in Heswall, Cheshire, with his second wife Rowena and pursues a career as a photographer.

165

SCREAMING LORD SUTCH Born on 10 November 1940, David Edward Sutch is one of British rock music's great eccentrics. He was nine years old when his father died in a motorcycle accident.

Sutch formed his group the Savages in 1958 and took his name from his inspiration – **Screamin' Jay Hawkins**. Initially, he presented an act that combined rock music and camp horror, being brought on to the stage in a coffin and appearing in a Jack The Ripper sketch.

Several leading musicians made early appearances in Sutch's bands. Members of the Savages included Nicky Hopkins, Jimmy Page, Jeff Beck and Ritchie Blackmore, while the members of his Roman Empire group between 1966 and 1967 included Ritchie Blackmore and Matthew Fisher.

His only US success was the album *Lord Sutch And Heavy Friends*, which included musicians such as Page, Hopkins and Blackmore.

In the early 1960s Sutch also entered politics, even standing for election against Prime Minister Harold Wilson in his Huyton ward in Liverpool. Sutch founded the Monster Raving Loony Party, which throughout the years has injected a much-needed dose of humour into the hustings.

In 1997, for the first time since the party was established, Sutch did not stand in the General Election, as he was caring for his sick mother, Annie Emily Sutch. She died on 30 April.

Screaming Lord Sutch remains a popular performer and is in constant demand. His autobiography, *Life As Sutch*, was published in 1991.

SCREAMIN' JAY HAWKINS This colourful American R&B singer, most noted for his version of 'I Put A Spell On You', a number he recorded when drunk. He was born Jalacy J. Hawkins in Cleveland, Ohio, on 18 July 1929 and began entertaining troops when he was a member of the US Air Force. For a time he was also a middleweight boxer.

When he was demobbed in 1952 Hawkins joined various bands, and in 1954 began a solo career, recording 'Baptise Me In Wine'. He developed an outrageous act, in which he dressed in a cape and rose from a coffin.

Although Hawkins only found record success with 'I Put A Spell On You', he was successful as a live performer, toured with the **Rolling Stones** and appeared in the movies *Mister Rock And Roll* and *Mystery Train*.

During the 1990s Screamin' Jay Hawkins signed with Demon Records, and in 1993 was commissioned to sing a **Tom Waits** composition, 'Heart Attack And Vine', in a television commercial for Levi jeans.

SCRITTI POLITTI Green Gartside (real name Green Strohmeyer-Gartside) was born on 22 June 1956. He formed the group Scritti Polliti as a trio in Leeds in 1977 with Nial Jinks on bass and Tom Morley on drums.

When Gartside became ill with heart trouble in 1980 he suspended the group for a while, then re-formed it without Morely. They initially found success in the indie chart, then their first album, *Songs To Remember*, became a hit in 1982. By the time of their second chart album, *Cupid & Psyche '85*, he had changed personnel again and brought in David Gamson on keyboards and Fred Maher on drums.

Scritti Politti's singles chart entries included: 'The Sweetest Girl', 'Faithless', 'Asylums In Jerusalem', 'Wood Beez (Pray Like Aretha Franklin)', 'Absolute', 'Hypnotize', 'The Word Girl', 'The Perfect Way', 'Oh Patti (Don't Feel Sorry For Loverboy)', 'First Boy In Town (Lovesick)' and 'Boom! There She Was'.

Gartside moved to Wales for two years to work on further material. Scritti Pollitti then charted with two more singles in 1992 – but instead of new material by Green, they were a version of the Beatles' 'She's A Woman' followed by 'Take Me In Your Arms And Love Me', a cover of the **Gladys Knight** hit.

The bank balance of Green Gartside, the group's mainstay, has received welcome shots in the arm via covers of his songs. Artists recording them include the late Miles Davis, Al Jarreau, Chaka Khan and **Madness**, but the last couple of years have produced little of note from the lad himself, bar a teaming-up with Shabba Ranks and then Sweetie Irie for respective singles.

SEARCHERS, The The Searchers were one of the best groups to emerge from the Mersey beat scene. Mike Prendergast and John McNally originally teamed up as an instrumental duo, naming themselves the Searchers after the John Wayne movie. Tony Jackson joined them on bass and vocals, and Norman McGarry on drums. The group began backing singer Johnny Sandon, who then went on to front another Mersey band, the Remo Four. When McGarry left to replace Ringo Starr in **Rory Storm** & the

Hurricanes, they were joined by Christopher Crummy. Mike adopted the surname Pender and Chris became known as Chris Curtis.

The Searchers were recorded live on stage at the Star Club in Hamburg and on their return to the UK were signed up by Pye Records, with Tony Hatch producing.

Their debut single, 'Sweets For My Sweet', topped the UK hit parade in 1963, and a Star Club track, 'Sweet Nothins', was rush released, entering the lower end of the chart. Their second Pye release, 'Sugar And Spice', proved to be another big hit, reaching No 3 in the chart. The group's other UK hits were 'Needles And Pins', which also topped the chart, plus: 'Don't Throw Your Love Away', 'Someday We're Gonna Love Again', 'When You Walk In The Room', 'What Have They Done To The Rain', 'Goodbye My Love', 'He's Got No Love', 'When I Get Home', 'Take Me For What I'm Worth', 'Take It Or Leave It' and 'Have You Ever Loved Somebody'.

In August 1964 Tony Jackson left for a solo career and Frank Allen, former member of **Cliff Bennett** & the Rebel Rousers, replaced him. Jackson formed a backing band called the Vibrations, but had only one hit, 'Bye Bye Baby'.

Chris Curtis left the band in 1966 suffering from nervous exhaustion, and John Blunt replaced him. Later that year, Billy Anderson was to replace Blunt.

They almost cracked the chart again in 1981, following their signing with Sire Records and the release of two highly acclaimed albums. Unfortunately, due to some complications, further copies of the albums were not pressed to cope with the demand and their potential return to the chart was stifled.

Mike Pender split from the band at the end of 1985 and was to form a breakaway group, Mike Penders' Searchers. Spencer James, former lead singer with First Class, replaced him.

Both outfits now tour the world and the Searchers appear regularly on the nationwide Solid Silver Sixties Tour concert tours organized by Flying Music.

In 1964 Tony Jackson, the lead voice on 'Sweets For My Sweet' and 'Sugar And Spice', formed a band called Tony Jackson & the Vibrations and had one minor chart hit, 'Bye Bye Baby'. On the proceeds of his career, he and his wife established a golf and leisure club.

In the 1990s Jackson returned to the music scene to appear on the sixties nostalgia circuit, although he began to suffer from ill health with arthritis, asthma and very poor eyesight. He lost his business, then his arthritis became so bad that he could no longer play guitar. In December 1996 Jackson was found guilty of possessing an imitation weapon and was sent to prison, but was released in 1997. In January 1998 he appeared in the UK television series *Rock Family Trees* and decided to return to live performances.

The Searchers went off to the Middle East in February 1997, while Mike Pender's Searchers appeared in Switzerland that month, prior to a tour of South Africa.

Now retired from the Civil Service, Chris Curtis has resurfaced in Liverpool venues as half of a duo called Jimmy. In a 1998 edition of *Record Collector* magazine, he gave his first interview since the mid-1960s.

SEDAKA, Neil Singer-songwriter Neil Sedaka was born in Brooklyn, New York, on 13 March 1939. While at school, he entered a songwriting partnership with Howard Greenfield and the two penned 'Stupid Cupid', which became a major hit for **Connie Francis**. Sedaka also became a recording artist, charting in 1959 with his first single for RCA records, 'The Diary'. Hit followed hit for almost 20 years.

His chart singles included: 'Oh! Carol', 'Stairway To Heaven', 'Calendar Girl', 'Happy Birthday Sweet Sixteen', 'Breaking Up Is Hard To Do', 'Next Door To An Angel', 'Laughter In The Rain', 'Bad Blood' and 'Steppin' Out'.

Songs by Sedaka and Greenfield have continued to be recorded over the years by a variety of artists including Skeeter Davis, Tom Jones and **Tony Christie**. Sedaka split the partnership when he settled in London with his wife Leba and children Dara and Marc in 1972, teaming up with new lyricist Phil Cody.

Due to living in London, he had hits in the UK but no releases in the US. He discussed the situation with Elton John, who issued Sedaka's 'Laughter In The Rain' on his Rocket Records – and it went on to top the US chart.

In 1997 a duet with his daughter Dara, 'Should've Never Let You Go', entered the US Top 20.

Sedaka's autobiography, *Laughter In The Rain*, was published in 1987. A 1991 compilation album, *Timeless: The Very Best Of Neil Sedaka*, still does brisk business in foyers during his ongoing international concert itinerary. The album

167

entered the UK Top 10 and a further album, *Classically Sedaka*, charted later the same year.

Throughout the 1990s Sedaka has toured both the UK and US annually.

SEEGER, Pete This influential American folk singer and songwriter was born on 3 May, 1919. Although his records made no impact on the charts, several numbers he composed were hits for other artists. These included 'We Shall Overcome' and 'Where Have All The Flowers Gone'.

Exemplified by *Can't You See This System's Rotten Through And Through* in 1986, Pete Seeger still releases albums that are as politically committed as those issued at the start of his career.

In 1997 a star-studded album of covers of his songs was released as a tribute.

SEEKERS, The This Australian group, formed in 1963, comprised Athol Guy (vocals and double bass), Keith Potger (vocals and guitar), Bruce Woodley (vocals and guitar) and Ken Ray (lead vocals and guitar). The following year Judith Durham became their lead vocalist and the group travelled to London, where they signed with the powerful Grade Agency, which had links with every field of British showbusiness. As a result, they appeared on *Sunday Night At The London Palladium*, a television show with such a vast audience that it virtually created stars overnight.

Tom Springfield stepped in to offer his services as a songwriter and producer, and the group's run of hits began.

Their chart singles included: 'I'll Never Find Another You', 'A World Of Our Own', 'The Carnival Is Over', 'Someday One Day', 'Walk With Me', 'Morningtown Ride', 'Georgy Girl', 'When Will The Good Apples Fall' and 'Emerald City'.

The Seekers' hits eventually seemed to dry up and the group made a farewell appearance on a television show. Judith became a solo artist, but had only one further hit, 'Olive Tree', while Keith Potger formed the **New Seekers**.

Members of the original group re-formed in 1975 without Durham, adding Dutch singer Louisa Wisseling as lead vocalist. They had one final entry, a chart-topper in Australia, 'The Sparrow Song'.

The original group re-formed once again in 1994 for an anniversary tour of Australia and a live album (it was 25 years since they originally disbanded). The four also performed two concerts at the Royal Albert Hall in London.

In January 1998, Readers Digest began a massive advertising campaign to promote a 3-CD set of 60 songs, *The Very Best Of The Seekers*.

SEX PISTOLS, The Formed in London in 1975, the Sex Pistols were the creation of Malcolm McLaren. They comprised Steve Jones (guitar), Paul Cook (drums), Glen Matlock (bass) and Wally Nightingale (vocals). John Lydon was then brought in as lead singer, with McLaren giving him the name Johnny Rotten.

Their rise to fame can be focused on a television chat show on which they appeared on 1 December 1976. Interviewer Stuart Grundy initially patronized the band, then goaded them into swearing. As a result, the Sex Pistols hit the headlines and Grundy's career was over.

Matlock left early in 1977 and was replaced by **Sid Vicious**.

The band recorded only one album, *Don't Forget The Bollocks*, and after they disbanded in 1978 Rotten formed Public Image Ltd. Jones and Cook took McLaren's advice and went to Rio to make a record with great train robber Ronnie Biggs.

McLaren also produced a film of the Pistols called *The Great Rock 'n' Roll Swindle*.

The original line-up of Lydon, Jones, Cook and Matlock re-formed in 1996 for a world tour, a 'live' album called *This Is Crap* and, most iconoclastically of all, an appearance on the UK television show *Top Of The Pops*. A Glen Matlock solo album was released at the same time, and one by Johnny Rotten was issued in 1997.

SHAKIN' STEVENS Born Michael Barrett on 4 March 1948, Shakin' Stevens initially began playing with groups in the 1960s, including the Denims and Shakin' Stevens & the Sunsets. In 1977 he starred in the West End stage production of *Elvis*.

His first chart single, 'This Ole House', appeared in 1980, followed by 'You Drive Me Crazy', 'Green Door', 'Oh Julie', 'The Shakin' Stevens EP', 'A Love Worth Waiting For' and 'Merry Christmas Everyone'. He also charted when he recorded a duet with Bonnie Tyler, 'A Rockin' Good Way'.

Shakin' Stevens lives in Surrey with his wife, two sons and one daughter.

WHERE ARE THEY NOW?

SHAM '69 Created by Jimmy Pursey in 1976, this five-piece band comprised Pursey on vocals with Albie Slider (bass), Neil Harris (lead), Johnny Goodfornothing (rhythm) and Billy Bostick (drums).

Within a short time, Pursey was changing the personnel and brought in Dave Parsons on guitar, Dave Treganna on bass and Mark Cain on drums. This is the line-up that entered the chart with the singles 'Angels With Dirty Faces', 'If The Kids Are United', 'Hurry Up Harry', 'Questions And Answers', 'Hersham Boys', 'You're A Better Man Than I' and 'Tell The Children'. They also had three chart albums – *Tell Us The Truth*, *That's Life* and *The Adventures Of The Hersham Boys*. Pursey then left the band in 1978 to go solo.

With Pursey once again at the helm, Sham '69 re-formed in the 1990s and today play their greatest hits to ageing punks, but still bring out an occasional new album such as *Soapy Water And Mr Marmalade* in 1995.

SHAPIRO, Helen Born in London's East End on 28 September 1946, it was while Helen Shapiro was taking singing lessons at the Maurice Berman School of Singers that recording manager John Schroeder spotted her. He wrote the number 'Don't Treat Me Like A Child' specially for her and it became her first hit, while she was still at school. The number topped the UK chart – and she was still only 14 years old. Schroeder also wrote 'Walking Back To Happiness' for her, which was another UK chart-topper. Her other hits included 'You Don't Know', 'Tell Me What He Said' and 'Little Miss Lonely'.

She also appeared in the films *It's Trad Dad* and *Play It Cool*.

During 1961 and 1962 Helen was voted No 1 Female British Singer, and on her major UK tour one of the support acts was the Beatles – whose subsequent rise to superstardom caused the beat music explosion, which probably caused the end of her run of hit records. While travelling with Helen on the coach, they offered her one of their songs, 'Misery', to record, but her recording manager turned it down.

Later in her career she became a jazz singer.

Helen, whose autobiography was called *Walking Back To Happiness*, featured on the Solid Silver Sixties Tour in February and March 1998 with the **Searchers** and the Swinging Blue Jeans. On 23 February 1998 EMI issued the CD *Helen Shapiro At Abbey Road*.

SHAW, Sandie This British singer (real name Sandra Goodrich) was born in Dagenham, Essex, on 26 February 1947. She originally worked for the Ford Motor Company, but was discovered by **Adam Faith**. He recommended her to his own manager Eve Taylor, who signed her up and gave her the name Sandie Shaw. Taylor also devised the gimmick of having Sandie sing in her bare feet, a ploy that continued to generate column inches for several years to come.

Sandie topped the chart with her second release, '(There's) Always Something There To Remind Me'. Between 1964 and 1986 she had 19 hits, including another chart-topper, her 1967 Eurovision Song Contest entry 'Puppet On A String', which won the contest and sold over four million copies worldwide. Several of her other hits were penned by songwriter Chris Andrews.

Sandie had no chart entries in the 1970s. Between her 1969 hit 'Think It Over' and 'Hand In Glove', which charted in 1984, there was a 15-year gap. 'Hand In Glove' was a version of the **Smiths'** first single and Sandie recorded it with the band. Several major British artists also contributed to her album *Hello Angel* in 1988.

Helen Shapiro

169

In her personal life, Sandie married fashion designer Jeff Banks in 1968, but they were divorced and she later married Nick Powell of Palace Records. Her autobiography, *The World At My Feet*, was published in 1991.

Sandie had another minor hit with 'Nothing Less Than Brilliant' in 1994 and currently lives in London, where she combines writing with infrequent recording and performances. She is also a qualified therapy counsellor and a practising Buddhist. As to her future as an entertainer, she is, she says, 'playing it by ear'.

A television biography of Sandie Shaw was transmitted in the UK on 29 November 1997 as part of the *Britgirls* series.

SHELTON, Anne   This singer (real name Patricia Sibley) was born in Dulwich, south London, on 10 November 1927. When she was only 12 years old she made her radio debut singing with the Bert Ambrose Orchestra, and became resident singer with them when she was only 14. While still in her teens, she sang a duet of 'Easter Parade' with Bing Crosby when he was appearing at the Queensberry Club in London. In 1950 she sang with **Perry Como**.

Anne recorded and had a hit with 'Lili Marlene' in 1946 and 'The Wedding Of Lili Marlene' in 1949. At that time, the only chart was the sheet-music one, which she topped for seven weeks with the latter.

Anne had a number of big-selling records prior to the establishment of a UK chart, and she even entered the US chart in 1949 with 'Be Mine'. Once the UK chart began, Anne's hits included 'Arrivederci Darling', 'Seven Days', 'Lay Down Your Arms', 'Village Of St Bernadette' and 'Sailor'.

She sang 'I'll Be Seeing You' in the 1979 film *Yanks* and also performed for the Queen Mother on her eightieth birthday in 1980, when she sang 'You'll Never Know'.

Anne Shelton is married to David Reid and lives in south-east London. She is the entertainment officer for the Not Forgotten Association, which looks after wounded and disabled ex-servicemen from World War I to the present. Among her duties is the organization of two annual concerts held in the grounds of Buckingham Palace.

SHIRELLES, The   Doris Kenner (real name Doris Coley) founded this girl group, who were originally called the Poquellos and made their record debut in 1958. Also in the group was lead singer Shirley Alston (real name Shirley Owens) and **Adie Harris**, whose nickname was Micki.

During the height of the 'girl group' era at the beginning of the 1960s, their hits included: 'Tonight's The Night', 'Will You Love Me Tomorrow', 'Dedicated To The One I Love', 'Mama Said', 'Big John', 'Baby It's You', 'Soldier Boy', 'Welcome Home Baby', 'Stop The Music', 'Everybody Loves A Lover', 'Foolish Little Girl' and 'Don't Say Goodnight And Mean Goodbye'.

Doris left the group in 1968 and returned in 1975, when Shirley left.

Despite Adie Harris's fatal heart attack after a 1982 performance in Atlanta, the Shirelles have continued to tour constantly on the nostalgia circuit.

SHOWADDYWADDY   Basically a rock 'n' roll revival group, re-recording some of the rock 'n' roll classics, this group was formed in Leicester in 1983. The members were Dave Bartram and Billy Gask (vocals), Russ Fields and Trevor Oakes (guitar), Al James and Rod Teas (bass), and Romeo Challenger (ex-Black Widow) and Malcolm Allured (drums).

Their UK hit singles included: 'Hey Rock And Roll', 'Rock 'n' Roll Lady', 'Hey Mr Christmas,' 'Sweet Music', 'Three Steps To Heaven', 'Heartbeat', 'Heavenly', 'Trocadero', 'Under The Moon Of Love', 'When', 'You Got What It Takes', 'Dancin' Party', 'I Wonder Why', 'A Little Bit Of Soap', 'Pretty Little Angel Eyes', 'Remember Then', 'Sweet Little Rock 'n' Roller', 'A Night At Daddy Gee's', 'Why Do Lovers Break Each Other's Hearts', 'Blue Moon', 'Multiplication', 'Footsteps' and 'Who Put The Bump'.

A Showaddywaddy perform frequently at nostalgia festivals in Europe, principally in Germany, while Gask and Allured also play rock 'n' roll revivalist music with the Teddys.

SIFFRE, Labi   Singer-songwriter Labi Siffre was born in London. His father was Nigerian, his mother English. After a variety of jobs, he joined a number of bands before turning solo.

His UK hit singles included: 'It Must Be Love', 'Crying Laughing Loving Lying', 'Watch Me', '(Something Inside) So Strong' and 'Nothin's Gonna Change'.

Madness reached the UK Top 10 in 1981 with a revival of Labi Siffre's 'It Must Be Love'. In 1995 he topped the bill at an outdoor festival in the abbey ruins at Reading in Berkshire.

As a songwriter with a powerful grasp of lyrics, Siffre also turned to poetry and has had two collections published in the 1990s – *Nigger* and *Blood On The Page*.

SILVER CONVENTION A studio recording by producers Silvester Levay and Michael Kunze in Munich, Germany, resulted in a UK chart entry for 'Save Me', under the name Silver Convention. The producers' next single, 'Fly Robin Fly', went on to top the US chart.

As a result, Levay and Kunze then formed a female vocal trio to perform the hits live and also to record further material.

Linda Thompson, Ramona Wulf and Penny McLean then went out as Silver Convention and had further hits in the UK chart – 'Get Up & Boogie', 'Tiger Baby' and 'Everybody's Talkin' 'Bout Love'.

After their final UK entry, the girls battled on for another year, highlighted by their performance of 'Telegram', West Germany's entry in the 1977 Eurovision Song Contest.

Showaddywaddy

SIMON DUPREE & THE BIG SOUND

Originally an R&B outfit based in Portsmouth, Hampshire, this group was initially called the Howlin' Wolves and then the Roadrunners. They included three brothers – Ray, Derek and Phil Shulman – together with Eric Hine, Tony Ransley and Peter O'Flaherty. The group changed their name to Simon Dupree & the Big Sound when they signed to Parlophone records in 1966. Derek adopted the name Simon Dupree.

After the release of their debut single, 'I See The Light', they then turned professional. Their follow-up was 'Reservations' and they next hit the UK Top 10 with 'Kites'. They followed with 'Whom The Bell Tolls', but had strayed so far from their R&B roots that there was disharmony in the band and they split in 1969. The Shulman brothers formed Gentle Giant, a 'progressive' group which had some success on the European college circuit.

SIMON, Paul

Paul Simon was born in Newark, New Jersey, on 13 October 1941 and began his partnership with Art Garfunkel in 1964. In the meantime, he also recorded under various names, including Paul Kane, Jerry Landis and True Taylor.

As Simon & Garfunkel, they topped the charts in 1965 with 'The Sounds Of Silence'. The duo's other hit singles included: 'Homeward Bound', 'I Am A Rock', 'The Dangling Conversation', 'A Hazy Shade Of Winter', 'At The Zoo', 'Fakin' It', 'Scarborough Fair', 'Mrs Robinson', 'The Boxer', 'Bridge Over Troubled Water', 'Cecilia' and 'My Little Town', the latter charting a few years after the duo split up in 1970.

They were major album sellers and charted ten times, beginning with *Sounds Of Silence* and ending with *The Concert In Central Park*. Their most famous LP was *Bridge Over Troubled Water*.

Garfunkel, born in Forest Hills, New York, on 5 November 1941, spent a brief time in Scotland following the split, then returned to the West Coast. He appeared in a number of films, including *Carnal Knowledge*, *Catch 22* and *Bad Timing*, and continued recording. His hit singles included 'All I Know', 'I Shall Sing', 'Second Avenue', 'I Only Have Eyes For You' and 'Break Away'. He also charted with '(What A) Wonderful World', which he recorded with **James Taylor** and Paul Simon in 1978.

Simon & Garfunkel teamed up for a special concert in New York's Central Park in 1981, which resulted in another hit for the duo, 'Wake Up Little Susie'.

Simon was more successful as a solo act on record than Garfunkel and his hit singles included: 'Mother And Child Reunion', 'Me And Julio Down By The Schoolyard', 'Kodachrome', 'Loves Me Like A Rock', 'American Tune', '50 Ways To Leave Your Lover', 'Still Crazy After All These Years', 'Slip Slidin' Away', 'Late In The Evening', 'One Trick Pony' – and he charted when he duetted with Phoebe Snow on 'Gone At Last'.

He also released several albums, the most critically acclaimed being *Graceland* in 1987, which he recorded with a number of South African musicians and followed with a world tour.

His 1980 film *One Trick Pony* was screened in the UK in January 1998.

Simon's new rock musical, the $11 million *The Capeman*, opened in New York in January 1998. It concerned an adolescent Puerto Rican immigrant killer of the 1950s. Simon's treatment of the illiterate double murderer Salvador Agron, who became a published poet during his gaol term, gathered criticism because of its sympathetic portrayal of a person many regarded as a thug. The 56-year-old Simon appeared on television to answer criticism of the show and said: 'I think I did good work.' Sadly, *The Capeman* was to prove the biggest flop in New York history, with a loss of approximately £7 million before it closed on 28 March 1998 after only 68 performances.

Simon's 12-track album *Songs From The Capeman* was issued in December 1997.

In June 1998 Art Garfunkel and his musicians toured the UK to raise money for cystic fibrosis. His band comprised Eric Weissberg, Warren Bernhardt, Steve Gadd and Kim Bullard. The tour included a Royal Gala Performance at the London Palladium in the presence of HRH Princess Alexandra.

SIMONE, Nina

Singer-songwriter Nina Simone (real name Eunice Waymon) was born in Tryon, North Carolina, on 21 February 1933.

Her hits included: 'I Put A Spell On You', 'I Loves You Porgy', 'Ain't Got No – I Got Life/Do What You Gotta Do', 'To Love Somebody' and 'My Baby Just Cares For Me'. Her version of 'I Put A Spell On You' entered the UK chart in 1965 and 1969.

'My Baby Just Cares For Me' became popular when used in a television commercial for

Chanel perfume. Her songs have since been used regularly, the latest being 'I Loves You Porgy' on a mobile phone advertisement in 1998.

Nina Simone remains a dependable in-person attraction and still produces atmospheric concert albums such as *Live At Ronnie Scott's* in 1989.

SIR DOUGLAS QUINTET Doug Sahm formed this group in the early 1960s. Sahm was born in Texas in 1943 and started playing steel guitar at the age of six. He was performing in the famous Louisiana Hayride Show at the age of nine.

The group, known for their Tex-Mex sound, had a big hit in 1965 with 'She's About A Mover'.

At one point in his career, Sahm called the outfit the Sir Douglas Quintet Plus Two. By the time of the chart hit 'Mendicino' in 1969, he had augmented his band and the line-up and personnel were: Doug Sahm (vocals and guitar), Franklin Morin (tenor sax), Wayne Talbert (piano), Martin Fierro (alto sax), Bill Atwood (trumpet), Mel Barton (baritone sax), Terry Henry (trumpet), Whitney Freeman (bass) and George Mains (drums).

Their other chart single was 'The Rains Came' in 1966.

Sahm had changed the line-up of the band several times and in 1973 broke them up again to lead Doug Sahm & Band.

He re-formed the Sir Douglas Quintet in 1981 and spent most of the 1980s touring with the band.

As a member of the Texas Tornados, in late 1995 a heavily bearded Doug Sahm was planning a world tour. Along with such great sidekicks as Augie Myers and Freddie Fender, his new band featured his son Shawn on guitar. It is quite likely that, true to form, Sahm will revive the name Sir Douglas Quintet for further live shows.

SLADE Wolverhampton quartet Slade comprised Noddy Holder (guitar and vocals), Dave Hill (guitar), Jimmy Lea (bass) and Don Powell (drums).

In 1969, former **Animals** member Chas Chandler, who was managing the **Jimi Hendrix** Experience, took over the group and they had an incredible string of hits between 1971 and 1991, including five chart-toppers.

Their hits were: 'Get Down And Get With It', 'Coz I Luv You', 'Look Wot You Dun', 'Take Me Back 'Ome', 'Mama Weer All Crazee Now', 'Gudbuy T'Jane', 'Cum On Feel The Noize', 'Merry Xmas Everybody', 'Skweeze Me, Pleeze Me', 'My Friend Stan', 'Everyday', 'Bangin' Man', 'Far Far Away', 'How Does It Feel', 'In For A Penny', 'We'll Bring The House Down', 'Lock Up Your Daughters', 'My Oh My', 'Run Run Away', 'All Join Hands' and 'Radio Wall Of Sound'.

'All Join Hands' entered the chart in 1984 and their next hit, 'Radio Wall Of Sound', in 1991. The group played together for the last time in April 1991, when they performed for fans at a twenty-fifth anniversary party. In 1992 Hill and Powell launched Slade II, making their debut in a restaurant in Umea, Sweden.

Noddy Holder became a disc jockey, hosting golden oldies' shows in Manchester and Sheffield, commuting from his home in Cheshire. By 1997 he was also an actor, appearing in *The Grimleys*, a television drama set in 1975 and also featuring Nigel Planer and comedian Jack Dee. 1997 also saw Noddy featured on *This Is Your Life*.

In June 1973 Powell was in a car accident in which his girlfriend, who was driving, was killed. Don was in intensive care and the doctors gave him just 24 hours to live. He survived, but found his memory had gone – although doctors advised that he keep on playing with the band as good therapy. It took him two years to get back into the swing of things, although he had lost his senses of smell and taste.

In 1997 Noddy commented: 'The band were upset when I left, but Dave and Don are touring and Jim would have liked to have carried on, but wouldn't do it without me.'

When Jimmy Lea left he studied to become a psychiatrist, then formed a pub band called the Rockin' Wrinklies in 1995. Dave Hill became a Jehovah's Witness, but continued to perform along with Don Powell and some new members in Slade II, with Steve Whalley providing lead vocals and bass guitarist Trevor Holliday completing the line-up.

SLEDGE, Percy This singer was born on 25 November 1940 in Leighton, Alabama. He first began performing with a group called the Esquires Combo while he was still a teenager. During the mid-1960s he began to enjoy a successful solo career with hits such as 'When A Man Loves A Woman', 'Warm And Tender Love' and 'Take Time To Know Her'.

After a reissued 'When A Man Loves A Woman' came within an ace of topping the UK chart in 1987, Percy Sledge's concert and recording spectrum broadened considerably.

His most recent album, *Blue Night*, released in 1994, featured contributions from Steve Cropper, Bobby Womack and ex-**Rolling Stone** Mick Taylor.

SLITS, The   This female punk band was formed in 1976. The original members were Kate Kaos (guitar), Suzy Gutz (bass), Palmolive (drums) and Arianna Forster (vocals). When Kaos and Gutz left, Viv Albertine and Tessa Pollitt replaced them. Singer Forster then changed her name to Ari Up. When Palmolive left to join the Raincoats she was replaced by Pete Clarke, known as Budgie. When Budgie left to join Siouxsie & the Banshees, Bryce Smith replaced him.

The group toured with punk bands such as the Clash and had a minor hit with 'I Heard It Through The Grapevine'. They disbanded in 1981.

Bass guitarist Tessa currently studies martial arts. Ari is living in Jamaica. Palmolive is playing drums in a Christian rock band in Massachusetts and Viv is now a film director.

SLY & THE FAMILY STONE   At the age of four, Sylvester Stewart made his first recording with the Stewart Four, his family's group. Over the years he appeared in several other outfits until, in 1967, he formed Sly & the Family Stone.

As vocalist, keyboards player and guitarist, he called himself Sly Stone. The other members were Freddie Stone (guitar), Rosemary Stone (vocals and piano), Cynthia Robinson (trumpet), Jerry Martini (sax), Larry Graham (bass) and Greg Errico (drums).

The group's hit singles included: 'Dance To The Music', 'M'Lady', 'Everyday People', 'Family Affair' and 'Runnin' Away'.

Their album hits included: *Stand!*, *Greatest Hits*, *There's A Riot Goin' On*, *Fresh*, *Small Talk*, *Heard You Missed Me – Now I'm Back*, *Back On the Right Track* and *Ain't But The One Way*.

Major changes occurred when Graham left the band to form his own Graham Central Station. Rusty Allen replaced him. The same year also saw Andy Newmark replace Errico and a further member, Pat Ricco, joined them on sax.

Throughout his career Sly suffered from drugs problems, which led to the cancellation of a UK tour and his arrest on several occasions. In 1989 he received a gaol sentence for drugs offences.

His picturesque marriage to Kathy Silva – which took place on stage at Madison Square Garden in 1974 – broke down and the couple was divorced. Sly, who had filed for bankruptcy, was also later arrested for failing to pay maintenance.

Larry Graham's Graham Central Station disbanded in 1980, and his solo output has since produced a solitary US hit in 'One In A Million You', released that year.

As for Sylvester 'Sly' Stewart, his latter-day career has continued to be blighted by drugs problems and ill-fated projects like *Ten Years Too Soon*, a disco re-mix of his hits with the Family Stone.

A CD anthology, *Takin' You Higher – The Best Of Sly & The Family Stone*, was issued in 1995.

SMALL FACES, The   This group was formed in London in 1965 and comprised **Steve Marriott** (vocals and guitar), **Ronnie 'Plonk' Lane** (bass), Ian McLagan (organ) and Kenney Jones (drums). They signed with Decca and had a minor chart hit with their debut single, 'Give Her My Regards'. They were popular with the 'mods' at the time and took their name from the fact that all the members were short in stature.

Their hit singles were: 'Whatcha Gonna Do About it', 'Sha La La La La Lee', 'Hey Girl', 'All Or Nothing', 'My Mind's Eye', 'I Can't Make It', 'Here Comes The Nice', 'Itchycoo Park', 'Tin Soldier', 'Lazy Sunday', 'Universal' and 'Afterglow Of Your Love'.

They also had three chart albums: *Small Faces*, *From The Beginning* and *Ogden's Nut Gone Flake*.

Marriott left the band to team up with Peter Frampton in Humble Pie in February 1969 and the Small Faces disbanded. Lane, Jones and McLagan brought in guitarist Ron Wood and vocalist **Rod Stewart**, and relaunched themselves as the Faces. They disbanded at the end of the year.

In 1976 Marriott re-formed the group with Jones and McLagan and began to tour the UK, but the group split the following year. Jones was later to join the **Who**.

Ronnie Lane had contracted multiple sclerosis and moved to a Florida hospital for treatment. Marriott had formed a group called Steve Marriott & His Packet Of Three in 1991, but died the same year in a fire at his cottage.

In 1996 Jones, McLagan and Wood received a Lifetime Achievement Award at the Ivor Novello Awards ceremony.

Ronnie Lane died in 1997. Ian McLagan is currently a highly paid international session musician; Kenney Jones is a businessman, horse owner and keen polo player. In 1995 he wrote a foreword to a Small Faces biography by Paolo Hewitt.

SMITH, Hurricane Norman Smith was a recording engineer at Abbey Road studios, assisting George Martin on Beatles recordings. He subsequently went on to produce records with other major British acts such as the **Pretty Things** and Pink Floyd.

In 1971, at the age of 49, he decided to make a record himself, using the name Hurricane Smith, which was the title of a film starring Yvonne DeCarlo, which he had seen in 1952. His hit singles included 'Don't Let It Die', 'Oh Babe What Would You Say?' and 'Who Was It'.

Hurricane Smith then decided to retire from the music business and now runs a medical equipment company in Surrey.

SMITH, Patti Born in Chicago on 30 December 1946, singer-poet Patti Smith lived in Paris, London and New York. She began to make a name for herself among the New York creative set and in 1974 recorded 'Hey Joe/Piss Factory'. That same year she formed her Patti Smith Group, and her debut album, *Horses*, was issued by Arista Records the following year.

Patti had several books of poetry published, issued albums such as *Wave* and toured Europe. In 1980 she married her childhood sweetheart, former MC5 player **Fred 'Sonic' Smith**, and settled in Detroit to raise their two children, Jesse and Jimmy.

Eight years later she came out of retirement to record 'People Have The Power' and the album *Dream of Life*, which were produced by Fred Smith and Jimmy Iovine.

Sadly, Fred died at the end of 1994. It was a tragic time for Patti, as she had also recently suffered the death of her brother and several close friends. Although she continues to spend most of her time raising her children, she emerged with a new album, *Gone Again*, in 1996 and embarked on her first UK tour for 17 years.

SMITHS, The Vocalist Stephen Patrick Morrissey was the recent author of the book *James Dean Isn't Dead* when he was approached by guitarist John Marr to join a group. Together with other Manchester musicians Andy Rourke on bass and Mike Joyce on drums, they formed the Smiths in 1982.

The group's chart singles were: 'This Charming Man', 'What Difference Does It Make', 'Heaven Knows I'm Miserable Now', 'William It Was Really Nothing', 'How Soon Is Now', 'Shakespeare's Sister', 'That Joke Isn't Funny Anymore', 'The Boy With The Thorn In His Side', 'Big Mouth Strikes Again', 'Panic', 'Ask', 'Shoplifters Of The World Unite', 'Sheila Take A Bow', 'Girlfriend In A Coma', 'I Started Something I Couldn't Finish' and 'Late Last Night I Dreamt That Somebody Loved Me'.

Their album hits included: *The Smiths*, *Hatful Of Hollow*, *Meat Is Murder*, *The Queen Is Dead*, *The World Won't Listen*, *Louder Than Bombs*, *Strangeways Here We Come* and *Rank*.

Morrissey was a man who was always seeking to pay tribute to his idols and influences, as could be found in the images on many of the group's record sleeves, and in 1984 they recorded 'Hand In Glove' with **Sandie Shaw**.

An additional guitarist, Craig Gannon, was added to the line-up in 1986, but he only remained with the Smiths for only a few months.

When Marr left in 1987, Joyce, Morrissey and Rourke soldiered on briefly as a trio before Morrissey embarked on a solo career that began well but has since oscillated, despite a re-acquaintance with his old group's X-factor, Marr, in 1994.

Marr has, in fact, collaborated with and appeared on records by a host of other artists, including Paul McCartney, **Talking Heads**, Bryan Ferry, and the Pet Shop Boys.

The reputation of the Smiths has only grown and 1995 saw a shoal of releases of past singles and albums, a number of which re-entered the charts.

SMOKE, The Formed in 1967, this group consisted of Mick Rowley (vocals), Mal Luker (guitar), John 'Zeke' Lund (bass) and Jack Gill (drums). The BBC banned their single 'My Friend Jack', as it was presumed that the line 'my friend Jack eats sugar lumps' referred to the ingestion of LSD. It became a hit on the Continent and some years later an even bigger one for **Boney M**.

After their next single, 'If The Weather's Sunny', they moved to Island Records and issued 'It Could Be Wonderful' and 'Utterly Simple'.

Following various personnel changes, the band persevered until the 1970s.

A CD retrospective, *My Friend Jack*, was issued in 1988.

SMOKIE This group originally started life as a trio called the Elizabethans. By 1968 they had changed their name to Kindness, and when they signed with Rak Records they became known as Smokey, but changed that to Smokie to avoid confusion with Smokey Robinson. The members were Chris Notman (vocals), Terry Utley (guitar), Alan Silson (bass) and Peter Spence (drums).

In the hands of hit songwriters Nicky Chinn and Mike Chapman, the group had a number of commercial songs at their disposal and their hit singles included: 'If You Think You Know How To Love Me', 'Don't Play Your Rock 'n' Roll To Me', 'Something's Been Making Me Blue', 'I'll Meet You At Midnight', 'Living Next Door To

Alice', 'Lay Back In The Arms Of Someone', 'It's Your Life', 'Needles And Pins', 'For A Few Dollars More', 'Oh Carol', 'Mexican Girl' and 'Take Good Care Of My Baby'.

Their album hits included: *Smokie*, *Greatest Hits*, *The Montreaux Album* and *Smokie's Hits*.

Norman was also to have a Stateside hit when he duetted with **Suzi Quatro** on 'Stumblin' In' in 1978.

Norman and Spencer had taken over from Chinn and Chapman in penning hits for the band and were also to provide the numbers 'Head Over Heels' for Kevin Keegan and 'This Time We'll Get It Right' for the England World Cup Squad.

When Norman went solo, **Alan Barton** replaced him – but Barton was killed in 1995 in a road accident during the group's German tour.

Chris Norman currently lives on the Isle of Man, from where he commutes to a crowded concert schedule in Eastern Europe. He produced Cynthia Lennon's 1995 revival of **Mary Hopkin's** 'Those Were The Days'.

In 1996, Smokie appeared on UK television's *Top Of The Pops* for the first time in years – to promote a somewhat risqué remake of 'Living Next Door To Alice' with comedian Roy 'Chubby' Brown.

SOFT CELL This group was formed in Leeds in 1979, vocalist Marc Almond having originally met up with keyboards player Dave Ball at Leeds Polytechnic.

Their singles hits included: 'Tainted Love', 'Bed Sitter', 'Say Hello Wave Goodbye', 'Torch', 'What', 'Where The Heart Is', 'Numbers/ Barriers', 'Soul Inside' and 'Down In The Subway'. 'Tainted Love' has entered the UK chart on three occasions.

Their hit albums have included: *Non-Stop Erotic Cabaret*, *Non-Stop Ecstatic Dancing*, *The Art Of Falling Apart* and *This Last Night in Sodom*.

In 1983 Ball issued a solo album, *In Strict Tempo*.

The duo disbanded in 1984 following a farewell tour.

Dave Ball collaborated with Cabaret Voltaire and the Virgin Prunes, and is a central figure in the Grid, initially a studio entity that reached the UK Top 10 in 1994 with 'Swamp Thing'.

Since the sundering of Soft Cell in 1984, Marc Almond's success has been more profound via a solo career that has embraced torch songs, Gallic *chanson* and 1960s revivals, notably

'Some-thing's Gotten Hold Of My Heart', an amused duet with Gene Pitney, that topped the charts in 1989.

SOFT MACHINE, The This progressive British group was originally formed in 1966, taking their name from a novel by William Burroughs. There were many personnel changes over the years, but the classic line-up was established in 1967 with Robert Wyatt, Kevin Ayres and Mike Ratledge. Another prominent line-up was one formed in 1970 with Wyatt, Ratledge, Hugh Hopper and Elton Dean. The following year Wyatt left to form Matching Mole. There were various other changes and Ratledge left in 1976. A new line-up of the band was brought together for a season at Ronnie Scott's club in 1984.

Robert Wyatt, who lives in Lincolnshire, is still an active recording artist. Bass guitarist Hugh Hopper lives in Canterbury and writes short stories, music instruction manuals and pamphlets such as *Thirty Kent Churches*. Mike Ratledge lives in London and has fingers in various musical pies, including advertising jingles. Saxophonist Elton Dean is a mainstay of London's avant-garde jazz scene.

SOUL, David Singer-actor David Soul (real name David Solberk) was born on 28 August 1943. He started out as a folk singer in the 1960s but found eventual success as an actor, portraying police detective Ken Hutchinson in the television series *Starsky And Hutch* from 1975 to 1979. He then had a series of hit singles in the charts – 'Don't Give Up On Us', 'Going In With My Eyes Open', 'Silver Lady' and 'Let's Have A Quiet Night In'.

David currently lives in California, but visited the UK several times during 1997 to appear on radio and television shows. His bank balance is buoyed as much by *Starsky And Hutch* repeats as by record royalties.

SOUNDS INCORPORATED Formed in Kent in 1961, this group became the most famous instrumental band in the UK next to the Shadows and regularly backed the visiting rock 'n' roll stars such as Little Richard. They were signed to **Brian Epstein** in 1964 and appeared on tour with the Beatles in the States. They also played on 'Good Morning Good Morning' on the *Sgt Pepper* album.

The members were Alan Holmes (flute and sax), Griff West (sax), John St John (guitar),

Barrie Cameron (keyboards), Wes Hunter (bass guitar) and Tony Newman (drums).

Sounds Incorporated had two minor hits on the Columbia label, 'The Spartans' and 'Spanish Harlem'. Their other singles included 'William Tell' and 'My Little Red Book'.

After the group called it a day in the late 1960s, most of the personnel became session musicians. Saxophonist Alan Holmes, for instance, played a part in many **Kinks** sessions. However, the most conspicuous ex-member was drummer Tony Newman, who served **Jeff Beck** and David Bowie before forming Boxer with the late Mike Patto in the mid-1970s. He moved to the US and in the 1990s backs artists such as the **Everly Brothers** and is currently writing his autobiography.

SPANDAU BALLET This group were trailblazers in the 'new romantic' movement at the beginning of the 1980s, which presented groups wearing exotic clothes and appearing at fashionable clubs where the audience also dressed in stylish and sometimes bizarre fashions.

The members were Gary Kemp (guitar), Martin Kemp (bass), Tony Hadley (vocals), John Keeble (drums) and Steve Norman (rhythm).

The group had problems over the years with two of their record companies, Chrysalis and CBS – blaming Chrysalis for their lack of success Stateside and breaking away from CBS because the company refused to release their album *Heart Like A Sky* in the US.

Their chart singles included: 'To Cut A Long Story Short', 'The Freeze', 'Muscle Bound Glow', 'Chant No 1 (I Don't Need This Pressure On)', 'Paint Me Down', 'She Loved Like Diamond', 'Instinction', 'Lifeline', 'Communication', 'True', 'Gold', 'Only When You Leave', 'I'll Fly For You', 'Highly Strung', 'Round And Round', 'Fight For Ourselves', 'Through The Barricades', 'How Many Lies', 'Raw' and 'Be Free With Your Love'.

Their hit albums were: *Journey To Glory*, *Diamond*, *True*, *Parade* and *The Singles Collection*.

While the combo has never split officially, each member has drifted into solo activity, and there have been no new releases since 1989's *Heart Like A Sky*.

Gary and Martin Kemp took the title roles in the acclaimed movie *The Krays* in 1989, and the two, who trained at a stage school when they were young, have since branched out into acting, with Martin appearing in several US television series and Gary taking the role of

Whitney Houston's manager in *The Bodyguard* in 1992.

Gary also released a solo album, *Little Bruises*, in 1995.

Tony Hadley gained a solo recording contract with EMI in 1992 that has yet to reap commercial dividends.

SPARKS Two brothers, originally teenage models, formed this duo in Los Angeles in 1968. Initially known as the Halfnelson, they recorded unsuccessfully with **Todd Rundgren** in 1971. Like the **Walker Brothers**, they then found fame by relocating to the UK, where they had success with their debut single, 'This Town Ain't Big Enough For Both Of Us'. Other hit singles in 1974 and 1975 included 'Amateur House', 'Never Turn Your Back On Mother Earth', 'Something For The Girl With Everything', 'Get In The Swing' and 'Looks, Looks, Looks'.

Russell Mael, bass guitarist and vocalist with a distinctive falsetto voice, was born Dwight Russell Day on 5 October 1953. Ron Mael, on keyboards, with his deadpan expression and Hitler moustache, was born Ronald Day on 12 August 1948. The duo enjoyed two hit albums under the aegis of Muff Winwood – *Kimono My House* and *Propaganda*; their third album, *Indiscreet*, produced by Tony Visconti, did not fare so well.

Despite being voted Brightest Hope For 1975 in a *Melody Maker* poll, their success as recording artists faltered and they made their way back to California in 1976. The duo then returned to the UK with a different style and a new release, 'Number One Song In Heaven', which entered the chart, and they followed with two further hits, 'Beat The Clock' and 'Tryouts For The Human Race'. The two found additional success in Europe, particularly France, where they became a popular live attraction.

Sparks entered the UK chart again in 1995 with 'When Do I Get To Sing "My Way"', and the same year released a further album, *Gratuitous Sax And Senseless Violins*. They also wrote the soundtrack to Francis Ford Coppola's movie *Mai The Psychic Girl*.

In December 1997 Sparks appeared in concerts in London.

SPECIALS, The This group was made up of a blend of black and white musicians from Coventry who attempted to combine elements of punk and Jamaican ska.

They formed in 1977 and comprised Terry Hall (vocals), Neville Staples (percussion), Jerry Dammers (keyboards), Lynval Golding and Roddy Radiation (guitar), Sir Horace Gentleman (real name Horace Panter) (bass) and John Bradbury (drums). The band initially called themselves the Coventry Specials, then the Special AKA. When they signed with Chrysalis Records they shortened their name to the Specials.

Their UK chart singles included: 'Gangsters', 'A Message To You Rudy/Nite Club', 'Too Much Too Young', 'Rad Race/Rude Buoys Outa Jail', 'Stereotype/International Jet Set', 'Do Nothing/Maggie's Farm', 'Ghost Town', 'Racist Friend', 'Nelson Mandela' and 'What I Like Most About You Is Your Girlfriend'.

Their chart albums were *Specials* and *More Specials*.

Dance Crazy, a film documentary about the Specials, also spawned a soundtrack album.

Golding, Hall and Staples formed **Fun Boy Three** in 1981. Hall was later the leader of Colour Field, before embarking on a solo career that included a revival of Charles Aznavour's 'She' and a 1997 album.

Until 1984 Dammers kept the Specials in the public eye – and the charts – as Special AKA (the group's original name) before he took up his greatest involvement, in Artists Against Apartheid. By 1993 he was running a club in London's Covent Garden.

Golding re-formed the group in 1995, with Staples, Panter and Radiation. During 1996 they had a minor hit with 'Hypocrite', released a new album, *Today's Specials*, and began a UK tour.

SPEDDING, Chris Guitarist-singer-songwriter Chris Spedding was born in Sheffield, South Yorkshire, on 17 June 1944.

In the late 1960s and early 1970s he was a member of various groups including the Vulcans, Pete Brown's Battered Ornaments, the Jack Bruce Band and Sharks. In his own right, he had a chart hit in 1975 with 'Motor Bikin''.

Spedding became one of the UK's leading session guitarists and has worked with numerous acts including **Lulu**, **Dusty Springfield**, Elton John, **Tom Waits**, **Gilbert O'Sullivan** and **Harry Nilsson**.

In the 1990s Chris Spedding relocated to Los Angeles, where he continues to perform as an in-demand session guitarist.

SPENCER DAVIS GROUP, The This R&B group was formed in Birmingham in 1962. Spencer Davis, a guitarist who was influenced by folk and blues music, shared the bill in a pub with the Muff Woody Trad Jazz Band. He was impressed by the guitarist, Muff Winwood, and Winwood's 15-year-old brother Stevie, who played piano. He approached them both and they agreed to form a band. Spencer played rhythm, Muff turned to bass, Stevie handled vocals and lead guitar, and the three were joined by drummer Pete York.

As the Spencer Davis Group, they were spotted by Chris Blackwell and signed to Island Records.

Their hit singles included: 'I Can't Stand It', 'Every Little Bit Hurts', 'Strong Love', 'Keep On Running', 'Somebody Help Me', 'When I Come Home', 'Gimme Some Loving', 'I'm A Man', 'Time Seller' and 'Mr Second Class'.

When Stevie Winwood reached the age of 18 he formed another band called Traffic with Dave Mason, Chris Wood and Jim Capaldi. Without Stevie, the Spencer Davis Group eventually disbanded in 1969.

In more recent years, Pete York and Spencer Davis have been participating in both York's Blues Reunion tours of Europe (with the likes of **Zoot Money**, **Chris Farlowe** and Brian Auger) and occasional new editions of the Spencer Davis Group for events such as the Birmingham Jazz Festival. When Spencer Davis, now a resident in the US, arrived to play a series of dates in Birmingham in May 1996, the other members of his band included Miller Anderson on vocals and Colin Hodgkinson, a former member of Whitesnake, on bass.

Based in London, Muff Winwood is high up the executive ladder of Sony Records. Stevie Winwood has homes in Gloucestershire and Tennessee and, since a brief re-formation of Traffic in the 1990s, has resumed a successful solo career.

SPOTNIKS, The This Swedish group was originally formed in 1957 by Bo Winberg under the name the Frazers. They had several hits in their native country and four UK chart entries in 1962 and 1963 – 'Orange Blossom Special', 'Rocket Man', 'Hava Nagila' and 'Just Listen To My Heart'.

Apart from lead guitarist Winberg, other members included Bob Lander (guitar and vocals), Bjorn Thelin (bass) and Ole Johannsson (drums).

At one time, the group's gimmick was to wear spacesuits.

When Johannsson departed to become a priest, Londoner Derek Skinner replaced him. When Skinner left in 1965 **Jimmy Nicol**, who had been Ringo Starr's replacement on a Beatles tour, stepped in. Nicol left in 1967 to be replaced by Tommy Tausis. Over the years there have been further personnel changes.

To date, the group's most recent album of new material was *Love Is Blue* in 1988, but the Spotniks were still touring Scandinavia in the 1990s – albeit with only Bo Winberg left from the original line-up.

SPRINGFIELD, Dusty Born Mary O'Brien in Hampstead, London, on 16 April 1939, this singer initially began her career with the Lana Sisters. In 1960, together with her brother Dion and a friend, Tim Field, she became a member of the folk trio the Springfields, changing her name to Dusty Springfield, with Dion becoming Tom Springfield. Their second record, 'Breakaway', entered the UK chart, and they followed up with the hits 'Bambino', 'Island Of Dreams', 'Say I Won't Be There' and 'Come On Home', although Field left the group in 1962 and was replaced by Mike Hurst. Having been voted Best UK Vocal Group, the Springfields disbanded in 1963 when Dusty embarked on a solo career.

Hurst was to become a record producer and produced **Showaddywaddy** in the 1970s. Tom Springfield became a composer and wrote the hits 'The Carnival Is Over' and 'Georgy Girl' for the **Seekers**.

Dusty was noted for her bell-shaped skirts with starched petticoats, a blonde bouffant hairstyle and long, black mascara-laden eyelashes.

Her UK hit singles between 1963 and 1979 were: 'I Only Want To Be With You', 'Stay Awhile', 'I Just Don't Know What To Do With Myself', 'Losing You', 'Your Hurtin' Kind Of Love', 'In The Middle Of Nowhere', 'Some Of Your Lovin'', 'Little By Little', 'You Don't Have To Say You Love Me', 'Going Back', 'All I See Is You', 'I'll Try Anything', 'Give Me Time', 'I Close My Eyes And Count To Ten', 'Son Of A Preacher Man', 'Am I The Same Girl', 'How Can I Be Sure' and 'Baby Blue'.

In 1968 she travelled to Memphis to record her album *Dusty In Memphis* and decided to relocate to Los Angeles in 1972.

Her chart days were virtually over and she

179

became a session singer, providing back-up vocals on records for artists such as Anne Murray. She was later to say that she 'lost nearly all the 1970s in a haze of booze and pills', admitted sleeping with both men and women, and became a virtual recluse for some years.

In 1984 Dusty duetted with **Spencer Davis** on 'Private Number', returned to the UK the following year to record 'Sometimes Like Butterflies', but found her biggest hit for years when she was a guest singer on the Pet Shop Boys' 'What Have I Done To Deserve This'. She then sang the theme to the British movie *Scandal*, which was also penned by the Pet Shop Boys.

When British comedian Bobby Davro portrayed her as a drunk on his show, she sued and received £75,000 damages.

After returning to the UK chart in the late 1980s with 'What Have I Done To Deserve This', Dusty made her way back from Los Angeles to live in England once more. In 1994, she and Cilla Black duetted on a single, 'Heart and Soul'. She also recorded the album *Dusty In Nashville*, 25 years after her LP *Dusty In Memphis*. A few months later she was diagnosed as having cancer of the breast and a lump was removed. Following the operation, Dusty spent months receiving chemotherapy and radiotherapy,

which was successful at the time. However, in February 1998 the 58-year-old singer, now living in a luxury home in Hurley, Berkshire, discovered that the cancer had returned.

SPRINGSTEEN, Bruce The singer-songwriter who came to be referred to as the 'Boss' was born in Freehold, New Jersey, on 23 September 1949. He first began playing guitar when he was 14 years old and joined his first group, the Castiles, in 1965. By 1969 he was in a group called Child, who changed their name to Steel Mill, and in 1971 he formed his own band, Dr Zoom & Sonic Boom, who then became the Bruce Springsteen Band. He was soon to form the backing outfit that became known as the E Street Band.

Springsteen's impact in the 1970s and 1980s was considerable, particularly in the States.

His debut album, *Greetings From Asbury Park*, was issued in 1973, and succeeding albums included: *The Wild The Innocent & The E Street Shuffle*, *Born To Run*, *Darkness On The Edge Of Town*, *The River*, *Nebraska*, *Born In The USA*, *Live 1975–1985* (a 5-album set), *Tunnel Of Love*, *Human Touch*, *Lucky Town*, *Greatest Hits* and *The Ghost Of Tom Joad*.

His hit singles include: 'Hungry Heart', 'The River', 'Dancing In The Dark', 'I'm On Fire/Born In The USA', 'Glory Days', 'Santa Claus Is

Dusty Springfield with The Springfields

Comin' To Town', 'War', 'Fire', 'Born To Run', 'Brilliant Disguise', 'Tunnel Of Love', 'Tougher Than The Rest' and 'Spare Parts'.

In his personal life, Springsteen married Julianne Phillips, an actress and model, in 1985. When he began an affair with his backing singer Patti Scialfa, she sued for divorce, which was finalized in 1989. By 1994 Scialfa, whom he had married, had provided Springsteen with three children.

Although he has suffered gradual commercial decline since his fattest years in the mid-1980s, he has no financial worries, and could enjoy a dotage rich in material comfort without having to play another note of music. However, he seems a determined and committed artist, whose music still reflects the content and concerns of his idol **Woody Guthrie**.

STARDUST, Alvin Born Bernard Jewry in London in 1942, this singer changed his name to Shane Fenton, led a group called the Fentones, and enjoyed four chart entries – 'I'm A Moody Guy', 'Walk Away', 'It's All Over Now' and 'Cindy's Birthday'. He moved away from the pop scene for a while after marrying Iris Caldwell, sister of Liverpool legend **Rory Storm**.

The singer re-emerged under the new name of Alvin Stardust, dressed in black leather and exuding a moody persona, and had a string of hits over an eight-year period. They were: 'Coo-Ca-Choo', 'Jealous Mind', 'Red Dress', 'You You You', 'Tell Me Why', 'Good Love Can Never Die', 'Sweet Cheatin' Rita', 'Pretend', 'A Wonderful Time Up There', 'I Feel Like Buddy Holly', 'I Won't Run Away', 'So Near To Christmas' and 'Got A Little Heartache'.

Alvin divorced Iris and married television actress Lisa Goddard, but that marriage also ended.

As a writer, he has had two autobiographies published and has also completed his first novel. He joined the committee of the Save The Children Fund, presented and narrated the UK television documentary *Countdown Apollo* and was chosen as the subject of a *This Is Your Life* programme.

In 1987 he was presented with the Music Business World Diamond Award. The same year he worked with Andrew Lloyd Webber and Tim Rice on their collaboration *Cricket*. In 1988 he starred in the UK tour of their musical *Godspell*.

In 1994 Alvin appeared with **Showaddy-waddy** and the **Rubettes** on the Solid Silver

Seventies Tour, and topped the bill on the second tour the following year, which also featured **Mud** and the Glitter Band.

During the autumn of 1995 he joined the cast of the new UK television soap opera *Hollyoaks* and released an album in Europe through CMC Records.

In 1996, Alvin played Gaston in *Beauty & The Beast* at the Millfield Theatre in London and starred as Sir Billy Butlin in the new musical *The Butlin's Story* at the London Palladium. Later in the year he toured with the concert show *The Birth Of Rock 'n' Roll* and recorded a live album of the same name over four nights at Ronnie Scott's jazz club.

For the 1996–7 Christmas season he appeared as Robin Hood in *Babes In The Wood* in Hull, and in March 1997 appeared on another seventies nostalgia tour.

STARGAZERS, The The line-up of this British vocal group, originally formed in 1949, consisted of **Dick James**, Cliff Adams, Marie Benson, Bob Brown, Fred Datchler and Ronnie Milne.

Between 1953 and 1956 they had a string of UK chart hits. These were: 'Broken Wings', 'I See The Moon', 'Happy Wanderer', 'Somebody', 'Crazy Otto Rag', 'Close The Door', 'Twenty Tiny Fingers' and 'Hot Diggity'.

Cliff Adams is a mainstay of the long-running UK radio series *Sing Something Simple*, which he devised in 1959. Fred Datchler's son Clark was a member of the 1980s hitmakers Johnny Hates Jazz. Ronnie Milne emigrated to Canada and Dick James died following a heart attack in 1986.

STARR, Edwin Born Charles Hatcher on 21 January 1942 in Nashville, Tennessee, this singer formed his first band in Cleveland, Ohio, before enrolling in the US Army and being posted to Europe. He formed another group and began performing at gigs in European clubs in his spare time.

On his return to the States he joined the Bill Doggett Combo, before going solo and making his recording debut with 'Agent Double O Soul' in 1965. Other hits included 'Headline News' and 'SOS – Stop Her On Sight'.

Most of his work in the latter part of the 1960s was in the UK and Europe. He then had another US hit in 1969 with '25 Miles' and topped the chart in 1970 with 'War (What Is It Good For)'. He toured the UK and Europe with **Marvin Gaye** in 1980.

181

Edwin Starr is still a popular attraction in the UK, and together with his 11-piece band he appeared at the Jazz Café in Camden Lock, north London, in December 1997.

During April, May and June 1998 he was the headline attraction in Flying Music's nationwide UK tour Dancing In The Streets.

STARR, Kay This singer of American Indian descent was born Katherine Starks in Dougherty, Oklahoma, on 21 July 1922. She began to sing with various bands, including those led by Glen Miller and Bob Crosby, and turned solo in 1940. Her hits included: 'Comes A-Long A-Love', 'Side By Side', 'Changing Partners', 'Am I A Toy Or A Treasure', 'Good And Lonesome', 'Rock And Roll Waltz', 'Second Fiddle' and 'My Heart Reminds Me'.

Kay Starr continues to perform and in 1993 she toured the UK with **Pat Boone**.

STATUS QUO This band was originally formed in London in 1962 as the Spectre. The line-up comprised Francis Rossi (guitar and vocals), Alan Lancaster (bass and vocals), John Coghlan (drums) and Rick Parfitt (guitar and vocals)

They changed their name to Status Quo when they recorded 'Pictures Of Matchstick Men' in 1967.

Their subsequent hit singles included: 'Ice In The Sun', 'Are You Growing Tired Of My Love', 'Down The Dustpipe', 'In My Chair', 'Paper Plane', 'Mean Girl', 'Caroline', 'Break The Rules', 'Down Down', 'Roll Over Lay Down', 'Rain', 'Mystery Song', 'Wild Side Of Love', 'Rockin' All Over The World', 'Again And Again', 'Accident Prone', 'Whatever You Want', 'Living On An Island', 'What You're Proposing', 'Lies', 'Something 'Bout You Baby I Like', 'Rock 'n' Roll', 'Dear John', 'She Don't Fool Me', 'Caroline (Live At The NEC)', 'Ol' Bag Blues', 'A Mess Of The Blues', 'Marguerita Time', 'Going Down Town Tonight', 'The Wanderer', 'Rollin' Home', 'Red Sky', 'In The Army Now', 'Dreamin'', 'Ain't Complaining', 'Who Gets The Love', 'Running All Over The World' and 'Burning Bridges'.

Their hit albums have included: Piledriver, The Best Of Status Quo, Hello, Quo, On The Level, Down The Dustpipe, Blue For You, Live, Rockin' All Over The World, Can't Stand The Heat, Whatever You Want, 12 Gold Bars, Just Supposin', Never Too Late, Fresh Quota, 1982, From The Makers Of..., Status Quo Live At The NEC and 12 Gold Bars Volume 2.

The group split in 1984, but Rossi and Parfitt re-formed it in 1986 without Lancaster, who was unhappy about their decision to leave him out of the band. However, he joined Australia's Party Boys. The new Status Quo included John Edwards on drums and Jeff Rich on bass.

The group celebrated the thirtieth anniversary of their debut single, 'I (Who Have Nothing)', in 1996 with a new album, Don't Stop.

Status Quo's career continues and their Whatever You Want tour, with Paul Rodgers on the bill, featured at Wembley Arena in December 1997.

STEELEYE SPAN This folk group underwent several changes in personnel when they first formed in 1969. They eventually settled down with a line-up comprising Maddy Prior (vocals), Tim Hart (vocals, guitar and dulcimer), Peter Knight (fiddle, mandolin and vocals), Bob Johnson (vocals), Rick Kemp (bass and vocals) and Nigel Pegrum (drums and flute).

They had two hit singles, 'Gaudette' and 'All Around My Hat', both in 1973.

The group were more successful in the album field, which produced such chart entries as: Please To See The King, Below The Salt, Parcel Of Rogues, Now We Are Six, Commoner's Crown, All Around My Hat and Rocket Cottage.

Steeleye Span embarked on a twenty-fifth anniversary tour of the UK, celebrating their first recording, in 1997 and toured again the following year, when they issued a new album, The Wandering Nomads.

STEPPENWOLF This Canadian hard rock band was originally known as Sparrow. They decided to move to San Francisco and Los Angeles at the height of the West Coast Sound boom in 1966 and renamed themselves after the Herman Hesse novel Steppenwolf, which was a campus favourite at the time. The line-up comprised John Kay (lead vocals), Michael Monarch (lead guitar), **Jerry Edmonton** (drums), Goldy McJohn (organ) and Rushton Moreve (bass). John Russell Morgan replaced Moreve in 1968.

Edmonton's brother Daniel, known as Mars Bonfire, composed the number 'Born To Be Wild', which was the group's biggest hit. Another massive seller was 'Magic Carpet Ride'. Their other singles hits were: 'Rock Me', 'Move Over', 'Monster', 'Hey Lawdy Mama' and 'Straight Shootin' Woman'. They also had a series of chart albums.

Kay disbanded the group in 1972, turning solo and issuing the album *Forgotten Songs And Unknown Heroes*. He also had a hit single with 'I'm Movin' On'. He re-formed the group in 1974 with McJohn, Edmonton and other musicians.

Steppenwolf disbanded again in 1978 and was reborn again in 1981 as John Kay & Steppenwolf.

Mars Bonfire is a member of the Los Angeles-based Stars New Seeds Band. The outfit includes former personnel from the Seeds, Iron Butterfly and the Fraternity of Man.

John Kay remains leader of a re-formed Steppenwolf and they continue to tour North America and Europe, albeit with a middle-aged joviality replacing the outlaw chic of old. Kay's autobiography, *Magic Carpet Ride*, was published in 1993.

Rushton Moreve and Jerry Edmonton both died in car accidents – in 1981 and 1993 respectively.

A John Kay & Steppenwolf album, *Rise And Shine*, was issued in 1993, the same year as *Born To Be Wild – A Retrospective*.

STEVENS, Cat   A major British singer-songwriter, Cat Stevens (real name Steven Georgiou) was born in London on 21 July 1947. For a ten-year period from 1967 to 1977 his hits included: 'I Love My Dog', 'Matthew And Son', 'I'm Gonna Get Me A Gun', 'A Bad Night', 'Kitty', 'Lady D'Arbanville', 'Moon Shadow', 'Morning Has Broken', 'Can't Keep It In', 'Another Saturday Night' and 'Old School Yard'. He also had nine chart albums, which included: *Mona Bone Jakon*, *Tea For The Tillerman*, *Teaser And The Firecat*, *Catch Bull At Four*, *Foreigner*, *Buddha And The Chocolate Box* and *Izitso*.

In December 1977 he converted to Islam, changed his name to Yusuf Islam and has dedicated himself tirelessly to the Muslim community. He retired from a music world that he considered was a place of 'sin and greed'. Almost 20 years later, in 1995 he recorded a mostly spoken-word narration of the life of Muhammad called *The Life Of The Last Prophet*, and contributed to the 1998 compilation *I Have No Cannons That Roar*.

Late in 1997, a song Yusuf had written called 'Afghanistan' began to be aired in Kabul. Yusuf had originally written the number as a freedom song for the Muslims fighting against the Soviet Army. When the Taliban regime of fundamentalist fighters took over Kabul in September 1996, all music was outlawed, and tapes and instruments were destroyed. Eventually, a bootleg tape of 'Afghanistan' was found and allowed to be broadcast, as it urged a religious revolution. The Taliban justified playing it over and over again on the radio, explaining that under Koranic law, Yusuf's songs were not 'music' since they included no instruments and were religious in content.

STEWART, Rod   Born Roderick David Stewart in London on 10 January 1945, Rod was his parents' fifth child. His father Robert, born in Edinburgh, had settled in the south of England to work as a master builder and married Elsie, a cockney.

As he grew up, Rod had two obsessions: football and Al Jolson. His parents collected Jolson records and Rod listened to them constantly at home as a child. When he was old enough, his parents took him to see *The Jolson Story* and *Jolson Sings Again*.

The influence of Jolson has remained with him. Rod noted Jolson's dislike of having empty seats in his audience, his sheer professionalism, and the fact that he could sing without a microphone while remaining audible to two thousand people.

On leaving school, Rod's first job was with a printing firm. Brentford Football Club then signed him as an apprentice, but he couldn't take the training regime, which would often cause him to vomit. He left after several months.

In the early 1960s he became a beatnik, and at the age of 16 hitchhiked his way to France. After being arrested three times in marches supporting the Campaign For Nuclear Disarmament, Rod teamed up with a noted beatnik, Wizz Jones, to hitch around Belgium, France, Italy and Spain. The pair supported themselves by busking for money, with Rod playing banjo. They were arrested as vagrants by the Spanish police, who forced the British consulate to repatriate them.

Rod returned home to Highgate, worked in his father's shop for a while and then became a gravedigger at Highgate Cemetary.

At this time he had his first serious romantic relationship, with a girl called Jan Donaldson. She bore him a daughter, Katie, in 1963, although Rod made it clear that her had no intention of marrying her.

Rod joined Jimmy Powell & the Five Dimensions in 1963. He then became a member of **Long John Baldry** & the Hoochie Coochie Men, then the Soul Agents, followed by Steampacket, in which he shared vocal honours with Julie Driscoll and Long John Baldry. In 1966 he became a member of Shotgun Express, sharing vocals with Liverpool singer Beryl Marsden. By this time he had picked up the nickname 'Rod The Mod.'

He then became a member of the **Jeff Beck** Group, and then of the Faces. As he had a solo contract to record, he was able to run parallel careers, recording both as a solo artist and a member of the Faces.

After joining the Faces, Rod had a high-profile romance with live-in girlfriend Dee Harrington, although he received even greater press coverage when, in 1975, he abandoned her for Britt Ekland, the former wife of actor Peter Sellers.

His name was also linked with models Paulene Stone, Debbie Doranck and Kathy Simmonds, and actresses Joanna Lumley and Mai Britt.

With the Faces, Rod recorded four albums and ten singles. The group embarked on their first US tour in the spring of 1970, playing support to other bands. By the following year they were a headline act and in 1972 enjoyed two successful tours of the States, one of which lasted for three months and covered 60 cities.

However, a degree of disharmony began to creep into the outfit when Stewart achieved international success with his solo chart-topper 'Maggie May' in 1971. The group backed him on his numerous television appearances to promote the single, but were unhappy at the new billing of Rod Stewart & the Faces.

Midway through a tour of the States in 1974, Ronnie Lane decided to quit after completing the band's remaining engagements there and in the UK. Japanese guitarist Tetsu Yamauchi replaced him.

The group had toured the States twice a year for four consecutive years and made a policy decision to spent 1974 on a world tour, taking in the Far East, Australia and New Zealand, along with two UK tours.

1975 was the final year for Rod Stewart & the Faces. Rod had quit the UK for tax purposes and settled in Los Angeles. Ronnie Wood had begun touring the States with the **Rolling Stones**, and the remnants of the Faces joined Stewart for the last time on a US tour to promote the singer's latest solo single, *Atlantic Crossing*.

In December of that year Rod announced that he was quitting the group, Ronnie Wood officially joined the Rolling Stones, and the Faces split up – ironically at a time when the re-release of 'Itchycoo Park' reached No 9 in the chart.

The following year Kenney Jones and Ian McLagan, together with **Steve Marriott**, re-formed the **Small Faces**, but the reunion was unsuccessful and Jones joined the **Who** in 1979.

Rod's hit singles include: 'Maggie May', 'Tonight's The Night (Gonna Be Alright)', 'The First Cut Is The Deepest', 'You're In My Heart, (The Final Acclaim)', 'Da Ya Think I'm Sexy?', 'Passion', 'Young Turks', 'Infatuation' and 'Some Guys Have All The Luck'.

His album hits include: *Gasoline Alley, Every Picture Tells A Story, Never A Dull Moment, Sing It Again Rod, Smiler, Atlantic Crossing, A Night On The Town, Best Of Rod Stewart, Foot Loose And Fancy Free, Blondes Have More Fun, Greatest Hits, Foolish Behaviour, Tonight I'm Yours, Absolutely Live, Body Wishes, Camouflage, Every Beat Of My Heart* and *Out Of Order*.

1990 saw the release of a Rod Stewart retrospective including both solo and group recordings, called *Storyteller/The Complete Anthology: 1964–1990*. The same year saw the release of *Downtown/Selections From Storyteller*. Other albums included the 1991 release *Vagabond Heart, The Best Of Rod Stewart & The Faces* in 1992, *Rod Stewart: Lead Vocalist* and *Unplugged – And Seated* in 1993 and *A Spanner In The Works* in 1995.

Rod then married Alana Hamilton, the former wife of actor George Hamilton, in 1979 and she bore him two children, Sean and Kimberley. They divorced in 1984 and Rod lived next with Kelly Emberg from 1985 until 1990; she bore him a daughter, Ruby. He then met New Zealand model Rachel Hunter, whom he married in December 1990. The couple were to have two children, Renée and Liam McAllister.

Rod ended 1997 hosting a New Year's Eve party in Melbourne, Australia. In December of that year he had been frequently in the press threatening to sue a number of lookalikes who were making his life a misery. The Stewart imposters were bedding women, turning up at restaurants and trying to buy cars, all using his name.

May 1998 saw the release of a new single, 'Ooh La La', and the announcement of a new album, *When We Were The New Boys*, in which Rod featured the songs of current bands such as Oasis, Primal Scream and Skunk Anansie.

Rod, who was 55 years old in January 1999, appeared on a series of Earls Court concerts from 9 to 16 December, 1998. He has houses in Epping Forest and Los Angeles.

STRANGLERS, The

This group was formed in 1974 as the Guildford Stranglers. They comprised Hugh Cornwell (guitar and vocals), Jean-Jacques Burnel (bass and vocals), Dave Greenfield (keyboards) and Jet Black (drums).

The Stranglers began to attract attention when they were the support act on a **Patti Smith** tour of the UK in 1976.

Their hits included: '(Get A) Grip (On Yourself)', 'Peaches (Go Buddy Go)', 'Something Better Change/Straighten Out', 'No More Heroes', 'Five Minutes', 'Nice 'n' Sleazy', 'Walk On By', 'Duchess', 'Nuclear Device (The Wizard Of Aus)', 'Don't Bring Harry', 'Bear Cage', 'Who Wants The World', 'Thrown Away', 'Let Me Introduce You To The Family', 'Golden Brown', 'La Folie', 'Strange Little Girl', 'European Female', 'Midnight Summer Dream', 'Paradise', 'Skin Deep', 'No Mercy', 'Let Me Down Easy', 'Nice In Nice', 'Always The Sun', 'Big In America', 'Shakin' Like A Leaf' and 'All Day And All Of The Night'.

They made their album debut with *The Stranglers IV: Rattus Norvegicus*, and followed with *No More Heroes*, *Black & White*, *Live (X Cert)*, *The Raven*, *Themeninblack*, *La Folie*, *The Collection 1977–1982*, *Feline*, *Aural Sculpture*, *Off The Beaten Track*, *Dreamtime*, *All Live And All Of The Night*, *Wolf* and *10*.

In 1979 both Cornwell and Burnel issued solo albums, Cornwell with *The Raven* and Burnel with *Euroman Cometh*.

In August 1990, Cornwell quit the group for a solo career. Paul Roberts replaced him in 1991 and guitarist John Ellis also joined the group, but opinion has been divided as to whether the Stranglers have remained as effective a force without Cornwell. Black also left in 1992 and Tikake Tobe replaced him.

In 1992 Cornwell formed a new band, CCW, with Roger Cook and Andy West.

No Mercy: The Authorized And Uncensored Biography Of The Stranglers by David Buckley was published at the end of 1997.

STRAWBS, The

This group was originally formed in London in 1967, under the name the Strawberry Hill Boys. The original line-up of Dave Cousins (guitar and banjo), Tony Hooper (guitar) and Arthur Phillips (mandolin) began playing folk music and were joined by vocalist Sandy Denny and bassist Ron Chesterton. Denny then left them to join Fairport Convention.

Phillips also left the group, which became a trio in 1969. Their debut album, *Strawbs*, was well received, and they followed up with *Dragonfly*. Chesterton was replaced by John Ford, and Richard Hudson and Rick Wakeman joined the line-up.

Following their 1971 album *From The Witchwood*, Wakeman left to join **Yes** and was replaced by an ex-member of **Amen Corner**, Blue Weaver. By 1972 Hooper had been replaced by Dave Lambert.

After an unsuccessful US tour, Hudson, Ford and Weaver left to be replaced by Rod Coombes, Chas Cronk and John Hawken. The group disbanded in 1978, but re-formed in 1983.

The Strawbs remain a recording entity – but only just – and they also hold regular reunion concerts and appear at folk festivals. Dave Cousins, who lives in Devon, is still the group's mainstay. Richard Hudson has his own publishing company and also does session work, while still remaining a Strawb. John Ford lives in Nassau and is a solo acoustic act. Blue Weaver is a leading session musician, based in London, and Dave Lambert lives in Austria, where he functions as a solo artist.

STRAY CATS, The

This trio, formed on Long Island, New York, in 1979, consisted of Brian Setzer (guitar and vocals), Lee Rocker (double bass) and Slim Jim Phantom (drums).

They based themselves in London in 1980 and had their first UK hit that year, taking their record debut, 'Runaway Boys', into the Top 10.

Other UK hits included 'Rock This Town', 'Stray Cat Strut', 'You Don't Believe Me' and '(She's) Sexy And 17'.

When the group split up shortly after '(She's) Sexy And 17' was a minor hit in 1983, the former members returned to the States. Rocker and Phantom (who is married to actress Britt Ekland) amalgamated – as Phantom, Rocker & Slick – with guitarist Earl Slick, with whom they reappeared in the UK on a star-studded televised tribute to **Carl Perkins**, organized by **Dave Edmunds** in 1985.

Phantom, Rocker & Slick released their eponymous debut album in 1985 and their second album, *Live Nude Guitars*, the following year. In the meantime, Brian Setzer entered the US chart with his album *The Knife Feels Like Justice* in 1986, the year in which he portrayed Eddie Cochran in the movie *La Bamba*.

The Stray Cats united for a 35-date tour of the States in 1988 and recorded a new album together called *Blast Off*. Both the album and a single taken from it, 'Bring It Back Again', entered the US chart. They issued a further album, *Let's Go Faster*, in 1991 and another, *Choo Choo Hot Fish*, in 1992.

By this time the group had split again. In 1993 Slim Jim Phantom joined Cheap Dates.

In 1996 there was a CD anthology, *Back To The Alley – The Best Of Stray Cats*, was issued, and during that year Brian Setzer took to the road with his own 16-piece orchestra.

STREISAND, Barbra   Singer Barbara Joan Streisand was born in New Jersey, New York, on 24 April 1942. She appeared in the Broadway musical *I Can Get It For You Wholesale*, which also featured Elliott Gould, and the two were married in 1963.

Barbra has had 37 gold US albums and received two Oscars – for Best Actress in *Funny Girl* and for Best Song, for 'Evergreen' in *A Star Is Born*.

Her hit singles include: 'People', 'Stoney End', 'The Way We Were', 'Evergreen', 'My Heart Belongs To Me', 'The Main Event' and 'Woman In Love'. She has also charted in duets with various other singers, including Neil Diamond, Barry Gibb, Donna Summer and Celine Dion.

In tandem with her recording and performance career, Barbra has also continued a movie career as an actress and director. Among the films in which she has featured are: *Funny Girl, Hello Dolly!, On A Clear Day You Can See Forever, The Owl & The Pussycat, What's Up Doc?, Up The Sandbox, The Way We Were, For Pete's Sake, Funny Lady, A Star Is Born, The Main Event, All Night Long, Yentl, Nuts, Places You Find Love* and *Listen Up*.

Barbra Streisand is now back on the road and appeared in London on a major concert tour in November 1997 as a special tribute to her fans in the UK. It was her first UK appearance since 1994 and coincided with her latest album, *Higher Ground*. Accompanying the 55-year-old

star to London at the time was her fiancé, actor James Brolin.

SUPERTRAMP   When they formed in 1969, this group rejected the suggestion of Daddy as a name in favour of Supertramp, inspired by the book *The Autobiography Of A Supertramp*. Vocalist and keyboards player Richard Davies had met Swiss millionaire Sam Miesegaes, who agreed to bankroll the band. Davies advertised and was joined by Roger Hodgson on bass, Richard Palmer on guitar and Bob Miller on drums.

With the addition of sax player Dave Winthrop, they debuted in 1970 with the album *Supertramp*. By January 1971 both Palmer and Miller had quit and been replaced by Frank Farrell on bass and Kevin Currie on drums. Before the end of the year the other members left, leaving only Davies and Hodgson. In 1973 John Helliwell joined them on sax, Dougie Thomson on bass and Bob C. Benberg on drums.

Supertramp enjoyed their first chart single, 'Dreamer', in 1975. Their other hit singles included: 'Give A Little Bit', 'The Logical Song', 'Breakfast In America', 'Goodbye Stranger' and 'It's Raining Again'.

Their hit albums included: *Crime Of The Century, Crisis? What Crisis?, Even In The Quietest Moments, Breakfast In America, Paris, Famous Last Words* and *Brother Where You Bound*.

When Hodgson left to embark on a solo career in 1982, the band remained a quartet. Hodgson enjoyed minor chart success with the album *In The Eye Of The Storm* and the single 'Had A Dream (Sleeping With The Enemy)'.

Supertramp had enjoyed major success as a touring band on both sides of the Atlantic and their compilation album *The Autobiography Of Supertramp* was issued in 1986, with 1987 seeing the release of a new LP, *Free As A Bird*, followed the next year by *Supertramp Live '88*. 1992 saw the release of the compilation *The Very Best Of Supertramp*.

In September 1997, to promote their new album release, *Some Things Never Change*, Supertramp embarked on their It's About Time tour of major UK venues such as the Nynex in Manchester, Sheffield Arena, Glasgow SECC and London's Royal Albert Hall

SWEET   Prominent figures in the British glam rock movement of the 1970s, the members of Sweet wore make-up, lip gloss, huge platform shoes – the whole caboodle. Singer **Brian**

Connolly first teamed up with drummer Mick Tucker in 1966 in a group called Wainwright's Gentlemen. The two left to form Sweetshop with bass guitarist Steve Priest and guitarist Frank Torpey, the latter soon being replaced by Andy Scott. The group then truncated their name to Sweet.

It was the songwriting team of Nicky Chinn and Mike Chapman who provided them with a string of hit singles.

Their chart entries with Chinnichap songs were: 'Funny Funny', 'Co-Co', 'Alexander Graham Bell', 'Poppa Joe', 'Little Willy', 'Wig-Wam Bam', 'Blockbuster', 'Hell Raiser', 'Ballroom Blitz', 'Teenage Rampage', 'The Six Teens' and 'Turn It Down'. The group then broke away from the songwriting team to pen their own material, and the singles hits which followed were 'The Run', 'Action', 'Lies In Your Eyes', 'Love Is Like Oxygen' and 'It's The Sweet Mix'.

Between 1971 and 1979 the band sold 50 million records.

Connolly split from the band for a solo career in 1979 and was replaced as lead vocalist by Andy Priest. New member Gary Mobeley also joined on keyboards.

Connolly claimed that it was Andy Scott who began to undermine his position as the group's frontman. He says that the other members of the band laid down the backing tracks to their last album in a key in which he wouldn't be able to sing. He said: 'I didn't understand why I couldn't get the high notes, why my voice was going.'

Scott, Connolly said, was jealous of the attention he received as lead vocalist. He commented: 'It was his idea to give Steve Priest vocals to sing, so that the camera would have to shift away from me. And on one tour he got me playing keyboards, even though all I was doing was pressing the odd button. It was just to get me away from centre stage.'

Connolly later formed his own backing band, which he named the New Sweet, and later Brian Connolly's Sweet.

From 1982 Sweet have appeared in various incarnations, with some original members joined by new musicians. One line-up in 1985 included Paul Mario Day on lead vocals and keyboards player Phil Lanzon.

Brian Connolly re-recorded his hits with his group on a Dutch album and toured the European nostalgia circuit before his death in 1997. In October 1996, a few months before he died, a documentary about him called *Don't Leave Me This Way* was screened on UK television.

Andy Scott leads an entity called Andy Scott's Sweet which has released many Germany-only records. Steve Priest lives in the US. Mick Tucker is a London-based record producer.

SWINGLE SINGERS, The A vocal octet, the Swingle Singers were formed in Paris in 1963 by American session musician Ward Swingle. They became an enormous success in France and had clothes created for them by Yves St Laurent and Pierre Cardin. Italian composer Luciano Berio wrote for them and Christine Legrand, sister of composer Michel Legrand, was the group's soprano.

Their debut album, *Jazz Sebastian Bach*, was awarded two Grammy Awards for Best New Artist and Best Vocal Group. The album also entered the UK chart.

Swingle disbanded the French group in 1973 and moved to London, where he formed a new group recruited from students from the *conservatoires* and choral scholars from cathedrals and colleges.

Ward Swingle left the group in the 1980s, but they have continued from their base in Walthamstow, London E17, although most of their 100 performances a year are outside the UK. The group also continues to make CDs which, although they don't make an appearance in the charts, still sell thousands of copies.

TAJ MAHAL This singer and multi-instrumentalist was born Henry Saint Clair Fredericks in New York on 17 May 1942, the eldest of nine children. His father was a jazz pianist, but was killed. He taught himself to play piano, guitar, harmonica, vibraphone, mandolin, dulcimer, Jew's harp and many other instruments.

In 1965 he moved to California and formed the band Rising Sons with Ry Cooder, then played with **Canned Heat** prior to cutting his first solo album, *Taj Mahal*, in 1968. The following year he issued a double-album, *Giant Step/De Ole Folks At Home*.

For a time in the early 1970s he toured Europe and had further success with the double album *Real Thing*. Other hit albums included *Happy To Be Like I Am* and *Recycling The Blues And Other Related Stuff*. In 1979 he travelled around Africa on a state department tour.

In 1995, Taj Mahal appeared in the film *When We Were Coloured*. In 1996 he released a new album, *Phantom Blues*, with guest musicians that included Bonnie Raitt and Eric Clapton.

In 1991 his album *Like Never Before* was released and he toured the UK in November of that year. Edsel Records were also to issue an early album, *The Natch'l Blues*, on CD.

His latest album, *Taj Mahal & The Hula Blues*, was issued in 1998.

TALKING HEADS Guitarist and vocalist David Byrne, bass guitarist Tina Weymouth and her boyfriend, drummer Chris Frantz, initially formed a trio in 1974. After rejecting several other names, they found the term 'talking heads' in a television listings magazine and adopted it. In 1976 they were joined by keyboards player Jerry Harrison and made their debut disc, 'Love Goes To Building On Fire', later that year. During 1977 they toured Europe, made their first album, *Talking Heads '77*, and Tina and Chris were married.

Their singles hits included: 'Take Me To The River', 'Burning Down The House', 'Once In A Lifetime', 'And She Was', 'Road To Nowhere' and 'Wild Wild Life'.

Album hits included: *Fear Of Music*, *Remain In Light*, *The Name Of This Band Is Talking Heads* and *Speaking In Tongues*.

In 1981 Weymouth and Frantz created a new group, the Tom Tom Club, although they continued as members of Talking Heads. The band was to release several singles and albums. Byrne also involved himself in numerous projects,

including writing and featuring in the 1986 film *True Stories*. He also became involved in producing records by other artists and composing film soundtrack music. 1995 saw the publication of a book of his photographs, *Strange Ritual*.

After a long lay-off, Chris Frantz and Tina Weymouth headed a 1991 edition of Talking Heads for what amounted to a nostalgia tour – with the **Ramones** and Debbie Harry – before an announcement from *de jure* leader David Byrne that the group was finished. Since then, Byrne has continued a low-profile if critically acclaimed solo career while Weymouth, Frantz and Jerry Harrison were heard on the soundtrack to the 1995 movie *Virtuosity*.

TANGERINE DREAM This group was founded in Germany in 1967. The three improvisational musicians who performed under the name Tangerine Dream were Edgar Froese (synthesizer, keyboards and guitar), Christopher Franke (synthesizer) and Peter Baumann (synthesizer, keyboards and flute).

Their debut album, *Electronic Meditation*, was issued only in Germany in 1970. After further albums issued there – *Alpha Centuri*, *Zeit* and *Atem* – they signed with a British label, Virgin Records. Tangerine Dream's first two albums for them were *Phaedra* and *Rubycon*.

The trio had begun to appear in as many cathedrals as possible following their initial performance at Rheims Cathedral in 1974. With the release of their third Virgin album, *Ricochet*, in 1975 they embarked on a UK tour which took in the cathedrals of York, Coventry and Liverpool.

Froese also began recording solo albums such as *Aqua* and *Epsilon In Malaysian Pale*.

Edgar Froese compiled and re-mastered a Tangerine Dream boxed set for Virgin Records in 1994. The group toured the UK in October and November 1997 to promote the release of their new album, *Tournado*.

TAYLOR, James Singer-songwriter James Taylor was born in Boston on 12 March 1948. He began writing songs when committed to a psychiatric hospital for several months suffering from depression.

1966 saw him join a New York band, the Flying Machine, but by 1968, in an attempt to rid himself of his heroin addiction, he moved to London and met up with Peter Asher, who signed him to the Apple label.

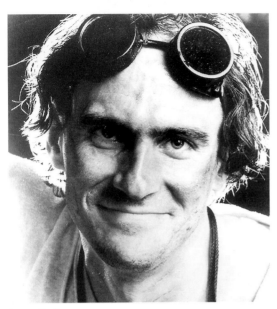

James Taylor

was 'You're So Vain' and she also penned and sang 'Nobody Does It Better', the theme song to the James Bond movie *The Spy Who Loved Me*.

In 1998, at the age of 52, Carly – who is prone to claustrophobia, agoraphobia and anxiety attacks and visits a therapist every week – revealed that she was undergoing chemotherapy for a malignant tumour in her breast, which was diagnosed in October 1997.

During 1998 she was working on a new album containing character sketches of New York women. She said that she had scrapped her memoirs, commenting: 'You can do it as a song because you don't have to name the people you are writing about. But in an autobiography they want names and action.'

TEARDROP EXPLODES, A This Liverpool band was formed in 1978 with members Julian Cope (vocals and bass), Michael Finkler (guitar), Paul Simpson (keyboards) and Gary Dwyer (drums). Dave Balfre replaced Simpson the following year.

Their hit singles included: 'When I Dream', 'Reward', 'Treason (It's Just A Story)', 'Passionate Friend', 'Colours Fly Away', 'Tiny Children' and 'You Disappear From View'.

Album hits included *Kilimanjaro* and *Wilder*.

There were various personnel changes, with Alan Gill replacing Finkler in 1980 and Balfe being replaced by Jeff Hammer later that same year. In 1981 there were substantial changes, with only Cope and Dwyer remaining out of the originals and new recruits Alfie Agius on bass and Troy Tate on guitar. Balfe also rejoined the band and Cope took up rhythm guitar.

In 1982 Agius was replaced by Ron Francois, who quit a few months later, along with Tate. The same year Cope split up the band, setting out on a solo career and taking Dwyer with him.

Troy Tate joined Fashion, while Dave Balfe worked in an administrative capacity for Food Records – whose flagship act is Blur. Meanwhile, from his base in rural Wiltshire, Julian Cope's solo career has embraced fluctuating chart success, a book about krautrock and a practical interest in neolithic monuments.

TEARS FOR FEARS This British duo teamed up in 1980. They comprised Curt Smith, born in Bath on 24 June 1961, on vocals and bass, and Roland Orzabal, born in Portsmouth on 22 August 1961, on guitar and keyboards. They took their name from a chapter heading in

Apple released his debut album, *James Taylor*, but his relationship with the label didn't last long and he returned to the States, booking himself into a hospital to rid himself of the drugs addiction. Asher followed him to the US and became his manager.

Over the years Taylor's album releases have included: *Sweet Baby James, Mud Slide Slim And The Blue Horizon, One Man Dog, Gorilla, In The Pocket, Dad Loves His Work, That's Why I'm Here, Never Die Young, Life Is Good, New Moon Shine* and *James Taylor Live*.

His singles included: 'Carolina On My Mind', 'You've Got A Friend', 'Don't Let Me Be Lonely Tonight', 'How Sweet It Is (To Be Loved By You)', 'Your Smiling Face', 'Honey Don't Leave LA', 'Never Die Young' and 'Copperline'.

In his personal life, Taylor married singer Carly Simon in 1972, but the couple divorced in 1982 and he married Kathryn Walker in 1985.

In breaks in his concert and recording schedule, Taylor works occasionally in the Caribbean as a crew member on board a mariner friend's boat.

As James Taylor & His Band, he began a UK tour in 1998 which was a sell-out, resulting in additional dates which caused The Hourglass Tour to extend from January to March.

Taylor's ex-wife Carly married poet James Hart in 1987, although the two continued to live in separate homes. Carly's biggest hit record

Prisoner Of Pain, a book by Arthur Janov, the originator of 'primal therapy'.

At the time of their debut single, 'Suffer Little Children', in 1981 they also engaged Manny Elias on drums and Ian Stanley on keyboards to back them on live appearances.

Their 1982 release 'Mad World' reached No 3 in the UK chart. It was followed by a series of hit singles: 'Change', 'Pale Shelter', 'The Way You Are', 'Mother's Talk', 'Shout', 'Everybody Wants To Rule The World', 'Head Over Heels', 'Suffer The Children', 'I Believe', 'Sowing The Seeds Of Love', 'Woman In Chains' and 'Advice For The Young At Heart',

Their album hits were: *The Hurting*, *Songs From The Big Chair* and *The Seeds Of Love*.

Despite their great success, in 1992 Smith and Orzabel decided to split. Smith moved to New York and Orzabel continued under the Tears For Fears name, releasing a new album, *Raoul And The Kings Of Spain*, in 1995. Smith issued a solo album unsuccessfully in New York, but decided to have another crack at solo success with *Reach Out*, released in April 1998. By that time he had also formed a new band called Mayfield.

TELEVISION This American group was originally formed in 1973 and comprised Tom Verlaine (real name Thomas Miller; vocals and lead), Richard Lloyd (rhythm), Richard Hell (real name Richard Myers; bass) and Billy Ficca (drums).

Fred Smith replaced Hell, who left to join the Heartbreakers in 1975.

The group found more success with their albums in the UK than in the US, charting with *Marquee Moon* and *Adventure*. Their singles 'Prove It' and 'Foxhole' also entered the UK chart.

Television split up in 1978. Verlaine and Lloyd began solo careers, Smith joined **Blondie** and Ficca joined the Waitresses.

Richard Hell lasted a year in the Heartbreakers with ex-New York Doll Johnny Thunders, before leading the Voidoids and then retiring from the music business for nearly ten years, returning in the 1990s for occasional new albums, spoken-word performances and the publication of a novel, *The Voidoid*.

Meanwhile, the other focal point of Television, Tom Verlaine, pursued fame in his own right, before re-forming the group in the early 1990s for a one-shot eponymous album. It received favourable reviews, but neither prefaced any permanent reunion nor heightened Verlaine's profile when he resumed his solo career with the 1996 retrospective double album *A Miller's Tale*.

TEMPERANCE SEVEN, The This jazz band was one of several to find recording success in the trad jazz boom. All their hits occurred within one year – 1961. They were: 'You're Driving Me Crazy', 'Pasadena', 'Hard Hearted Hannah' and 'Charleston'.

The Temperance Seven

The group was more of a dance band, playing music with a 1930s ambience, than a jazz group playing traditional Dixieland jazz. The members were Paul McDowell (vocals), Cephas Howard (trumpet and euphonium), John Davies (trombone and sax), Frank Paverty (sousaphone), Philip Harrison (alto and baritone sax), Alan Swainston-Cooper (clarinet, soprano sax, phonofiddle, swanee whistle and pedal clarinet), Colin Bowles (piano and harmonium), Brian Innes (drums) and John Gieves-Watson (banjo).

The Temperance Seven were re-formed in the 1970s by Ted Wood, brother of Art of the Artwoods and **Rolling Stone** Ronnie, although they had little success and soon broke up.

10 CC Under the name Frabjoy & Runcible, Kevin Godley and Lol Crème cut a single called 'I'm Beside Myself' in 1969 with Eric Stewart and Graham Gouldman backing them. The four, all born in Manchester, next recorded a hit, 'Neanderthal Man', under the name Hotlegs. It was **Jonathan King** who gave the group the name 10 CC in 1972 when he signed them to his UK Records label.

Their hit singles included: 'Donna', 'Rubber Bullets', 'The Dean And I', 'Wall Street Shuffle', 'Silly Love', 'Life Is A Minestrone', 'I'm Not In Love', 'Art For Art's Sake', 'I'm Mandy Fly Me', 'Things We Do For Love', 'Good Morning Judge', 'Dreadlock Holiday' and 'Run Away'.

Their album hits included: *10 CC, Sheet Music, The Original Soundtrack, Greatest Hits Of 10 CC, How Dare You, Deceptive Bends, Live And Let Live, Bloody Tourists, Greatest Hits 1972–1978, Look Here* and *Window In The Jungle*.

In 1976 Godley and Crème left the group and continued as a duo, while Gouldman and Steward continued 10 CC as a trio, with the addition of Paul Burgess. The following year they added additional musicians – Rick Fenn on guitar, Tony O'Malley on keyboards and Stuart Tosh on drums.

In the meantime, Godley & Crème had completed a triple album, *Consequences*, and their singles hits included 'Under Your Thumb', 'Wedding Bells' and 'Cry'. Gouldman was also to have chart success in his own right with the single 'Sunburn'.

Godley, Crème, Gouldman and Stewart all became involved in various ventures, ranging from production to songwriting. And in 1982 Stewart teamed up with Paul McCartney on several collaborations, including performing on the album *Tug Of War*.

In 1991 Stewart and Gouldman teamed up again to re-form 10 CC and recorded an album, *Meanwhile In New York*, with contributions from Godley and Crème.

In 1995 Gouldman and Stewart re-formed 10 CC once more for an album called *Mirror Mirror*, and took on a promotional tour of Japan. Later the same year a double CD anthology of 10 CC material was issued, entitled *The Things We Do For Love*.

These days, Kevin Godley and Lol Crème are in-demand producers of pop videos.

TEN YEARS AFTER Guitarist Graham 'Alvin' Lee was a member of groups such as the Jailbreakers and the Square Caps. He teamed up with bass guitarist Leo Lyons and they appeared at Hamburg's famous Star Club as the Jaymen. They were then joined by drummer Ric Lee (no relation to Alvin) and Chick Churchill on keyboards. When Chris Wright became their manager, they changed their name to the Jaybirds, then Blues Trip and Blues Yard. When it came to a decision regarding a permanent name, they had to choose between Life Without Mother and Ten Years After. They became Ten Years After in 1967.

The group's album hits included: *Undead, Stonehenge, Ssssh, Cricklewood Green, Watt, Space In Time, Rock And Roll* and *Recorded Live*. Despite being primarily an album and performing band, they had one UK Top 10 hit in 1970 with 'Love Like A Man'.

Their final album was *Positive Vibrations*, released in 1974. Ric Lee and Churchill then came out with solo albums and that same year Lee formed his own outfit, Alvin Lee & Co. Later, Ten Years After were to re-form for a tour of the US, but they disbanded again in 1980.

After a brief regrouping in 1989 that produced one album, *About Time*, Alvin Lee resumed a solo career that hinged on much the same sort of music – dominated by lengthy guitar work-outs – heard on 1995's Ten Years After retrospective, *Pure Blues*.

Another reunion took place and they issued a further album, *Live In Vienna*, in 1996, the year Chrysalis Records issued two Ten Years After compilations. During 1997 they appeared at European festivals and made their first visit to South America.

A boxed set is planned for 1998.

THOMPSON TWINS, The Singer-keyboards player Tom Bailey founded the Thompson Twins in 1977, naming them after the two detectives in Hergé's famous cartoon series *Tintin*.

Born in Halifax on 18 June 1957, Bailey had various different personnel in the band until 1981, when he invited his girlfriend Alannah Currie – a singer, a songwriter and a multi-instrumentalist – to join them, together with the group's former road manager, Joe Leeway, who became singer, synthesizer player and percussionist. Alannah was born in New Zealand on 20 September 1957. Joe was also born on 20 September – but in 1949.

The outfit was pruned down to a trio in 1982 and their singles hits in the UK included: 'Lies', 'Love On Your Side', 'We Are Detective', 'Watching', 'Hold Me Now', 'Doctor Doctor', 'You Take Me Up', 'Sister Of Mercy', 'Lay Your Hands On Me', 'Don't Mess With Doctor Dream', 'King For A Day', 'Revolution', 'Get That Love' and 'In The Name Of Love '88'.

When Joe Leeway left in 1986, the Thompson Twins actually became a duo, both professionally and personally. Becoming an 'item', Tom Bailey and Alannah Currie also became parents for the first time in 1988, and in 1993 began recording again under the name Babble, the trio being made up by Keith Fernley. They issued a single, 'Chale Jao', and their debut album, *The Stone*, was released later that year. Babble have now disbanded.

THREE DEGREES, The The members of this American vocal group were Fayette Pickney, Sheila Ferguson and Valerie Thompson. They topped the UK chart with 'When Will I See You Again' in August 1974, which reached No 2 in the US. Their other UK singles hits were: 'Year Of Decision', 'Get Your Love Back', 'Take Good Care Of Yourself', 'Long Lost Lover', 'Toast Of Love', 'Givin' Up Givin' In', 'Woman In Love', 'The Runner', 'The Golden Lady', 'Jump The Gun', 'My Simple Heart' and 'The Heaven I Need'.

The group proved more popular in the UK than in the States and had only two entries in the US chart – apart from 'TSOP', a No 1 hit in 1974, which was the theme song from the television show *Soul Train*. The hit was credited to 'MFSB featuring the Three Degrees'. MFSB stood for Mother Father Sister Brother.

At one time, the Three Degrees were touted as being Prince Charles' favourite group.

Now resident in the UK, the new formation of Three Degrees are fixtures on the country's variety and cabaret circuit. Sheila left for a solo career, became an actress and also writes cookery books.

THREE DOG NIGHT This vocal and instrumental group was formed in Los Angeles in 1968 by vocalist Danny Hutton, who wanted to establish a group with three lead vocalists. The two singers he recruited were Cory Wells and Chuck Negron, and the other members were Mike Allsup (guitar), Jimmy Greenspoon (organ), Joe Schermie (bass) and Floyd Sneed (drums).

The group's name was derived from an Australian phrase referring to a cold night in the outback when dogs provided warmth – and a 'three dog night' is the coldest of all.

Their first album, *Three Dog Night*, was issued in 1968 and they charted with the single 'Try A Little Tenderness' the following year.

Their other hits in the US singles chart were: 'One', 'Easy To Be Hard', 'Eli's Coming', 'Celebrate', 'Mama Told Me (Not To Come)', 'Out In The Country', 'One Man Band', 'Joy To The World', 'Liar', 'An Old Fashioned Song', 'Never Been To Spain', 'The Family Of Man', 'Black & White', 'Pieces Of April', 'Shambala', 'Let Me Serenade You', 'The Show Must Go On', 'Sure As I'm Sittin' Here', 'Play Something Sweet (Brickyard Blues)' and 'Til The World Ends'.

They weren't as successful in the UK as some other major American bands and had only two chart entries – 'Mama Told Me (Not To Come)' and 'Joy To The World'.

Hutton left the band in 1976 and Jay Gruska replaced him, but the group split up at the end of the year.

The three vocalists reunited in 1981 for live work and also charted with the single 'Joy To The World'. They had a backing group that included original members Mike Allsup on guitar and Jimmy Greenspoon on keyboards. In the mid-1980s Chuck Negron went solo, and Danny Hutton and Cory Wells carried on without replacing him. The outfit's schedule of concert dates is listed regularly on the Internet by Three Dog News, the quarterly newsletter from the band's still-functioning fan club.

A 43-track double *CD Celebrate: The Three Dog Night Story* was issued in 1993.

THUNDERCLAP NEWMAN This group was formed in 1969 and had a relatively short career. Former post office engineer, keyboard player Andy 'Thunderclap' Newman, had met Pete Townshend of the **Who** at art college. The two became friends and it was Townshend who suggested the group to Newman after spotting lead guitarist **Jimmy McCulloch**. They were joined by drummer John 'Speedy' Keen, who also penned 'Something In The Air'. The number became their debut single and topped the UK chart. Unfortunately, their live appearances didn't live up to expectations and they split up in 1970 following one further single, a minor hit called 'Accident', and an album, *Hollywood Dream*.

Andy Newman issued an album, *Rainbow*, in 1971 before retiring from the record business. Jimmy McCulloch joined Blue, Stone The Crows and then Wings. He died in mysterious circumstances in 1979. Speedy Keene released some solo albums as a vocalist before concentrating on songwriting and production.

TILLOTSON, Johnny Born in Jacksonville, Florida, on 20 April 1939, this singer initially became a disc jockey, then a country music performer. He was then launched as a teen singer with his self-penned debut record, 'Well I'm Your Man', reaching No 87 in the US chart. Following other minor hits such as 'True True Happiness' and 'Why Do I Love You So', he received international acclaim for 'Poetry In Motion' in 1961. This was his biggest hit and a transatlantic chart-topper, selling more than one-and-a-half million copies.

Tillotson's chart hits included: 'Dreamy Eyes', 'Jimmy's Girl', 'It Keeps Right On A Hurtin'', 'Send Me The Pillow You Dream On', 'I Can't Help It', 'She Understands Me', 'Talk Back Trembling Lips', 'Out Of My Mind' and 'Heartaches By The Number'.

In 1968 he moved to California for a time, where he appeared in nightclubs and indulged in some television acting roles.

Tillotson bestrode the line between straight popular music and country music, finally moving into mainstream country music in the 1980s.

His last tour of Europe took place in 1993 and was aimed mainly at the nostalgia market, although his regular work is performing before American country music audiences. He is also particularly popular in US air bases in Europe.

Currently, Johnny Tillotson presents a networked television programme, *Nashville Today*, with **Brenda Lee**.

TORNADOS, The This instrumental outfit was formed by independent producer **Joe Meek**. The members were Alan Caddy and George Bellamy (guitar), Clem Cattini (drums), Roger LaVern (keyboards) and Heinz Burt (bass). The group had a massive hit in 1962 with their debut disc, 'Telstar', although – despite legal wrangles – they received scant royalties for their transatlantic chart-topper, the first record by a British group to hit the No 1 spot in the US and the biggest-selling instrumental of all time.

At the height of their fame, the band were earning just £25 per week each. Their legal battle to win their rights took 29 years and lasted until 1991.

The Tornados' other hits included 'Globetrotter', 'Robot', 'The Ice Cream Man' and 'Dragonfly'.

Following Meek's suicide in 1967, the group disbanded. In the mid-1970s Bellamy, Burt, Cattini and LaVern teamed up again as the Original Tornados and re-recorded 'Telstar', but they broke up soon afterwards.

Clem Cattini became a successful session drummer with more than 40 No 1's behind him, before re-forming a new Tornados in 1989, introducing some glamour in the shape of Lynn Alice on keyboards and vocals. The other members are Dave Harvey (bass), Dave Graham (lead and vocals) and Bip Wetherell (keyboards and vocals).

Of the other original members, pianist Roger LaVern went bankrupt in an attempt to wrest royalties from Meek's publishing company. He married eight times and had children with another four women. In the mid-1970s he set off for Mexico, where he appeared in numerous television commercials and played piano on television and in top hotels and nightclubs. He says: 'I was known as El Lobo Plateado, The Silver Wolf.' In 1986 his hands seized up with a crippling disease and he could no longer play. He then married Maria-Esther, his eighth wife, who was 20 years his junior.

After a short career as a musician, Heinz Burt worked on the assembly line at the Ford car plant in Dagenham, painted trains for British Rail, and then fell victim to multiple sclerosis.

George Bellamy became a builder in Devon and Alan Caddy's whereabouts are unknown.

TRAVELING WILBURYS, The This unique project, which was launched in Los Angeles in 1988, teamed some of the biggest names in rock music, all of whom had previously worked together at some time or other. The musicians were George Harrison, **Bob Dylan**, **Roy Orbison**, **Tom Petty** and Jeff Lynne.

The result was the creation of a mythical band, the Traveling Wilburys, and their first album, *Traveling Wilburys Volume 1*, was released that year.

Harrison was Nelson Wilbury, Dylan was Lucky, Orbison Lefty, Lynne Otis and Petty Charlie. A hit single from the album was 'Handle With Care'.

After the sudden death of Roy Orbison in 1988, certain media folk speculated on who would replace him in the Traveling Wilburys. In the running, apparently, were Roger McGuinn, **Carl Perkins** and **Del Shannon**. However, the group settled for the simpler expedient of continuing as a quartet for a second album, *Traveling Wilburys Volume 3*, in 1990, before the participants again went their separate ways – although a third coming has never been out of the question.

TREMELOES, The   The Tremeloes originally formed in 1959 as a quintet: Rick West (guitar), Alan Blakely (rhythm), Alan Howard (bass) and Dave Munden (drums) They auditioned for Decca Records on the same day as the Beatles – New Year's Day 1961 – with their lead singer **Brian Poole**. Decca rejected the Beatles and gave a three-year contract to the Tremeloes, who then had eight hits before parting company with front man Poole.

They continued as a quartet and went on to score a further series of hits, including: 'Here Comes My Baby', 'Silence Is Golden', 'Even The Bad Times Are Good', 'Be Mine', 'Suddenly You Love Me', 'Helule Helule', 'My Little Lady', 'I Shall Be Released', 'Hello World', '(Call Me) Number One', 'By The Way', 'Me And My Life' and 'Hello Buddy'.

The Tremeloes also acted as producers and session band for Jeff Christie on a song called 'Yellow River', which sold over nine million copies. They then decided to cease live performances for a while.

Each member began to work on solo projects for a while, but they then drifted back together again.

The current line-up features two of the original members of the band, Dave Munden and Rick West. They are joined by Davey Freyer (bass and lead vocals) and John Gillingham (keyboards and vocals).

Former member Chip Hawkes, who had joined in 1966, was to see his son Chesney experience a meteoric rise to fame when he starred in the pop film *Buddy's Song* and topped the chart with 'The One And Only'. A few years later, in 1997, Chesney was leading a London band called The Ebb. Alan Blakely lost a long battle against cancer in 1996.

TROGGS, The   This group was originally formed in Andover, Hampshire, in 1964 under the name the Troglodytes. By the following year their line-up comprised Reg Ball (vocals), Chris Britton (guitar), Pete Staples (bass) and **Ronnie Bond** (drums).

In 1966, now managed by Larry Page, they truncated their name and saw the release of their first single, 'Lost Girl', which was unsuccessful.

They next recorded 'Wild Thing', which reached No 2 in the UK and also became a chart-topper in the States. By this time, Ball had changed his surname to Presley.

The Troggs' other hit singles were: 'With A Girl Like You', 'I Can't Control Myself', 'Anyway That You Want Me', 'Give It To Me', 'Night Of The Long Grass', 'Hi Hi Hazel', 'Love Is All Around' and 'Little Girl'. Both 'Wild Thing' and 'Anyway That You Want Me' were penned by Chip Taylor, brother of American actor Jon Voight.

The group split up in 1969 and Presley and Bond recorded solo singles, which did not have any chart success. Britton's solo album venture also failed to register.

Presley and Bond teamed up in 1972 to re-launch the Troggs with new members Richard Moore and Tony Murray.

In recent years Peter Lucas and Dave Maggs have joined Presley and Britton, following the departure of an ailing Ronnie Bond – Britton rejoined in the 1970s after running a club in Portugal.

In 1995 Reg Presley became a near-millionaire after Wet Wet Wet had an international chart-topper with his 'Love Is All Around'. He is a known authority on crop circles and similar mysterious matters. Reg still lives in Andover – as does Chris Britton who, like Reg, is likely to remain a Trogg until the grave. Pete Staples has an electrical business in Basingstoke. Ronnie Bond died in 1992, the year that his former group recorded the *Athens To Andover* album with members of REM.

TUBES, The   This outrageous, erotic, camp group was formed in San Francisco in 1972. Former drama student Fee Waybill (real name John Waldo) teamed up with Bill Spooner and Roger Steen (guitar), Vince Welnick (keyboards), Rick Anderson (bass), Michael Cotton (synthesizer), Prairie Prince (drums) and Re Styles (dancer). Their costumes were sensational, with Re wearing transparent basques, while Waybill was in the habit of exposing his penis on stage. They had three album hits in the UK – *What Do You Want From Life*, *Remote Control* and *Outside Inside* – and the same number of hit singles – 'White Punks On Dope', 'Prime Time' and 'Don't Want To Wait Anymore'. The group was known mainly for their exotic stage shows, visual extravaganzas that were so energetic that in one incident Waybill fell off stage and broke his leg – but he continued performing.

Their albums ceased to sell and the group eventually disbanded in 1986. Fee Waybill began to concentrate on songwriting, notably for Richard Marx and Toto, and he was featured in the movie *Bill & Ted's Excellent Adventure*.

Original members Rick Anderson, Prairie Prince and Roger Steen re-formed and currently appear on the US club circuit. Bill Spooner teaches at San Francisco's Blue Bear School Of

Music. Vince Welnick was a member of the Grateful Dead and now works as a computer programmer, while Re Styles is a full-time landscape gardener.

TURTLES, The Mark Volman, together with Howard Kaylan (real name Howard Kaplan), formed a band called the Nightriders in 1961, in which Kaylan was lead singer. They later renamed it the Crossfires and made their first recording in 1963.

They changed their name to the Turtles in 1965 and then experienced record success with hits such as: 'It Ain't Me Babe', 'Let Me Be', 'Happy Together', 'You Baby', 'You Know What I Mean', 'She's My Girl', 'Sound Asleep', 'You Showed Me', 'She'd Rather Be With Me', 'You Don't Have To Walk In The Rain', 'Love In The City', 'Elenore' and 'Lady-O'.

Other members of the band included Allan Nichol (lead), Jim Tucker (guitar) and Charles Portz (bass). Drummer John Barbata joined the group in 1966 and was present on their biggest hits. He then moved over to **Crosby, Stills, Nash & Young**, replacing Dallas Taylor. In 1974 he joined Jefferson Starship. He also appeared as a session musician on various records by artists such as John Sebastian and Ry Cooder. John Seiter replaced him.

Portz left in 1966 and was replaced by Chip Douglas, who was in turn replaced by Jim Pons.

The band split up in 1970 and Volman and Kaylan, together with Pons, joined the Mothers Of Invention. In 1972 they teamed up as a duo to make records as Phlorescent Leech & Eddie, then as Flo & Eddie, but with Pond still in their backing band. The duo also sang back-up vocals on **John Lennon's** 'Some Time In New York City'.

Pons moved to Nashville and a publishing deal with Chappell, while Volman and Kaylan continued as Flo & Eddie, also acting as a vocal duo for sessions on albums by artists as diverse as **Blondie** and **Alice Cooper**.

Through the offices of US promoter David Fishoff, a water-testing nostalgia tour in 1983 led to a permanent if sporadic re-formation of the Turtles, fronted as always by Howard Kaylan and Mark Volman.

TWINKLE Born Lynne Annette Ripley in Surbiton, Surrey, on 17 July 1947, as a 17-year-old this singer-songwriter penned 'Terry', which she recorded in 1965. Her only other hit was 'Golden Lights'. In the late 1960s she retired to become a housewife. Her husband Graham Rogers was once the James Bond-esque hero of the Cadbury's Milk Tray UK television commercial. The couple have two children, Amber and Michael.

Twinkle recorded again in 1972, when she covered the **Monkees** hit 'I'm A Believer'. The **Smiths** covered her hit 'Golden Lights', which once again encouraged her to begin live appearances, and she returned to the stage in 1993.

Twinkle intends to release a CD single in 1998 featuring an up-to-date dance version of 'Terry', along with another of her self-penned numbers, 'Holiday Romance'.

Twinkle (centre) with Billy Hatton and Mike Millward of the Fourmost

UFO   The original personnel of this hard rock band, formed in London in 1969, included Phil Mogg (vocals), Pete Way (bass) and Andy Parker (drums). Michael Schenker of the Scorpions joined them in 1973. Following a gig in 1977, Schenker disappeared. Many believed him dead, but he turned up six months later, confessing that he had merely wanted to quit the band but didn't know how to explain it. One of several lead guitarists to pass through the band was Paul Chapman.

When Way left in 1982, the group seemed unable to recover and split up in 1983. They were revived in 1985, when Mogg led a UFO with different personnel. That band split in 1988. Mogg and Way revived the band in 1991, but they too disbanded.

The latest incarnation, as a five-piece with original members, formed in November 1997 to tour the UK and promote a new release, their *Walk On Water* album, which had originally been issued in Japan in 1995. The UK album contained three new tracks: 'Written In The Sand', 'Raw Material' and 'Edge Of The World'.

Between 1980 and 1985, UFO had a number of hit albums, including: *Lights Out, Obsession, Strangers In The Night, No Place To Run, The Wild The Willing And The Mechanix, Making Contact, Headstone – The Best Of UFO* and *Misdemeanours*.

They also had a series of entries in the singles chart between 1978 and 1983: 'Only You Can Rock Me', 'Doctor Doctor', 'Shoot Shot', 'Young Blood', 'Lonely Heart', 'Let It Rain' and 'When It's Time To Rock'.

ULLMAN, Tracey   This British actress-singer was born in Slough, Berkshire, on 30 December 1959. She attended the Italia Conti stage school at the age of 12 and continued in showbusiness, appearing in the West End stage show *Elvis*. After featuring in some dramatic roles, she starred in the UK television comedy series *Three Of A Kind*, which was hugely popular.

Tracey met the wife of the head of Stiff Records at the hairdresser. As a result, she was given a recording contract with the company, which produced a string of hit singles. They included: 'Breakaway', 'They Don't Know', 'Move Over Darling', 'My Guy', 'Sunglasses' and 'Helpless'. Paul McCartney featured in her video for 'They Don't Know'.

Tracey married television producer Allan McKeown in 1983 and the couple moved to Los Angeles, where he became a media mogul who

sold one of his companies in 1997 for $40m – which is around the same amount that Tracey has earned as a major television star in the States.

In 1987 she launched *The Tracey Ullman Show*, which was awarded two Emmys. Further awards followed for her succeeding shows, which included *Tracey Takes On*.

Tracey and Allan have two children, Mabel and Johnny, and houses in Los Angeles and Mayfair, London.

Tracey Ullman returned to the UK in 1998 to promote the screening of her latest television series.

ULTRAVOX   Formed in 1976, this group comprised John Fox (guitar and lead vocals; later replaced by Midge Ure), Billy Currie (synthesizer and piano), Chris Cross (bass and synthesizer) and Warren Cann (drums).

They made their chart breakthrough in 1980 with 'Sleepwalk' and for the next six years their chart singles included: 'Passing Strangers', 'Vienna', 'Slow Motion', 'All Stood Still', 'The Thin Wall', 'The Voice', 'Reap The Wild Wind', 'Hymn', 'Visions In Blue', 'We Came To Dance', 'One Small Day', 'Dancing With Tears In My Eyes', 'Lament', 'Love's Greatest Adventure', 'Same Old Story' and 'All Fall Down'.

After John Fox and Midge Ure left in 1984 to pursue solo careers – which included a UK chart-topper for Ure – the group struggled on for three more years. Then Billy Currie and latter-day guitarist Robin Simon kept the faith with U-Vox, before reverting to Ultravox in 1993.

John Fox lives in Oxfordshire.

UNDERTONES, The This group from Northern Ireland was formed in 1978 by vocalist Feargal Sharkey, who was born in Londonderry on 13 August 1958. The other members were John O'Neill and Damian 'Dee' O'Neill (guitar), Michael Bradley (bass) and Billy Doherty (drums).

They made their recording debut with 'Teenage Kicks', which was the first of several hits by the band. Other singles chart entries included: 'Get Over You', 'Jimmy Jimmy', 'Here Comes The Summer', 'You've Got My Number', 'My Perfect Cousin', 'Wednesday Week', 'It's Going To Happen' and 'Julie Ocean'. Their last chart entry was a reissue of 'Teenage Kicks' in 1983, released when the group disbanded.

The Undertones had toured extensively in the UK and the States, and when they decided to disband EMI also issued a 30-track album, *All Wrapped Up*, which reached the charts. Their other chart albums had been *The Undertones*, *Hypnotized*, *Positive Touch* and *The Sin Of Pride*.

Initially, Sharkey teamed up with Vince Clarke and the two had a big hit with 'Never Never', although Sharkey then decided to go solo and had several hits, including: 'Listen To Your Father', 'Loving You', 'A Good Heart', 'You Little Thief', 'Someone To Somebody' and 'More Love'. He also had an album entry with *Feargal Sharkey*.

In his personal life, 1986 proved to be a dramatic year. In Londonderry, his mother and sister were held at gunpoint by terrorists for four hours, and in August he separated from his wife and moved to Los Angeles in an attempt to revive his career.

In 1993, Feargal Sharkey returned to the UK to become an A&R man with Polydor, and the following year was promoted to head up a new interactive label for the multimedia company ESP.

John and Damien O'Neill joined That Petrol Emotion and had a number of hits, until they disbanded in 1994. Billy Doherty was a member of the Saw Doctors for a while, and Michael Bradley is a BBC radio producer back home in Londonderry.

UNIT FOUR PLUS TWO This group was originally formed in 1964 as a quartet under the name Unit Four, and changed their name when another two members were added. They comprised Buster Meikle (vocals and guitar), Tommy Moeller (vocals, tambourine, piano and guitar), Peter Moules (vocals, autoharp, guitar and banjo), Rodney Garwood (bass) and Hugh Halliday (drums).

The group made their chart debut with 'Green Fields' in 1964 and topped the chart with their next release, 'Concrete And Clay'. They had two further chart singles, 'You've Never Been In Love Like This Before' and 'Baby Never Say Goodbye'.

They disbanded in 1969.

A Unit Four Plus Two were at large in the UK in 1992, when Tommy Moeller and other members of the 1960s edition were involved in the writing and production of a London musical play about Leonardo Da Vinci.

U2 This band was formed in Dublin in 1976 with members Bono (real name Paul Hewson; vocals), the Edge (real name David Evans; guitar), Adam Clayton (bass) and Larry Mullen Jnr (drums).

They topped the Irish chart in 1980 and began to make inroads into the UK the same year. International tours followed, in which they gradually emerged as one of the leading attractions in the rock world. They also had formidable hits in both the singles and albums charts.

Hit singles included: 'Fire', 'Gloria', 'Celebration', 'New Year's Day', 'Two Hearts Beat As One', 'Pride (In The Name Of Love)', 'The Unforgettable Fire', 'With Or Without You', 'I Still Haven't Found What I'm Looking For', 'Where The Streets Have No Name', 'In God's Country', 'Desire', 'Angel Of Harlem All I Want Is You', 'The Fly', 'Even Better Than The Real Thing', 'Who's Gonna Ride Your Wild Horses' and 'Hold Me Thrill Me Kiss Me Kill Me'.

Album hits included: *Boy*, *October*, *War*, *Under A Blood Red Sky*, *The Unforgettable Fire*, *Wide Awake In America*, *The Joshua Tree*, *Rattle & Hum* and *Achtung Baby*.

In 1996 Clayton and Mullen arranged and performed a new version of the *Mission Impossible* theme for the Tom Cruise movie of the same name.

Early in 1997, U2 completed their world tour PopMart, which earned the group members £100 million. Bono, Adam Clayton, the Edge and Larry Mullen were already among the richest people in the Irish Republic. Bono entertains with lavish parties, Mullen has his collection of expensive Harley Davidson motorbikes, the Edge runs Dublin's trendiest hotel and Clayton once spent £1 million on an engagement ring for model Naomi Campbell, his fiancée at the time.

VALANCE, Ricky   Despite having only one hit record – and that way back in 1960 – Ricky Valance is still actively performing today.

Born David Spencer in Ynysddu, Wales, the eldest of seven children, he spent three years in the Royal Air Force, during which time he married his wife Evelyn, before establishing himself as a singer in clubs in northern England.

Under his new name, Ricky Valance, he signed with **Norrie Paramor** at Columbia and his debut disc was a cover version of Ray Peterson's US hit, 'Tell Laura I Love Her'. A controversial 'death' disc, it was banned by the BBC but went on to sell over 250,000 copies in the UK, topping the chart and bringing Valance a silver disc. It also went on to top the charts in several other countries, rewarding Valance with over a million sales and earning him a platinum disc.

He began touring with a backing band, the Lucky Strike, but failed to make any impact with follow-up discs, becoming something of a one-hit wonder. He continued recording with Columbia for two years, cutting several other singles – including another 'death disc', 'Bobby' – without success.

Valance became an actor, appearing in UK television series such as *The Planemakers*, *No Hiding Place* and *Maigret*. In 1967 he went to Dublin to front a show band called the Chessmen, and later turned to country music. Throughout the 1970s he was back on the cabaret circuit and released a number of C&W discs, before embarking on another spell as an actor, making appearances in stage shows such as *Wuthering Heights* and *Lead Into Heaven*.

Ricky Valance began to headline several sixties revival shows during the 1980s and is still performing in the 1990s, after almost 40 years as an entertainer.

VANGELIS   Born Evangelos Papathanassiou in Volos, Greece, on 29 March 1943, this musician left his country in 1967 when the military junta took control, initially moving to Paris. He later moved to London and became a member of Aphrodite's Child with **Demis Roussos** and Lucas Sideras. When the group split in 1972 he went solo and has had tremendous success ever since, particularly in his work composing film soundtracks. He was awarded an Oscar for his soundtrack for *Chariots Of Fire*.

In 1980 he teamed up with Jon Anderson, former lead singer of **Yes**, and as Jon & Vangelis they had hits with the singles 'I Hear You Now', 'I'll Find My Way Home' and 'He Is Sailing'.

Vangelis has had a number of chart albums throughout the 1980s and 1990s, and in 1989 issued *Themes*, which contained 14 highlights from his soundtracks for films such as *Blade Runner* and *Mutiny On The Bounty*.

He teamed up with Jon Anderson once again in 1991 for the album *Page Of Life* and continued with soundtrack releases such as *1492 – Conquest Of Paradise*. Vangelis' album *Portrait (So Long Ago, So Clear)* entered the UK Top 20 in 1996.

VAUGHAN, Frankie   Born Frank Ephraim Abelson in Liverpool on 3 February 1928, this singer was the first Liverpool artist ever to top the chart when he recorded 'Garden Of Eden' in 1957. He made his chart debut with 'My Sweetie Went Away', and among almost three dozen chart entries for him between 1954 and 1968 was another No 1 record, 'Tower Of Strength', and hits such as 'Green Door', 'Hello Dolly' and his theme tune, 'Give Me The Moonlight'. Vaughan starred in movies such as *These*

Frankie Vaughan with Marilyn Monroe   199

Dangerous Years and appeared with Marilyn Monroe in *Let's Make Love*. He also had two hit records with the Kaye Sisters.

A major British recording artist of the late 1950s, he then became a popular cabaret performer.

Vaughan devoted much of his spare time to working with the National Association Of Boys' Clubs, in particular the Merseyside and North Wales Variety Club, based in Liverpool, for which he was awarded an OBE. In 1997, almost 30 years later, when he was 68, he was awarded a CBE.

Frankie Vaughan lives with his wife Stella in High Wycombe, Buckinghamshire, and in 1993 was made deputy lieutenant of the county. Liverpool's John Moores University also awarded him an honorary fellowship in 1988.

VEE, Bobby Following the tragic air crash in February 1959 which killed **Buddy Holly**, **Ritchie Valens** and **J. P. Richardson** (the 'Big Bopper'), 15-year old Bobby Vee with his band the Shadows was booked to step in and appear on the show the stars were to perform in that night in Vee's home town of Fargo.

Born Robert Thomas Velline on 30 April 1943, the singer has since notched up nearly 40

hits, including ten entries in the UK Top 10. They include: 'Devil Or Angel', 'Rubber Ball', 'Stayin' In', 'Take Good Care Of My Baby', 'Run To Him', 'Please Don't Ask About Barbara', 'Sharing You', 'Punish Her', 'The Night Has A Thousand Eyes', 'Charms', 'Be True To Yourself', 'Come Back When You Grow Up', 'Beautiful People' and 'My Girl'.

Vee currently lives in Minnesota with his wife Karen and is still an active performer and recording artist. He is backed by the Richochets, whose personnel include his three sons Jeff, Tommy and Rob, and he toured the UK with them once again in March and April 1998 on the Solid Silver Sixties Tour.

A CD of all his 1960s albums, *The Essential Bobby Vee*, was issued in 1998, the same year he recorded an album of Buddy Holly songs and one of self-penned numbers with his sons.

VELVET UNDERGROUND, The This was an influential group, despite an initial lack of success. They originally formed in New York in 1965, taking their name from a pulp novel. The members were Lou Reed (guitar and vocals), John Cale (bass, viola and vocals), **Sterling Morrison** (guitar) and Maureen Tucker (drums).

Andy Warhol produced their first album and included female singer **Nico** in their line-up. Following the release of the album *The Velvet Underground And Nico*, she left to pursue a solo career. The rest of the group completed a second album, *White Lightning/White Heat*, released in December 1967. Following its release, John Cale left the band. Doug Yule replaced him and a third album, *The Velvet Underground*, was released in 1969. Their final album, *Loaded*, was issued in 1971. Lou Reed had already left the band prior to the album's release and the group disbanded later that year.

Maureen Tucker continued with a solo career, in between giving birth to five children, while Morrison took a doctorate in English at Austin University before becoming captain of a ferryboat.

In the years following the split, the Velvet Underground became a popular cult band and their albums influenced numerous major artists. Following the death of Andy Warhol, the group re-formed to record a tribute record, *Songs For Drella*, and undertook a European tour in 1992. They then toured the States as support to **U2** and an album of their live show, *Live MCMXCII*, was issued.

Bobby Vee (left) with Billy Fury

Nico died in 1988 and Sterling Morrison in 1995. Following Morrison's death, Lou Reed decided that the Velvet Underground could no longer exist, although he continues to pursue a solo career. In 1997 he enjoyed great success when his number 'A Perfect Day' was made into a four-minute television promotional video by the BBC at a cost of £2 million. It featured Reed and a host of stars ranging from **Dr John** to Bono, Elton John to Tom Jones, singing the number – which then became a chart smash. In April 1998 a television documentary about Reed called *Rock And Roll Heart* was screened in the US, and the following month his album *Perfect Night*, originally recorded at the Royal Festival Hall in 1996, was issued.

VENTURES, The   This American instrumental group was formed in 1960 with members Nokie Edwards (lead), Don Wilson (guitar), Bob Bogle (bass) and Howie Johnson (drums).

The Ventures' biggest-selling single was their first, 'Walk Don't Run', a million-seller which reached No 2 in the US chart. They followed with 'Perfidia' and 'Ram-Bunk-Shush'. In 1964 they recorded 'Walk Don't Run '64', which became a Top 5 hit. They followed this with 'Slaughter On Tenth Avenue' and 'Hawaii Five-O'.

The group fully exploited the market for instrumental sounds with a range of albums, including *The Ventures, Twist With The Ventures, Going To The Ventures' Dance Party* and *The Ventures In Space*. They even teamed up with **Bobby Vee** to record *Bobby Vee Meets The Ventures*.

In 1965, the Ventures toured Japan and became so popular there that they aimed much of their product specifically at the Japanese market, and continued to tour the country on a regular basis for more than ten years.

They adapted their instrumental albums to varying trends over the years with *Play Guitar With The Ventures, Guitar Freakout* and *The Ventures Play The Classics*.

While paying heed to contemporary trends on new releases, the Ventures are still very popular in Japan, where the bulk of their stage engagements take place.

VERNONS GIRLS, The   This female vocal group from Liverpool was originally formed in December 1961, sponsored by the local football pools firm, Vernons.

Featured on the television shows *Oh Boy!, Boy Meets Girl* and *Wham!*, their hits included 'Lover Please', 'You Know What I Mean', 'Funny All Over', 'Do The Bird' and 'Loco-motion'.

There were various permutations of numbers and personnel in the group and at one time they slimmed down to a trio, calling themselves Maureen & the Vernons Girls. They appeared on an all-Merseyside edition of the television show *Thank Your Lucky Stars* and toured for five weeks with the Beatles.

In 1990 Maggie Stredder decided to re-form the Vernons Girls as a trio, with Sheila Bruce and Penny Lightfoot. Sheila, Paul McCartney's original girlfriend, was at one time married to singer Tommy Bruce. The Vernons Girls are currently appearing on the sixties nostalgia circuit and often turn up on television variety shows.

VILLAGE PEOPLE, The   This group was conceived and assembled in 1977 by French producer Jacques Morali. Inspired by the gay clubs of Greenwich Village in New York, he decided to dress his vocal act as various images – a motorcycle rider, a policeman, an American Indian, a GI and a cowboy.

The group consisted of lead vocalist Victor Willis with David Hodo, Felipe Rose, Randy Jones, Glenn Hughes and Alex Briley.

Aimed at the disco market, their first release, 'San Francisco (You've Got Me)', was a minor hit, as was their debut album, *Village People*.

They entered the Top 30 with 'Macho Man', followed by two major hits, 'YMCA' and 'In The Navy', and an album hit, *Go West*.

There were some personnel changes in the late 1970s when Willis left, to be replaced by Ray Simpson.

They charted again with the title track for *Can't Stop The Music*, a 1980 feature film in which the group starred. There were then some minor personnel changes as the group continued to perform throughout the decade, occasionally changing their image.

A boost to their fortunes occurred in 1994, when the Pet Shop Boys had a big hit with their cover of 'Go West'. Suddenly, interest in the Village People was back on the agenda. A 'YMCA '93 Re-mix' entered the UK chart, followed by their album *The Best Of The Village People* and an 'In the Navy 1994 Re-mix'.

The group performed 'In The Navy' on an edition of the *Rikki Lake* television show show in the UK in 1997.

VINTON, Bobby Born Stanley Robert Vinton in Canonsburg, Pennsylvania, on 16 April 1935, this singer made his recording debut in 1962 with a No 1 hit in the US chart, 'Roses Are Red'.

He followed with: 'Rain Rain Go Away', 'I Love You The Way You Are', 'Trouble Is My Middle Name', 'Let's Kiss And Make Up', 'Over The Mountain', 'Blue On Blue', 'Blue Velvet', 'There! I've Said It Again', 'My Heart Belongs To Only You', 'Tell Me Why', 'Clinging Vine', 'Mr Lonely', 'Long Lonely Nights', 'L-O-N-E-L-Y', 'What Colour (Is A Man)', 'Satin Pillows', 'Dum-De-Da', 'Coming Home Soldier', 'Please Love Me Forever', 'Just As Much As Ever', 'Take Good Care Of My Baby', 'Halfway To Paradise', 'I Love How You Love Me', 'To Know You Is To Love You', 'The Days Of Sand And Shovels', 'Every Day Of My Life', 'Sealed With A Kiss', 'My Melody Of Love' and 'Beer Barrel Polka'.

'My Melody Of Love', composed by Bobby Vinton himself, gave him one more US No 1, in 1974. His arrangement of 'Blue Moon' was included on the soundtrack of the 1981 film *An American Werewolf In London*, but it was the use of 'Blue Velvet' in both a 1989 television commercial and a movie of the same name that triggered a chart-topper two years later in the UK, where Vinton became omnipresent until the failure of a re-released 'Roses Are Red' in 1993.

VISAGE This group helped to establish the vogue for 'new romantics' in the early 1980s. They were conceived by Steve Strange (real name Stephen Harrington), who was born on 28 May 1959.

The first group he was involved with was called the Moors Murderers. He next joined a band called Photon, then opened a fashionable club called Blitz.

Strange formed and led Visage, and between 1980 and 1984 their hit singles were: 'Fade To Grey', 'Mind Of A Toy', 'Visage', 'Damned Don't Cry', 'Night Train', 'Pleasure Boys' and 'Love Glove'.

After the group petered out in the mid-1980s, he opened a disco called Camden Palace and then formed another romantic-style band named Strange Cruise, but they proved unsuccessful.

VISCOUNTS, The This British vocal trio was formed in the late 1950s with members Gordon Mills, Ronnie Wells and Don Paul. The group began appearing on several pop package shows

and they charted in 1960 with 'Short'nin Bread' and in 1961 with 'Who Put The Bomp'.

Gordon Mills left the Viscounts shortly before the group split in 1964. A most successful songwriter and pop manager – whose clients included Tom Jones and Engelbert Humperdinck – Mills died from cancer in 1996.

Don Paul also had a career in pop management, at one time co-managing Paddy, Klaus & Gibson with Tony Stratton-Smith, until the act was bought from them by **Brian Epstein** on the recommendation of **John Lennon**. Ronnie Wells recorded – as Darren Wells – for Mills' MAM label. Mills' replacement in the Viscounts, Johnny Gentle, who also recorded for MAM, now has a carpentry business in Kent.

WAITS, Tom Born in Pamona, California on 7 December 1949, this gruff-voiced singer's songs visit the seamier side of life. Despite his lack of chart success, Waits has a large cult following.

A songwriter and pianist, Waits began playing in Los Angeles clubs in 1971 and did not cut his first album, *Closing Time*, until 1973.

His releases generally hovered outside the Top 100, although 'Heart Attack And Vine' reached No 96 in 1980. Like many other American artists who gain popularity in the UK, he found himself in the Top 20 with his album *Frank's Wild Years* – although it reached only No 115 in the US.

As a songwriter, Waits found success through artists covering his numbers, such as **Rod Stewart** with 'Downtown Train'. He also earned a crust composing movie soundtracks and acting in various films, ranging from *Down By Law* to *Dracula*.

In 1993, Waits released *Black Rider*, a reworked soundtrack to a comic opera he had co-written with William Burroughs.

1995 saw the release of the soundtrack of *The 12 Monkeys* which included Tom Waits' tracks, as did *Music From And Inspired By The Motion Picture Dead Man Walking* in 1996.

WAKEMAN, Rick Born on 18 May 1949, This songwriter-pianist was originally a member of the **Strawbs** and then joined **Yes**.

From 1972, he worked for some years as a session musician, appearing on various albums by artists such as Elton John, David Bowie and Lou Reed. He teamed up with Yes once again in 1989 to record a new album.

In his own right, he had a succession of hit albums, including: *The Six Wives Of Henry VIII*, *Journey To The Centre Of The Earth*, *The Myths And Legends Of King Arthur & The Knights Of The Round Table*, *No Earthly Connection*, *White Rock*, *Criminal Record*, *Rhapsodies*, *1984*, *Beyond The Planets* and *The Gospels*.

In 1997, after three decades as a performer, Wakeman, who had been living in the Isle of Man for ten years, began touring with his 23-year-old son Adam and was planning a concert tour of his original hit concept *Journey To The Centre Of The Earth*.

Rick Wakeman married his second wife Nina (half of the Blonde On Blonde duo) in 1983. In 1997 he was commissioned by the BBC to produce the score for the run-up to the 1998 World Cup.

WALKER BROTHERS, The Born in Hamilton, Ohio, in 1944, Scott Engel was the bass guitarist with a Californian group called the Routers until 1964, when he joined John Maus and Gary Leeds in a trio they called the Walker Brothers.

The group decided to move to the UK and they settled in London. Their second single, 'Love Her', became a hit in 1965, and the trio soon became major stars with a string of further hits. Their chart singles included: 'Make It Easy On Yourself', 'My Ship Is Coming In', 'The Sun Ain't Gonna Shine Anymore', '(Baby) You Don't Have To Tell Me', 'Another Tear Falls', 'Deadlier Than The Male', 'Stay With Me Baby' and 'Walking In The Rain'.

Conflicts between Scott and John eventually resulted in the trio splitting up. Gary charted with 'You Don't Love Me' and 'Twinkie Lee', John with 'Annabella' and Scott with 'Jackie', 'Joanna' and 'Lights Of Cincinatti'.

They re-formed briefly in 1976, hitting the chart with 'No Regrets'.

In 1992 a CD collection, *No Regrets – The Best of the Walker Brothers 1965–1976*, reached No 4 in the UK chart.

In 1995 Scott Engel recorded his first new album in 11 years, *Tilt*, and performed a track on the UK television show *Later With Jools Holland*, his first such appearance in over a decade. The album entered the chart at No 27. He lives in west London.

John Maus lives near San Diego, California, with his third wife Randy and daughter Nicholle. He is an inspector for a software company.

Gary Leeds lives in east London and in 1994 was working as a motorcycle courier.

WAR In 1969 Eric Burdon was looking for a group to back him on recordings and approached an American band called Night Shift. They decided to join him and the name War was adopted.

Initially, the band consisted of Burdon, Howard Scott (guitar and vocals), Harold Brown (drums), Lonnie Jordan (keyboards), Peter Rosen (bass), Charles Miller (sax and clarinet) and Lee Oskar (harmonica).

A few weeks after they got together, Rosen died from a drugs overdose and was replaced by B.B. Dickerson. Keyboards player Papa Dee Allen also joined them.

The group's debut album, released in 1970, was called *Eric Burdon Declares War*, and was followed by *The Black Man's Burdon* the next year.

In the middle of a tour, Burdon decided to leave and the group continued without him. They were successful on their own, with a range of releases between 1971 and 1979 which included the albums *All Day Music*, *Greatest Hits*, *Platinum Jazz*, *Galaxy* and *Music Band 2*.

Their singles included 'Slippin' Into Darkness', 'Me And Baby Brother' and 'Why Can't We Be Friends'.

The group was still active in the 1990s, although the line-up is in more of a state of flux than ever before.

WARWICK, Dionne This American singer was born on 12 December 1940 in East Orange, New Jersey. She made her debut on the Scepter label with the Burt Bacharach-Hal David composition 'Don't Make Me Over'. The songwriters were to provide her with a number of hits, including 'Anyone Who Had A Heart' and 'Walk On By'. Her other hits stretched into the early 1980s and included: 'You'll Never Get To Heaven', 'Reach Out For Me', 'You Can Have Him', 'Valley Of The Dolls', 'Do You Know The Way To San José', 'Heartbreaker', 'All The Love In The World', 'Yours' and 'I'll Never Love This Way Again'.

Over the years Dionne received a number of accolades, including a star on Hollywood's Walk Of Fame, tributes from New York City for her work for AIDS charities, a Key Of Life Award in Los Angeles, a Humanitarian Award and various Grammy Awards.

Dionne Warwick continues to appear as a performer on the international stage, toured Europe with Burt Bacharach in 1995, and in June 1997 sang her classic songs with the BBC Concert Orchestra at the Royal Festival Hall in London.

Dionne Warwick

WEATHER REPORT This jazz-rock outfit was formed in New York in 1970. Throughout their initial 16-year career there were numerous personnel changes, although the main stalwarts were keyboards player Joe Zawinul and saxophonist Wayne Shorter.

Their eponymous debut album was issued in 1971 and the other musicians included Airto Moreira (percussion), Miroslav Vitous (bass) and Alphonse Mouzon (drums).

Their second album was *I Sing The Body Electric*, on which they were augmented by Eric Gravatt on drums and Um Raman on bass. Other releases were *Sweetnighter*, *Mysterious Traveller* and *Tale Spinnin'*. In 1976, with their *Black Market* album, **Jaco Pastorius** joined them on bass. Other new personnel who followed included Alejandro Neciosup Acuna (percussion) and Chester Thompson (drums).

Heavy Weather and *Mr Gone* followed, and new drummer Pete Erskine joined while Pastorius departed. With Procession in 1983 and the inclusion of Manhattan Transfer singer Janet Siegel, they included vocals for the first time. For their *Domino Theory* album they included vocals by Carl Anderson.

The group's final album, *This Is This*, was issued in 1986, when Joe Zawinul formed Weather Update and then the Zawinul Syndicate. The other mainstay of Weather Report, Wayne Shorter, continues with a solo career that had been underway long before the outfit split.

Jaco Pastorius, who had left the group in 1980 to form his own band, Word Of Mouth, later became an alcoholic. He died in a fight in a bar in 1987.

WEEDON, Bert This famous British guitarist was born in London on 10 May 1920. A self-taught musician from the age of 12, he began playing with the major big bands of the late 1940s and early 1950s as a soloist, and in 1956 began leading his own quartet. Between 1959 and 1961 he had a string of chart entries, including 'Guitar Boogie Shuffle', 'Nashville Boogie', 'Big Beat Boogie', 'Twelfth Street Rag', 'Apache', 'Sorry Robbie', 'Ginchy' and 'Mr Guitar'.

Weedon wrote a guitar manual, *Play In A Day Guide To Modern Guitar Playing*, which sold more than two million copies and inspired a generation of guitarists, including Eric Clapton, **Jeff Beck** and George Harrison.

The Shadows wrote 'Mr Guitar', his last hit, for him – and when the Beatles made their debut on the children's television show *The Five O'Clock Club*, on which Weedon was resident, they also wrote a number for him – although it was allegedly lost in the post!

Now in his late seventies, Bert Weedon lives in Buckinghamshire with his wife Maggie – and still tours with his one-man show.

WEST, Keith This singer was born Keith Hopkins in Dagenham, Essex, on 6 December 1943. Originally a member of the In Crowd, he then joined Tomorrow. He was still with the group when he embarked on a solo project, as lead singer for the ambitious album *A Teenage Opera*. His debut single was 'Grocer Jack Or Excerpt From A Teenage Opera'. It reached No 2 in the UK chart, being prevented from hitting the top spot by Engelbert Humperdinck's 'The Last Waltz'. Keith was in good company: Humperdinck also kept the Beatles from the top spot with 'Penny Lane/Strawberry Fields Forever' with his 'Release Me'.

West's second single from *A Teenage Opera*, 'Sam', failed to register and he withdrew from the project. He had no success with his third single, 'On A Saturday', and abandoned his musical career for a while.

West began recording again in 1973 and also founded a new group, Moonrider, but never repeated his earlier success – and could therefore be tagged with the label 'one-hit wonder'.

He still records – although he has remained incognito on some football club recordings. In 1997 he appeared on two soccer CDs for Cherry Red for the Wimbledon and Fulham teams, singing on the tracks 'The Dons Are Coming' and 'Victory'.

Keith West lives in Weybridge in Surrey with his wife Pat and has three grown-up daughters. He is a marketing manager for the Burns Guitar Company and also writes songs and jingles for television.

WHAM! This super duo brought together George Michael (real name Georgios Kyriacos Panayiotou), born on 25 June 1963 in Finchley, north London, and Andrew Ridgeley, born on 26 January of the same year in Windlesham, Surrey.

With Michael as the main songwriter and vocalist and Ridgeley on guitar, the duo enjoyed incredible success, and in 1982 were joined by backing vocalists Shirlie Holliman and Mandy Washburn, the latter being replaced by Dee C.

Lee, who left the following year and was replaced by Pepsi, to form **Shirlie & Pepsi**.

The duo's hits included four chart-toppers. Their singles successes were: 'Young Guns', 'Wham Rap', 'Bad Boys', 'Club Tropicana', 'Club Fantastic Megamix', 'Wake Me Up Before You Go Go', 'Freedom', 'Last Christmas', 'I'm Your Man' and 'The Edge Of Heaven'.

Wham! also became the first pop group ever to be invited to appear in China, where they performed at the Workers' Gymnasium in Beijing in April 1985.

It was inevitable that George Michael should opt for a solo career, which he did the following year, although the two remained firm friends.

Andrew Ridgeley went into semi-retirement and tried a spell at acting and motor racing. He rejoined Michael for a special concert in Rio in 1991.

George Michael continued a successful career as an international superstar and in November 1997 a new compilation album, *Wham! If You Were There*, was issued, containing 15 tracks from their two chart-topping albums, *Fantastic* and *Make It Big*.

In 1997 the 35-year-old singer was arrested in Los Angeles for an alleged sex act in a public toilet. He revealed that he was gay and was able to put his point of view across in a television interview on the *Parkinson* show in December 1998, soon after the release of his new album compilation, *Ladies And Gentlemen: The Best Of George Michael*.

WHISTLING JACK SMITH 'I Was Kaiser Bill's Batman' was a number penned by Roger Greenaway and Roger Cook and recorded by the Mike Sammes Singers. It was released as a single under the name Whistling Jack Smith – who did not exist. In order to promote it, Decca Records approached singer Billy Moeller, who had been recording under the name Coby Wells. He was given the name Whistling Jack Smith in order to promote the song on a UK tour.

Moeller was born in Liverpool on 2 February 1946 and never had a hit in his own right. Whistling Jack Smith fell into the category of 'one-hit wonders'. 'I Was Kaiser Bill's Batman' entered the UK Top 5 and US Top 20 in 1967.

Billy Moeller now lives in Hertfordshire.

WHITE, Barry This singer-songwriter, born on 12 September 1944, played from the age of 16 in the Upfronts, an R&B band in Los Angeles. He penned the number 'Harlem Shuffle' for Bob & Earl in 1964.

His own string of hit singles stretched from 1973 to 1988. They included: 'I'm Gonna Love You Just A Little Bit More Baby', 'Never Never Gonna Give Ya Up', 'Can't Get Enough Of Your Love Babe', 'You're The First The Last My Everything', 'What Am I Gonna Do With You', 'I'll Do Anything You Want Me To', 'Let The Music Play', 'You See The Trouble With Me', 'Baby We Better Try And Get It Together', 'Don't Make Me Wait Too Long', 'I'm Qualified To Satisfy', 'It's Ecstasy When You Lay Down Next To Me', 'Just The Way You Are', 'Sha La La Means I Love You' and 'Sho' You Right'. In 1988 a re-mix of his second hit, 'Never Gonna Give You Up', re-entered the charts.

White's backing singers Love Unlimited recorded in their own right and their hits included 'Walkin' In The Rain With The One I Love' and 'It May Be Winter Outside (But In My Heart It's Spring)'. White also led the Love Unlimited Orchestra, which had a major hit with' Love's Theme' in 1974.

From 1989 Barry White became active as a performer once more and currently tours on the lucrative international cabaret circuit.

WHO, The One of the major British rock groups of all time, the line-up of the Who – Pete Townshend (guitar), Roger Daltrey (vocals), John Entwistle (bass) and **Keith Moon** (drums) – was finalized in 1964, the year Peter Meadon took over their management and established them as the leading group for the 'mods'. They were known as the High Numbers at the time, but when Kit Lambert and Chris Stamp took over the management from Meaden later that year, Lambert changed the group's name to the Who.

Over the years their hit singles have included: 'I Can't Explain', 'Anyway Anyhow Anywhere', 'My Generation', 'Substitute', 'A Legal Matter', 'I'm A Boy', 'The Kids Are Alright', 'Happy Jack', 'Pictures Of Lily', 'The Last Time/Under My Thumb', 'I Can See For Miles', 'Dogs', 'Magic Bus', 'Pinball Wizard', 'The Seeker', 'Summertime Blues', 'Won't Get Fooled Again', 'Let's See Action', 'Join Together', 'Relay', '5:15', 'Squeeze Box', 'Who Are You', 'Long Live Rock', 'You Better You Bet', 'Don't Let Go The Coat', 'Athena' and 'Ready Steady Who'.

Their hit albums have included: *My Generation*, *A Quick One*, *The Who Sell Out*,

Tommy, Live At Leeds, Who's Next, Meaty, Beaty, Big & Bouncy, Quadrophenia, Odds And Sods, The Who By Numbers, The Story Of The Who, Who Are You, The Kids Are Alright, Face Dances, It's Hard, Who's Last and *The Who Collection*.

Keith Moon died in 1978. In the 1990s, John Entwistle – one of Ringo Starr's All-Starr Band in 1995 – and trout farmer Roger Daltrey have been seen performing at Who fan club conventions. They were also involved when Pete Townshend supervised latter-day presentations of the group's rock operas *Tommy* and *Quadrophenia*.

WIGAN'S OVATION   This British group had three hits in 1975 – 'Skiing In the Snow', 'Per-So-Nal-Ly' and 'Super Love'.

Wigan's Ovation disbanded in 1976, but *Northern Soul Dance*, a CD of their collected works, was issued in 1992.

WILDE, Marty   One of Britain's longest-performing rock 'n' roll stars, Marty Wilde (real name Reginald Leonard Smith) was born in London on 15 April 1936. Lionel Bart spotted him performing at a London club and tipped off **Larry Parnes**, who changed the singer's name – taking the first name from the Ernest Borgnine movie *Marty*.

Wilde began to appear on UK television shows such as *6.5 Special* and *Oh Boy!*, and had a series of chart hits from 1958 to 1962. They included: 'Endless Sleep', 'Donna', 'A Teenager

In Love', 'Sea Of Love', 'Bad Boy', 'Johnny Rocco', 'The Fight', 'Little Girl', 'Rubber Ball', 'Hide And Seek', 'Tomorrow's Clown', 'Jezebel' and 'Ever Since You Said Goodbye'.

Wilde resisted Parnes' efforts to steer him into an acting career, although he did appear in the West End production of *Bye Bye Birdie* and in films such as *The Hellions* and *That'll Be The Day*.

He married Joyce Baker, a member of the **Vernons Girls**, and they then settled in St Albans, Hertfordshire, and had two children, Rick and Kim. Rick was to become a songwriter and producer while Kim became a star in her own right, surpassing her father's success as a chart artist. On 3 January 1997, at the age of 35, she gave birth to a son, Harry Tristan. She had married Hal Fowler, with whom she had appeared in the stage musical *Tommy* two years previously.

Marty became a songwriter and penned 'Ice In The Sun' for **Status Quo**, managed Rick's career for a while and continued to perform as a rock artist. In September 1997 he embarked on a four-month nationwide UK tour along with **Joe Brown**, **John Leyton**, **Eden Kane** and the **Vernons Girls**.

In January 1998 Marty Wilde was banned from driving for 15 months following a drink-driving offence.

WILLIAMS, Danny

Singer Danny Williams was born in Port Elizabeth, South Africa, on 7 January 1942. During a tour of England in 1959 he was spotted by A&R man Norman Newell, who signed him to the HMV label, issuing his debut single, 'Tall A Tree', the same year.

In 1961 Williams topped the UK chart with 'Moon River' and followed with further chart entries 'Jeannie' and 'Wonderful World Of The Young'. During this time he also toured on the same bill as the Beatles. Although his 1964 release 'White On White' wasn't a UK chart entry, it gave him a Top 10 hit in the States. More than a decade was to pass before he entered the charts again with a minor hit, 'Dancing Easy', in 1977.

These days, now with a shaven head and married for the second time, Danny Williams has an international cabaret schedule that stretches years into the future. He also has a hands-on involvement with a charity called Dream Flight, which arranges trips to Disneyland for terminally ill children.

WILSON, Mari

This attractive female singer, born on 29 September 1957, became known as the 'Neasden Queen Of Soul'. With a tongue-in-the-cheek approach, she wore her hair in a bouffant style and dressed in 1950s fashions. She enjoyed success in the UK chart in 1982 and 1983, her hit singles being: 'Beat The Beat', 'Baby It's True', 'Just What I Always Wanted', '(Beware) Boyfriend', 'Cry Me A River' and 'Wonderful'.

Currently, Mari Wilson fronts a critically acclaimed jazz quartet.

WINTER, Edgar

This American singer-songwriter-pianist was born in Beaumont, Texas, on 28 December 1946. The younger brother of **Johnny Winter**, he played in his sibling's band, Johnny & the Jammers, when he was 13 years old. The group changed its name to Black Plague and the brothers then went their separate ways as solo artists, with Edgar forming White Trash and then the Edgar Winter Group. The latter, with members Rick Derringer, Ronnie Montrose and Dan Hartman, had hits with 'Frankenstein', 'Free Ride' and 'River's Risin''.

The group split in the 1970s and Edgar continued as a solo artist for a time, then teamed up with his brother for another period and also appeared on records by a number of artists, including Bette Midler and Meatloaf.

By the 1990s, Edgar Winter's output on disc had placed him as much in the field of jazz as rock, and a hit as enormous as 1973's 'Frankenstein' seems unlikely.

WINTER, Johnny

This blues guitarist-singer-songwriter was born John Dawson Winter III in Leland, Mississippi, in 1944. He first began playing with his own band Johnny & the Jammers, then teamed up with his brother **Edgar Winter**.

He received critical acclaim with his debut album, *Johnny Winter*, released in 1969. He then began touring and appearing at festivals with a backing band which included Edgar, guitarist Rick Derringer, bassist Randy Jo Hobbs and drummer Randy Z. Edgar left and was replaced by Bobby Caldwell. Johnny never had any hit singles, but his 1971 album *Live/Johnny Winter And* became a million-seller.

Johnny always had problems arising from being an albino, and his career then suffered setbacks due to his increasing dependency on drugs.

Since recovering from drug addiction and suicidal depression, Johnny Winter has become a prominent accompanist to black blues legends – he produced the last major albums by his blues idol Muddy Waters on the Blue Sky label – while continuing to issue workmanlike albums, of which 1987's *Third Degree* received most critical acclaim.

WINWOOD, Stevie Still performing after 30 years, Stevie Winwood was born in Birmingham on 12 May 1948 and joined the **Spencer Davis Group** in 1963 at the age of 15. In 1967 he joined Traffic and was also to become a member of **Blind Faith** and Ginger Baker's Airforce. From 1974 he went solo and issued his first solo album, *Stevie Winwood*, in 1976. Since that time he has released a number of further albums and his seventh, *Junction Seven*, was issued in June 1997, when he embarked on another UK tour.

Winwood was divorced from his first wife, Nicole, in 1986 and married Tennessee-born Eugenia Grafton in Nashville in January 1987. Currently, Stevie, Eugenia and their four children live in Gloucestershire.

WISHBONE ASH This group was formed in London in 1969 and comprised Andy Powell and Ted Turner (guitar), Martin Turner (bass and vocals) and Steve Upton (drums).

They had a series of chart albums in the UK: *Wishbone Ash*, *Pilgrimage*, *Argus*, *Wishbone Four*, *There's A Rub*, *Locked In*, *New England*, *Front Page News*, *No Smoke Without Fire*, *Just Testing*, *Live Dates II*, *Number The Brave* and *Both Barrels Burning*.

Over the years there were changes in personnel. Ted Turner left in 1974 and Laurie Wisefield replaced him. In 1980, the last of the original members, Martin Turner, also left and was replaced by John Whetton. With further changes, the group has continued to perform on tours of the States.

November 1997 saw the release on the German label Repertoire of a 56-track, 4-CD Wishbone Ash compilation called *Distillation*.

WRECKLESS ERIC Wreckless Eric was the name by which Eric Goulden, born in Newhaven, Sussex, was known when he signed with Stiff Records during the pub-rock and punk era of the late 1970s. He received critical success – but not hit status – with album releases which included *Wreckless Eric*, *The Wonderful World Of Wreckless Eric* and *Big Smash*, plus the single 'Whole Wide World'.

Under his own name, he formed the Len Bright Combo.

Eric now lives in France, where he has formed Le Beat Group Electrique with drummer Catfish Truton and moonlighting Bootleg Beatle André Barreau. As well as overseeing this group's record releases, the undervalued Eric also tours regularly in a solo capacity.

WYNTER, Mark This British singer (real name Terence Lewis) was born in Woking, Surrey, on 29 January 1943. One of the many handsome, clean-cut solo singers who were popular shortly before the Beatles revolution, he was spotted singing in a Co-op Hall in London. He began recording for Decca and had a four-year run of hits with 'Image Of A Girl', 'Kicking Up The Leaves', 'Dream Girl', 'Exclusively Yours', 'Venus In Blue Jeans', 'Go Away Little Girl', 'Shy Girl', 'It's Almost Tomorrow' and 'Only You'.

In 1995 Mark Wynter was seen in the musical *Phantom Of The Opera* in London's West End and heard narrating a BBC radio programme about the life of Danny Kaye. This led to further radio work – including a regular Saturday noon slot, *Wynter's Weekend Collection*. He is now firmly ensconced in generalized showbusiness, including pantomimes, children's television and cabaret.

YARDBIRDS, The This group originally formed as the Metropolitan Blues Quartet at Kingston Art College in 1963. The members were **Keith Relf** (guitar and harmonica), Paul Samwell-Smith (bass), Chris Dreja (guitar), Jim McCarty (drums) and Anthony Topham (guitar). By the end of the year Eric Clapton had replaced Topham.

As the Yardbirds, they enjoyed a string of hits, including: 'For Your Love', 'Heart Full of Soul', 'Over Under Sideways Down' and 'Happenings Ten Years Ago'.

Clapton left in March 1965, unhappy with recording numbers such as 'For Your Love', and **Jeff Beck** replaced him. Later that same year Jimmy Page joined them on guitar, while Dreja switched to bass. A few months later, Beck left.

The group split in July 1968. Page then formed the New Yardbirds, who evolved into Led Zeppelin. Dreja became a photographer and Relf and McCarty appeared together in Renaissance. The two were actually planning a new band when Relf died in an accident in 1976, electrocuted by faulty wiring on his guitar.

For a time in the early 1980s Dreja, McCarty and Samwell-Smith teamed up once again in under the banner Band Of Frogs.

The Yardbirds were inducted into the Rock & Roll Hall Of Fame in 1992.

In 1997, almost 30 years after the original split, two of the groups' founder-members, Chris Dreja and Jim McCarty, decided to re-form the Yardbirds, together with three new members – John Idan (vocals), Gypie Mayo (guitar) and Laurie Garman (harmonica). They launched their new career with a six-week tour of the States in July and began to record a new studio album.

YES This group was originally formed in London in 1968 and comprised Jon Anderson (vocals), Steve Howe (guitar), Tony Kaye (keyboards), Chris Squire (bass) and Bill Bruford (drums).

They began their career supporting artists such as **Cream** and **Janis Joplin** at the Royal Albert Hall and made their recording debut with 'Sweetness' in 1969. During a ten-year period from 1977 they had half a dozen entries in the singles chart: 'Wonderous Stories', 'Going For The One', 'Don't Kill The Whale', Owner Of A Lonely Heart', 'Leave It' and 'Love Will Find A Way'.

Their chart albums were: *Time And A Word*, *The Yes Album*, *Fragile*, *Close To The Edge*, *Yessongs*, *Tales From Topographic Oceans*, *Relayed*, *Yesterdays*, *Going For The One*, *Tormato*, *Drama*, *Yesshows* and *90125*.

Their album covers were also noted for the distinctive science-fantasy designs by artist Roger Dean.

In 1971 Kaye left to form a group called Badger and was replaced by **Rick Wakeman**, former member of the **Strawbs**. The following year Bruford joined **King Crimson** and was replaced by Alan White.

Wakeman, who had entered the chart with a solo album, *The Six Wives Of Henry VIII*, in 1973, followed with another successful solo album, *Journey To The Centre Of The Earth*, which reached No 1 in the UK chart and No 3 in the States. Soon after, he was hospitalized with a suspected coronary disease. He then went on to enjoy an extremely successful solo career.

Patrick Moraz, former member of Mainhorse, replaced Wakeman in 1976, but Wakeman returned to the band later the same year. In 1980 both Wakeman and Anderson left Yes and were replaced by Trevor Horn and Geoff Downes of Buggles. In the meantime, Anderson had success recording with Greek musician **Vangelis** under the name Jon & Vangelis.

Yes disbanded in 1981, with the various members involved with other bands and projects. Squire and White formed a band called Cinema with South African guitarist Trevor Rabin. They re-formed two years later, with

The Yardbirds

members continuing to be involved with outside projects. By 1989 there were legal wrangles regarding the rights to the name Yes, and four of the members recorded and performed under the name Anderson Bruford Wakeman & Howe. The legal problems were resolved in 1991 and the group, now including Howe, Kaye, Anderson, Squire, Rabin, Bruford and Wakeman, embarked on a world tour.

Further changes were made and by 1994 the group comprised Anderson, Rabin, Squire, Kaye and White.

There was a reunion of the late-1970s line-up of Yes early in 1997 comprising Jon Anderson, Chris Squire, Steve Howe, Alan White and Rick Wakeman. This is the line-up which recorded albums such as *Tales Of Topographic Oceans*, *Going For One* and *Tormato*. During their reunion get-together they took disc jockeys and journalists to Paris on a day trip by Eurostar, entered their handprints on the Wall Of Hands at Rock Circus in Piccadilly and began work on a new album.

A Yes line-up comprising Jon Anderson, Steve Howe, Billy Sherwood, Chris Squire and Alan White recorded a new studio album, *Open Your Eyes*, late in 1997 and appeared in concert in Nottingham, Bournemouth and London in March 1998.

YOUNG, Paul Singer Paul Young was born in Luton, Bedfordshire, on 17 June 1956. He first began playing in local bands in 1979 and that year formed a group called Streetband which entered the chart with 'Toast'.

They split up the following year and Young took two of the members, John Gifford and Mick Pearl, with him to form an eight-piece outfit called Q Tips. They had a minor hit with 'SYSLJFM (The Letter)'.

Young made his solo recording debut with 'Iron Out The Rough Spots' in 1982 and topped the chart in 1983 with 'Wherever I Lay My Hat (That's My Home)'. Other hits which followed included: 'Come Back And Stay', 'Love Of The Common People', 'I'm Gonna Tear Your Playhouse Down', 'Everything Must Change', 'Everytime You Go Away', 'Tomb Of Memories', 'Wonderland', 'Some People', 'Why Does A Man Have To Be Strong', 'Softly Whispering I Love You', 'Oh Girl', 'Calling You', 'Don't Dream It's Over', 'What Becomes Of The Broken-hearted', 'Now I Know What Made Otis Blue', 'Hope In A Hopeless World' and 'It Will Be You'.

In 1998, 15 years after he sang with the Q Tips, Paul Young was back working with his songwriting collaborator Drew Bartfield.

YOUNG RASCALS, The Organist Felix Cavaliere, percussionist Eddie Brigati and drummer Dino Danelli were members of Joey Dee & the Starliters when they met up with guitarist Gene Cornish. He completed a quartet who broke away from the Starliters, initially called themselves Felix & the Escorts and then settled on the Young Rascals. They were to top the US chart with 'Good Lovin''. Their biggest hit, 'Groovin'', was followed by 'How Can I Be Sure' and a third US chart-topper, 'People Got To Be Free'. By this time, in 1968, they had truncated their name to the Rascals.

Brigati and Cornish left the group in 1971 and Ann Sutton, Robert Popwell and Buzzy Feiten joined, although the group disbanded the following year. Cavaliere went solo and Danelli and Cornish formed the group Bulldog and then Fotomaker.

Cornish, Cavaliere and Danelli teamed up again for a tour of the States in 1988. There was then another schism in the re-formed Young Rascals.

Felix Cavaliere is now billed as 'formerly of the Young Rascals', while Gene Cornish and Dino Danelli are mainstays of an entity called the New Rascals. The precise whereabouts of Eddie Brigati is unknown, but he is thought to be living in New Jersey.

ZAGER & EVANS Denny Zager and Rick Evans, two guitarists from Nebraska, were originally with a band called the Eccentrics. In 1960 they decided to split from the group and try their luck as a duo. In 1964 Evans penned a song called 'In The Year 2525'. They were unable to record this until November 1968, when they borrowed $500 dollars to do so, pressing 1,000 copies on their own label, Truth Records. It came to the attention of RCA Records, who signed them up and issued the single in June 1969. It became a US chart-topper, selling over a million copies within eight weeks. It also topped the UK chart and eventually sold over four million copies.

This was to be the duo's only chart success and they split as an act in 1970. However, they remained conjoined professionally by their jointly owned production company in Texas.

ZAVARONI, Lena This singer was born on the island of Rothesay, Scotland, on 4 November 1963. She shot to fame at the age of ten when she appeared on the television talent show *Opportunity Knocks* in 1973 and entered the UK Top 10 with the single 'Ma He's Making Eyes At Me'. She followed with 'Personality', which also charted. She had another chart entry with the album *Ma*.

Despite such a minor recording life, Lena became a well-known celebrity, appearing on numerous television variety shows. She then suffered from anorexia and her career floundered.

On 5 March 1998, when she was 34, a fire destroyed her seventh-floor flat and all her memorabilia. At the time, Lena was living on benefit in a bedsit in Hoddesdon, Hertfordshire.

ZOMBIES, The This group was formed by keyboards player Rod Argent while he was still at St Albans Grammar School in 1963. The other members were Hugh Grundy (drums), Paul Atkinson (guitar), Colin Blunstone (vocals) and Paul Arnold (bass). Chris White soon replaced Arnold.

In 1964 the group were to win a local beat group competition, which led to a Decca Records audition and a contract. On leaving school that year they recorded their debut single, 'She's Not There', a number penned by Argent.

*The
Zombies*

The group's proposed tour of the US was reduced to a series of gigs in New York due to a ban by the immigration authorities, then worried about the number of British bands performing in the States.

Their second single, 'Tell Her No', was their final UK hit, although it prevented them from being tagged 'one-hit wonders'.

They were finally able to tour the States in 1965, when they had two minor hits with 'She's Coming Home' and 'I Want You Back Again'. The following year they appeared in the film *Bunny Lake Is Missing* and toured Europe and the Far East.

Due to their apparent lack of chart success at home, the group disbanded in 1967.

A previously unreleased track, 'Time Of The Season, was issued in the US in 1969, where it became a million-seller, reaching No 3 in the chart.

Atkinson and Grundy went on to work as A&R men at CBS Records, while Argent and White teamed up to become record producers and Blunstone continued with a solo career.

Colin Blunstone lives in Surrey. In 1997 he toured the UK to promote a new album. He has also sung with a re-formed Zombies that contains Hugh Grundy on drums and Chris White on bass.

Paul Atkinson and Rod Argent, a music equipment shop owner and colossus of New Age music, put in guest appearances on a 1993 Zombies album, *New World*, recorded after 'Time Of The Season' had been included on the soundtrack of the movie *Awakenings*, reviving interest in the band. In October 1997 *Zombie Heaven*, a 4-CD boxed set compiled by Alec Palao, was released.

To mark the launch of the retrospective CD package, the 1964 line-up of the Zombies re-formed for a performance at the Jazz Café in London in December 1997.

In May 1998 Blunstone issued a brand-new album, *The Light Inside*, and embarked on a UK concert tour.

Z Z TOP This group was formed in El Paso, Texas, in 1969 with members Billy Gibbons (guitar and vocals), Dusty Hill (bass and vocals) and Frank Beard (drums).

The boogie-rock trio developed a huge cult following and their hit singles include: 'Tush', 'I Thank You', 'Gimme All Your Lovin'', 'Legs', 'La Grange', 'Pincushion' and 'Breakaway'. Album hits include: *Fandango, El Loco, Eliminator, Afterburner* and *One Foot In The Blues*.

Their cult appeal lies in their bizarre image, initially developed in a series of videos for their singles. These featured sexy, leggy girls in stockings and suspenders and short tight skirts, in a series of brief storylines, while the group's distinctive car was also featured, along with the incredible face fungus of Gibbons and Hill and the visual trick of rotating guitars.

The original trio was still together and on the boards in 1996, when they recorded their most recent album, *Rhythmeon*.

HOPE I DIE BEFORE I GET OLD

Pete Townshend, 'My Generation'

IVE FAST, die young and leave a good-looking corpse,' said John Derek in the film *Knock On Any Door*. He could well have been discussing the fate of dozens of rock 'n' roll stars.

While our memoriam of artists covers mainly rock and pop performers, we have included a select number of blues, gospel, middle of-the-road and country music artists. The performers in the latter categories seem to live to a ripe old age – into their sixties, seventies and even eighties – while a large number of the rock artists mentioned here suffered premature deaths in their twenties and thirties.

The stresses and strains of rock 'n' roll have taken their inevitable toll: artists suffering depression and hanging or shooting themselves; deaths through a surfeit of drugs or alcohol; artists travelling thousands of miles to their gigs by plane and never reaching their destination; punished bodily systems, with very young men suffering heart attacks; the pace of the road, with crashes in cars and on motorbikes. All this is in stark contrast to the veteran blues, jazz and country music artists quietly dying in bed after reaching their allotted three score years and ten.

A major tragedy of the rock 'n' roll scene occurred on 2 February 1959 when Buddy Holly, Ritchie Valens and the Big Bopper were all killed in a plane crash. A nine-month period at the beginning of the 1970s also shocked the music world, when three major rock icons died in quick succession: Jimi Hendrix on 18 September 1970, Janis Joplin a few weeks later on 4 October and Jim Morrison several months after that on 3 July 1971. However, the rock death which really shocked the world occurred on 8 December 1980, when John Lennon was murdered.

And tragedies continue to occur, including the death of John Denver in a plane crash and the suicide of Michael Hutchence of INXS, both in 1997, and in 1998 the deaths of Carl Perkins in January and Carl Wilson in February, both from cancer.

ACE, Johnny   American R&B star, born John Marshall Alexander Jnr on 29 June 1929 in Memphis, Tennessee. Ace topped the US R&B charts with his debut single, 'My Song', in 1963. On 24 December 1954 he was playing Russian roulette backstage at a concert in Houston in order to impress a girl and accidentally shot himself. Ace was 25 years old. His biggest hit was the posthumous single 'Pledging My Love'.

ACLAND, Chris   Drummer for the band Lush (who recorded for Reprise), born in Lancaster. He killed himself in 1996, when he was 30 years old.

ADAMS, Justin   Guitarist born in New Orleans, who played on classic 1950s records by **Fats Domino**, Little Richard and others. Prior to his death in 1991, Adams had been playing with Dave Bartholemew's Big Band. He was 68 years old.

ALEXANDER, Arthur   Songwriter-R&B singer born on 10 May 1940 in Florence, Alabama. Among his songs, which were to be recorded by groups such as the Beatles and the **Rolling Stones**, were 'Anna', 'Soldier Of Love', 'A Shot Of Rhythm & Blues', 'You'd Better Move On' and 'Go Home Girl'. Heart troubles and respiratory problems resulted in Alexander's death on 9 June 1993.

ALLIN, G.G.   Punk-rock singer with the Murder Junkies, who died from a drugs overdose on his release from prison in 1993. He was 36 years old.

ALLISON, Luther   Blues guitarist who made an impact at the 1969 and 1970 Ann Arbor Blues Festivals. Allison died on 12 August 1997 at the age of 57.

ALLMAN, Duane   Guitarist born on 20 November 1946 in Nashville, Tennessee, who in 1969 formed the Allman Brothers Band with his brother Greg. Their eponymous album was issued the following year. Eric Clapton invited Duane to join him on recording sessions for Derek & the Dominoes. The Allman Brothers Band made their chart debut in 1971 with 'Revival (Love Is Everywhere)', but Duane was killed in a motorcycle crash later the same year on 19 October in Macon, Georgia, when he attempted to avoid a lorry. He was only 24 years old.

AMES, Vic   Singer born on 20 May 1926 who was a member of the Ames Brothers, a highly successful American vocal group comprising the four brothers: Ed, Gene, Joe and Vic.

They topped the chart twice in 1950 with 'Rag Mop' and 'Sentimental Me', and followed with four more million-sellers: 'Undecided', 'You You You', 'The Naughty Lady Of Shady Lane' and 'Melodie d'Amour'. They had further US Top 20 entries with: 'Can Anyone Explain', 'Put Another Nickel In', 'Stars Are The Windows Of Heaven', 'Oh Babe!', 'Wang Wang Blues', 'I Wanna Love You', 'Auf Wiedersehn Sweetheart', 'Stay Along', 'My Favourite Song', 'The Man With The Banjo', My Bonnie Lassie, 'It Only Hurts For A Little While', 'Tammy', 'A Very Precious Love' and 'Pussy Cat'.

The group disbanded in 1960 and Vic was killed in a car crash in Nashville in 1978.

ANGLIN, Jack   Country music singer born on 13 May 1916, who was one half of the duo Johnny & Jack. He was killed in a car crash on 7 March 1963 while on his way to the funeral of **Patsy Cline**.

ARMSTRONG, Louis   Premier jazzman, born in New Orleans on 4 June 1900. Armstrong invented the 'scat' style of singing and had numerous jazz hits in the 1920s and 1930s, before becoming a mainstream entertainer and appearing in a variety of films ranging from *Diamond Lil* to *High Society*. He had several major hits, including: 'Takes Two To Tango', 'Theme From The Threepenny Opera', 'The Faithful Hussar', 'Mack The Knife', 'Hello Dolly', 'What A Wonderful World' and 'Sunshine Of Love'. Armstrong died in New York on 6 July 1971.

ASHMAN, Matthew   Guitarist with several British bands, including Adam & the Ants and Bow Wow Wow. He teamed up with former **Sex Pistol** Pete Cook in Chiefs Of Relief. Matthew died on 21 November 1995 from complications caused by diabetes. He was 35 years old.

ATWELL, Winifred   Pianist, born in Tunapuna, Trinidad, in 1914, Winifred arrived in the UK in 1954 and became the first black person to top the UK chart with her medley 'Let's Have Another Party' in December 1954. Between 1952 and 1959 she had 15 chart hits, including: 'Coronation Rag', 'Brittania Rag',

'Flirtation Waltz', 'Let's Have a Party', 'Rachmaninoff's 18th Variation On A Theme By Pagnini', 'Let's Have A Ding Dong', 'Poor People Of Paris', 'Port Au Prince', 'Left Bank', 'Let's Rock 'n' Roll', 'Let's Have A Ball', 'Summer Of The Seventeenth Doll', 'Piano Party' and 'Flirtation Waltz.' Winifred died in Sydney, Australia, on 28 February 1983.

BALLARD, Florence Female vocalist born on 30 June 1943 and one of the founder members of the Motown recording group the Supremes in 1959. Florence was fired from the group in July 1967. Unable to make a success as a solo singer, she was reduced to poor circumstances, having only been paid a salary during the time the group had ten No 1 singles in the 1960s. Florence died following a heart attack at Mount Carmel Mercy Hospital in Detroit on 22 February 1976. She was 32 years old.

BAR-KEYS, The Six-piece soul band who scored with numbers such as 'Soul Finger'. They were hired to back **Otis Redding** on tour and four of the members died in the crash that killed Otis on 10 December 1967. There was only one survivor, Ben Cauley, and he teamed

John Belushi (left) with Aretha Franklin and Dan Aykroyd

up with the one member who was booked on another plane, James Alexander, to continue with the group name from 1968, although they enjoyed only one further hit, 'Shake Your Rump To The Funk'.

BARRETT, Carlton   Drummer with Bob Marley's Wailers who was shot dead outside his own home in Kingston, Jamaica, on 17 April 1987. He was 36 years old.

BARTON, Alan   Singer with Black Lace, noted for their hit single 'Agadoo'. He later joined **Smokie** as lead singer and was killed in a car crash in Germany on 23 March 1995 while the band were on tour.

BATORS, Stiv   Vocalist born in 1949 who sang with the Cleveland-based group Dead Boys. When the group disbanded in 1978, Bators joined the London-based Wanderers and later became a member of Lords Of The New Church, before moving to Paris. In 1990 he was on his way to the recording studio when he was knocked down by a car and died the same night from a brain haemorrhage.

BELL, Chris   Founder member of the Memphis group Big Star, born on 12 January 1951. The group formed in 1971, but disbanded in 1975 after creating a style called 'power pop'. Bell died in a car accident on 27 December 1978. He was 27 years old.

BELLAMY, Peter   British folk artist born in Norfolk on 8 September 1944, who was a founder member of Young Tradition. He committed suicide in Keighley, West Yorkshire, on 24 September 1991.

BELUSHI, John   Actor who teamed up with Dan Aykroyd as the Blues Brothers. They appeared as the musical duo on the US television show *Saturday Night Live* and in the feature film *The Blues Brothers*. Their chart hits included 'Soul Man', 'Rubber Biscuit', 'Gimme Some Lovin'' and 'Who's Making Love'. Belushi died from a drugs overdose on 5 March 1982. He was 33 years old.

BELVIN, Jesse   R&B singer born on 15 December 1933 in Texarkana, Arkansas, whose first hit was 'Dream Girl' in 1953 when he was half of the team Jesse & Marvin. Belvin turned solo and his hits included 'Goodnight My Love', 'Funny' and 'Guess Who'. He also co-penned 'Earth Angel' and appeared with several doo wop groups such as the Sheiks, Three Dots & A Dash, the Cliques and the Sharptines. Belvin died in a car crash in Los Angeles on 6 February 1968, aged 27.

BENNETT, Duster   British blues performer, born Anthony Bennett on 23 September 1946. He signed to Mike Vernon's blues label and his debut single was 'It's A Man Down There'. His album releases included *Smiling Like I'm Happy*, *Bright Lights* and *12 DBs*. Bennett was killed in a car accident on 25 March 1976, aged 30.

BENNETT, Wayne   Guitarist who played on hits by Bobby Bland, including 'Stormy Monday' and 'Turn On Your Love Light'. He died in 1991, aged 58.

BENTON, Brook   Singer, born Benjamin Franklin Peay in South Carolina on 19 September 1931. He had numerous hits, including 'So Many Ways', 'Kiddio', 'Think Twice', 'The Boll Weevil Song' and 'Hotel Happiness'. He also duetted with Dinah Washington on the hits 'Baby (You've Got What It Takes)' and 'A Rockin' Good Way'. Benton died in New York on 9 April 1988.

BLACK, Bill   Bass player for Sun Records, born on 17 September 1926 in Memphis, Tennessee. He also played as backing musician to **Elvis Presley** for five years before forming his own outfit, the Bill Black Combo, which saw success with hits such as 'Smokie Part 2' and 'White Silver Sands'. Black retired from touring in 1962, but his band continued to play under that name, even after Black died on 21 October 1965 as the result of a brain tumour. He was 39 years old.

BLISS, John   Founder member of American punk band Powertrip and also their drummer. Bliss died as the result of a heart attack in Los Angeles on 7 July 1988, aged 32.

BLOOM, Bobby   Singer whose biggest hit was 'Montego Bay'. He also wrote 'Heavy Makes Happy' for the Staple Singers. Bloom shot himself in the head at a Hollywood hotel on 28 February 1974, although it was presumed to be an accident. He was 28 years old.

BLOOMFIELD, Mike   Guitarist born on 28 July 1944 in Chicago, who initially joined the Paul Butterfield Band in 1965 but left them in 1967 to form the Electric Flag in 1967. Bloomfield died in San Francisco from a drugs overdose on 15 February 1981, aged 39.

BLUE, David   American folk singer, born David Cohen on 18 February 1941. He was a contemporary of **Bob Dylan**, and also toured with Dylan as part of the Rolling Thunder Revue and recorded eight albums. Blue died as the result of a heart attack while jogging in New York on 2 December 1982.

BOLAN, Marc   Singer-songwriter-guitarist-poet, born Marc Field in London on 30 September 1947. He initially appeared as Toby Tyler, then Marc Bowland and finally Marc Bolan, and made his recording debut with 'The Wizard' in 1966. He joined John's Children in 1967, then teamed up with Steve Peregrine Took in Tyrannosaurus Rex later the same year. Took suffered from drugs problems and was replaced by Mickey Finn in 1968. The group truncated their name to T. Rex and became a quartet, issuing a string of major hits, including: 'Ride A White Swan', 'Hot Love', 'Telegram Sam', 'Children Of The Revolution' and 'The Groover'.

In 1970 Marc married his girlfriend June Child, but the couple were to split three years later when he fell in love with Gloria Jones, an American singer, with whom he had a child, Rolan.

Tragedy occurred on 16 September 1977. Bolan, who had never learned to drive because he hated cars, was on his way home, with Gloria at the wheel. The car swerved off the road and crashed into a tree on Barnes Common in London. He was killed instantly. It was two days before his thirtieth birthday and, bizarrely, he had always believed he would not reach the age of 30.

Twenty years after his death, Marc Bolan remains a star. The tree on the common has become a shrine, there are regular conventions held in his honour and several fan clubs still exist. In addition, there are re-releases of his recordings on a regular basis.

The diminutive singer with the distinctive hairstyle developed a somewhat effete image, which caught on in the era of 'glam rock' in the UK but did not bring him major stardom in the States. It was even said that at the time of his death he had passed the peak of his popularity and 'Bolanmania' was on the wane.

A special memorial at the site of his death was unveiled in 1997. His son Rolan followed in his father's footsteps and although reared in Los Angeles, began making appearances in Britain during 1998.

BOLIN, Tommy   Guitarist born in Sioux City, Idaho, on 1 August 1951, who joined the James Gang, then moved to the UK to replace Ritchie Blackmore with **Deep Purple** in April 1975. When the band initially disbanded in July 1976, he returned to the States to form the Tommy Bolin Band. He died from a heroin overdose on 4 December 1976 at a hotel in Newport, Miami. He was 25 years old.

BOND, Graham   British R&B musician born in Romford, Essex, on 28 October 1937. Bond was a Dr Barnardo's orphan who began his musical career in 1961. By 1964 he had established himself as a major British R&B figure, leader of the Graham Bond Organization. Sadly, he became hooked on heroin, which caused him to have a nervous breakdown. He was hospitalized and later killed when he fell under a train at Finsbury Park station on 8 May 1974, aged 37. Suicide or an accident? The jury is still out.

Marc Bolan (right) with Elton John

BOND, Johnny   Country singer, born Cyrus Whitfield Bond on 1 June 1915, who had a No 1 hit in the US chart in 1960 with 'Hot Rod Lincoln' and a second hit with 'Ten Little Bottles' in the country chart in 1965. His autobiography was called *Reflections*. Bond died on 12 June 1978.

BOND, Ronnie   Drummer, born Ronald Bullis in Andover, Hampshire, on 4 May 1943, who founded the **Troggs**. They went on to have nine hits in the UK and three in the States. Together with Reg Presley, Bond continued recording at different times over the years and in the late 1980s made a Rhino release album with members of REM. He died at Winchester hospital on 13 November 1992, survived by a wife and three sons.

BONHAM, John   Drummer born in Bromwich, Staffordshire, on 31 May 1948. Bonham developed a passion for the drums at the age of five and had his own kit by the age of 15. His first group was the Band Of Joy, a Birmingham outfit whose lead singer was Robert Plant. In July 1968 Robert invited him to join a band he was in called the New Yardbirds, later to be known as Led Zeppelin. The quartet became superstars, with a string of multi-million-selling albums and a film, *The Song Remains The Same*, to their credit.

Led Zeppelin were noted for their outrageous behaviour and Bonham's reputation was soon as notorious as that of **Keith Moon** of the **Who**. At one time he was barred from every hotel in London. A series of unfortunate incidents of a personal nature plagued the band, so in 1977 they decided to take a sabbatical and Bonham was able to spend time with his wife and family on their farm.

The group decided to go back on the road again in 1980 and began rehearsing. Bonham spent the day and evening drinking vodka and was so drunk that he had to be carried to his bed. He was found dead the next morning, 25 September 1980, having choked on his own vomit. He was 32 years old.

John's son Jason has also become a drummer.

BONO, Sonny   Singer-songwriter, born Salvatore Bono in Detroit, Michigan, on 16 February 1935, who originally found fame as one half of the duo Sonny & Cher, with Cherilyn Sarkasian, who became his wife. Their biggest hit was 'I Got You Babe'; others included: 'Baby Don't Go', 'All I Really Want To Do', 'Laugh At Me', 'Just You', 'But You're Mine', 'Little Man' and 'The Beat Goes On'. They also appeared in two films, *Good Times* and *Chastity*.

The two split up and Cher became tremendously successful as both a solo singer and a film actress. Sonny became a politician and was elected mayor of Palm Springs. He later opened a restaurant with his fourth wife and in 1991 his autobiography, *The Beat Goes On*, was published.

Sonny was a Republican Congressman when he died in a skiing accident at Lake Tahoe during the first week of January 1998.

BOON, Dennis Dale   Singer-guitarist who founded the Minutemen, a Los Angeles group, in the late 1970s. He was killed in a car crash in December 1985.

BOULET, Gerry   Rock singer born in Quebec who was lead singer with Offenbach before becoming a major solo star. He died from cancer in 1990 at the age of 44.

BOYCE, Tommy   Songwriter, born on 29 September 1944, who was also part of the Boyce & Hart songwriting team with Bobby Hart. Boyce originally co-penned hits such as 'Under The Moon Of Love' and 'Pretty Little Angel Eyes'. The two even had a hit in their own right with 'I Wonder What She's Doing Tonight' in 1967. In 1965 he auditioned unsuccessfully as one of the **Monkees**, but together with Hart co-wrote and produced a great deal of the Monkees' material, including 'The Monkees Theme' and 'Last Train To Clarksville'. In the 1970s, Boyce and Hart teamed up with Mickie Dolenz and Davy Jones to perform as the Monkees.

Early in 1997, Boyce committed suicide in Nashville by shooting himself.

BRADLEY, Owen   American pianist-arranger-band leader, born on 21 October 1915. His major hit was 'Blues Stay Away From Me' in 1949. He led Owen Bradley & His Quintet, who recorded with acts such as the Mills Brothers and the Four Aces. Bradley opened the Nashville division of Decca Records, where he recorded numerous artists including Kitty Wells, Loretta Lynn, **Patsy Cline**, **Brenda Lee**, Ernest Tubb and Webb Pierce. He died in January 1998.

BREL, Jacques   Singer-songwriter born in Brussels, Belgium, on 8 April 1929. He composed his songs in French and several were translated and recorded in English by various artists, including 'Seasons In The Sun' and 'If You Go Away'. Brel spent some time in semi-retirement in the Polynesian Islands before returning to Paris for treatment for lung cancer, which eventually killed him on 9 October 1978.

BRIGGS, David   Record producer born in Douglas, Wyoming, on 29 February 1944. He produced records by artists such as **Alice Cooper**, Nils Lofgren and Spirit, and had a long association with Neil Young. Briggs died on 25 November 1995 following a long illness.

BRILLEAUX, Lee   Singer, born Lee Green in Durban, South Africa, in 1953, who became vocalist and harmonica player with **Dr Feelgood**, the British band formed in 1971 on the 'pub rock' scene. They had six UK chart hits, their biggest being 'Milk And Alcohol'. Brilleaux died from pancreatic cancer on Canvey Island on 7 April 1994.

BROWN, Buster   American singer-songwriter born on 15 August 1911, who had a chart entry with 'Fannie Mae' in 1960. He died on 31 January 1976.

BROWN, Roy   R&B singer, born in New Orleans on 10 September 1925, who recorded the original version of 'Good Rockin' Tonight' in 1947. His hits included: 'Hard Luck Blues', 'Boogie At Midnight', 'Love Don't Love Nobody', 'Long About Sundown', 'Big Town', 'Party Doll' and 'Let The Four Winds Blow'. He died as the result of a heart attack on 25 May 1981.

BUCHANAN, Roy   American rock guitarist, born on 23 September 1939. Buchanan began life as a session guitarist and also recorded in his own right. He was asked by the **Rolling Stones** to act as a replacement for Brian Jones, but turned them down. He was arrested for being drunk and hanged himself in his cell on 14 August 1988.

BUCKLEY, Jeff   Son of **Tim Buckley**, who became a well-respected songwriter following the release of his album *Grace* in 1994 and originally established his reputation as a performer at the Café Sin-e in New York. Jeff drowned in May 1997. He was last seen floating in the Mississippi River on his back, singing and still holding his guitar. He was 30 years old.

BUCKLEY, Tim   American folk artist, born in Washington, DC, on 14 February 1947. Buckley began recording with the Elektra label and released 11 albums. He died in hospital in Santa Monica, California, on 29 June 1975 from an overdose of heroin and morphine. He was 28 years old.

BURNETTE, Dorsey   Singer-songwriter, born on 28 December 1932, who initially began performing with his brother **Johnny Burnette** and Paul Burlison in the Johnny Burnette Trio. Later the brothers teamed up as songwriters, penning hits for artists such as **Ricky Nelson**. Dorsey's biggest hit was '(There Was A) Tall Oak Tree'.

Dorsey died as the result of a heart attack at Canoga Bay, California, on 19 August 1975. His son Billy became a successful country music artist.

BURNETTE, Johnny   Singer-songwriter, born in Memphis, Tennessee, on 25 March 1934, who had a string of five consecutive hit records in the States in 1960 and 1961. These included his biggest-selling single, 'You're Sixteen'. On 14 August 1964 he drowned when he fell from a ferryboat while fishing. He was 30 years old.

Johnny's brother **Dorsey Burnette** was also a hit artist, as was his son Rocky, who in turn hit the chart with 'You're Sixteen'.

BUTTERFIELD, Paul   Vocalist and highly influential blues harmonica player, born in Chicago, Illinois, on 17 December 1942. He formed the Paul Butterfield Blues Band in 1965. The group was successful, had a number of hit albums and appeared at the Newport Folk Festival and at Woodstock. They disbanded in 1971 and Butterfield formed a band called Better Days, but could not repeat his earlier success. He tried again in 1976 with the Danko-Butterfield Band, which also failed to register.

Suffering from bowel problems, Butterfield underwent two operations and became too ill to pursue a career. He died on 4 May 1987.

BYRON, David   Singer born on 29 January 1947 who was a founder member of Uriah Heep. He was the lead singer on ten of their albums before being sacked in 1976. Byron made further recordings with his own outfits, but died on 28 February 1985. He was 38 years old.

CALDWELL, Tommy Lead guitarist with the South Carolina outfit the Marshall Tucker Band who was born in Spartanburg, South Carolina, in 1948. The other band members included his brother Toy (bass), Doug Gray (keyboards and vocals), George McCorkle (rhythm), Jerry Eubanks (sax and flute) and Paul Riddle (drums). The group had a number of hits, including 'Fire On The Mountain' and 'Heard It In A Love Song'. Caldwell died in a car crash in Spartanburg on 28 April 1980, aged 32.

CALIFORNIA, Randy American musician, born Randy Craig Wolfe in 1951. He played with **Jimi Hendrix**, who gave him the name Randy California. He travelled to England with Hendrix, but it was decided he was too young to be a member of the Jimi Hendrix Experience. He later joined Spirit. Randy suffered a nervous breakdown in 1972. While on holiday in Hawaii, he was surfing with his 12-year-old son when they were swept away by a rip tide and Randy died saving his son's life.

CALVERT, Eddie British trumpeter born in Preston, Lancashire, on 15 March 1922. He joined the Preston Silver Band at the age of 11 playing cornet, and eventually began recording in 1951, releasing 'Oh Mein Papa' in 1953. His version of the number chalked up over three million sales, the biggest volume for any instrumental record up to that date. Other hits included: 'Cherry Pink And Apple Blossom White', 'Stranger In Paradise', 'John And Julie', 'Zambesi', 'Mandy' and 'Little Serenade'. Calvert eventually went to live in South Africa and died as the result of a heart attack in Johannesburg in 1978.

CAMPBELL, John Blues artist noted for his albums *One Believer* and *Howlin' Mercy*. He died from heart failure at his home in New York on 13 June 1993.

CARPENTER, Karen Singer born on 2 March 1950 in New Haven, Connecticut, who teamed up with her brother Richard to form the Carpenters. They hit the charts with a version of 'Ticket To Ride' in 1970 and had a string of hits for the next decade, including: 'Close To You', 'Yesterday Once More', 'Please Mr Postman' and 'Calling Occupants Of Interplanetary Craft'. They proved to be the most successful brother and sister act in recording history.

The Carpenters – Karen and Richard

Dark-haired, dark-eyed Karen had reputedly been unlucky in love, despite the fame and adulation the Carpenters enjoyed. They had received Grammy Awards for Best New Artist and Best Vocal Performance, and had their own television series, *Make Your Own Kind Of Music*, but the fame brought them anxiety and stress.

Despite the popularity of Karen's strong, clear and distinctive vocals, critics regarded the Carpenters as a bland duo and dismissed them for creating run-of-the-mill pop music. However, the passage of time has caused their recordings to be reappraised and the twosome is now highly regarded.

The unhappy Karen became ill with the slimmer's disease in the 1970s and continued to suffering from anorexia until she died. In December 1975 she weighed only 41kg (90lb) and had to cease touring and take a two-month rest.

On 3 February 1983 Karen was found lying unconscious in her parents' home in Downey, California. She was immediately rushed to the nearby Downey Community Hospital, but died from cardiac arrest at 9:51am. She was 32 years old.

The coroner announced that the cause of death was 'heartbeat irregularities brought on by chemical imbalances associated with anorexia nervosa'.

CARR, Eric American drummer born on 7 July 1950. He replaced Peter Criss in **Kiss** in 1981 and died ten years later on 24 November 1991.

CARTER, Stanley American country music artist, born on 27 August 1925. He died on 1 December 1966.

CHAPIN, Harry Folk-rock storyteller, born in Greenwich Village, New York, on 7 December 1942. He originally formed an act with his brothers Tom and Stephen called the Chapin Brothers, which ceased when his brothers left the country to avoid the draft.

Initially Harry attempted to become a film-maker and won an Oscar for *Legendary Champions*, his documentary about boxers. His gifts as a storyteller led him to compose songs and he became a folk singer, making his recording debut in 1971 with the Elektra album *Heads And Tails*. He then conceived a musical revue, *The Night That Made America Famous*, which received two Tony nominations.

Harry's No 1 hit was 'Cat's In The Cradle', while other chart hits included the songs 'Taxi' and 'W-O-L-D'.

During his brief career, he was committed to raising money – a total of more than $5 million – for charity and he co-founded WHY (World Hunger Year) in 1975.

Harry Chapin was killed in a road accident in Jericho, New York, on 16 July 1981, when the petrol tank of his car exploded. He was 39 years old.

CHARLES, Charlie Former drummer with **Ian Dury** & the Blockheads. He died from cancer at the Park Royal Hospital in London on 5 September 1990.

CHASE, Bill Leader of the jazz-rock band Chase, whose only chart hit was 'Get It On'. Along with three other members of his group, Bill died in a plane crash in Jackson, Minnesota, on 9 August 1974. He was 39 years old.

CHENIER, Clifton American king of zydeco, Louisiana's black R&B-influenced form of cajun, born on 26 June 1925. He died on 12 December 1987.

CHEVALIER, Maurice French crooner, born on 12 September 1888, who became a major film star and received a special Academy Award in 1958. He appeared in a number of Hollywood musicals and is remembered for singing 'Every little breeze seems to whisper Louise...' in his US film debut. Another memorable movie moment was his rendition of 'Thank Heaven For Little Girls' in *Gigi*. He died as the result of a heart attack on 1 January 1972.

CIPOLLINA, John Guitarist born in Berkeley, California, on 24 August, 1943, who was a founder member of **Quicksilver Messenger Service** in 1964. He left the band in October 1970 and died on 29 May 1989.

CLARK, Dee Singer, born Delectus Clark in Arkansas on 7 November 1938. He moved to Chicago and joined the Hambone Kids. Their big hit was the novelty number 'Hambone'. After singing with another outfit, the Goldentones, Clark turned solo and had six Top 40 hits between 1959 and 1961, including 'Nobody But You' and 'Raindrops'. His final hit was a UK chart entry in 1975, 'Ride A Wild Horse'. He died on 7 December 1991 following a series of heart attacks.

CLARK, Gene Singer-guitarist-songwriter, born in Tipton, Missouri, on 17 November 1941. He became a founder member of the Byrds in 1964. The group had a number of major hits including 'Mr Tambourine Man' and 'Turn! Turn! Turn!'. Over the years there were various permutations in personnel and a number of offshoots, such as Dillard & Clark and McGuinn, Clark & Hillman.

Clark died from natural causes at his home in Sherman Oaks, California, on 24 May 1991, the year the group were inducted into the Rock & Roll Hall Of Fame.

CLARK, Steve Guitarist born in Hillsborough, South Yorkshire, on 23 April 1960. He joined Def Leppard as joint lead guitarist and also composed the music to Joe Elliott's lyrics. The band gained superstardom in the States.

In 1984 drummer Rick Allan lost his arm in a road accident. A custom-built drum kit was constructed and he rejoined the band six months later.

Despite mega-hit albums such as *Pyromania* and *Hysteria*, Clark became a heavy drinker and had to join Alcoholics Anonymous. The drink finally killed him on 8 January 1991. He was 30 years old.

CLARKE, Michael American drummer born on 3 June 1943. He was a member of the Byrds, the **Flying Burrito Brothers** and Firefall. He also worked as a drummer on numerous recording sessions for various artists. He died from liver failure on Treasure Island, Florida, on 19 December 1993.

CLINE, Patsy Legendary country singer, born Virginia Patterson Hensley in Winchester, Virginia, on 8 September 1932. She became the first female artist to be inducted into the Country Music Hall Of Fame, albeit posthumously in 1973.

Patsy first began recording in 1956 and her hits included 'Walkin' After Midnight', 'I Fall To Pieces', 'Crazy' and 'She's Got You'.

She was very young when she married Gerald Cline and he divorced her for having an affair with her manager. Throughout her career she gained a reputation for promiscuity. She next married Charlie Dick, who often physically beat her, and she retired briefly from showbusiness to give birth to a child. When Dick was drafted she resumed her career.

On 5 March 1962 Patsy appeared in a benefit concert in aid of the late Cactus Jack's widow – Jack had been a popular Nashville disc jockey who was killed in a car accident. She was returning from the concert in a small plane, along with Cowboy Copas and **Hawkshaw Hawkins** and, despite warnings about bad weather conditions, they were all killed in the subsequent crash. Patsy was only 30 years old.

Since her death there have been several posthumous chart entries. *Sweet Dreams* was the name of the 1985 film biopic in which Jessica Lange starred as Cline.

COBAIN, Kurt Leader of **Nirvana**, born in Aberdeen, Washington, on 20 February 1967. He formed Nirvana with bassist Chris Novoselic in 1987, and originally played drums himself. Several drummers then joined them until they settled for Dave Grohl in 1990. Nirvana recorded their first album, *Bleach*, in 1989 and followed with another impressive album, *Nevermind*. On 24 February 1992 Cobain married **Courtney Love** of Hole and the couple had a daughter, Frances Bean, on 18 August. Cobain's uncompromising songs and performances attracted a cult following and he became a major rock icon of the 1990s.

In March 1994 he was taken to hospital in a coma, having suffered a drugs overdose. A few weeks later he obtained a Remmington .20 shotgun from a friend and committed suicide by shooting himself in the head on 5 April 1995. He left a note reading: 'It's better to burn out than fade away.' He also left a message to his wife: 'Please keep going, Courtney, for Frances, for her life which will be so much happier without me.'

A visiting electrician found his body in his Seattle home four days later. Cobain was 27 years old.

The following year Grohl formed a new band, the Foo Fighters.

COCHRAN, Eddie Seminal rock 'n' roll star, born Ray Edward Cochrane in Albert Lea, Minnesota, on 3 October 1938. He initially teamed up with another singer, Garland Perry, who called himself Harry Cochran, and they billed themselves as the Cochran Brothers. They split when Harry wanted to turn to country music while Eddie, having seen **Elvis Presley** perform, turned to rock 'n' roll. At the age of 18 he made his movie debut in *The Girl Can't Help It*. He also appeared in the films *Untamed Youth* and *Go, Johnny Go*. Because of the latter film, he had to turn down the opportunity

Eddie Cochran

of joining a tour with **Buddy Holly** – and might well have been among the victims of the notorious plane crash.

Eddie's hits included: 'Sittin' In The Balcony', 'Jeannie, Jeannie, Jeannie', 'Summertime Blues', 'C'mon Everybody' and 'Three Steps To Heaven'.

Touring the UK, he was in a car with his girlfriend Sharon Sheeley and **Gene Vincent** when it crashed into a lamp-post. Gene and Sharon suffered injuries, but Eddie had gone through the windscreen and sustained brain damage. He died the following day, 17 April 1960. He was 21 years old.

COGAN, Alma   Singer born in London on 19 May 1932, who became the most successful British female artist of the 1950s. Known as the 'girl with the giggle in her voice', Alma had a string of 18 chart hits, including 'Hernando's Hideaway', 'Sugartime' and 'Where Will The Dimple Be'. She also topped the chart with numbers such as 'Dreamboat'.

Alma numbered many prominent celebrities among her close friends. She even became a friend of the Beatles and her last records were covers of Lennon & McCartney songs, including 'Yesterday', 'Eight Days A Week' and 'Help!'. John and Paul actually attended her recording session for 'Eight Days A Week'. Alma died from cancer on 26 October 1966. She was 34 years old.

COLE, Brian   Bass guitarist born in 1944, who was a founder member of the Association, the Californian sextet which was formed in February 1965. The group had seven chart hits, including: 'Along Comes Mary', 'Cherish', 'Windy', 'Never My Love' and 'Everything That Touches You'. Cole died from a heroin overdose on 2 August 1972, aged 28.

COLE, Nat King   Singer born in Montgomery, Alabama, on 17 March 1917. He first found success with his own trio, before turning solo and receiving his first gold disc in 1948 for 'Nature Boy'. Throughout his career he was subject to racist attacks, but became a major artist with a formidable canon of hits, including 'Mona Lisa', 'Too Young', 'When I Fall In Love', 'Let There Be Love' and 'Those Lazy, Hazy Days Of Summer'. Cole died from cancer on 14 February 1966.

COLLINS, Albert   Noted American blues guitarist, known as the 'King Of The Telecaster'. He was born in Leona, Texas, on 3 October 1932 and died in Las Vegas, Nevada, from lung cancer in November 1993.

COLLINS, Allen   Lead guitarist with **Lynyrd Skynyrd**, born on 19 July 1952. Allen survived the air crash that killed Ronnie Van Zant and Cassie and Stevie Gaines. He teamed up with other colleagues from the band – Gary Rossington, Bill Powell and Leon Wilkinson – to form the Rossington Collins Band. They disbanded in 1982 and he continued with the Collins Band.

Collins was involved in a car accident in 1986 which left him paralysed from the waist down and he died from pneumonia on 23 January 1990.

Nat King Cole

COLLINS, Rob Keyboards player with the Charlatans, born in Manchester in 1967. He was also the group's main songwriter. The band were the recipients of five gold discs.

Collins was killed when he crashed his car in July 1996 after drinking more than twice the legal limit. The coroner said he was satisfied that alcohol was the cause of the accident. Collins had previously served four months in gaol for driving a getaway car during a bank robbery. He was 32 years old when he died.

CONNOLLY, Brian Lead singer with **Sweet**, born in Hamilton, Scotland, on 5 October 1949. Connolly was brought up in Scotland until his family moved to Middlesex when he was 12. He was 18 years old when he discovered he had been adopted. Years later, he also found out that actor Mark McManus, who starred in the Scottish police detective television series *Taggart*, was his half-brother.

Connolly, the father of two daughters and a son, was divorced from his wife Marilyn. In 1981 he suffered 14 heart attacks in 24 hours. After that he was a physical wreck. He died on 10 February 1997 in hospital in Slough, Berkshire, suffering from renal failure following another series of heart attacks.

COOKE, Mike British drummer, known as 'Cookie', who was a member of several bands from the 1960s to the 1990s, including Blue Rondos, Home and Groundhogs. He died on 7 February 1995.

COOKE, Sam Singer born on 22 January 1935 in Clarksdale, Mississippi, and raised in Chicago, Illinois. His father was a minister and encouraged his children to sing in church, with four of them, including Sam, calling themselves the Singing Children. In 1950 Sam became lead tenor with a gospel group called the Soul Stirrers.

He then turned solo and his brother Charles wrote a number, 'You Send Me', which Sam recorded. It became the first of a string of hits, which included 'Chain Gang', 'Cupid', 'Another Saturday Night' and 'Twistin' The Night Away'.

Mystery surrounds the death of the singer, who had been happily married since 1959 to his childhood sweetheart. He was a prominent black celebrity, who fought for black rights and was an icon among the black community. Therefore, when a motel manageress shot him and then cudgelled him to death at the Hacienda Motel in Los Angeles on 10 December 1964, a lot of questions remained unanswered. Although her reasons remained unclear, she made an assertion that he was trying to rape a girl. Despite no substantial evidence to prove it, the court verdict was 'justifiable homicide'.

Several posthumous hits were released, including 'Shake' and 'Wonderful World'.

CORDELL, Denny Record producer, born in Buenos Aires, Columbia, who produced the first albums and hit singles by the **Moody Blues**, **Procol Harum**, the **Move**, **Joe Cocker** and Tyrannosaurus Rex. After working for Island Records, he formed the Deram, Regal Zonophone and Fly labels. Cordell then moved to the US, where he formed the Shelter and Mango labels, then transferred to Ireland where he became a horse breeder. He also signed the Cranberries. Cordell died in Dublin from lymphoma in 1995. He was 51 years old.

COSTA, Don Music entrepreneur, born on 10 June 1925, who founded DCP Records (Don Costa Productions). Costa discovered Paul Anka and produced numerous major artists. He also had hits in his own right with 'Theme From The Unforgiven' and 'Never On Sunday'. Costa died on 19 January 1983.

COUNT BASIE One of the major figures in the world of jazz music, born William Basie in New Jersey on 21 August 1904. He became a band leader in 1935 and his big band were very influential, with many major artists working with them, including singer **Billie Holiday**. Count Basie died on 26 April 1994.

COWAP, Peter Vocalist and guitarist, born in Middleton, who formed the Country Gentlemen. Cowap was to back a number of artists on tour, including **Marty Wilde**, **Billy Fury** and Ike & Tina Turner. He replaced Peter Noone in **Herman's Hermits** in 1971 and recorded two singles with the band, before leaving the following year to form another outfit, the Grumble. Cowap later performed as a solo C&W artist. He died in August 1997 from pneumonia, aged 53.

CRANE, Vincent British singer-songwriter-musician, born Vincent Rodney Chessman on 21 May 1943. An original member of the **Crazy**

World Of Arthur Brown, Crane penned the group's chart-topper 'Fire'. He then formed Atomic Rooster and survived many line-up changes, before eventually disbanding the group and later joining Dexy's Midnight Runners. Crane committed suicide by taking an overdose of sleeping tablets while in a state of depression in February 1989.

CREED, Linda Philadelphia songwriter whose material was part of the 'Philly Sound'. A number of her compositions were written with Thom Bell and many of her songs were recorded by the Stylistics.

Following her death from cancer on 10 April 1986 at her home in Ambler, Philadelphia, 'The Greatest Love Of All', a number she wrote with Michael Masser, topped the US chart in a version by Whitney Houston.

CROCE, Jim Singer-songwriter born in Philadelphia on 10 January 1943. He and his wife Ingrid moved to New York as folk singers, releasing an album, Jim And Ingrid Croce, in 1969.

He later teamed up with guitarist Maury Mulheisen and had a series of hits, including: 'You Don't Mess Around With The Operator', 'One Less Set Of Footsteps', 'I've Got A Name', 'Time In A Bottle', 'I'll Have To Say I Love You In A Song' and 'Workin' At The Car Wash Blues'. His biggest hit was the chart-topper 'Bad Boy Leroy Brown'.

On 20 September 1973, Croce, Mulheisen and four others were killed when their charter plane crashed into a tree on take-off. Croce was 30 years old.

CRUDUP, Arthur 'Big Boy' Influential blues artist, born in Forest, Mississippi, on 24 August 1905. His recordings of his own songs 'That's Alright Mama', 'My Baby Left Me' and 'So Glad You're Mine' were all covered by Elvis Presley, but Crudup received no royalties whatsoever until very shortly before his death, in relative poverty, as the result of a stroke on 28 April 1974.

CUGAT, Xavier Popular band leader, born in Spain on 1 January 1900. He moved to Cuba, then the States, and was credited with introducing the rhumba to that country. Cugat's hits included 'The Lady In Red', 'Perfidia' and 'Brazil'. He died on 27 October 1990.

CURTIS, Ian Singer, born on 15 July 1956, who was lead vocalist with the post-punk band Joy Division, which was formed in 1976 as the Stiff Kittens, changed their name to Warsaw, then decided to call themselves Joy Division, the name of the concentration camp band in the novel House of Dolls. The group built up a following with releases such as the album Unknown Pleasure and singles 'Love Will Tear Us Apart' and 'Transmission'. Curtis, who suffered from epilepsy, hanged himself on 18 May 1980, aged 24, and the group changed their name to New Order.

CURTIS, King Famous session musician, born Curtis Ousley on 7 February 1934 in Fort Worth, Texas. He made his debut at New York's Apollo Theatre and moved to the Big Apple permanently when he was 20 years old. Known as the 'King Of The Tenor Saxophone', Curtis was a former member of the Coasters, and his hits with them included 'Charlie Brown', 'Yackety Yak', 'Poison Ivy' and 'The Chipmunks Song'. He also recorded for John Lennon on his Imagine album. The saxophonist was stabbed to death outside his New York apartment on 13 August 1971 in a fight with a Puerto Rican youth, Juan Montanez, who stood trial for his murder. Curtis was 37 years old.

CYMBAL, Johnny Musician-songwriter, born in Scotland on 3 February 1945 and raised in Canada, who recorded the hits 'Mr Bass Man' and 'Cinnamon' under the name Derek. He also produced the Partridge Family and David Cassidy. Cymbal died as the result of a heart attack in 1993.

DARIN, Bobby   Singer, born Walden Robert Cassotto in New York on 14 May 1936. His father died before he was born and his mother was so young that Bobby was told she was his sister and believed his grandmother was his actual mother until later in his life. One of his first records was a cover of Lonnie Donegan's 'Rock Island Line'.

Darin began his career as a teen idol with hits such as 'Splish Splash', 'Queen Of The Hop' and 'Dream Lover'. He then decided to widen his appeal, and among his 21 chart entries were: 'Mack The Knife', 'Beyond The Sea', 'Multiplication', 'Things', '18 Yellow Roses' and 'If I Were A Carpenter'.

Darin fell in love with Connie Francis and the two wanted to get married, but her father prevented it. He then married 1960s teen icon Sandra Dee and the two appeared in three films together. Darin proved to be a good actor and received an Oscar nomination for his performance in *Captain Newman, MD*.

Bobby and Sandra divorced and he married again, but it was to last just a few months. He also changed direction and began to sing folk songs.

Darin had suffered from ill health throughout his life and died during a heart operation on 20 December 1973. He was 37 years old.

DAVIES, Cyril   British blues harmonica player, born in 1932, who worked with Chris Barber's jazz band in the mid-1950s, together with **Alexis Korner**. The two left and founded Blues Incorporated, in which Davies was the main vocalist. He left the band to form the Cyril Davies All Stars in 1962. Davies died from leukaemia on 7 January 1964, aged 32.

DAVIS, Jesse Ed   Famous session guitarist who worked on albums for a host of artists ranging from the **Monkees** to **Rod Stewart**. He also appeared on *The Concert For Bangladesh*. Davis died from a drugs overdose in Venice, California, on 22 June 1988. He was 43 years old.

DAVIS, Rev 'Blind' Gary   Blind blues and gospel performer born on 30 April 1896, who spent much of his early life as a street singer in South Carolina. He achieved fame after appearing at the Newport Jazz Festival in 1964. Davis died as the result of a heart attack in New Jersey on 5 May 1972.

DAVIS Jnr, Sammy   Singer born into a vaudeville family in New York on 8 December 1925 who made his professional debut at the age of two. His hits included 'What Kind Of Fool Am I' and 'As Long As He Needs Me'. Sammy's biggest hit was the chart-topper 'Candy Man' in 1972. He died from throat cancer in May 1990.

DAY, Bobby   Texas-born musician (real name Robert James Byrd Jnr) who reached No 2 in the chart with 'Rockin' Robin'. Bobby, who formed the Hollywood Flames, was the first artist to record 'Little Bitty Pretty One', which later became a hit for Thurston Harris and **Clyde McPhatter**. The flipside of Day's 'Rockin' Robin' was 'Over And Over', which later became a hit for Thurston Harris and the **Dave Clark Five**. He died from cancer in 1990, aged 60.

DE FREITAS, Peter   Drummer with **Echo & the Bunnymen**, a Liverpool band originally formed in 1977. De Freitas, who was born in Port of Spain, Trinidad, on 2 August 1961, joined the Bunnymen in September 1979. He was killed in a traffic accident on 15 June 1989, aged 27.

DENNY, Sandy   Folk singer, born on 6 January 1941, who left the **Strawbs** to join Fairport Convention in July 1968 and remained with the group until January 1976. Sandy turned solo and released an album, *Rendezvous*. She died from a brain haemorrhage following a fall down a flight of stairs on 21 April 1978. She was 37 years old.

DENVER, John   Singer-songwriter, born Henry John Deutschendorf in Roswell, New Mexico, on 31 December 1943. He adopted the name Denver after his favourite city. John was initially interested in folk music and in 1965 joined the folk group the Chad Mitchell Trio. Later he was to turn to country music and had more than 15 hits, including: 'Take Me Home, Country Roads', 'Rocky Mountain High', 'Sunshine On My Shoulders' and 'Annie's Song'. The latter was written for his first wife, Ann Martell, whom he married in 1967. His records were to bring him 11 gold albums and five platinum discs.

Later in his life, the Denver clean-cut image was tarnished by revelations that he went on a rampage with a chainsaw when not quite so besotted with Annie, and that some of his songs were written under the influence of drugs. He married again and penned an autobiography,

Take Me Home. His last concert in the UK was in March 1997.

John Denver was killed on 12 October 1977 when his light aircraft crashed off the coast of California.

DEWITT, Lew Member of the Statler Brothers, a gospel/country band from Virginia. The group's biggest hit was 'Flowers On The Wall', which reached No 4 in the chart in 1965. DeWitt died in 1990. He was 53 years old.

DIMWIT Drummer (real name Ken Montgomery) from Vancouver who played with a variety of bands including the Subhumans, DOA, Pointed Sticks, the Moderaires and the Four Horsemen. He was one of a large group of people, reputed to be 220 in number, who overdosed on China White in Vancouver in 1994.

DINGLEY, Nicholas 'Razzle' Drummer born on the Isle of Wight, who played with American band Hanoi Rocks and died in a car crash in California on 8 December 1984. The car, a Ford Pantera sports model, was driven by Vince Neil, lead singer with **Motley Crue**. Two other people were also injured and Neil was jailed, fined and sentenced to community work. Dingley was 24 years old when he died.

DINNING, Mark Singer born on 17 August 1933 who first hit the charts with 'Teen Angel'. His other hits included 'A Star Is Born', 'Lovin' Touch' and 'Top 40, News, Weather & Sport'. Dinning died at home as the result of a heart attack on 23 March 1986.

DONNER, Ral American singer, born on 10 February 1943. He was known as the 'Chicago Elvis' and was Elvis' voice in the film *This Is Elvis*. Ral's hits included: 'Girl Of My Best Friend', 'You Don't Know What You've Got (Until You Lose It)', 'Please Don't Go' and 'She's Everything'. He died from cancer on 6 April 1984.

DORSEY, Lee Singer, born in New Orleans on 24 December 1924, and a former professional boxer who fought under the name Kid Chocolate. Dorsey had his first hit, 'Do Re Me' in 1962. He also had five chart entries, including 'Ya Ya', 'Ride Your Pony' and 'Working In The Coal Mine'. He died from emphysema on 1 December 1986.

DOUGLAS, Steve Session saxophonist (real name Steve Kreisman) who originally backed **Ritchie Valens**, then Duane Eddy. He appeared on a number of Phil Spector hits and several by the **Beach Boys** and Jan & Dean. Steve also played on sessions for **Elvis Presley**, **Dion**, Frank Sinatra and many others, and toured with **Bob Dylan**, Eric Clapton and John Fogerty. He died from heart failure during a recording session for a Ry Cooder album. He was 55 years old.

DRAKE, Nick British folk singer-guitarist, born in Burma on 18 June 1948. He returned to England with his parents when he was five years old. After attending Marlborough public school, Drake became interested in music and began recording in 1968. Three albums established his reputation: *Five Leaves Left*, *Bryter Layter* and *Pink Moon*.

Drake suffered a nervous breakdown in April 1972 and was hospitalized. He died in bed at his home in Tamworth, Staffordshire, from an overdose of prescribed antidepressants on 25 October 1974, aged 26. He retains a significant cult following.

DRUMMOND, Don The Jamaican trombone player with the Skatellites, a group of session musicians who formed the band in June 1964. They were noted for numbers such as 'Guns of Navarone' and backed many Jamaican artists in the recording studios. Drummond died on 21 March 1971 in Kingston's Bellevue Mental Hospital after being incarcerated there for murdering his common-law wife.

DYSON, Ronnie Singer from Washington, DC, who appeared in the stage musical *Hair*. He had a big chart hit with 'If You Let Me Make Love To You' and several entries in the R&B chart. Dyson died from the effects of drugs use in 1991. He was 40 years old.

EASY-E Rap artist (real name Eric Wright) who was born in Compton, California. Easy-E was a member of the gangsta rap group NWA with Ice Cube and Dr Dre. He died from an AIDS-related illness in 1995, aged 31.

ECKSTINE, Billy Singer and orchestra leader, born William Clarence Eckstein on 8 July 1914. He began singing with the Earl Hines band in 1939 and charted with 'Stormy Monday Blues' in 1943. For a time Eckstine led his own band, and then turned solo in 1945. His hits included: 'A Cottage For Sale', 'Prisoner Of Love', 'My Foolish Heart' and 'I Apologize'. Eckstine died on 8 March 1993.

EDMONTON, Jerry Drummer with Toronto-based band Sparrow, who then joined **Steppenwolf** and had 13 chart records during his time as a member. His brother Dennis, also known as Mars Bonfire, penned 'Born To Be Wild'. Jerry died in 1993 in a car crash near Santa Barbara.

EDWARDS, Bernard Musician-producer born in 1952 who, together with partner Nile Rogers, created the disco group Chic. They had a string of hits, including 'Dance, Dance, Dance', 'Le Freak' and 'Good Times'. As a producer, Bernard worked with Robert Palmer, the Power Station and **Rod Stewart**. While Chic was touring Japan in 1996, Rogers found his partner dead in his hotel room.

EDWARDS, Tommy Singer born in Richmond, Virginia, on 17 February 1922, whose hits included the popular 'Morning Side Of The Mountain' and 'It's All In The Game', both of which charted in 1951. Other hits were: 'Love Is All We Need', 'Please Mr Sun', 'My Melancholy Baby' and 'I Really Don't Want To Know'. When Edwards' career seemed to be slipping, 'It's All In The Game' was re-released and topped the chart in 1958. He died on 23 October 1969.

ELLIOTT, Cass Singer, born Ellen Naomi Cohen in Baltimore, Maryland, on 19 September 1941. She eschewed her parents' plans for her to be educated at an important girl's college and moved to New York to enter showbusiness, joining a folk outfit called the Big Three. She then began singing with the Mugwumps.

John Phillips approached Cass to join the Mamas & Papas in 1965 and they had their first hit with 'California Dreamin'' the following year. Other hits, such as 'Monday Monday', 'Words Of Love' and 'Dedicated To The One I Love' followed. More familiarly known as Mama Cass, the rotund singer did not seem unduly worried about her weight, commenting that she'd never be mistaken for Jane Fonda. When the Mamas & Papas disbanded, she embarked on a solo career in 1968, with records such as 'Dream A Little Dream Of Me'. She appeared frequently on television and had an acting role in the series *Pufnstuf*. In the 1970s she began to work with English musician Dave Mason and they issued an album, *Dave Mason And Cass Elliott*.

In her personal life, Cass became addicted to drugs, was often heavily in debt and got married for the second time in 1971 – to a German baron.

Cass Elliott died alone in a London flat after choking on a sandwich and inhaling vomit on 29 July 1974, with the pathologist stating the cause of death as a heart attack. She was 31 years old.

An album, *Don't Call Me Mama Any More*, was issued posthumously.

ELLISON, Jim Guitarist from Chicago who was the front man for Material Issue, who began recording in 1987. They had three albums issued on Mercury. Ellison killed himself with carbon monoxide in 1996. He was 31 years old.

EPSTEIN, Brian Manager of the Beatles, born in Liverpool on 19 September 1934. Brian discovered the group in 1961 when he began contributing record reviews to the local music paper **Mersey Beat**, which he stocked in his family music store, Nems. He signed the Beatles, created Nems Enterprises and also went on to manage a host of other artists including **Gerry & the Pacemakers**, Cilla Black, **Billy J. Kramer & the Dakotas**, the **Fourmost** and Tommy Quickly & the Remo Four. Many people, including **Colonel Tom Parker**, believed he should have stuck to managing just the Beatles, and he was to be unsuccessful with a number of the acts he personally signed such as the Rusticks, the Silkie and Michael Haslam. He also suffered financial losses when he bought the Saville Theatre in London's West End to promote rock shows.

Brian Epstein (right) with Billy J Kramer

Epstein's autobiography, *A Cellarful Of Noise*, ghosted by Derek Taylor, was published in 1964. He also desired a high profile for himself, appearing on numerous UK television and radio shows ranging from *Juke Box Jury* to *Desert Island Discs*. At one time he even hosted a US television show, *Hullabaloo*.

Epstein was troubled by his homosexuality and became increasingly addicted to drugs, resulting in his death from an accidental overdose on 25 August 1967. He was 32 years old.

EVANS, Mal   Road manager with the Beatles, who died in his forties. After the group broke up, Mal left his wife and son and moved to California, settling in with a new girlfriend, Fran Hughes. On 5 January 1976 she telephoned the police, saying: 'My old man has a gun and has taken Valium and is totally screwed up.' When they arrived, the police saw that he had a rifle in his hands and fired six shots, four of them hitting Mal and killing him instantly. The rifle was not loaded.

EVANS, Tom   Bass guitarist and vocalist with Badfinger. Born in Liverpool on 21 June 1947, he originally backed Liverpool singer **David Garrick** before joining the Iveys. They changed their name to Badfinger and were the second most successful act after the Beatles on the Apple label.

Badfinger's biggest hit was the Paul McCartney-penned 'Come And Get It'. Evans co-wrote 'Without You', a million-seller and No

1 hit for **Harry Nilsson**. Plagued by financial troubles and a lengthy and unsuccessful battle to receive his fair royalty for 'Without You', he hanged himself in 1983. He was 36 years old.

EVERETT, Kenny   British disc jockey and television personality, born Maurice James Christopher Cole in Liverpool. His career began on the pirate ship Radio London and in 1967 he joined Radio 1. The BBC sacked him over a controversial remark he made and he joined Capital Radio. His *Kenny Everett Video Show*, which he launched in 1978, was an inspiration for MTV. His autobiography, *The Custard Stops At Hatfield*, was published in 1982.

The madcap Kenny, who came out of the closet to admit that he was gay, suffered from AIDS and died in 1995. He was 50 years old.

FAITH, Percy Orchestra leader born in Toronto, Canada, on 7 April 1908. He had major hits with the theme tunes from the films *Moulin Rouge* and *A Summer Place*. Faith died in Los Angeles on 9 February 1976.

FARINA, Richard Folk singer-songwriter, born in 1937. Farina penned songs such as 'Pack Up Your Troubles' and 'Hard Lovin' Loser', and married Joan Baez' younger sister Mimi. It was during the launch party for his novel *Been Down So Long It Looks Up To Me* on 30 April 1966 that he took a ride on his motorbike and was killed in a road accident. He was 29 years old.

FARNDON, Pete American bass guitarist born on 12 June 1952, who originally played with the Bushwackers, an Australian band. He became a founder member of the **Pretenders** in 1972 but drugs problems led to him being replaced by Malcolm Foster four years later. Farndon was found dead in his bath in his London home on 16 April 1983. He was 30 years old.

FARRELL, Wes Composer (real name Wes Fogel) who was born in the Bronx. He co-wrote 'Hang On Sloopy' with Bert Berns. Farrell's other hits included 'Boys' and he produced several groups, including the Cowsills and Every Mother's Son. He also wrote the music for the Partridge Family. Farrell died from cancer in 1996. He was 56 years old.

FILAZ, Yafu Member of the rap group Outlaw Immortalz, who was shot in the head in New Jersey in November 1996.

FITZGERALD, Ella Legendary jazz singer born in Newport News, Virginia, on 25 April 1918. During her career she had 90 hit records, including the smash 'Mack The Knife' and her cover of the Beatles' 'Can't Buy Me Love'.

Ella had begun her career as a teenager, singing with Chick Webb's band. She was also to record with **Louis Armstrong**. Her reputation grew from 1956, when she recorded two volumes of Cole Porter songs and began a series of 'songbook' albums, dedicated to the work of leading American songwriters such as Cole Porter, Irving Berlin and Rogers & Hart.

Ella Fitzgerald died in 1996.

FOGERTY, Tom Singer born in Berkeley, California, on 9 November 1941. Tom began his career with brother John as lead singer with the Blue Velvets, formed in 1959. They changed their name to the Golliwogs and recorded seven singles. By 1968 the group had changed their name to **Creedence Clearwater Revival**. Tom quit in 1971 and the group disbanded the following year. Tom recorded five solo albums and two LPs with the group Ruby. He died from tuberculosis in 1990.

FOLEY, Red Country music singer, born Clyde Julian Foley on 17 June 1910, who hosted the television show *Ozark Jubilee*. Foley had the chart-topper 'Chattanoogie Shoe Shine Boy' in 1950 and his other hits included 'Smoke On The Water' and 'Dancing Pig'. He was **Pat Boone's** father-in-law. Foley died on 19 September 1968.

FORD, Clarence Saxophonist who played alto or baritone with **Fats Domino** from the early 1950s until 1970, appearing on a total of 66 of Domino's hits. He died in 1995, aged 64.

FORD, Mary American singer, born Colleen Summer in Pasadena, California, on 7 July 1928. Mary met guitarist **Les Paul** in the 1940s and they began recording together as a duo. When they married they had a series of million-sellers, including: 'Mockin' Bird Hill', 'How High The Moon', 'The World Is Waiting For The Sunrise' and 'Vaya Con Dios'. They divorced in 1963 and Mary died on 30 September 1977.

FORD, Tennessee Ernie Singer, born Ernest Jennings in Bristol, Tennessee, on 13 February 1919. He first became a recording artist in 1948. After recording 'I'll Never Be Free' and 'Nobody's Business' with **Kay Starr**, he had his first solo hit in 1955 with 'Sixteen Tons'. Other hits included 'Mule Train' and 'Shotgun Boogie'. Ford recorded more than 80 albums and had his own television show, which he hosted from 1956 to 1961. He then turned to gospel music. Ford died on 17 October 1991.

FOXX, Charlie R&B singer, born in Greeensboro, North Carolina on 9 September 1939. He teamed up with his sister Inez in an act called Charles & Inez Foxx and they had an American top ten hit with 'Mockingbird' in 1963. The record did not enter the British charts until 1969. Other hits included 'I Stand Accused' and '(1-2-3-4-5-6-7) Count The Days'. Charlie died on 18 September 1998.

FRANÇOISE, CLAUDE   Major French pop singer of the 1960s, who died in Paris in March 1978. At one point it seemed as if he would have success in the UK chart following his entry with 'Tears On The Telephone' in 1976. Françoise accidentally electrocuted himself when changing a light bulb while having a bath. He was 39 years old.

FRANKLIN, Carolyn   Singer-songwriter, sister of soul singer Aretha Franklin. Carolyn penned two of Aretha's biggest hits, 'Ain't No Way' and 'Angel'. She was a singer in her own right and recorded several albums. Together with her other sister, Emma, she sang on Aretha's 1987 album *One Lord, One Faith, One Baptism*. Carolyn died on 25 April 1988 in Bloomfield Hills, Michigan, aged 43.

FRANKLIN, Melvin   Alabama-born singer, a founder member of the Temptations. He provided the bass voice in the group from its formation in 1960. Following the deaths of **Paul Williams** in 1973, **Dave Ruffin** in 1991 and **Eddie Kendricks** in 1992, Franklin was the only surviving member, but died from heart failure on 23 February 1995 at Cedars-Sinai Medical Centre in Los Angeles. He was 52 years old.

FREED, Alan   Famous American disc jockey, born on 15 December 1922. It was he who created the term 'rock 'n' roll'. As a disc jockey, he popularized the music on his show *Moondog's Rock 'n' Roll Party*, on which he played black R&B records that appealed to his young white audience. Freed's career was destroyed by accusations that he received payola. He was reduced to penury, became a chronic alcoholic and died from uraemia on 20 January 1965. A film biopic, *American Hot Wax*, was released in 1978 with Tim McIntyre portraying Freed.

FULLER, Bobby   Lead singer-guitarist with the Bobby Fuller Four, a rock band from El Paso, Texas, born on 22 October 1943. The group's biggest hit was 'I Fought The Law'. Fuller was found dead in his car on 18 July 1966. He was 22 years old.

FURY, Billy   The first Liverpool rock 'n' roll star, born Ronald Wycherley on 17 April 1941. He approached impresario **Larry Parnes** during the latter's visit to Merseyside, was signed to his stable and was given the name Billy Fury. At one time the Beatles attended an audition to become Fury's backing band, but weren't chosen. His hits included: 'Colette', 'Wondrous Place', 'Halfway To Paradise' and 'I Will', and he starred in the films *Play It Cool* and *I've Gotta Horse*.

Fury had been plagued by illnesses since he was a child, and rheumatic fever had left him with a damaged heart. He retired due to ill health in 1967.

Fury was attempting a comeback when he died from heart failure on 28 January 1983. He had recently entered the charts with 'Devil Or Angel'.

  Billy Fury

GAINSBOURG, Serge The French singer-songwriter, born on 2 April 1929, who originally penned the number 'Je T'Aime' for Brigitte Bardot. He then recorded it with British actress Jane Birkin in 1969. The record became an international hit and caused a great deal of controversy because of its sexual nature. The two then lived together for a number of years. Gainsbourg died on 2 March 1991.

GALLAGHER, Rory Guitarist born in Ballyshannon, Eire, on 2 March 1949. Gallagher came to prominence with his trio Taste in 1968. Following success with albums such as *Taste* and *On The Boards*, there were internal disputes within the band and they broke up in October 1970. Gallagher then turned solo. He died following a liver transplant in June 1995. He was 46 years old.

GANSER, Marge Singer (real name Marguerite Dorste) from Queens, New York, who was a member of the Shangri-Las. They had six chart hits, including the chart-topper 'Leader Of The Pack'. Marge died from an accidental drugs overdose in 1976, in her late twenties. Her identical twin sister **Mary Ann Ganser** had died in 1971.

GANSER, Mary Ann Singer with the Shangri-Las, a female singing quartet formed in New York in 1964. The other members were Mary Ann's twin sister **Marge Ganser** and the sisters Mary and Betty Weiss. They made their chart debut with 'Remember (Walkin' In The Sand)', followed by 'Leader Of The Pack', 'Give Him A Great Big Kiss', 'Give Us Your Blessings', 'I Can Never Go Home Anymore' and 'Long Live Our Love'. Mary died from encephalitis in 1971.

GARCIA, Frankie Singer from Los Angeles who was the 'Cannibal' in Cannibal & the Headhunters, a band which had a hit with 'Land Of 1,000 Dances' in 1965. That same year, the group toured the States with the Beatles. Garcia died in 1996.

GARCIA, Jerry Leader and founder member of the Grateful Dead, born Jerome John Garcia in San Francisco on 1 August 1942. He originally formed Mother McCree's Uptown Jug Champions in 1963, which changed to the Warlocks in 1965 and became the Grateful Dead later that same year. Known as Captain Trips, Garcia built up his group until they developed a large following which lasted for over three decades. They were known as 'Deadheads'. The group appeared at major festivals such as the Monterey Jazz Festival and Woodstock, and had a series of record hits. They almost disbanded in the 1980s due to Garcia's heroin addiction, but he joined a drugs diversion programme and the group continued to record and perform until he died in his sleep on 8 August 1995.

GARDINER, Paul Former bass player with **Gary Numan**, who died from a heroin overdose in 1984. That same year, Numan launched his own label Numa Records and the first release was Gardiner's 'Venus In Furs'.

GARDNER, Ron Sax player who also sang with the Wailers, a band from the north-west US who recorded numbers such as 'Out Of Our Tree'. Gardner died in a fire in Tacoma in 1992, at the age of 45.

Jerry Garcia

GARNES, Sherman Bass singer with **Frankie Lymon** & the Teenagers, born on 8 June 1940 in New York. He died in prison in 1977, aged 37.

GATTON, Danny Guitarist from Newburg, MD, who began his career in a local band at the age of 14. Gatton played with **Roger Miller** and Robert Gordon and recorded for numerous indie labels. He shot himself in 1994 at the age of 49.

GAYE, Marvin Major Motown artist, born Marvin Penz Gay in Washington, DC, on 2 April 1939. He joined the US Air Force, but was incompatible and was given an honorable discharge after one year. He then joined the Marquees vocal group, followed by Harvey Fuqua & the Moonglows. When they disbanded in 1960, Marvin went to Detroit and acted as a session musician at Motown. He married Berry Gordy's sister, Anna, who was 17 years his senior, and she encouraged him to become a solo singer. He added an 'e' to his surname and made his recording debut with 'Let Your Conscience Be Your Guide'.

Marvin had 28 chart hits, including: 'Stubborn Kind Of Fellow', 'Pride and Joy', 'How Sweet It Is To Be Loved By You', 'I Heard It Through The Grapevine' and 'Sexual Healing'. He also had a number of successful singles duetting with **Tammi Terrell**. When she died in 1970 he became depressed and could not work, and his marriage broke down due to his wife's infidelity. He fell in love with Janis Hunter, who was 17 years his junior. Anna sued for divorce and he married Janis, but she also left him. Marvin was plagued with financial troubles and became a drug addict. When the tax authorities pursued him for two million dollars, he fled to Hawaii.

On his return home Marvin had an argument with his father, a Pentecostal minister, who used to beat him as a child. On 1 April 1984, his father shot him once in the heart and once in the shoulder, and left him to bleed to death.

GEORGE, Lowell Guitarist leader of **Little Feat** and former member of the Mothers Of Invention, born on 13 April 1945. George was a member of the Standells and the Seeds, before joining the Mothers Of Invention. **Frank Zappa** encouraged him to form his own band and he founded Little Feat in 1970; they made their record debut with 'Strawberry Flats'. The band broke up in 1973 and re-formed the following year. Lowell died as the result of a heart attack brought on by drug abuse, on 29 June 1979. He was 34 years old.

GEORGE, Samuel Lead singer-drummer with American band the Capitols, whose Top 10 hit in 1966 was 'Cool Jerk'. He was stabbed to death on 17 March 1982, aged 40.

GIBB, Andy Youngest of the Gibb brothers, born in Manchester on 5 March 1958. Andy's siblings had established themselves as the **Bee Gees** and in the late 1970s Andy approached Robert Stigwood and signed to RSO Records, having massive hits with 'I Just Want To Be Your Everything', '(Love Is) Thicker Than Water' and 'Shadow Dancing'.

Andy began a romance with Victoria Principal, beautiful star of the hit television series *Dallas*, but his addiction to cocaine was a principal cause of their split. He tried to get to grips with the addiction and entered the Betty Ford Clinic, then joined his brothers in Florida. He was in the UK when he succumbed to a viral infection and died as the result of a heart attack in an Oxfordshire hospital on 11 March 1988. He was 30 years old.

The Bee Gees' 1989 album *Ordinary Lives* was dedicated to Andy.

GILMORE, John Tenor sax player from Summit, Mississippi, who was a member of Solar Arkestra from 1953. When Sun Ra died in 1993, Gilmore took over the group. He died in 1996, aged 63.

GODCHAUX, Keith Keyboards player, born 14 July 1948, who replaced Ron 'Pigpen' McKernan as a member of the Grateful Dead in 1971.

His wife Donna joined him, although they were forced to leave the group in 1979. Godchaux died in a car crash in Marin County on 23 July 1980, aged 32. Donna became Donna MacKay and established herself as a singer of Christian music.

GODFREY, Kevin Paul Drummer-pianist, born in 1959, who was also known as Epic Soundtracks. He joined various bands, including Swell Maps, who disbanded in 1980. He next joined Crime & the City Solution and then left them to form These Immortal Souls. Godfrey died on 6 November 1997, aged 38.

GOETTEL, Dwayne Keyboards player from Alberta, Canada, who was a member of Vancouver band Skinny Puppy from 1985. He recorded the band's ninth album with them in 1995, the year that he died after overdosing on heroin. Goettel was 31 years old.

GOINS, Glen Former vocalist and lead guitarist with Bootsy Collins' Parliament-Funkadelic Set-Up. Goins died from complications caused by Parkinson's Disease on 30 July 1978. At the time he was producing a new group, Quazar, and leading his own band, Mutiny. He was 24 years old.

GOODSON, Ronnie Singer with Ronnie & the Hi-Lites, whose only hit was 'I Wish That We Were Married', in 1962. He died on 4 November 1980, at the age of 33.

GRANT, Earl Singer-keyboards player whose big hit was 'The End'. Earl died on 10 June 1970, at the age of 39.

GRANT, Peter Former British road manager to **Gene Vincent** and **Chuck Berry**, who managed the **New Vaudeville Band** before becoming manager to Led Zeppelin and leading them to success with legendary management techniques, which were sometimes of a strong-arm nature. The group's career ended following the death of drummer **John Bonham** and Grant went into semi-retirement with heart and drugs problems. He died at his home in Sussex on 21 November 1995, aged 60.

GRASCOCK, John Former bass player with **Jethro Tull**. Grascock left the group following heart surgery and died soon afterwards, on 17 November 1979. He was 27 years old.

GRECH, Rick Singer-bass guitarist, born in France on 1 November 1946. Grech played bass, electric violin and cello with **Family** and recorded two albums with them, before leaving in 1968 to join **Blind Faith**. He then joined Ginger Baker's Airforce before re-forming Traffic. Grech then moved to the States and did session work with the Crickets and KGB. His only solo album, *The Last Five Years*, was released in 1973. He died on 17 March 1990.

GREENBERG, Florence Female record impresario born in Passaic, New Jersey. Florence ran the Scepter and Wand labels, discovered the **Shirelles** and released many hits by artists such as **Dionne Warwick**, the Kingsmen, and the Isley Brothers. She also penned the Shirelles' hit 'Soldier Boy'. Florence died in 1996, aged 82.

GREENE, Lorne American actor, born in 1914, who starred in the television cowboy series *Bonanza*. He recorded an album, tied in with the series, called *Welcome To The Ponderosa*. One of the tracks, 'Ringo', about the notorious gunslinger Johnny Ringo, was issued as a single and topped the US chart. Greene died on 11 September 1987 after developing pneumonia following an operation for a perforated ulcer, shortly before he was to appear in a spin-off movie, *Bonanza: The Next Generation*.

GROSSMAN, Albert Major American manager whose clients included **Bob Dylan**, Joan Baez, **Janis Joplin**, **Peter, Paul & Mary**, Gordon Lightfoot, Ritchie Havens and the Electric Flag. Grossman died on a flight to the MIDEM Conference, an annual music festival, in Cannes on 25 January 1986.

GUNTER, Arthur Louisiana bluesman, best known for his Excello record of his own song 'Baby Let's Play House', which was covered by **Elvis Presley**. He died on 16 March 1976, at the age of 50.

GUTHRIE, Woody Major American folk artist, born Woodrow Wilson Guthrie in Okemah, Oklahoma, on 16 April 1912. He was to influence most of the prominent folk artists of the 1960s, including **Bob Dylan**, Joan Baez, **Phil Ochs** and **Pete Seeger**. One of his more popular hits was 'This Land Is Your Land'. Woody died from Huntington's Chorea in 1967. David Carradine starred in the film biopic of his life, *Bound For Glory*, in 1976. Woody's son Arlo also became a folk singer.

HALEY, Bill   Singer born in Detroit, Michigan, on 6 July 1925. With his group the Comets he produced some of the earliest rock 'n' roll hits, beginning with 'Rock Around The Clock' in 1954. Other hits followed, including 'Razzle Dazzle', 'See You Later, Alligator' and 'Rockin' Through The Rye'. Haley continued to tour internationally through the 1960s and 1970s, although he was ill for much of the latter decade. He had to cancel a proposed tour of the UK in 1980 through illness and died as the result of a heart attack on 9 February 1980 in Harlington, Texas – as commemorated in the Tom Russell-Dave Alvin song 'Haley's Comet'.

HAM, Pete   Guitarist-pianist-vocalist with Badfinger, born in Swansea, South Wales, on 27 April 1947. Formerly the Iveys, the group were dubbed Badfinger by Paul McCartney, who wrote their first hit, 'Come And Get It', which was the theme tune for the film *The Magic Christian*. After they left Apple Records, the band suffered financial difficulties and Ham hanged himself on 23 April 1975, at the age of 28.

HAMILTON, Dean   Musician-songwriter-session man, who was a member of the T Bones when they had a major hit with 'No Matter What Shape' in 1965. Dean was also a member of Hamilton, Joe Frank & Reynolds, who had three chart entries with 'Don't Pull Your Love', 'Fallin' In Love' and 'Winners And Losers'. He died in 1995, aged 48.

HAMILTON, Roy   R&B/gospel singer, born in Leesburg, Georgia, on 16 April 1929. He reached No 1 in the R&B chart with 'You'll Never Walk Alone' and also had chart entries with 'You're Gonna Need Magic', 'Unchained Melody', 'Don't Let Go' and 'You Can Have Her'. Hamilton contracted tubercular pneumonia in 1956, spent nine months in hospital and was unable to sing for two years. He died as the result of a stroke on 20 July 1969.

HARDIN, Tim   Singer-songwriter, who was born in Eugene, Oregon, on 23 December 1941. Tim was a descendant of the notorious gunfighter, John Wesley Hardin. On leaving the US Marines, he began singing in folk clubs and his recording career started in 1964. Many artists, including **Bobby Darin** and **Rod Stewart**, were to cover the numbers he featured on his albums, which included 'Misty Roses', 'Reason To Believe' and 'If I Were A Carpenter'. Ironically, the only chart hit he had in his own right was penned by Bobby Darin – 'Sing A Simple Song Of Freedom'. Hardin was plagued by drug and alcohol problems and died in Hollywood from a drugs overdose on 29 December 1980.

HARPO, Slim Bluesman (real name James Moore), born 11 January 1924, who was originally known as Harmonica Slim. Noted for his Excello recordings of numbers such as 'King Bee' and his chart hits 'Rainin' In My Heart' and 'Baby Scratch My Back', he died as the result of a heart attack on 31 January 1970.

HARRIS, Adie Singer, born in New Jersey on 22 January 1940. Adie became a member of the vocal quartet the **Shirelles**, while she was still at school. The group made their recording debut in 1958 and they had a dozen chart singles in the US. Adie collapsed and died as the result of a heart attack on 10 June 1982.

HARRISON, Wilbert Musician born in Charlotte, North Carolina, on 6 January 1929. His major hits included 'Kansas City' and 'Let's Work Together'. Harrison toured as a one-man band and also with Creedence Clearwater in 1969. He died as the result of a stroke in 1995.

HARTMAN, Dan Musician born in Harrisburg, Pennsylvania, who was a member of the Edgar Winter Group from 1972 to 1976. After he left the band he had four solo chart hits, including 'Instant Replay', 'I Can Dream About You' and 'We Are Young', in addition to writing or performing hit songs for the films *Streets Of Fire*, *Flashdance* and *Rocky IV*. He also produced Tina Turner's album *Foreign Affair*. Hartman died on 22 March 1994 at his home in Bridgeport, Connecticut, from an AIDS-related illness. He was 43 years old.

HARVEY, Alex Leader of the Sensational Alex Harvey Band, born in Glasgow, Scotland, on 5 February 1935. He first became a musician in 1955 and formed Alex Harvey's Soul Band. In 1963 he performed in Hamburg, Germany, and then moved on to London where he formed various bands. He founded the Sensational Alex Harvey Band, which became a major attraction in the 1970s, although he disbanded the group and embarked on a solo career in 1977. Harvey died as the result of a heart attack on 4 February 1982.

HARVEY, Les Younger brother of **Alex Harvey**, born in 1947. He formed Power with his girl-friend Maggie Bell; they changed their name to Stone The Crows and were managed by **Peter Grant**. Les was lead guitarist with the group. He was electrocuted on stage at the Top Rank in Swansea on 3 May 1972 and the group then broke up. Les was 25 years old.

HARVEY, Rick Blues guitarist who performed with numerous artists, including Sam The Sham & the Pharoahs, Little Milton, B.B. King and **Albert King**. Harvey died in 1993, aged 43.

HARVEY, Tony British guitarist, a former member of Nero & the Gladiators and Vince Taylor's Playboys. Harvey died from cancer in 1993.

HATHAWAY, Donny Singer, born on 1 October 1945, who charted with three records on which he duetted with Roberta Flack – 'You've Got A Friend', 'Where Is The Love' and 'The Closer I Get To You.' Hathaway plummeted to his death from the fifteenth-floor window of a hotel in New York on 13 January 1979. He had been recording further material with Roberta, which was to be released the following year. He was 33 years old.

HAWKINS, Hawkshaw Country music singer, born Harold F. Hawkins in Huntingdon, West Virginia, on 22 December 1921. Hawkshaw was killed along with **Patsy Cline** and Cowboy Copas in an air crash on 5 March 1962. His 'Lonesome 7-7203' was a posthumous chart-topper.

HAWKINS, Ted Acoustic guitarist-street ballad singer born in Lakeshore, Mississippi, who found himself a cult following in the UK after the release of two of his albums there. A new album on the Geffen label was issued in 1994, shortly before his death as the result of a stroke. Hawkins had had an amazing life, travelling in boxcars and spending time in a number of prisons, and a film biopic is being mooted.

HAYNES, Henry D. Guitarist born on 27 July 1918, the Homer of Homer & Jethro, who had a US hit in 1959 with 'The Battle Of Kookamonga', a parody of 'The Battle Of New Orleans'. His partner Jethro's real name was Kenneth C. Burns. The duo first teamed up in 1932. Haynes died as the result of a heart attack on 7 August 1971.

HAYS, Lee Folk artist born in Little Rock, Arkansas, in 1914. With **Pete Seeger**, Ronnie Gilbert and Fred Helermane, he was co-founder in 1949 of folk group the Weavers. They became the States' major folk attraction, with hits such as 'Goodnight Irene' and 'On Top Of Old Smokey', before they broke up in 1952. The group reunited in 1955 to have hits with several other folk tunes, including 'Kisses Sweeter Than Wine', 'Rock Island Line', 'Wimoweh' and 'Guantanamera'. They held their farewell performance at the Orchestral Hall, Chicago, on 29 November 1963. Hays died as the result of a heart attack on 26 August 1981.

HAZEL, Eddie Brooklyn guitarist who played in bands such as George Clinton's Parliament and Funkadelic. He went on to work for Motown records and penned songs under the pseudonym G. Cook. Hazel's most noted track was 'Maggot Brain'. He died in 1992, aged 42.

HIEROWSKI, Zenon de Fleur Guitarist with the group Count Bishops, who died as the result of a heart attack on 17 March 1979. He was 28 years old.

HENDRIX, Jimi World-famous guitarist, born James Marshall Hendrix in Seattle, Washington, on 27 November 1942. Jimi enlisted as a paratrooper but was discharged due to a back injury.

Jimi Hendrix

238

The youth was left-handed, but taught himself to play guitar upside down. On leaving the service, he became a backing musician for numerous artists including Little Richard, **Sam Cooke**, B.B. King and the Isley Brothers.

Hendrix moved to New York, where he formed his own band, Jimmy James & the Blue Flames. In 1966 he was discovered playing in New York's Café Wha by Chas Chandler of the **Animals**, who became his manager, took him to London and teamed him with Mitch Mitchell and Noel Redding to form the Jimi Hendrix Experience. He began to make an impact with records such as 'Hey Joe' and 'Purple Haze', and the group made their US debut at the Monterey Pop Festival in June 1967. A series of bestselling albums and singles established Hendrix as one of the premier guitarists in the world.

Sadly, he became addicted to drugs, trying as many as possible from alcohol to LSD, sniffing cocaine and heroin, popping pills – and was arrested in Toronto, Canada, in 1969 for possessing heroin. He was acquitted. The group split up that year and Hendrix appeared at the Woodstock Festival before forming a new group, the Band Of Gypsies. It was not a successful outfit and disbanded within a relatively short time.

Hendrix was found dead on 18 September 1970 in London, aged 27, having choked to death by inhalation of vomit due to barbiturate intoxication. He was once heard to say: 'Once you're dead, you've got it made.'

HERBERT, Greg Saxophonist who joined Blood, Sweat & Tears in 1977. Herbert died from a drugs overdose in Amsterdam during the group's European tour on 31 January 1978.

HEWHOCANNOTBENAMED Guitarist with the San Francisco band the Dwarves. He was stabbed to death in Philadelphia in 1963.

HEYWOOD, Eddie American pianist-songwriter, born on 4 December 1915. As an orchestra leader, he had his first million-selling record with 'Begin The Beguine' in 1945. 'Canadian Sunset', a number he wrote, became a big hit for Hugo Winterhalter, and he also had a solo hit in 1956 with 'Soft Summer Breeze'. Heywood died on 2 January 1989 following a long illness.

HINTON, Eddie Songwriter, Muscle Shoals session guitarist and recording artist. His songs were recorded by a variety of acts, including the

Box Tops, **Percy Sledge** and UB40. After releasing some solo albums, Hinton died in 1996, aged 50.

HINTON, Joe Soul singer, born in 1929, whose major hit was 'Funny (How Time Slips Away)' in 1964. He died in Boston on 13 August 1968, aged 39.

HITE, Bob Vocalist-harmonica player with **Canned Heat**, nicknamed the 'Bear', who was born on 26 February 1945. The group was formed in 1966 and appeared at the Monterey Pop Festival the following year. Their biggest hit was 'On The Road Again'. Hite died as the result of a heart attack in Venice, California, on 5 April 1981. He was 36 years old.

HOBBS, Elsberry Singer from New York City, who was the bass vocalist with Ben E. King's Five Crowns, the group that became the new Drifters in 1959. Hobbs sang on several of their hits, including 'There Goes My Baby', but was drafted in 1960 and replaced. He rejoined a revised Drifters in 1969. He died from cancer in 1996, at the age of 59.

HODDER, Jimmy Drummer with Steely Dan from 1969 to 1974. Jimmy was found dead at the bottom of his swimming pool in 1990. He was 42 years old.

HOLIDAY, Billie Tragic jazz/blues singer, born Eleanora Fagan in Baltimore, Maryland, on 7 April 1915. Billie began singing with big bands and started her recording career in 1935. She had a number of hits, including 'Porgy' and 'Loverman', but became hooked on drugs and drink.

Billie became known as 'Lady Day' when she joined Artie Shaw's band, before moving to New York to appear in the clubs there. She married Jimmy Monroe in 1941, but it didn't work out and in 1945 she married Joe Guy, a trumpeter. Billie also went to Hollywood to appear in the movie *New Orleans*. She was imprisoned for possession of drugs and on her release became romantically involved with a club owner, John Levy. The two were arrested, again for possession of drugs, but she was acquitted. She then married Louis McKay, who had become her manager.

Billie's alcohol intake increased to such a point that she was hospitalized with cirrhosis of the liver. She died in hospital from heart failure on 17 July 1959. Diana Ross starred in the movie biopic based on Holiday's autobiography, *Lady Sings The Blues*.

HOLLIDAY, Michael Liverpudlian singer, born Michael Miller on 24 November 1928, who topped the chart with 'Starry Eyed'. Holliday was the first Liverpudlian to have two No 1 hits; his other chart entries included 'The Story Of My Life', 'Stairway Of Love' and 'Skylark'. He even had his own television show. Sadly, he apparently could not cope with his success and committed suicide by shooting himself on 29 October 1963, aged 34.

HOLLY, Buddy Singer-songwriter-guitarist, born Charles Hardin Holley in Lubbock, Texas, on 7 September 1936. He was to become one of the most influential of the rock 'n' roll stars of the 1950s and was noted for the dark-rimmed spectacles that he wore. Holly penned a string of

Buddy Holly

239

influential hits, which he recorded with his backing band, the Crickets. They included: 'That'll Be The Day', 'Oh Boy', 'Maybe Baby', 'Peggy Sue', 'Think It Over' and 'Rave On'. His influence was immense.

Holly met and married Maria Elena Santiago in 1958. Due to disputes with his manager Norman Petty over the handling of his finances, Holly broke away from him. The Crickets decided to remain with Petty and Holly turned solo, recording 'It Doesn't Matter Any More'. It was to be his last major recording. Together with **Ritchie Valens** and **J. P. Richardson** (the 'Big Bopper'), he was killed when their plane crashed on 3 February 1959. Holly was 22 years old.

Holly's influence remains tremendous. A stage musical, *Buddy*, has been showing to packed houses in London from the late 1980s through the 1990s; a film biopic, *The Buddy Holly Story*, won an Oscar and every year Paul McCartney holds a special Buddy Holly celebration on Buddy's birthday. His former backing band the Crickets are still active performing artists.

HOLTON, Gary Singer with the Heavy Metal Kids, who actually rose to fame as a member of the cast of the UK television series *Auf Wiedersehen, Pet*. Gary had problems with drugs and died on 25 October 1985, aged 32.

HONEYMAN-SCOTT, James Former guitarist with the **Pretenders**, who died as a result of his cocaine and heroin addiction on 16 June 1982. He was 25 years old.

HOOKER, Earl Blues virtuoso instrumental guitarist born in Clarksdale, Mississippi, on 15 January 1930. He died from tuberculosis in 1970.

HOON, Shannon Lead singer of Blind Melon who was born in Lafayette, Indiana. The group's debut album in 1992 sold two million copies. Hoon died from an accidental drugs overdose in 1995. He was 28 years old.

HOPKINS, Nicky The UK's most famous keyboards session man, born in London on 24 February 1944. A pianist trained at the Royal Academy of Music, he joined **Screaming Lord Sutch's** Savages at the age of 16. Hopkins appeared on over 500 albums by the world's top groups, including the Beatles, the **Rolling Stones** and the **Who**, and also had spells as a member of groups such as the **Jeff Beck** Group and **Quicksilver Messenger Service**. He endured a lengthy spell in hospital in 1963, when he lost his gall bladder and left kidney – he also had a collapsed lung. Hopkins died on 6 September 1994 in a Nashville hospital following a stomach operation.

HORTON, Johnny Country rock singer born in Los Angeles on 3 April 1929. Horton's hit records included 'Battle of New Orleans', 'North To Alaska', 'Honky Tonk Man' and 'When It's Spring Time In Alaska', all of which came within a four-year period. Horton, who married **Hank Williams'** widow Billie Jean Jones, was killed in a car crash on 5 November 1960, aged just 31.

HOUSTON, David Country singer whose No 1 country hit was 'Almost Persuaded'. He also had a hit with his duet with **Tammy Wynette**, 'My Elusive Dreams'. Houston died in November 1994 as the result of a stroke. He was 57 years old.

HOWLIN' WOLF Singer (real name Chester Arthur Burnette), born in West Point, Mississippi, on 10 June 1910. Among his memorable songs were 'Smokestack Lightnin'', 'Sittin' On Top Of The World' and 'Spoonful'. During the 1970s, Howlin' Wolf experienced a series of heart attacks and was also involved in a car crash, which damaged his kidneys. He died from cancer on 10 January 1976.

HUDSON, Keith Jamaican reggae star who died from lung cancer in New York on 14 November 1984.

HUEY, Baby Singer of huge physical proportions, who died from a drugs overdose in Chicago on 28 October 1970.

HULL, Alan Main songwriter-vocalist with Lindisfarne, born on 20 February 1945. His numbers, based very much on his Geordie roots, included 'Meet Me On The Corner', 'Fog On The Tyne' and 'We Can Swing Together'. The group broke up in 1972, but re-formed later in the decade. Hull had just completed a new solo album when he died from heart failure at his home in Newcastle-upon-Tyne on 17 November 1995.

HUNTER, Alberta Blues singer, born on 1 April 1895. During her career she used several names, including Helen Roberts, Josephine Beatty and May Alix. Her biggest hit under her own name was 'Beale Street Blues'. Alberta died in New York on 17 October 1984.

HUNTER, Ivory Joe R&B singer born 10 October 1914. His hits included: 'Blues At Sunrise', 'Pretty Mama Blues', 'I Almost Lost My Mind' and 'Since I Met You Baby'. Hunter died from lung cancer on 8 November 1974.

HUTCHENCE, Michael Australian singer-songwriter, born on 22 January 1960, who was a founder member of INXS. The band made their recording debut in 1980 and went on to achieve international success. Their hits included: 'What You Need', 'Need You Tonight', 'Devil Inside', 'New Sensation' and 'Never Tear Us Apart'.

Hutchence hanged himself by a leather belt from a door in his hotel suite in Sydney on 22 November 1997, on the eve of a major tour to celebrate the band's twentieth anniversary.

Hutchence had spent nearly ten years playing crowded bars on the pub rock circuit in Australia before the band became international stars with records such as 'Suicide Blonde'. He had a serious drugs problem, used methodone on a daily basis and had also recently begun using Rohypnol, the so-called date rape drug that can induce amnesia. He was also a heavy drinker.

Hutchence's sexual conquests included singer **Kylie Minogue**, actress Kym Wilson and model Helen Christianson. He had begun an affair with Paula Yates, estranged wife of Bob Geldof, and the couple had a baby daughter, Heavenly Hiraani Tiger Lily, who was 16 months old when he died.

The suicide was puzzling, as Hutchence had seemed in good spirits on the eve of the tour and had announced his plans to marry Paula in the New Year on the island of Bora Bora. He had just sung the title song of the new John Travolta movie *Face/Off* and had been invited to Hollywood by Michael Douglas to discuss film roles.

Michael Hutchence was 37 years old when he died.

ISLEY, O'Kelly One of the famous Isley Brothers, born in Cincinatti, Ohio, on 25 December 1937. O'Kelly first began recording in 1958 with two of his brothers, Ronald and Rudolph. Two other brothers, Marvin and Ernie, plus their cousin, Chris Jasper, later augmented them. They had 30 chart hits, including: 'Shout', 'Twist and Shout', 'It's Your Thing', 'That Lady', 'Fight The Power' and 'Love The One You're With'. O'Kelly died as the result of a heart attack at his home in New Jersey on 31 March 1986.

ISLEY, Vernon When the Isley Brothers first formed in 1955 they were a vocal quartet consisting of Rudolph, Ronald, **O'Kelly** and Vernon Isley. Soon afterwards, Vernon was killed in a motorcycle accident and they became a trio.

IVES, Burl Folk singer-actor, born Burle Icle Ivanhoe Ives in Hunt, Illinois, on 14 June 1909. He was also a banjo player and was originally a member of the Weavers. He became estranged from the mainstream, leaving the US folk movement during the McCarthy era. Ives had nine chart hits in his own right, including: 'Lavender Blue', 'Riders In The Sky', 'On Top Of Old Smokey', 'Funny Way Of Laughin'', 'A Little Bitty Tear', 'Call Me Mr In-Between' and 'Mary Ann Regrets'.

Ives experienced tremendous success as an actor both on Broadway and on the big screen, appearing in more than 35 films. These included *East Of Eden*, *The Miracle Worker*, *Desire Under The Elms* and *Cat On A Hot Tin Roof*. He won an Oscar for his role in *The Big Country*. Ives died in 1996.

JACKSON, Al Drummer with **Booker T. & the MGs**, born on 27 November 1935. He was shot dead in his home in Memphis on 1 October 1975. Jackson's wife, who had been arrested for shooting him in the chest a few months earlier, was questioned in connection with the murder. The group had hits in their own right and also backed artists such as **Wilson Pickett**, **Otis Redding** and **Sam & Dave**.

JACKSON, Walter R&B singer, born in Florida, who had a number of hits in the 1960s including 'It's All Over'. Jackson contracted polio and was to die from a cerebral haemorrhage in New York on 19 June 1983. He was 45 years old. His 'When The Loving Goes Out Of Loving' was released posthumously two days later.

JAMERSON, James Noted Motown bass guitarist whose work appeared on scores of Motown hit records. His reputation among bass guitarists was immense. Motown head Berry Gordy referred to Jamerson as 'an incomparable bass player who pumped lifeblood into hundreds of our Motown hit records'. He died as the result of a heart attack on 2 August 1983, at the age of 45.

JAMES, Dick Music publisher, born Richard Leon Vapnick in the East End of London in 1921. He began as a vocalist at the age of 17 with big bands and continued to perform when he joined the Medical Corps during World War II. He changed his name to Dick James in 1945.

James began to record in the mid-1950s: his A&R man was George Martin and he had chart hits with 'The Ballad Of Davy Crockett' and 'Garden Of Eden'. His biggest hit was 'Robin Hood', the theme from the UK television series *The Adventures Of Robin Hood*. He ceased singing professionally in 1959 and it was George Martin who made the introductions that led to James becoming music publisher to the Beatles, and later to Elton John. He died following a heart attack on 1 February 1986.

JAMES, Elmore Blues artist – the ultimate slide guitar innovator and inspirer – born in Richland, Mississippi, in 1918. He initially teamed up with Sonny Boy Williamson, then formed his own band, the Broomdusters. James hit the charts in 1952 with 'Dust My Broom'. Other influential recordings included 'Shake Your Moneymaker', 'Bleeding Heart' and 'Done

Somebody Wrong'. James died as the result of a heart attack in May 1963.

JAMES, 'Fat Larry' American musician and former member of the Delfonics and Blue Magic. He led his own outfit, Fat Larry's Band, and they had three UK chart hits between 1977 and 1982 – 'Center City', 'Looking For Love Tonight' and 'Zoom'. James died in Philadelphia on 5 December 1987. He was 38 years old.

JEFFREY, Mike Co-manager of **Jimi Hendrix** who died in a plane crash over France on 5 March 1973.

JEFFREYS, Paul Avron Bass guitarist with **Cockney Rebel**, born on 13 February 1952. The group formed in 1973. Their hits included 'Sebastian', 'Judy Teen' and 'Mr Soft'. Jeffreys was one of the victims of the Lockerbie air disaster on 21 December 1988.

JENSEN, Ken Drummer with DOA, a punk band from Vancouver. He replaced **Dimwit** (Ken Montgomery), who died in September 1994, but died himself in a house fire four months later.

JOHN, Little Willie R&B singer, born William J. Woods in Camden, Arkansas, on 17 November 1937. He was only 15 when he made his record debut and his original version of 'Fever' reached No 1 in the R&B chart in 1956. His other hits included 'Talk To Me', 'Need Your Love So Bad' and 'Sleep'. John died on 27 March 1968 in Washington State Penitentiary from pneumonia. He had been sentenced to three years on a manslaughter charge for stabbing a man to death. He was 31 years old.

JOHNSON, Allen Pittsburgh-born singer, a baritone vocalist with doo-wop group the **Marcels** (of which his brother Fred was a founder member) who had four chart hits. However, Allen, who joined in 1961, was not on their biggest hit, the chart-topper 'Blue Moon'. Later, he became a professional soldier. He died from cancer on 28 September 1995.

JOHNSON, Marv Motown artist, born Marvin Earl Johnson in Detroit on 15 October 1938. He began performing at the age of 13 with his own group, the Serenaders. Berry Gordy Jnr discovered him and Johnson had four chart hits, including 'You Got What It Takes'. He died as the result of a stroke in 1993, while he was performing on stage. He was 54 years old.

JOHNSON, Robert   Legendary blues singer and superb guitarist who was to inspire many British blues bands in the 1960s, ranging from the **Rolling Stones** to **John Mayall's** Bluesbreakers. Johnson was born on 8 May 1911. He recorded 27 songs, including 'Love In Vain', 'Crossroads', 'From Four Till Late', 'Dust My Blues' and 'Rambling On My Mind'. He died on 16 August 1938 – his girlfriend was said to have poisoned him – aged 26. Johnson was the inspiration behind the 1986 feature film *Crossroads*.

JONES, Brian   Founder member of the **Rolling Stones** born in Cheltenham, Gloucestershire, on 26 February 1944.

Jones first arrived in London in 1962 and began playing guitar with **Alexis Korner's** Blues Incorporated. He decided to form a group and recruited **Ian Stewart**, Geoff Bradford and Mick Jagger. Jagger brought Keith Richard and Dick Taylor with him and they called themselves the Rollin' Stones. By 1963 Charlie Watts and Bill Wyman had become part of the outfit and **Andrew Loog Olham** became their manager, getting rid of Stewart and adding a 'g' to the Rollin'. Oldham brought Mick Jagger and Keith Richard to the forefront by having them compose the group's material. Disenchanted, Jones took to drink and drugs and left the group in June 1969.

Jones was arrested on a drugs charge and sent to prison, but his medical state was such that he was released and sent for treatment in a clinic. On 3 July 1969 he was found dead in the swimming pool of his home. He was 25 years old. The death has always been the subject of controversy and books have been published which allege that Jones had been murdered.

JONES, Linda   Singer whose major hit was 'Hypnotized'. Linda died on 24 March 1972, aged 26.

JONES, Michael 'Busta Cherry'   Bass guitarist who joined Albert King when he was 17. He was to work as a musician, songwriter and producer with **Chris Spedding**, Eno, Stevie Wonder and David Byrne, and toured with **Talking Heads**. Jones died in 1995, aged 44.

JOPLIN, Janis   Rock singer born in Port Arthur, Texas, on 19 January 1943. Although a pretty child, her looks altered as she grew older and she convinced herself that she was ugly. As a result she became a tomboy, took to drinking and was reputed to be promiscuous.

During a spell at the University of Texas, Janis began to sing in clubs in the evenings, inspired by the blues artist Bessie Smith. However, classmates proved cruel and when, in 1963, she was voted the 'Ugliest Man On Campus' she could stand the humiliation no longer and left for Los Angeles. She began singing in local coffee houses and became involved in drugtaking, until she was addicted. She returned home briefly in an effort to kick the habit, but found Port Arthur boring and returned to Los Angeles, where she became lead singer with Big Brother & the

Janis Joplin

Holding Company in June 1966, appearing with them at the Monterey Pop Festival the following year.

Janis left the band in December 1968 and formed her own outfit, the Kozmic Blues Band, then another group, the Full Tilt Boogie Band. By this time drugs and alcohol controlled her life completely, although she still managed to record a number of bestselling albums as well as singles.

Janis, who had had a romance with **Kris Kristofferson**, fell in love with a student, Seth Morgan, and the two talked of marriage. She made a determined effort to rid herself of drugs, but sadly died from an overdose of heroin on 4 October 1970 in a Los Angeles motel. She was 27 years old.

Janis was cremated and her ashes were scattered along the California coast. A posthumous album, *Pearl*, became one of her biggest sellers. The 1979 film *The Rose*, starring Bette Midler, was said to be based on Janis' brief life. In 1998 there was talk of two film biopics being made of her short but turbulent life.

JORDAN, Louis Major singer of the 1940s and prime mover of early R&B born in Brinkley, Arkansas, on 8 July 1908. Jordan led his own band and also played alto sax. His songs included: 'School Days', 'Blue Light Boogie', 'Caldonia' and 'Let The Good Times Roll'. He died from pneumonia on 4 February 1975.

JUDGE DREAD Controversial artist, born Alex Cox in Brixton, south London. Judge Dread blitzed the UK chart during the 1970s with a series of hit singles that were lewd, sexist, littered with *double entendres* and proved to be a lot of fun. His hits in that decade were: 'Big Six', 'Big Seven', 'Big Eight', 'Je T'Aime (Moi Non Plus)', 'Big Ten', 'Christmas In Dreadland/Come Outside', 'The Winkle Man', 'Y Viva Suspenders', '5th Anniversary', 'Up With The Cock/Big Punk' and 'Hokey Cokey/Jingle Bells'.

When Dread issued his first single, 'Big Six', in August 1972, it was banned by the BBC – and controversy followed him from then on.

A former doorman at the Ram Jam club and a professional wrestler under the name the Masked Executioner, he had recorded a demo costing him £8 on which he performed 'Little Boy Blue'. He was playing it to a friend when it came to the attention of Trojan Records, who decided to release it. Cox changed the name of the record to 'Big Six' after a Prince Buster number and also took the name Judge Dread from a Buster record.

Over the years he recorded under several different names – the Dreadnoughts, J.D. Alex and Jason Sinclair.

When Trojan Records went bankrupt in 1975, Dread bought the rights to all his recordings for £10,000 and licensed them to various budget labels from then on.

He performed in cabaret throughout Europe and in early 1997 recorded his first studio album in 12 years, *Dread, White And Blue*. On Friday, 13 March 1998, while appearing at the Penny Theatre in Canterbury, Kent, he collapsed at the end of his act and died of a suspected heart attack.

KAEMPFERT, Bert Composer-songwriter-record producer, born in Hamburg, Germany, on 16 October 1923. He was the first person to produce a record featuring the Beatles and composed hits such as 'Spanish Harlem', 'Strangers In The Night' and 'Danke Shoen'. Kaempfert also had success with his own orchestra with hits such as 'Wonderland By Night'. He died in Spain while on holiday on 22 June 1980.

KAHN, John Bass guitarist who was featured on many albums, including *The Live Adventures Of Mike Bloomfield* and *Al Kooper*. He also performed live with numerous artists and backed **Jerry Garcia** on almost all his live and recorded non-Grateful Dead work. He died from a drugs overdose in 1996. He was 48 years old.

KATH, Kerry Vocalist-songwriter-bass guitarist, born on 31 January 1946. He began his career as a member of Jimmy & the Gentlemen and then became a founder member of Chicago. Kath accidentally shot himself on 23 January 1979, unaware that the gun was loaded. He was 32 years old.

KENDRICKS, Eddie Singer born in Hot Springs, Alabama, who became the founder and lead tenor singer with the Temptations. They had 25 hits, including 'The Way You Do The Things You Do' and 'Just My Imagination'. After he left the group in 1971 he had a series of hits, including 'Keep On Truckin'' and 'Boogie Down'. He died from lung cancer at the Baptist Medical Centre, Birmingham, on 5 October 1992, aged 52.

KENNER, Chris Singer-songwriter, whose major hit was 'I Like It Like That' in 1961. He died on 25 January 1976, at the age of 46.

KENNY, Bill Singer born in 1915, who was to become the last remaining original member of the Ink Spots, the legendary singers of the 1940s who became the first black group also to appeal to the white record-buying public. They were former New York City Paramount Theatre porters and their first hit was 'If I Don't Care' in 1939. They had a million-seller when they duetted with **Ella Fitzgerald** on 'Into Each Life Some Rain Must Fall'. Kenny was the tenor and the other members were Ivory 'Deek' Watson (tenor), Charlie Fuqua (bass and guitar) and Orville 'Hoppy' Jones (bass and cello). The group had enjoyed 50 years in showbusiness by the time of Kenny's death on 23 March 1978.

KIDD, Johnny Singer-guitarist, born Frederick Heath in London on 23 December 1939. He wore a patch over his eye and called his band

Johnny Kidd (front) and the Pirates

the Pirates. Kidd's classic rock track 'Shakin' All Over' reached No 2 in the UK chart and his other hits included 'A Shot Of Rhythm & Blues' and 'I'll Never Get Over You'. He was killed in a car crash in Lancashire on 7 October 1966, at the age of 26.

KING, Albert Blues singer-guitarist (real name Albert Nelson) who was born in Indianola, Mississippi. Before becoming a blues guitarist, he played drums for **Jimmy Reed**. King began singing and playing guitar in 1953 and his songs include 'Born Under A Bad Sign' and 'Oh Pretty Woman'. Famous for his flying guitar, his albums in the 1960s were released on the Stax label and **Booker T. & the MGs** backed him. King continued recording until 1984 and was still touring up to his death in 1991. He was 69 years old.

KING, Freddie Blues guitarist, born Freddie Christian on 3 September 1934. He originally formed a band in Chicago called the Every Hour Blues Boys. King later went solo and his major hit was 'Hide Away'. He died as the result of a heart attack while performing on stage on 27 December 1976.

KING, Phil Erstwhile front man for Blue Oyster Cult, who was to become a promoter. King was shot three times in the head during a fight in New York on 27 April 1972, by a gambling associate who owed him money.

KING, Teddi Singer whose biggest hit was 'Mr Wonderful'. He died on 18 November 1977, aged 48.

KOELLEN, Helmut Member of the German rock band Triumvirat. Koellen committed suicide on 27 May 1977. He was 27 years old.

KORNER, Alexis Blues musician, born in Paris on 19 April 1928. He formed Blues Incorporated in 1962 and encouraged the **Rolling Stones** in their early career. The veritable godfather of British blues, in 1969 Korner sang vocals with CCS. He died from cancer on 1 January 1984.

KOSSOFF, Paul Son of television personality David Kossoff, born in London on 14 September 1950, who was a founder member of Free in May 1968. The group was to top the charts with 'All Right Now'. Free split in 1971 to explore individual projects, but re-formed the following year. Kossoff's drugs problems led to him being replaced on the group's Japanese tour in 1972, but he rejoined them for their UK tour. He left soon afterwards to form another band, Back Street Crawler. Kossoff died as the result of a heart attack, his second, while on a transatlantic flight on 19 March 1976. He was 25 years old.

LAKIND, Bobby Percussionist with the Doobie Brothers. Lakind died from inoperable brain cancer on 24 December 1992, several weeks after members of the group gathered to play a benefit concert for his children. He was 47 years old.

LAMBERT, Kit Co-manager, along with Chris Stamp, of the **Who**. Lambert died after a fall at his mother's house on 7 April 1981.

LAMBLE, Martin Drummer with Fairport Convention, born in St John's Wood, north London, on 28 August 1949. Lamble was killed when the group's van was involved in a crash on 14 May 1969. He was 19 years old. Also killed was Jeanne Franklin, nicknamed 'Genie The Tailor', who designed clothes for rock stars such as **Jimi Hendrix**, **Lovin' Spoonful**, **Donovan** and the Mamas & Papas, and was the inspiration for Jack Bruce's album *Songs For A Tailor*.

LANCE, Major Chicago singer, born on 4 April 1941, who had 19 R&B hits between 1963 and 1975, including the Top 10 entries 'Monkey Time' and 'Um, Um, Um, Um, Um, Um'. Lance was imprisoned from 1978 to 1981 for dealing in cocaine and died in 1995.

LANE, Ronnie Bass guitarist with the **Small Faces**, born in Plaistow, London, on 1 April, 1946. Nicknamed 'Plonk', he was a founder member of the band in 1965. After the group originally disbanded, Lane refused to join them again when they re-formed in 1976. He contracted multiple sclerosis and battled against the disease for 20 years, being confined to a wheelchair almost permanently for the latter part of his life. He died at his home in California on 4 June 1997.

LA ROCK, Scott Hip-hop/rap star who was killed in a gangland shoot-out on a New York street on 25 August 1987, shortly after the release of his debut album, *Criminal Minded*.

LEANDER, Mike British producer-arranger-A&R man, who also penned hits for **Gary Glitter**. Leander was musical director at Decca records in the 1960s, working with artists such as the **Rolling Stones**, **Marc Bolan**, **Joe Cocker**, **Lulu** and the **Small Faces**. He also arranged the Beatles' 'She's Leaving Home' on the *Sgt Pepper* album. He died from cancer on 18 April 1996, aged 54.

LECKENBY, Derek 'Lek' Bespectacled lead guitarist with **Herman's Hermits**, born in Leeds on 14 May 1946. Apart from their successful record career, the group appeared in the movies *Go Go Mania*, *When The Boys Meet The Girls*, *Hold On!* and *Mrs Brown You've Got A Lovely Daughter*. Lek remained with the Hermits after Peter Noone left in 1972. He died in 1996.

LEDFORD, Lily May Country music song-writer-banjo player, who also led the all-female band the Coon Creek Girls. Lily began her musical career in 1936 and cut several albums. She died in Lexington, Kentucky, on 14 July 1985, aged 68.

LENNON, John Legendary musician born at Oxford Street Maternity Hospital in Liverpool on 9 October 1940. While at Quarry Bank School he founded the Quarry Men, a skiffle group that evolved into the Beatles, who became the biggest trendsetters, superstars and most influential group in the history of popular music.

Together with Paul McCartney, he penned a number of songs which established them as among the leading songwriters of pop music this century. They were also to write many numbers singly which they credited to both their names. Lennon wrote a series of classic numbers, including 'Help!' and 'Strawberry Fields Forever'.

Lennon had married his art-school girlfriend Cynthia Powell and the couple had a baby son, **Julian**.

He later met Yoko Ono, a Japanese avant-garde artist, and they fell in love, although both were married at the time. Her influence then began to play a dominant role in his life and career.

The Beatles split and John developed The Plastic Ono Band with Yoko, whom he married. In his solo recordings, he continued to produce classics like 'Imagine'.

The couple moved to the States and settled in New York. They split up for a while when John moved to Los Angeles with their former secretary, May Pang. After what he called his 'lost weekend,' he was reunited with Yoko and they had a son, Sean, to whom John dedicated himself for the next five years, virtually retiring from music.

Lennon had recently become re-inspired and had started recording again, when a man claiming to be a fan shot him dead on 8 December 1980.

No other rock star's death, including **Elvis Presley's**, had such a momentous effect on the world population – and many people compare it to the universal mourning following President John F. Kennedy's assassination.

LEONETTI, Tommy Singer whose biggest hit was 'Free' in 1959. He died on 15 September 1979.

LERNER, Alan J. Playwright-lyricist whose musicals included *Brigadoon*, *Paint Your Wagon*, *Camelot*, *My Fair Lady* and *Gigi*. Lerner died in New York on 14 June 1986, aged 67.

LIGGINS, Joe Singer-songwriter who was also a band leader. Liggins was born on 9 July 1916 and had a series of million-selling singles: 'The Honeydripper', 'Got A Right To Cry' and 'Pink Champagne'. He died on 1 August 1987.

Frankie Lymon (centre) and the Teenagers

LITHMAN, Phil American singer-guitarist-pianist with Chilli Willi & the Red Hot Peppers, a band which was formed in London in 1971. After the group disbanded in 1975 Lithman joined the Residents, a band from California, with whom he recorded five albums. He died from heart problems in 1987.

LITTLE WALTER Musician, born Manon Walter Jacobs in Marksville, Louisiana, on 1 May 1930, who was famous for his ground-breaking amplified blues harmonica. He had instrumental hits with 'Juke' in 1952 and 'My Babe' in 1955, and was also noted for his song 'Confessin' The Blues'. Little Walter also played in **Muddy Waters'** band. He died following a bar fight on 15 February 1968, when he suffered a cerebral haemorrhage during the beating and was then stabbed. Little Walter was 37 years old when he died.

LONG, Shorty Soul singer (real name Frederick Earl Long), born in Detroit on 20 May 1940. He recorded the original version of 'Devil With A Blue Dress On' and had hits with 'Function At The Junction' and 'Here Comes The Judge'. Long drowned in a boating accident in Ontario on 29 June 1969. He was 29 years old.

LONGHAIR, Professor Archetypal New Orleans pianist, born Ron Byrds in Bogalusa, Louisiana, on 18 December 1918. 'Fess' died at his home in New Orleans on 18 December 1980.

LORDAN, Jerry British songwriter, born Jeremiah Patrick Lordan in London on 30 April 1934. A wide range of artists – including the Shadows, **Cliff Richard**, Matt Monro, Cleo Laine, Cilla Black, **Petula Clark** and the **Fortunes** – recorded his compositions. Hits he penned include 'Apache', 'Wonderful Land', 'Diamonds' and 'A Girl Like You', and as a singer he enjoyed three chart hits in his own right: 'Who Could Be Bluer', 'Sing Like An Angel' and 'All My Own Work'. He died from acute liver and renal failure on 24 July 1995.

LOWELL, George Singer-songwriter-guitarist and former member of the Mothers Of Invention, who helped to form **Little Feat** in 1969. The group built a reputation as a touring band and their albums included *Little Feat, Dixie Chicken* and *Feats Don't Fail Me Now*. In 1979 Lowell left the group to record his solo album *Thanks, I'll Eat It Here* and began touring with an eight-piece band. That year, on 29 June, he died as the result of a heart attack, aged 34.

LUCAS, Harold Founder member of the Clovers, who had 13 R&B hits during the 1950s including 'One Mint Julip' and 'Devil Or Angel'. Another of their hits was 'Love Potion No 9'. Lucas died in 1994, aged 61.

LUC-GABRIELLE, Sister Belgian nun (real name was Janine Deckers), born in 1928. She began singing to young girls at her convent near Brussels in 1961 and had a hit with 'Dominique' in 1963. Her hit album of that year was called *The Singing Nun*, a title by which she became commonly known. Sister Luc-Gabrielle left the convent in October 1966 and committed suicide in 1985.

LUMAN, Bob An American country-style singer whose biggest hit was 'Let's Think About Living'. Luman died on 27 December 1978 at the age of 40.

LYALL, Billy Latter-day member of the **Bay City Rollers**. Lyall contracted AIDS and died in 1989.

LYMON, Frankie Singer born in Washington Heights, New York, on 30 September 1942, who became lead vocalist with the Premiers. They changed their name to Frankie Lymon & the Teenagers with the release of their hit 'Why Do Fools Fall In Love?' in 1956. Other hits included 'I'm Not A Juvenile Delinquent' and 'Little Bitty Pretty One'. Lymon died from a heroin overdose in New York on 28 February 1968. He was 25 years old.

LYNARD SKYNARD American group formed in 1965, who had a number of bestselling albums before tragedy struck on 20 October 1977 shortly after they had received a gold album for their *One More For The Road*. Singer Ronnie Van Zant, guitarist Steve Gaines, his sister Cassie – who was one of the three back-up singers – and the group's manager Dean Kilpatrick were killed when their single-engined plane crashed. The other members of the band were seriously injured, but recovered and re-formed the band.

LYNCH, David Singer, born in St Louis in 1929. Lynch was a member of the **Platters** when they first formed in 1954. He died from cancer on 2 January 1981.

LYNOTT, Phil Guitarist born in Dublin on 20 August 1951 of Brazilian and Irish parents who formed the group Thin Lizzy in 1969. They had a number of successful albums and singles during the 13 years of their existence, including the single 'Whiskey In The Jar' and albums such as *Jailbreak* and *Live And Dangerous*. Lynott, who married Caroline Crowther, daughter of UK television personality Leslie Crowther, suffered from drugs problems and died in Salisbury, Wiltshire, on 4 January 1986. He had been in a coma for a week following a drugs overdose and died from heart failure and pneumonia. Lynott was 36 years old.

MACKENZIE, Billy Singer born in Dundee, Scotland, on 2 March 1957. MacKenzie teamed up with guitarist Alan Rankine in 1976 to form a duo called the Absorbic Ones, which evolved into the Edinburgh band the Associates. They received acclaim for their debut album, *The Affectionate Punch*, but the group suffered when Rankine left in 1983. MacKenzie signed with Nude Records in 1996, but his body was found in his garden shed in Dundee on 23 January 1997, a suspected suicide. He had signed a six-album record deal only a few weeks previously. MacKenzie was 39 years old. On 9 October 1997 his posthumous album *Beyond The Sun* was released, containing ten new songs.

MACLENNAN, Gene Canadian songwriter, born in Val d'Or, who penned numerous hits for Canadian artists, including 'Snowbird' for Anne Murray and 'Put Your Hand In The Hand' for Ocean. MacLennan hanged himself in 1995. He was 54 years old.

MANCINI, Henry Leading film and television composer who received four Oscars and 20 Grammy Awards for his compositions. His hits included: 'Mr Lucky', 'Moon River', 'Just You And I', 'Don't Cry Out Loud', 'Pretty Girls', 'Fire In The Morning' and 'You Should Hear How She Talks About You'. Mancini also composed the rock score for the US television series *Peter Gunn*. He died in 1994 at the age of 70.

MANN, Michael Musician who replaced Dave Alvin on lead guitar in Los Angeles group the Blasters. Known as Michael 'Hollywood Fats' Mann, he died as the result of a heart attack in 1986, He was 32 years old.

MANTOVANI Famous orchestra leader, born Annunzio Paolo Mantovani in Venice, Italy, in 1905. He had many hits, including million-sellers such as 'Charmaine', 'Cara Mia', 'Swedish Rhapsody', 'Theme From Moulin Rouge', 'Around The World In 80 Days' and 'Theme From Exodus'. Mantovani died on 29 March 1980.

MANUEL, Richard Singer-pianist, born in Stratford, Canada, on 3 April 1944. Manuel was originally a member of the Hawks, who changed their name to the Band when they backed **Bob Dylan** on a world tour. The group made their farewell performance in November 1976. Manuel became depressed in later years and hanged himself on 6 March 1986.

Bob Marley

MARLEY, Bob   First reggae superstar, born Robert Newton Marley in St Anne, Jamaica, on 5 February 1945. His father was a soldier from Liverpool. Originally a member of the Wailers, Marley later became leader of the group, who signed with Island Records.

Eric Clapton had a hit with Marley's 'I Shot The Sheriff' and Marley began to have major hits in his own right with a series of bestselling albums and singles, including 'No Woman No Cry' and 'Three Little Birds'. He was awarded Jamaica's Order Of Merit and died from lung cancer and a brain tumour at the Cedars Of Lebanon hospital in Miami on 11 May 1981. He was 36 years old. There were a number of posthumous hits, including the single 'One Love' and the album *Legend*.

MARRIOTT, Steve   Lead singer with mod group the **Small Faces**, born on 30 January 1947 in Bow, east London. The group had a series of successful singles, including 'Whatcha Gonna Do About It', 'Sha-La-La-La-Lee', 'All Or Nothing', 'Tin Soldier' and 'Lazy Sunday', plus hit albums such as *Itchycoo Park* and *Ogdens Nut Gone Flake*. Marriott left the group in 1969 to join Humble Pie and in later years attempted a solo career. He died in a fire at his home on 20 April 1990.

MARTIN, Dean   Singer, born Dino Crocetti in 1917, who was part of the successful movie comedy team of Dean Martin and Jerry Lewis, but embarked on a solo recording career. He had a string of major hits over a number of years, including 'That's Amore', 'Memories Are Made Of This' and 'Everybody Loves Somebody'. He also enjoyed a successful solo film career, was part of the Frank Sinatra clan and had his own US television series from 1965 to 1974. A heavy drinker, Martin suffered from lung cancer and mental deterioration and died on Christmas Day 1995.

McCOY, Van   Singer-songwriter, born on 6 January 1944, who originally sang with the Marylanders and the Starliters. As a producer he was involved with the **Shirelles'** recordings, produced **Gladys Knight** and worked with the **Drifters** and Leiber & Stoller. McCoy also launched his own record company. As a recording artist in his own right, McCoy's biggest hits were 'The Hustle' and 'The Shuffle'. He died from a heart attack on 6 July 1979. He was 38 years old.

McCULLOCH, Jimmy   Scots guitarist, born on 13 August 1953. Formerly with **Thunderclap Newman**, McCulloch then joined **John Mayall**, Stone The Crows, Wings and the **Small Faces**. He was found dead in his flat in Maida Vale, west London, on 28 September 1979. He was 26 years old.

McDANIEL, Floyd   Guitarist with Chicago group Four Blazes, who had three R&B hits in 1952–3. They went on to back **Sam Cooke**, the Ink Spots and Willie Dixon. McDaniel died in 1996, aged 80.

McGHEE, Brownie   Blues guitarist born in Knoxville, Tennessee. From 1939 he partnered Sonny Terry, and the two made numerous albums and appeared in the films *Festival* and *The Jerk*. McGhee died in 1996. He was 80 years old.

McINTOSH, Robbie   Drummer with the Average White Band, born in Glasgow, Scotland, in 1950. McIntosh joined the band on their formation in 1972, having previously been with Oblivion Express. He died in Los Angeles from a heroin overdose on 23 September 1974. He was 24 years old.

McLEAN, Daniel   Vocalist-drummer born in Carmel, California. McLean first began to play in the Crawdaddy's in the late 1970s, appeared solo as Country Dick Montana and then joined the Beat Farmers. He had recently completed a new solo album when he collapsed on stage during a concert in British Columbia in 1995 and died from an aneurysm. He was 40 years old.

McNAIR, Harold   Sax player and jazz flautist who joined Ginger Baker's Airforce. McNair had also played on recording sessions backing **Donovan**. He died from lung cancer on 26 March 1971.

McPHATTER, Clyde   Singer born in Durham, North Carolina, on 15 November 1933. McPhatter became lead singer with the Dominoes on hits such as 'Do Something For Me', but left the group in 1953 to form the **Drifters**. He left them when he was drafted into the US Army in May 1954 and turned solo on his return to civilian life, having 20 further hits, including 'Lover Please'. He suffered from drink and drugs problems and died in Teaneck, New

Jersey, on 13 June 1971 from complications caused by heart, liver and kidney diseases. He was 37 years old.

McPHERSON, Don Leader of New York soul band the Main Ingredient, born in Indianapolis, Indiana, on 9 July 1941. The group's hits included 'Everybody Plays The Fool', 'Just Don't Want To Be Lonely' and 'Happiness Is Just Round The Bend'. McPherson died from leukaemia on 4 July 1971. He was 29 years old. His replacement in the band was Cuba Gooding.

MEEK, Joe The UK's first major independent record producer, born in Gloucester on 5 April 1929. Meek built his own studio above a shop in Holloway, London, in 1960 and produced hundreds of records, including numerous hits. Artists he recorded included **John Leyton**, **Mike Berry** and the **Honeycombs**. He hit the top of the charts on both sides of the Atlantic with 'Telstar' by the **Tornados**. Meek shot his landlady in the back and turned the shotgun on himself on 3 February 1967. He was 37 years old.

Some 30 years after Meek's death, a number of his former recording artists gathered to perform at a special tribute concert in his memory at the Lewisham Theatre. They included the Tornados, **Screaming Lord Sutch**, **Mike Berry**, the **Honeycombs**, **Cliff Bennett**, the Moontrekkers, Danny Rivers and **Heinz**.

MELVIN, Harold Leader of the Philadelphia soul quartet Harold Melvin & the Blue Notes, whose hits included 'If You Don't Know Me By Now', 'The Love I Lost', 'Bad Luck' and 'Wake Up Everybody'. The group's lead singer, Teddy Pendergrass, was paralysed in a car crash on 18 March 1982. Melvin died on 24 March 1997, aged 57.

MELVIN, Jonathan Keyboards player for the Chicago-based band the Smashing Pumpkins. Melvin overdosed in a New York hotel room on 12 July 1996 shortly before their series of sell-out Madison Square Gardens concerts. His sister Wendy was keyboards player with **Prince**. Melvin was 34 years old when he died.

MENSON, Michael A member of the rap group Double Trouble, whose one hit was 'Street Tuff' in 1989. Menson died that year, after a gang soaked him in petrol and set it alight. He was 29 years old.

MERCURY, Freddie Vocalist with Queen, born Frederick Bulsara in Zanzibar on 5 September 1946. Mercury teamed up with Brian May and Roger Taylor to form the group in 1970 and they were joined by bass guitarist John Deacon the following year. The group were a major success internationally and their hits included: 'Seven Seas Of Rhye', 'Bohemian Rhapsody', 'We Are The Champions', 'Bicycle Race/Fat Bottomed Girls', 'A Kind Of Magic' and 'Who Wants To Live Forever'.

Mercury also recorded 'Barcelona', a theme to tie in with the 1992 Olympic Games, with opera singer Montserrat Caballé. Mercury's final record with Queen was 'The Show Must Go On', released a month before his death. Mercury had contracted AIDS and died from bronchial pneumonia on 24 November 1991.

MERRILL, Bob Songwriter who began composing in 1949 and penned hits such as 'How Much Is That Doggie In The Window', 'If I Knew You Were Coming I'd Have Baked A Cake', 'Sparrow In The Treetop' and 'Mambo Italiano'. Merrill also wrote the music for the film version of the musical *Funny Girl*, composing numbers such as 'People' and 'Don't Rain On My Parade', and penned the script for the Diana Ross movie *Mahogany*. Merrill contracted cancer and shot himself outside his Beverly Hills home in February 1998. He was 77 years old.

MIAMI SHOWBAND, The An Irish band, several members of which were killed when Protestant gunmen in Northern Ireland shot them in an ambush on 31 August 1975.

MILLER, Jacob 'Killer' Lead singer of the reggae band Inner Circle born on 4 May 1956, who died in Jamaica in a motorcycle accident on 21 February 1980, aged 23. He appeared in the film *Rockers* and his hits included 'Each One Teach One', 'We Are Rockers' and 'Tenement Yard'.

MILLER, J.D. Record producer, born James Denton in El Campo, Texas. Based in Crowley, Louisiana, from the 1940s on, Miller owned the Excello label and produced a host of artists including **Lightnin' Slim**, **Slim Harpo** and Doug Kershaw, in addition to cajun, rockabilly, country and blues music. He also penned Kitty Wells' No 1 country hit 'It Wasn't God Who Made Honky Tonk Angels'. He died in 1996, aged 74.

MILLER, Jimmy Brooklyn-born singer who travelled to England in the early 1960s and became the record producer for a host of bands, including the **Spencer Davis Group**, Traffic and **Blind Faith**. He produced all the **Rolling Stones'** albums from 1968 to 1973, ranging from *Beggar's Banquet* to *Goat's Head Soup*. In all, Miller produced over 100 gold albums. He died in October 1994 from liver failure. He was 52 years old.

MILLER, Roger Singer-songwriter, born in Forth Worth, Texas, on 2 January 1936. Miller had a dozen hits in the 1960s, including 'King Of The Road', 'Dang Me', 'Chug-A-Lug', 'Engine Engine', 'Little Green Apples' and 'England Swings'. He also wrote 'Little Swiss Maid' for **Del Shannon** and 'You Don't Want My Love' for Andy Williams. Miller died from lung cancer on 25 October 1992.

MILLER, Seagram Member of a rap group who, like several other members of such groups, was gunned down. A drug dealer, he was shot to death in Oakland, California, in August 1996.

MILLS, Harry One of the famous Mills Brothers, the others being Herbert and Donald. The vocal group was originally formed in 1930 and their hits included 'Queen Of The Senior Prom', 'Get A Job' and 'Cab Driver'. Mills died on 28 June 1982, aged 68.

MILLS, Mrs (Gladys) Popular British pianist, whose major chart hit was 'Mrs Mills' Medley' in December 1961. She died on 25 February 1978.

MILLWARD, Mike Guitarist, born in Bromborough, Cheshire, on 9 May 1942. Millward joined Liverpool band the **Fourmost** in November 1961. The group became part of the **Brian Epstein** stable and their hits included 'Hello Little Girl', 'I'm In Love', 'A Little Lovin'' and 'Baby I Need Your Loving'. Millward developed leukaemia and died in April 1966, aged 23.

MR C. Member of the Californian rap group RBL Posse, who was shot dead during a drug deal in 1995.

MONRO, Matt Former London bus driver, born Terry Parsons on 1 December 1932. He came to fame impersonating Frank Sinatra on Peter Sellers' album *Songs For Swinging Sellers*. Monro had a string of hits throughout the 1960s, including: 'Portrait Of My Love', 'My Kind Of Girl', 'Softly As I Leave You', 'From Russia With Love', 'Yesterday' and 'Born Free'. He died from cancer in Cambridge on 7 February 1985.

MONROE, Bill Country music artist, born on 13 September 1911. He was known as the 'Father Of Blue Grass Music' and was leader of the Blue Grass Boys. The vocalist-mandolin player proved influential, not only to fellow country artists, but to a range of other musicians including **Elvis Presley**, **Bob Dylan**, the Byrds and the Grateful Dead. He penned 'Blue Moon Of Kentucky' and his biggest hit was 'Kentucky Waltz'. He died on 9 September 1996.

MOON, Keith Drummer with the **Who**, born in London on 19 May 1945. The group was tremendously successful and Moon's wild image and alcoholism were legendary. He blew up his drum kit on *The Smothers Brothers Show*, causing Bette Davis to faint, accidentally killed his chauffeur when he ran over him and collapsed on stage several times. Moon died from an overdose of chlormethiazole, prescribed to combat his alcoholism, on 8 September 1978. He was 32 years old.

MORALI, Jacques French producer who conceived the **Village People** and formed the group in 1977. He died from an AIDS-related illness in Paris on 15 November 1991, aged 44.

MORGAN, George Country music star, born in Waverly, Tennessee, on 28 June 1924. His first No 1 record, 'Candy Kisses', which he wrote, became his signature tune. Morgan's other hits included 'Room Full Of Roses', 'Almost' and 'Slippin' Around'. He died on 7 July 1975 from complications arising from heart surgery.

MORRISON, Jim Leader of and vocalist with the **Doors**, born in Melbourne, Florida, on 8 December 1943. Morrison first formed a group in 1965 and named them the Doors in 1966 after being inspired by Aldous Huxley's book *Doors of Perception*. They had a series of singles and album hits, including 'Light My Fire', 'Hello I Love You', 'Riders On The Storm' and 'Touch Me'.

Morrison was arrested on a number of occasions for lewd behaviour and played his last

Jim Morrison

concert with the group in November 1970, before moving to Paris to write poetry. He died from a heart attack in his bath on 3 July 1971, aged 27, and was buried in the Père Lachaise cemetery in Paris. Oliver Stone was to direct a film biopic of his life, *The Doors*.

MORRISON, Sterling   Guitarist with the **Velvet Underground**, who was born in East Meadow, New York. After the band split up, following the recording of four albums, in 1971, Morrison went on to achieve a PhD in English Literature, before becoming a tugboat captain based in Houston. He returned to the Velvet Underground for their reunion tour in 1993. Morrison died in 1995 from non-Hodgkins lymphoma. He was 53 years old.

MURCIA, Billy   Drummer with the New York Dolls. While he was asleep on 6 November 1972, a girl poured coffee down his throat and he suffocated to death. He was 21 years old.

MURPHY, Alan   Guitarist with **Level 42**, who died from an AIDS-related illness on 19 October 1989.

MURRAY, Don Ray   Drummer from Inglewood, California, who began his career with the surf instrumental band the Crossfires in 1963. The group changed their name to the **Turtles** in 1965 and Murray played on their early hits, including 'It Ain't Me Babe', 'Let Me Be' and 'You Baby'. He was replaced in 1967. Murray then went on to form a computer graphics company. He died in 1996, aged 50.

MURRAY, Ruby   Belfast-born singer, once voted the UK's favourite female vocalist. Ruby first entered the chart with 'Heartbeat' in February 1954 and set a record of having five singles in the Top 20 at the same time – a feat equalled only by **Elvis Presley** and **Madonna**. Her second release, 'Softly Softy', topped the chart and her other hits were: 'Happy Days And Lonely Nights', 'Let Me Go Lover', 'If Anyone Finds This I Love You', 'Evermore', 'I'll Come When You Call', 'You Are My First Love' and 'Real Love'. Ruby's final hit, 'Goodbye Jimmy Goodbye', was in 1959. Frank Sinatra once told her: 'You're a hell of a great singer and I am your greatest fan', and her name was immortalized as Cockney rhyming slang for a curry.

In 1960 Ruby married Bernie Burgess, a member of the Jones Boys, a vocal group. She then gave up most of her singing career to spend time on her marriage and the raising of her two children. There was an acrimonious divorce 14 years later.

For years Ruby battled against alcoholism, and she died in a Torquay hospital on 17 December 1996 from complications associated with liver cancer. She was 61 years old.

MYDLAND, Brent   Keyboards player, born in Munich to American military parents, who in 1979 replaced Keith Goodcheaux in the Grateful Dead. Mydland died from a drugs overdose in 1990. He was 38 years old.

NEGRONI, Joe   Baritone singer with Frankie Lymon & the Teenagers, born in New York on 9 September 1940. Negroni died from cerebral haemorrhage in 1978.

NELSON, Nate   Leader of Chicago R&B group the Flamingos, born on 10 April 1932. The group's hits included 'I Only Have Eyes For You' and 'Nobody Loves Me Like You'. Nelson later became a member of the Platters and died on 1 June 1984.

NELSON, Ricky   A singer who entered show-business in his parents' television series, *The Adventures Of Ozzie And Harriet*. Born Eric Hilliard Nelson in Teaneck, New Jersey, on 8 May 1940, he began singing on his parent's show, released a single and found immediate success. Nelson became a recording artist in his own right, with 36 major chart hits including 'A Teenager's Romance', 'Be-Bop Baby', 'Stood Up', 'Never Be Anyone Else But You,' 'It's Late', 'Hello Mary Lou Poor Little Fool', 'Travelin' Man' and 'Young World'. Nelson died along with his fiancée Helen Blair and members of his band when a private plane caught fire and crashed on 31 December 1985.

NICO   Former model-singer (real name Christa Paffgen) with the **Velvet Underground**, born in Cologne, Germany, on 16 October 1938. Startlingly beautiful facially, she inspired a song by **Bob Dylan**, a story by Ernest Hemingway, a film by Andy Warhol and a poem by Jean Baudrillard. It was Warhol who decided she should become the singer with the group when he became their manager in 1965. She later left the Underground to embark on a solo career and made seven albums and 17 films. Later in life she became a heroin addict, put on weight and lost her looks. She died from a brain haemorrhage, caused when she fell off her bike during a holiday in Ibiza on 18 July 1988.

NILSSON, Harry   Singer, born Harry Edward Nilsson III in Brooklyn, New York, on 15 June 1941. His debut album, *Pandemonium Shadow Show*, brought him to the attention of the Beatles. He enjoyed a total of ten chart entries and had a major hit with 'Everybody's Talkin'' from the film *Midnight Cowboy*. Nilsson's biggest hit was 'Without You'. **John Lennon** produced his album *Pussy Cats*, he appeared in two films with Ringo Starr and composed a number of songs which were recorded by various artists. Nilsson died in Los Angeles on 15 January 1994, having suffered a heart attack the previous year from which he never fully recovered.

NOLAN, Jerry   Drummer with the New York Dolls, the pre-punk group from New York which was formed in 1972. Nolan died as the result of a stroke on 14 January 1992. He had been undergoing treatment for pneumonia and meningitis. He was one of four members of the group to die prematurely.

NOLAN, Jimmy   Guitarist who backed artists such as **James Brown** and Johnny Otis. Nolan died as the result of a heart attack on 18 December 1983, aged 47.

NOTORIOUS BIG   Brooklyn rapper (real name Christopher Wallace) who was shot dead in his car in Hollywood in March 1997.

NOWELL, Brad   California-born lead vocalist-guitarist with the ska-punk group Sublime. Nowell overdosed in Los Angeles in 1996, a few months before the band's first album was released by MCA. He was 28 years old.

NYRO, Laura   Singer-songwriter, born in New York on 18 October 1947. Laura penned hits for a number of artists including **Blood, Sweat & Tears**, **Three Dog Night**, **Barbra Streisand** and the Fifth Dimension. She was a recording artist in her own right with a series of introspective albums, including *More Than A New Discovery*, *Eli And The Thirteenth Confession*, *New York Tendaberry* and *Christmas And The Beads Of Sweat*. Laura originally retired from music when she married, but when her marriage broke up she began to record again in 1975. She died in May 1997 from ovarian cancer.

OAKLEY, Berry Former bass guitarist with the Allman Brothers Band, born in Jacksonville, Florida, on 4 April 1948. Oakley died in a motorcycle accident on 11 November 1972, a mile from the spot where **Duane Allman** had been killed in a similar accident a year earlier.

OCHS, Phil Folk singer, born in El Paso, Texas, on 19 December 1940. One of the core of Greenwich Village folk artists in New York who received national acclaim, Ochs signed to the Elektra label and released a series of albums. Joan Baez recorded his 'There But For Fortune'. His voice was affected when he was nearly strangled during a tour of Africa. He became an alcoholic and hanged himself at his sister's house when in a state of depression on 9 April 1976, aged 35.

O'KEEFE, Johnny Singer, known as the 'Elvis Presley Of Australia'. He died as the result of a heart attack on 6 October 1978, at the age of 43.

ORBISON, Roy Major singer-songwriter, born Roy Kelton Orbison in Wink, Texas, on 23 April 1936, who formed the Wink Westerners in his teens. Orbison moved on from country music, but was particularly interested in ballads. Moving to Nashville, he began to write songs for music publishers Acuff-Rose. They included 'Claudette', named after his wife, which was recorded by the **Everly Brothers**. Orbison, who always wore dark glasses, had a string of more than two dozen hits in his own right, including: 'Only The Lonely', 'Blue Angel', 'Dream Baby', 'Running Scared', 'Blue Bayou', 'Oh Pretty Woman' and 'Walk On'. In 1988 he teamed up with George Harrison, **Bob Dylan**, Jeff Lynne and **Tom Petty** in the **Traveling Wilburys**.

There was tragedy in Orbison's life. He divorced Claudette in 1964 when he discovered she was having an affair. They were remarried in 1966, but several weeks later, when the two were returning from a drag race meeting on their motorbikes, she was hit by a truck and died in hospital an hour later. Then, in 1968, while he was touring the UK, Orbison's house was destroyed by fire, killing two of his three sons, Roy Jnr and Tony. The following year he got married again, to Barbara Wellhonen, a woman he had met in Leeds.

Orbison died as the result of a heart attack on 7 December 1988.

OWENS, Donnie Musician, born in Pennsylvania, who appeared on albums by artists such as Duane Eddy and Lee Hazelwood, and had his own chart hit, 'Need You', in 1958. Owens was shot dead by his girlfriend in 1995. He was 62 years old.

PANOZZO, John Chicago-born drummer who, together with his twin brother Chuck, formed TW4 in the 1960s. They changed their name to Styx and had 16 hit singles and numerous chart albums.

Their hits included: 'Lady', 'Come Sail Away', 'Babe', 'The Best Of Times', 'Too Much Time On My Hands', 'Mr Roboto' and 'Don't Let it End'. John was a chronic alcoholic and died in 1996, at the age of 47.

PAPPALARDI, Felix Former producer of **Cream** and bass guitarist with Mountain (a group he formed in July 1969), born in the Bronx in 1939. Pappalardi was shot dead by his wife Gail Collins in their New York apartment on 18 April 1983. He was 43 years old.

PARAMOR, Norrie A&R man and orchestra leader, born in 1914, who recorded numerous hits for EMI's Columbia label. The artists Paramour recorded include **Cliff Richard**, **Frank Ifield**, **Helen Shapiro** and the Shadows. He also had some orchestra hits in his own right, including 'Theme From A Summer Place' and 'Theme From Z Cars'. He died on 9 September 1979.

PARKER, Colonel Tom **Elvis Presley's** manager, born Andreas Cornelis Van Kuisk in Holland in 1909. He emigrated to the States illegally in 1929. Parker became involved with travelling carnivals, founded a pony circus and developed an act called Colonel Parker & His Dancing Chickens. In the 1950s he became manager to acts such as Tommy Sands, Hank Snow and Eddy Arnold. He then signed up Elvis Presley in 1953 and managed him for the rest of his life.

Being interested solely in the money, Parker placed Elvis in a number of second-rate films – and turned down some quality movies that would have enhanced his career. He also prevented Elvis from touring the world because he was afraid of leaving the country, as he would have had to apply for a passport and might have been unveiled as an illegal immigrant. One of the worst deals Parker made for Elvis was to sell his entire catalogue to RCA Records in 1976 in exchange for $6 million, half of which he pocketed himself.

Elvis once said: 'Parker is a rude, crude, son of a bitch, and you can quote me.'

Parker died on 21 January 1997.

PARNES, Larry British impresario, born in Willesden, north London, in 1930. He became the leading pop group manager of the 1950s, creating colourful names for the range of singers he managed. They included Tommy Steele, **Marty Wilde**, Lance Fortune, **Dickie Pride**, Johnny Gentle and **Duffy Power**. Parnes died on 4 August 1989.

PARSONS, Gram Singer-songwriter-guitarist-banjo player, born Cecil Connor in Winterhaven, Florida, on 5 November 1946, who was originally a member of the Byrds, but quit the group in 1968 to form the **Flying Burrito Brothers**. Parsons left them in 1970 and was later to turn solo. He died from heart failure following a drugs overdose in Joshua Tree, California, on 19 September 1973 at the age of 26. His road managers stole his body and took it into the desert where they buried it, claiming they were simply following Parsons' wishes.

PASKOW, Bruce Musician, born in Elizabeth, New Jersey, who was a member of various groups in New York City including the Invaders and the Washington Squares. Paskow died in 1994, aged 36.

PASTORIUS, Jaco American bass guitarist, born in 1951. A former member of **Weather Report**, he also backed **Joni Mitchell** and led his own band, Word Of Mouth. Pastorius was badly beaten up by a bouncer when trying to enter a club in Fort Lauderdale on 12 September 1987 and fell into a coma, dying nine days later. He was 35 years old.

PATTO, Mike Singer, born Michael McCarthy on 22 September 1942. He formed his first band, Mike Patto & the Breakaways, and then sang with the Bow Street Runners and Chicago Line Blues Band. He formed Timebox in 1966 and the group became Patto in 1973. He then formed another band, Boxer, in 1975, but died from throat cancer on 3 March 1979. He was 36 years old.

PEERS, Donald Singer, born Donald Rhys Hubert Peers in Ammanford, Wales, in 1909. Peers was a popular performer, known as the 'Cavalier Of Song', whose big hits included 'Please Don't Go' and 'Give Me One More Chance'. He was also famous for songs like 'In A

Shady Nook (By A Babbling Brook)', 'Dear Hearts And Gentle People', 'Music! Music! Music!', 'Enjoy Yourself', 'It's Later Than You Think', 'In A Golden Coach' and 'If I Knew You Were Comin', I'd've Baked A Cake'. Peers died on 9 August 1973.

PERETTI, Hugo Songwriter-record producer who penned 'Can't Help Falling In Love' and 'The Lion Sleeps Tonight'.

Peretti founded Avco Records with his partner Luigi Creatore and also produced a host of artists, including the Stylistics, the Isley Brothers and Sam Cooke. He died on 1 May 1986, at the age of 68.

PERKINS, Carl A seminal rock 'n' roll singer-guitarist-songwriter, born on 9 April 1932. He was on the way to appear on *The Ed Sullivan Show* with his brothers Jay and Clayton when he was involved in a car crash and was hospitalized. From his hospital bed, he was able to see Elvis Presley make a huge impact on the show with Perkins' number 'Blue Suede Shoes'.

Perkins was a major influence on the Beatles, who recorded three of his songs – 'Matchbox', 'Everybody's Trying To Be My Baby' and 'Honey Don't' – and they invited him to the studio while they recorded them. George Harrison had originally used the name Carl Harrison on a tour of Scotland in 1960.

In 1986 Perkins recorded the album *Class Of '55* with **Roy Orbison**, **Jerry Lee Lewis** and Johnny Cash. He was inducted into the Rock 'n' Roll Hall Of Fame in 1987, but was to suffer from throat cancer in 1990. He beat it and continued to perform and record, his two sons Greg and Stan also appearing with him.

Perkins' last album was *Go Cat Go*, released in 1996, on which guest artists such as **Paul Simon**, Bono and Willie Nelson joined him.

Four months before his death, Perkins was appearing in London in a special charity concert to raise money for the volcano-stricken island of Montserrat. Also on the bill were Paul McCartney, Mark Knopfler and Sting.

Perkins died on 19 January 1998 in a hospital in Jackson, Mississippi, following a series of strokes.

PERRIN, Steve Singer with the group Children and a writer for **Z Z Top**. Perrin choked on his own vomit on 9 August 1973. He was 28 years old.

PERRYMAN, Willie Famous R&B pianist, also known as Piano Red, whose hits between 1950 and 1958 included 'Rockin' With Red', 'Red's Boogie' and 'Wrong Yo Yo'. In 1962 he adopted the pseudonym Dr Feelgood and with his band the Interns recorded hits such as 'Dr Feelgood' and 'Right String But The Wrong Yo Yo'. Following a long illness, Perryman died in Atlanta, Georgia, on 25 July 1985. He was 73 years old.

PFAFF, Kristen Bass player with **Courtney Love's** group Hole. Kristen overdosed in 1994, two months after the death of Courtney's husband, **Kurt Cobain**. She was 27 years old.

PHILLIPS, Esther Singer, born Esther Mae Jones in Houston on 23 December 1935. Under the name Little Esther, she began singing with the Johnny Otis Revue at the age of 13. She ceased using the 'Little' in 1962. Her hits included 'Release Me' and 'What A Diff'rence A Day Makes'. Esther died on 7 August 1984.

PICKETT, Kenny Singer-songwriter with the Mark Four, who changed their name to Creation in 1966. Although not a major hit band, they were well respected and their single releases included 'Making Time' and 'Painter Man', both penned by Pickett, who also received an Ivor Novello Award for 'Grandad'.

Pickett left the group in 1967 and then rejoined it in February 1968, although the group was to disband just a few months later. He teamed up with Eddie Phillips in the early 1990s to re-form Creation and sign a deal with Creation Records.

Pickett died on 10 January 1997 and was cremated at Mortlake Cemetery on 27 January.

PIERCE, Jeffrey Lee Singer-guitarist born in El Monte, California. A former music reviewer, Pierce formed the Los Angeles-based group Gun Club, which later moved to the UK. They recorded 11 albums, beginning with *Fire Of Love* in 1981.

Pierce also recorded two solo albums. A Buddhist, he died from a brain haemorrhage in 1996. He was 37 years old.

PILATUS, Rob Member of Milli Vanilli who was found dead from a surfeit of alcohol and pills on 2 April 1998. Pilatus was 32 years old.

POMPILLI, Rudy Sax player who joined **Bill Haley's** Comets in September 1955. He died on 5 February 1976, aged 48.

POMUS, Doc Famous US songwriter, born on 27 June 1925, who penned a number of rock classics with co-writer Mort Shuman. They included 'Teenager In Love', 'Sweets For My Sweet' and 'Little Sister'. The songwriting partnership came to an end in 1966 after Pomus was disabled and confined to a wheelchair following a fall. He died on 14 March 1991.

POPE, Joseph Lee Singer born in Atlanta, Georgia, on 6 November 1933. He was a member of the Tams, who entered the US Top 10 in 1964 with 'What Kind Of Fool'. Pope also appeared in the movies *Mondo Daytona* and *Weekend Rebellion*. He died in 1996. The group is still active and is led by Pope's brother Charles.

PORCARO, Jeff Drummer and percussionist, born in Los Angeles on 1 April 1934. Together with his brother Steve, he founded Toto in 1978.

The group had a string of hits, including 'Rosanna', 'Africa' and 'I Won't Hold You Back'. Their album *Toto IV* was awarded seven Grammys. Jeff died from heart failure on 5 August 1992, possibly caused by cocaine use.

PORTER, Dick Lead singer with the Ink Spots, a popular American vocal group whose hits included 'Address Unknown', 'We Three', 'I'm Making Believe', 'Into Each Life Some Rain Must Fall', 'The Gypsy' and 'To Each His Own'. Porter died on 6 January 1978, aged 46.

POWELL, Cozy Songwriter-drummer, born Colin Powell on 29 December 1947. A former member of the Ace Kefford Stand and the Jeff Beck Group, Powell formed his own outfit, the Beast, in 1969. They changed their name to Bedlam but eventually split up in 1974.

By that time Powell had issued two hit singles, 'Dance With The Devil' and 'Na Na Na'. He launched Cozy Powell's Hammer, then joined groups such as Strange Brew, **Black Sabbath** and Rainbow. He also joined Emerson Lake & Palmer for one album.

Cozy Powell

Over the years Powell was much in demand as a session musician, in addition to his regular live appearances with **Donovan**, the **Who's** Roger Daltrey, Gary Moore and Brian May of Queen.

He was also a major artist in Japan, where he was voted in as No 1 drummer in a major poll in 1997. At the beginning of 1998, Powell began a world tour with Yng Wie Malmsteen, voted the No 1 guitarist in Japan. The duo began their tour in March, but Powell injured his foot and returned to the UK where, on 6 April, he was killed when his car smashed into barriers on the M4 near Bristol.

POWELL, William   Singer with the O'Jays, born on 20 January 1942. The American vocal group had eight hits between 1972 and 1983, including Love Train, I Love Music, Brandy and Sing A Happy Song. Powell was replaced in the group by Sam Strain in 1976 and died from cancer on 26 May 1977, aged 35.

PRATER, David   One half of the soul team **Sam & Dave**, born in Ocilla, Georgia, on 9 May 1937. Together with Sam Moore, he began recording for the Stax label in 1965 and the duo had a string of hits, including 'Hold On! I'm Coming', 'Soul Man' and 'I Thank You'. Prater died on 9 April 1988, when his car crashed into a tree near Sycamore in Georgia.

PRESLEY, Elvis   Single most influential solo figure in popular music, born in Tupelo, Mississippi, on 8 January 1935, who was dubbed the 'King Of Rock 'n' Roll'. Elvis first began recording for Sun Records in 1954 with 'That's Alright Mama'. Throughout the 1950s he continued to release classic rock 'n' roll cuts – 'Good Rockin' Tonight', 'Baby Let's Play House', 'Mystery Train', 'Blue Suede Shoes' – and became a music phenomenon. After a stint in the US Army, Elvis embarked on a movie career, although his series of films throughout the 1960s were rather lightweight, mainly due to the avarice of his manager **Colonel Tom Parker**, who was primarily interested in the fees and didn't even bother to read the scripts.

Elvis Presley

Elvis' recording career continued to produce classic tracks, including 'GI Blues', 'Return To Sender', '(You're The) Devil In Disguise' and 'Heartbreak Hotel', although the releases from his later movies were disappointing.

The next stage of his career created the Las Vegas image of outlandish stage wear, popular with Elvis impersonators.

Elvis' body was found on the floor of his bathroom on 16 August 1977 by his girlfriend Ginger Alden. He had been sitting on the toilet reading *The Scientific Search For The Face Of Jesus*. He was pronounced dead from heart failure. Some 75,000 people attended Elvis' funeral ceremony.

PRIDE, Dickie Singer-guitarist, born Richard Kneller in London. He was given his stage name by **Larry Parnes** and appeared on Jack Good's television rock shows, including *Oh Boy!*. Nicknamed the 'Sheik Of Shake', he recorded a hit version of 'Primrose Lane' in 1959 and other notable singles included 'Slippin' And Slidin'', 'Betty Betty' and 'Frantic'. Pride died in 1969 from drugs-related maladies. He was 27 years old.

PRIMA, Louis American band leader, born on 7 December 1912, whose hits included 'Wonderland By Night'. He was married to singer Keely Smith and the two hit the chart with 'That Old Black Magic'. They were divorced in 1962. Prima died in New Orleans on 24 August 1978.

PRIOR, Les Singer with the Manchester rock-comedy group Alberto Y Lost Trios Paranoias. Their album successes included *Alberto Y Lost Trios Paranoias*, *Italians From Outer Space* and *Skite*. Prior died from leukaemia on 31 January 1980. The group never recovered from his death and folded soon afterwards.

PTACEK, Rainer Blues guitarist, born in 1959, who died from a brain tumour at his home in Phoenix, Arizona, on 12 November 1997. He was 38 years old.

RAM, Buck Songwriter-manager-record producer, born in Chicago on 18 December 1908. Ram penned 'I'll Be Home For Christmas' for Bing Crosby and several hits for the Platters, one of the groups he managed. He died in in on 1 January 1991.

RAMIREZ, Bobby American musician, a member of **Edgar Winter's** White Trash. Ramirez was killed in a bar brawl in Chicago on 24 July 1972. He was 23 years old.

RAPP, Danny Singer, born in Philadelphia on 10 May 1941. Rapp became leader of **Danny & the Juniors**, whose first major hit was 'At The Hop' in 1957. Their follow-up was 'Rock & Roll Is Here To Stay'. They continued recording until their break-up in 1963. Rapp was found dead from self-inflicted gunshot wounds in Parker, Arizona, on 5 April 1983.

RAY, Johnny Singer born in Dallas, Oregon, on 10 January 1927. Despite becoming partially deaf at the age of nine, Ray began a musical career and enjoyed a string of hits, including 'Cry', 'The Little White Cloud That Cried' and 'Such A Night', and had three chart-toppers in the UK. He was dubbed the 'Nabob Of Sob', the 'Cry Guy', the 'Tearleader' and the 'Prince Of Wails'. Ray appeared with Marilyn Monroe in the musical *There's No Business Like Showbusiness*. He later suffered financial problems and began to drink too much. Ray died from liver failure on 24 February 1990.

REDDING, Otis Soul singer, born in Dawson, Georgia, on 9 September 1941. Redding began singing with an R&B group, Johnny Jenkins & the Pinetoppers, in 1959. He initially started recording R&B material and crossed over to the mainstream chart with 'I've Been Loving You Too Long (To Stop Now)' in 1965, following with 'Respect'.

Redding had a string of hits during the 1960s and appeared at the Monterey Pop Festival. He recorded '(Sittin' On) The Dock Of The Bay' on 7 December 1967 and died a few days later, on 10 December, when the twin-engined plane carrying him and his backing band, the **Bar-Keys**, crashed into Lake Monoma in Wisconsin. '(Sittin' On) The Dock Of The Bay', released posthumously, became his biggest hit.

Some years after his death, in 1980, his sons Dexter and Otis Redding III, together with their

Otis Redding

cousin Mark Locket, formed a band called the Reddings.

Otis Redding was inducted into the Rock & Roll Hall Of Fame in 1989.

REED, Jimmy Blues singer-guitarist, born on 6 September 1925, whose hits included 'Honest I Do' and 'Baby What You Want Me To Do'. Reed was also a songwriter and the **Rolling Stones**, every British blues group in the 1960s and **Elvis Presley** sang some of his numbers, including 'Big Boss Man' and 'Ain't That Loving You, Baby'. He died on 29 August 1976.

REED, Phil Guitarist with Flo & Eddie, who fell from the window of his hotel room in Salt Lake City on 25 October, 1976.

REEVES, Jim Country singer, born in Galloway, Texas, on 20 August 1923. He originally had aspirations to become a baseball pro, but a broken ankle laid that dream to rest. Reeves' first country music hit was 'Mexican Joe' in 1953 and his follow-up, 'Bimbo', was also a chart hit.

Reeves, who was inducted into the Country Music Hall Of Fame in 1967, had almost 30 chart singles, many of them charting posthumously and the majority of them in the UK. They included: 'He'll Have To Go', 'You're The Only Good Thing', 'Welcome To My World', 'I Love You Because', 'Distant Drums' and 'Nobody's Fool'. Reeves also starred in a South African film, *Kimberley Jim*.

Reeves died on 31 July 1964 in a plane crash in Nashville, along with his manager, Dean Manual.

In addition to the posthumous hits, he was paired with **Patsy Cline** on 'Have You Ever Been Lonely' in 1981, followed by the two paired again on 'I Go To Pieces' the next year. In 1983 'The Jim Reeves Medley' was issued, featuring four of his numbers. Another pairing resulted in three Top 10 singles in 1979 and 1980. Reeves was also paired on duets with singer Deborah Allen, who was 11 years old at the time of his death.

RELF, Keith Singer-guitarist, born in Richmond, Surrey, on 22 March 1943. Relf formed his first band, Metropolitan Blues Quartet, in 1963; they were to change their name to the **Yardbirds**. The group had a number of hit singles, including 'Good Morning Little Schoolgirl', 'For Your Love', 'Heartful of Soul', 'Shapes Of Things' and 'Happenings Ten Years Time Ago', before they disbanded in 1969. Relf was found dead from electrocution at his home on 4 May 1976, aged 32. He was holding a live guitar.

REYNOLDS, Malvina American folk singer-songwriter, two of whose songs – 'Little Boxes' and 'What Have They Done To The Rain' – reached the charts. Malvina died in March 1978. She was 77 years old.

RHODES, Randy Guitarist with Blizzard Of Ozz, a group led by Ozzie Osbourne. Rhodes was killed when the light aircraft in which he was travelling crashed in Orlando, Florida, on 19 March 1982.

RICH, Charly American country music singing star, born in Colt, Arkansas, on 24 December 1932. Rich, who came to be known as the 'Silver Fox', had a succession of hits from 1958, including 'Lonely Weekends', 'Behind Closed Doors', 'The Most Beautiful Girl', 'A Very Special Love Song' and 'Pictures And Paintings'. He suffered from drink problems and died as the result of a stroke in a motel in late July 1995.

RICHARDSON, J.P. Singer-songwriter, born in Sabine Pass, Texas, on 29 October 1932. Known as the 'Big Bopper', he became a disc jockey before recording his biggest hit, 'Chantilly Lace', followed by 'The Big Bopper's Wedding' and 'Little Red Riding Hood'. Richardson died on 3 February 1959, aged 26, in an air crash with **Buddy Holly** and **Ritchie Valens**. Ironically, he had persuaded Waylon Jennings to give up his seat on the plane to him. As a songwriter, some of Richardson's compositions found posthumous chart success, including 'Running Bear', which he had written for his friend **Johnny Preston**.

RIPPERTON, Minnie Singer with a five-octave range, born in Chicago on 8 November 1947. Minnie was a former member of Rotary Connection who joined Stevie Wonder's Wonderlove. Her biggest hit was the US chart-topper 'Lovin' You', written and produced by Stevie. Minnie died from cancer on 12 July 1979. She was 31 years old.

RITTER, Tex Country singer, born Woodward Maurice Ritter in Panula County, east Texas, on 11 January 1906. Ritter's hits included 'The Wayward Wind', 'I Dreamed Of A Hill-Billy Heaven' and 'Theme From High Noon'. He died as the result of a heart attack on 2 January 1974.

RIVERS, Jerry Nashville artist who was a member of the Drifting Cowboys, who toured and recorded with **Hank Williams**. Rivers was later to tour and record with a host of country music stars including Johnny Cash, Loretta Lynn and Hank Williams Jnr. He died in 1997, at the age of 68.

RIVERS, Rick Guitarist with the group New York Dolls, which was formed in 1972. Rivers died in 1982 from a combination of drugs and alcohol. Other members of this ill-fated group who died prematurely included **Billy Murcia** and **Jerry Nolan**.

ROBBINS, Marty Country singer, born Martin David Robinson in Glendale, Arizona, on 26 September 1925. Following a three-year spell in the US Navy, Robbins took various jobs ranging from digging ditches to working in the oil fields, and began to play guitar. He started recording in 1948 and had a hit in the country chart every year from 1956. These included: 'Singing The Blues', 'A White Sports Coat (And A Pink Carnation)', 'El Paso', 'Don't Worry' and 'Devil Woman'. Robbins died as the result of a heart attack on 8 December 1982.

ROBI, Paul Member of the **Platters**, born in New Orleans in 1931. Robi died in 1989.

ROBINSON, Darren 'Buffy' Brooklyn-born member of the Fat Boys rap trio, who recorded seven albums and had 12 R&B hits, including remakes of 'Wipeout' and 'The Twist'. Robinson also appeared in the movies *Knights Of The City*, *Krush Groove* and *Disorderlies*. He weighed 205kg (32 stone/450lb) and died in 1995, aged 28.

ROMERO, Tony Songwriter who penned the Partridge Family hit 'I Think I Love You'. Romero died in 1996, aged 56.

RONSON, Mick Noted British guitarist, born in Hull, Yorkshire, on 26 May 1947. Ronson played with various musicians including Ian Hunter, **Bob Dylan**, Van Morrison and Morrissey. He was noted for his work with David Bowie and had a musical partnership with Ian Hunter that lasted for 15 years. He died in 1993 from lung cancer, following a long illness.

The next year, the Mick Ronson Memorial Concert took place at the Hammersmith Apollo featuring artists such as Steve Harley, Ian Hunter, Roger Taylor, Roger Daltrey, the Rays, Dana Gillespie and Gary Brooker. The concert raised enough money to construct a Mick Ronson memorial stage in his home town.

ROSS, Jack American singer whose only chart hit was 'Cinderella' in 1962. Ross died on 16 December 1982, at the age of 66.

ROSTILL, John Guitarist, born in Birmingham on 16 June 1942, who joined the Shadows in October 1963 and remained with them until they disbanded in December 1968, although they agreed to play a tour of Japan together the following year. For a time, Rostill backed Tom Jones in Las Vegas, but he returned to the UK and was electrocuted while playing his guitar at home on 26 November 1973. He was 31 years old.

ROTHCHILD, Paul Main record producer for Elektra Records, who produced records by artists such as the Butterfield Blues Band, **Phil Ochs** and **Love**. Rothchild recorded the first six **Doors** albums and **Janis Joplin's** *Pearl*. He also recorded the soundtrack for the 1991 film *The Doors* and even appeared in the movie. Rothchild died from lung cancer in 1996, at the age of 59.

RUFFIN, David American gospel singer, born on 18 January 1941, who became lead singer with the Temptations from 1964 to 1968 and sang on hits such as 'My Girl'. When he left the group for a solo career, Ruffin charted with 'My Whole World Ended (The Moment You Left Me)' and 'Walk Away From Love'. He collaborated for a while with his brother Jimmy, and also teamed up with former Temptations member **Eddie Kendricks**, the duo touring with Hall & Oates in 1988. Ruffin died as the result of a drugs overdose at the hospital of the University of Pennsylvania on 1 June 1991.

RUSSELL, Devon Jamaican vocalist and former member of the Tartans. He died in London on 19 June 1997.

RYAN, Paul Singer born in London on 24 October 1948, along with his twin brother Barry. They were the sons of singer **Marion Ryan** and entered the chart with their debut single, 'Don't Bring Me Your Heartaches', in 1965. Other hits included 'Have Pity On The Boy', 'I Love Her' and 'Eloise'. Paul was also a songwriter and his composition 'I Will Drink The Wine' was recorded by Frank Sinatra. He died from cancer in 1992.

SADLER, Barry Singer-songwriter, born in New Mexico in 1941. Sadler joined the US Army, became a Staff Sergeant and fought in Vietnam. He penned the hit song 'The Ballad Of The Green Berets', recorded it and found himself at the top of the chart. Sadler was charged with and acquitted of murdering songwriter Lee Emerson Bellamy, and three years later was found not guilty of shooting his former business partner. He died from heart failure in Tennessee on 5 November 1989.

SAKAMOTO, Kyu Japanese singer, born Kawasaki in 1941. He had 15 hit singles and eight hit albums in Japan, in addition to numerous film and television roles. His 'Sukiyaki' became a No 1 hit in the US in 1962 and his other international hit was 'China Nights', the following year. Sakamoto was killed on 12 August 1985 when a jumbo jet in which he was travelling crashed into a mountain, killing 520 people.

SANDERS, Felicia Singer, whose one chart hit was 'Blue Star', from the US television series *Medic*, in 1955. Felicia died on 7 February 1975.

SANDON, Johnny Liverpool singer (real name Bill Beck) who was lead vocalist with Mersey Beat groups the **Searchers** and the Remo Four, before turning solo. Sandon recorded for Pye, but had no hits and was later to become a taxi driver. In a state of depression, he hanged himself on Christmas Day 1996.

SCOTT, Bon Lead singer with Australian-based Scottish heavy metal band AC/DC, born Ronald Bilford in Kirriemuir, Scotland, on 9 July 1946. Scott joined AC/DC in March 1974. He died from alcoholic poisoning in a London hospital on 21 February 1980, aged 33.

SECUNDA, Tony British entrepreneur who discovered and promoted the **Moody Blues** and the **Move**. Together with producer **Denny Cordell**, he formed Straight Ahead, a company which had hits with **Joe Cocker**, **Procol Harum** and T Rex. Secunda, who was also a music publisher, managed **Steeleye Span** and produced John Cale and Motorhead. He died in San Francisco just one week prior to the death of his former partner Cordell, in 1995.

SEVILLE, David Singer-songwriter, born in Fresno, California, on 27 January 1919. Seville entered the US chart in 1958 with 'Witch Doctor'. He then devised the Chipmunks, who hit the chart in 1959 with 'Ragtime Cowboy'. Seville died in Beverly Hills in January 1972.

SHAKUR, Tupac   Bronx-born rap artist (real name Lesane Crooks), whose hits included 'Me Against The World', 'All Eyez On Me', 'Apocalypse Now' and 'Strictly For My NIGGAS'. Shakur also appeared in the films *Juice, Poetic Justice, Above The Rim, Bullet, Gang Related* and *Gridlock*. Gunmen shot him fatally on 7 September 1996 in an ambush while he was on his way to a charity function. At the time, he was on bail after serving an eight-month prison sentence for sexual abuse. Shakur was 25 years old when he died.

SHANNON, Del   Singer, born Charles Westover in Coopersville, Michigan, on 20 December 1939. Shannon had nine US chart hits, including 'Runaway', 'Hats Off To Larry', 'Handy Man' and 'Little Town Flirt'. The first artist to have a Lennon & McCartney cover issued in the States, he seemed on the brink of a comeback when he was found dead at his home in Santa Clarita, California, on 8 February 1990, the victim of suspected self-inflicted gunshot wounds.

SHEPPARD, James 'Shep'   Lead singer of the Heartbeats and Shep & the Limelites, having founded the latter group in 1961. His hits included 'Daddy's Home', 'A Thousand Miles Away' and 'Three Steps To The Altar'. Sheppard was found beaten to death in his car on Long Island on 24 January 1970.

SHERMAN, Allan   Comedian, born in Chicago on 30 November 1924. In 1962, Sherman had a million-selling album with *My Son, The Folk Singer*, and followed this with *My Son, The Celebrity*. He also had a No 1 single with 'Hello Muddah, Hello Faddah', a number he wrote with Lou Busch, which was set to the music of Ponchielli's *Dance Of The Hours*. Sherman died from respiratory problems on 20 November 1973.

SHINES, Johnny   Blues guitarist-singer from Tennessee. A companion of the legendary **Robert Johnson** in his youth, Shines later moved to Chicago and was nominated for a Grammy Award in 1980. He died in 1992, at the age of 76.

SILL, Leslie   An American music publisher-entrepreneur who was associated with Phil Spector's Philles label. He died early in 1997 at the age of 76.

SILVA, Jimmy   Singer-songwriter, born in San Mateo, California. Silva based his career in Seattle and recorded four solo albums. His songs were covered by a variety of artists including the Smithereens and the Young Fresh Fellows. Silva died in 1995 from complications arising from chicken pox. He was 42 years old.

SLIM, Lightnin'   Blues performer and Excello recording star, born Otis Hicks in St Louis in 1913. Slim died from stomach cancer in Detroit on 27 July 1974.

SLIM, Memphis   Blues pianist, born Peter Chapman in Memphis, Tennessee, on 3 September 1915. He had lived in Paris since 1961 and died there from kidney failure on 24 February 1988.

SLIM, Washboard   One-man blues band from Texas, who was still active and playing in the Philadelphia area when he died in 1990 at the age of 89.

SLOVAK, Hillel   Founder member of the Red Hot Chilli Peppers, and the group's lead guitarist. Born in Haifa, Israel, he died in Hollywood on 27 June 1988, aged 25.

SMITH, Frank Elser   Keyboards player with Air Supply. The group had a number of hits, including 'All Out Of Love', 'The One That You Love' and 'Making Love Out Of Nothing At All'. Smith died from pneumonia in 1991.

SMITH, Fred 'Sonic'   Former guitarist with the MC5, who recorded albums such as *Kick Out The Jams* and *Back In The USA*. He married singer **Patti Smith**, who wrote her hit 'Frederick' about him. In the late 1980s they co-produced the album *Dream Of Life,* and were collaborating on Patti's latest album when Fred died as the result of a heart attack early in 1997. He was 45 years old.

SMITH, George   Member of the vocal group the Manhattans, a soul outfit who were formed in Germany with members of the US Air Force in 1962. Their hits included the songs 'Don't Take

Your Love', 'Kiss And Say Goodbye' and 'Shining Star'. Smith died in 1970 from spinal meningitis.

SMITH, Ray American rock 'n' roll singer, born on 31 October 1934. Smith's big hit was 'Rockin' Little Angel'. He committed suicide on 29 November 1979.

SOHL, Richard 'DNV' Pianist with the **Patti Smith** Group until 1977. He was featured on Patti's albums *Horses* and *Radio Ethiopia*. Sohl returned to join her on her comeback album in 1988 and died in 1990.

SOVINE, Red Singer (full name Woodrow Wilson Sovine), who had one chart hit, 'Teddy Bear', in 1976. He died on 4 April 1980, aged 61.

SPANN, Otis Blues musician-pianist-singer, who was also house pianist at Chess Records in Chicago and long-time pianist for **Muddy Waters**. Spann contracted liver cancer and died from heart failure on 25 April 1970, aged 40.

SQUIRES, Dorothy Singer, who between 1953 and 1970 had several hits, including 'I'm Walking Behind You', 'For Once In My Life', 'Till' and 'My Way'. She also had a chart entry when she teamed up with pianist Russ Conway for the single 'Say It With Flowers' in 1961.

Born Edna May Squires on 25 March 1918 in a travelling caravan parked in a field in Llanelli in Wales, Dorothy was a major star, particularly in the 1940s and 1950s, appearing regularly on radio shows such as *Variety Bandbox*. Some of her early hit songs, including 'I Close My Eyes' and 'Gipsy', were penned by accordionist Billy Reid, with whom she lived for 11 years, before she met actor Roger Moore. Roger, 17 years her junior, was married at the time, but as soon as his divorce came through in 1953 he married Dorothy. The singer was a multi-millionairess and they settled into a large house in Bray, in Berkshire. Moore's star began to ascend following his roles in the television series *The Saint* and as James Bond, and he met a 29-year-old Italian lady, Luisa, whom he married after his divorce from Dorothy was finalized in 1969.

Dorothy made a comeback in 1970, filling the London Palladium and touring, and often appearing at three clubs per night. However, the very high cost of litigation as she pursued writs over a variety of matters caused her to lose her fortune and she was evicted from her home in 1987, moving into bed-and-breakfast accommodation in Maidenhead before settling in Yorkshire.

The contents of her house was sold in November 1990 and she was provided with a cottage in Trebanon by one of her fans.

Despite her divorce from Moore, Dorothy considered their marriage a happy one and Moore paid all the hospital bills when she was diagnosed as having cancer of the bladder.

Moore also came to her aid in October 1997 when she became involved in litigation once again. She had a legal dispute with Castle Communications regarding the release of their album *The Best Of Dorothy Squires*. She claimed she held the rights to five of the songs, which were hers. She said: 'They do not own any of these recordings. Every one of the recording sessions was set up, produced and paid for by me.' The 70-year-old Moore, now involved with Swiss socialite Christina Tholstrop, commented: 'These songs are hers, financed by her. I have complete recall of these facts as, at the time, I was married to Dorothy Squires.'

Dorothy died from cancer on 14 April 1998.

STAFFORD, Terry Singer born in Hollis, Oklahoma, and based in Amarillo, Texas. Stafford reached No 3 in the US chart with 'Suspicion' and his other chart hit was 'I'll Touch A Star'. He also had six hits in the country chart. Stafford died in 1996.

STANSHALL, Vivian Lead singer with the Bonzo Dog Doo Dah Band, born in Shillingford, Oxfordshire, on 21 March 1943. The group of former art students originally got together as a band in 1965. After the Bonzos had disbanded in 1970, Stanshall appeared in the film *Sir Henry At Rawlinson's End*, which was based on one of his solo albums, and staged a play at London's Bloomsbury Theatre in 1988. Addicted to tranquillizers and struggling with alcoholism, he was confined to a mental hospital in Crouch End for a time. Stanshall also became a voice-over artist, but died in a fire at his flat in London in March 1995.

STARR, Ruby Groupie (real name Constance H. Mierzwiak) who also acted as back-up singer on numerous albums by artists such as Black Oak Arkansas and Ruby Jones. She died from cancer in 1995, aged 44.

STEPHENS, Robert Lead singer for the **Village People** in the mid-1980s. He sang the theme song for the film *Cat's Eye*. Stephens died in 1990, aged 35.

STEWART, Billy Soul singer, born in Washington, DC, on 24 March 1937, who, with three members of his band, was killed when their car crashed over a bridge in North Carolina on 17 January 1970. His major records included 'Summertime', 'Secret Love' and 'Sitting In The Park'. Stewart was 32 years old when he died.

STEWART, Ian Pianist who joined the **Rolling Stones** in 1962. When **Andrew Loog Oldham** took over management of the group, he decided that Stewart didn't have the right image for them and demoted him to roadie and backing musician. He remained with the band throughout their career and was often referred to as 'the sixth Stone'. Stewart died as the result of a heart attack in a Harley Street clinic on 12 December 1985. He was 47 years old. The Stones dedicated their 1986 album *Dirty Work* to his memory.

STINSON, Rob Musician from Waconia, Minneapolis. He was co-founder of Minneapolis-based band the Replacements, who recorded for Twin Tone in the 1980s, but was fired in 1986 and appeared with several other groups before he died from a drugs overdose in 1995.

STORM, Rory Legendary Liverpool singer (real name Alan Caldwell). The original drummer with Rory Storm & the Hurricanes was Ringo Starr – their other drummers included Keef Hartley and Ainsley Dunbar. Storm was found dead on 27 December 1972, aged 32, allegedly a suicide. He was suffering from a medical condition and it is probable that he died from an accidental combination of drink and drugs while mourning the recent death of his father.

STRUNK, Jud Singer-comedian, born Justin Strunk Jnr on 11 June 1936, whose biggest hit was 'Daisy A Day' in 1973. He died in a plane crash on 15 October 1981.

SUN RA Musician, born Sonny Blount in Birmingham, Alabama, in 1914. He began his career as a pianist with the Fletcher Henderson Band in the 1940s, then led his own band, Solar Arkestra, and recorded over 200 albums. Sun Ra died in 1993.

Rory Storm

SUTCLIFFE, Stuart Guitarist-artist, born in Edinburgh on 23 June 1940. He joined **John Lennon's** group the Quarry Men, who went through a number of name changes before settling on the Beatles. As the Beatles' bass guitarist, he toured Scotland with them and joined their season in Hamburg in 1960. He fell in love with a German girl, Astrid Kirchherr, and elected to remain in Germany to study art, leaving the band following their Top Ten club season in 1961. Paul McCartney took over on bass. Stuart died from a brain haemorrhage on 10 April 1962, probably caused by a fall he had had some months earlier. A film biopic, *Backbeat*, was released in 1993.

SZELEST, Stan Pianist, based in Woodstock, who played on stage for a number of artists, including Neil Young, and also recorded with **Stevie Ray Vaughan**, Lonnie Mack and members of the Band. He died in 1991, aged 48.

TARESSENKO, Ivan One of the drummers with the Mutoid Waste Company. Taressenko was a victim of the King's Cross station fire in London and died in hospital on 22 November 1987.

TAYLOR, Alex American singer, the older brother of **James Taylor**. He died as a result of a heart attack in 1992, aged 47.

TAYLOR, Mel Brooklyn-born drummer who became a session musician in California. Taylor played on 'The Monster Mash' hit and on early **Herb Alpert** recordings. In 1962 he joined the **Ventures**, then left the group in 1967 but rejoined in 1978. The band recorded a reputed 150 albums, several of which entered the chart. Taylor died from cancer in August 1996, aged 62. His son Leon has replaced him in the Ventures, and his younger brother Larry was bass guitarist with **Canned Heat**.

TAYLOR, Vince Cult British rocker, born in Middlesex in 1939, who formed the Playboys in 1958. Taylor appeared regularly on the *Oh Boy!* television show and composed and recorded a British rock classic, 'Brand New Cadillac'. He moved to France in 1961 and remained there for the rest of his career. He died in 1991.

TAYLOR, Vinnie Latter-day guitarist (real name Chris Donald) with Sha Na Na, a group formed in 1968 to perform 1950s rock 'n' roll. They rose to fame at the Woodstock Festival and released half a dozen albums. Taylor died from a heroin overdose on 17 April 1974 in Charlottesville, Virginia. He was 25 years old.

TERRELL, Tammi Motown singer, born in Philadelphia on 29 April 1945. She initially recorded a number of R&B hits, before becoming partner to **Marvin Gaye** on a string of hit singles between 1967 and 1969. These included: 'If I Could Build My Whole World Around You', 'Ain't Nothing Like The Real Thing', 'You're All I Need To Get By', 'You Ain't Livin' Till You're Lovin'', 'Good Lovin' Ain't Easy To Come By' and 'Onion Song'. Tammi died in the Graduate Hospital, Philadelphia, on 16 March 1970 following several operations to remove a brain tumour. It was rumoured that her brain disorders had originally been sparked off by beatings she had been given by the hierarchy at Motown. Tammi was 24 years old when she died.

TERRY, Sonny Blues vocalist-harmonica player, born Saunders Terrill in Georgia in 1911, who teamed up with **Brownie McGhee** in 1939, a partnership which was to last for 35 years. The duo was to influence many of the British blues performers in the 1960s. Terry died in New York on 12 March 1986 following a long illness.

TEX, Joe Soul singer, born Joseph Arrington in Rogers, Texas, on 8 August 1933. He came to prominence with 'Hold What You Got' in 1965. Between 1965 and 1977 he had nine hits in the States, including 'Skinny Legs And All' and 'I Gotcha'. Tex converted to Islam and changed his name to Yusuf Hazziez in 1966. He died as the result of a heart attack on 12 August 1982.

THAIN, Gary Bass guitarist, born in New Zealand, who moved to the UK and left the Keef Hartley Band to join Uriah Heep in 1972. Thain remained with them until 1975, when he was sacked for being unreliable and died on 19 March the following year from a drugs overdose.

THARPE, Sister Rosetta Gospel singer and pioneer female electric guitarist, who died in Philadelphia on 9 October 1973. She was 57 years old.

THIELE, Bob Brooklyn-born record producer-executive, who produced numerous hits in the 1950s. Thiele signed **Buddy Holly** & the Crickets in 1957 and produced Holly's New York City sessions. His fourth wife was singer Teresa Brewer. Thiele died in 1996, aged 73.

THUNDERS, Johnny American guitarist, born John Genzale in New York in 1952, who started his career as Johnny Volume. When he was approached to join the New York Dolls in 1971, he changed his name to Thunders and switched from bass to lead guitar. He was also to become leader of the Heartbreakers (*not* the Tom Petty band). A heroin addict, Thunders died at the St Peter Guest House, New Orleans, on 23 April 1991. Two other members of the ill-fated New York Dolls – **Billy Murcia** and **Jerry Nolan** – were to die prematurely.

TIL, Sonny Singer, born Earlington Tilghman in Baltimore on 18 August 1925. He formed the Vibranaires, who changed their name to the Orioles after the Maryland State bird in 1948. Til was the group's lead singer and the other members were George Nelson, Alexander Sharp and Johnny Reed. Their biggest hits were 'Tell Me So' in 1948 and 'Crying In The Chapel' in 1953. The original group disbanded in 1954; Nelson died from asthma in 1959 and Sharp as the result of a heart attack in 1970. Til also died following a heart attack, on 9 December 1981.

TILLEY, Sandra   Former member of the Velvelettes, who joined Martha Reeves & the Vandellas in 1971. Sandra died in 1982.

TILLMAN, Georgeanna Marie   Singer with the Marvelettes, one of Motown's female vocal groups. Georgeanna died following a long illness in Inkster, Michigan, on 6 January 1980, aged 46.

TINY TIM   Eccentric singer-ukelele player, born Herbert Buckingham Khaury in New York City on 12 April 1925. He had a major hit in 1968 with 'Tiptoe Thru' The Tulips', recorded several albums and toured the world. Tiny Tim married Victoria May Budinger on the UK television show *Tonight*, although they were later divorced due to his prudish attitude towards sex. He died in 1997.

TOOK, Steve Peregrine   Percussionist and singer, born 28 July 1949, who became the co-founder of Tyrannosaurus Rex with **Marc Bolan** in May 1967. The duo made their recording debut with the single 'Debora' and the album *My People Were Fair And Had Sky In Their Hair*. Took left in October 1969 and was replaced by Mickey Finn. He died from asphyxiation in London on 27 October 1980, aged 31.

TOSH, Peter   Singer-percussionist (real name Peter McIntosh), born in Jamaica on 19 October 1941. One of the founders of the Wailers in 1963, after splitting with **Bob Marley** in 1973 he had several hit albums, toured the States with the **Rolling Stones** and received a Grammy Award for Best Reggae Artist with his album *Captured Live*. Tosh and two friends were shot dead in his home in Kingston, Jamaica, by three armed raiders on 11 September 1987.

TRAVIS, Merle   Country singer, born in Rosewood, Kentucky, on 29 November 1917. Travis was the composer or co-writer of several country classics, including 'Sixteen Tons' and 'Smoke Smoke Smoke (That Cigarette)'. He was also renowned for his finger-picking style of guitar playing. Travis' chart-topping country singles included 'Divorce Me COD' and 'So Round, So Firm, So Fully Packed'. He was inducted into the Country Music Hall Of Fame in 1997.

Travis died as the result of a heart attack in Oklahoma on 20 October 1983.

TUCKER, Luther   Blues guitarist, born in Mississippi, who played with a host of Chicago blues bands and artists such as **Muddy Waters**, John Lee Hooker, James Cotton and **Little Walter**. He died in 1993, aged 57.

TUCKER, Tommy   Singer (real name Robert Higgenbotham) born in Springfield, Ohio, on 5 March 1933. His biggest hit was 'Hi Heel Sneakers' in 1964. Tucker died as a result of poisoning in New York on 17 January 1982.

TURNER, Big Joe   Singer, born in Kansas City on 18 May 1911, who was arguably the first artist to cut a rock 'n' roll disc when he recorded 'Shake Rattle & Roll' in 1954. During his lengthy career, which began in the 1930s, Turner recorded nearly 200 albums. He also worked with a number of jazz giants such as Duke Ellington and **Count Basie**. Turner died in Inglewood, California, on 23 November 1985.

TWITTY, Conway   Singer born Harold Lloyd Jenkins in Friars Pond, Mississippi, on 1 September 1933. Twitty had a series of hits, including 'It's Only Make Believe', 'Story Of My Love', 'Hey Little Lucy' and 'Mona Lisa'. He also appeared in the films *Platinum High School*, *Sex Kittens Go To College* and *College Confidential*. Twitty was taken to Cox South Memorial Centre in Springfield, Missouri, on 4 June 1993 and died the following day from an aortic aneurism – a blood clot on his abdomen.

TYNER, Rob   Singer with the MC5, born 12 December 1944. The band was originally formed in 1965 and the other members included Wayne Kramer (guitar), **Fred 'Sonic' Smith** (guitar) and Bob Gasper (drums). Their albums included *Kick Out The Jams*, *Back In The USA* and *High Times*. The group disbanded in 1972 and Tyner was found dead on 18 September 1991. Kramer was jailed for cocaine dealing, and Fred Smith died in 1997.

VALENS, Ritchie Singer-songwriter-guitarist, born Richard Steven Valenzuela in Pacoima, Los Angeles, on 13 May 1943. Valens originally doted on Mexican-American style chicano music, but on hearing Little Richard fell in love with rock 'n' roll. He formed his first band, the Silhouettes, while still at high school and made his recording debut with 'Come On Let's Go', a Top 50 entry, in October 1958. Valens' biggest hit in an all-too-brief career was the follow-up, 'Donna/La Bamba'. He made several television appearances and had a guest part in the film *Go Johnny Go*.

Valens died in a plane crash with **Buddy Holly** and **J. P. Richardson** (the 'Big Bopper') on 3 February 1959. He was 15 years old.

It was a stroke of bad luck that Valens, who was afraid of flying because he had had premonitions that he would die in a plane crash, persuaded guitarist Tommy Allsup to give him his seat on the journey. Valens was the subject of a film biopic, *La Bamba*, in 1987.

VALENTI, Dino Folk singer (real name Chester Powers), born in Danbury, Connecticut, who wrote the Youngbloods' hit 'Get Together'. Valenti formed **Quicksilver Messenger Service** in 1965, but was arrested for possession of drugs and sent to gaol before they recorded. He later recorded a solo album in 1978, then rejoined Quicksilver, recording 'Fresh Air' and 'What About Me'. He died in 1994, aged 51.

VALENTINE, Dickie British singer, born Richard Bryce on 4 November 1929. His most successful year in the UK chart came in 1955 with five Top 10 hits, including two chart-toppers – 'Finger Of Suspicion' and 'Christmas Alphabet'. Valentine was still performing to full-house audiences when he died in a car crash on 6 May 1971.

VAN DYKE, Earl Keyboards player at Motown Records, who performed on countless hits. He died in 1992, aged 62.

VAN ZANDT, Townes Singer-songwriter, born in Fort Worth, Texas, who teamed up with fellow Texan Guy Clark to write songs. They formed a quartet, along with Peter Rowan and John Stewart.

Van Zandt's songs, which included 'Pancho' and 'Lefty', were covered by a number of artists, including **Bob Dylan**, Emmy Lou Harris, Merle Haggard and Willie Nelson.

Van Zandt, who was institutionalized in his teens as a 'manic depressive with schizophrenic tendencies', died as the result of a heart attack on New Year's Day 1997. He was 52 years old.

VAUGHAN, Stevie Ray Blues-rock guitarist, born in Dallas, Texas, on 3 October 1954. Vaughan joined his first band, Blackbird, at the age of 14; his other bands included the Chantones and A Cast Of Thousands. He moved to Austin and began appearing with various blues bands; eventually, he formed his own outfit, Double Trouble, in May 1979.

Vaughan's first major album, *Texas Flood*, was released on Epic in 1983. He recorded with a number of noted artists and appeared on David Bowie's *Let's Dance* album. He had just completed a new album with his brother Jimmie, a former member of the Fabulous Thunderbirds, when he was killed in a helicopter crash in August 1990. He was 35 years old.

VAUGHN, Billy Originally a big band leader, born in Glasgow, Kentucky. With his orchestra, Vaughn had a string of 12 middle-of-the-road chart hits, including 'Melody Of Love', 'The Shifting Whispering Sands', 'Raunchy' and 'Sail Along Silvery Moon'. He became musical director of Dot Records, arranging and conducting for artists such as **Pat Boone**, Lawrence Welk and Liberace. Vaughn died in 1991, aged 72.

VICIOUS, Sid Singer-bass guitarist, born John Simon Ritchie in London on 10 May 1957, who replaced Glen Matlock in the **Sex Pistols** in February 1977. The outrageous punk band, led by Johnny Rotten, became even more subversive with the inclusion of Vicious, who would cut himself on stage with razors, broken glass or knives.

Together with his American girlfriend Nancy Spungen, Vicious was arrested on a drugs charge, but was later released. He was then taken to hospital following an overdose. The Sex Pistols folded, and Vicious recorded 'My Way' and gave a farewell concert in London called Sid Sods Off, before leaving for New York.

He stabbed Nancy to death on 11 October 1978 at the Chelsea Hotel in New York. Bailed out of prison, he then died from an overdose of heroin on 2 February 1979. He was 21 years old.

Vicious was the subject of the film biopic *Sid And Nancy* in 1988, with Gary Oldman portraying the punk rock star.

VINCENT, Gene Singer, born Vincent Eugene Craddock in Norfolk, Virginia, on 11 February 1935. Vincent was disabled in a motorcyle accident in 1955, but went on to record hits such as 'Be Bop A Lula' with his group the Blue Caps, who appeared with him in the film *The Girl Can't Help It*. Other hits included 'Race With The Devil' and 'Blue Jean Bop'.

At the age of 21 Vincent married a teenage girl, but they soon broke up. He continued to suffer pain from his leg and had to have a metal brace placed on it. His star began to wane in the States following financial problems, drinking and the withdrawal of his Musicians' Union card for 'unprofessional conduct'. He decided to move to England.

Vincent arrived in the UK in 1960 and developed an image by wearing a black leather outfit and emphasizing his limp. He survived a road accident in which **Eddie Cochran** was killed.

Vincent was to appear with the Beatles in Liverpool's Cavern club and Hamburg's Star Club, and with **John Lennon** at the Toronto Rock 'n' Roll Festival.

By 1965 his life was falling apart again. He continued to experience financial problems, and was now married for the fourth time, constantly ill and putting on too much weight.

Vincent returned to the States, where he died as the result of a bleeding ulcer on 12 October 1971. He was 36 years old.

VOGEL, Janet American vocalist, born on 10 June 1942, who was a member of the Skyliners. Janet committed suicide on 21 February 21 1980, aged 37.

VON PALLANDT, Baron Frederick Male half of singing duo Nina & Frederick. The Danish baron and his wife had a number of hits in the late 1950s with 'Mary's Boy Child' and 'Little Donkey'. The couple split up in 1969 and Frederick went to live in Ibiza, while Nina became a cabaret artist. They were divorced in 1976 and Frederick went to live in Manila in the Philippines, where an assassin shot him dead in May 1994.

Gene Vincent and his Blue Caps

WAITE, Patrick Bass guitarist with British reggae band Musical Youth, who had a single chart hit, 'Pass The Dutchie' in 1982. The group had no further hits and Waite became involved in criminal activities, including armed robbery. He died mysteriously in 1993, aged 24.

WALKER, Aaron T Bone Highly influential pioneer electric blues guitarist, born in Linden, Texas, on 28 May 1910. Walker began recording with Trinity River Blues in 1929 and his biggest hit was 'Stormy Monday' in 1947. He died from bronchial pneumonia on 16 March 1975.

WALKER, Junior Leader of Junior Walker & the All Stars, born Autry de Walt Jnr in Blytheville, Arkanasas, in 1942. Walker was also a leading Motown saxophonist and one of the label's major instrumentalists. His hits included 'Shotgun' and 'What Does It Take?'. Walker died from cancer in late November 1995.

WALKER, Randy 'Stretch' Member of the rap group Live Squad, who was murdered in November 1995.

WARD, Jeff Drummer who played with a number of bands, including Low Pop Suicide, Ministry and Nine Inch Nails. He died in 1993, at the age of 30.

WASHINGTON, Dinah Singer, born Ruth Jones in Tuscaloosa, Alabama, on 29 August 1924, who was known as the 'Queen Of The Blues'. Most of her hits were in the 1950s and included 'What A Difference A Day Makes' and 'Unforgettable'. Her final chart entry was 'September In The Rain' in 1961. Dinah said: 'When you get inside a tune, the soul in you should come out.' The six-times married singer died from a heart seizure caused by an overdose of sleeping pills at her home in Detroit on 14 December 1963. She was 39 years old.

WATERS, Muddy Legendary blues guitarist-singer-songwriter, born McKinley Morganfield in Rolling Fork, Mississippi, on 4 April 1915. Waters' songs were an inspiration during the British blues boom in the 1960s and included numbers such as 'Got My Mojo Working', 'Mannish Boy', 'I'm Ready' and 'Hoochie Coochie Man'. Following a heart attack, he passed away in his sleep in Downers Grove, Illinois, on 30 April 1983.

WATSON, Johnny 'Guitar' Guitarist, born in Houston, Texas, on 3 February 1935, who made his first record – 'Motorhead Baby' – as a teenager in 1952. Between 1955 and 1984 Watson had 18 R&B chart hits, including 'Those Lonely', 'Lonely Nights' and 'A Real Mother For Ya'. He died as the result of a heart attack while on stage in Yokohama, Japan, in 1996.

WATSON, Merle Country music singer-guitarist, the son of blind guitarist Doc Watson. Father and son performed as a team. Merle was killed on 23 October 1985, when a tractor he was driving on his farm in North Carolina overturned.

WAYNE, Thomas Singer with the DeLons, whose biggest hit was 'Tragedy'. Wayne was killed in a car crash on 15 August 1971. He was 29 years old.

WEBER, Joan Singer, born in Paulsboro, New Jersey, in 1936. Joan's only hit was 'Let Me Go Lover', which topped the US chart in December 1954. When she recorded it, she was an 18-year-old pregnant housewife. Joan died on 13 May 1981.

WELLS, Mary Singer, born Mary Esther Wells in Detroit on 13 May 1943, Mary first started singing when she was ten. She made her debut with Motown, singing her own composition 'Bye Bye Baby'. She had 21 hits, including 'The One Who Really Loves You', 'You Beat Me To The Punch', 'Two Lovers' and 'My Guy'.

Mary travelled to the UK and toured with the Beatles. She also appeared on the television special *Around The Beatles* and recorded an album, *Love Songs To The Beatles*.

Mary died from cancer in August 1992.

WEST, Dottie Country music singer-songwriter, born in McMinnville, Tennessee, on 11 October 1932. Dottie's biggest hit was 'What Are We Doin' In Love', a 1981 release with Kenny Rogers on backing vocals. Dottie also appeared in the movies *Second Fiddle To A Steel Guitar* and *The Road To Nashville*. Her hits in the country chart included 'Here Comes My Baby', 'Country Sunshine', 'Every Time Two Fools Collide' and 'All I Ever Need Is You'. She died on 4 September 1991 from injuries sustained in a car crash.

WHITE, Carol Member of the novelty vocal group the Rivingtons, whose hits included 'Papa-Oom-Mow-Mow' in 1962 and 'The Bird's The Word' in 1963. The other members were Al Frazier, Rocky Wilson and Sonny Harris. White died at his home in Los Angeles on 7 January 1980, at the age of 48.

WHITE, Clarence American guitarist, born on 7 June 1944, who joined the Byrds in November 1968. White was killed in a car accident in Lancaster, California, on 14 July 1973, aged 29.

WHITE, Robert Musician, born in Billmeyer, who was originally a member of the Moonglows, a group that recorded for Chess in the 1950s. White became a session guitarist for Motown Records and featured on many hits of the 1960s by groups such as the Temptations and the Miracles. He died in 1995, aged 57.

WHITE, Ron Singer, born in Detroit on 5 April 1939. White was a founder member and baritone singer of the Miracles, who originally formed in 1955 as the Matadors and became the

*Dinah
Washington*

Miracles in 1958. Their hits included: 'You Really Got A Hold On Me', 'Mickey's Monkee', 'The Tracks Of My Tears' and 'The Tears Of A Clown'. White, who was credited with discovering Stevie Wonder and co-wrote 'My Girl' and 'My Guy', died from leukaemia at the Henry Ford hospital in Detroit on 26 August 1995.

WHITFIELD, David Most successful British male artist of the 1950s, born in Hull on 2 February 1926. Whitfield was a builders' labourer earning £7 a week when had his first hit with 'Bridge Of Sighs'. His next recording was 'Cara Mia', which topped the UK chart, making him the first British male singer to win a gold disc. Whitfield's other the chart-topper was 'Answer Me', and further releases included 'Beyond The Stars', 'Adoration Waltz', 'My September Love' and 'Smile'. He died on 15 January 1980 in Sydney, Australia.

WHITTEN, Danny Member of Neil Young's backing group, Crazy Horse. Young invited Whitten, Billy Taylor and Ralph Molina to join him on his album *Everybody Knows This Is Nowhere* and the group began to tour with him. Their relationship suffered and ended due to Whitten's drugs dependency, and he died from a heroin overdose on 18 November 1972, aged 29.

WHITTEN, Jesse Guitarist from Chicago, Illinois, who played with London-based disco band Heatwave. Their hits included 'Boogie Nights', 'Always And Forever' and 'The Groove Line'. Whitten was stabbed to death in 1977 during a visit to Chicago.

WHYTON, Wally Former folk disc jockey who became leader of the Vipers skiffle group which, in 1957, enjoyed three chart hits – 'Cumberland Gap', 'Don't You Rock Me, Daddy-O' and 'Streamline Train'. Whyton later became a radio and TV presenter. He died in January 1997, at the age of 67.

WILLIAMS, Billy Singer, born on 28 December 1916. Williams was a member of the Charioteers, whose major hit was 'I'm Gonna Sit Right Down And Write Myself A Letter'. He died on 17 October 1972.

WILLIAMS, Eddie Musician, born in San Augustine, Texas, who was the bass fiddle player with Johnny Moore's Three Blazers, based in Los Angeles. The group had 16 entries in the R&B charts between 1946 and 1955, including 'Merry Christmas Baby' and 'Groovy Movie Blues'. Williams died in 1996. He was 83 years old.

WILLIAMS, Hank Legendary country singer, born in Mount Olive, Alabama, in 1923, who first began recording in 1946. Williams became the first country singer to have a succession of hits in the pop charts, which included 'Lovesick Blues', 'Your Cheatin' Heart', 'Rootie Tootie' and 'Jambalaya'. He died from heart failure brought on by overdosing on pills in the back of his car on New Year's Day 1953, when he was 29 years old. The film biopic *Your Cheatin' Heart* was released in 1964 with George Hamilton playing Williams.

WILLIAMS, Lamar Bass player with the Allman Brothers Band, who died from cancer in Los Angeles on 25 January 1983, aged 36.

WILLIAMS, Larry Singer-songwriter, born on 10 May 1935, whose hits in the 1950s included 'Dizzy Miss Lizzy', 'Short Fat Fanny' and 'Bony Moronie'. Williams died in Los Angeles from gunshot wounds to the head on 2 January 1980. Whether he was murdered or committed suicide remains a mystery.

WILLIAMS, Paul Singer, born in Birmingham, Alabama, on 2 July 1939. Williams joined the Elgins in 1960 and the following year they changed their name to the Temptations and signed with Motown Records. The vocal group had tremendous success with chart-topping albums and a run of hit singles, including 'The Way You Do The Things You Do', 'My Girl', 'Ain't Too Proud To Beg' and 'You're My Everything'. Due to his alcoholic problems, Williams was forced to leave the group in June 1971. Plagued by financial and matrimonial troubles, he was found dead in his car on 17 August 1977, having shot himself in the head. He was 34 years old.

WILLIAMS, Rozz Singer with Christian Death, a group who first rose to fame in 1982 with the release of their debut album, *Only Theatre Of Death*. Williams hanged himself in his Hollywood home in April 1998. He was 34 years old.

WILLIAMS, Tony Singer, born in Elizabeth, New Jersey, on 5 April 1928. Williams was the original lead singer with the Platters and appeared on 20 of their hits, including 'Only You' and 'The Great Pretender'. He left the group in 1961. Williams died in 1992, suffering from diabetes and emphysema.

WILLIAMS, Tony Drummer with the group Lifetime, who died early in 1997, aged 52.

WILLIAMS, Wendy O. New York-born punk singer of what she dubbed 'pornography rock'. Wendy led a band called the Plasmatics and in 1980 they were banned from performing in London because of their controversial stage act. Wendy used to appear on stage in body stockings or skimpy bottoms, with her chest naked but for black sticky tape and bits of whipped cream. She was dubbed the 'Queen Of Shock Rock' and was nominated for a Grammy in 1985 as Best Female Rock Vocalist. Her songs included 'Sex Junkie', 'Pig Is A Pig' and 'Living Dead'. Her body was discovered on 6 April 1998 by her manager and lover Rod Swenson in a wood near their home in Storrs, Connecticut. She had committed suicide by shooting herself with a shotgun. At the time of her death, she had not performed with the Plasmatics for several years. Wendy was 48 years old when she died.

WILLIS, Chuck Singer-songwriter, born in Atlanta, Georgia, on 31 January 1928. Willis had a series of R&B hits from 1952 and his records included 'The Stroll', 'C.C. Rider', 'Betty And Dupree', 'Hang Up My Rock And Roll Shoes' and 'What Am I Living For'. He also penned over 50 songs, which were recorded by a number of artists ranging from **Ray Charles** to **Dean Martin**. Willis died from a perforated ulcer at the Hugh Spalding Hospital in Atlanta, Georgia, on 10 April 1958. He was 30 years old.

WILSON, Al A guitarist-vocalist-harmonica player, born on 4 July 1943. A member of Canned Heat, he was nicknamed 'Blind Owl'. Wilson died from a drugs overdose on 3 September 1970, and his body was found in the backyard belonging Bob Hite, his fellow group member. Wilson was 27 years old when he died.

WILSON, Buster Singer with the Coasters, whose dismembered body was found in Modesto, California, in May 1980. The Coasters' former manager Patrick Cavanaugh was convicted of his murder on 8 December 1984.

WILSON, Carl Guitarist-vocalist with the **Beach Boys**, born in Hawthorne, California, on 21 December 1946. In 1967 he refused to be drafted, claiming to be a conscientious objector. He was arrested and a legal case ensued which continued for years, until it was settled by his agreement to do community work. Carl left the group in 1981 to tour with his own outfit, the Carl Wilson Band, and also released an eponymous album. He returned to the Beach Boys the following year. Despite suffering from liver cancer, Carl toured with the group in 1997 and died in February 1998.

WILSON, Dennis Drummer-vocalist with the **Beach Boys**, born in Hawthorne, California, on 4 December 1944. The original group comprised his two brothers, Brian and **Carl**, their cousin Mike Love and friend Al Jardine. They became one of the major groups of the 1960s with a string of bestselling singles, including classics such as 'Good Vibrations' and 'God Only Knows'. Dennis became the first Beach Boy to record a solo album, but it didn't chart. He died while swimming from his boat in a harbour on 28 December 1981 and was given a burial at sea. Dennis was 37 years old when he died.

WILSON, Jackie Singer, born Jack Leroy Wilson in Detroit, Michigan, on 9 June 1934. He began a solo singing career with Reet Petite in September 1957. After several further hits, Wilson was shot by a fan and later discharged from hospital with a bullet still lodged in his back. He had a number of million-sellers, including '(Your Love Keeps Lifting Me) Higher And Higher', and then suffered a heart attack while singing on stage on 29 September 1969, when he was 35. He fell into a coma, suffering from brain damage, and never regained consciousness, finally being declared dead on 21 January 1984.

WILSON, Ricky Guitarist, born on 19 March 1953, who was a founder member of the **B52s**, a group formed in Athens, Georgia, in 1976. Ricky's sister Cindy Wilson, together with another female vocalist, Kate Pierson, wore bouffant hairstyles, which gave the group its name.

The band had several album releases which sold well, but their biggest hit, 'Rock Lobster' came after Ricky had died from lymph cancer on 13 October 1985. He was 32 years old.

WILSON, Ron Vocalist-drummer, born in 1945. He was a member of the Surfaris, whose hits included 'Wipe Out', 'Surfer Joe' and 'I'm A Hog For You'. Wilson died in 1989 from a brain haemorrhage.

WOLFMAN JACK American disc jockey, born Robert Weston Smith in Brooklyn. He became legendary as a disc jockey, appeared as himself in the film *American Graffiti* and was the subject of songs by Todd Rundgren and Guess Who. He also recorded several albums. Wolfman Jack died as the result of a heart attack in 1996. He was 57 years old.

WOLTERS, John Christian Drummer, born in Pompton Lakes, New Jersey, on 28 April 1945. Wolters joined **Dr Hook** in 1975, recording nine albums with the band and touring with them until their One And Only Farewell Tour in 1985. When the group disbanded he played with various bands, before becoming an executive with the record company Hearts Of Space. Wolters died from liver cancer at his home in San Francisco on 16 June 1997.

WOOD, Andy Singer with Mother Love Bone, a group from Seattle formed in 1988. They were on the brink of success when Wood died from a heroin overdose in March 1990. The group then disbanded.

WOOD, Chris Musician, born in Birmingham, England, on 24 June 1944. In 1967 he was invited by Stevie Winwood to join his newly formed Traffic on sax and flute. Wood remained with the group until they split in 1974 after a series of hits, including 'Hole In My Shoe'. He died from liver failure on 12 July 1983, aged 39.

WYNETTE, Tammy Country music queen, born Virginia Wynette Pugh on a cotton farm in Mississippi. Tammy had 20 chart-topping hits in the States, including 'Stand By Your Man' and 'D-I-V-O-R-C-E'. She won the Country Music Association's award for Female Vocalist Of The Year in three successive years from 1968, and sold more than 30 million albums. Tammy returned to the UK chart in 1991 with 'Justified And Ancient', on which she appeared with KLF. Tammy led a turbulent and flamboyant life, being married five times and giving birth to five daughters and a son. She became addicted to painkillers and was once kidnapped and beaten by a masked assailant. The singer suffered years of ill health and underwent major surgery in 1992. She died from a blood clot on 6 April 1998, aged 55.

WYNNE, Phillipe Lead singer with the Spinners, the hit American band, originally formed in Detroit in 1957. Born on 3 April 1938, Wynne replaced G.C. Cameron in the group in January 1971. He left in 1977. The Spinners had 16 entries in the US chart, including 'I'll Be Around', 'Could It Be I'm Falling In Love', 'The Rubberband Man' and 'Working My Way Back To You'. He died as the result of a heart attack on stage at San Francisco's Ivey club on 14 July 1984.

YANA Glamorous British singer, born Pamela Guard in Romford, Essex, on 16 February 1932. She had several major record releases in the 1950s, including 'Climb Up The Wall', 'Something Happened To My Heart' and 'My Wonderful'. Yana had her own television series and appeared in many West End musicals. She died from throat cancer in 1988.

YOUNG, Faron Country music star, born in Shreveport, Los Angeles. Young, who founded *Country Music News* magazine, entered the country chart 89 times between the years 1983 and 1989. He also had a pop chart entry, 'Hello Walls', in 1961. Young shot himself in 1997, at the age of 64.

YOUNG, Johnny One of only two famed American blues mandolin players, who died following a heart attack in Chicago on 18 April 1974, aged 56.

ZAPPA, Frank Singer-guitarist-songwriter, born in Baltimore on 21 December 1940. Zappa first formed a group at high school called the Blackouts. In 1964 he formed the Muthers, changing the name to the Mothers the following year – and the year after that to the Mothers Of Invention.

Frank Zappa

Their albums included *We're Only In It For The Money*, *Cruising With Ruben And The Jets* and *Uncle Meat*. In the UK, Zappa filmed *200 Motels* and spent nine months in a wheelchair after being pushed off stage at the Rainbow Theatre. He was to receive a Grammy in 1988 when his *Jazz From Hell* album was named Best Rock Instrumental. He died from a terminal illness in December 1993.

Former members of Zappa's Mothers Of Invention began touring in the 1980s as the Grandmothers, and were touring the UK in early 1998. Members included Don Preston, Bunk Gardner and Jimmy Carl Black.

WHEN I FIRST LAUNCHED the newspaper *Mersey Beat* in 1961, local fans began taking out advertisements for fan clubs for groups such as the Beatles and Gerry & the Pacemakers. Brian Epstein then took over management of the Beatles and decided to place the fan club on a more professional footing, and Freda Kelly was placed in charge. When I moved offices at *Mersey Beat*, Freda and her club were located just down the hall.

One day I noticed several tea chests crammed with books stacked along the corridor. I asked Freda what they were and she told me that Ringo had mentioned in an article that he liked science fiction – and literally thousands of science-fiction books had been sent in from fans around the world. I began to notice that Mr and Mrs Harrison, George's parents, were regular visitors to the fan club office, and that the quantity of gifts sent to the Beatles was staggering, the items ranging from hand-knitted dolls to full china dinner services. This was just a sample of how devoted fans can be to their idols.

The majority of fan clubs are non-profit making, and the standard of their product for fans vary from newsheets to glossy full-colour magazines. Various goodies, such as photographs and badges, are also usually available to members. Since the clubs are non-profit making, it is essential that you send a stamped, addressed envelope (or an International Reply Coupon) when you are making enquiries.

Incidentally, I am curious as to why the Netherlands, which appears to have no major pop music stars of its own, is so active in the fan field. Their clubs are well run and the publications they produce are absolutely fascinating.

The fan clubs listed here are for artists with their own entries in the Where Are They Now? and In Memoriam sections of this book. *Record Collector* and *The Beat Goes On* magazines are excellent sources of information regarding fan clubs for other artists mentioned in the text.

Abba
1 Barrow Hill Road, Shirehampton, Bristol BS11 9QT.

Bangles, The
Bangles And Mash, 4455 Torrance Boulevard, Torrance, California 90503, US.

Barron Knights, The
Phil Black, 92 Heol Yr Odyn, Ely, Cardiff CF5 5QX, Wales.

Beach Boys, The
Beach Boys Stomp, 22 Avondale Road, Wealdstone, Middlesex HA3 7RE.

Freaks United, PO Box 842282, Los Angeles, California 90073, US.

Bee Gees, The
Renée Schreiber, PO Box 249, Miami Beach, Florida 33140, US.

The Bee Gees

Berry, Mike
Ken Coombs, 37 Spartley Drive, Highridge, Bristol BS13 8DQ.

Bolan, Marc
The Bolan Society, PO Box 297, Newhaven, East Sussex BN9 9NX.

Brooks, Elkie
Lorraine Osbourne, Mapleleaf, Stapleford Road, Stapleford Abbots, Romford, Essex RM4 1EJ.

Brown, Joe
Ray Johnson, PO Box 4, Haverhill, Suffolk CB9 0JQ.

Cassidy, David
The Old Post House, The Street, Litlington, Polegate, East Sussex BN26 5RD.

Clark, Petula
Terry Young, 38 Elmley Way, Margate, Kent CT9 4ES.

Costello, Elvis
28 The Butts, Brentford, TW8 8BL.

Creedence Clearwater Revival
Peter Koers, Schopperhofstrasse 74, 90789 Nurnberg, Germany.

D'Arby, Terence Trent
The Hardline Society, PO Box 910, London NWI 9AQ.

Deep Purple
Deep Purple Appreciation Society, PO Box 254, Sheffield, South Yorkshire S6 5FL.

Dylan, Bob
PO Box 18, Bury, Lancashire BL9 OLX.

East 17
PO Box 153, Stanmore, Middlesex, HA7 2HF.

Everly Brothers, The
Sue Goodwin, 3 Everest Close, Hyde, Greater Manchester SK14 4DY.

The Beehive, The Fun Club For Fans Of The Everly Brothers, PO Box 3933, Seattle, Washington 98124-3933, US.

Farlowe, Chris
c/o 60 Babbacombe Road, Bromley, Kent BRI 3LW.

Fortunes, The
John Holman, PO Box 220, Swanley, Kent CT6 8BB.

Fury, Billy
Clare Mehmet-Nugent, 36 Manbey Grove, Stratford, London E15 1EX.

Glitter, Gary
37 Blacksmith Lane, Rainham, Essex EM13 7AD.

Gerry & The Pacemakers
Phil Tucker, Boroughbridge Garden Centre, Kirby Hill, Boroughbridge, York YO5 9DE.

Hendrix, Jimi
Jimi Hendrix Information Management Institute, PO Box 374, Des Plaines, Illinois 60016, US.

Herman's Hermits
Mary Dyer, 151 Great Preston Road, Ryde, Isle of Wight PO33 1AZ.

Hollies, The
Chris and Sheila Bowen, 12 The Aspens, Kingsbury, near Tamworth, Staffordshire B78 2JY.

Human League
c/o Smerch, PO Box 1AP, London WIA 1AP.

Jones, Howard
102 Green Street, High Wycombe, Buckinghamshire, HP11 2RE.

Kane, Eden
Sue Vale, 16 Morris Avenue, Studd Hill, Herne Bay, Kent CT6 8BB.

The Fortunes

279

Kinks, The
The Official Kinks Fan Club, PO Box 30, Atherstone, Warwickshire CV9 2ZX.

Kiss
The Kiss Army, PO Box 840, Westbury, New York 11590-0840, US.

Laine, Frankie
Tony Cooper, 24 Napier Crescent, Seamer, Scarborough, North Yorkshire YOI2 4HY.

Frankie Laine

Lee, Brenda
Les Wright, Flat 4, Ash Lodge, 80 Kildas Road, London N16 5BY.

Leyton, John
Jacky Cain, 3 Bushey Lane, Sutton, Surrey SMI 1QL.

Madonna
8491 Sunset Boulevard, 485 West Hollywood, California 90069, US.

Manfred Mann
29 Lyndhurst Road, Wallasey, Merseyside L45 6XB.

Manilow, Barry
PO Box 40, Epsom, Surrey KT1 9EF.

Merseybeats, The
Maureen Hillyer, 20 North Court, Leighton Buzzard, Bedfordshire LU7 8DJ.

Minogue, Kylie
PO Box 292, Watford, Hertfordshire WD2 4ND.

Mitchell, Guy
The Guy Mitchell Appreciation Society, 30 Kingston Road, Portsmouth, Hampshire PO1 5RZ.

Monkees
6 Pinfolds, Warwick Court, Teviott Avenue, Aveley, Essex RM15 4QA.

Moody Blues
53 High Street, Cobham, Surrey KT11 3D.

Petty, Tom
890 Tennessee Street, San Francisco, California 94107, US.

Presley, Elvis
Official Fan Club, PO Box 4, Leicester, LE3 5HY.

Elvis Presley Fan Club Osterreich, Pete Baumann, Offenes Fach 543, A -1101 Wien, Austria.

Nicole Marechal, Graceland Elvis Presley Fan Club, 62 Rue Aux Grands Champs, 4950 Beauchamps, Belgium.

International Elvis Presley Fan Club, Hubert Vindevogel, Pijlstraat 15, 2739 Zwinjndrecht, Belgium.

Elvis Presley Fan Club Of Denmark, Kate Jorgensen, Enghave Plads 14, 1640 Kobenhavn V, Denmark.

Elvis Presley Fan Club Of Finland, Box 21, 03601 Karkkila, Finland.

Treat Me Nice Elvis Presley Fan Club, Jean-Marc Gargiulo, 306 Rue de Belleville, 75020, Paris, France.

Elvis Presley Gesellschaft eV, Helmut Radermacher, Postfach 1264, D-8430 Neumarkt 1, Germany.

Peter Haan, It's Elvis Time, Postbus 27015, 3003 LA Rotterdam, Netherlands.

Always Elvis Fan Club, Postbus 60, 6990 AB Rheden, Netherlands.

Prince
PO Box 858, Old Chelsea Station, New York, NY 10012, US.

Richard, Cliff
PO Box 2BQ, London WIA 2BQ.

International Cliff Richard Movement, PO Box 94164, 1090 GD Amsterdam, Netherlands.

Rubettes, The
PO Box 2896, Billericay, Essex CM11 1QW.

Searchers, The
Tim Viney, 123 Laburnum Grove, North End, Portsmouth, Hampshire PO2 OHE.

The Searchers

Searchers, Mike Penders'
Anne and Roger Askey, 14 Goldfields Close, Greetland, Halifax, West Yorkshire HX4 8LD.

Seekers, The
Friends Of The Seekers, PO Box 62, Westerham, Kent TN16 2ZT.

Shannon, Del
c/o Flat 2, 3 Sands Lane, Birdlington, Yorkshire YO15 2JG.

Shapiro, Helen
Gay Wiggins, 63 Arnold Road, Clacton-on-Sea, Essex CO15 1DQ.

Simon, Paul
PO Box 32, Kendal, Cumbria LA9 7NP.

Slade
The Slade And Slade II International Fan Club, PO Box 4YD, London W1A 4YD.

Springsteen, Bruce
PO Box 319, Reading, Berkshire RG2 8QS.

Shakin' Stevens
158 Camden Road, London NWI 9HJ.

Stewart, Rod
The Official Rod Stewart Fan Club, PO Box 475, Morden, Surrey SM4 6AT.

PO Box 4000, Los Angeles, California 90046, US.

Streisand, Barbra
Lynne Pounder, 17 Adrian Place, Peterlee, Co Durham SR8 5SR.

Tornados, The
Tom Hammond, 73a East Street, Blandford Forum, Dorset DT11 7DX.

Tremeloes, The
Julie Chapman, 85 Ridley Road, Bury St Edmunds, Suffolk IP3 3JA.

Troggs, The
Jacky Ryan, 56 Waite Davies Road, Lee, London SE12 OND.

U2
PO Box 48, London N6 5RU.

Vangelis
Vangelis Appreciation Society, Mark Griffin, Smithy Croft, Ythanbank, Elton, Aberdeenshire AB41 7UA, Scotland.

Vee, Bobby
John McPhee, St Ives, Eden Road, Gordon, Berwickshire TD3 6JA, Scotland.

Walker Brothers, The
Lynne Goodall, 71 Cheyne Court, Glengall Road, Woodford Green IG8 ODN.

Young, Paul
PO Box 4UB, London W1A 4UB.

Z Z Top
PO Box 19744, Dept TN, Houston, Texas 77224, US.

WELCOME TO THE WORLD of fanzines, an alternative form of publishing which is richly rewarding. I have found fan magazines to be among the most interesting and innovative of publications and have been involved with them all my life. Currently, I contribute to a range of Beatles 'zines – and my son Sean produces his own publication, *The Claudia Christian Chronicle*.

I was around ten years old when I launched my first fanzine, *Biped*, which I conceived when I was introduced to the world of science-fiction fandom. I began to explore the much wider phenomenon of fandom when I introduced a fan club section into my magazine *Idols* in the late 1980s. Corresponding with the various clubs, I discovered in excess of 700 different fan clubs in the UK alone – and perhaps I was just scratching the surface. The Elvis Presley Fan Club had over 20,000 members and there were over 4,000 dedicated Marc Bolan followers. (Incidentally, I also traced more than 30 different *Star Trek* fan clubs.)

There were fan clubs of every kind, and it became obvious that the sheer devotion of fans to their subjects produced magazines that often contained far more interesting and exclusive material than many mainstream publications, particularly in the field of music. There were even magazines dedicated to particular decades or genres, such as 1950s artists and rock 'n' roll in general.

If you are really interested in a specific artist, it is well worth subscribing to a fanzine. In its pages you will find more information about your idol than anywhere else. Unfortunately, from time to time the editors of fanzines give up and the publication folds. At the time of writing, all those listed below are thriving. Some have been in existence for many years, but it is always best to check that a publication is still being produced before sending off your subscription. If any of the fanzines detailed below take your fancy, send along a letter, together with a stamped, addressed envelope (or an International Reply Coupon) for details.

As for the future, many fanzines are now transferring to web sites on the Internet and it is likely that this will become the main forum for fanzines in the years to come.

The fanzines listed here are for artists with their own entries in the Where Are They Now? and In Memoriam sections of this book. As with fan clubs, *Record Collector* and *The Beat Goes On* magazines are excellent sources of information regarding fanzines for other artists mentioned in the text.

Abba
Agnetha, Benny, Bjorn, Frida
Katherine Courtney-O'Neill, ABBF Fan Club, 1 Barrow Hill Road, Shirehampton, Bristol BS11 9QT.

The Cartoon
54 Grampian Avenue, Glenburn, Paisley PA2 8DW, Scotland.

After Abba
Nicholas Thornhill-Faltskog, Australian Abba Fan Club, PO Box 299, Canterbury, Victoria 3126, Australia.

Ant, Adam
Red Antz International
Rob Lesman, Snoekstraat 42, 6833EE Arnhem, Netherlands.

Bangles, The
Banglemania
John Edwards, 24 Weaponness Valley Road, Scarborough, North Yorkshire YO11 2JF.

Barclay James Harvest
Nova Lepidoptera
117 De Haviland Close, Yeading, Northolt, Middlesex UB5 6RZ.

Barron Knights, The
Knightly News
Phil Black, 92 Heol-Yr-Odyn, Ely, Cardiff, Wales.

Beach Boys, The
Beach Boys Stomp
22 Avondale Road, Wealdstone, Middlesex HA3 7RE.

Black Sabbath
Southern Cross
Peter Scott. PO Box 177, Crewe, Cheshire CW2 7SZ.

Blondie
Picture This
Francois Wintein, 57 Church Avenue, Humberston, Grimsby, Humberside DN36 4DJ.

Bolan, Marc
Electric Boogie
Barry Smith, 11 Medoc Close, Wymans Brook, Cheltenham, Gloucestershire GL50 4SW.

Mainman
Terry Hughes, FDS, RAF Stafford, Beaconside,
Stafford, Staffordshire ST18 OAQ.

Rumblings
Tyrannosaurus Rex Appreciation Society,
PO Box 297, Newhaven, East Sussex
BN9 9PN.

Precious Star
A. Lauchlan, 36 Crummock Street, Beith,
Ayrshire KA15 2BD, Scotland.

The Never Ending Waltz
Aled Wilding, Flat 4, 29 Christchurch Road,
Newport, Gwent NP9 SLN, Wales.

Brotherhood Of Man
Midnight Express
S. Jacks, 15 Upton Court, Lincett Avenue,
Tarring, Worthing, West Sussex
BN13 IBJ.

Captain Beefheart
Apocalypso
P. Brown, 18 Fitzgerald Court, Leyton Grange,
London E10 5HT.

Cocker, Joe
Civilized Man
PO Box 43, Torquay, Devon TQ2 5XB.

Cogan, Alma
Alma-Holics
Stephen Woods, 9 Canterbury Avenue,
Bowerham, Lancaster LA1 4AU.

Costello, Elvis
Beyond Belief
Mark Perry, 6 Hillside Grove, Taunton,
Somerset TAI 4LA.

Information Service
Richard Groothuizen, Primulstraat 46,
1441 HC, Purmerend, Netherlands.

Creedence Clearwater Revival
Fan Club
Peter Koers, Schopperhofstrasse 74, 90789
Nurnberg, Germany.

Dave Clark Five, The
Bits & Pieces
71 The Mead, Darlington, Co Durham
DLI 1WU.

Deep Purple
Darker Than Blue
Cee Dee Mail DP, PO Box 14, Stowmarket,
Suffolk IP14 4UD.

De Shannon, Jackie
Newsletter
Peter Lerner, 7 Sheppards Close, St Albans,
Hertfordshire AL3 5AL.

Dexy's Midnight Runners
Keep On Running
Neil Warburton, 56 Apollo Road, Oldbury,
Warley, West Midlands B68 9RS.

Dion (& The Belmonts)
Yo Frankie
Gordon Watson, 185 Cairngorm Drive,
Kincorth, Aberdeen AB12 5PN, Scotland.

Donovan
Donovan's Friends
PC Publications, PO Box 1119, London
SW9 9JW.

The Hurdy Gurdy Man
PO Box 17, Rye, East Sussex TN31 6ZY.

Doors, The
Collector's Magazine
Three Dimensional Marketing Inc,
PO Box 1441, Orem, Utah 84059-1441, US.

Drake, Nick
Pink Moon
J. Creed, 34 Kingsbridge Road, Walton-on-
Thames, Surrey KT12 2BZ.

Dylan, Bob
Freewheelin'
My Back Pages, PO Box 117, Carlisle, Cumbria
CA1 2UL.

Isis
PO Box 132, Coventry, West Midlands
CV3 5RE.

Eagles, The
Natural Progressions, 177 South Norwood Hill,
London SE25 6DH.

Echo & The Bunnymen
Return Of Voodoo Billy
Voodoo Billy, Willow House, Coaley, Nr Dursley,
Gloucestershire GL11 5EG.

Eddie & The Hot Rods
Writing On The Wall
Alan Heaven, 8 George Frederick Road, Street,
Sutton Coalfield, West Midlands B73 6TB.

Electric Light Orchestra (ELO)
Destination Unknown
PO Box 365, Stafford ST18 0RY.

Face The Music
PO Box 718, Sidcup, Kent DA15 7UD

Kings Of The Universe
A. Heath, 18 Hawthorn Avenue, Stone,
Staffordshire ST15 0AX.

Starlight
PO Box AB, Almere, Netherlands.

Family
Weaver's Answer
Patrick Little, 425 8th Street, Ann Arbor,
Michigan 48193, US.

Fleetwood Mac
Crystal
Aine Foley, 46 St John's Avenue, Clondalkin,
Dublin 22, Eire.

Genesis
Dusk
Mario Giammetti, PO Box 10, 82100
Benevento, Italy.

Harper, Roy
Hors d'Oeuvres
Dave Carlin, 11 Dover Road, Botanical
Gardens, Sheffield, South Yorkshire
S11 8RH.

Hawkwind
Hawkeye and *Worldwide Discography*
A. Parr, 6 Conifers Close, Teddington,
Middlesex TW11 9JG.

Hendrix, Jimi
Jimpress
108 Warrington Road, Penketh, Warrington,
Cheshire WA5 2JZ.

Univibes
Caesar Glebeek, Coppeen, Enniskeane,
Co Cork, Eire.

Voodoo Child
Box 20361, Indianapolis, Indiana 46220, US.

Hollies, The
Carousel Newsletter
12 The Aspens, Kingsbury, Nr Tamworth,
Staffordshire B78 2JY.

Incredible String Band, The
Be Glad...
Raymond Greenoaken, 11 Ratcliffe Road,
Sheffield, South Yorkshire S11 8YA.

Jefferson Airplane
Holding Together
Bill Parry, 89 Glengariff Street, Clubmoor,
Liverpool L13 8DW.

Grace Slick of Jefferson Airplane

Jethro Tull
A New Day
D. Rees, 75 Wren Way, Farnborough,
Hampshire GU14 5TA.

King Crimson/Robert Fripp
Book Of Saturday
PO Box 221, Leeds LS1 5LW.

We'll Let You Know
Darren Woolsey, 3 Kings Drive, Wrose,
Bradford, West Yorkshire BD2 1PX.

Kinks, The
Newsletter
The Official Kinks Fan Club, PO Box 30,
Atherstone, Warwickshire CV9 2ZX.

Kiss

Strike
Ray Paul, 32 Seymour Road, Lower Edmonton, London N9 0SE.

Kiss Kollector
Joop Van Pelt, Herenweg 109, 1244 PZ Ankeveen, Netherlands.

Kissaholic Madness
Andy Guttman, PO Box 364, Mitcham 3132, Melbourne, Victoria, Australia.

Kraftwerk

Aktivitat
108 Cummings Park Crescent, Northfield, Aberdeen AB16 7AR, Scotland.

Lewis, Jerry Lee

Fire-Ball Mail
Barrie Gamblin, 16 Milton Road, Wimbledon, London SW19.

Little Feat

Feat Prints
PO Box 603, Mt Airy, Maryland 21771-0603, US.

Love Affair

Steve Ellis' Love Affair
Sarah Coleman, 40 Alverstone Avenue, East Barnet, Hertfordshire EN4 8EB.

Steve Ellis' Love Affair

Madness

Nut Inc
Stuart Wright, 15a Clarence Street, Southend, Essex SS1 1BN.

Madonna

Absolute Ciccone
Stephen Jones, 39 Marlborough Close, Grays, Essex RM16 2SU.

Dita
Lisa Walters, 109 Dock Road, Little Thurrock, Grays, Essex RM 17 6EY.

Manfred Mann

Platform End
The Manfred Mann Fan Club, 29 Lyndhurst Road, Wallasey, Merseyside L45 6XB.

Marriott, Steve

Steve Marriott International
A. Steel, 1 Wellington Avenue, St Ives, Cambridgeshire PE17 6UT.

Meek, Joe

Appreciation Society Newsletter
JMAS, 242 Brodie Avenue, Garston, Liverpool L19 7NG.

Minogue, Kylie

International Kylie Network
Stephen O'Donaghue, 12 Donegal Avenue, Whitehead, Co Antrim BT38 9NB, Northern Ireland.

Mitchell, Guy
Mitchell Music
5 Heathside Way, Hartley Wintney, Hampshire
RG27 8SG.

Mitchell, Joni
Shadows & Light
Alan Beadle, 103 Boxgrove, Goring-by-Sea,
Worthing, West Sussex BN12 6LX.

Monkees, The
Band 6
19 Skipsey Avenue, East Ham, London E6 4HW.

Head
D. Inquieti, 39 Long Mallows Rise, Ecton Brook,
Northamptonshire NN3 5AR.

Mungo Jerry
Mungo For It
A. Taylor, 24 Nafferton Place, Fenham,
Newcastle-upon-Tyne NE5 2QR.

Nazareth
Razamanewz
Joe Geesin, Headrest, Scotsford Road,
Broad Oak, Heathfield, East Sussex TN21 8TU.

Newton-John, Olivia
Only Olivia
5 Finchley Road, Ipswich, Suffolk 1P4 2HX.

Nirvana
Mangled Mind
Adrian T'vell, PO Box 1888, Wood Green,
London N22 6NF.

Numan, Gary
Asylum
Daniel Turner, 100 Oakshott Court,
Polygon Road, Somers Town, Euston, London
NW1 1ST.

Photograph
N. Lunn, 55 Belvere Avenue, Blackpool,
Lancashire FY4 2LW.

The Side Parting Is Dead
Survival Records, 29 Townhall Street,
Inverkeithing, Fife KY11 1LX, Scotland.

Orbison, Roy
In Dreams
A.J. Bishop, 105 Whippingham Road, Brighton,
East Sussex BN2 3PF.

Petty, Tom (& The Heartbreakers)
Makin' Some Noise
Amanda Saladine, 69 Crofthill Road, Slough,
Berkshire SL2 IHG.

Powell, Cozy
NaNaNa
Joe Geesin, Headrest, Scotsford Road,
Broad Oak, Heathfield, East Sussex TN21 8TU.

Presley, Elvis
Elvis: The Man And His Music
Now Dig This, 19 South Hill Road, Bensham,
Gateshead, Tyne & Wear NE8 2XR.

Fan Club Magazine
PO Box 4048, Milton Keynes, Buckinghamshire
MK8 0JH.

Pretty Things
SF Sorrow
Joop de Ligt, Vlasstraat 30, 1773 AM
Kreilroord, Netherlands.

Prince
Funky Design
Christian Murison, 27 Newport Street,
Millbrook, Torpoint, Cornwall PL10 1BW.

Interactive Experience
Interactive Productions, PO Box 541, Sheffield,
South Yorkshire S9 4YN.

7 Magazine
PO Box 363, Chadstone Centre, Victoria 3148,
Australia.

Procol Harum
Shine On
John Grayson, 75 Clarence Way,
Camden Town, London NW1 8DG.

Quatro, Suzi
Suzi And Other Four Letter Words
Faren Short, 20 Grants Avenue, Bournemouth,
Dorset BH1 4NR.

Ramones, The
UK Fan Club Newsletter
Veronica Kofman, 100 Albion Hill, Brighton,
East Sussex BN2 2PA.

Richard, Cliff
Cliff United
28 Blenheim Road, Sutton, Surrey SMI 2PX.

Constantly Cliff
William Hooper, 17 Podsmead Road, Tuffley, Gloucester GL1 5PB.

Dynamite International
The International Cliff Richard Movement, PO Box 94164, 1090 GD, Amsterdam, Netherlands.

Rolling Stones, The
Shattered! International
J. Hoeksma, PO Box 3723, London SE15 1HW.

Sticky Fingers
John Carr, 12190 1/2, Ventura Boulevard, Box 411, Studio City, California 91604, US.

Basement News
Gunter Beetz, Waldstr. 59, 63110, Rodgau 6, Germany.

It's Only Rock 'n' Roll
Bjornulf Vik, Vabraten 111, N-1392 Vettre, Norway.

Respectable
Erik Engholm, Furugata 19, S-753 24 Uppsakam, Sweden.

Rundgren, Todd/Utopia
Special Interest
Lino Terlati, Ple Moroni 9/5, 17100, Savona, Italy.

Scritti Politti
Scritti Politti
James Lawrence, 7 Hazely, Tring, Hertfordshire HP23 5JH.

Sex Pistols, The
Never Trust A Hippie
J.W. Henderson, 25a Grange Road, Bidford-on-Avon, Alcester, Warwickshire B50 4BY.

The Filth And The Fury
Scott Murphy, 24 Muirside Street, Bailliestonm, Glasgow, Scotland.

Simon, Paul (& Garfunkel)
The International Simon & Garfunkel Newsletter
Rob Oudshoorn, Rooseveltlaan 166a, NL 622 CW, Mastricht, Netherlands.

Slade
Feel The Noize!
Dave Jewell, Cardiff Community Enterprise Centre, Roath House, 22a City Road, Cardiff CF2 2ER, Wales.

Small Faces, The
Darlings Of Wapping Wharf Laundrette
John Hellier, 29 Hollidge Way, Dagenham, Essex RM10 9SP.

Small Faces International
Andrew Steel, 1 Wellington Avenue, St Ives, Cambs PE17 6UT.

Smiths, The
I Really Don't Care
Euan Forrest, 29 Auchinbaird, Sauchie, Clackmannanshire FK10 3HA, Scotland.

Sparks
Looks Aren't Everything
Tony Machin, 16 Dale Valley Road, Southampton, Hampshire SO16 6QR.

Spedding, Chris
Guitar Graffiti
T. Nomura, 3-9 Nakadono-cho, Nishinomiya, 662, Japan.

Chris Spedding

Springfield, Dusty
Bulletin
Dusty Springfield Bulletin, PO Box 203, Cobham, Kent KT11 2UG.

Stewart, Rod
Smiler
The Official Rod Stewart Fan Club, PO Box 475, Morden, Surrey SM4 6AT.

Sweet
Cut Above The Rest
C. Cimino, 52 Ashbank Road, Bucknall, Stoke-on-Trent, Staffordshire ST2 9DR.

Sweet Fanny Adams
Vreny Thommen, PO Box 167, CH-4013 Basel 13, Switzerland.

10 CC
Headline Hustler
Phil Loftus, 45 Windsor Road, Droylsden, Manchester M43 6WB.

10 CC

UFO
Misty Green And Blue
120b Auckland Terrace, Shildon, Co Durham DL4 1AZ.

U2
Silver And Gold
PO Box 159, Southend-on-Sea, Essex SSO 9SP.

The Zooropean
PO Box 12940, London N8 0WA.

Vangelis
Albedo
Vangelis Appreciation Society, Mark Griffin, Smithy Croft, Ythanbank, Ellon, Aberdeenshire AB41 7UA, Scotland.

Vee, Bobby
Vee News
John McPhee, St Ives, Eden Road, Gordon, Berwickshire TD3 6JA, Scotland.

Ventures, The
Resurgence
Ventures International Club, 13 Limetree Close, Grove, Wantage, Oxfordshire OX12 0BJ.

Who, The
Generations
P. Hopkins, 1 Egbert Road, Meols, Wirral, Merseyside L47 5AH.

Naked Eye
PO Box 7331, London E18 1TE.

Wishbone Ash
Hot Ash
The Official Wishbone Ash Fan Club, 186 Herschel Crescent, Littlemore, Oxford OX4 3TZ.

Yes
The Revealing
Ian Hartley, 35 Field Lane, Oldswinford, Stourbridge, West Midlands.

Yes Music Circle
Progressive Society, PO Box 310, Guildford, Surrey GU2 5WH.

Zappa, Frank
T'Mershi Duween
Fred Tomsett, PO Box 86, Sheffield, South Yorkshire SO16 8XN.

The Arf Dossier
Jos Schoone, Arf Society, Sekretariat, Am Markt 3, 18209 Bad Doberan, Germany.